# *Facilities* Economics

*INCORPORATING 'PREMISES AUDITS'*

by Bernard Williams Associates

Published by:

Building Economics Bureau Limited
Kings House
32 –40 Widmore Road
Bromley
Kent
BR1 1RY

Tel:  0181 464 5418
Fax:  0181 313 3363

First Edition 1994
Reprinted 1995
Revision (1) 1996
Reprinted 1997, 1999

ISBN: 0 904237 168

Cover Design & typeset by Ken Ticehurst
Graphics design & typeset by Andrew Hayward
General design & typeset by Ken Ticehurst & SOS Graphics

Printed in Great Britain by Anthony Rowe Ltd, Chippenham, Wilts.

ACKNOWLEDGEMENTS:

The editors are grateful to the many business colleagues and members of BWA who have
offered helpful advice and constructive criticism in the course of preparation of this text.
The sections dealing with property funding and taxation are based extensively on material
provided by Geoffrey Parsons MSc, BSc, ARICS IRRV, AILAM.

## THE AUTHORS

Bernard Williams Associates - **BWA** - is a firm of Chartered Surveyors specialising in Facilities and Building Economics offering comprehensive advice on all financial and management aspects of providing and using land, buildings and business support services.

Founded in 1969 there are now three divisions each specialising in particular aspects of their work - Project Services, Facilities Consultancy and Building Cost Consultancy.

They have an extensive client base of national and multi-national corporations as well as Central Government and Local Authorities and each division boasts a broad range of internationally prestigious commissions and projects.

As well as its mainstream activities **BWA** has specialists in capital allowances, value-added taxation and development grants and assistance and has an ongoing programme of Research and Development.

In the field of facilities management **BWA** has what is believed to be Europe's largest independently audited data base of facilities costs and data, all analysed in accordance with set rules of classification and measurement. They also edit the Premises and Facilities Data Service set up in conjunction with the IML Group, publishers of 'Premises and Facilities Management'.

The editor-in-chief, Bernard Williams, wrote the original 'Premises Audits' book in 1986 and was until recently external examiner to the MSc Degree in Facilities Management at the Centre for Facilities Management at the University of Strathclyde. He, and other senior members of the practice write and lecture extensively on all aspects of facilities and building economics and are authors of a number of standard reference works including:

- Property Development Feasibility Tables

- Design Economics for Building Services in Offices

- Property Expert's Guide to VAT

- Development Grants and Other Assistance

- Building and Development Economics in the EC (Financial Times Management Reports).

# Contents

# PART D SUPPORT SERVICES

## SECTION 7 BUSINESS SUPPORT

## SECTION 8 STAFF SUPPORT COSTS

# PART E RELOCATION

## SECTION 9 RELOCATION

## SECTION 10 THE DEVELOPMENT OPTION

# PART F TAXATION

## SECTION 11 TAXATION CONSIDERATIONS

# PART G BENCHMARKING

## SECTION 12 THE PREMISES AND FACILITIES AUDIT

# PART H INDEX AND LIST OF FIGURES

# INTRODUCTION

Adam Smith in 'The Wealth of Nations' defined economics as the 'study of man's efforts to create wealth'.

The authors of this work have linked this definition to the modern concept of facilities in defining **'facilities economics'** as **'the study of man's efforts to create wealth through the provision, use and management of facilities'**.

This broad description encapsulates the interests of both provider and user and takes a lead from the authors' earlier definition of **'building economics'**: **'the study of man's efforts to create wealth by building'** [1]. Insofar as **'building economics'** embraces **'all the financial and management aspects of providing and using land and buildings'** [2] it is concerned with the wealth created by any or all of developer, builder, financier, consultant, user and investor as a consequence of their involvement with a building at one stage or another in its life-cycle.

'Building economics' is an amalgam of the principal ingredients of the surveying disciplines - ie: valuation, cost control, development, investment and property management - and is concerned with their influence on the performance and *profitability generated* throughout the premises life-cycle from inception to demolition.

But 'facilities economics' **embraces** building economics, supplementing the 'built premises' component with non-premises business support services such as 'security', 'catering', and 'office services' and extending the consideration of the interface between non-core and core business activity. Further consideration of the concept of core and non-core activities and the full gamut of services potentially falling within the definition of facilities is discussed more fully in the following chapters. **Suffice it here to remind the reader that 'facilities economics', by the authors' definition, is so widely drawn as to bring into question whether it is reasonable for an individual who has not received a thorough grounding across the whole spectrum of the discipline to take full responsibility for decisions made in the course of its application.**

Of course, some individuals holding the post of 'facilities manager' may survive on a knowledge of office services and simple running and maintenance applications and may never have to concern themselves with issues of building development and investment - but they are already becoming the exception, anachronisms.

On another front the building industry and its maintenance and services sub-sets are choc-a-bloc with highly trained specialists who have absolutely no idea of the contribution made by a building and its operational management to the profitability, efficiency and satisfaction of its occupiers.

And what about the investor and his real estate advisors who value portfolios by reference to historic comparables flawed by a misconception of building quality and by the incestuous nature of the ill-informed conventional wisdom prevailing in this market sector?

Just about everyone of the players on the 'facilities economics' stage has a unilateral view of its implications whereas 'facilities economics' is a concept which desperately needs to be tackled holistically.

This work strives to achieve just this.  Each facet has been covered in sufficient depth to enable the reader to gain a command of all the relevant cost and value 'drivers' and the management context in which they are framed without reliance on depth of technical knowledge or experience.

———————

(1) Bernard Williams - 'Premises Audits' (Bulstrode Press - 1988)

(2) Bernard Williams - 'Asset Management & Financial Control (SBIM - 1990)

# PART A

# FACILITIES AND THEIR MANAGEMENT

# SECTION 1

# FACILITIES AND THE CORPORATE PLAN

# CHAPTER 1.1 – THE SCOPE OF FACILITIES

## 1.1.1 DEFINITIONS

*Facilities*

The term 'facilities' in a business context has been defined as **'the premises and services required to accommodate and facilitate business activity'**. [1]

*Facilities management*

Facilities management has been defined as **'the process by which an organisation delivers and sustains agreed levels of support service in a quality environment at appropriate cost to meet the business need'**. [2]

Facilities management in fact has three facets – **sponsorship, intelligence** and **service management (FIG 1.1.A)**..

**FIG. 1.1.A:** *3 facets of facilities management*

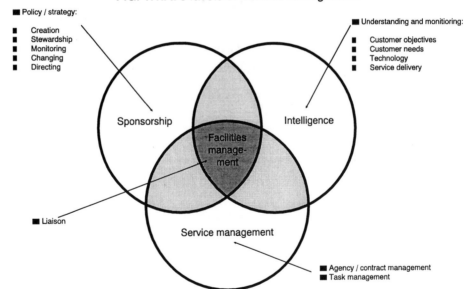

All facilities operations involve all 3 facets; although the service management is capable of being carried out by either contractors or in-house staff - often a mixture of both - the sponsorship and intelligence must always, by definition, belong exclusively in-house.

*Facilities sponsorship*

Facilities sponsorship is the essence of the intelligent/informed client function (ICF); it emerges more clearly as a smaller - but critical - separately identifiable function as responsibility for facilities service management is devolved from in-house to external resources. In the less devolved, hybrid models the sponsorship role is not usually a separate function other than for capital projects where it is well established.

The term sponsorship in respect of facilities implies the ownership of responsibility for the facilities provision, the stewardship of the organisation's policy for the provision, maintenance and allocation of resources for the accommodation and services required to facilitate corporate objectives.

*Intelligence*

The 'intelligence' facet is actually both introspective and outward looking: introspective as the eyes and ears of the facilities management function with regard to core business needs and outward-looking in respect of the effectiveness of service delivery (see below) and new techniques and technology available in its support.

The sponsorship and intelligence functions of facilities management are unquestionably 'core' activities (ie: directly contribute to the productive output) even though some facilities service management firms offering 'partnering' arrangements will suggest they can cope with this aspect as well. **In fact, the 'intelligent client' facets need to be identified and separately established in-house regardless of the location of service management**.

The 'intelligent client function' is discussed in more detail in Chapter 2.1

*Service Management.*

It is most important to understand clearly the distinction between the line management of a particular service or task (such as 'cleaning' or 'distribution') and the overall direction and co-ordination of all the services which is defined here as 'facilities service management'. Both the individual services and the facilities service management contribute to **facilities service delivery** but the relationships via which this is effected are many and various as are their economic implications. Again, this third and equally important facet of facilities management is discussed at greater length in Chapter 2.1

However, before reviewing the critical inter-relationships of the three facets of facilities management it is first necessary to consider the scope of facilities services and the way that they relate to corporate objectives and impact upon the bottom line - be that drawn in terms of profit, efficiency or, more likely, both.

## 1.1.2 SERVICE MANAGEMENT STRUCTURE

There is no absolute concensus as to what activities facilities management should or should not embrace. Even if there were, there would never be universal agreement as to the responsibility for and control of the generic cost centres.

Even old-established functions like personnel, finance, sales and marketing frequently turn up in different titles, regimes and hierarchical structures and facilities management itself, unless - exceptionally - holding down a discrete upper management position, may be found reporting to any of these and other disciplines or a combination thereof. The most broadly drawn facilities management division might be as **FIG 1.1.B** which defines scope and cost centres rather than dynamic function.

Note that information technology is shown as an 'optional' component of the facilities hierarchy.

In practice it is common for the IT facilities management and general facilities management to co-exist rather than come under one level of middle management. For the purposes of this text, however, IT has been treated as one of the **business support services** components of facilities (see chapter 7.5). Nevertheless such treatment is not in any way to imply that its significance in the scheme of things is other than as depicted in the diagram below.

**Fig. 1.1.B:** *Broadly drawn scope of facilities management*

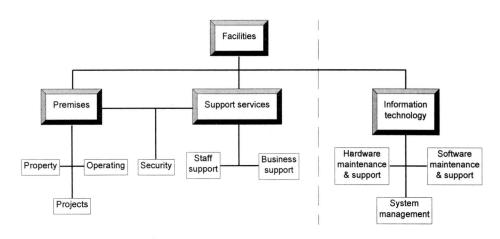

## 1.1.3 FACILITIES COST CENTRES

Within each of these management divisions costs might be collected under the following cost centres – not an exhaustive list but representing those most commonly found in practice.

### 1. FACILITIES MANAGEMENT

- Administrative and technical staff ie: 'white collar' workers
- Facilities management consultants (other than those providing specialist out-source services) eg: space planning, maintenance management
- Service charge component

### 2. PREMISES

Property
- Rents
- Rates
- Insurance
- Depreciation
- Service charge component

Projects
- Design
- Supervision
- Cost Control

Operating Costs
- Maintenance of fabric
- Maintenance services
- Cleaning/housekeeping
- Energy
- Water and sewerage
- Waste disposal
- Internal landscaping
- External landscaping
- Service charge component

## 3. SUPPORT SERVICES

Security
- Reception
- Guarding

Staff support
- Catering
- Sports/social and Trade Union facilities
- Health, Safety & Welfare

Business support
- Reception/porters/messengers
- Storage/archiving
- Communications systems
- Data cabling support
- Office furniture
- Stationery, printing & reprographics
- Churn
- Motor transport
- Disaster recovery

Service charges, which are described in more detail in Chapter 3.2, occur on leasehold properties and are in respect of facilities and services procured on behalf of tenants by the landlord and re-chargeable to the tenant in accordance with the terms of the lease.

Typically service charges will comprise such items as repairs to the fabric, maintenance of common services, cleaning of common areas such as foyer, staircases etc. It is important that costs of these re-chargeable items plus any charges in respect of management, should be analysed into the appropriate facilities cost centres **as if they were directly incurred by the tenant on his own behalf**. This is to facilitate benchmarking against costs and performance of facilities in owner/occupation regimes.

The argument in favour of drawing the management of facilities services as (or nearly as) widely as depicted above is that

- it embraces the whole concept
- it provides a bigger cost-base in support of appropriate calibre of management.

Against the case is the obviously uneasy mixture of the highly technical aspects of building design and management and the predominantly administrative character of much of Support Services activity. There is of course no reason why management cannot cope with both aspects but cultural difficulties may cause internal rivalries with counter-productive consequences.

Historically, non-technically skilled administrators have tended to rise above professionally qualified specialists on the management ladder eg: the Civil Service in the UK. Given the particularly complex and critical inter-relationship between premises and their occupants such a tendency toward the non-technological in any facilities management structure needs to be the subject of careful appraisal in the context of personnel, their experience and management capabilities.

## 1.1.4 THE FACILITIES MISSION

Every department within an organisation should have a mission statement in support of the main business objective.

A mission statement should always relate to the corporate goal and describe the intentions of the facilities providers in pursuit of their own supportive contribution.

An example of a facilities mission statement is:

**'to provide and maintain accommodation and support services to the standards required to facilitate and promote the business productivity with minimum risk to efficiency and personal safety, pro-active financial control and asset management, and to be constantly prepared for change'**

Whether the mission statement is in the form of a 'charter' within an 'internal market' arrangement such as described in Chapter 1.2 below or whether it is merely internal to the facilities management department is not important. Its very existence in a dedicated group will focus minds and effort on quality of provision, which must be to the good.

## 1.1.5 FACILITIES AND THE CORPORATE PLAN

This relationship between the aspirations of facilities management and the business goal is expressed theoretically in **FIGS 1.1.C** and **1.1.F**.

**FIG 1.1.C** tracks the connection between the premises strand of facilities and the business plan. It emphasises the fact that the way in which the operational requirements are accommodated should be directed by a 'premises policy'.

**FIG. 1.1.C:** *Facilities and the corporate plan - premises policy*

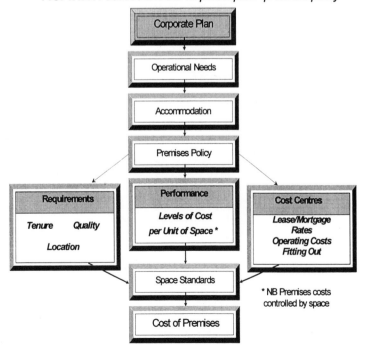

*The premises
policy*

This should determine the objectives for accommodation in terms of

- location

- quality

- performance

- tenure

- space

- management

- service delivery

- cost

The performance of premises is discussed in more detail in Chapter 1.2. Suffice it here to say that the combined effects of location, quality and tenure will determine the price the organisation must pay per unit of space occupied. How the organisation uses the space in terms of fitting out and premises management will impact upon the overall performance of the premises; however, the numbers of persons/ pieces of equipment accommodated will have a very high impact on the premises economics. Provided that the density of space use is not so intense as to have an adverse effect upon the efficiency of the occupants then higher densities will reap economic benefits to the organisation in terms of cost-effective premises.

Increased density will affect operating costs right across the board. More people per square metre of available space means more wear-and-tear, greater cooling loads, earlier replacement of components and so on.

However in nearly all cases the property costs (ie: rent/mortgage etc) will be far more significant than the operating costs (eg: maintenance, cleaning, energy); so, although the operating costs per capita will increase with greater density of occupation, the reduced cost per capita of the property costs will more than outweigh this cost-penalty (see **FIG. 1.1.D**).

**FIG. 1.1.D:** *Effect of varying density of space use on operating and property costs per capita*

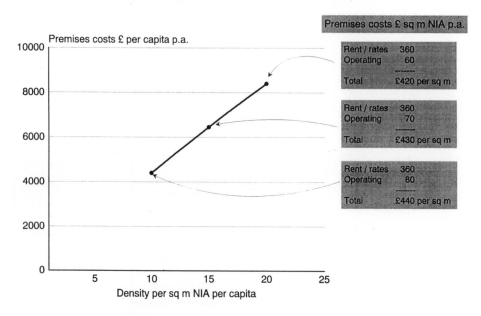

Space use will always be the cost driver in any premises cost equation. However, the performance of the space in terms of the business requirement will be more critical than the cost of providing and maintaining the premises.

Premises costs are rarely more than 5% of turnover (or revenue expenditure in the case of administrative organisations) - see **FIG 1.1.E**. Of that figure the property costs make up the great majority - say 80:20 property:operating costs. The property costs are comparatively fixed - any movement usually being upwards on rent reviews - whereas operating costs are to some extent controllable, if only by further deferral of the inevitable once full economic efficiency has been achieved. Consequently the premises manager must try to minimise the amount of fixed cost space in use, looking out continually for opportunities to get rid of space surplus to requirements. The surplus may, of course, be with reference to inadequate quality or performance as well as quantity.

**FIG. 1.1.E:** *Premises costs in the context of turnover*

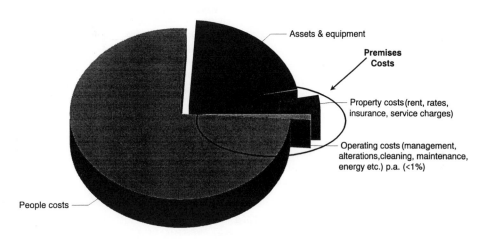

The premises policy should be in writing and formally accepted by the Board of Management. It should envisage and state the principal strategy in pursuit of the mission and identify alternative strategies and sub-strategies to deal with changes in business requirements.

For instance, a cornerstone of a company's premises policy might be to come together from several sites into one freehold building in Central London within, say, 7 years. The principal property strategy concerning acquisition and disposal would therefore be to avoid commitments to new long leases whilst rationalising use of existing space to facilitate disposal of the least marketable assets. A sub-strategy in the event of temporary unforeseen reductions in staff numbers might involve 'mothballing' the least efficient space in terms of operating costs - mindful always of the all-important factor of the effects of location and quality on business productivity.

Once part of the corporate business plan the premises policy and its accompanying strategies can be implemented without constant reference back to the Board; reactive decision-making and its dire economic consequences can thus be reduced or eliminated completely.

The various components of the premises policy are discussed in detail in their relevant Chapters below.

*The support
services policy*

**FIG. 1.1.F** shows similarly how the Support Services policy must accommodate the business needs. Space does not generally drive the costs of these services although it can be a significant factor in such cost centres as catering, security and staff facilities. However, the amount of resource consumed by the operation will in most cases drive the costs the hardest; for instance, the amount of stationery consumed per capita, the numbers of vehicles in the transport fleet and average time spent on the telephone are the sort of critical benchmarks against which to target and monitor the effective provision of support services.

**FIG. 1.1.F:** *Facilities and the corporate plan - support services policy*

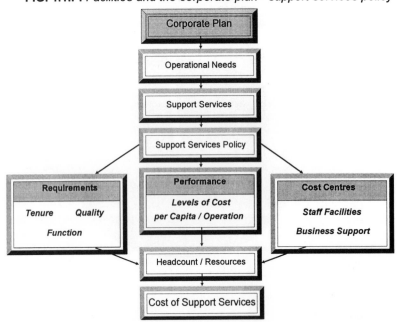

The support services policy will link much more obviously with the mainstream business activity and will be more easily understood and readily accepted than its premises counterpart. However, both policies are likely to be equally significant in their overall impact on the bottom-line year-end result.

## 1.1.6 CORE AND NON-CORE ACTIVITIES

There is a perception amongst modern business managers - and one which has the increasing support of government policy - that any activity which does not directly contribute to income (or productive external output) should be considered as 'non-core' ie: does not lie at the heart of the raison d'être of the organisation.

Therefore, the solicitor who drafts the conveyancing document has a 'core' function whereas the person who types it has a 'non-core' function.

The salesman closing the deal is 'core' but the person keeping the loos in his office clean and resistant to spread of disease is not.

This fairly clear distinction between the relative contribution of production and support services is not universally accepted but is axiomatic on most Business Studies courses. If there is a blurring at the edges it occurs most obviously at management level of support services and support level of production services. For example, the non-core office services manager who has responsibility for ensuring that reports are typed correctly and despatched on time can genuinely feel part of the production process; within the core the sales director's p.a. – in a secretarial mode – is, at best, no more productive than the office services manager.

However, the inspection of needle-ends to check up on numbers of dancing angels is definitely a non-core activity!

Suffice to say that one of the primary reasons for drawing the 'core' v 'non-core' distinction is to attempt to concentrate the attention of an organisation's management on those activities forming an essential part of the end-product. The corollary of this axiom is that any other activity not involving or requiring the core skills of the business could and should be provided and managed by external contractors.

Extreme proponents of this view, such as Drucker [3], would out the whole of the typing pool and its management. Naturally, facilities management goes via the same window.

The Drucker theory is that managers of 'non-core' service functions cannot aspire to top-level management positions in an organisation which is, or should be, dominated by the skills of 'core' activity managers.

The head of security services will not make MD in the conglomerate which employs him so will lack motivation; however as MD of his own security services contracting company he can be a big fish in a smaller pond and have both status and investment opportunity to spur him on to higher performance and productivity.

Of course, contracting productivity is a two-edged sword: on the one hand competitive bidding can save the customer money while on the other hand the benefits of production efficiencies should go to the service provider - if sound, free-market, economic theory is to prevail. If it does not then providers will cut standards to compete, to the customer's detriment.

The logic of out-sourcing non-core activity and the benefits thus obtained are clearly not of the black-and-white variety - there are too many examples of good and bad in both in-and-out-source approaches for the arguments to go away completely, or even recede. Insofar as facilities management is the subject of consideration for out-sourcing the debate is frequently fuelled by a perceived lack of credibility in the facilities personnel and their efficiency; where problems do exist they spring from a legacy of almost universal absence of training and education in the discipline.

In most parts of the Western world the recession of the early 90's has encouraged very many private and public concerns to latch eagerly, nay desperately, on to the 'non-core' activity concept. Sometimes this is for genuinely philosophical grounds but too often it is an excuse to overcome internal problems of staffing levels and, even worse, it can be used to justify the killer blow to end internecine management struggles.

Even where well-respected departments have been externalised real cost savings have been identified (in the short-term at least) giving further justification to those who just want to get rid of the function without reference to any philosophical opinions to the contrary.

However the core v non-core argument should always be the determining factor unless the organisation's reason is that:

- the existing structure and/or calibre of the organisation is inadequate, and

- it does not wish to use internal resources or funds to rectify the situation, or

- it simply wishes to reduce staff numbers as a matter of principle, and/or

• it seeks the cash flow advantage of a deferred payment for facilities services to the extent permitted by the contract or to a greater extent as necessary from time to time.

In this context the rapid growth of the competence and status of the 'new breed' of facilities management emerging during the past decade forms a fascinating back-drop to the developing out-sourcing scenario.

There is now a clearly identifiable and highly motivated discipline within facilities management spawning masters degrees and doctorates and demanding a place on the board of management. The distinction between 'core' and 'non-core' within facilities is acknowledged by its own academia; however the aggressive view that the direction of facilities (as opposed to management of services) constitutes a core function justifying top-level representation is a war that is far from won in the battlefields of commercial and administrative management at large.

One thing is nevertheless clear: in the course of elevating from Maintenance Manager to Facilities Director the role (and its players) have changed beyond recognition. And just as well too. To use an analogy from another industry, if an aircraft falls out of the sky it may be the fault of the designer, the constructor or the maintenance gang - but in the end it will be sales of flights which will suffer. So with business facilities; if they are badly managed (whether internally or by an out-sourced agent) or if their quality does not marry up to the business objectives, profits will undoubtedly be adversely affected over time.

Properly implemented proactive facilities management can become integral to production sales and marketing whilst value engineering its own function. Yet it must never be forgotten that badly administered reactive (or worse, inactive!) facilities management will equally hold back business efficiency while wasting the valuable resources at its disposal.

---

(1) Keith Alexander – The Centre for Facilities Management, University of Strathclyde

(2) Keith Alexander – The Centre for Facilities Management, University of Strathclyde

(3) 'Managing the Future - the 1990's and beyond' (Butterworth – Heinemann 1992) et al.

# CHAPTER 1.2 – THE PERFORMANCE OF FACILITIES

## 1.2.1 THE CONCEPT OF PERFORMANCE

Performance, in business terms, means the manner or quality of functioning.

Modern management theory seeks to target and measure the performance of individuals, work-groups and equipment. This principle is now becoming enshrined in the facilities management culture, with the development and use of performance indicators (PI's) across the whole range of cost centres.

## 1.2.2 MANAGEMENT AND PERFORMANCE

**FIG.1.2.A:** *Facilities management performance criteria*

---

- **The extent to which facilities support or can be adapted to the changing needs of an organisation**

- **The contribution that facilities make to organisational effectiveness**

- **The value added by effective management**

- **Improvements in service and environmental quality**

- **The risks associated with using facilities**

---

Source: The Centre for Facilities Management

The facilities management function must expect to be tested like any other aspect of business activity. **FIG 1.2.A** suggests the features which need to be assessed in the process of measuring this performance.

*Performance indicators*

A performance indicator is a tool used by management to measure the efficiency achieved in the process of carrying out a function.

It comprises a description of the function, the targets to be achieved and the degree of success in meeting them. The targets may relate to time, quality, cost or any combination thereof.

For example, an organisation may run a bus service to remote stores. Its published timetable sets out the targets; the numbers of occasions over a month on which the service is more than (say) 5 minutes late on leaving from base and arriving at the destination might be described in percentage terms. Thus, in the month of January 87% of departures and 76% of arrivals were within a period of 5 minutes after schedule, compared with targets of 85% and 80% respectively!

*Service level agreements - the internal market*

The publication of the timetable and the performance targets is effectively an offer of service to the customer using that part of the facilities service. Some organisations now seek to formalise such missions in 'Service Level Agreements' (SLA's) which are pseudo-contracts within what is sometimes described as an 'internal market'. This pseudo-contract commits the provider to the level of service described in a published document and may, or may not, be accompanied by a cross-charge by the provider to the beneficiary of the service ('the customer').

A critical aspect of facilities economics is the identification of the **appropriate service level requirement** prior to formalising any agreement.

There is sometimes confusion between service level agreements, service level commitments (SLC's) and mission statements. A mission statement is a general statement of intention, such as 'to provide an adequate and reliable bus service'. There is little point in incorporating such a generality in a service level agreement - although it may provide some motivation to the provider if he is reminded of it from time to time when standards obviously fall.

Many organisations moving towards a complete internal market regime stop short of SLA's, relying upon the service level commitment and relevant performance indicators to be established and managed by the provider; individual performance related financial incentives and publication of achievements against target do certainly act as a stimulus to efficiency as long as the commitments and targets are sharply defined and meaningfully measurable. Customer satisfaction should also be monitored in a formal way, even though the customer may not be directly charged for the service.

## Cross-charging

The important step-up from the service level commitment to the SLA should be the penultimate stage in completion of a full internal market - ie: it should ideally be the prelude to a cross-charging of facilities. In terms of facilities economics the process whereby the cost of service provided has to be borne as an overhead by the internal customer is an optimum arrangement. Such cross-charging should be in the context of a pseudo-contract based upon a SLA which is in turn bolstered by an agreed set of performance indicators. The benefits of such an arrangement to the organisation are threefold:

- it can sit neatly within a written facilities policy correctly identifying and costing the relationship between facilities performance and the corporate plan as described in Chapter 1.1.

- it encourages the purchaser to be more aware of his consumption of the business' resources and so more judicious in his demands as to the extent of the facilities provided

- it makes the facilities provider accountable for the cost and quality of the service which is delivered.

*'Back-to-back' agreements*

It is still uncommon for facilities managers to pass SLA's and PI's across to external contractors, although the logic for doing so is overwhelming. For example, a SLA which commits to performance targets in respect of response time to emergency maintenance, down-time of lifts etc, can easily be written into the external contract - even if the only financial penalty for failure is not to have the contract renewed on expiry.

Often it is the trend towards over-bureaucracy which makes facilities managers hold back from this total commitment to measured performance, and it is essential that any PI regime should be manageable whilst having the desired economic effect. 'Pareto's principle' ie that 80% of the cost, value or resource consumed is contained in 20% of the constituent parts, is always worth following and is a good basis upon which to decide which items to target and measure - and also to decide upon the classification of tolerance bands. It may be better to accept delays of 10 rather than 5 minutes in the Bus Service if that eases the problem of collecting data thereby reducing the time spent in measurement. There is still nothing to prevent the provider aiming for higher targets, thereby keeping the customer happy to accept a less stringent 'contract' condition. The right balance is essential if the system is to work to the common good.

*Quality of service*

Quality management is discussed in detail in Chapter 2.2. Suffice it here to say that if a contractor has a commitment to Quality Assurance to BS EN ISO 9000 , Total Quality Management, the Citizens Charter etc, there is a good case for the performance indicators and checking processes enshrined in those procedures to be referred to or fully incorporated into the external contract or internal SLA.

*Implementing the full internal market*

Although the culture in many organisations may present resistance to the concept of a full internal market there can be little doubt that the practice will become the norm sooner than the objectors might hope or expect.

There is at least one organisation in the UK which cross-charges each employee with the facilities he or she uses within the office - if they work from home they do not get charged. It may be that this Orwellian 'Big Brother' connotation may prove to be unacceptable in the large majority of organisations. However home-working will become more and more a feature of business strategy and may itself require some form of performance-related penalties as well as positive incentives in pursuit of premises efficiency.

Home-working is considered in greater detail in Section 4 - Space Management.

*Benchmarking*

A close relative of the performance indicator is the 'benchmark'. Taken from the process of marking datum levels in land surveying the term benchmark, in the context of facilities economics, means a cross-reference to achievements in a particular field of activity by a comparable internal or external source. The concept of benchmarking costs and performance is discussed in Section 12 - The Premises and Facilities Audit.

## 1.2.3 THE PERFORMANCE OF BUILDINGS

*The significance of building performance*

The quickest route to recognition as an intellectual in the world of property and building these days is to drop the word 'performance', in a reasonably relevant manner, into as many sentences as possible.

The concept of performance specification has been fairly familiar to people on the construction side of the fence for many years. Many building materials are specified by their performance characteristics and, indeed, there are a number of institutions specialising in the appraisal of the performance of buildings and materials in use, eg the Building Performance Research Unit subsequently subsumed into the Centre for Facilities Management at the University of Strathclyde.

Property people (being more conservative traditionally) have inevitably been slower to introduce this terminology into their already jargon-filled vocabulary. In fact, since they consider buildings from a very different angle, the performance they are concerned with is more likely to be that of value rather than construction - as if there were in fact no correlation whatsoever between the two.

It is submitted that understanding and acceptance of the concept of performance will be the most critical development in property and building in the next decade and the fact that the term means all things to all men at present is an unfortunate obstacle which has to be overcome in using the concept to help us to achieve the ultimate efficiency for which we are all striving.

Of course, it is one thing to understand what is meant by performance and another to be able to measure it. Lord Kelvin is quoted as saying, in the context of measurement generally, 'if you cannot measure it you cannot understand it' and Harrington equally believes that 'if you cannot measure it you cannot improve it'.

What they are both actually arguing for is the need to make sense of complexity, not necessarily by fully calculating costs and benefits but by recognising patterns of relationships.

This text discusses the concept of building performance and its applications in property and building and considers what must be done to facilitate the measurement which clearly is a condition precedent to understanding and improving performance of property.

*The three facets of building performance*

Building performance is normally associated with building quality. It is a complex issue and difficult to define. It is currently considered primarily in terms of physical integrity and durability and the associated capital and revenue costs, but the reality is that it goes infinitely deeper than that.

Buildings are simply a means to an end. They are variously concerned with:

- people

- processes

- places

- spaces

- support systems

- costs

- income

- profitability

A building's response to accommodating these requirements represents its performance.

Performance of buildings is therefore defined here as '**the contribution made by a building or estate to the functional and financial requirements of the occupiers and the associated physical behaviour of the fabric, services and finishes over time**'.

From this it follows that there are three components of performance, ie: functional efficiency, physical efficiency and financial efficiency (**FIG. 1.2.B**).

**FIG. 1.2.B:** *The three facets of building performance -
interrelationships*

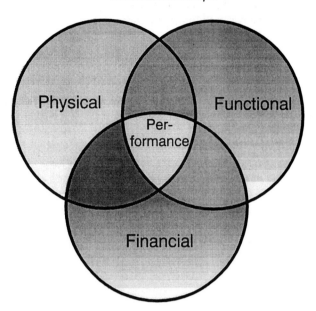

**Physical** performance relates to the behaviour of the fabric, services and finishes embracing physical properties such as structural integrity, internal environment (heating, lighting etc) energy efficiency, cleanliness, maintainability, durability and environmental impact.

**Functional** performance is the term used to describe the properties afforded by the building to the benefit (or otherwise) of the occupier. Examples are space (quantity and quality), layout, ergonomics, image, ambience, amenity, movement/communications, security, health & safety and flexibility.

The **financial** performance is a combination of capital and revenue expenditure, rate of depreciation, investment value and contribution to profitability/efficiency. It springs from the physical and functional performance of the building and the way in which it is used.

These three facets are inextricably linked, although the significance of this relationship is frequently missed by those whose pre-occupation is with one particular facet only eg: property developers, maintenance managers or space planners each ploughing their individual furrow oblivious of their part in the overall scheme of things.

Techniques exist for evaluation, at design stage, of the likely cost of maintaining a building's physical performance over its life-cycle, although the data presently available upon which to base the necessary forecasts of life, deterioration, maintenance and associated costs is so sparse and unreliable as to cast serious doubt on the validity of such an exercise for investment appraisal. Nonetheless, life-cycle cost appraisal is an important discipline encouraging designers to justify their decisions to the future occupier.

However, whereas the physical costs (including capital depreciation) over a building's life-cycle are unlikely to be more than about 5% of an organisation's total costs, the functional performance impacts directly on the efficiency of the organisation's core activities - which can account for some 80-90% of its total costs. Consequently it is likely that the functional performance will have a much greater impact on profitability and efficiency than the tangible costs attributable only to the physical operation of the premises.

## 1.2.4 THE PHYSICAL PERFORMANCE OF BUILDINGS

An inherent function of the performance of the building is its physical performance ie: its rate of deterioration, the operations required to maintain and run it and the replacement of the components, elements and finally the building over time (see Chapter 10.4 - Whole-life Economics.

Design teams must be encouraged by the client or his project manager to deliver a life-cycle cost plan at the same time as the capital budget is presented. An example of such a life-cycle cost plan is given in Chapter 10.4. In order to produce such a plan the design team must clearly have access to good data on performance and cost-in-use. Such data does not exist in any measure of sophistication at present but important moves are being made to overcome this shortcoming. A study carried out by the Building Research Establishment in association with The University of Strathclyde and Arup R+D entitled 'Building Performance and Cost-in-Use' has delivered a methodology whereby designers, building owners and occupiers will be able to access good historical data on the performance of buildings in use, enabling a meaningful conversation to take place around the life-cycle cost plan when design proposals are submitted.

Although the operating, maintenance and replacement costs are not a significant part of the investment valuation (see Chapter 5.1) they do assume very considerable importance during the life of a building where money has to be found for them. Equally important, of course, is the fact that maintenance and refurbishment costs absorb almost half of the output of the construction industry in the UK in any one year.

## 1.2.5 THE FUNCTIONAL PERFORMANCE OF BUILDINGS

Most decisions to spend money on buildings in the name of higher quality cannot be formally justified in terms of return on investment because the 'benefit' side cannot be quantified or evaluated. Thus, natural stone facing is perceived as higher quality than the reconstituted variety: we know the cost differential in both capital and life-cycle terms but what value does natural stone add to bottom-line profit (assuming that the options are both permissible)? The same question-mark hangs over investment in faster, bigger lifts, comfort cooling and so on right through the elements.

**FIG. 1.2.C:** *Zero-based budget – added cost/benefit analysis*

| Subject: | Partitions | Estimated Cost |
|---|---|---|
| Location: | Cellular Offices | |
| Zero-base | Metal stud and plasterboard | £10,000 |
| Proposal | Proprietary demountable | £25,000 |
| Subjective Evaluation | | |
| Effect of proposal on functional performance | Perceived quality | Better |
| | Visual Ambience | Better |
| | Comfort | - |
| | Ergonomics | - |
| | Flexibility | Better |
| | Safety | - |
| Effect of proposal on operating costs | Cleaning | - |
| | Energy | - |
| | Maintenance & Repairs | Better |
| | Security | - |
| | Insurance | - |
| | Replacement | Worse |
| | Management | Better |

Anecdote abounds, but good hard data is difficult, if not impossible, to find. There can be little doubt that higher perceived quality in a building can, in many cases, improve the efficiency of the operation going on within it. However, techniques enabling clients to make decisions on performance are not in proliferation. One rather simple pragmatic method is illustrated in **FIG 1.2.C** whereby the client and the design team may sit around and review some of the more significant items of expenditure and consider the financial, physical and functional implications without necessarily getting involved in cost/benefit analysis of a complex nature.

That is not to say that the cost/benefit analysis should not be carried out. Indeed, the concept whereby all design decisions are made on the basis of justification of expenditure over and above a zero base is at the heart of the new thinking on value-engineering. The problem here again is one of measurement and valuation: you can measure the payback on energy efficiency measures but how do you value the comfort implications of the sound reduction qualities of double glazing.

An answer to that could, in the first instance, be approximated by the use of sensitivity analysis of variations in efficiency; over time, the constant flow of such calculations would encourage the necessary research to take place in order that the quantification process should become more scientific and valid.

This brings us to the consideration of how the functional efficiency of the building influences the overall productivity of an organisation by the way it accommodates it. Chapter 1 discusses the theory by which the level of performance of premises should extend from the business requirement and suggests that the cost of achieving such performance should also be enshrined in the business plan. To achieve such mathematical correlation requires a level of understanding of the concept of the functional value of buildings which is totally missing from current practice and procedure in cost estimating and investment valuation.

## 1.2.6 THE FINANCIAL PERFORMANCE OF BUILDINGS

*Building performance and costs*

As yet there exists no common language between building professionals and their clients whereby the performance required of buildings can be described in terms which are exclusive of specification and design parameters. A quantity surveyor who recently produced a £10m capital expenditure budget for a new headquarters for a firm of chartered accountants was asked whether the building proposed was equivalent to a Vauxhall Cavalier, Ford Scorpio, BMW or Rolls Royce. They were comforted by a Ford Scorpio analogy, although few around the table realised the inaccuracy of such subjective assessment.

However, if we are to get away from budgeting for new buildings on the basis of what older ones have cost - essential if we are to start to achieve value for money - then we have to invent an alternative language; indeed, not only do we have to invent the language but we have to create a series of cost analyses which accurately reflect the expenditure required to achieve the described performance.

Performance is of course a key to the ability to value-engineer building solutions. In its simplest but most profound definition, value-engineering is the 'elimination of redundant performance' ie: the avoidance of expenditure on any item of construction which does not add value to the product or which makes the product achieve more than is required. (see Chapter 2.2).

Although the operating costs must be taken into account in building design and specification, value engineering must look beyond the cost consequences of physical performance if the building is to have a real impact on the organisation's efficiency and hence profitability. That means that decisions about cost levels must be related to functional values rather than physical costs. Techniques being developed in Finland by the University of Tampere are breaking new ground in this respect by producing costed schedules of alternative qualities of specification and performance achievement across all the building elements.

*Building performance and valuation*

Professional valuers tend not to understand functional values - or, if they do, they disregard their formal consideration in the process of the 'black art'.

Property developers and investors are guided by these valuers and their first cousins the estate agents who purport to know 'what the market demands'.

Generally speaking, as discussed in Chapter 3.3 - Investment Valuation, market valuation is made by reference to 'comparative valuation' ie having regard to current transactions involving similar property. There is nothing at all wrong with that apart from the fact that the computation supporting the transaction underlying the comparable valuation may itself be inaccurate. It may well be a case of the blind leading the blind.

What we therefore need is for someone to produce a valuation of a property which reflects its performance in terms of the business requirement - one of which features may well be the location; however, in spite of the old myth, propounded by estate agents, that the three most important features of a property are 'location, location and location' this may not be the principal determining factor.

Several methodologies of performance evaluation are already available. For instance the Building Quality Assessment (BQA) procedure which originated in Australia and New Zealand is now being validated by the Building research Establishment for UK and European application. It consists of a sophisticated software program with market weighting for various performance characteristics established by reference to consultants, users and property owners. The output is an Index of Performance which can be used on a comparative basis to assess the relative usefulness of one building to another.

The concept of 'serviceability', developed by Gerald Davies in Canada, is also helping users to measure the usefulness of a building's capacity in the context of their own specific needs.

Frank Duffy et al in studies of 'Intelligent Buildings' and 'The Responsible Workplace' have also shown a way forward in understanding the true worth of well-designed premises and facilities and Frank Becker and Robertson Ward Jnr in the USA are among others who are also helping to enlighten the conventional wisdom.

Inevitably as the necessary data is made available the appraisal of buildings will have to become more technical, more scientific whether from a construction, valuation or occupation viewpoint. It is crucial that such data covers performance in all its aspects - functional efficiency, physical efficiency and financial efficiency.

In quest of better methods of building performance evaluation the inter-action between the building, its occupants and the activities they carry out within it must become a critical area for consideration. Equally importantly, however, the relationships between building-related costs and other expenditure of organisations must be examined to identify the likely scope for added value, or savings in general costs and the factors that may influence such benefits.

A first step towards a new method for building performance assessment is being researched [1] which will bring together currently available information and expertise so that a comprehensive, coherent approach can be developed. This will require a wide range of expert inputs. Major tasks will be to ensure that due weight is given to the various aspects of performance and that the method is sufficiently flexible to cover a wide variety of buildings and occupancies.

When fully developed and evaluated the method should be capable of assessing the performance capabilities of proposed new buildings at the sketch design stage and be equally applicable to refurbishment of existing buildings. In due course it should lead to improvements in functional design and evaluation and result in buildings that meet more closely the requirements of the organisations that occupy them. This, in turn, will lead to considerable savings to the industry and its clients. It is, of course, absolutely vital that the investment valuation process is informed by this new level of understanding of building performance and takes it properly into account.

## 1.2.7 BUILDING PERFORMANCE AND THE FACILITIES MANAGER

The tools are coming into place : the quality assessment programs emerging from current research will all play their part in making it possible, as never before, to measure and value the performance of buildings.

The growing awareness of the need to operate and manage facilities effectively and an inevitable increase in the involvement of facilities managers in the design process will make a fundamental difference to the way buildings are commissioned, designed, maintained and refurbished. More and more the Facilities Manager and his consultants will become involved in life-cycle cost analysis, projecting their asset plans, and reviewing project proposals in the context of the overall business requirement. Inevitably this will impact upon property rents, yields and hence on values.

Most of all, however, the facilities manager's informed involvement should contribute to the delivery of valuable buildings which exactly meet the business need at exactly the right price.

---

[1]    'The functional performance of buildings' (BWA / Oxford Brookes University / BRE)

# SECTION 2

# FACILITIES MANAGEMENT

# CHAPTER 2.1 – FACILITIES AND CORE BUSINESS MANAGEMENT

## 2.1.1 SCOPE OF FACILITIES MANAGEMENT

*The emergence of facilities management*

The term 'facilities management' originated in the USA. Thankfully, under the persistent preaching of the UK space-planning pioneers, particularly Dr. Francis Duffy and Professor John Worthington, the term gained acceptance in the UK and was adopted by the emerging professional and educational bodies. This acceptance was prodded hard by the publication of the UK's first sector-dedicated journal 'Facilities' [1]

[From the outset 'Facilities' contained a regular feature on the subject of facilities economics written by the authors of this work. Demand for increasing data led to the series 'Premises Audits' which was subsequently published as a book [2], the basic tenets of which are herein incorporated]

In spite of this institutional acceptance of the title the function (or part of it) is still found hidden under a bewildering array of alternative titles eg:

- Facilities and Premises Manager

- Facilities, Premises and Offices Services Manager

- Director of Administration Services

- Head of Services

- etc.

The term 'facilities' used in this work categorically subsumes both 'premises' and 'support services'; however, significantly, facilities management as now defined includes a level of strategic responsibility patently missing from the patchwork structures of a decade ago. These **sponsorship** and **'intelligence'** facets of facilities management were introduced in Chapter 1.1 and are further considered below.

The facilities management role has clearly come a long way from the simple service delivery rôle of the maintenance manager and office services manager who, quite independently, used to look after 'patches' which few recognised as having any common theme or policy – even where grouped, for administrative convenience, under common line management.

*The mission statement*

The concept of 'service provision' was discussed in principle in Section 1. The facilities department's mission statement (frequently confused with a 'facilities policy' from which it is several thousand light years removed) should embrace property, premises, support services, risk, cost and change. A further example from real-life is shown at **FIG 2.1.1.A**.

FIG 2.1.1.A: *Facilities management mission statement*

| Quality | Pursue continual improvement of the operating requirement in terms of premises and support services |
|---|---|
| Value | Add or maintain the value of the premises in terms of real estate and contribution to productivity. |
| Risk | Control performance (e.g. safety, efficiency) and costs and be ready for change. |

The mission statement is, however, only a flag-waving exercise; the proof of the pudding is in the eating. Which is not to say that a rallying-call is not a valid contribution in a well-structured management strategy, provided the team members at whom it is directed understand and own the performance level and concept that it is underwriting.

*The facilities management challenge*

The raison d'être of facilities management is summarised in **FIG 2.1.1.B.** Whether such responsibility can reasonably be handed over lock, stock and barrel to an outside agency is one of the major issues facing all organisations seeking to downsize their non-core staff complement.

FIG. 2.1.1.B: *The facilities management challenge*

- **Support effectiveness of organisation, operating units and individuals**

- **Create conditions for continuous quality improvement of service, environment and process**

- **Create and sustain the total workplace**

- **Adapt easily to changing needs and patterns of work**

- **Harness advanced technology**

- **Add value to the organisation**

- **Use resources effectively**

- **Protect the environment**

Source: The Centre for Facilities Management

*Scope of responsibilities*

In its widest definition facilities management embraces the provision and operation of:

- premises

- business support (including I.T.)

- staff support.

The management process involves planning, executing and monitoring the performance of its sector. Performance is judged internally with reference to quality, cost, time and risk and externally on its contribution to the organisation's productivity or profitability.

The cost centres under the control of this broadly drawn management regime are described in Chapter 1.1 and considered individually in detail in the following chapters. The alternative management structures to handle these responsibilities are discussed below together with the economic implications.

*Skill
requirements*

The most important attributes of the prototypical facilities manager emerging in the 1990's are leadership and communication skills. The facilities in a large organisation will be able to function efficiently under a non-technical manager provided that there is an appropriate level of technical proficiency reporting to him - whether from an in-house or an out-sourced regime.

All of the technical skills required in support of facilities management are available externally, if required, either via facilities management contractors or from independent specialist consultants.

Among the more obvious management and specialist skills which facilities management needs to possess or to have access to are:

- business management
- man management
- building design
- interior design
- space management
- 'house' management
- office services management
- energy management
- building maintenance management
- services maintenance management
- property management
- grounds management
- security management
- health & safety management
- catering management
- purchasing management
- motor fleet management
- IT management
- legal advice
- facilities audit
- project management
- financial management
- tax management
- risk management

An amusing film 'The trick is co-ordination' [3] projects the image of the facilities manager as a juggler - 'juggling with the constraints of facilities management' - and sometimes a magician pulling a rabbit out of the hat to meet the demands of some unforeseen crisis. The film is virtual reality, particularly when it stresses the wide range of activities over which the facilities manager has to preside.

There is a general presumption that a modern-day facilities manager cannot - indeed should not - possess all the skills required to make the function happen. Although that may be true, there is an equally strong argument in favour of the facilities manager having sufficient in-depth knowledge of all the activities to know their significance, complexity and cost drivers; most importantly - he must have the knowledge and ability to present and argue a coherent case for each and every corner at top management level.

In the same way that building economics has grown into an amalgam of all the strategic financial and management attributes of surveying so facilities management should eventually subsume the discipline of building economics to add a thorough understanding of premises and real estate to the rather less technical support services skills most have already mastered.

## 2.1.2 MANAGEMENT STRUCTURES

*Facilities management organisation*

Dr. Craig Anderson [4] argues that, since organisations are dynamic self-organising systems, charted structures merely indicate the formal lines of communication rather than what the organisation as a whole is there to do or its organic state. Accepting his argument that a key function of facilities management is the 'brokerage' of knowledge distributed throughout the organisation as much as resource allocation or service management and that this function is not explicit by viewing organisational charts it is nevertheless useful to trace the generic patterns of the organisation of facilities management in the post-World War era in the light of developments in technology and management science.

In the early days there were many organisations who directly employed all the staff needed to run and maintain premises and business support services. It is possible that one or two examples of 100% in-house operation still exist, but probably not on a large scale. The structure at **FIG 2.1.2.A** relates to a traditional **premises management** function in which the core premises management comprised engineer/technology - trained personnel in charge of a direct labour force which carried out nearly all the work except really specialist tasks such as lift maintenance.

**FIG 2.1.2.A:** *Direct labour organisation - minimal outsourcing*

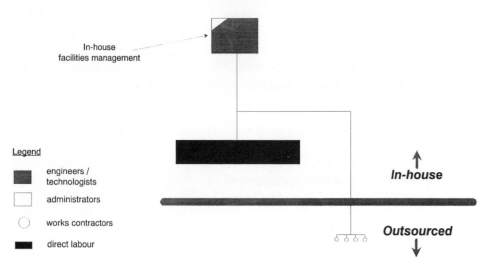

In-house
facilities management

Legend

- engineers / technologists
- administrators
- works contractors
- direct labour

In-house

Outsourced

By the mid-1980's most large organisations outside of the public sector - and many within it - had moved across to out-sourcing of one shape or another.  There are four main versions of the out-sourcing syndrome:

- out-tasking some of the services on separate contracts

- out-tasking all services on separate contracts

- contracting-out on a commercial contract

- a management type of contract

The term 'total facilities management' discussed below is a concept which may or may not apply to the latter two versions.

In the arrangement at **FIG 2.1.2.B** certain of the non-engineering operations such as cleaning and security are out-sourced (as 'contracted-out' used to be called before jargon invaded facilities management), with tasks such as the maintenance of heating, air-conditioning and electrical services and the repair and maintenance of the 'fabric' retained as an in-house operation.

**FIG. 2.1.2.B:** *Outsourcing some of the premises services*

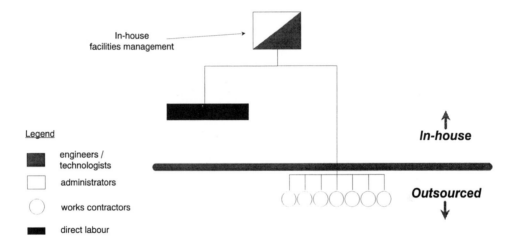

This arrangement has three main perceived advantages:

- specialist contractors can do their work without the need for dedicated in-house supervision

- in-house maintenance teams can respond quickly to emergency service requirements

- the core premises management team can shed its 'blue-collar' image by replacing technicians/technologists with non-specialist administrators

However, by the end of the 1980's most premises departments in larger organisations looked like the set-up in **FIG 2.1.2.C**:  just a small handyman gang to sort out 'special' problems, with all main delivery of accommodation services being provided by individual specialist works contractors or small - 'part-bundled' - groups of specialist contractors under a main contractor.

This arrangement sometimes extended, and still extends, to the provision of general and engineering maintenance on site by resident contractors on either a lump sum contract, some form of schedule of measured rates or cost reimbursement.  It has been accompanied by a shrinking of the core premises management team - both technical and administrative - but with an increase in the calibre of the non-technical staff supporting the interface of the core business and the out-sourced service delivery.

**FIG 2.1.2.C:** *Outsourcing virtually all premises services on separate or 'bundled' contracts*

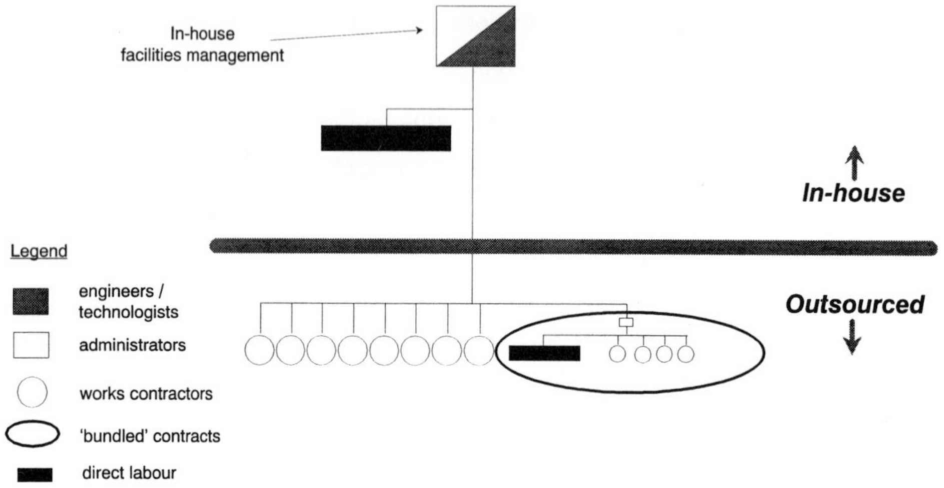

Commercial contracting, ie: the provision of predetermined accommodation services for a single price per annum, schedule of rates, or both, as depicted at **FIG 2.1.2.D**, is liable to lead to the employer losing control of the costs and quality of the services provided; this, together with the inevitable non-scheduled works, claims and conflict of interests intrinsic to any lump sum contract arrangement, explains why the process of task-contract management is becoming a more popular alternative.

**FIG. 2.1.2.D:** *Outsourcing on a commercial contract*

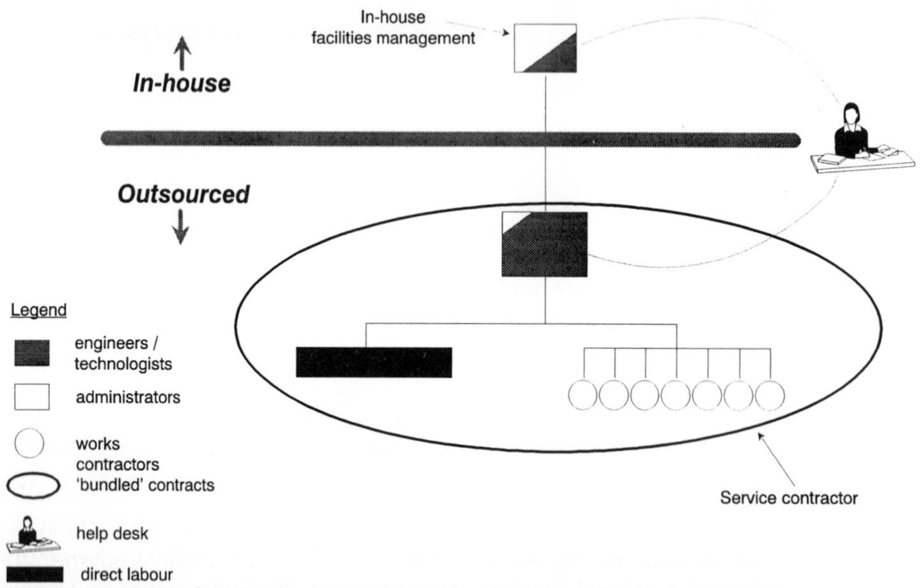

The process depicted at **FIG 2.1.2.E** is similar to the management contracting and construction management routes applying in construction work and described in more detail in Chapter 6.3. Basically, they involve payment of a lump sum or percentage or sliding scale fee to a contractor or management company to organise and manage the tasks to an agreed specification and budget; the employer will sometime enter into direct contract with the works contractors using a **managing agent** to co-ordinate the service provision, or the principal management contractor may interpose contractually and as the paying agent. However, in both cases the employer is committed to pay the price charged by the works contractors and is at direct risk of their default, albeit that the managing agent or management contractor will work to mitigate problems.

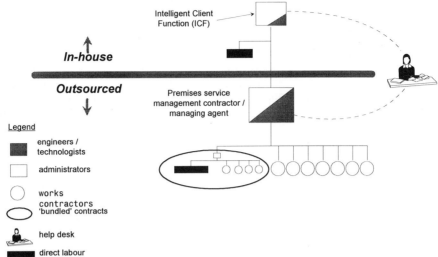

FIG. 2.1.2.E: *Outsourcing on a management contract*

FIGS 2.1.2.F and G extend the two generic variants of the total out-sourcing of premises to embrace support services thereby generating not only a **facilities management** regime but also the concept of **total facilities management.**

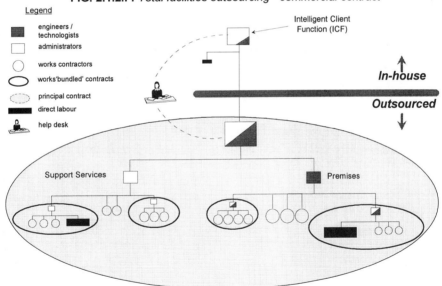

FIG. 2.1.2.F: *Total facilities outsourcing - commercial contract*

FIG. 2.1.2.G: *Total facilities outsourcing - management contract*

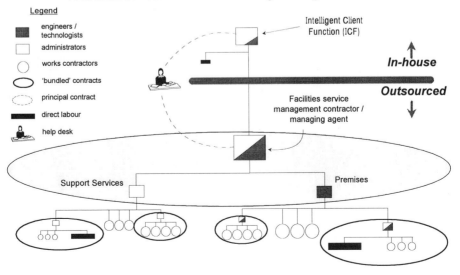

Here again the service management arrangement may either involve the client in direct contract with all suppliers of services using a managing agent to effect delivery or the service manager may himself interpose as the principal. In either case the service manager will receive a fee geared to his management; payment to service suppliers will be on an open-book cost reimbursement basis.

All of these regimes require in-house management teams of varying sizes. However, the total management package of the latter two genres need only a small kernel of core staff to liaise with the out-source partner - and some organisations are now questioning whether a simple Board Director/contractor relationship could be appropriate, thereby eliminating **all** non-core facilities personnel. Although this may be appropriate for smaller firms, in general failure to institute a robust **'Intelligent Client Function' (ICF** – see below and also Chapter 1.1) is a recipe for total disaster.

*Structures for in-house management*

The on-going protracted debate about out-sourcing (see below) has possibly disguised the fact that for many years facilities have been managed on a part-in/part-out-house basis. Contract services for work such as 'cleaning', 'maintenance', and 'security' have for long been acceptable as an alternative to the payroll liability for teams of Mrs. Mops' and Bill Bloggs'.

Where the in-house direct labour structure prevails in a substantial form there is a need for well qualified management, both blue and white collar, to brief and supervise their work. This can amount to a sizeable overhead, especially if their reimbursement is linked to general salary scales within the organisation which may result in payment at higher-than-open-market levels for their skills. Furthermore, in practice, the contractor's equivalent manager may well find himself supervising a larger volume of work on different sites; 'Parkinson's Law' is always a threat to the economic efficiency of in-house regimes.

At the in-house operatives' end of the issue the problem of uncompetitive wage levels also applies, and management may have to deal directly with Trade Union disputes, representations and working practices. A premises audit carried out in a Financial Services organisation a few years back uncovered a building services maintenance cost three times the sector norm. Further investigations uncovered plumbing fitters with salaries linked to the Bank's general scales working a shift system affording them an income of £35,000pa; this, together with a complete absence of either stock control or financial management, produced a level of expenditure in line with the worst abuses of the in-house process.

**FIG 2.1.2.H:** *Traditional hierarchical management structure*

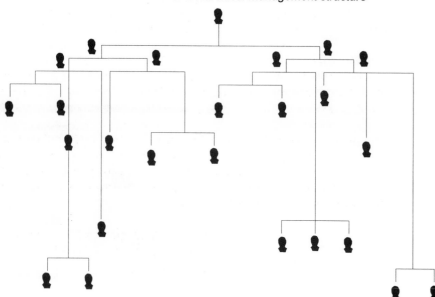

An in-house team set up to provide any services on a directly managed basis should identify that component of staff which could be replaced by contractors and 'market-test', either formally - as with Government, Local Authority and some corporate commercial departments – or by benchmarking using the services of a facilities auditor.

There are as many structures for in-house departments as there are departments. However, **FIG 2.1.2.H** gives a generic model based on the 'pyramid' style of mainly in-house management currently being questioned (and frequently replaced) by proponents of the 'flatter' management structures appropriate to a re-engineered 'intelligent client' status.

*The 'intelligent client'*

**FIG 2.1.2.J** shows how such a flatter structure can be obtained in facilities management by simplifying the management hierarchy within the department, outsourcing the day-to-day running of the facilities services and rationalising the former middle management into more of a 'team' structure.

**FIG. 2.1.2.J:** *'Flatter' and slimmer management structure*

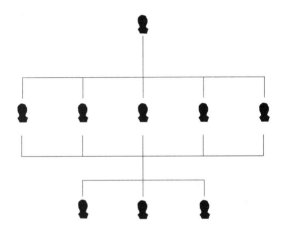

**Regardless of the shape of the network it is imperative that strategic responsibility for the overall function lies within the organisation, that the personnel entrusted with sponsoring that responsibility have the appropriate levels of skill and motivation and that they have control over and have unrestricted access to all essential data - including costs - and systems.**

It is extremely important to recognise that as well as husbanding resources the strategic role of the facilities manager equally involves intelligence gathering; he must constantly be aware of the way the business is developing and the consequential effects on the facilities policy and the strategies in place for its delivery.

**In a fully devolved outsourced regime the residual 'intelligent client' remains the creator and guardian of the facilities policy, constantly looking inwards to the core activity, picking up signs of change to be accommodated, prompting alternative but efficient changes in procedure which will reduce and/or add value to the facilities overhead.**

In a less black-and-white structure this strategic function must be recognised and given its reign (preferably independence) even amidst the hurly-burly of day-to-day contract administration and man-management.

Ideally, in the larger organisation, the facilities manager should be a Board appointment. It has historically been quite common for 'property' to command a Board position, so, if the thesis proposed here ie: that property asset management should be a sub-set of facilities, and given that some or all of the other non-core services can be provided in the global structure being considered, then the level of expenditure and scope of responsibilities being managed in such a regime would clearly justify representation.

When facilities have to report through the Director of Finance, Property, Personnel, Legal or any other discipline, there is always the danger that their case may not be properly understood or appreciated.

Certainly many of the older school of Finance Directors still see facilities as a necessary evil, the first port of call at times of adverse cash flow; no way will they argue a case to increase facilities budgets to generate increased overall productivity.

Property directors have traditionally put the emphasis on premises as real estate investments rather than admitting their real function which is as an invaluable piece of 'plant' to accommodate the activities envisaged by the corporate plan.

In many respects, if facilities has to get to the Board via another discipline an obvious spokesperson would be the Personnel Director, given the interaction with people which is at the heart of the facilities manager's mission. However, as has been stressed several times elsewhere in this text, it is the calibre of the people that counts, much more than the regime in which they find themselves, always provided that such regime does not physically or philosophically impede delivery of the required facilities performance.

## 2.1.3 OUTSOURCING

### The objectives

The arguments in respect of core v non-core activities have already been developed in Section 1 and the sort of facilities management structures suitable to deal with the outsourcing of large parts of the facilities management activities were described earlier in this Chapter.

Aside from the philosophical arguments about core/non-core activities there are a number of practical reasons why out-sourcing may, in certain cases, work to the core business advantage. These concern:

- cost
- quality
- motivation
- flexibility
- availability of skills.

In theory, there is no reason why a fully resourced in-house team should not carry out its functions as efficiently as any external agent - and save the company the contractor's mark-up for profit and risk (not overheads, however, for they will be common). In practice, however, there are few examples of such efficiency; the advent of benchmarking as a near-standard procedure has shown many in-house set-ups to be uncompetitive in financial and performance terms. Unfortunately for them the general reaction of core management has been to go straight to an outsourced solution rather than afford an opportunity to re-engineer the old team structure.

In such cases the objectives often have as much to do with getting rid of an internal management problem such as Trades Union negotiations, difficult personalities and committed, inflexible cash-flow as any real belief in the added value promised by the contractors.

*Cost issues*

The costs of a fully-resourced in-house team - ie: one which directly employs all, or substantially all, of the management, technical and operational staff required to carry out the facilities activities - are usually higher than those emanating from an out-sourced solution.

The reasons for this are many and varied, but stem from two main sources:

- the lack of competition
- over-provision

Lack of competition, as has been discussed earlier, can be addressed by market testing and benchmarking. Nevertheless, there are issues aside from the market place which can cause the in-house regime to be more expensive:

- size of operation
- in-house pay structures
- trades union activity
- experience

Of all these issues it is the size of the operation which is the most critical. An organisation running all its own facilities will need the resources of all the management skills described earlier in the Chapter. Even if these were available in-house the likelihood of every one being 'best of breed' or fully gainfully occupied would be remote. A good example of this is considered under 'Health & Safety at Work' in Chapter 8.2. Here it is seen that, once the project stage of implementing the new legislation is over, the rationale of having a full-time Health & Safety Officer often recedes; 'sharing' becomes a viable option, or specialist consultancy services can take a lot of responsibility off the facilities manager's shoulders.

The key danger is that the organisation's needs will not exactly fit the **optimum** resource required to service this. So, a qualified services engineer running the in-house maintenance team may only need to be 70% occupied in that role given the scale and nature of the activity; nevertheless the chances are that he will either

- work at only 70% efficiency

or

- work at 100% efficiency and over-provide services

'Right sizing', to use the jargon, is the problem here because, in a similar position with a contractor, he would be given responsibility for other sites and thus add to his organisation's bottom line profit.

Linking trades management and operations to in-house pay structures will, in most cases, result in wages and salaries higher than the levels available to the building services and general labour sectors of the external / commercial workforce. Add to this the propensity for non-competitive, unbenchmarked management of in-house departments and Trades Union demands (reasonable or otherwise) in respect of working practices and it is not difficult to see how the in-house effort could cost two, or even three, times the external market norm.

Another major problem for the in-house team is the rate at which their accumulated experience gets out of date once they are removed from the fertile, competitive, cross-company contracting environment which is so essential to the ability of any individual to retain his market-edge in knowledge and pragmatism. The mere fact of being separated from day-to-day contact with one's peer group is enough to result in fall-off in ability, including loss of confidence, within a matter of months rather than years. An even worse problem is the prolonged application of increasingly out-dated concepts to the organisation's changing requirements.

---

These problems mainly relate to the qualified middle-management tier of facilities ie: the level which can easily be replaced by an external counterpart. At the operational level formal training programmes can do the trick, and at senior management level there should be sufficient daily contact with core management to guarantee keeping abreast of new management techniques; in any event, technology changes many times faster than management principles

Some facilities departments have moved over to becoming a profit centre in their own right - either externally structured with parent company equity participation or wholly owned in-house. This concept of saving costs for - whilst earning a profit from – the parent organisation has its attractions as a concept, especially where contracting non-core services to other companies is part of the business plan. Such examples are, however, still in their early years; it remains to be seen, over time, how the core business will fare within the new regime as core and non-core services diverge commercially accompanied by replacement of original facilities personnel.

## Quality issues

The trade-off between cost and quality of service is critical and is the most important factor in the outsourcing decision. Well-managed in-house departments frequently run up costs of facilities way above the outsourced norm simply by **over-providing** quality of service. This feature is particularly common in the more affluent companies where the cost of facilities is not seen as significant and the excuse given for exceeding cost benchmarks is that the higher quality is appropriate to their business needs and status. However, wasted resources are wasted resources wherever they surface and all companies have a moral obligation to make the best use of whatever resources they bring to bear on the operation of their business.

Insistence on quality in facilities management has to follow through into any outsourcing arrangement. BS EN ISO 9000, or a commitment to it, may be relevant to some contracts but much more important is a perceived and proven dedication to

- customer's satisfaction
- training
- continuous improvement
- flexibility
- systems
- controls
- procedures
- management.

These qualities, together with the supplier's financial status, can easily be checked out by references. Whether quality is delivered will, in the event, be less dependent upon the management regime than the calibre of the people given responsibility for the mission. Nevertheless the people responsible for delivery must be made properly aware of the quality required if under- or over-provision of quality is to be avoided in any of the delivery structures.

## Motivation

Examples of the state of inertia which used to prevail in many parts of the public sector and the large corporate commercial organisations have considerably reduced in the past decade. The big in-house facilities teams are far better motivated than of yore, partly due to the sense of being part of and contributing to the evolution of a new discipline. Better education in the subject area, an elevation in its perceived importance and an increasingly higher calibre of senior facilities managers have improved motivation enormously across the board. Gone is the sinecure for the line manager who screwed up but could not be fired; he has been (or soon will be) replaced by a dedicated, highly motivated go-getter who may or may not be a salaried member of staff.

The man-and-boy 'company man' is now an anachronism, although the few examples of the 'one-firm firm' continue this philosophy to good advantage. Elsewhere, the modern facilities workforce is motivated by prospects of reward and advancement. In the out-sourced facilities company both are easier to come by than in the in-house equivalent which is part of a non-core department perceived as an **overhead** rather than a **profit-centre**.

The first serious wave of examples of transfers of in-house staff to contractors indicate that motivation can be enhanced by a change in management style, and working environment.

## Flexibility

The well-structured external contract should afford the requisite level of response to emergency change without the employer being unduly exposed to financial risk.

The directly employed workforce is, in theory at least, able to be moved from project to project, emergency to emergency, under the direct control of the organisation and without risk of contractual claims for disruption, out-of-sequence working, etc. Where it is inflexible is where companies need to cut back temporarily on expenditure on facilities provision. In times of reduced demand, the contractor can usually re-deploy spare operatives on other sites, where he is probably operating slightly below projected resource quotas to optimise efficiency. Likewise, the contractor or consultant can usually find the resource required for a special task or project.

However, in-house teams sometimes do not have the authority to take on temporary relief staff as easily as their external counterparts.

## The availability of skills

The multiplicity of skills needed in facilities management cannot all be reasonably brought in-house, so some out-sourcing is virtually inevitable.

The problem is more exaggerated where the organisation has smaller facilities requirements, in which case full-time appointments of specialists such as space planners, quantity surveyors, health & safety experts, engineers etc is not viable.

In the large organisations, where it may be financially feasible to employ expensive qualified professionals, the costs incurred may be lower than the comparable consultants' fees but this benefit may be offset by:

- difficulty of efficiently matching resource to tasks
- lack of cross-fertilisation of ideas.

The problem of over-resourcing particular functions was discussed earlier in this chapter. Under-resourcing is also a problem where the task outgrows the resource, in which case outsourced assistance is usually needed to complement either numbers, or skills, or both.

A major weakness of the in-house professional appointment is the difficulty of enticing high-flying specialists away from a lucrative consulting career. Of course, not every post needs a high-flyer but pursuit of excellence demands good quality personnel in all key posts.

A good professional will look for good ideas as he goes about his business. As he finds them he will tend to plug them into other regimes where similar functions are being handled less efficiently. Consequently, the biggest problem with plucking a consultant or contracting professional out of his familiar environment and inserting him into a cross-disciplined team is the rapid loss of contact with his peer group which means that the **cross-fertilisation of ideas** which the external consultant transfers from one client to another, one project to another, is lost.

## 2.1.4 DEVOLVED RESPONSIBILITY

*Procurement
and the budget*

A common water-shed in terms of the in/out-source syndrome is the location of the **'budget holder'**. Some organisations hand over the budget completely to the out-source agent and only want to know if things are going wrong. Others want to control everything in-house on a 'open-book' basis; some 'profit-sharing', or 'savings over existing levels' deals are carried out on this basis.

The concept of allowing contractors or consultants to share in the saving they make over existing budgets is seriously flawed. It is a route sometimes adopted by facilities managers who do not have authority to spend money on consultancy fees; it usually results in the sum given away being many times greater than would have been paid to a consultant to help get the level of existing costs down by application of the three facets of cost control discussed in Chapter 2.2 below.

It is imperative that the **cost** and **performance** of the facilities which are to be provided is thoroughly benchmarked before the out-sourced arrangement is put in place. That way the contractor will be bidding on the quality of the services he will deliver and manage, not on the degree of sloppiness featuring in the current cost and management regime.

*The partnership
approach*

However, facilities management is not, or should not be, just about money. In recognition of this, most serious contenders for the innumerable varieties of out-sourcing are now extolling the virtues of a 'partnership' approach; this longer-term relationship again entails the in-house facilities manager in an ICF rôle briefing and monitoring the performance of the external manager, being responsible for all strategic decisions and forming an essential interface between the external team and the core-business activity.

In this case, the facilities service manager will be seeking a long-term partnering arrangement whereby both he and his client can benefit from a continuing improvement of performance in both camps over time.

*The devolved
risk*

Stephen Harrup's [5] lucid illustration of the extent to which core business is put at risk through inadequate provision of facilities the further away from 'in-house' the provision of non-core service functions stretches is given at **FIG 2.1.4.A**

The key features in risk management in procuring outsourced service functions are:

- tight, professionally constructed contracts (and that does not necessarily mean by lawyers - many lawyers are very bad at drafting contracts for technologically-based services)

- tight, professionally constructed specifications

- full investigation of potential contractor's financial standing, track record, management and training procedures and control systems

- insistence on full disclosure of all data - to be available on client's premises at all times

- employer's right to choose or reject key personnel

- quality control procedures

- performance levels, indicators, methods of measurement, bonuses and penalties

- mechanisms for dispute resolution.

**FIG 2.1.4.A:** Devolution of service function from the core function – degree of risk

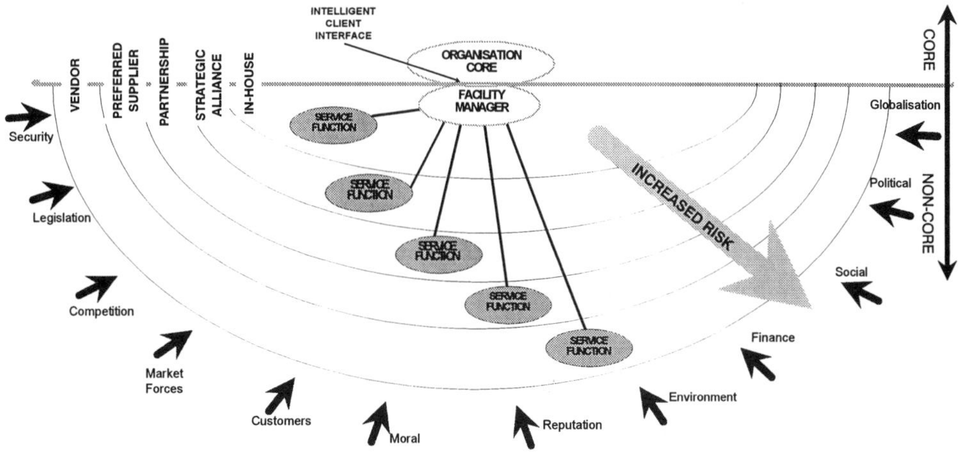

Source: Stephen Harrup

The 'partnership management contract' approach particularly aims to avoid disputes and undoubtedly, given the right personnel, can elevate the contracting-out process to a much more professionally committed plane.

## The help desk

The days when the premises manager used to pin up notes of telephone requests to deal with problems are long gone. In place of the pin-board it is normal to have either a formal manual register or a computerised help desk system.

Apart from the obvious need to find out what emergencies are about and how they are being handled, the help desk has two other most important functions – public relations and customer satisfaction.

The corollary of those functional activities is that the interposition of this agency of facilities management should not distance the managers from personal contact with their customers.

A personalised approach, either by way of a formal physical enquiry point, a dedicated telephone help-line team, or both, can be an invaluable help to the facilities management team to gain the respect and confidence of their customers.

Performance targets and achievements should be publicly displayed - this will help the team to a better performance as well - and customer feed-back on the quality of service delivered, both at the helpdesk and the coal-face, actively encouraged.

The system will have three key operating functions:

- incident reporting
- workload processing
- process monitoring.

Whether the help-desk is manned by the in-house or the out-sourced team may not be too significant provided that both have access to it for reference. Insofar as it can also function in a performance-monitoring capacity it may usefully form the focal point for any performance-related remuneration for an out-sourced service manager or vendor.

(1)  'Facilities' – (formerly the Bulstrode Press, now MCB University Press)

(2)  'Premises Audits' – (The Bulstrode Press – now out of publication)

(3)  Steelcase - Strafor

(4)  'A facilities evaluation praxis for knowledge generation in social systems.' (PhD. thesis)

(5)  Stephen Harrup MSc (Facilities Management) – CFM University of Strathclyde – extract from thesis

# CHAPTER 2.2 – FACILITIES MANAGEMENT FUNCTIONS

## 2.2.1 FINANCIAL MANAGEMENT

*The principles*

Financial management is the process of ensuring that the funds available to an organisation for the purposes of running its business are used effectively, readily accessible and properly accounted for.

Accounting for funds is a re-active function whereby moneys earned and expended and assets bought, sold and depreciated are accounted for according to a pre-scribed convention at agreed intervals.

The facilities manager will need to understand these conventions and be able to interpret the financial position of his own and other organisations from scrutiny of their trading accounts.

However, this text is not concerned with the re-active accounting process. The facilities manager must first and foremost understand the pro-active component of financial management ie: ensuring effective use of financial resources and making sure that necessary funds are readily available.

Although the facilities manager cannot control the amount of money the business has available at any one time he can make sure that, for his part, there is enough money available in his sector of the overall budget to meet the commitments emanating from his facilities policy and strategies. So, when he does commit the company to expenditure on facilities, it should be on the basis that it is:

- the right amount
- at the right price
- for the right service
- within budget.

**FIG. 2.2.1.A:** *Three facets of cost control - inter-relationships*

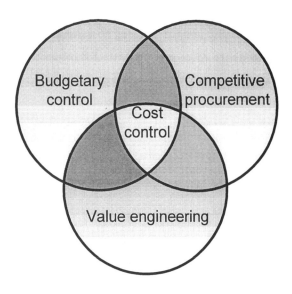

These requirements can only be met with proper application of the principles of financial control ie: with thorough application of competitive procurement, value engineering and budgetary control.

These three facets of financial control are inter-dependent; the absence or misapplication of any one of them will put financial control at risk. **FIG 2.2.1.A** illustrates this inter-dependence.

*Competitive procurement*

This term describes **the process whereby products are created or purchased at or below the general price level at which similar products may be purchased in the market place.**

It does not mean that every project, service or item of office equipment has to be put out to tender; it merely means that the price paid has to be that which is known to be competitive in the market-place.

The facilities manager may be responsible for procurement of a wide range of facilities in widely differing market conditions. In many cases he may delegate the procurement process to specialists, eg to the Purchasing Departments for office stationery, to the quantity surveyor for the fitting-out project. Nevertheless, he must accept overall responsibility for the efficiency of the procurement of facilities and always have a considered and well informed opinion as to the most suitable purchasing procedure and a well referenced list of potential suppliers.

The procurement of fitting-out projects is discussed in detail in Section 6 and new construction in Section 10.

*Value Engineering*

Value engineering is **the process whereby products and services are provided to the required performance for the least cost. It requires the elimination of any 'redundant performance'**, ie should not permit the design or specification of a product or service to impute costs in respect of performance criteria which are not necessary to support the business requirement.

Examples might be:

- cleaning down the internal partitions twice a week when once a month is adequate

- using white envelopes to send out overdue credit reminders when brown manila would do

- designing building floors to carry a superimposed loading of 6KN/sq.m when 5KN/sq.m is perfectly suitable.

All these examples presume that the excess provision does not add value to the business. It is this process of value analysis which makes value engineering such an important feature of facilities economics.

There is a school of thought which suggests that there is a process called 'value management' which subtends value engineering. The implication is that value management considers financial **strategies** whereas value engineering is only concerned with the use of economical **tactics**. However, without wishing to waste the reader's time with undue didactics, the quest in search of value for money permeates all business decisions and the process of achieving it does not change from one level of the business hierarchy to another.

Setting a budget which is dependent upon value engineering for achievement may be called value management, but it is nonetheless an essential and integral part of the process of value engineering.

Far more important than terminology is the concept of 'value' which has to be properly understood before the value engineering process can be implemented.

In the context of physical performance value can be assessed in terms of a return on an investment delivering cost reductions. So, investing £10,000 in an energy conservation tool which saves £2,500 pa in electricity costs, shows a return on initial investment of 25% p.a. before tax. If the organisation's criterion rate of return for such an investment is 15% then value has been added; similarly, where £1m spent on refurbishment of the headquarters building results in the asset value being increased by £2m.

However, if the organisation's public relations image is damaged by the distribution of 'payment overdue' reminders in brown manila envelopes instead of the snappy, crisp embossed parchment enclosing its normal missives then the saving in cost may well produce a **negative return** - but how can anyone prove it?

This is the real problem with value engineering. Most individual centres of non-core business expenditure are of little significance in isolation in the context of overall turnover, yet any modification to the service they are financing, either upwards or downwards, may well have an impact on the business at the point of interaction many times in excess of the money saved or spent - see **FIG 2.2.1.B**.

**FIG. 2.2.1.B:** *Typical turnover, profit and facilities costs (excluding I.T.)*

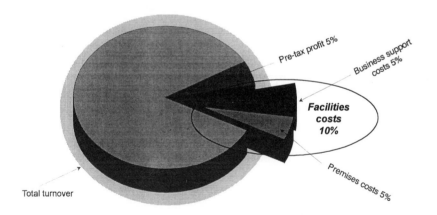

This interaction between facilities and the efficiency of core activity is vastly under-researched and un-documented. **Until such time as good data on benefits and disbenefits emanating from facilities decisions is available value engineering appraisal will needs be restricted, in many cases merely to sophisticated objective optimisation of trivial issues on the one hand and crude subjective assessments of major issues on the other.**

Perhaps the time will come when the added cost of 'image' in the 'name architect's' eccentric design will come out of the marketing director's budget; a comprehensive performance assessment built up on similar lines to the real life example in **FIG 2.2.1.C** would certainly focus the mind of the Board when commissioning their new Headquarters. In fact, the concept of zero-base budgeting as a means of applying value engineering techniques to all aspects of financial appraisal - not just for facilities - has much to commend it.

**FIG 2.2.1.C:** *Performance appraisal - zero-based budget approach*

| Subject: | Rooflights | **Estimated cost** |
|---|---|---|
| Location: | Restaurant/bar | |
| Zero-base | No rooflights | Nil |
| Proposal: | 5 No of rooflights | £20,000 |
| **Subjective Evaluation** | | |
| **Effect of proposal on functional performance** | Perceived quality | Better |
| | Visual ambience | Better |
| | Comfort | - |
| | Ergonomics | - |
| | Flexibility | - |
| | Safety | - |
| **Effect of proposal on operating costs** | Cleaning | Worse |
| | Energy | Better |
| | Maintenance & repairs | Worse |
| | Security | Worse |
| | Insurance | - |
| | Replacement | Worse |
| | Management | Worse |

*Budgetary Control*

This is **the process whereby appropriate budgets are calculated and agreed, and expenditure against them monitored before and after commitment, to ensure that once budgets are set they are neither under-spent nor exceeded other than to meet variations in the performance criteria or market conditions upon which they were based.**

Some of the words used in the definition are particularly significant.

**Appropriate** budgets means that they should be suitable for the service to be provided. They must presume that the procurement and value engineering processes will be efficient and not allow any slack which might allow default in either or both facets to go unnoticed.

Monitored **before commitment** implies a pro-active process in which the budget controller assesses the potential impact of a prospective financial event upon the planned cost for that particular cost centre. First of all comes the idea, then the quotation; they can both be tested in the **pro-active** phase. Any invoice resulting from commitment will be processed in the **reactive** phase ie will be recorded to compute the extent of any under- or over-expenditure. These two distinct phases of budgetary control are illustrated in **FIG 2.2.1.D**. Although most budgetary control systems in facilities and general management are of the reactive variety it is clearly unsatisfactory to have to rely upon a system which tells you how much you have over-spent when it is too late to do other than pay the bill - assuming the money can be found from elsewhere to do so.

**FIG. 2.2.1.D:** *Pro-active v reactive styles of cost control*

| Proactive Phase | Reactive Phase |
|---|---|
| Planned cost ● | Last date to influence outcome |
| Anticipation of change ● | |
| Decision to change ● | |
| Revised cost agreed ● | |
| Cost incurred | ● |
| Unplanned change ● | |
| Unplanned cost incurred | ● |

The first truly proactive system of budgetary control to be developed in the UK is believed to be the 'Journal System' (c)[1] of cost control of building design and construction, the principles of which have since been enshrined in the '*prem*FINANCE' (c) Facilities Financial Control System.[2]

An underlying tenet of both these programs is that , for budgetary control to be effective, the basis of the forecast must be presented in such a way that both financial controller and purchasers can readily identify potential changes; such presentation will also ensure that purchasers accept responsibility for the adequacy of the specifications supporting the budget figures for work under their direction. **This 'ownership' of the budget is critical; the financial controller must stand up and be counted for his estimating but must not assume responsibility for reading the minds** of those who are going to spend his - no, **their** - budget.

When the budget is formulated it must be expressed in such a way that potential change for a significant item is obvious. For example, if the stationery budget is based upon a headcount of 850 persons it might be expressed as in **FIG 2.2.1.E**. Any increase in numbers during the year should be accompanied by a budget review in advance of commitment to increased expenditure. The detail behind this build up is given in Chapter 7.3 at **FIG 7.3.D**.

**FIG 2.2.1.E:** *Presentation of budget proposals - stationery cost*

| Office services budget 1994/95 | | | |
|---|---|---|---|
| **Cost centre : Stationery** | | Date | Quantity |
| **Benchmark data** | No. of full time employees | 30/9/94 | 850 |
| | No. of executives | 30/9/94 | 100 |
| | No. of wp operators | 30/9/94 | 40 |
| **Budget proposals** | | | £ |
| General office paper products | | | 153,000 |
| Personal desk consumables | | | 51,000 |
| Storage stationery | | | 25,000 |
| Presentation materials | | | 13,000 |
| Administration | | | 5,000 |
| **Total** | | | **247,000** |
| **Total per capita** | | | **290.00** |

Where important budgeted items are not shown explicitly in any documentation their existence and identifying features must always be described. For example, in the design stage for a capital project the engineer might have decided that steel sheet piling may be required in part of the foundations.

**FIG. 2.2.1.F:** *Presentation of budget proposals - calculation and expression of assumptions: extract from the JOURNAL system*

| LOCATION | SPECIFICATION | SOURCE | QUANTITY | UNIT | RATE £ | TOTAL |
|---|---|---|---|---|---|---|
| Generally | Oversite strip including excavating and transporting topsoil to spoil heaps | Site visit | 2,485 | m² | 3.00 | 7,455 |
| Generally | Excavate to reduce levels and dispose material off site including all necessary working space, earthwork support and compacting bottom of excavation | Site visit | 2400 | m³ | 10.00 | 24,000 |
| Generally | 450mm diameter reinforced driven concrete piling average 10m deep | Engineer 16/10/94 | 274 | No. | 200.00 | 54,800 |
| N.W. Corner | Heavy duty steel sheet piling say 80m girth - provisional allowance | Engineer - 25/10/94 | Allowance | - | - | 10,000 |
| | | | | | Rounding Factor | 45 |
| | | | | | ELEMENT TOTAL TO SUMMARY £ | 290,000 |

PROJECT: *Example* — COST STUDY No.2 — DATE: October 1994 — ELEMENT : Substructure

FIG 2.2.1.F shows how the 'Journal' system deals with this, as yet undocumented, potential cost event. When the engineer sets about his detailed design he will refer to this part of the budget (which he has already 'signed off' in principle) and can therefore inform the cost controller as soon as he can confirm, or otherwise, the real extent of the work provisionally predicted. Failure to observe this procedure could mean that:

- project tenders containing a far greater amount of sheet piling than originally envisaged will fall way outside of the cost plan (see chapter 6.3)

or

- incorporation of desirable design features might be obstructed by the financial controller during the design stage only for the team to find out later that the cost of sheet steel piling was not needed after all.

Under-spending the budget, possibly as the result of such a default, can have an adverse effect on performance, possibly even more serious than over-expenditure.

Facilities managers are often heard to claim that calculation of budgets from first principles is pointless given the propensity for change in this volatile business. Actually this argument is self-defeating; it is the risk to financial control inherent in this uncertain regime which renders the recording of 'best-estimate' assumptions a pre-requisite of the pro-active financial control essential to management of that risk.

Chapter 6.3 contains an anecdote of the consequences of under-expenditure resulting from the other major crime in budgetary control - inaccurate estimating. Estimating is a skilled job, and one in which few facilities managers have adequate training, so they should either seek training to do it scientifically or make sure that they have professional help to hand when predicting the costs of substantial commitments.

*Interdependence of the three facets*

When proposing a budget for a project or for the annual expenditure the facilities manager should be anticipating:

- competitive procurement

- value engineering

- efficient budgetary control.

The value engineering exercise, with its basis in anticipated out-turn benefits and costs, is heavily dependent on the cost savings (resulting from getting rid of unwanted performance) turning up in the final analysis - not frittered away in poor procurement or sloppy estimating/budgetary control.

And what is the point of having the world's most efficient Purchasing Department if they buy the wrong product at the best price available - especially if there was no budget for it in the first place?

In order to get value for money in procurement of any component of facilities all three facets of financial control must be actively pursued and diligently applied. Budgeting at the 'right' level will make some of this happen, but knowing what the 'right' level is will continue to present problems until much more research is carried out on the subject of the interaction between facilities and core business activity.

In the meantime benchmarking costs and performance to the 'best of breed' should guarantee a general trend towards added value.

*Financial appraisal techniques*

Premises last a long time, and it is often necessary to compare options involving both initial and future costs. Equally it is necessary to provide funds to replace an asset at the end of its useful life.

Management accountants use the concept of **compound interest** on money invested to enable them to carry out various aspects of investment appraisal. However, whereas replacement funds (sinking funds) are calculated by reference to **accumulation** of compound interest, evaluation of future expenditure is made using the reciprocal of compound interest to discount its value. This technique is known as **discounted cash flow (DCF).**

DCF works on the principle that in order to calculate future payments alongside up-front investments it is necessary to allow for the fact that, for every pound of deferred payment, an investor has the use of that pound and can earn either interest or a commercial return on it in the interim.

Therefore, if £1 is invested at 10% pa by the end of one year it will have earned 10p interest; when the investor has to spend £1 in one year's time he can deduct the 10p from the cost, giving a discounted value of £(1 - 0.1) = £0.9.

If the expenditure were deferred two years 21p interest would be earned making the future payment worth only £(1 - 0.21) - £0.79.

The principle of this computation is fed into tables of DCF factors per £1 known as the 'Present Value of £1' table. The factors may then be extracted relative to any future years and any rate of interest and applied to the total amount of expenditure in each future year. **FIG 2.2.1.G** is an extract from the 'Present Value of £1' tables.

FIG 2.2.1.G: *The present value of £1*

| Years | Rate Per Cent | | | | |
|---|---|---|---|---|---|
| | 9.5 | 10 | 10.5 | 11 | 12 |
| 1 | 0.9132420 | 0.9090909 | 0.9049774 | 0.9009009 | 0.8928571 |
| 2 | 0.8340110 | 0.8264463 | 0.8189841 | 0.8116224 | 0.7971939 |
| 3 | 0.7616539 | 0.7513148 | 0.7411620 | 0.7311914 | 0.7117802 |
| 4 | 0.6955743 | 0.6830135 | 0.6707349 | 0.6587310 | 0.6355181 |
| 5 | 0.6352277 | 0.6209213 | 0.6069999 | 0.5934513 | 0.5674269 |
| 6 | 0.5801166 | 0.5644739 | 0.5493213 | 0.5346408 | 0.5066311 |
| 7 | 0.5297868 | 0.5131581 | 0.4971232 | 0.4816584 | 0.4523492 |
| 8 | 0.4838236 | 0.4665074 | 0.4498853 | 0.4339265 | 0.4038832 |
| 9 | 0.4418480 | 0.4240976 | 0.4071360 | 0.3909248 | 0.3606100 |
| 10 | 0.4035142 | 0.3855433 | 0.3684489 | 0.3521845 | 0.3219197 |

Taking a simple example of three equal annual payments of £2,000, the **net present value** - NPV (ie: net of all discount) of those transactions is calculated as shown in **FIG 2.2.1.H**.

FIG 2.2.1.H: *Calculation of the net present value (NPV) using discount tables*

| | Year 1 £ | Year 2 £ | Year 3 £ | cumulative £ |
|---|---|---|---|---|
| Payment | 2,000 | 2,000 | 2,000 | 6,000 |
| Present value of £1 @ 10% | ×0.909 | ×0.826 | ×0.751 | - |
| Present value for the year | 1,818 | 1,652 | 1,502 | 4,972 |
| Net present value (NPV) cumulative total | | | | 4,972 |

This 'Present Value' table is also the basis of another very important table - the 'Present Value of £1 per Annum'. This gives the accumulation of the net present values of all future annual expenditure (of equal amounts) discounted at the same rate of interest, saving the need to calculate each year as was shown in **FIG 2.2.1.H**. The same calculation but extracting the appropriate figure from the 'Present Value of £1 per Annum' table at **FIG 2.2.1.J** finds the NPV more simply as shown in **FIG 2.2.1.K**.

FIG 2.2.1.J: *An extract from ' present value of £1 per annum' tables*

| Years | Rate Per Cent | | | | |
|---|---|---|---|---|---|
| | 8.75 | 9 | 9.5 | 10 | 11 |
| 1 | 0.9195 | 0.9174 | 0.9132 | 0.9091 | 0.9009 |
| 2 | 1.7651 | 1.7591 | 1.7473 | 1.7355 | 1.7125 |
| 3 | 2.5426 | 2.5313 | 2.5089 | 2.4869 | 2.4437 |
| 4 | 3.2576 | 3.2397 | 3.2045 | 3.1699 | 3.1024 |
| 5 | 3.9150 | 3.8897 | 3.8397 | 3.7908 | 3.6959 |
| 6 | 4.5196 | 4.4859 | 4.4198 | 4.3553 | 4.2305 |
| 7 | 5.0755 | 5.0330 | 4.9496 | 4.8684 | 4.7122 |
| 8 | 5.5866 | 5.5348 | 5.4334 | 5.3349 | 5.1461 |
| 9 | 6.0567 | 5.9952 | 5.8753 | 5.7590 | 5.5370 |
| 10 | 6.4889 | 6.4177 | 6.2788 | 6.1446 | 5.8892 |

**FIG 2.2.1.K:** *Calculation of example at FIG 2.2.1.H using 'present value of £1 per annum table'*

| Annual payment for each of 3yrs £ | Present value of £1 per annum @10% for 3yrs | Net present value (NPV) cumulative total £ |
|---|---|---|
| 2,000 | × 2.487 | 4974* |
| * The slight difference results from rounding the factors in the previous example to 3 decimal places. | | |

The same calculation will apply to income receivable as well as amounts payable and forms the basis of the 'Years purchase' calculation used by valuers to value income-bearing properties. This process is described in detail in Chapter 3.3 - 'Investment valuation'. The tables, along with those for the sinking fund, mortgage payments and others, all have alternatives calculated for the effect of tax at different rates in the £ - fair enough, because tax is payable on investment returns whether manifesting themselves as interest or profits.

A major application of DCF in facilities is in the appraisal of building investment options, particularly with regard to whole-life costs of alternative designs of buildings and their components. Chapter 10.4 - 'Whole-life economics' considers in depth the application of DCF to such option appraisal and also uses the examples to explain DCF in more detail from first principles.

One further appraisal technique using DCF is known as the **Internal Rate of Return - IRR**. This is a process used when there is both positive and negative cash flow over time. A calculation is made of the interest rate at which the sum of the discounted present values of both positive and negative cash flows are equal. This rate of interest is then compared with the organisation's criterion rate of return for such investments; if it is better than the criterion rate the project may go ahead, and vice-versa. Computer programs can work these calculations easily (most spreadsheet programs have them built-in) or the figures can be worked by using 'trial and error' interest rates until the figures balance at the IRR percentage. However the system is considered by many mathematicians to be unreliable where amounts of positive and negative cash flow are irregular, so the technique has not been used in any of the examples in this work.

## 2.2.2 INFORMATION AND APPLICATION MANAGEMENT

*Facilities
information and
applications*

Any management task comprises two distinct phases

- application management

- information management.

So, for example, arranging for the boilers to be serviced is a management **application** whereas knowing their location, condition and history requires management of **information**.

Management applications are described elsewhere in their various sections. Here we deal predominantly with the management of information, a process which is fundamental to the success of the dependent application.

Both phases are mutually informative so it is essential that any facilities management system - be it manual or electronic - must be arranged so as to facilitate feedback and feed-forward of data with the minimum of effort and risk of misplacement. Ideally this system should be automatic, so in principle a computerised data base system will certainly be warranted in any sizeable facilities management operation.

Chapter 7.5 considers the management of information technology on a business-wide basis; this section considers technology available for the day-to-day management of facilities.

**FIG 2.2.2.A** illustrates the concept of a 'data-spine' in which all the information emanating from the design of the building, the provision of supplier services and inventories (ie: short-term assets - see 'Asset Management' below) is retained and set up to receive and disseminate information emanating from the various facilities management applications.

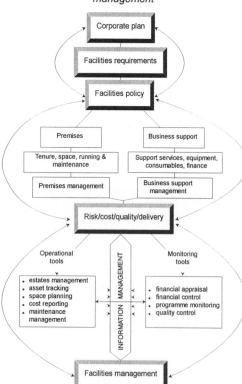

**FIG. 2.2.2.A:** *Facilities management - an integrated approach to information and application management*

This concept of integrating information and application management via a data-spine has been researched and in some cases developed for individual facets of facilities management eg: the 'performance-and-cost-managed-building' study carried out by CFM/BRE/Arup R+D described in Chapter 1.3. Also there are numerous maintenance management packages which link the information from a condition survey to and from on-going maintenance activity to ensure that application and information work in tandem. However, maintenance is only a minor component of facilities management in financial terms and a system to handle the arrangement at **FIG 2.2.2.A** has yet to be fully developed in respect of the whole gamut of facilities management applications.

*CAD-based
facilities
management
systems*

Computer-aided design/draughting systems are becoming increasingly evident in facilities management for three reasons:

- more and more buildings are being designed, and as-built working drawings produced on CAD

- space planning lends itself readily to CAD applications

- data-bases linked to CAD have been developed for facilities management applications

The latter systems are generically referred to as computer-aided facilities management systems (CAFMs) and by the authors as CAFOMs - computer-aided facilities operational management systems. They have the advantage over simple databases in that they can hold facilities data graphically on a full-sized scalable model. To date development of these systems has been geared to the more common applications, particularly:

- maintenance

- space planning

- security

- energy

- property management

- inventory tracking

- personnel tracking and records

- move management.

More recent packages have addressed the thorny problem of cable management, and some of the more sophisticated CAD systems can provide speedy review of all 'as designed' systems facilitating feasibility appraisals by testing at the screen the impact of any proposed modifications without corrupting the base schematic data.

The principal disadvantages of the present generation of CAFOM systems are:

- they comprise add-on applications to simplify existing facilities management functions rather than addressing applications from first principles and integrating application and information requirements

- the cost of systems and, more importantly the resources (including training) required to operate them and keep the data up-to-date is considerably greater than currently generally available to facilities management departments; justifying the additional costs by reference to increased efficiency is difficult in other than a medium to long-term scenario

- the inflexibility of most systems which will not permit the plotting of a **prospective** change without the user either making another copy of the database (a recipe for total confusion) or irrevocably changing the database in advance of real-time developments

- time taken to maintain the accuracy of databases can distract resources from day-to-day hands-on management of the facilities.

There are just too many examples of CAFOM systems lying around unused - certainly under-utilised - because of inadequate understanding of how CAFOM systems might or might not facilitate FM activities and the resource required to operate them.

*Facilities information management systems (FIMS)*

The principal objective of a FIMS is to enable a strategic approach to facilities management by providing a framework integrating data-collection/dissemination with applications in a model similar to that depicted in **FIG 2.2.2.A** above. **Pro-active financial management systems** have to have access to all information needed by a facilities manager to run his activities in a similarly pro-active mode; the introduction of such pro-active systems, which rely on their success on the ability of the facilities manager to identify potential change at a time when it is still possible to influence its implementation and consequence will, over time, forge the missing link between all the applications incorporated in **FIG 2.2.2.A** and the pro-active management strategy portrayed in **FIG 2.2.2.B**

**FIG. 2.2.2.B:** *Pro-active v reactive management strategy*

| Proactive Phase | Reactive Phase |
|---|---|
| Anticipation ● | Last date to influence outcome |
| Planned action ● | |
| Situation under control ● | |
| Unplanned event ● | |
| Awareness | ● |
| Reaction | ● |

However, at the present time **none** of the commercially available CAFOM systems has anything approaching a pro-active financial control system so delivery of a FIMS deriving from such a concept may be some time coming.

*The economics of computer-aided facilities management systems*

The cost of CAFOMS will vary considerably depending on the commercial deal available. However, a typical real-life example of the cost of acquiring and running a dedicated networked 4-node system connected into an existing local area network is suggested at **FIG 2.2.2.C**; **FIG 2.2.2.D** shows this expenditure in the context of the total cost of full in-house administration of the facilities function.

To consider the cost as additional is a bit unfair since the level of competence and quality achievable using these systems properly is very much enhanced, leading to improvements and savings across many fronts.

A popular feature available from most systems is the cross-charging of space-related costs. However, the CAD component of the package is by no means essential to this important function which the database component or a financial package like *prem*FINANCE copes with perfectly adequately.

**FIG. 2.2.2.C:** *Typical annual equivalent cost of acquiring and operating a dedicated CAFM system*

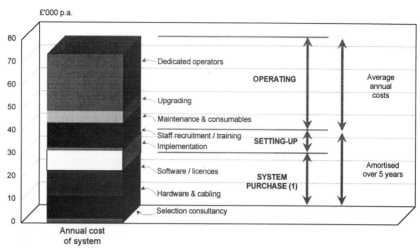

Note (1): A 4-node system with dedicated network and file server

**FIG. 2.2.2.D:** *The cost of CAFM in context of overall facilities administration*

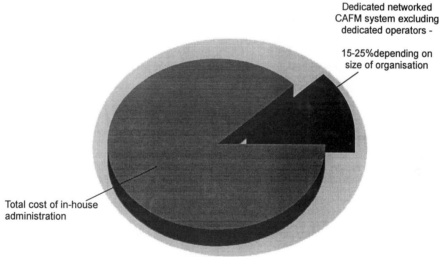

Facilities management contracting companies are now able to offer these CAFOM applications as part of their service. Obviously modern operating systems and hardware can cope with data from many different organisations under management and dedicated trained staff can service a number of organisations more efficiently than an individual organisation can set up and service its own bespoke system.

That is fine, but it is absolutely essential that the internal FM team owns and has in-house access to all the data concerning their organisation's applications. Losing control of and access to the data in an out-sourced situation is the worst possible scenario which will undoubtedly nullify any other benefits derived from the strategy.

The potential contribution of an effective FIMS to decision-making, quality, financial and risk management cannot be over-stated. **Until suitable systems become available facilities managers need to be wary of purchasing CAFOM tools to facilitate and perpetuate generically inadequate application techniques.** The IT industry must instead be encouraged to develop the integrated CAFOM/CAFIM systems which are essential for the provision of quality managed facilities (QMF) discussed under 'Quality Management' below.

### 2.2.3 ASSET MANAGEMENT

*Categories of
assets*

An asset has been defined an '**anything valuable or useful**'[3].

Although facilities management is as much concerned with optimising (facilitating the performance of) human assets, as with physical assets the **management** of **human resources** falls to the personnel director whereas **management of physical assets** should be down to the facilities manager.

Should be, but in practice not always in their entirety.

The physical assets of an organisation comprise some or all of the following

- buildings and their services
- fitting out components
- furniture and fittings
- office equipment and consumables
- vehicles
- production plant and machinery
- work in progress
- raw materials
- finished goods.

A further classification of these assets is necessary for a number of reasons, including tax liability, depreciation and management techniques. Therefore:

- property — buildings and their services
- inventories
- premises — fitting out components

  — furniture and fittings
- office services — office equipment and consumables
- transport — vehicles and parts
- production — production plant and machinery

  — raw materials

  — work in progress

  — finished goods

**Property assets** are usually of a long-term nature and may well appreciate in value during the early part of their useful lives - and in some cases for the greater part of their life possibly abetted by inflation, refurbishment or both.

**Assets in inventories** have short-term life spans - up to say 5 years, but much shorter in the case of office consumables, raw materials and (hopefully) finished goods. Those that survive in the balance sheet at the year end will either be valued at cost, if of the consumables variety, or at their depreciated value in the case of equipment, fitting out components etc expected to last for a few years.

The facilities manager will not normally be concerned with the management of production assets but ought to be concerned with the management of the property, office services and other business support assets.

*Property asset*
*management*

However, it is not uncommon for management of property assets to be split into two distinct operations:

• property management

• premises management.

This distinction is highly significant for facilities managers to recognise in that it represents and highlights the dichotomy facing many organisations whose property asset values underpin balance sheets and borrowings. These valuations reflect (or should do) the institutional investors' view of the price obtainable for a property in the open market; this may have no relevance at all to the usefulness of the property as **'premises' - defined as a 'piece of land together with its buildings, esp. considered as a place of business'** [4]

Whereas the facilities manager's objective is to ensure that the premises accommodate the requirements of the business plan in a cost-effective manner, a property director working independently of facilities management may have other designs on the asset value of the stock, its disposal and/or replacement.

The significance of property and inventory assets in the context of the balance sheet is shown typically at **FIG 2.2.3.A**. Property values have dropped by as much as 50% in the period from 1988 to 1993, so the 1988 version of this balance sheet, also shown in the Figure shows how important a good property asset can be in support of business stability. Conversely, the impact of a severe drop in market values on businesses being propped up largely by property assets is only too evident.

**FIG. 2.2.3.A:** *Balance sheet assets - 1988 to 1993 transition*

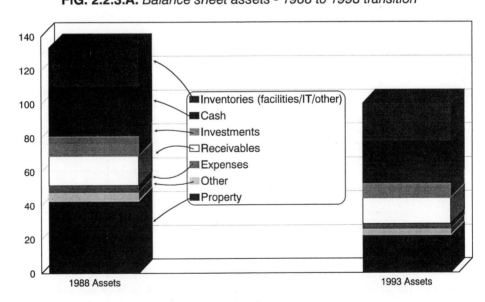

Nevertheless, the arguments for the management of property assets to be closely alongside, if not within, facilities management are very strong, especially in the context of the impact of premises on productivity discussed in Chapter 1.3.

A particularly good example of the close liaison between property and facilities management relates to an organisation in the financial services sector whose facilities management, by successfully creative space planning, managed to reduce its stock of office space from 840,000 sq ft to 700,000 sq ft over a 5-year period.

In most cases the space reductions were timed to coincide with break clauses in leases, and the right balance was struck between retention of useful buildings and disposal of expensive ones. In this example the property management was part of the facilities function, albeit staffed and directed by highly qualified property professionals.

The process of property management is described more fully in Chapter 3.8. Suffice to say here that the preservation of the property asset in terms of its market value does not necessarily reflect the business accommodation requirement, and vice-versa. Eg: a building about to be demolished may invite a property maintenance strategy invoking 'rubber bands and sticking plaster' whereas the potential impact of such a regime on business efficiency might well dictate a modification to, if not abandonment of, this extreme solution in spite of its direct benefits to cash flow.

Maintenance of property assets is considered in detail in Chapter 5.2. It is best considered over a reasonable time-span. The process of forecasting maintenance costs over a medium period - say 10-15 years - must not be confused with the forecast accompanying planned preventative maintenance (PPM - see Chapter 5.2), although the calculations may be identical in outcome. Making a forecast need not (probably should not) generate a commitment to expenditure for it may merely act as an aid to financial and strategic planning. In particular, exposure to major expense in terms of replacement of important components such as boilers, chillers, roof coverings etc should be tracked ahead so that redundant maintenance may be avoided. Alternatively, maintenance can be slotted into the replacement works programme and/or replacement can be tailored to coincide with works of alteration.

An illustration of this point is the example of a 10-year forecast of maintenance and replacement incorporating a programme of capital works shown at **FIG 2.2.3.B**. Extending the replacement of the roof-mounted chillers from year 1 as originally planned to year 3 as depicted under 'Space heating and air treatment' incurs increased 'holding' maintenance and repair but allows the replacement cost to be reduced by a far greater amount - as well as discounting it for the further 2-year period.

**FIG 2.2.3.B:** *Asset management – maintenance plan incorporating capital works (ABSTRACT)*

| Ten year planned maintenance programme | | | | | | | | | | | | |
|---|---|---|---|---|---|---|---|---|---|---|---|---|
| BUILDING B: (all costs current as at 3rd quarter 1988 and exclusive of VAT | | | | | | | | | | | | |
| Sub-element | 198 | 1989 | 1990 | 1991 | 1992 | 1993 | 1994 | 1995 | 1996 | 1997 | 1998 | Total |
| | £ | £ | £ | £ | £ | £ | £ | £ | £ | £ | £ | £ |
| SUBSTRUCTURE | 0 | 0 | 0 | 0 | 0 | 0 | 0 | 0 | 0 | 0 | | 0 |
| SUPERSTRUCTURE | | | | | | | | | | | | |
| Frame | 0 | 748 | 2264 | 352 | 43640 | 319 | 748 | 3683 | 264 | 35009 | 319 | 87346 |
| Upper floors | 0 | 99 | 0 | 0 | 0 | 0 | 0 | 0 | 0 | 0 | 0 | 99 |
| Roof | 0 | 45000 | 0 | 0 | 0 | 0 | 0 | 0 | 0 | 0 | 0 | 45000 |
| Stairs | 0 | 0 | 429 | 166 | 0 | 31528 | 0 | 429 | 252 | 0 | 342279 | 67083 |
| External walls | 0 | 0 | 0 | 0 | 0 | 0 | 0 | 0 | 0 | 0 | 0 | 0 |
| SERVICES (Cont'd) | | | | | | | | | | | | |
| Heat source | 0 | 0 | 0 | 0 | 0 | 0 | 0 | 0 | 0 | 0 | 0 | 0 |
| Space heating and air-treatment | 0 | 3760 | 284880 | 3500 | 0 | 0 | 0 | 30000 | 0 | 0 | 0 | 322140 |
| Ventilating systems | 0 | 0 | 0 | 0 | 0 | 0 | 0 | 0 | 0 | 0 | 0 | 0 |
| Electrical installations | 0 | 99137 | 41269 | 40041 | 3016 | 10640 | 0 | 3016 | 0 | 0 | 10516 | 207635 |
| Drainage | 0 | 0 | 0 | 0 | 0 | 0 | 0 | 0 | 0 | 0 | 0 | 0 |
| External Services | 0 | 0 | 0 | 0 | 0 | 0 | 0 | 0 | 0 | 0 | 0 | 0 |
| CAPITAL PROJECTS | | | | | | | | | | | | |
| Roof works | 0 | 184500 | 195450 | 0 | 0 | 0 | 0 | 0 | 0 | 0 | 0 | 379950 |
| Toilet areas | 0 | 0 | 49500 | 49500 | 49500 | 0 | 0 | 0 | 0 | 0 | 0 | 148500 |
| Reception areas | 0 | 0 | 0 | 99000 | 0 | 0 | 0 | 0 | 0 | 0 | 0 | 99000 |
| TOTAL (£) | 0 | 385167 | 745168 | 192769 | 102295 | 58571 | 35866 | 192295 | 38776 | 40291 | 170858 | 1962056 |

Whole-life appraisal of asset maintenance and replacement is particularly important at building design stage, and should form the basis of medium term budget projections for purposes of property asset management. Whole-life appraisal techniques are discussed fully in Chapter 10.4. However, forecasting the incidence of replacing components for any sort of period ahead is fraught with problems, although there is data available which, used with care and constantly monitored against actual, can be used as a satisfactory working-base.

**FIG. 2.2.3.C** gives typical life-spans for some of the more common materials and components as an example of the conventional wisdom.

**FIG 2.2.3.C:** *Typical economic life of some common components*

| Building fabric components / materials | | Estimated life - years | Building services components | Estimated life - years * |
|---|---|---|---|---|
| Walls | Stone | 50 + | Steel boilers | 15-20 |
| | Brickwork | 50 + | | |
| | Concrete blocks | 40-60 | Gas burners | 15-20 |
| | Reinforced concrete | 50 + | | |
| | Rendering | 20-40 | Calorifiers | 20-25 |
| | Timber framing | 40-50 | | |
| | Timber cladding | 30-40 | Steel radiators | 15-20 |
| | Curtain walling | 20-40 | | |
| | | | Pipework | 25-30 |
| Doors / windows | Softwood | 25-40 | | |
| | Hardwood | 40-60 | Control equipment | 15-20 |
| | Galvanised steel | 30-40 | | |
| | UPVC | 20-30 | Tanks (depends on material) | 15-30 |
| | Aluminium | 20-35 | | |
| | | | Water chillers | 15-20 |
| Roofs | 3-layer felt / chippings | 15-30 | | |
| | Asphalt | 15-50 | Cooler batteries | 15-20 |
| | Slate | 60 + | | |
| | Clay tiles | 30 + | Pumps | 20-25 |
| | Concrete tiles | 20 + | | |
| | Copper | 100 + | Heater batteries | 15-20 |
| | Aluminium | 30-60 | | |
| | UPVC | 15-25 | Cooling towers (depends on materials) | 10-25 |
| | | | | |
| Finishes | Carpet | 5-10 | Air handling units | 8-15 |
| | Vinyl | 10-20 | | |
| | Woodblock | 40-70 | Main cables | 25-30 |
| | Terrazzo | 40 + | | |
| | Quarry tiles | 50 + | Switchgear | 25-30 |
| | Plaster | 40-60 | | |
| | Plasterboard | 20-40 | Electric motors | 20-25 |
| | Mineral tiles | 15-40 | | |
| | | | * Source: CIBSE | |

The condition of property assets should be recorded early in the life of a new building and immediately on taking occupation of newly acquired existing premises. The condition survey should concern itself with the major components, leaving minor items to be dealt with on a routine ad hoc basis. Ideally the data in the survey should be entered into a computerised data-base coded up to enable instant retrieval of component data (including maintenance histories); large, beautifully bound, expensive reports growing out-of-date on inaccessible shelves are worse than useless and they are a monument to the failure of the commissioner to understand what asset management is all about.

Recent software developments [5] enable the condition survey to be updated using a touch-screen portable computer with the material being downloaded direct to the data-base to update the original condition survey without further keyboard entry.

## Inventory asset management

Unlike property assets the inventory assets are almost invariably in a depreciating mode from the date of acquisition.

As discussed above some or all of such inventories as fitting-out components (partitions, carpets, light fittings etc) furniture and fittings, office equipment (eg: PC's, photocopiers), consumables (such as stationery, reference books) and vehicles may come under the facilities manager's responsibility throughout their limited life-span.

His duties in their respect may involve

- purchase
- distribution
- installation/placement
- inventory
- maintenance
- storage
- disposal.

He may also be the budget-holder for these items responsible for all three facets of financial control in their respect.

These inventory assets are either semi-fixed – eg: suspended ceilings, carpets – or 'loose', such as PCs, motor vehicles etc. The semi-fixed items demand less resources in terms of asset management than the 'loose' items which are apt to 'go walkies' unless their disposition is tightly monitored; they are also likely to suffer from the 'out-of-sight-out-of-mind' syndrome in regard to abuse, lack of maintenance and re-allocation.

The principles of procurement, financial control, maintenance and storage described elsewhere in this work apply equally to loose inventories. Generally, however, it is essential to set up an asset register identifying the following (where applicable) in respect of each component:

- code identification reference
- title
- date of purchase
- name of manufacturer
- model, series, colour, material and manufacturer's reference numbers
- initial (and subsequent) location
- areas served (eg: photocopiers)
- internal market ownership
- maintenance periods, servicing contractor & history
- operator's maintenance instructions
- warranty/guarantee data
- condition
- other relevant data.

The modern-day asset register must surely be set up on a computerised data-base preferably linked to a CAD program - with inventory assets bar-coded to be instantly traceable and their location and records up-dated.

Such systems, discussed earlier in this Chapter, do not only enable efficient control of inventories; they also greatly facilitate the process of cross-charging equipment etc to the beneficial user.

*Asset
depreciation*

All company expenditure must either:

- add to the value of the assets in the balance sheet

(capitalised), or

- be charged in the profit and loss account (expensed)

**Capital expenditure** on projects creates assets such as new or improved plant or buildings.  The objective is to maintain or increase profits.  Due to use, the passage of time and obsolescence these assets lose value, ie: depreciate, though, as discussed above, property assets may behave erratically in this respect throughout their life span.

Any amount that can be capitalised will increase profit directly, in the year in which it is incurred, by the amount capitalised - but at the expense of the profits in future years when (increased) capital values will require (increased) depreciation.

The lower the charge for depreciation in a year, the higher the book value of the fixed assets and the higher the profits for that year.

**Revenue expenditure** includes premises operating costs and business support services costs.

An effective and efficient maintenance strategy will extend the economic life of assets thereby reducing depreciation as an annual expense.  It is therefore important for facilities managers to work closely with their accounts departments to ensure that capital expenditure, such as major improvements or adaptations, are recognised as such and not charged as an expense on the profit and loss account instead of being capitalised on the balance sheet.

Further consideration and worked examples of depreciation in respect of property are given in Chapter 3.7, and Chapter 11.2 looks at the impact of depreciation on taxation.

The application of reserve, contingency and sinking funds to preserve and replace assets via service charges is reviewed in Chapter 3.2.

*Asset stripping*

Some organisations have assets - particularly of the property variety - which are valuable out of proportion to the business they accommodate.

The increase in the status of commercial property as a valuable investment through the '70s and '80s saw a number of shrewd entrepreneurs make their fortunes buying ailing companies at a price reflecting their business performance but not recognising the underlying property values which the accountants were allowed to include on a 'written-down' basis on the balance sheets.  The subsequent break up of the businesses to enable realisation of the real-time property values caused much concern in genuine business circles but also alerted corporate owner-occupiers and their accountants to the dangers of not keeping a regular check on the current market value of their freehold and long-leasehold premises.

The current property value down-turn of the early '90s may be expected to lull many erstwhile property-rich companies into a depressed sense of security from the stealthy attacks of the asset strippers.

Enough said!

## 2.2.4 QUALITY MANAGEMENT

*The meaning of quality*

Quality is a noun meaning basic character or nature. It is often linked to adjectives such as 'high' or 'low' - to qualify or benchmark levels of achievement; nevertheless, on its own the noun 'quality' is strictly **not** a parameter, although in modern times it has come to be used more and more frequently as a modifying word indicating a degree of excellence or superiority eg: 'quality managed facilities'.

The imperfections of syntax in this particular matter can be a source of confusion to those seeking improved efficiency in industry; the term 'performance' is less open to misinterpretation than 'quality' since it is not used as a modifier on its own account. The concept of performance considered in Chapter 1.2 could be read as 'quality'. However the terms 'quality control', 'quality assurance' and 'total quality management' are now enshrined in business management jargon and have found their way in recent times into theory and practice of facilities management. As such the terms cannot be expunged from the vocabulary so it is very important that the term 'quality', where used in facilities management, is always in its 'relative' rather than 'absolute' modifying form, thereby discouraging inadvertent pursuit of **absolute excellence** with attendant acquisition of **redundant performance**.

Although this distinction between 'performance' and the popular understanding of quality may seem to be pedantic it does serve to highlight the critical significance of the **degree** of quality sought and achieved in the process of optimising the cost and value of any contribution to productivity.

'Quality', where used in a mission statement to imply the required level of performance, may render that statement inappropriate – possibly harmful – if what is delivered is in excess of the business requirements whilst having incurred greater costs eg: excessive maintenance for the sake of a high standard **engineering performance** to the financial detriment of more strategically critical cost centres.

*Quality management in facilities*

The quality of facilities, ie: the performance of facilities, should be enshrined in the facilities policy supporting the corporate plan. Chapter 1.1 discusses the relationship between the cost of premises and support services and the business requirement; quality management is the process by which these relationships are forged - hopefully optimised.

'Hopefully', because although management implies the skilful use of resources it does not imply success, only the application of techniques.

**Quality management** in facilities is primarily dependent upon a willingness by top management to accept the contribution of appropriate facilities to the productivity of the core business; quality truly does start at the top. However, down the line any facilities manager unable to identify the relationship between his own goals (sic!) and corporate requirements will be unlikely to make any proactive contribution even if top management is enlightened enough to be seeking it.

Seeking an improvement in the quality of facilities performance must be accompanied by an educational process both within the organisation - two ways - and from within the discipline itself. The internal customer must know what he may expect, and agree with it - possibly pay against results. On the other hand the facilities manager must not only understand the importance of communications within the 'internal market' but also have the skills and resources to achieve agreed objectives to time and budget.

Quality management must apply both to the performance of the in-house team, who should be empowered, well qualifed and fully trained, and of any suppliers whom they engage.

The various Quality Assurance (QA) standards such as BS EN ISO 9000 can be usefully applied either to part of the whole of a facilities organisation's work; equally they may insist upon compliance from suppliers. However, the burden of compliance may be counter-productive for smaller vibrant outfits such as consultancies whose resources may be best directed towards creative problem-solving rather than pushing paper around. Most of such firms engage fully qualified professionals whose basic training affords some guarantee of competence (though rather less than one would hope in many cases). Smaller firms are probably best judged by extensive reference-taking rather than slavish compliance with a standard geared towards the lower common denominators.

The larger firms can afford and may well benefit from BS EN ISO 9000 compliance though the facilities manager should treat that as an added bonus in support of his own investigations into their standards of quality delivery.

The concept of total quality management (TQM) involving a corporate culture of performance delivery is now becoming increasingly popular in business and its extension to facilities is described by Keith Alexander under the term 'Quality Managed Facilities' (QMF).

QMF describes how a total quality management framework can be used to enable facilities managers to provide services of a quality appropriate to meeting corporate objectives. The approach demands a thorough understanding of the corporate culture and setting up of a framework for managing customers, services and assets at every level from strategic to operational. The difference between such an approach - which is also subjected to performance monitoring - and the simpler QA process is vast and has already been highly successful in a number of major organisations in which it has been instituted.

The pace of change in corporate goals and applications puts a considerable strain on facilities and those who have responsibility for managing them. Identifying the appropriate quality of performance and negotiating intelligently for the resources with which to achieve it are tasks for well-trained personnel of the right quality; their success, or otherwise, will be dependent on similar characteristics in the management to whom they report.

*Measuring quality*

The measurement of quality is only possible where there are parameters: performance indicators are discussed in Chapter 1.2. Sometimes such indicators may seem crude relative to the significance or nature of the service being measured eg: the cost of providing and running libraries per book! Nevertheless these indicators, however crude they seem, provide a starting point from which at least some discussion can take place; they can provide a basis on which **cross-benchmarking can replace unsupported assertions** by those whose power and/or position is threatened by objective assessment or who do not understand the purpose and principles of benchmarking performance achievements.

People who do not **want** to plan will try to scupper the planning process by instancing the prevalence of unforeseen change. In the same mode those averse to performance quality measurement denigrate benchmarking by trying to identify and highlight the deficiencies of the chosen parameters.

The negative attitude in both cases is wrong even though the arguments may seen persuasive at first hearing; those who do not plan, like those who will not benchmark, have nothing against which their performance may be judged so have only their personal commitment and judgement to support their actions. That may in fact be totally adequate but is totally lacking in accountability, so who can tell?

In the same way that a business overdraft is afforded against imperfect perform-ance indicators related to the historic profit-and-loss accounts and balance sheet and the conduct of the account, so the amount of borrowing sought will almost certainly be geared to financial projections whose basis may change significantly over the period. Nevertheless, the process by which both parties make their decisions will lead to a better understanding of the people, the problems and the risks than would be possible in an analytical vacuum.

As the comedian Leon Cortez might once have said, with apologies to the bard, 'tis better to have planned and screwed up than not to have tried in the first place!'

The same goes for quality measurement.

Internally imposed benchmarking of quality may be informal or may be the subject of public scrutiny using one of the public standards set by the European Commis-sion eg: BS EN ISO 9000. Internal benchmarking is linked to results whereas external monitoring is geared to slavish adherence to agreed procedures.

Although the procedures in the standard accreditation processes are agreed in advance by the applicant they are generally geared to avoidance of error rather than enhancement of service. Organisations (or departments) which do not make mistakes in established procedures may provide comfort to their customers but risk the impact of bureaucracy on the creativity (always short of resources) which is the real source of quality (and risk) control.

A happy medium of sound procedure and proactivity is essential to the process of producing the relevant level of quality in facilities. Just like financial control and building performance, quality management is dependent upon a trinity of facets - **FIG 2.2.4.A**

**FIG. 2.2.4.A:** *Three facets of quality control - inter-relationships*

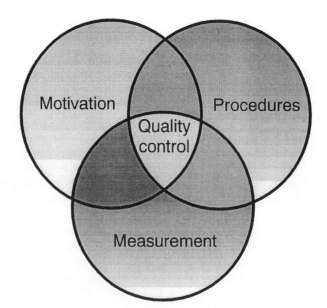

As with all trinities (religious or otherwise) you cannot expect the whole to be present in the absence of any one of the components.

The procedural aspect of quality management is covered by the formal standards to the exclusion of the other two which are of themselves essentially more significant. In the same way the better understood **physical performance** of buildings is in reality subordinate to the far more important **functional and financial performance** discussed in Chapter 1.3 and **competitive procurement** is emphasised bureaucratically in financial control whilst in economic reality being subservient to **budgetary control and value engineering** (which is explained in Chapter 2.2 below).

Actually, **FIG 2.2.4.A** in turn describes the control mechanisms for the all important value engineering component of financial control, so it can be seen that the formally controlled, simple quality assurance processes in effect have a relatively small contribution to make to the real quality/value outcome of quality management processes as a whole. The application of TQM should generate much better results.

Quality must be motivated by top management, guided by procedures and measured by results. In facilities management, as in all production processes, the results will find their way, sooner or later, to the bottom line.

*Quality and economics*

As discussed in Chapter 1.2 the delivery of the 'right' performance at the right price is the ultimate economic aim in facilities. The rider is that 'right' performance means **exactly** what is required by the organisation to achieve its corporate goals; 'right' price is the consequence of a fully cost-controlled operation involving the three facets of which the value-engineering process will have properly identified the level of performance needed.

The more conventional view of the economics of quality management is that it can be measured by the cost of non-provision (including corrective action) as well as by the beneficial effects of a pro-active application. The latter is probably much more difficult than the former which tends to show up clearly in staff attitude towards the organisation and their role in it.

Given typical profit margins of between 3% and 10% of turnover in commercial organisations it seems reasonable that high quality performance throughout an organisation, achieved at little or no additional cost, will impact on profitability by some measure within these bands - possibly much higher in a 'turn-around' situation. British Rail announced in July 1994 that it had reduced its losses from £183m to £108m in the financial year whilst substantially achieving the 'Passengers' Charter' performance targets for punctuality and availability of services. Although other factors than quality management probably made a big contribution to the BR achievement of almost halving the loss while improving performance, this is a good example of how quality measurement against financial performance may be used to review trends in success or otherwise of business strategies, including customer satisfaction and bottom-line profitability.

Although decisions to invest in physical and human resources in pursuit of excellence may well produce the necessary financial return, a change in the culture of an organisation - the way it sees and treats itself and its customers -may well be achieved with no investment other than a shift in management attitude and direction, which may cost nothing more than a few confrontations with the diehards.

Equally, judicial financial investment coupled with application of Total Quality Management procedures - both efficiently measured against performance criteria - will bring optimum benefit to an organisation. One form of investment without the other is likely to put the planned improvement process into a low gear - or stall it completely when the going is uphill.

## 2.2.5 RISK MANAGEMENT

*Risks facing
facilities
managers*

Risk is '**the possibility of incurring misfortune or loss**' [6]. The facilities manager is confronted with a wide array of such potential problems in respect of persons, property and money. Some of the risks can be managed internally within the facilities department direct, while risks emanating from third party involvement have to be countered, in part, by extension of obligations to suppliers via their contracts or by insurance, or both.

Risks to persons for which the facilities manager may have responsibility include:

- health & safety at work

- physical injury or death through disaster

- environmental pollution

- loss of or damage to personal property.

Risks to property can comprise:

- disaster damage

- deterioration

- loss of amenity

- faulty or onerous legal title

- technical failure.

Both the above categories have attendant financial risks, such as fines, loss of value, cost of reinstatement, loss of productivity etc. Additionally the organisation may suffer financially - directly or indirectly - from one or more of:

- project failure or inefficiency

- failure of premises policy to support business strategies

- loss of reputation - externally

- loss of confidence - internally.

Many of these risks have become more of a burden as the result of legislation emanating originally at home and latterly via the European Commission. The Health & Safety at Work Acts, Environmental Pollution Act, Food Safety Act etc are just a few examples of legislation which have placed the facilities manager (and his employers) at risk to severe penalty for failure to observe and monitor risk to employees, visitors and passers-by.

*Risk
management
process*

The extent of all the risks described above and measures to counter them are fully described in their various chapters elsewhere. Here we are concerned with the principles to be observed in risk management, which involve yet another trinity - see **FIG 2.2.5.A.**

The process of **identification** is more a legal obligation with regard to personal safety. Facilities managers must not only be alert to the possibilities of danger to persons, property and finance, but, having traced the risk, they must analyse the likely consequence in terms of the extent and effect of the hazard to which the organisation may be exposed.

**FIG. 2.2.5.A:** *Three facets of risk management - inter-relationships*

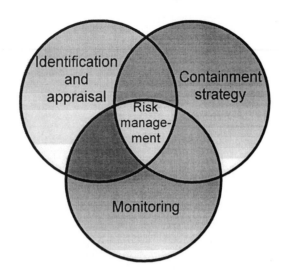

The facilities manager's strategy for containment of the risk will stem from his facilities policy which should spell out the risk management philosophy of the organisation as a whole and the facilities manager's commitment thereto.

In a properly constituted internal market (see Chapter 1.2) there should be a service level agreement in support of a policy statement specifically relevant to risk management. The tactic for managing the risk will derive from the risk appraisal eg: low risk situations may merely be subjected to a **monitoring** procedure whereas high risks such as imminent structural failure may require immediate preventative or, in most cases, corrective action.

Generally speaking the facilities manager will have greater discretion in the tactics he adopts for dealing with hazards threatening productive output, than where persons or property are at risk.

Most organisations now have a **crisis management** strategy which should be in addition to a **disaster recovery** plan and embrace all three facets described in **FIG 2.2.5.A** above.

Having identified and appraised the risk and implemented a strategy for containing or eliminating it, the facilities manager must then make sure that the processes he has instituted are monitored regularly - both internally as part of the quality management process and externally by the engagement of auditors. The facilities audit described in Section 12 can be extended to cover all management procedures as well as simply financial management, either via one consultant or using independent specialists in areas such as health & safety, environmental pollution, energy consumption etc.

In some circumstances the facilities manager can **transfer** the risk management function eg: some consultants can offer a complete risk management service in specific fields such as the 'Health & Safety at Work' package described in Chapter 8.2. This provides a form of preventative insurance which is the only type of insurance a facilities manager must rely upon in matters relating to avoidable misfortune or loss.

Which is not to say that appropriate insurance cover should not be in place to cover the financial consequences of disaster, avoidable or otherwise.  So, as shown in Chapter 3.6, building contracts will provide for cover against loss or damage to persons and property through fire, negligence, non-negligence etc and building contents insurance may cover loss through theft, vandalism etc.

Sometimes the term 'transfer of risk' is used in reference to contracting services or taking out insurance.  This is a misconception for the risk will always remain with the facilities manager however widely he is able to 'lay off' responsibility for management or compensation.

*Risk management economics*

Where risks are insurable the cost of risk management can be calculated by costing up the savings on the annual premium against the annual cost of the tactic (eg: depreciation and maintenance on a sprinkler installation) plus the staff and consultants' time involved in the risk management process.

An example of such a calculation involving management of the risk of fire is shown at **FIG 2.2.5.B**.

**FIG 2.2.5.B:** *The cost of managing the risk of fire*

| | Sprinkler installation | | £ |
|---|---|---|---|
| Capital cost | 5,000 sq m @ £10 per sq m (inc fees & finance) | £50,000 | |
| Annual costs | Amortised cost over 15 years - say | £5,000 p.a. | |
| | Maintenance - say | £1,000 p.a. | |
| | Staff / consultants' time - fire risk management | £2,000 p.a. | |
| | Total costs of fire risk management p.a. | | £8,000 p.a. |
| | | | |
| Insurance cost implications | All-risks insurance - 5,000 sq m @ £3 per sq m p.a. | £15,000 | |
| | Premium reduction for sprinkler installation - say 10% | | £1,500 p.a. |

Financial risk assessment can be quite an involved process particularly in the case of major projects.  An example of appraisal of the risk inherent in a range of options to an organisation in refurbishing its leased headquarters is shown at **FIG 2.2.5.C**. The two options involve:

- Option A - the tenant finances and commissions the work taking advantage of a lengthy and favourable remainder of lease not subject to rent reviews

- Option B - the landlord undertakes and finances the work in exchange for a modern lease.

The back up calculation to one of the risk items  - 'delay to lease negotiations' in the landlord-led Option (B) is shown at **FIG 2.2.5.D.**

The extent to which the organisation is exposed to cost and time risk throughout the duration of the project are shown graphically at **FIG 2.2.5.E** and **2.2.5.F** respectively.  In both cases the organisation is at greater risk in the landlord-led option (B) except for the time parameter for a brief period during the client lead-in phase; this is the consequence of 'delay to lease negotiations' at item A1 in the Risk Appraisal Summary (**FIG 2.2.5.C**) and amplified in **FIG 2.2.5.D**.

**FIG 2.2.5.C:** *Risk appraisal summary - headquarters refurbishment options*

| Event | | Option A: tenant led project | | | Option B: landlord led project | | |
|---|---|---|---|---|---|---|---|
| | | Quantified | | Opportunity costs | Quantified | | Opportunity costs |
| | | Time wks | Cost £,000's | | Time wks | Cost £,000's | |
| **A.** **Legal** | Delay to lease negotiation | 13 | 300 | Add rent £3,570,000* | 4 | 100 | Add rent £1,190,000* |
| | Delay to landlord's approvals | 6 | 150 | Add rent £1,785,000* | 2 | 50 | Add rent £595,000* |
| | Blurred definition of base build/fit out | - | - | - | - | 100 | - |
| | Incompatability between base build/fit out | - | - | - | - | 500 | - |
| **B.** **Statutory Approvals** | Planning permission delay | 8 | 200 | Add rent £2,380,000* | 2 | 50 | Add rent £595,000* |
| | Building Regulations delay | - | - | - | - | - | - |
| | E C Directives | - | - | - | - | - | - |
| **C.** **Design** | Fee levels | - | 150 | - | - | - | - |
| | Design period | - | - | - | - | - | - |
| | Cost control | - | - | - | - | - | - |
| | Specification | - | - | - | - | 150 | Add running costs £150,000 pa |
| **D.** **Construction** | Existing structure constraints | - | - | - | - | - | - |
| | 'Unknowns' | 2 | 70 | Add rent £595,000* | - | 50 | - |
| | Market conditions | - | 300 | - | - | 50 | - |
| | Late instructions | -- | 100 | -- | 2- | 200- | Add rent £595,000*- |
| | Delay by contractor | - | - | - | - | - | - |
| | Delay by the design team | - | - | - | - | - | - |
| | Insured peril | - | - | - | - | - | - |
| | Programme | - | - | - | 4 | - | Add rent £1,190,000 |
| | Commissioning | - | - | - | - | - | - |
| **E.** **Client** | In-house approvals | 4 | 100 | Add rent £595,000* | 4 | 100 | Add rent £1,190,000 |
| | Funding availability | - | - | - | 4 | 100 | Add rent £1,190,000 |
| | Phasing | - | - | - | 8 | 200 | Add rent £1,190,000 |
| | Capital allowances | - | - | - | - | - | - |
| **Totals** | | 33+ | 1,370++- | - | 30+ | 1,650++ | |

\* Property costs only - loss of productivity due to delay excluded
+ Delay not necessarily consecutive  ++ Costs not necessarily cumulative

Some risks or benefits do not lend themselves easily to financial evaluation. Cost/ benefit analysis involves a lot of risk appraisal and is often criticised as a technique because of the essentially subjective nature of evaluation of human issues such as a poor ambience, excessive noise, loss of life etc. Nevertheless, to quote Harrington again 'if you can't measure it you cannot understand it!' so, having a good shot at evaluation will at least enable one to understand the risks and benefits involved and get some sort of handle on their relative significance thereby facilitating a fully discursive and informed decision-making process.

**FIG 2.2.5.D:** *Risk appraisal - back-up calculation to Option 'B' appraisal of 'delay to lease negotiations'*

| Event | Risk evaluation | | | Commentary | Risk control mechanism | Potential effect |
|---|---|---|---|---|---|---|
| | Time | Cost | Quality | | | |
| A. Legal 1. Delay to lease negotiations | / | / | × | Time not of the 'essence' so far as the landlord is concerned | Agree cut-off dates with landlord but little opportunity to impose penalties if these are not achieved. | Assume Landlord proves intransigent - allow for 3 month delay. The majority of buying would take place during a period when tender prices are projected to be increasing at 4% pa (0.33% per month). Additional construction costs would therefore be: £30,000,000 × 3 months × 0.33% = £300,000, whilst additional rent and rates on the Tenant's existing buildings would amount to: 3 months @ £1,190,000 = £3,570,000 |

**FIG. 2.2.5.E:** *Risk appraisal - financial loss exposure*

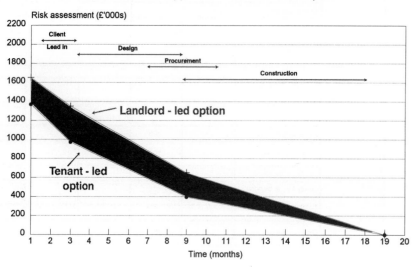

**FIG. 2.2.5.F:** *Risk appraisal - time delay exposure*

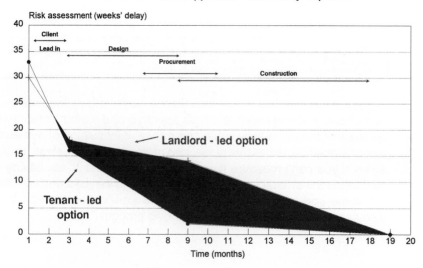

## 2.2.6 PROJECT MANAGEMENT

*Facilities
projects*

Project management in facilities relates to tasks which are, generally speaking, outside of the routine management functions carried out by the department. Such tasks normally involve significant change, but may not always involve the physical upheaval attendant upon fitting-out, alteration or relocation.

For example, introduction of management regimes to cope with the rigours of new legislation (Health & Safety at Work etc) and introduction of IT processes may be substantially non-physical in their nature whilst still requiring the vision, tenacity and negotiating skills needed to deal with installation projects.

Very often the facilities manager will not have the relevant experience to deal with certain types of project. He must recognise and admit this fact and bring on board additional resources with the necessary skills. This may entail adding to the staff complement if a full-time involvement is expected over a long term, but in most cases a better solution will involve the appointment of consultants specialising in management of the particular types of project. Not only does this avoid staff appointments which may turn out to be unwarranted or superfluous, but it also brings access to the resources of a specialist organisation upon which the organisation may draw for experience and manpower at critical stages of a project.

*Objectives*

The project manager's objective is to deliver the project in accordance with the requirements of the brief which should stipulate **cost, quality and time**. In the process he must manage the risk so as to keep exposure to failure in respect of any of these criteria to an acceptable and pre-agreed level.

Again, a trinity is present and **FIG 2.2.6.A** illustrates how risk management as described above is central to successful avoidance of failure in respect of the three critical facets of any project; it is axiomatic that failure in respect of one facet will aggravate, and most likely render futile, attempts to be successful in the other two.

**FIG. 2.2.6.A:** *Project risk exposure*

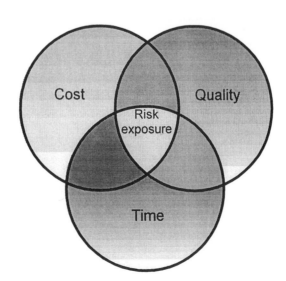

*Programme
management
tools*

The principles of financial, quality and risk management and various tools to facilitate their application are discussed elsewhere in this section and specifically in respect of fitting-out, construction and development projects in Sections 6 and 10 respectively.

However there are a number of programme management software programs available commercially which are generically applicable to any project, as well as those specifically geared to the more common types of project encountered by construction and development specialists.

Fitting the complexity of the software to the problem in hand is important but there are few projects of consequence facing the facilities manager which would not benefit to some extent from an IT application - even if only on a spreadsheet.

The principal generic types of programming tools are:

- milestone charts
- the Gantt chart
- network analysis (CPM/PERT)
- float analysis
- resource allocation (labour/plant/materials)
- operational schedule
- work breakdown structure (WBS)
- progress analysis and control - 'S' curves
- line of balance.

*Milestone chart*

This is a simple planning and control tool which is often used as a summary plan.

As **FIG 2.2.6.B** demonstrates milestones are specific and readily identifiable points of achievement marking the start and/or completion of stages (either major, minor or intermediate) of a project.

**FIG. 2.2.6.B:** *A 'milestone' chart*

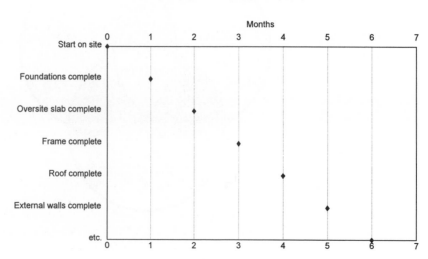

The technique, which was the forerunner of the Gantt chart described below, is still sometimes used to present a report which schedules programmed milestone dates against those actually achieved.

## The Gantt chart

This is probably the oldest and most common planning technique in use today. Developed during World War I by Henry Gantt its chief advantages are that it is: easy to understand, easy to construct with little training and can be used to show progress. Like the 'milestone' chart which pre-dated it, the Gantt chart is concerned with beginning and end dates and is particularly suitable for projects where activities are more or less consecutive, each one being dependant upon one logical predecessor. As **FIG 2.2.6.C** illustrates it does not show interrelationships between activities which are not immediately linked and on large and/or complex projects this can lead to problems in co-ordination of the work.

**FIG 2.2.6.C:** *A gantt chart for the fitting-out of a relocation project*

| Ref | Activity | Duration | May | Jun | Jul | Aug | Sep | Oct | Nov | Dec | Jan | Feb | Mar | Apr |
|---|---|---|---|---|---|---|---|---|---|---|---|---|---|---|
| 1 | Feasibility report submitted | 0w | | ● | | | | | | | | | | |
| 2 | Project Board Meeting | 0w | | ● | | | | | | | | | | |
| 3 | Further study undertaken | 7w | | ▬ | | | | | | | | | | |
| 4 | Accommodation selected | 0w | | | ● | | | | | | | | | |
| 5 | Lease negotiations | 6w | | | ▬ | | | | | | | | | |
| 6 | Develop project brief | 2w | | | | | ▪ | | | | | | | |
| 7 | Approval to proceed | 0w | | | | | ● | | | | | | | |
| 8 | Detailed design development | 4w | | | | | ▬ | | | | | | | |
| 9 | Site investigation | 4w | | | | | ▬ | | | | | | | |
| 10 | Prepare tender documents | 2w | | | | | | ▪ | | | | | | |
| 11 | Tender period | 4w | | | | | | | ▬ | | | | | |
| 12 | Tender analysis | 1w | | | | | | | | ▪ | | | | |
| 13 | Client approvals | 1w | | | | | | | | ▪ | | | | |
| 14 | Contractor mobilisation | 4w | | | | | | | | | ▬ | | | |
| 15 | Site enabling works | 4w | | | | | | | | | ▬ | | | |
| 16 | Construction period | 13w | | | | | | | | | | ▬▬▬ | | |
| 17 | Building regs. approval | 6w | | | | | | | ▬ | | | | | |
| 18 | Landlord approvals | 8w | | | | | | | ▬▬ | | | | | |

A compromise on simple projects is the vertical linking of activities by means of a dotted line; however, once this process gets profuse the whole presentation gets more confusing than helpful.

## Critical path method (CPM/ PERT) - network analysis

The Programme Evaluation and Review Technique (PERT) identifying the 'critical path' through a project was developed in the USA in the late 50's / early 60's to overcome the Gantt chart's deficiency in dealing with interrelationships between activities. Consequently it is used primarily for the more complex projects.

Its method of calculation identifies those activities which are critical to completion of the project and additionally shows the extent to which these activities have spare or 'float' time for their completion.

The process involves identification and numbering of **events** and **activities**.

In the diagram of a project network at **FIG 2.2.6.D** the events are numbered 1,2,3 etc; the activities needed for achievement of the events are described by the relationship between two consecutive events eg: 1-2 and 5-9.

**FIG. 2.2.6.D:** *Network analysis diagram*

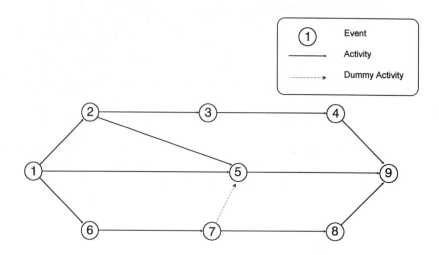

In this example the following relationships are important:

- Activities 1-2, 1-5, 1-6 can all start together

- Activities 2-3, 2-5 can start when activity 1-2 is finished

- Activities 2-5, 1-5, 7-5 must all be complete before activity 5-9 can be started

- Activity 7-5 is a dummy activity

Dummy activities are necessary to indicate a logical relationship - in the example above, activity 5-9 is dependant on activity 6-7, with activity 7-8 being dependant upon activity 6-7 but not on activities 1-5 or 2-5, hence, the need exists for a logical link that does not tie activity 7-8 to event 5.

Whilst a dummy will not usually have a duration it can be of use to delay the start of following activities.

The numbering of the activities can be in random sequence, but it makes sensible practice to use ascending numbers, leaving gaps of (say) 10, between event numbers, for the later insertion of extra activities as required.

It is important to note that the length of the activity line does not need to correspond to the duration. When first drawing the network logic, it would be almost impossible to draw it to a timescale - the important thing is to construct a logically correct plan and then analyse this for decision purposes. Computerised programs such as PLANTRAC offer a feature of plotting the network, with or without a timescale, after analysis, thus obviating the need for formalised drawing of networks.

The **critical path** through the network traces those events whose late completion will cause delay to start of activities required to achieve another event whose completion date is equally critical to the overall programme time.

Once time is added in to the network it is possible to see the minimum possible programme time for activities leading to critical path events and where there is any 'space' or 'float' time in any of the activities. So, in the example, if events 1, 5 and 9 are on the critical path and activities 1-2, 2-3, 3-4 and 4-9 are estimated to take 20 days, whereas activities 1-6, 6-7, 7-8 and 8-9 are estimated to take only 15 days there is a 'float' time of 5 days in the latter sequence in the network - more if the sum of 1-5 and 5-9 is **greater than** 20 days.

*Float management*

Although this 'float' time is spare as a contingency, if the activities in the sequence 1-6, 6-7, 7-8, 8-9 were to slip to, say, 22 days then the critical event No.9 would be 2 days late, even if the upper and central sequences on the network were delivered within 20 days. Therefore float management deals with the management of the so called 'non-critical' activities to ensure that any slippage that does occur does not delay start of activities on the project's critical path.

*Resource allocation*

This technique is often allied to network analysis and involves forecasting resource requirements (in terms of labour, materials and plant) from the initial project plan and comparing these requirements with those either available or which can be made available. These factors may impose restraints on the project plan and require it to be modified to take into account, for example:

- resource limitations

- avoidance of undue fluctuations in resource requirements

- the overall resource pattern and its effect on productivity.

**FIG 2.2.6.E** illustrates the resources which are required in terms of men per week given either a timely or late build-up of the resources needed to complete the activity to schedule.

FIG. 2.2.6.E: Resource allocation chart

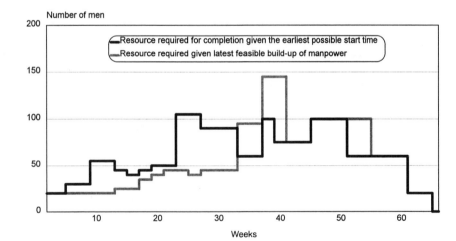

*Operational scheduling*

Again, this is a step beyond basic network analysis which goes on to designate not only start and finish times for an activity but also who does what and when.

Operational scheduling therefore combines network analysis with resource and time scheduling.

*Work
breakdown
structure
(WBS)*

WBS is a structured method of identifying the work to be carried out on a project and the procedure involves breaking the work down logically and systematically into its component parts to:

- enable the planning to be done effectively by defining the work required to complete the project and to sub-divide it into manageable tasks that can be planned, controlled and budgeted

- assign responsibility for the completion of those tasks to designated personnel/organisations to integrate the work to be done with the overall organisation structure

- design and integrate the control and information systems with the work to be done and who is responsible for it.

*'S' curve
progress
analysis chart*

An 'S' curve is a graph of the cumulative value of man hours, percentage complete, or cost against time. The graph generally takes the form of an 'S' because most activities (projects) have a slow start followed by a longer period of relatively constant activity and finally a falling off of activity.

The 'S' curve is a very sensitive tool for the analysis and control of progress. **FIG 2.2.6.F** from a construction project shows how the planned 'S' curve in terms of contract expenditure (on the vertical scale) per month's activity (horizontal scale) was not being achieved when tested against the monthly payment certificates under the contract; consideration of the 'S' curve needed to achieve completion and the resources it would demand would be a good indicator of the possibility of avoiding a delayed completion.

**FIG. 2.2.6.F:** *The 'S' curve used to test project progress*

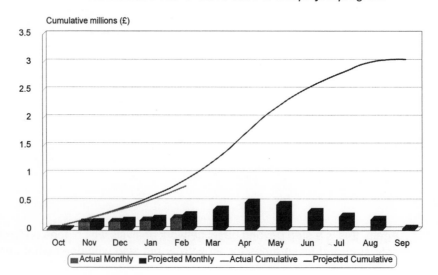

*Line of balance
(LOB)*

This technique developed by the US Navy in the early 50's is a graphical method of scheduling designed to improve the planning and reporting of an on-going production process.  It is particularly useful where:

- the project is made up of a number of identical units eg: fitting-out repetitive floors of a multi-storey office block

or

- the project consists of first the design and then the production of a limited number of units from that design eg: 'customised' toilet pods

or

- on a one-off project to give a concise presentation of progress against plan.

**FIG 2.2.6.G** presents a 'line-of-balance' analysis of progress on fitting-out repetitive floors in an office building.  It shows the actual state of completion of each stage against projections enabling a complete overview of the project to be taken at any point in time.

**FIG. 2.2.6.G:** *'Line of balance' chart for completion of fitting-out repetitive floors of an office building*

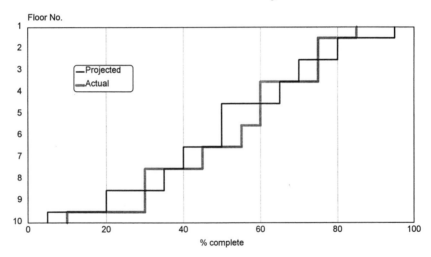

*Computerised
applications*

There are many programme management software packages available, many of which combine some or all of these techniques in one program.  Most of these packages are structured on network analysis but can output as Gantt chart, milestones, resource allocation histograms, etc;  most spreadsheet programs can produce 'S' curves against a plotted cash flow configuration.

---

(1)         'The Journal System of Capital Cost Control' – BWA

(2)         '*prem*FINANCE' Facilities Financial Control System – BWA

(3) (4) & (6)     The Collins English Dictionary

(5)         First Move Management (FM$^2$) Swindon

# PART B

# REAL ESTATE

# SECTION 3

# COMMERCIAL PROPERTY

# CHAPTER 3.1 – INTERESTS IN PROPERTY

## 3.1.1 UK PROPERTY LAW AND BUSINESS PREMISES

The Law of Property Act 1925 established the principles of property ownership in England and Wales;  Scotland was afforded the perceived benefit of one or two minor variants of the common theme.  Under that famous statute it was ordained that there would be but two categories of ownership of land and buildings:

- Fee simple absolute in possession (freehold)

and

- Leasehold

In 1927 Part (1) of the Landlord and Tenant Act afforded commercial or professional business tenants rights for compensation for improvements and 'goodwill' created by them during their tenancy;  1954 saw a further landlord and Tenant Act, Part (II) of which introduced security of tenure provisions which are mandatory except by a joint application from landlord and tenant under the Law of Property Act 1969.

Various attempts in recent times to interfere with the normal market processes of owning, buying and selling land have come crashing round the ears of their proponents:  Community land and the accompanying Development Land Tax in 1974 fared little better in attempting to frustrate property speculation than the Betterment Levy unsuccessfully planted under the land dealers by the Land Commission Act of 1967.

At present there is no legislation aimed at prevention of or punishment for successful dealings in land or buildings other than the tax regime which, by and large, impacts on all businesses in equal measure, although the exempt funds, ie: pensions, insurance etc do get favourable tax treatment.

So, for the time being, facilities managers need only concern themselves with the 1925 and 1954 legislation insofar as it impacts upon the 'tenure' component of the premises policy for which they will, hopefully, have received a formal blessing from their top management.

## 3.1.2 FREEHOLD INTERESTS

In theory the owner of freehold property owns it outright and in perpetuity.  Deterioration or demolition of any building upon the land in no way changes the perpetual nature of the title.  The owner may do anything he wishes upon it subject only to any rights others may possess either conferred by the owner or imposed by Statute.

In practice, there is little to differentiate between a medium/long lease and a freehold.  In most cases there is a mortgagor who is very interested in what happens to his security and the accountants are quick to pounce upon any modification to property having an adverse effect on the balance sheet.

Certain statutes concerning Town and Country Planning, Public Health, Local Bye-laws and building regulations may in any case restrict a freeholder's ability to develop or alter property and may impose obligations upon him as to keeping buildings in repair.

A freeholder must respect the 'natural rights' of others such as rights of light or support; he has occupier's liability to occupants and visitors and the land may also be subject to rights or restrictions, to the benefit of others, which are conditions of entitlement to ownership.

A major benefit of owning the freehold is the ability to create lesser interests in all or part of a piece of land. These interests are leaseholds; in certain cases they may take the form of licences to occupy, creating no interest in the land as such. However, the freeholder's common law right to take back physical possession at the expiry of a lease is severely curtailed by statute – in particular, for business tenancies, the Landlord and Tenant Act 1954.

### 3.1.3 LEASEHOLD INTERESTS

*Types of lease*

A leasehold affords the lessee (or leaseholder) exclusive use of the property for a specific period, either a term of years or periodic eg: quarterly, monthly etc. In return he usually has to pay a rent and accommodate and observe any rights or restrictions incorporated in the legal agreement. His rights in respect of use of the land will usually be quite restricted and specifically laid down in the agreement.

A lease will normally be either a 'building lease' or an 'occupation lease'.

*Building leases*

These are granted to developers by freeholders who wish to retain ownership in perpetuity while enjoying a rental income from land developed for use by others. The rent paid by the developer (lessee) to the landlord (lessor) is known as a ground rent, and relates to the development value of the land but excluding the value of any buildings erected thereon.

Such leases are, for obvious reasons, normally for substantial periods, say 99 years; the buildings revert to the landowner on expiry of the lease subject only to statutory rights of the tenant.

*Occupation leases*

This type of lease is for exclusive occupation of the tenant and can be for any period, but normally not more than 20 years with 'break' clauses (options to end the agreement) at specific periods - say 5 and 10 years. **These break periods must not be confused with the 'rent review' periods discussed below, although they often coincide.**

*Sub-leases*

Anyone who has a leasehold interest may, subject to the terms of his own lease - which usually requires his landlord's consent - sub-let the property at any rent he can obtain but only for a period expiring before his own lease period expires. The sub-lessee may enjoy similar protection under statute as his own immediate landlord; the latter will be responsible for any default by his tenant with regard to obligations passed on to the sub-tenant from the main lease.

The landlord and his tenant may however make a joint approach to the courts to restrict the security of tenure provisions of the Landlord and Tenant Act 1954 (Part 2).

*Assignments*

Subject again to the usual requirement of landlord's consent a leaseholder may hand over the remaining portion of his lease to a third party; an assignment can only be at the current passing rent and all existing conditions of the lease will be transferred to the assignee.

Because there is **privity of contract** between the original parties to a lease an assignor may yet be liable for a default of the assignee.

## 3.1.4 LICENCES

*The nature of a licence*

Whereas a lease, however short, creates an interest in the land a licence does not.

A licence may be either:

•       to occupy land,

or

•       to use land

and it may be granted orally or in writing and for any period.

*Licences to occupy*

Case law on the subject of when a right to occupy is a lease as opposed to a licence is voluminous and beyond the scope of this work. In most cases facilities managers will only consider taking premises under a licence agreement for a short period eg: during refurbishment or relocation - and then only as a last resort.

The licence agreement should make it clear that no lease or tenancy is to be created, but even explicit wording may yet fail to prevent the courts - or the VAT man - from construing the agreement differently.

The most significant issues about lease v licence are that the latter provides no statutory right of security of tenure, does not breach any covenant against subletting and may not give exclusive rights to possession.

*Licences to use*

These are rights to use land either to carry out some operation or to use specialised facilities eg: storage. Rights over land eg: rights of way are in effect licences to use; if they are accompanied by consideration then there may be VAT implications.

## 3.1.5 RESTRICTIVE COVENANTS

It is quite common for the user of both freehold and leasehold property to be subjected to restrictions formally set down in the deeds.

These 'restrictive covenants' emanate from the action of a previous owner in attempting to protect his own or others interests from some detrimental use by succeeding users, eg: restrictions as to the nature of a manufacturing process to be carried out on the land, or categories of business activity.

In some circumstances the vendor or lessor may be merely trying to protect his own enjoyment of adjacent property, whereas in other situations he may be concerned to maintain the general level of values in the adjoining property - eg: where he owns substantial investment properties.

Over time these restrictive covenants often mar the value or development potential of the property by restricting what is by then appropriate use of the site.

Rights to enforce these covenants may be forfeited if the beneficiary has been seen to permit breaches or allowed them to go unchallenged.

Under the Law of Property and Lands Tribunal Acts a freeholder may seek to have restrictive covenants set aside or modified and the Landlord and Tenant Act of 1954 allows similar action where leases of more than 40 years duration have at least 25 years elapsed.

The Lands Tribunal may also grant an order to compensate the beneficiary of any restrictive covenant who would suffer as the result of their adjudication.

# CHAPTER 3.2 – LEASEHOLD CONDITIONS

## 3.2.1 THE CONSTRUCTION OF A LEASE

A typical leasehold or sub-lease agreement will contain specific provisions, in particular with regard to:

- details of the demised areas and the parties to the agreement - including any 'superior' landlord; eg: in the case of a sub-lease the sub-lessor's landlord (who may himself be a leaseholder to the owner of the freehold) will be named in the sub-lease and his interest in the arrangement defined

- the period of the lease and any break points

- the rent, payment details and any rent review provisions

- any covenants (ie: obligations) to be observed (see Chapter 3.1)

- permitted uses

- landlord's obligations and any means of recovering costs from the tenant in their respect eg: service charges, further rent etc in respect of works to maintain the 'common parts'

- other obligations of the tenant in respect of the premises eg: maintaining in 'good and tenantable repair'

- conditions relating to any alterations and/or improvements, including obtaining landlord's approvals

- alienation

- provisions in respect of value added tax (see Chapter 11.4)

- landlord's rights to enter and inspect and actions he may take in respect of default

- notices

- rights to redevelop or refurbish.

## 3.2.2 RENT

*The nature and payment of rent*

Rent is the amount paid by a leaseholder or tenant for the use of land (ground rent) or buildings. It is usually set at an annual figure payable by quarterly instalments; in periodic tenancies eg: quarterly, monthly etc rent is usually paid per period at a time. In all cases rent is conventionally paid in advance.

The quarterly rent is due on the traditional 'quarter days'. In England and Wales these are:

- Lady Day        -      25 March
- Mid-summer Day   -      24 June
- Michaelmas      -      29 September
- Christmas       -      25 December

A rental level set at, or near, the full market value is known as a '**rack rent**'. Where significantly less than the rack rent it may give rise to a valuable interest to an occupation lessee subject to the timing of the next rent review.

Sometimes, particularly in retail premises, rents are geared to a percentage of turnover. These 'turnover rents' are often applied in new locations, such as new shopping centres, to encourage take-up of leases in advance of proven establishment of a successful trading location.

Another form of incentive to secure tenants in new locations, but less fashionable in this day and age, is the 'rising rent' where the levels are pre-set for a number of years at a time.

*Failure to pay rent*

Most leases permit the landlord to enter and repossess the property if the tenant fails to pay up on the due date, but they must go to court to do so legally. The tenant is obliged to pay the rent, and any 'further rent', even if his landlord is in default in respect of his own obligations under the agreement.

*Rent reviews*

Modern leases invariably contain provisions for the level of rent to be reviewed at regular intervals and reset to the level prevailing in the current market.

The conventional period is 5 years; 7 and even 14 may be found in older leases while just prior to the 1990's recession some landlords were trying to introduce 3-yearly reviews because of the high inflation in rents for the limited amount of high quality space then available.

Many of these rent review clauses have wording to ensure that in the event of market levels dropping (as has happened dramatically in the early 1990's) rents cannot go below the passing level.

However, new leases are certainly being negotiated on tough terms for the investors who obviously have to make sure that not only is the future rent guaranteed but also that the value of the property is not further reduced due to any lack of certainty with regard to upwards only rent review..

The timing of the rent review is sometimes set to coincide with dates in the lease at which either party may terminate the agreement. The provisions setting down the rights and obligations of the parties in this respect are commonly known as 'break clauses'. It is quite common for lay people to fall into the trap of thinking that the rent review period is also a potential break-point, which it most often is **not.**

### 3.2.3 REPAIR AND MAINTENANCE

*Fully repairing and insuring lease*

Under a lease the liability of the parties for maintaining, repairing, decorating and insuring the premises will be set down - although historically definitions of terms, rights and obligations have left much to be desired.

Who does what is largely determined by the practicality of the situation. So, if the building is let entirely to one leaseholder, then it is likely that the 'fully repairing and insuring' type of lease will apply. In this case the tenant will have full responsibility for upkeep of the property including not only repair and maintenance, redecoration, insurance, all fuel bills and other running costs but also the replacement of defective plant, materials and structure and reinstatement to its original condition on expiration of the lease. In the latter situation it is common for this liability to be commuted to a payment based on a 'schedule of condition' prepared at the end of the lease. Where a lease is assigned or sub-let during its course a schedule of condition is usually produced at the commencement of the assignment or sub-lease as well as on expiration to enable the assignor's or sub-lessor's compensation to be calculated.

*Multiple occupation leases*

Where premises are in multi-occupation the usual arrangement is for the landlord to keep responsibility for maintenance and insurance of the 'common parts', with the tenants reimbursing him by way of a 'service charge' type of arrangement as discussed below.

The term 'common parts' usually embraces:

- the external envelope ie: foundations, external walls, windows, doors and roof.
- main entrance
- common staircases and lifts
- main services and utilities
- HVAC central plant and distribution
- atria
- external grounds.

The leaseholder usually has to maintain the 'tenanted area' ie: that which he occupies exclusively and pay all the bills specifically relating to his occupation and identifiable as such. So, he will pay his own internal cleaning bills, any metered gas or electricity and internal repairs/redecoration and the like. Whereas the insurance of his own goods and chattels will probably be his own direct contract he will have to pay (via the service charge) his agreed share of insuring the property against fire and other forms of damage.

*Dealing with obsolescence*

The lease or agreement covenants both parties to their obligations in this area and the substantial increase in the engineering and electronic content of modern buildings has brought increasing difficulties in determining where obsolescence takes over from dilapidation. More and more the chosen route through this dilemma has been to restructure the lease to take account of modernisation to standards acceptable to both landlord and tenant. In this case either the landlord or the tenant may carry out the refurbishment, with the terms of the lease reflecting the risks and benefits to both parties. The example of 'risk analysis' in Chapter 2.2 takes these two alternatives as options for evaluation of risk accruing to the existing lease-holder.

*Enforcement of
the repairing
covenants*

The ability of the landlord to insist upon repair of buildings is governed by statute, in particular the Leasehold Property Repair Act 1938 and the Landlord and Tenant Act 1927; additionally, the landlord's ability to ensure that the condition of premises does not fall below defined minimum standards is framed in the Defective Premises Act 1957 and Occupiers' Liability Act 1984. Current Health & Safety legislation clearly impinges on the rights and obligations of landlord and tenant in this respect (see Chapter 8.2).

### 3.2.4 SERVICE CHARGES

*The purpose*

The service charge as a distinct cost centre is peculiar to leasehold premises. It exists normally to provide for services which are common to tenants in a multi-tenanted building. It can also, however, be found in single tenanted buildings, when the landlord wants to maintain physical control of the condition of the building.

In some cases it can also incorporate - sometimes by ex-contractual agreement - such items as general office cleaning, lighting and other 'workplace' services, which the tenant wishes to delegate to the landlord, his agents and contractors.

Without doubt this is the single most complicated cost centre of the premises budget. First, the content of the charge is so significantly varied as to render inter-building comparisons virtually meaningless. Second, the level of expenditure is beyond the control of the tenant. Third, the legal framework surrounding rights and liabilities of landlord and tenant is a complex mass of case law in contract and tort.

Such is the under-development of the science of premises cost control that few facilities managers have a clear idea of whether or not they are paying the right price for the services provided by their landlord. It is still common for facilities managers to fail to take account of items of maintenance, cleaning, fuel and the like masked by the title 'service charge' when attempting to compare their cost centres to published data. Equally, they can render such data useless when they do not unscramble service charges from other information they have provided in response to questionnaires.

*Key financial
issues*

The facilities manager must pay particular attention to the following issues when addressing the liability to pay a service charge:

- the extent to which the service offered (and performed) safeguards the financial and environmental interests of the tenant

- the total financial implications of the service contract

- the tenant's rights of enforcement in terms of performance and price

- the apportionment of the charge between tenants in a multi-tenanted building

- the relationship of the service charge to the total cost of operating the premises.

*Scope of the*
*service contract*

The form of words in the lease will have a significant bearing on the rights, duties and liabilities of the parties and this aspect is further discussed below.

The headings under which expenditure is incurred closely follow the cost centres of a tenant's own operating costs - for example cleaning, energy, maintenance, alterations, insurance, planting, security, porterage, administration and reserve/ sinking fund.

The lessor should be able to recover the reasonable cost of carrying out his obligations under the lease. There are, however, question marks over certain costs where legal advice is sometimes needed.

Particularly contentious areas are:

- interest - on money borrowed to meet expenditure where a shortfall of reserve funds exists

- management fee charged for landlord's personal activities in the field

- replacement, as opposed to repair of components.

The question of 'reasonableness' and common law duty of care may impinge upon contractual terms in determining the scope of the service.

*Cost Levels*

Perhaps the commonest area of misconception in considering operating cost levels is to assume that the level of the service charge expenditure in any one building - or group of buildings - can be viewed in isolation from the total operating costs of the premises. In making external comparisons there are also countless variables influencing both the total operating cost level and the proportion of it taken by the service charge.

- **The scope** of the service is dictated by the terms of the lease and any independently negotiated extensions or exclusions. This means that, for example, the cleaning contract may extend to the 'demised areas', 'small' power and/or lighting may or may not be separately metered. The proportion of common areas and the nature of the fabric will also greatly vary the scope of such items as internal cleaning, window cleaning, fabric repairs and external decorations.

- **The quality** of the building will also dictate both the amount of services required to operate it and the standards to be achieved in each cost centre. For instance, marble-clad buildings should require less external cleaning than, say, precast concrete panels - but it is also likely to be very important that the marble be kept in peak condition because of the aspirations of tenant and landlord alike. Quality of specification will normally demand quality of maintenance, regardless of inherently cost-saving characteristics of materials and design.

- **Design**, that somewhat amorphous ingredient of the building's character, embraces quality as well as specification, style, size, shape and 'operability'.

- **Operability** - a piece of jargon coined to cover the inherent capacity of the building to be operated efficiently and economically - for example, are the lift doors wide enough, and the storage areas large enough, to facilitate the access of the big, modern, cleaning machines so essential to fast, efficient cleaning operations?

- **Administration** costs in the service charge will normally cover the fees paid to managing agents - sometimes embracing the collection of rents - as well as his auditors', accountants' and surveyors' fees. Note that time spent by the landlord **in person** is not normally recoverable unless it is charged as fees via a separate firm employing his services for the purpose of administration.

  The calibre of administration will have a marked effect on the total level of service charge, although variations above and below the norm may each be caused as much by diligence as by neglect. Regular and thoroughly planned maintenance - as opposed to crisis management - may lead to higher charges; but so can irregular maintenance procured in the profligate manner. The lessor has a duty to exercise his obligations to the letter of the lease and may have an implied responsibility to carry out - or have an agent carry out - the necessary functions in a proper and efficient manner. This includes cost control.

- **Historic factors** such as performance by the administrator in looking after the works covered by the service agreement will bear largely on the frequency and cost level of future operating expenditure.

  Buildings over 20 years old are especially liable to sudden bouts of economic outpouring due to inadequate maintenance or deferred improvements. With new technology such an important feature of the facilities manager's daily problems, even buildings just a few years old can be found wanting in many (expensive) respects - such as flexibility of communications, capacity of services etc

- **Inflation** is variable from one cost centre to another. Building Maintenance Information Ltd publishes a series of indexes showing historical trends in inflation of operating cost centres such as cleaning, energy and maintenance. Note that contract prices will be more closely geared to the market conditions than direct operations which more closely follow labour-and-material inflation; however, over a period of three years or more any divergencies will be naturally adjusted as, for example, direct labour is 'poached' by contractors in a 'bull' market, forcing up in-house basic rates.

- **Location** impinges on general cost levels in two ways. On the one hand, original cost level and local market conditions vary the base price of certain specific operations from one place to another. At the same time the quality of buildings and the aspirations of the parties to a lease also vary substantially across the country.

  Not only are premises operating standards usually higher in, say, the West End of London than in the provincial centres, but also certain cost centres such as security and 'housekeeping' appear as identifiable cost centres in their own right the more prestigious the building.

  Prestige normally goes with location; there are, of course, many out-of-town headquarters buildings, but these are usually owner-occupied and not subject to service charges.

- **Air-conditioning** affects the level of service charge in two ways. First, the costs of energy and plant maintenance and replacement are considerably higher than in a non-air-conditioned building. Second, air-conditioned buildings are most usually found in prestigious city centre locations so there tends to be a statistical correlation between air-conditioning and higher quality (and hence more expensive) operating performance and management.

Service charges analysed during an audit of 100 branch offices of a major financial institution are given at **FIG 3.2.4.A**. The tenancies were mostly between 2,500 and 5,000 sq ft NIA and there is no distinction in this particular sample between air-conditioned and non-air-conditioned buildings.

**FIG. 3.2.4.A:** *Service charge analysis - survey of 100 branch offices*

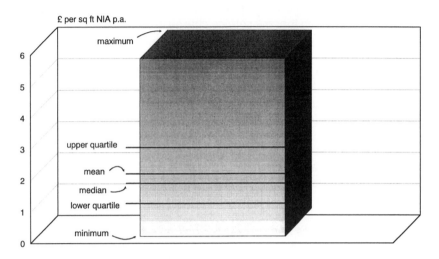

However, the figure does show the wide range of costs across the sample, and by showing the service charge in the context of total operating costs (see **FIG 3.2.4.B**) the danger of looking at the service charges in isolation from total operating costs is clearly emphasised.

**FIG. 3.2.4.B:** *Service charges in the context of total operating costs*
*- average of survey of 100 branch offices*

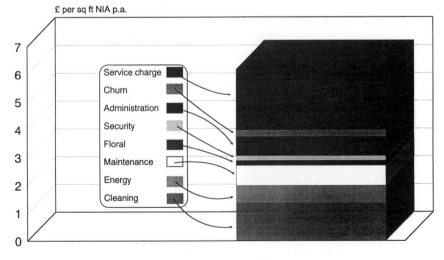

It is rather easier to forecast the operating costs level, and hence the likely level of service charge, in new buildings, but it must be remembered that the policy for dealing with depreciation and reserve funds will greatly affect whether future service charges grow faster than inflation or start at a higher, most cautious, figure which does not catch the tenant out in later years.

## Reserve funds and sinking funds

Although these two funds sound alike, their effect on the level of service charge is markedly different.

**The reserve fund** is sometimes set up by the lease to make sure there is normally some money available to meet regularly occurring revenue expenditure, such as decorating the common parts, repairs, modernisations. It is normally a regular contribution, so that the service charge in total equalises out occasionally expected but not totally determined future expenditure.

**The sinking fund** is usually created to pay for the replacement, from time to time, under capital expenditure, of components such as central heating/air-conditioning plant, lifts and roof coverings which may not actually be needed in the timespan of a particular tenant's occupation of the building.

Some leases as a variant of the same theme allow the lessor to claim depreciation on his capital expenditure. Tenants (and owner-occupiers) should be wary of sinking funds set to accumulate too rapidly due to a highish (risk-bearing) interest rate or a too short writing-down period. In the latter connection both tenants and owner-occupiers must distinguish clearly between writing-down rates and periods for tax purposes and realistic replacement programmes. Let the premises budget - including the service charge and sinking funds - stand on its own two feet, regardless of the tax regime presently prevailing.

To summarise, the **reserve fund** is a way of evening out short-term, regular commitments whereas the **sinking fund**, if it appears in the service charge, may cover eventualities outside of the tenant's probable occupation period - and sometimes at a penal rate.

Whether or not the funds are held in trust by the landlord is a most important point of detail. Stated or implied trust status for the fund may help avoid trouble if the landlord becomes bankrupt but it can cause problems with tax avoidance since payment by the tenant into his own trust fund may not be allowable as an expense.

The more usual way of paying reserve funds and sinking funds is as 'further' or 'additional' rent against future expenditure. No real tax problems lurk here for the tenant but the landlord may get caught making an extra profit rent because he expends the money in a future accounting year and he may also get taxed on any interest earned on deposited reserves.

## Service charge and the terms of the lease

As a general principle, the landlord is only obliged to provide the services specifically stipulated in the lease - and there are nearly as many one-off clauses as there are buildings to let. The lease is normally framed in one of two ways. The first involves landlords making very wide-ranging covenants including provision and maintenance of future services which are not definitely known to be required - such as, say, local area network. He is then empowered to levy a service charge in respect of work carried out in performance of the covenants.

The second method is more detailed, listing the likely heads of expenditure against which service charges can be levied. This means that the landlord is only covenanted in respect of the headings listed, although he may be empowered, by a 'landlord's discretion' clause, to do a lot more than his covenant obliges.

**Quality and
type of work**

There will be no liability for the tenant to pay for any work of a type which is not included specifically in the lease - for example, unless renewal is covered either specifically or implicitly then it cannot be charged. Obviously, if a repair job would be more expensive or otherwise uneconomical then the parties would be well advised to waive any restrictive wording.

On the matter of repair, in the absence of wording to the contrary in the lease, the duty of the landlord to repair extends only to putting the component back into 'good working order; how he does it is up to him.

Case law remains, as always, fairly inconsistent on issues such as whether he has to do the repair in a reasonably cost effective manner where the lease does not specifically so require. Some help may be available to the tenant under recent Statute Law - such as the Unfair Contract Terms Act 1977 and the Supply of Goods and Services Act 1982. Nevertheless the safest remedy for the tenant is to try to get a 'reasonable care and skill' clause inserted in the lease at the outset. Whether or not the landlord will agree to this will probably depend on how the market is at the time and how badly he needs the tenant.

**Disputes**

Sometimes clauses in leases require an annual certification by surveyors or accountants relating to the expenditure incurred and charges levied. Such certificates cannot be binding and conclusive where they involve interpretation of the contract - such as the definition of repair and scope of covenants, which are a matter of law. Arbitration clauses are common and generally desirable although this may limit the right to refer questions of law to only those prescribed in the Arbitration Act 1979.

**Apportionment
of charges**

The lease will sometimes be quite specific as to how the service charge should be split between tenants in a multi-tenanted building, a percentage being expressed or calculable in each of the demised areas.

The percentage will usually be related to floor area or rateable values. It is sometimes, however, left as variable by the landlord or his agents eg: 'a fair and reasonable proportion' (watch out for this) and sometimes a fixed percentage is payable. Differential percentages relating to certain heads of expenditure are sometimes given as between one tenancy and another in a building - usually where some tenants have an obviously substantially greater or lesser requirement for the service; parts of the building, for example, which are heated but not air-conditioned may have a differential percentage on energy costs and maintenance and repair of plant. As long as such differentials are fair and are clearly expressed then that is fine - but vagueness can lead to all sorts of niggling disputes with neighbouring tenants as well as with the landlord.

**Insurance**

Insurance will normally be required in respect of reinstatement of all or part of the building, loss of rent, and loss of service charge. Charges for premiums should be 'dead net' after deduction of any discounts. If the landlord or his agent acts as the insurance agent he should not include any commission in the insurance charge as this is likely to be in contravention of the Prevention of Corruption Act 1906.

### 3.2.5 LANDLORD'S APPROVALS

*Alienation*

Most leases will require that any proposal by a tenant to transfer ownership of the interest to a third party will require the landlord's consent and some may specifically prohibit sub-letting or assignments. Clearly undesirable or unsubstantial tenants are apt to be detrimental to the landlord's interest whether in terms of management, investment value or both. The Landlord and Tenant Act 1988 obliges the landlord to act reasonably and promptly with applications and puts the onus upon him to prove that he has so acted.

*Alterations and improvements*

Some leases may absolutely prohibit alterations (but the Landlord and Tenant Act 1927 may come to the rescue of certain business occupiers) or they may be silent on this issue; in the latter case, provided the tenant observes the normal statutory controls and delivers the premises back in good repair he has absolute freedom to make whatever changes he wants.

Consent to 'improvements' must not be unreasonably withheld even if it has an adverse effect on the value of the property - the landlord may recover compensation and may require reinstatement if that is a reasonable thing to do.

On the other hand, if a business tenant's improvements enhance the value of the property or its 'lettability' he may, having been given notice to quit on expiration of his lease, be able to recover all or part of this costs under the Landlord and Tenant Act 1927, typically a figure equivalent to the rateable value. This right of recovery will be lost if the improvements are carried out as part of a contractual liability with the landlord in respect of works which are **not** required to comply with statutory requirements.

Correct observation of procedures for applying for consent and securing notice is imperative - starting work in anticipation of approval is a common occurrence with impatient tenants who may not realise the possibility that they may have to pull it all down again if the landlord reasonably refuses consent -even if he had originally given an informal nod (maybe not in possession of all details).

A tenant making improvements with the landlord's consent may find himself paying for his trouble when the rent comes to be reviewed under the terms of the lease, unless the terms expressly provide against it or he has received a licence authenticated by the landlord's solicitor. If the lease is renewed under the Landlord and Tenant Act 1954 (eg: where the tenant agrees to occupy refurbished premises) improvements made voluntarily in the course of the previous agreement (ie: not required by a covenant of the lease) and either by the current tenant or completed (by whomever) within the 21 years preceding application for a new tenancy, must be disregarded in computing the new rent. However this is an area of property law which is bedevilled by conflicting case law so the safest way for a tenant to go about substantial upgrading is to do a deal with the landlord on a new lease effecting an appropriate compromise of both parties' interests.

If there is a long lease to run at historic rents without rent reviews (many fortunate tenants and unfortunate investors still enjoy/suffer these relics from the past) the tenant should be able to get the best deal by undertaking the improvements under his own steam - with the landlord's approval and a formal licence of course!

A real life example of the financial implications of these two options on a Central London office building is discussed in Chapter 2.2.5 (Risk management) and the financial appraisals of the options are illustrated in **FIG 3.2.5.A**

**FIG.3.2.5.A:** *Rentalisation v amortisation of refurbishment - financial appraisal of options*

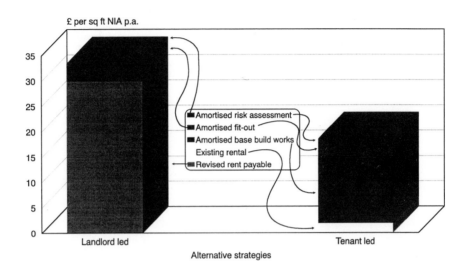

In the example the tenant was the beneficiary of a long remainder of an existing lease with no rent review for several years. In spite of the obvious financial advantage to the tenant in undertaking the refurbishment on his own account the decision went with the landlord-led option on grounds which were not dictated by pure facilities economics.

## 3.2.6 REDEVELOPMENT AND REFURBISHMENT

Some leases may contain provisions entitling the landlord to take repossession for the purposes of redevelopment or refurbishment and the Landlord and Tenant Act 1954 reinforces this right provided that the intention is registered in the County Court by **both parties**.

The Act permits the landlord to offer to re-house the tenant either in the new development or in suitable alternative accommodation and he must compensate him for any loss or inconvenience thereby caused. In certain circumstances the landlord may get a declaration from the courts that the tenancy is terminated in which case compensation will be payable in normal circumstances.

FACILITIES ECONOMICS

3 – 16

# CHAPTER 3.3 – INVESTMENT VALUATION

### 3.3.1 THE PRINCIPLES OF REAL ESTATE VALUATION

*Types of valuation procedure*

The value of a vacant plot of land or a developed site will be required to be established for a variety of purposes using different procedures as appropriate.

In general the valuation will have regard to one or more of the following criteria:

- open market value

- replacement cost (see Chapter 3.6 - Property insurance)

- development or redevelopment value (see Chapter 10.2 - Development economics)

- profitability.

The open market price will involve an appraisal of market place transaction comparables, whereas replacement entails estimates of construction costs; the residual valuation essential for the development or redevelopment options require both estimates of cost and forecasts of market value on completion.

### 3.3.2 OPEN MARKET VALUE

*The property investment market*

This is not the place for detailed review of one of the most complex concepts facing qualified valuers, so discussion is limited to the principles and issues most likely to influence the valuer's decision in respect of any particular piece of real estate.

Apart from residential freehold property where a widespread selection of comparables is normally available to the valuer (and, indeed, the prospective purchaser) most property transactions relate to business premises either in owner-occupation or leased by an investor to a business occupier. Provided such property is of a type and in a location to attract a purchaser or tenant when offered to the market then its value will be geared to the 'investment value' rather than to any intrinsic value it may have to the existing or prospective occupier.

There is normally no direct relationship between investment value and cost. The important relationship between building performance and value is considered in detail at Chapter 1.2. For present purposes, however, the conventional view of factors influencing rents and the valuation multipliers thereof must be considered as the norm, and explained.

The value of a property investment, as will be examined and calculated in detail below, is most commonly perceived and expressed as a product of multiplying the passing (current) or predicted rent by a multiplier - commonly known as the '**Years Purchase**' (**YP**).

## The rental level

The level of rent is either the passing rent ie: what is currently being paid under a lease (to be reviewed at some point in the future) or a prediction of what a tenant would be prepared to pay for a term of years in occupation of the premises.

Local comparables will be sought by the valuer whose appraisal will have regard to many critical factors including particularly

- location - especially 'prime' or 'secondary' status, access to public transport, motorways etc

- quality of design and construction - including methods of environmental control, special features etc

- proposed lease terms - especially rent review periods, term of years, covenants and break clauses

- current supply and demand for similar property.

## The 'Years Purchase' multiplier

This term is really a misnomer since, although the factor manifests itself as a multiplier of the annual rent (whence the phrase) it does not derive from a period of time but from the return sought by a real estate investor from his capital invested in an income-producing property.

This return is conventionally expressed relative to the '**initial yield**', which is a percentage of the initial rent to the capital invested. Therefore, a new property let at an initial rent of £100,000 pa for which an investor has paid £1m will give an initial return on investment of

$$\frac{£100,000}{£1,000,000} \text{ ie } 10\%$$

It can be seen that the investor has used a multiplier of 10 times the annual rent in deciding what the investment is worth ie: how much to pay for the right to receive **that** rental income from **that** tenant under **those** conditions in **that** building in **that** location etc for **that** length of time **and to receive an income in perpetuity thereafter**. This multiplier is the 'years purchase in perpetuity' and is calculated simply by taking the reciprocal of the investment yield percentage.

So, in the above example

$$\frac{100}{10} = 10YP$$

If the return were 8% the reciprocal would be

$$\frac{100}{8} = 12\frac{1}{2}YP \text{ and so on.}$$

**FIG 3.3.2.A** expresses these relationships graphically.

If he wishes to provide a sinking fund of £500,000 to replace the building after say 30 years the investor can, in theory, apply a factor of 0.015 x £500,000 to provide a sum of £7,500 pa which, invested at 5% for 30 years, would yield the sum of £500,000 required (ignoring any tax on the investment).

In this case his initial yield is

$$\frac{£(100,000 - 7,500)}{£1,000,000} \qquad \text{or } 9.25\%$$

In practice and as discussed further below, the sinking fund for building replacement a long time ahead is often ignored in calculations for freeholds and long leases.

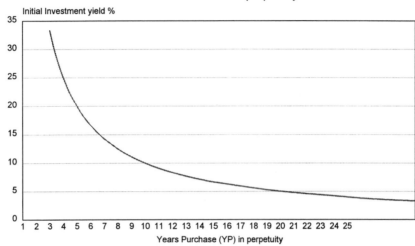

**FIG. 3.3.2.A:** *Graphic relationship between initial yield and 'Years Purchase in perpetuity'*

The decision the investor will make regarding the appropriate percentage return from his investment in a rented, or rentable, property embraces a highly complex set of factors, such as

* the length of lease and remaining period

* rental growth forecasts

* the 'covenant' of the tenant (will he be able to pay his rent through time)

* the frequency and conditions of rent reviews

* comparative impact of inflation on alternative forms of investment

* comparative returns/risks from other forms of investment

* the likelihood of any 'voids' in the income stream eg: rent-free periods, post-break empty periods

* the quality of the property

* any potential windfall gain eg: 'marriage value' with adjoining properties

* the liquidity of capital invested

* the amount of capital available and opportunities to invest.

Investment yields on prime commercial property fluctuate with the vagaries of the national economy but not always in strict tandem with the ups and downs thereof.

For example, in the inflationary period of 1972-74 in the UK rents doubled at a time when inflation was running at around 15% - 20% pa. This phenomenon was caused by a shortage of good property;  the perception of investment managers that property would provide a hedge against inflation brought vast tranches of funds to the market and the 'weight' of this money pushed initial market yields down to unprecedentedly low levels.

Yields of 5% on prime office buildings were commonplace so the 20 Years Purchase of the escalating rents occasioned enormous windfall profits to developers lucky enough to sell on their completed projects before the miners' strike, 3-day week, and the fall of the Heath government, brought the whole pack of cards tumbling down.

**FIG 3.3.2.B** shows how the developer might have 'cleaned up' over this period having purchased land on the basis of assumptions which, fortunately for him, turned out to be totally wrong as the project evolved.

**FIG 3.3.2.B:** *The effect of appreciating values on development profits*

| Capital value of completed development: 50,000 sq ft NIA: | 1971 projection £,000 | 1973 out - turn £,000 |
|---|---|---|
| @ £8 / sq ft x 15 YP | 6,000 | |
| @ £12 / sq ft x 20 YP | | 12,000 |
| Land including fees and finance | (2,750) | (3,000*) |
| Building and site development costs 60,000 sq ft GIA: @ £30/sq ft | (1,800) | |
| @ £40/sq ft | | (2,400) |
| Fees and finance on building etc | (360) | (480) |
| Residual profit | 1,090 = 22% on capital expenditure | 6,120 = 96% on capital expenditure |
| * Increase due to higher interest rates than predicted for the period of the development | | |

This scenario was, of course, seen in reverse in the period from 1989 to 1991/2.

**FIG 3.3.2.C** tracks the changes in investment yields in the UK since the 1960's against several key economic indicators.

**FIG 3.3.2.C:** *Variations in prime investment yields on office buildings 1965 - 1994*

| Date | Prime yield % | Prevailing economic and political situation |
|---|---|---|
| 1972 | 4½ | 'Barbour boom', 'weight of money' into property |
| 1974 | 8 | 3 - day week fall of Conservative government, Community Land Act, Development Land Tax |
| 1980 | 5½ | New Conservative government, institutional investment in property |
| 1987 | 6 | Rapid economic growth - shortage of good space |
| 1990 | 8 | World recession bites |
| 1994 | 7 | Recession slowly easing, property investors slowly returning |

*Inflation and
the investment
yield*

The underlying principles of investment in income-bearing property are diametrically opposed to fixed interest investment in gilts (although significantly influenced by their coupon levels) and quite different from investment in shares.

Whereas government stocks bear the same rate per annum for the life of the issue - say 15 or 25 years - and are redeemable at cost on expiry of the period, commercial property will bear a fixed return until the first rent review (say 5 years) and a higher (inflated) return for the next period.

Company shares overall will normally increase annually with inflation thereby increasing annually the percentage return on the initial investment. A successful company, like a successful property, will out-perform the market thereby not only 'hedging' against inflation but also generating a capital profit over and above inflation.

At **FIG 3.3.2.D** the relative performance of property, equity, shares and gilts is shown for the period 1971 - 1994. The yields for property, as with equities, are an average across all sectors. Prime shops and offices, like the blue-chip companies, command initial investment yields lower than the average. This is good for their owners, not bad, because the initial yield reflects the market-place view of an acceptable return at a moment in time; so the punter viewing an ordinary share as a 4% investment (anticipating good future growth) will pay 25 times the dividend per share for the privilege of getting on to the 'gravy train'. Similarly, low initial property investment yields produce high valuations. In the case of property the 'dividend' is the rental income which gets adjusted (usually upwards) every 5 or 7 years whereas the commercial company dividends vary (hopefully upwards) annually depending upon efficiency and market forces.

**FIG. 3.3.2.D:** *Comparative initial yields on property, equities and gilts - 1971/94*

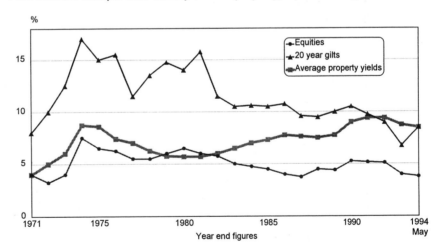

Source: ICHP/SAVILLS/DATASTREAM

Gilts, on the other hand, deliver only the investment yield promised on the 'coupon'. Inflation whittles away all the non-variable income stream and also the value of the capital investment when recovered at the end of the term. When interest rates are high gilts offer high returns making low initial property and equity yields look poor ; the latter then usually rise causing loss of value (the drop frequently fuelled by the poor economic conditions of which high interest rates are most often a symptom and an applied remedy). However, in the good economic times, the growth in property and equities will justify low initial yields, against high-yielding fixed interest investment, especially when the future income is discounted to present worth.

**FIG 3.3.2.E** tells an interesting story about how property has kept up with inflation since 1965 by compacting actual values at various points in time, with the theoretical values updated by the Retail Price Index from the base valuation in 1965. The boom cycles of the early 70's and late 80's both proved to bear false promise and, of course, those investing at those times missed out badly.

**FIG. 3.3.2.E:** *Actual values of a prime central London office building -*
*(1965 - 1994) compared with RPI - adjustment of 1965 value*

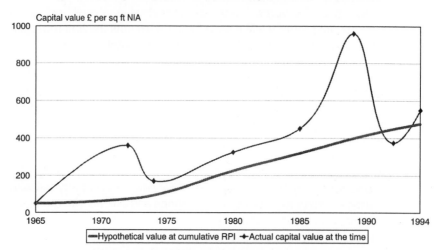

Given the substantial sums invested in property and volumes of evidence to indicate that values **do** go down as well as up (heresy to valuers and their institutional clients prior to the 1974 crash) it is not surprising that techniques of investment and risk appraisal have grown more sophisticated in the past couple of decades.

The concept of the equated yield is that the pattern of rent reviews and future growth can be isolated from the other factors influencing the 'all risks' initial yield discussed above. As such the 'equated yield' takes into account assumptions of growth rates and the rent review cycle which triggers the growth, and produces a yield which is directly comparable with fixed interest securities - as well as with other options available for property investment.

Tables of equated yields are available covering a wide range of initial yields, rent review periods and growth rates and provide an extremely useful tool for investment comparison and also sensitivity analysis on each of the factors.

*The sinking fund*

Where an income is receivable in perpetuity or for long periods such as 99 or 125 years it is not necessary to take into account the necessity to re-finance the capital investment via a sinking fund as described above. For one thing, the sinking fund factor over such periods is of a negligible amount, and it is far outweighed by the vagaries of inflation and market yield.

Nevertheless, where income is terminable in the medium term it is necessary to set aside a sum of money which will replace the original investment at expiry of the investment cycle so making the return directly comparable with an investment – bearing income in perpetuity.

The historic concept of a sinking fund was that it should be invested in absolutely safe and consequently low-yield situations. Consequently there would be a difference between the **accumulative rate** of the sinking fund and the **remunerative rate** of the yield percentage. So, rather than take the sinking fund out of the rental income as shown in the Years Purchase multiplier explanation above, the valuation tables treat it as a separate function of the multiplier, effectively reducing it by an amount equivalent to a reduction from the annual rent.

**FIG 3.3.2.F** illustrates how a remunerative rate of 10% and an accumulative rate of 2½% are combined by adding the interest at 10% per £ to the annual sinking fund per £ at 2½% and then taking the reciprocal to calculate the years purchase multiplier for a leasehold valuation.

The calculation uses **dual rates** and reflects the principle that the **remunerative rate** expresses judgement of the risk whereas the **accumulative** rate adjusts for the time factor.

The 'annual equivalent cost' referred to in the table is not a term used often in connection with real estate. It is, in effect, the annual cost of borrowing on a 100% mortgage and is used extensively in management accounting when capital sums need to be annualised and amortised in investment appraisal.

| Example: Years purchase factor calculation in respect of a non - recoverable investment bearing constant income over 20 yrs | |
| --- | --- |
| Sinking fund @ 2½% pa to redeem £1 capital invested over 20 yrs: | 0.0391471 |
| Interest @10% pa reserved on £1 capital invested in perpetuity (Years Purchase in perpetuity): | 0.10 |
| Annual equivalent cost (per £1) of purchasing the investment using a finance rate of 10% and a sinking fund of 2½%:   0.10 + 0.03915: | 0.13915 |
| **Years purchase dual rate** (10% + 2½%):        1 / 0.13915: | **7.187 YP** |

FIG 3.3.2.F: *Calculation of Years Purchase (dual rate) from first principles*

Most investors valuing a freehold interest will apply only the remunerative rate reflecting the fact that

- it will not be necessary to replace the capital - as in the purchase of a leasehold
- replacement or refurbishment of any building will be many years hence
- the low risk makes it reasonable to consider that the theoretical sinking fund for such works can be supported out of income at the remunerative rate

However, as discussed below in Chapter 3.7 - 'Depreciation' the need to make a positive allowance for upgrading buildings on a regular basis must be addressed positively in modern valuations.

Many of the buildings purchased by investors in the late 70's and early 80's at low initial yields with no apparent sinking fund provisions were found wanting in the Information Technology explosion which followed their construction. Consequently, later revaluations had to take into account the prematurely imminent cost of refurbishment. In some cases extensive voids or substantial rental discounts were overlaid on the sinking fund provision for refurbishment and the higher remunerative yield rates already pulling the valuations down.

Sinking fund provision can be made before or after tax; the necessity for precision in the calculation depends largely on the period of redemption - short terms are fairly critical - and the degree of obsolescence envisaged.

## 3.3.3 VALUATION OF FREEHOLD INVESTMENTS

The application of the simple Years Purchase (in perpetuity) multiplier in computing the valuation of a new freehold office building is shown at **FIG 3.3.3.A**.

Although the calculation is simple the processes of appraisal and risk analysis used by valuers in establishing the yield are likely to be highly sophisticated – indeed this example may be a simple portrayal of the result of a complicated statistical evaluation. Note that the application of a sinking fund to replace the building at the end of its 60-years expected life would only reduce the valuation by a nominal amount (cf. **FIG 3.7.2.C** below); however, this, plus likely future investments in refurbishment are already well covered by return from the remunerative rate calculation.

**FIG 3.3.3.A:** *Freehold valuation using years purchase in perpetuity*

| | |
|---|---|
| Rentable area NIA | 50,000 sq ft |
| | × |
| Annual rent per sq ft NIA | £30.00* |
| | × |
| Years purchase in perpetuity @ 7% | (1 / 0.07) or 14.286 YP** = |
| **Capital value of freehold property** | **£21,429,000** |

\* If required any cost of managing the investment may be deducted at this point
\*\* This figure is available direct from the valuation tables

## 3.3.4 VALUATION OF LEASEHOLD INVESTMENTS

The organisation buying a leasehold building for its own occupation will need to establish the market value using the same techniques as an institutional investor purchasing the building with the organisation as leaseholders for the same period. For instance, they must take into account that, should they vacate the premises, there may well be an extensive 'void' period before a new tenant can be found.

Although business judgements may overlay the level of their bid, in a competitive situation the owner/occupier must always have regard to the balance sheet and liquidity implications of turning cash into property or - at least - accepting liability for a commercial mortgage.

**FIG 3.3.4.A** shows how the valuation of the leasehold for 10 years would vary from that involving 40 years occupation at the same **single rate** of return.

**FIG 3.3.4.A:** *Comparative leasehold valuations - 10 and 40 years terms of occupation*

| **Rental income** | 50,000 sq ft NIA @ £30 = £1,500,000 | | **Capital value £,000** |
|---|---|---|---|
| 10 years legal interest: years purchase single rate capitalisation | $\frac{1}{(0.1* + 0.0627**)}$ or 6.146 YP*** | 6.146 YP × 1,500,000 | **9,219** |
| 40 yrs legal interest: years purchase single rate capitalisation | $\frac{1}{(0.1* + 0.0023**)}$ or 9.775 YP*** | 9.775 YP × 1,500,000 | **14,663** |

\* Remunerative rate @ 10%
\*\* Accumulative rate (sinking fund) @10% over the period
\*\*\* Also available direct from the valuation tables - years purchase single rate

## 3.3.5 REVERSIONS

A freeholder or leaseholder granting a lesser interest whereby, at the expiry of the term, a further valuable letting could be expected to be made may assess the value of this reversion alongside the value of the immediate income stream when computing an investment valuation of his property.

However, the value of the deferred income from the reversion must be subjected to the effect of discounting to present worth over the deferred period. Such a computation is only really relevant in older leases with no, or infrequent, rent reviews.

## 3.3.6 PREMIUMS

A premium is an incentive paid to the existing leaseholder or sub-lessee by a new tenant (or a renewing tenant) in respect of the benefit of a period at which the **rent is below the rack rental achievable in the market.**

A common example is where a leaseholder of a high-performing property wants to move on sometime between rent reviews and seeks a premium from the incoming sub-lessee or assignee who has the benefit of a level of rent well below the market. Similarly, a tenant wishing to renew his lease before the natural expiration date may pay a premium to the lessor **if the new rent ignores current market increases above that passing under the old lease.**

A simple calculation of the former looked at from the point of view of both parties is given at **FIG 3.3.6.A**. In practice, however, the matter will be one for negotiation, and particular business interests are likely to 'muddy the waters' of such a purist approach.

**FIG 3.3.6.A:** *Theoretical valuation of a premium from opposing viewpoints*

| Basis of valuation | Outgoing tenant's or landlord's valuation * | Incoming tenant's valuation * |
|---|---|---|
| Estimated rack rental pa | £1,500,000 | £1,350,000 |
| Passing rent pa | £1,000,000 | £1,000,000 |
| Estimated profit rental pa over (say) 5 years period to next rent review | £500,000 | £350,000 |
| Market value of profit rent pa for 5 years @ 7% single rate: × 4.098 YP | £2,049,000 | |
| Business value of profit rent for 5 years @ 10% single rate: × 3.788 YP | | £1,325,800 |
| * Excluding tax | | |

## 3.3.7 SURRENDERS

An occupier may be invited to surrender his leasehold interest to his landlord who may have plans for redevelopment or refurbishment putting the premises outside of the existing tenant's financial capacity. In this case the landlord will need to make an offer of compensation to the tenant reflecting:

- the tenant's investment in any improvements

- the 'profit rental' he would otherwise enjoy for the period to the next rent review (ie the difference between the passing rent and rack rent)

- any inconvenience or incidental loss likely to be suffered.

Typical calculations of the value from both standpoints as a prelude to agreement by negotiation is given at **FIG 3.3.7.A**.

**FIG 3.3.7.A:** *Theoretical valuation of surrender value from opposing viewpoints*

| Basis of valuation | Landlord's valuation | Surrenderer's valuation |
|---|---|---|
| Estimated rack rental pa | £1,500,000 | £1,650,000 |
| Passing rent pa | £1,000,000 | £1,000,000 |
| Estimated profit rent pa for the 5 years to next rent review | £500,000 | £650,000 |
| Market value of profit rent pa for 5 years @ 7% single rate: 4.098 YP × £500,000 | £2,049,000 | |
| Market value of profit rent pa for 5 years @ 6% single rate: 4.212 YP × £650,000 | | £2,737,800 |
| Compensation for improvements | £250,000 | £350,000 |
| **Estimated surrender value** | **£2,299,000** | **£3,087,800** |

### 3.3.8 REVERSE PREMIUM AND SURRENDER VALUES

Of course, when times are tough the boot may be on the other foot. So, the organisation taking on a lease where the passing rent is above the current market will be looking for a 'reverse premium' ie a cash sum to offset against the over-valued rental up to the next (presumably stabilising) rent review.

Equally, a leaseholder with no further use for a property which may have little or no prospect of early assignment or sub-lease may persuade his landlord to accept a surrender of the lease, compensating him by a tempting cash sum. However, such a deal is rarely acceptable to landlords of substance unless they have reservations about the tenant's covenant - possibly due to serious business difficulties which may be at the root of the need to surrender - or can see a refurbishment or redevelopment opportunity which the leaseholder may not have perceived.

### 3.3.9 THE 'CONTRACTOR'S VALUATION'

**FIG 3.3.9.A:** *Example of a 'contractor's valuation'*

| | |
|---|---|
| Land price | £500,000 |
| Land aquisition fees and costs | £25,000 |
| Finance on land etc for 1 year @ 10% | £52,500 |
| Building site and development costs: 2,000 sq m GIA @ £500 | £1,000,000 |
| Fees and finance charges on building etc | £150,000 |
| Total expenditure | £1,727,500 |
| Developer's margin for overheads, profit, & risk: say 15% | £259,125 |
| **Contractor's valuation** | **£1,986,625** |

Sometimes, when open market valuations are not available or are conflicting, valuers will use the 'contractor's valuation' as a double check on the figures they are proposing. The term describes a simple process of building up the total cost of a development on a 'green-field' or 'brown-field' site (as appropriate) as it would stand in the developer's books on completion of the project. **FIG 3.3.9.A** is an illustration of such a calculation, the detailed principles of which are fully explained in Chapter 10.2; the process of 'residual valuation' described in that Chapter derives from exactly the same kinds of cost centres and figures as are used here, but leaving either the land, the building cost or the profit to be calculated as a residual within the equation by deduction from the estimated open market value of the building on completion. The contractor's method is also used in certain rating assessments (see Chapter 3.5) and, with certain modifications and restrictions, in valuations for reinstatement for insurance purposes - described in Chapter 3.6 below.

### 3.3.10 PROFIT-BASED VALUATION

In some types of property, such as small private hotels, public houses, etc, it may be necessary to value the premises in terms of the profit an occupier will make out of using the premises for business purposes. Particularly relevant to rating assessment the technique is sometimes used for property valuation for one-off locations where comparables are difficult to establish; in such cases another valuation based on the 'contractor's valuation' described above is usually offered in support.

# CHAPTER 3.4 – PROPERTY INVESTMENT

## 3.4.1 PROPERTY AS AN INVESTMENT

*Introduction*

Chapter 1.1 explained the relationship between the premises policy eg tenure, costs, values, performance, and the business plan.

As well as considering the pros and cons of owner-occupation this chapter now looks outwards from the business to consider how property as an investment manifests itself to external investors, who they are and the issues which motivate them and influence their investment decisions.

*The nature of property as an investment*

Chapter 3.3 described the process by which property investment valuations are calculated using rental income and a capital multiplier.

Criteria influencing decisions in respect of property investment are considered in detail below. However, in general terms, an external investor in property is looking at four main factors:

- income stream over time
- appreciation or stability of capital value
- the inherent risk
- liquidity of the asset.

Property therefore has much the same considerations as any other income-bearing investment such as stocks and shares, gilt-edged securities, etc

The principal differences lie in the following factors:

- most modern leases have a rent review clause which has historically permitted an increase after 3, 5 or 7 years. Such increases have until quite recently tended to better the rate of inflation providing investors with particularly reliable inflation-proof returns over the term of years.

- Such growth in the sector or in an individual property enhances the market's view of its suitability as a medium for investment; this means that investors will accept a lower initial return on investment (anticipating future growth and stability of value) which in turn pushes up the market price in the manner described in Chapter 3.3.

- Sometimes this combination of upward increases in rent and the low initial yields (high capitalization factors) have a gearing effect upon values which generates high levels of profit for those whose good judgement, or luck, enables them to buy and sell efficiently.

- The down-side (apart from the now well established evidence that property is not guaranteed to perform in the foolproof manner suggested above) is that property is not a flexible investment, ie it is bought and sold in very large chunks. Compare this with the ability to move quickly in and out of stocks and shares - in the proportions deemed appropriate to the optimisation or safeguarding of the portfolio - to understand the property investors' main problem. Taking these matters all into account, general fund managers tend to limit the amount of property investments in their portfolios. Nevertheless there are many types of investment media which are 100% linked to property performance.

## Objectives of direct property ownership

Generally, direct property ownership in the private sector falls into four groups: investment, dealing, business occupation and residential occupation. Any owner may be a developer in the sense that land is acquired and one or more buildings built upon it. Therefore, the objectives of ownership are apparent in holding the property and letting (as an investor); selling the property perhaps after letting (as a dealer); or occupying the buildings (for business, residential or leisure purposes). Moreover, as discussed in Chapter 3.2, the occupier may be either the owner of the freehold or a lessee (who holds an equity in the property). Apart from financial or economic targets, such as profit from dealing or return from investment, those holding property may have cultural, ethical or social objectives as well.

The business decision to own and occupy will be made on two grounds:

- the policy of holding potentially appreciating assets to bolster the balance sheet

- the opportunity to create a 'bespoke' building tailored to specific user needs.

The appropriateness of these criteria in different circumstances is considered in more detail in Section 9 - 'Location and business performance'.

In the public sector, property ownership is 'functional', eg a sewerage works or railways, or 'objective' eg schools, colleges, clinics, hospitals and similar uses. (Of course, schools, hospitals and so on are also 'business' property in the private sector).

The distinctions made above are particularly important for reasons of taxation.

## Status of direct owner

Direct ownership in one of these ways (or perhaps a mix of them) may be undertaken by an individual or some other legal 'person', eg a company, a trust or a charity. It is always important to be sure of status since it prescribes what can or cannot be done in respect of property. For instance, in general, charities are unable to **deal** in property. Also, status among other factors may be an important matter affecting liability to taxation.

## Indirect property ownership

Persons with surplus funds may achieve indirect involvement in land and buildings in three general ways, one of which is to use a 'financial intermediary'. Thus a person may:

- share in the ownership by financial devices - for instance, by investing in the shares of an investment company which buys property or develops land for long term holding

- invest by holding units in a unit trust, by owning property bonds or by holding a pension policy (or life insurance policy) in a pension fund (or life insurance company) which has a proportion of its assets in property: such assets may be either by direct holdings or indirectly in some other vehicle, such as shares in a property company

- lend funds to another by mortgage or other device without the involvement of a financial intermediary, although this use of mortgages is probably not attractive to many investors.

Of course, individuals or companies who are dealers derive their income from the profits obtained from buying and selling property, or from buying land, building and selling on the completed development. Others may share in any profit from such operations by investing in the shares of companies which trade in this way, eg commercial property development companies which are quoted on the International Stock Exchange.

Other avenues for indirect investment in the field of property lie in such devices as company debenture stock or preference shares, some of which may be convertible to equities.

Similarly, mortgage bonds (when available), units in property (when they become available) and other devices, or variations of the above, afford opportunities for related investments.

## Categories of owner

Owners in the market for commercial land and buildings fall into following specific categories:

- businesses
- property investment companies
- property dealing companies
- pension funds
- insurance companies
- property bonds.

In many cases ownership will be by virtue of the purchase of an existing building. However those wishing to get involved in property development may enter into various forms of 'partnership', such as joint venture companies, straight partnerships, side by side leasing arrangements, forward funding or project management arrangements. Sharing the equity in the project is a prime issue in such ventures.

## Financial intermediaries

The pension funds and insurance companies together with the building societies, the banks and finance houses have another function as 'financial intermediaries' in that they are sources of funds which enable others to purchase existing property, to develop land or to refurbish or improve buildings.

These so-called 'financial intermediaries' have the function of gathering together savings and other funds which are surplus for the time being and allocating some of them to borrowers. (They may, or course, develop land themselves). In society at large some considerable financial advantages accrue from the processes by which the financial intermediaries operate. For instance, they enable:

- the development of expertise in structuring opportunities for savers to invest in ways which suit their particular requirements

- the switching by savers of funds from current investments into other investments when the need arises

- the structuring of opportunities to borrow funds or to participate in mixed borrowing and investment projects, eg by partnership arrangements

- a distancing between savers and borrowers which removes or reduces the prospects of conflict and dissonance between them.

This is not to suggest that financial intermediaries do not create problems. Thus, in property development, their investment criteria for new projects may not entirely suit the needs of users. Similarly, their prudent investment policy may delay or squash the advent of innovation in the property market.

Again, a general shift of policy on investment allocations between sectors, say from property to equities, may depress the property market and alter the fund-seekers' routes to suppliers.

## The 'property market'

It may be seen that in one sense the 'property market' comprises property owners on the one hand, and savers who provide funds on the others. The funds are, however, provided either directly or through a complex system of financial intermediaries. The financial intermediaries have a role of providing funds but some of them invest in property as well.

The other sense in which 'property market' is used pertains to the type of property in which interest is expressed, eg the office market, the industrial property market and so on. It is outside the scope of this work to review the property market (or markets) in detail.

Generally, the players in the market cluster into specific sectors. Thus, developers tend to specialise in one or other of house-building, developing industrial property, office development, leisure development and so on. On the other hand, investors, eg insurance companies, tend to spread their holdings in their portfolios into a number of market sectors so as to have a spread of offices, shops and industrial property. Nevertheless some specialise in a specific sector, eg some property unit trusts are 'in' agricultural property or 'in' industrial property in enterprise zones (in this instance so as to catch the taxation reliefs which are available).

A dynamic aspect of the property market is spotting trends in one or other of its sectors. These may result from the needs of users, eg hi-tech requirements, or from other factors, eg taxation reliefs generating investment in enterprise zones to pick up the capital allowances and rates exemption.

## Property investment criteria

The traditional criteria for investment are sufficient to indicate the general range of relative considerations which must be made in selecting a field or sector of investment as well as a particular property. Thus, (and in amplification of the main criteria given earlier in this chapter), the investor will have the following in mind:

- the prospect of capital being enhanced or at least maintained in real terms

- the prospect that income will be regularly received and will grow or be maintained in real terms

- management will be relatively inexpensive and the burden of outgoings may be shifted to tenants

- any national or local taxation incentives, exemptions, reliefs, and concessions are enjoyed to the full

- the degree of certainty (recognising that property is relatively illiquid) that the capital may be readily realised within a reasonable time at a reasonable expected cost

- whether opportunities for redevelopment or at least improvement will be achievable in due course

- whether the size in capital terms of any single property is suitable for a balanced portfolio

- the potential asset value of the property as security for borrowing

- the duration or lead-time to the effectiveness of decisions - eg development decisions, may need several years before fruit is borne, or disposal may take several months before net proceeds are received

- the spread of the investment both geographically and by sector (property or otherwise)

- the availability of short, medium or long-term funds for purchase or for development having regard to the risk and the size of the property

- the degree to which risks can be minimised or shifted to others, eg by taking out insurance policies against the happening of particular perils.

Professional property evaluation and management requires a wide and deep range of knowledge and skills in legal, financial, economic, technical and other areas. To the extent that individuals and other persons wish to invest indirectly in property the quality of advice and its application by those who manage the estate are of considerable importance.

Some facilities managers do find themselves in the position of managing (or being responsible for) the management of large estates. This aspect of their work is considered in detail in Chapter 3.8.

## Location and property investment

It is not only the general quality of the investment which should be considered by investors in property, but also the environment or society in which it exists. At an international level, broad issues of a country's stability, eg political, economic and social, require attention. In this context restraints on ownership of property by foreigners and relative currency fluctuations may be important.

Within a national boundary, location is paramount so that a review must be made and judgement formed on such factors as:

- population: size, socio-economic composition, age structure, mobility, health and morale

- workforce: composition, size, knowledge and skills, availability and mobility

- transport and communications infrastructure: road, rail, air and waterways, ports and airports, various utilities and their aggregate disposition

- planning, fiscal and other 'governmental' policies: structure and local planning policies, scope for implementation, Enterprise Zones, assisted area status, and so on

- amenities and attractions: range and quality of housing, shopping, educational and training facilities, leisure and tourist facilities, art, entertainment and other cultural resources

- accommodation: business, cultural, tourist and residential, particularly its composition, quality and quantity

- state of the property market: values (capital and rental), cost of development and the quality of its processes, eg political, planning and financial

- the effect of national, regional and local policies for economic development, planning and other governmental provisions

- the level of recent, past, current and planned capital investment in the area

- any predominance of employment opportunities which may be threatened by long-term structural changes in the economy

- the quality of the image and identity of the area.

The owner-occupier will, in addition, have due regard to the appropriateness of the location to his markets, distributors, distribution routes and competition.

## Quality of a property portfolio

The present conventional wisdom does not yet encompass a scientific method of evaluation (or even an appreciation of) the impact of the functional performance of buildings on the user's efficiency and hence on the quality and value of the investment. Various tools, such as the BQA system discussed in Chapter 1.2 are coming to bear on the issue but in most cases the quality of a property portfolio will still, in the investor's eyes, be reflected in the following:

- the age of its buildings, their condition and cost-in-use, their perceived ability to meet the needs of occupiers and the investment criteria of the owners

- the spread of holdings in different sectors, ie industrial, offices, shops, agricultural, forestry, leisure and others

- the geographical spread either internationally or within the United Kingdom

- the pattern of tenures, eg freeholds, long leases and short leases

- the ease of management, eg good security arrangements, rent reviews and full repairing insuring leases

- the abilities of the tenants in terms of paying the rent and meeting their obligations under their leases

- the financial acumen of management and the financial resources in hand or on call to meet immediate needs for repair and maintenance, and in the longer term, for expansion and rationalisation

- the gearing of the portfolio's underlying financial resources, ie as a measure of vulnerability to adverse income or capital changes

- the quality of the operations undertaken by management and professional advisers to improve the long-term standing of the estate with an achievable plan of operations.

Where the current performance of the portfolio is being measured, short-term considerations may outweigh a longer-term perspective.

## The owner-occupier's portfolio

The dichotomy facing many owner-occupiers is whether to move away from monolithic chunks of space to a more flexible, wider-distributed portfolio generally more appropriate to ready asset realisation or to come together from fragmented locations into one building providing greater efficiency in inter-departmental communications.

# CHAPTER 3.5 – BUSINESS RATES

### 3.5.1 THE NATURE OF BUSINESS RATES

*The evolution
of the rating
system*

Prior to 1990 the rates levy on businesses, as a contribution towards locally-based public services, was calculated and administered by the local authority. The amount of the levy was the product of the 'notional' value of the premises occupied to which a 'rating in the pound' - known as 'poundage' was applied annually. The resulting amount was billed to the occupier of the premises who might or might not be the owner.

The system had its origins in the Poor Relief Act of 1601; 389 years of application and contest resulted in a well tried and tested system albeit that only a few specialist surveyors understood how the complex system of hypothetical tenancies, hereditaments and valuation lists actually worked. The system was also seen as a facility for profligate local authorities to bail themselves out by pushing the business rate poundage beyond the limits of acceptability.

During the 1980's the business rates in Central London and many provincial cities started to make the overall level of occupancy costs, based on the very high passing rents, look excessive, leading to general discontent with the whole system, as well as its implementation. The Local Government Finance Act 1988, as substantially amended by the Local Government and Housing Act 1989, sounded the death-knell for the old system. Together with a plethora of secondary legislation they completely changed the basis of the levy in that:

- domestic rating was dropped completely out of the process

- the level of rates is calculated by central as opposed to local government

- the proceeds are distributed to the local authorities by central government.

The principles of liability to rating and methods of valuation have remained, although with a revised terminology built upon, but slightly differing from, the original.

Before going into the detail of how the levy is computed, it is first necessary to determine when liability, if any, exists.

*Liability to pay
business rates*

The tests of an organisation's liability to rates under the Uniform Business Rate (UBR) which took effect from 1st April 1990, are that:

- the organisation is in occupation of the premises in question

- the premises constitute a 'relevant non-domestic or composite hereditament'

- the premises are not exempt, or partially exempt, from UBR.

Clearly the non-rating expert needs to understand the precise legal meaning of some of these terms; the facilities manager's interest will lie particularly in any liability to pay rates on empty premises, temporary premises held under licence and sub-leased or assigned premises.

## Occupation and ownership

The historic concept that the rates charge was on the occupier of the property - who was not necessarily the owner - has survived the new order. So, although the charge is calculated on the value of the property upon which it is levied, payment of the levy is the liability of whomever is in occupation for the period of the **'chargeable financial year'** in question. The current occupier is not liable for any default of his predecessors or successors in occupation.

However, if the hereditament (ie: premises - see below) is empty it will be the **owner** who is liable to pay the rate on the empty building - the 'empty rate'.

In the context of the UBR, as in the general law of real estate, the **owner** is the person who is entitled to possession; but whereas 'possession' in land law is determined by a person's right to receive rents and profits arising from it, possession under the uniform business rate is based upon the person's right to take physical possession of the land.

The latter distinction is of particular significance where property is mortgaged and where leases are forfeited, surrendered or disclaimed.

Although a mortgagee (the one lending against the security) may be entitled to possession he will not be liable for the rates on a building while another party is in actual physical possession - even if the latter is in liquidation.

A landlord may become liable for rates on a building once he exercises a right of forfeiture under a lease, or takes a surrender or it is disclaimed by a liquidator. In all those circumstances he will be entitled to physical possession and thereby the owner for purposes of UBR; however, his liability for payment of rates does not arise until the building is 'empty'. The matter of 'empty rates' is discussed further below.

## A non-domestic hereditament

The Local Government Finance Act 1988 defines the term **hereditament** by reference to the definition in the General Rate Act 1967. Although the 1988 Act fully repeals the latter, it is necessary to resort to the 1967 Act to understand what the term 'hereditament' means in its current context.

In order to qualify as a hereditament - which of itself does not automatically invoke a current liability to rating - a property, (or unit within it) is one which is, or would fall to be, shown as a separate item in the **Rating List**.

The Rating List schedules all non-domestic (see below) properties, and units therein, which are liable to have a charge levied upon them, together with their respective **rateable values** ie: the amount upon which the **charging authority** (formerly the rating authority) levies its **non-domestic rating multiplier** (formerly poundage - see above!)

In order to attract uniform business rates premises have to classify as a **relevant non-domestic hereditament**. Although offices, manufacturing and mining premises clearly come into the category of **non-domestic**, the term can also include advertisement hoardings let out by the occupier or by the owner of otherwise empty land. What is non-domestic is established by reference to what the statutory instrument defines as **domestic**! To precis the position - which does seem fairly obvious in most cases - a hereditament is non-domestic if its principal use is as a place of business for persons who either do not live there, or whose principal place of residence is elsewhere.

Where people live and work in the same building but the business part is not self-contained, business rates can be levied on the latter part of a **'composite heredi-tament'**. Such properties as offices with an overnight residential suite or caretaker's flat, or shops with an integral flat may come into this category.

The issue of 'composite hereditament' as it affects people working from home - 'home-workers' - where the business takes over the accommodation to the extent that structural alterations have to be made to facilitate it, or the owner moves out to another main residence, is obviously one which will need to be carefully watched by those companies pursuing this employment policy.

A non-domestic hereditament is **relevant** if it is rateable (to use the old parlance), which means that it will appear in the Rating List.

## *Exemption from rating*

The 1988 Local Government Finance Act exempts certain types of business premises from liability, notably property in enterprise Zones (now just about phased out) certain agricultural and fisheries property and premises providing welfare services to the disabled.

## 3.5.2 RATES ON EMPTY BUILDINGS

## *Wholly-unoccupied property*

The rates levy on unoccupied buildings is only 50% of the full rate, so both developers and occupiers need to have their wits about them to ensure that they get their proper entitlement to this relief.

Again, the LGFA 1988 lays down the provisions as to when an 'unoccupied rate' (empty rate) is payable. In order for a liability (or indeed a concession) to arise, the following principal conditions must apply:

- the property must attract liability as a 'relevant non-domestic heredita-ment'

- no part of it must be occupied on a particular day (rates are calculated on a daily basis - see below)

- the hereditament must not be exempted from unoccupied rating by the legislation eg: certain defined industrial land and buildings, properties below a certain rateable value or properties prevented from occupation by some statutory or other official intervention

- an 'existing' hereditament has been wholly unoccupied for a continuous period in excess of three months (ignoring any periods of re-occupation of less than six weeks within the three months period). **FIG 3.5.2.A** gives an example of how this regulation would be applied given alternative re-occupation periods of under and over six weeks duration

- a new hereditament including merely a part capable of separate occupa-tion has been wholly unoccupied for three months following either:

    - the date of service by the Local Authority of a completion notice on a building or part thereof which has already been completed, or

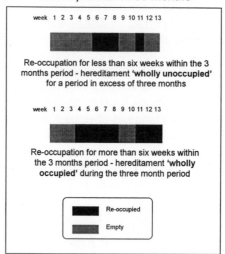

**FIG 3.5.2.A:** *Effects of re-occupation on definition of 'wholly unoccupied for three months'*

- the date given in the Local Authority's completion notice (forecast not more than three months ahead) when the building or part thereof is expected to be complete.

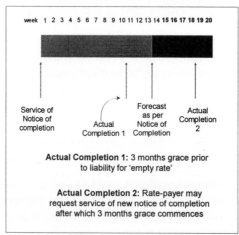

**FIG 3.5.2.B:** *Grounds for requesting service of a new notice*

Where the date of actual completion is within the three months forecast by the Authority and is agreed by the developer (or the future rate-payer) then it must stand; however, if the rate-payer disagrees and can prove completion was more than three months after the notice was served he can request service of a new notice. **FIG 3.5.2.B** illustrates the application of this concession.

*Partly-occupied property*

For general purposes of rating business premises a partly occupied hereditament is deemed to be wholly-occupied, but the **charging authorities** (formerly rating authorities) may, at their discretion, if the partial occupation is for a short period - as in gradual decanting - apportion the rateable liability as between the occupied and unoccupied parts enlisting the help of the Valuation Officer in making the calculation.

New properties filling up, existing premises decanting slowly over time or downsizing can all benefit from partial-occupation relief, but certain important procedures must be observed by the ratepayer in order to be reasonably sure of getting it. Absolutely critical is the establishment of a separate rating assessment for the unoccupied part. Among criteria the Valuation Office for the Inland revenue will take into account on receipt of an appeal in this respect are:

- whether the parts claimed to be unoccupied are **completely** empty - best not to leave **any** bits or pieces around in case they give rise to a suspicion of beneficial occupation

- the areas appealed should be clearly defined having independent direct access from the main core or direct from the street

- it must not be seen to be merely in a temporarily decanted state as part of a natural internal re-organisation

- there must be full compliance with statutory liabilities including Health & Safety at Work and Means of Escape (in case of fire).

Where there are a number of buildings in a complex care must be exercised to pick out discrete buildings which will qualify for 'empty rate' relief. Having done so, their complete separation from the complex must be maintained and not compromised by continuing to afford access to other parts or relying upon a common security regime.

### 3.5.3 THE RATEABLE VALUE

*The basis of valuation*

The definition in the LGFA 1988 perpetuates, or fails to discount, the concept of a 'hypothetical lease', which has become the cornerstone of the rating surveyor's discipline and fee income for specialists in the legal profession over the years.

It all boils down to something approaching the rack rental passing from year to year where a tenant is on a full repairing and insuring lease (see Chapter 3.2 - leasehold conditions). Although the definition implies a property to let with vacant possession the 'hypothetical tenant' can be the owner-occupier paying himself rent (as he often does in a 'notional rent' accounting convention). Although the hypothetical tenancy is from year to year this is probably only to keep the hypothetical rent at market level rather than to preclude the prospect of its continuance beyond the end of any one year.

*Alterations to the rating list*

The date of the current re-valuation for rating was 1 April 1990 and reflected values of 1 April 1988. The next revaluation will be in 1995. Government provisional estimates suggest that rateable values for office buildings in Central London will be less than half of the 1989 levels whereas provincial locations are expected to be up-valued by 50% or more. Given this uneven state of play the decisions on the level of the UBR to match the 1995 revaluation is awaited with concern by many business rate payers.

Since 1990 many appeals have been made and settled and time to appeal against the **original** assessment has long expired. However, there are certain circumstances affecting the rateable value which can be appealed - provided that the appeal is lodged within six months of the date when the effect on the value was first felt ie: the 'event'.

Such circumstances include:

- temporary falls in value due to disturbance from local building or civil engineering works

- permanent changes in the status of the locality caused by external factors such as closure of a railway station or a by-pass encroaching on the previously green-field curtilage

- reductions to rateable values of similar properties in the vicinity or other comparable locations. In the latter case, if the change sought follows the decision of a Valuation Tribunal, the right of appeal is automatic for a period of six months. On the other hand, if the base change decision emanates from agreement with the Local Valuation Officer there is no such right of appeal: the VO himself may - and should - take the necessary actions to correct the rateable values of comparable properties in the list.

Importantly, the Charging authority may now make proposals to the Valuation Officer in respect of alterations to the Rating List (eg as in the case of the short-term partial occupancy described above), as may any **'interested person'**; this term includes not just the occupier but also any other person owning a legal estate or some reversionary right of possession as well as subsidiaries, co-members of a group, associated companies and the like having a 'qualifying' connection with the occupier.

Properly registered **charities** using property essentially for charitable purposes are entitled to relief of 80% and the Charging Authority may have discretion to grant relief up to 100%.

Appeals must be made to the Local Valuation Officer within six months of the 'event' in writing, stating the extent of and reason for the alteration being sought and the date of the event causing the change in value.

The process of making proposals and appeals is a specialist area for the rating surveyors; in major issues the resources of legal specialists may be involved to ultimate advantage.

If negotiations fail the proposal may go to an appeal to the Valuation Tribunal involving yet more surveying and possibly legal fees – and an almost certainly **far better briefed VO!**

*Methods of valuation*

Apart from hereditaments in the 'central non-domestic rating list' which have to be valued on a statutory formula the Valuation Officer may use his absolute discretion in choosing the method of valuation.

The usual methods involve:

- comparison of rents

- extrapolation from cost using the contractor's valuation

- extrapolation from open market capital value

- valuation by reference to profits.

The principles underlying all these methods and their components are discussed and illustrated in Chapter 3.3

**FIG. 3.5.3.A:** *Rates as a proportion of business premises costs*

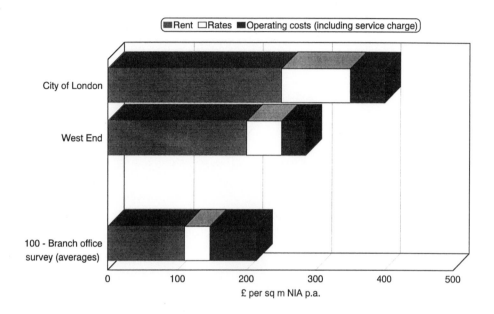

In nearly all cases the **comparative rent** method will be adopted as the Valuation Officers have a vast network of comparable data which is much easier to use in substantiation of values than the other more scientific, but relatively subjective approaches.

*The rate demand*

The rate demand must always be checked by a competent person to ensure that it has been properly calculated. Charging authorities are apt to make the odd error particularly where alterations to the rating list have taken place.

As **FIG 3.5.3.A** shows rates are still an important component of premises occupancy costs; unfortunately, because the process is not always understood by the facilities manager (especially in smaller organisations lacking direct access to competent professional advice) rates can often be over-charged in the occupier's complete ignorance. Fees for consultants helping to get rate relief are conventionally based on the savings achieved.

# CHAPTER 3.6 – PROPERTY INSURANCE

### 3.6.1 ALL RISKS INSURANCE

*Getting the right cover*

Any organisation occupying business premises must have adequate insurance cover against all risks. It may fall to the facilities Manager to ensure that the organisation is adequately covered against all reasonably foreseeable risks and is paying a reasonable insurance premium to obtain such cover with an insurance company of good standing.

Of course, this is the job of the insurance broker - but some companies do not use brokers, preferring to purchase direct (sometimes pocketing the broker's commission). Others have brokers, but the wrong ones - those who have their pet underwriters or who are too lazy to trawl the market for the best deal available.

In view of the fate which has befallen many of the Lloyds underwriters of property-related risks in recent years it is not surprising that nowadays the small print in every policy and details in every claim are very carefully scrutinized. The importance of dealing with the insurance provisions professionally has never been so great, especially when the risk of activities of terrorists and increasing employer's liability under the Health and Safety at Work Regulations comes to be appraised and indemnified.

*Material damage insurance*

Whoever is responsible for insurance of property will need to obtain cover for reinstatement in the wake of:

- fire
- lightning
- explosion
- aircraft
- riot
- civil commotion
- malicious damage
- earthquake
- storm
- flood
- burst pipes
- impact by road vehicles - (including your own)
- sprinkler leakage
- subsidence and heave
- damage to outside fascia, signs, special glass

*Insurance
premiums*

In the process of auditing premises costs, a quite staggering variation in the annual costs of material damage insurance per capita and per unit of floor area is revealed. The causes of the variations are frequently as much to do with purchasing - whether direct or by brokers - and post-codes as with the risks and values to be insured.

**FIG 3.6.1.A** indicates the typical costs for insuring against these perils in office buildings.

**FIG. 3.6.1.A:***Sample range of property (material damage) insurance premiums for office buildings*

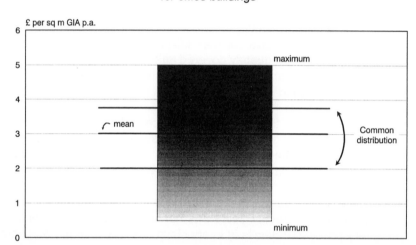

The figures are calculated from a generic sample of office buildings in Central London or provincial locations.

The insured values used in the formulation of these typical premium charges include demolition, reconstruction, professional fees and short-term finance charges.

Most companies will have to pay the final bill for insuring the building(s) they occupy against fire, and special perils. These days 'all-risk' insurance, to include subsidence and damage caused in the course of larceny, is generally available on reasonable terms and should be purchased as a matter of course.

Where property is tenanted, it is essential for the cover to include loss of rental during the reinstatement period - normally three years except in the largest buildings.

Recent spates of terrorism have caused the insurance market to exclude material damage and consequential loss resulting from such action. Substantial premiums can enable lifting of the exclusions, and because fire and explosion are perils against which insurance is obligatory in most leases, many have perforce taken out this additional cover; failure to do so may affect the tenant's repairing covenant, with potentially disastrous consequences. Of course, adequate formal security and disaster recovery regimes will help to convince the underwriter that the risk is worth taking though he may well charge heavily loaded premiums for sensitive companies and locations.

*Reinstatement
value*

The building owner and any tenants should be concerned to see that the total cost of reinstatement is covered - and that means everything from demolition to reconstruction, professional fees and finance charges. The finance charge is frequently overlooked but can be expensive unless the underwriter agrees (as he should) to meet the payments as they arise - professional fees when due and the builder's monthly payment on the architect's certificate.

The RICS publishes guidelines for the valuation of work for reinstatement following damage by fire and other perils. A typical calculation for reinstatement of an office building substantially damaged by fire is given at **FIG 3.6.1.B**

**FIG 3.6.1.B:** *Typical calculation for valuation of reinstatement costs*

| Insurance claim | | Amount of claim £ |
|---|---|---|
| Reinstatement costs | 1,000 sq m GIA @ £600 | 600,000 |
| Professional fees | 10% × £600,000 | 60,000 |
| Alternative accomodation (rent only)* | 850 sq m NIA @ £150 pa for 1½ yrs | 191,250 |
| Removals and charges | At cost | 6,000 |
| Betterment | No deduction | |
| VAT | Fully recoverable | |
| **Total claimed** | | **857,250** |

\* Rates, operating costs/service charge not recoverable as they would otherwise be incurred in the insured building in course of occupation

In building insurance there is always a dilemma as to which index to use for inflation purposes. But there is usually little or no correlation between general inflation (measured by the retail price index), the 'cost of building' indices and 'tender price indices' (prepared by the Building Cost Information Service of the RICS).

It is worth taking time to consider the relative merits of the latter two forms of building costs index:

- the 'general building cost' indices plot the source increases in the costs of labour, plant and materials over time. This method reflects, in theory, the prices which building contractors have to pay for the resources needed to carry out a building project

- the 'tender price index' reflects the charges made by building contractors for specified building operations - ie, the market price for building work.

It is not at all uncommon for there to be a startling contrast between cost increases theoretically incurred by builders and the prices charged to their clients.

Several years of suppressed demand and hardship have led to a loss of resources to the building industry which would catch the industry and its customers napping in the event of any upturn in the present depressed level of demand. This would have the effect of reversing the differential pattern of cost increases between tender price and general building cost, pushing tenders higher as builders get overloaded and also anticipate large cost increases.

The BCIS publishes an annual booklet on reinstatement costs for housing, but there is no comparable publication for commercial and industrial buildings. Given this volatile situation it would be sensible for building owners to seek the advice of a qualified quantity surveyor on the reinstatement value of their buildings for the coming year; the traditional general escalation clause clearly may leave the owner either unnecessarily exposed to risk of inadequate cover or paying an excessive premium for building insurance.

The tenant, in the conventional fully repairing and insuring lease, may feel that it is the landlord's worry as to whether the reinstatement value is correctly stated to the underwriters. This is a dangerous presumption - what if the landlord is hard hit financially as a consequence of under-insurance? The trading losses suffered by the tenants due to the inevitable delay due to arguing the toss and working out the liability for the deficiency will certainly not justify the meagre saving on premiums made prior to the catastrophe.

## Consequential loss

In order for an organisation to obtain effective cover against consequential loss it is essential that material damage insurance is in place in respect of the property and the primary risks upon which any consequential loss is dependent. The logic for this apparent imposition is to avoid the consequential loss claim from being expanded to cover business lost while the building lies in ruins awaiting possibly non-existent funds for reinstatement.

The level of cover for the material risk must also match the prospective consequential loss. For example, heavily networked premises may go completely out of action causing a business loss out of all proportion to the cost of reinstatement of what may possibly be only nominal interior damage.

Restricted or denied access due to damage to lifts, stairs or reception may, again, prove consequentially disastrous compared with the material damage. Loss of rent cover for these circumstances is very important. This knock-on effect of partial damage taking out whole areas is also relevant to key business features such as computer rooms, kitchens and critical reference libraries. Loss of rent cover against such parts of a property may be inadequate if the whole area becomes useless within a business context.

## Public Liability Insurance (PLI)

PLI is not mandatory but the organisation which does not carry appropriate cover (or ensure that its contractors and sub-contractors do) is courting disaster, particular with regards to breaches of the Occupiers' Liability Act.

PLI relates partly to property and partly to the organisation's business activities so, where possible, a split of the cost should be sought - often a problem with all-risks policies.

Cover is required against injury or death to visitors, passers-by, neighbours (near and far) and property, as the result of some malfunctioning or failure of the services and structure or execution of any construction works; in addition the hazard of pollution of air and water as a result of the way the building is constructed or run, or from its effluent, is now defined as a third party liability and solidly condemned in the statute book. Managing the risk of Health and Safety at Work is discussed in Chapter 8.2 but appropriate insurance cover is an important backstop. Importantly, basic cover against such risks only usually applies to one-off incidents; incremental, insidious damage by, for example, pollution needs to be separately insured - and cover is hard to get and expensive.

## Employer's Liability Insurance (ELI)

The public face of the Health and Safety law may be covered by PLI, but there is now a considerable increase in the cost of ELI as a result of employee claims under the same banner. The problems of RSI (Repetitive strain injury), eye strain and mental stress are all considered in Chapter 8.2.

Although the Facilities Manager must have a sound risk management programme in place to deal with the avoidance of the problem the size of settlements under the growing number of claims demands that adequate Employer's Liability insurance cover should be put in place by the organisation, its contractors and sub-contractors.

'Passive smoking' ie the inadvertent inhalation of another's tobacco fumes, is now well documented as a health hazard and will no doubt produce a defensive response from the underwriter of any loosely worded policy in its respect.

Cynics might say that the move towards controlling or banning smoking in public places is more a response to potential liability for claims in respect of passive smoking rather than a philanthropic attitude of employers and licensors. Anyway, the **Premises and Facilities Data Service**, in its 1994 annual report, showed that 95% of its subscribers either banned smoking completely or restricted it severely by location, time or both. **Fig 3.6.1.C** is the relevant extract from the Report; it is interesting that the 1993 comparable data put only 75% in this category. This is an area where insurance premiums can be saved without taking a risk, although historic risk may still be present.

**FIG.3.6.1.C:** *Smoking in offices - sample of company policies*

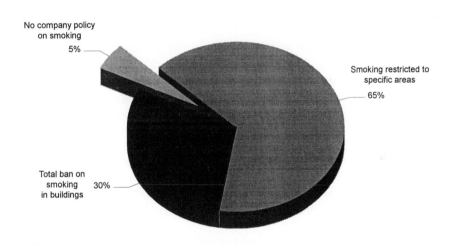

Source: Premises & Facilities Data - 1993/94 annual report

It should be noted that claims for insidious injuries or illness are on a **claims-occurring** basis ie the insurer covering the risk **when the damage is incurred** has to underwrite the loss. Contrast this with the **claims-made** basis of professional indemnity insurance considered below, where the insurer holding the baby when the claim is delivered has to respond. The problem with the 'claims-occurring' syndrome is that certain personal injury at work may be incremental, resulting in the need to claim on one or a number of previous policies - and who knows where they are or who underwrote them? This may well present a task for the Facilities Manager ie to take responsibility for storage and safe-keeping of **all** insurance documents, not just those which are property related.

*Contents insurance*

It can be argued that this cover is nothing really to do with 'premises', and the extent of cover needed is as variable as the reinstatement value of the buildings. However, such is the cross-relationship between 'pure' premises management and office services that it is naive to expect that there will always be a clear division of liability.

Most all-risks policies these days tend, in any case, to extend to contents, with an overall sum insured making a split of the costs between premises and contents difficult to establish. **FIG 3.6.1.D** gives an indication of the typical costs of covering the 'contents' risk in office buildings. Figures are calculated for a number of generic office building sizes either in central London or a provincial (South-east England) location.

**FIG. 3.6.1.D:** *Sample range of contents insurance premiums for office buildings*

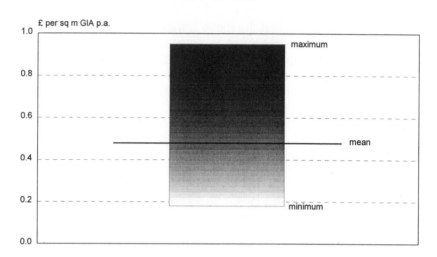

The insured values used to calculate these typical premium charges include demountable partitions (group space layout), furniture and fittings, general office equipment, employees; personal belongings and legal fees in respect of possible claim contests.

Excluded are any allowances for business interruption or engineering insurance, which can have a great effect on the amount insured as also allowances for public and employers' liability, for which a minimum of £1 million is recommended, although the nature of the business may cause this to vary significantly.

The policy should be checked for adequacy of cover against:

- material damage - including items temporarily removed
- public and employer's liability
- IT hardware
- IT software
- cash
- business interruption
- directors'/employees' personal effects
- engineering insurance - for hightech users
- legal expenses - to pay for defence in disputes.

## 3.6.2 PROFESSIONAL INDEMNITY INSURANCE (PI)

*Areas of risk*

The risk of loss to facilities through the negligence of a consultant is most commonly encountered in construction or fitting-out projects, although valuation surveyors, large maintenance contractors and others offering specialist advice from time to time are also potential sources of bad advice and consequential loss.

The facilities manager must ensure that each consultant carries a level of PI insurance relevant to any project he is carrying out on or in respect of the premises.

Now that out-sourcing is becoming more common companies are realising that many of the functions formerly carried out in-house were highly complex requiring the involvement of experienced and highly responsible managers and technologists.  At the same time they could not get insurance against their failure, or fraudulent activities, which they can if the works are contracted to a third party owing a duty of care.  The costs covered will include the legal costs of defending any claim - these may amount to 50% or more of the final payment.

The recently introduced CDM liability of a property occupier and his agent for the safety of construction operations carried out at his behest on his property is obviously a major risk centre for indemnity insurance.

PI claims are on a **claims-made** basis as defined above; the consultant's failure to disclose potential liability on **any** project when applying for cover may well result in the whole policy becoming unenforceable.  Consequently anyone relying upon a consultant's PI policy to manage to risk of a project should, in theory, make it his business to ensure that the consultant's cover application had been filled in honestly!

Clearly, this is a project manager's recurring nightmare, and proves that there really is no foolproof cover against poorly managed risk.

### 3.6.3 CLAIMS

*Planning and preparation*

Unless an insurance claim is prepared thoroughly and presented in accordance with the underwriter's requirements it will hold up and possibly prejudice the outcome.

First and foremost it is essential to make sure the premiums are up to date and that the loss claimed is in fact covered by the policy - otherwise everyone's time will be completely wasted.  The amount insured must always be kept under review, to make sure that it is in line with the level of financial risk involved.  Levels set too high bring no benefits at all.

Proper notes, photographs (if appropriate and humanly possible), and statements should be taken at the time of any incident, not left to the imperfections of the memory.

*Avoidance of claims*

The best way to avoid a claim is to manage the risk properly.  Too many claims will push up premiums, apart from which the accident-prone workplace will be *de facto* less efficient and its occupants less productive - or absent!

### 3.6.4 PROCURING INSURANCE

*Using a broker*

The cost of insurance relative to the risk of not having it - or not having enough - is reasonable.  Failure on the part of the facilities manager or his broker to get adequate cover at the right price is an inexcusable but frequent occurrence, with definite connotations of actionable negligence claims in the event of exposure to ill-covered perils.

And how do you recognise a good broker?  Check first if he is registered under the Insurance Brokers Act of 1977.  Then take up references.  And, finally, put him into competition with other brokers of comparable status.

# CHAPTER 3.7 – DEPRECIATION OF PROPERTY

## 3.7.1 THE CONCEPT OF DEPRECIATION

*Definition of depreciation*

The RICS definition of depreciation is given at **FIG 3.7.1.A**. Some pundits argue that depreciation is not automatically accompanied by a fall in value, and over part of an asset's lifetime this may be so - for a variety of reasons. The thesis probably turns on the matter of whether value relates to open market or intrinsic productive value.

**FIG. 3.7.1.A:** *Official definition of 'depreciation'*

> 'Depreciation is defined as the measure of the wearing out, consumption, or other reduction in the useful economic life of a fixed asset whether arising from use, effluxion of time or obsolescence through technological or market changes'
>
> Source: RICS 'Red Book' 1990

Before considering further the effects of depreciation on property values it is necessary to take a closer look at the factors accompanying, and causing, this phenomenon.

*The three facets of depreciation*

Yet another trinity of facets contributes to the total impact of depreciation, as shown in **FIG 3.7.1.B**.

**FIG. 3.7.1.B:** *The three facets of depreciation - inter-relationships*

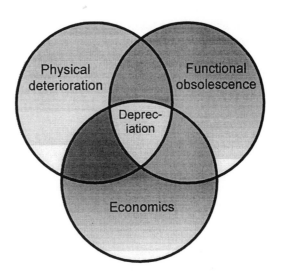

**Functional obsolescence** means the depreciation of the usefulness of the asset relative to its functional performance requirements. As discussed in Chapter 1.2 - 'The performance of buildings', the functional performance of the asset will be intrinsically linked to the physical performance in its as-designed condition.

As the technology available to the user advances - both for his business (external issues) and his facilities (domestic issues) - the asset, be it a building or some other piece of productive plant, will become functionally obsolescent in response to both 'external' and 'domestic' influences.

The inter-relationship between physical and functional performance described in Chapter 1.2 operates in an exactly complementary way in the process of depreciation; as the physical performance deteriorates below its designed standards so those aspects of functional performance dependent upon the delivery of the physical goods will falter, contributing to, but not necessarily allied to, any functional obsolescence coming about through external factors such as changes in business strategies.

The **physical deterioration** will result from the way the asset is used and maintained; its rate of depreciation can, in the short term, be measured by the capital and revenue resources it consumes in holding its value or in the process of value-damage limitation!

One aspect of the **economics** facet is the financial management approach to the resulting change in values which will depend partly on the accountancy conventions adopted. In the case of property the **current cost accounting convention** requires that open market valuation should always be reflected in the balance sheet; however, depreciated cost may be appropriate for relatively new buildings which are clearly provided on partly functional grounds without regard to property investment values. This might apply, for example, to a data-centre, or to a headquarters office building in a poor location uniquely useful to a particular employer.

The **historical accounting** convention requires the latter approach of including property assets in the balance sheet at depreciated cost; however, the 'modified' version of this alternative convention permits either of the two approaches.

Ignoring the accounting convention, the economic balance between the usefulness of an asset in its currently depreciated condition and an upgraded alternative must be keep under constant review. Life 'churn' (described in Chapter 7.8) or the upgrading of computer equipment, change is expensive, insidious, and usually avoidable. Measurement of the state of usefulness of an asset is a much better yardstick of value than an accountant's written-down figures using his standard conventions, although the latter can be a good 'zero-base' from which to appraise the costs and benefits of modernisation or renewal.

## 3.7.2 DEPRECIATION OF LAND AND BUILDINGS

*Value in context*

In the case of property, as has been discussed in Chapter 1.2 under -'The performance of buildings', the value to the user may be quite different from the value to the owner (who may be one and the same); equally, although both valuations will eventually depreciate, the rate - and the reasons therefore -will almost certainly be at considerable and continual variance.

Where there is no doubt that buildings and their fixtures and fittings will lose their usefulness over time until they fall into decay, become totally redundant and/or get demolished, the land upon which they are built may not necessarily have any depreciation at all; indeed, the land may well appreciate on demolition of an old building to make way for a new one.

*Depreciation of
land*

Because land exists in perpetuity, its value is less likely than any building upon it to be affected by the three facets of depreciation. Nevertheless interests in the land suffer from the effluxion of time - quite apart from that enemy's influence on the functional and physical facets of performance. The effects of time on leasehold interests is considered in Chapter 3.3, so here it is only necessary to review the **physical, functional and consequential financial** changes which time may bring to the perpetual resource.

**Physical deterioration** may come about by:

- pollution

- ground obstructions (from previous structures)

- encroachment/erosion by the elements.

**Functional obsolescence** will depend on the ability of a site to continue to accommodate a valuable user. Hindrances to such ability might be:

- local or regional economic decline (see also the **economics** facet)

- depreciation of local or regional infrastructure

- statutory intervention, eg: planning restrictions.

**Economics** will impact on the depreciation of land values through the laws of supply and demand which do, of course, dictate the use to which land can be put, the price it will fetch in the market, and the time it takes to realise that price.

*Depreciation of
buildings*

**Physical deterioration** of buildings may arise from one or more of the following causes:

- wear and tear

- lack of adequate maintenance and repair

- poor design

- poor construction

- accidental or malicious damage

- dereliction

- demolition (the ultimate in deterioration!)

**Functional obsolescence** in a building means that it has lost some of its ability to accommodate the business requirement in a manner appropriate to the corporate objectives. Causes of this worrying condition can be:

- changes in statutory requirements eg: fire regulations, control of pollution, health & safety at work

- changes in working practices eg: open-plan offices

- introduction of new technologies eg: electronic information technology

The **economic** impact on buildings will eventually be manifested in:

- construction economics eg: where the cost of refurbishment is greater than the added value thereby created

- development economics eg: where the potential land use has a greater value than the extant investment.

*Premature obsolescence*

The invasion of information technology in the 1980's had a dramatic impact upon the functional and physical performance requirements of commercial buildings across the developed world. In the UK particularly it had a dramatic effect since the extensive property development activity at the turn of the decade had mimicked the meanness of nearly all post-war commercial development ie: provided minimum floor-ceiling heights, inadequate or no air-conditioning and with planning grids related to substantially cellular offices.

Then along came the high-speed photocopiers, pc's and printers with all the attendant power and data cables and excessive heat, leaving owners and occupiers struggling to find the space and coolth to make the buildings fit for their revised production process and workplace arrangements.

The ORBIT[1] study first alerted the property world to the likely impact of this phenomenon on property values. The authors of 'Facilities Economics', in their role as building economists to that project, culled the term **premature obsolescence** to describe the reducing effect of the cost of the necessary upgrading works (raised floors or new floor trunking, new or modified air-conditioning etc) on the investment value of what, in many cases, were newly-completed buildings.

In some cases the building and engineering technologies of the time had no answer to the lack of adequate height to accommodate either ceiling trunking or false floors. Afflicted buildings were forecast to have a substantial drop in investment values; although these research findings were censored by some of those whose interests were not best served by the bad news, the property market soon got the message and values were adjusted - albeit gradually - over time.

*Calculation of depreciation*

The ORBIT example is a good illustration of the relationship between investment value and the cost of countering the depreciation caused by functional obsolescence. The computation used at the time to illustrate the point (adjusted for current values and costs) is given at **FIG 3.7.2.A.**

**FIG. 3.7.2.A:** *The cost of upgrading to cope with I.T. - 1984 'ORBIT' report*

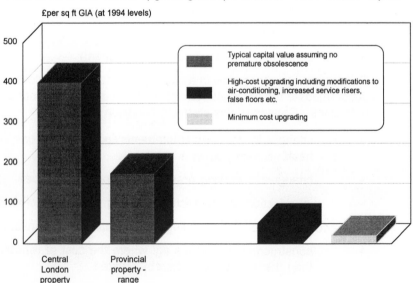

£per sq ft GIA (at 1994 levels)

This is a perfectly valid approach akin to a residual valuation of land, the reversion of a lease, the price of a derelict house or a motor car with a sound body but short of a good engine. Nevertheless, on top of the basic remedial costs is the 'hassle factor', which represents the bargaining discounts a willing buyer of a sub-standard article can negotiate in a buyer's market.

In practice the overall effect of obsolescence - premature or timely - is usually rolled up by the valuers into the rent and investment yield in such a way that, even if there were a scientific base to the computation, no one would ever know what it was, let alone if it was correct.

The way that property investment valuation works, with construction-related costs rarely a key ingredient in prime locations, as shown in **FIG 3.7.2.B**, means that allowances for periodic refurbishment should not have a serious impact; in the ORBIT example the problem was that the buildings afflicted were at a particularly early stage in their economic life at which, if anything, **appreciation** in value might have been anticipated.

**FIG. 3.7.2.B:** *The relationship of construction costs to investment values*

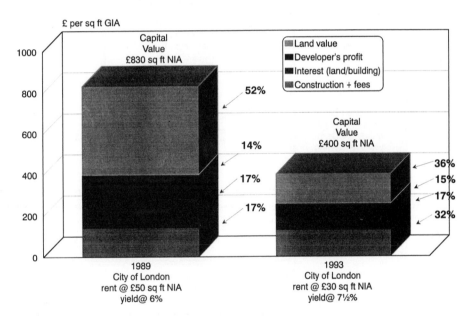

The whole episode focused the attention of investment fund managers on the need for better asset management and, in particular, for making financial provision in their valuations for timely replacement of major components and more frequent refurbishment.

Getting it exactly or even half right is a tall order. For instance, the high-energy pc's and bulky cables of the 1980's are being replaced by low-energy equipment and fibre-optic cables - even wireless networks; the VAV systems can now be replaced by much simpler devices doing much the same job at half the capital and running costs (see Chapter 5.4). All at once mean storey heights are acceptable - even a bonus, for they save on heating and cooling loads - and clever investors are refurbishing them to good advantage, as the example at **FIG 7.10.C** in Chapter 7.10 well depicts.

The process of allowing for refurbishment and eventual replacement of a building as part of a property valuation is given at **FIG 3.7.2.C** which builds upon the simple investment valuation example at **FIG 3.3.3.A** in Chapter 3.3 above. In this example choice of a 4% sinking fund results in the valuation dropping by about 5%; had a single rate (ie: 7% + 7%) been used the differential would have been negligible. Nevertheless, the general trend seems to be inexorably towards increasing pace of change in technology accompanied by increasing rate of functional obsolescence of assets. This must impact upon the way property assets are valued, in particular the depreciation assumptions built into any calculation.

**FIG 3.7.2.C:** *Incorporation of refurbishment/replacement of building in a freehold valuation*

| | | |
|---|---|---|
| **Capital value of freehold as FIG 3.3.3.A:** | 50,000 sq ft NIA @ £30 / sq ft = £1,500,000 pa × 14.286 YP: | **£ 21,429,000** |
| **Sinking fund - major refurbishment after 30 years (excluding inflation)** | 60,000 sq ft GIA @ £50 / sq ft (inc fees): £3,000,000 Sinking fund @ 4% for 30 years: (no income tax) to provide the funds in 30 years time: 0.0178 × £3,000,000 | £53,400 |
| **Sinking fund - replacement of the building after 60 years (excluding inflation)** | 60,000 sq ft GIA @ £100 / sq ft (inc fees): £6,000,000 Sinking fund @ 4% for 60 years: 0.0042 × £6,000,000 | £25,200 |
| **Revised capital value after allowing for sinking fund** | Value as if sinking fund payments in perpetuity: £1,500,000 - (£53,400 + £25,200) × 14.286 YP: | 20,306,120 |
| | ADD Reversion to perpetuity after sinking fund payments cease in 30 years: £53,400 × 1.877 YP : | 100,232 |
| | ADD Reversion to perpetuity after sinking fund payments cease in 60 years: £25,200 × 0.247 YP : | 6,224 |
| **Revised capital value** | | **20,412,576** |
| **Reduction in capital value: £21,429,000 - £20,412,576:** | | **1,016 424** |

\* Net present value of £1 receivable in perpetuity after 30 yrs
\*\* Net present value of £1 receivable in perpetuity after 60 yrs
NB Tables for years purchase dual rate 7% and 4% incorporating these deferred receipt calculations are available for simplicity

The combination of the adverse economic climate, the problems of escalating premature obsolescence and property's illiquid characteristics have brought severe depreciation to all property values in the early 1990's. **FIG 3.3.2.E** above hypothesised the value of a prime Central London site at the 'then' values over a 30-year period from 1965 - 1994 plotting it against the values it would have achieved if adjusted to the RPI over the same period. It would have been a very clever valuer who had forecast property **market** changes of this order let alone built in the right level of **modernisation** investment to cope with the asset depreciation.

### 3.7.3 INFLATION AND DEPRECIATION

Inflation may affect property values in three ways:

- supply and demand factors - adverse or favourable depending on whether viewed by tenant or investor - may push up rents

- the 'weight of money' seeking a home in property investments may force initial yields down and hence capitalisation factors up (a concept further discussed in Chapter 3.3 above)

- high inflation in the economy will raise the rental levels in the short term; however, any consequential economic adversity affecting business generally, and/or the property sector in particular, may well turn the situation on its head - witness the 1974 post-inflation slump in property values.

An important side effect is the propensity for inflation to mask the effects of depreciation of assets in real terms. Strong demand coupled with high inflation may keep the open market value of obsolescent properties at or near that of newish buildings. Conversely, when demand is weak the older building may be vulnerable, unsaleable or, probably, both. The lesson to be learned by investors or owner-occupiers from this scenario is that the troughs will get deeper, as the building ages, even though the peaks may retain some parity; so, selling an old building in a peak period would be a sensible strategy - if the peak could be identified as such at the time it materialised!

---

[1] 'The impact of information technology on office buildings' – DEGW / EOSYS 1984

# CHAPTER 3.8 – PROPERTY MANAGEMENT

## 3.8.1 THE PROPERTY MANAGEMENT ROLE

*Introduction*

There is a distinct difference in approach between property management which is concerned with investment assets, and premises management which is concerned with built facilities.

Nevertheless, many facilities managers will find themselves presiding over the management of all, or parts, of property assets leased out to their employer's tenants or sub-tenants, so a thorough understanding of the principles of investment property management is essential.

The owner, or prospective owner, of one or more properties who intends to hold the estate for a long period is faced with a number of activities which must be undertaken if the wealth sunk into the property is to be maintained or enhanced. In planning for these activities there may, however, be conflict between what is good long-term management and stewardship of an estate and what is evidence of good short-term performance.

*Performance appraisal*

Estate or portfolio standards are likely to require re-appraisal and the property management function requires knowledge of the environment in which the estate exists and the knowledge and skills to appraise the potential for development and re-development should needs or opportunities arise.

At a different level of conceptualisation, continued investment in the estate may be compared with other opportunities to invest eg: in equities or gilts. Similarly, where individual properties in the portfolio are not performing in a way commensurate with the risk involved, rationalisation of the holdings will be affected and new investments sought. In particular, this would appear to be the process undertaken by the financial institutions eg: the pension funds in making any relative shift from property to other investment sectors, or vice versa.

Of course, not all owners have the resources to appraise their estates as fully as may be suggested above, but the function is one which the financial institutions in particular have been concerned to develop and progress. It follows that an owner's criteria for investment should be fully established and appraised.

As far as valuations of property assets belonging to institutions and companies are concerned, the 1970's and later development of accounting standards was, and is, linked with the development of valuation and standards practice. Thus, the Assets Valuation Standards Committee of the Royal Institution of Chartered Surveyors has produced numerous Guidance Notes Background Papers on the subject.

*Ownership and professional advice*

Many large organisations have their own in-house team of property management specialists - usually chartered surveyors from the general practice division. It is less common to find the legal expertise in-house.

As out-sourcing comes more and more into vogue, both aspects of the property management function are likely candidates for the 'non-core' window exit.

*Property management functions*

Once buildings have been completed and occupied a new phase of their life begins. Property management is required on a planned basis to ensure that they meet occupiers' requirements and maintain their worth to the owner (who may be an investor or the owner-occupier). The management will involve both day to day activities and deeper study and action. The latter is sometimes referred to as 'active management' and requires the estate manager to spot opportunities for, say, redevelopment, major refurbishments, or acquisition of adjoining property, perhaps to realise 'marriage value' - see Section 10 - The Development Option.

Generally, investment property management includes:

- maintenance and repair of buildings, plant & machinery, and fixtures, fittings and furniture in 'common areas' of buildings

- insurance against numerous perils affecting buildings, occupiers and other persons, including fire insurance, consequential loss of rent, and employer's compulsory insurance

- assessment of rent on letting, on review or on renewal of leases

- obtaining possession from tenants for the purposes of redevelopment or for other reasons, including the settlement of compensation claims for disturbance and any improvements, if appropriate

- management of vacant property prior to re-letting, or demolition for redevelopment

- re-letting, or breaking of leases

- evaluations for improvements, redevelopment or disposal

- disposal by sales, assignments, or grants of leases, by gifts, or by other means

- funding acquisitions, repairs, maintenance, refurbishment and development projects

- planning to avoid or mitigate tax burdens and to take advantage of particular tax incentives eg: capital allowances.

What the owner-occupier does with the estate is derived from needs and pre-occupations of the business which gives rise to the strategies adopted in carrying out these activities in line with the premises policy - see Chapter 9.1

Property management requires a comprehensive property record system to include: rent roll, estate terrier, caution system, minor and major works programmes, storage arrangements for deeds, agreements and plans, and a library. Taxation records need to be kept, particularly for service charges and capital allowances. There are a number of excellent estates management programs now available either on a data-base or linked to computer-aided facilities management systems.

*The cost of investment property management*

External management of an estate may cost from 1% to 10% (typically 5%) of income from rents depending upon scale and complexity. Sometimes it is geared to the service charge - 10% is a common figure. Where the income is incidental to the basic business activity some time for the facilities manager liaising and negotiating with tenants and consultant surveyors will have to be added on.

# SECTION 4

# SPACE MANAGEMENT

# CHAPTER 4.1 SPACE - THE PREMISES COST DRIVER

### 4.1.1 THE USE OF SPACE

*Space and the organisation*

Buildings are essentially working platforms which are wholly or partially enclosed. The area of the platforms which is able to be used for production purposes is what the user pays for; however, included in the cost of providing the usable space are the costs of all the other platforms needed to support it eg: space for services plant, stairs, landings and fire escape routes.

Whether or not the user is a tenant or the freeholder does not influence this issue; the tenant's rent is usually linked to the lettable floor area - which is **not** the usable area as is shown below - and the freehold value is usually also geared to the rental value per unit of lettable area.

Both tenant and freeholder will endeavour to get as much usable space out of the area provided. The main difference in outlook is that the tenant is not concerned with the non-lettable space (although in theory he is paying for it in the building component of the rent) whereas the freeholder, if he is also the developer, will be seeking to optimise the proportion of the total built space which is lettable and therefore valuable.

Space use economics from the developer's viewpoint is discussed in Chapter 10.2 so this section is concerned primarily with the tenant's floor space (and the owner-occupier's equivalent thereof) and how it is used.

**FIG 4.1.A** is a reminder of how premises costs relate to 'people' costs per capita in a 'Flagship' and 'Back-office' location.

**FIG. 4.1.A:** *People costs v facilities costs per unit of area ('front' and 'back' office examples)*

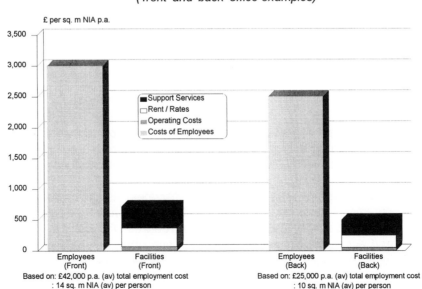

Different organisations have different work-cultures which influence the way they use their space. At the same time buildings have their own characteristics which impact upon the way they can be used and furniture systems and statutory provisions add a further set of benefits and constraints. Since the late '60's/early '70s the science of space planning has been developed to help building users through one of the most critical issues they have to undertake - how best to use the available space with regard to its cost and the productivity of the employees working in it. Since premises are a non-core overhead there is, and always will be, pressure on organisations to cut down on the costs of space and this is a reasonable challenge for the facilities manager. Nevertheless, the productivity issue should always drive the solution, for the consequences of reduced output will always be greater than any premises cost saving from which it results.

*Analysis of space use*

Terminology developed by facilities managers and space planners, while being appropriate for internal use, has often tended to conflict with terms used by quantity surveyors, letting agents, developers and planners. The building industry is concerned with the building shell as a container, while the space planner is concerned with the distribution of activities in the available usable space.

The definitions which follow are depicted graphically in **FIG 4.1.B**. They resolve the differences and provide a spectrum of categories ranging from those related to fixed properties of a building to varying categories geared to the organisation's use of a building.

The first three definitions are taken from guidelines published by the RICS.

**FIG. 4.1.B:** *Space use - definitions and typical proportions*

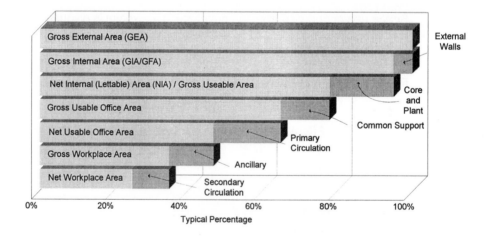

**Gross external area (GEA).** This describes the office floor space as per the Town and Country Planning Act (1971). It is the area measured from the outside face of the external walls - that is, the complete footprint on all floors.

**Gross internal area (GIA).** This describes the gross floor area which is the parameter frequently used by quantity surveyors and others estimating building costs at feasibility stage. It is measured between the inside face of the outside walls and across all circulation area voids and other non-office areas such as plant, toilets and enclosed car parks. It excludes the voids at structural floor levels in an atrium which must, however, be indicated separately when presenting figures for GIA.

**Net internal area (NIA).** This refers to the gross internal building area less the building core area and any other common areas such as plant rooms, toilets, lift structure and lift voids. This equates with the letting agents' 'lettable floor area'. As the **actual** lettable can be a negotiable term it is as well to use the term NIA in any formal presentation.

The net internal area is equally the **gross usable area.**

For ease of assessing the way that space may be most effectively used within the building shell, the space planner may use the following definitions.

**Gross usable office area.** This is the net internal (lettable) area (or gross usable area) less 'common support' which is a term used to describe space provided for the use of the whole or a substantial part of the organisation eg: 'special' areas like the library, restaurant, mainframe computer room, central storage, or 'auxiliary' areas essential for the running of the building, such as goods areas, workshops etc.

**Net usable office area.** This is the gross usable office area less the area of primary circulation routes within the office area. Whereas the 'landlord's' circulation comes off the gross internal area as described above, the deduction here is for the fire escape routes which have to be provided by law.

**Gross workplace area.** We are now down to the space in which the user can put workstations and local storage. However, first we must eliminate any space required for 'ancillary' purposes ie any space (open or enclosed) owned or managed by a department or group eg: filing, terminals or meeting space.

**Net workplace area.** This is the space totally dedicated to the individual including desk, personal filing and any meeting place. It is derived by eliminating from the gross workplace area the space linking it to the fire routes, known as 'secondary circulation'. Note that any circulation around the workplace eg: the space behind the workstation chair to enable movement about the workstation, or the whole of the open space inside a single-person room, is part of the net workplace area; it is sometimes described as 'tertiary' circulation.

The importance of using established rules of measurement for space use as well as any other parameter cannot be emphasised sufficiently. The pitfalls of failing to do so, or, worse still, not qualifying the unit of measurement at all (eg: 100 sq.ft. per person) is discussed under 'Benchmarking' in Section 12.

Having defined the terminology, it is possible to understand the implications of the results of any measurement. It must be remembered that whereas it is possible to prepare a preliminary budget for space by building up from these definitions (see below) the amount of space in each category provided in a plan will vary according to the design in the context of the building, the furniture and the user's requirements.

*The space budget*

Although state-of-the-art space management procedures eschew the concept of uniform space-standards it is usually necessary to get to grips with space requirements by assessing typical space consumption.

In establishing a space budget it may be useful to use simple rules of thumb, giving areas required per office staff member. This could be expressed according to several of the above definitions. **FIG 4.1.C** illustrates a notional space build up for providing a net workplace area averaging 7m² per person.

**FIG. 4.1.C:** *Typical calculation for space budgeting*

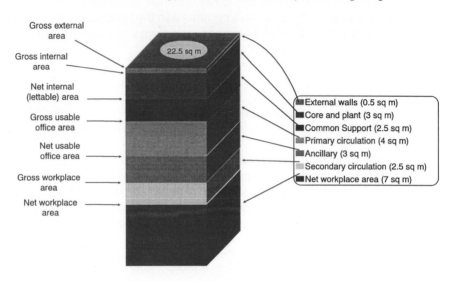

Gross external area
Gross internal area
Net internal (lettable) area
Gross usable office area
Net usable office area
Gross workplace area
Net workplace area

22.5 sq m

External walls (0.5 sq m)
Core and plant (3 sq m)
Common Support (2.5 sq m)
Primary circulation (4 sq m)
Ancillary (3 sq m)
Secondary circulation (2.5 sq m)
Net workplace area (7 sq m)

## Building assessment

The **tenant** need not be too concerned about the ratio of net internal to gross internal floor area; rent is paid on the net internal area and, in theory at least, rateable value is geared to rents. However, common services such as heating, air conditioning, window cleaning, maintenance and upkeep are all related to the gross amount of space and building volume, with the result that operating costs and service charges are sensitive to uneconomical gross building design. Developers, however, have the most to lose from not getting the maximum lettable (net internal) floor space out of the gross area, and work hard to achieve efficient gross-to-net ratios - sometimes at the expense of lettable-to-usable ratios, which are the prime concern of the final user.

When assessing the space available in a building as a rule of thumb one might expect a ratio of net internal area to gross internal area of between 70 - 87.5%

These proportions may vary dramatically depending on the number, depth and configuration of floors. The major reasons for the increasing proportion on non-lettable areas in larger buildings are:

- means of escape

- sizing of lifts and width of stairs

- capacity of ducts

- space for plant.

The impact of common support makes any attempt to benchmark net or gross usable office area to the net internal or gross internal areas quite fruitless; in practice, the ratio of usable space to gross internal area varies considerably over similar sized buildings, a point which should be well understood and not overlooked when reviewing an organisation's building stock.

## Planning efficiency

A large number of buildings seem to be designed for the benefit of the passer-by, the investor, the builder - anyone but the occupier, the user of the space.

The building design features which most influence the ability to use the space effectively are:

- window mullions, ceiling grids and structural bays, which influence where partitions can be located and the size of enclosed offices that can be provided. An organisation which has a high demand for enclosed offices moving into a building with an inflexible planning grid may find itself with larger offices than required and a major wastage of space. **FIG. 4.1.D** shows the effect of some traditional planning grids on space allocation, and maximum space utilisation (modern office buildings are most often designed to a 1.5m square grid which is not dictated by the fenestration modules.)

- depth of building, dimension from wall to wall, location of cores and configuration of floor plan, influence how efficiently the space may be utilised. The width of a building may be too great to provide for offices either side of a central corridor, or too narrow to accommodate enclosed offices, a workplace and a primary circulation route.

- the location of columns and service elements (HVAC units) may hamper efficient planning and reduce the effective space available

- the frequency and location of power and data outlets may also restrict planning flexibility.

**FIG.4.1.D:** *The effect of planning grids on cellular office space efficiency*

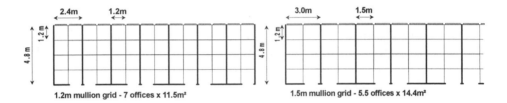

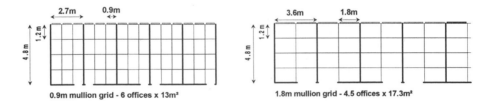

Source: 'Premises Audits'

In addition to the assessment of planning flexibility, the capacity of building shells should also be assessed against such criteria as:

- potential to accommodate enclosed offices
- adaptability to be planned for different styles of layout and size of working groups
- capacity to accommodate cables
- flexibility of air-conditioning to adapt to varying heat loads

*Matching organisations to buildings*

How much space an organisation needs to carry out its function is, or should be, determined by the organisation's business plan, with the guiding principles expressed in the company's premises policy statement. The premises policy may cover guidelines on the allocation of cellular offices, space standards and rules of thumb for support functions.

The space budget, or total amount of floor space needed, is the summation of the amount of space required for

- office space

- support space

- expansion space

The space budget is built up by multiplying the number of staff by predetermined average standards, and adding areas for support and expansion. The result is a space demand independent of the efficiency of a particular building.

Building shells, according to their configuration, depth and planning grids, suggest planning principles to make the most effective use of the space provided. Organisations, independent of building stock, establish space policies regarding size and dimensions of office and planning rules. To use the space available most effectively the constraints and opportunities of the building should be analysed and some questions posed.

**Space standards:** does current company policy concerning the amount and quality of space per person apply itself efficiently to the building areas available?

**Types of workplace:** could standards be varied to meet the effective use of the building without impairing the efficiency of the organisation? Organisations which apply rigid space policies regarding size of offices, allocation of enclosure and access to views may find themselves using space less and less effectively.

**FIG 4.1.E** shows an example of the comparative costs of tailoring space requirements to the space available.

**FIG 4.1.E:** *Comparative costs of tailoring space, by location & floor area*

| Option A | Gross usable space requirement 100,000 ft² | |
|---|---|---|
| Option B | Gross usable space requirement 80,000 ft² | |
| **Number of employees** | | 400 |
| **Gross usable space / employee A** | | 250 ft² |
| **Gross usable space / employee B** | | 200 ft² |
| **Around the UK costs - rents rates operating costs - would vary thus:** | | |
| | **Cost / Person / pa** | |
| **Location** | **Option A £** | **Option B £** |
| City of London | 16,000 | 12,750 |
| West End | 9,500 | 7,500 |
| London Suburbs | 5,750 | 4,500 |
| Good Provincial | 4,250 | 3,500 |

Applying space standards to create a theoretical space budget could result in an average of 220 sq.ft. per person. Option A has applied standards rigidly, never providing offices below the company space standards. In Option B the company has been prepared to adapt its standards to the module of the building, with a saving of £3,250 per annum per member of staff in the City of London.

### 4.1.2 THE COST OF SPACE

*Total premises costs in the context of turnover*

In Chapter 1.1 the relationship between premises and the total costs of an organisation were considered. **FIG 4.1.F** is a reminder that premises represent possibly one-third of the total cost of facilities - 5% or so of the total outgoings.

**FIG. 4.1.F:** *Typical turnover, profit, facilities and I.T. costs*

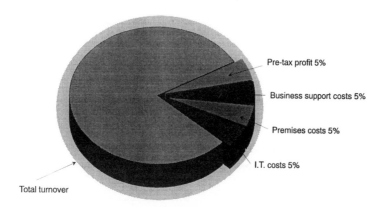

However, the whole of the premises costs figure is geared to the amount of space occupied.

Factors influencing the cost of space per unit of area include:

•       location

•       quality/performance (but see Chapter 1.2)

•       tenure

•       operating requirements

•       fitting out.

**FIG. 4.1.G:** *Prime office costs - regional variations*

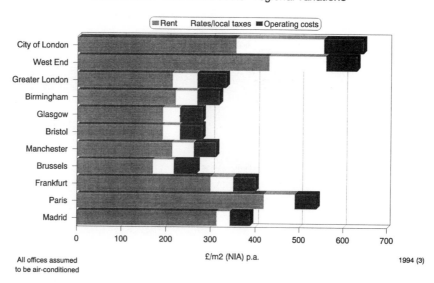

However, because the largest cost component in the premises cost equation is the rent (or mortgage equivalent) the location is generally regarded to be the major influential factor. Note in the owner-occupier model location is still a key factor as it influences the land price and also, to a certain extent, construction costs.

**FIG 4.1.G** shows typical relationships between rent and other premises costs in selected centres with the UK and other European centres.

*Regional variations*

Even in a tight little enclave like the European Union, costs in the various capital locations vary wildly; and it is not the building costs, nor the operating costs, which rule the day but the residual value of the land derived from the perceived market value of the investment - see **FIG 4.1.H**.

**FIG. 4.1.H:** *Residual land values, international standard offices, 1992*

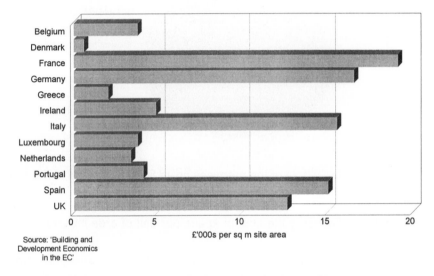

Source: 'Building and
Development Economics
in the EC'

**FIG 4.1.J** illustrates how the development budget splits down in all the major European locations, with the land values highest in the high rental, low investment yield areas. It is in these high rental value areas that top-management pressure can be brought to bear on space use - but only in those organisations whose economic performance has got out-of-sync with the premises cost regime of the location into which they find themselves hooked.

**FIG. 4.1.J:** *The development budget - international standard offices, 1992*

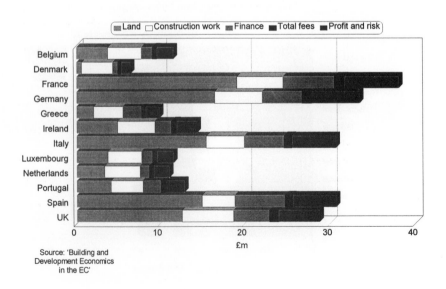

Source: 'Building and
Development Economics
in the EC'

As discussed elsewhere in this text the operating costs, though sometimes varying a little unaccountably between location, do not impact greatly, or at all, on the overall costs of premises.

## Effects of varying density

The state-of-the-art solution to mitigating the high cost of premises is to increase the number of employees using the space. This can be done in two ways:

- changing the layout to allow more workplaces per unit of space, and/or

- planning the space and its management to permit multiple use of 'non-territorial' workplaces.

Both strategies involve increased levels of operating costs, but the overall effect is to reduce premises costs per capita.

In the case of increased physical density, the cost of operating the space must increase; the doors will open and close more frequently, carpets will get more wear, cooling loads will demand more maintenance and consume more energy, security will become more of a problem, furniture costs may increase and so on. With 'just-in-time' (JIT) space solutions (see below) the extra cost of managing the space to keep it as efficient as the dedicated territorial version has to be deducted from the savings in what is nevertheless a premises-cost-efficient workplace solution.

The key issue relates to the impact of these cost- cutting strategies on the productivity of the workforce. JIT solutions show early signs of added value as well as cost-efficiency; this may have much to do with the thought and consultation which has gone into their creation - features which are frequently lacking when the unmitigated 'sardine-can' approach to space planning prevails.

## Effects of varying space requirements

Some job functions require more space than others. Other job functions need the status of more space and others receive it as a perquisite. **FIG 4.1.K** shows how traditional space use standards impact on premises costs; by and large the name of the space management game now is to get rid of these predetermined standards and replace them with the ad hoc, as required, functional allocations.

FIG 4.1.K: *Space use typical premises costs per capita pa*

| Job Function | sq m NIA* | UK Prestige HQ | UK Back Office |
|---|---|---|---|
| Clerical | 6 | 3,600 | 1,200 |
| Secretary | 7.5 | 4,500 | 1,500 |
| Executive | 15 | 9,000 | 3,000 |
| Executive Director | 20 | 12,000 | 4,000 |
| Managing Director | 30 | 18,000 | 6,000 |
| Waste Paper Basket | 0.1 | 60 | 20 |
| *Occupied area | | | |

Obviously reductions in space use per capita can effect premises cost savings, provided always that there is a reasonable chance of re-allocating or off-loading the redundant space.

The 'just-in-time' generic solutions have two main objectives:

• the de-dedication of workplace

• the increased intensity of workplace usage.

A necessary corollary of these strategies is that the employees must feel at least as comfortable, if not more so, in their new environment; a key feature in the achievement of this essential breakthrough is the involvement of the users in the concept - its planning, design and implementation. If they believe they own it they will appreciate it. Imposed solutions are destined to fail in any management scenario, and where the 'non-territorial' workplace solution is concerned all the available evidence supports this dictum.

**FIG 4.1.L:** *Dynamic space use -typical functional analysis per capita*

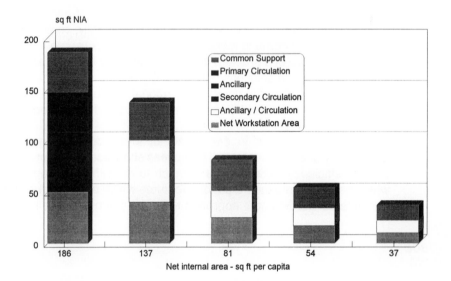

**FIG 4.1.L** illustrates how multiple use of space effects area distribution per capita compared with more conventional solutions. Even allowing for the additional management costs found to be necessary in some situations the economics are still startling, as in **FIG 4.1.M.**

**FIG 4.1.M:** *Dynamic space use - typical premises costs per capita p.a.*

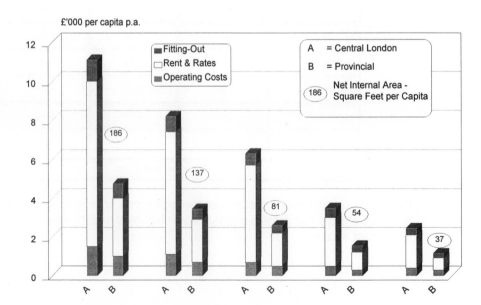

All workspace economies depend for their acceptance on improved facilities, whether on a better environment, greater workplace efficiency, more meeting rooms or other bonuses. Particularly, those who have lost a cellular office will need to be appeased by some tangible added benefit, and even then the consultative process will be a condition precedent to any chance of approval of the concept.

## 4.1.3 THE SPACE AUDIT

*The need to audit space*

Organisations are seldom static. The political, economic and technological climate surrounding them is changing, which affects the technology available to do their job, the markets they work in, the products they deal in and the activities they undertake. The result of this fluidity is a high rate of personnel turnover, shifts in the quality of staff employed, reorganisations of working groups and relationships, and possibly an increasing take up of office automation.

These changes are happening incrementally and are unplanned with the result that in many organisations dramatic changes have occurred without a clear premises strategy; often such changes are outside the control of the premises manager resulting from the initiative of individual departments or the information systems function.

The result is:

- uneven space standards, with gross over-crowding in areas
- a changing distribution of activities to space, as the spatial demand for new activities and equipment are felt
- inefficient usage of space, due to ad hoc planning.
- disjointed relationships between departments, and dislocation between buildings as annexes are taken over to meet unpredicted growth, or 'short-term' pressures
- deteriorating visual and climatic environment due to an increase in office automation equipment, with the proliferation of cables, noise and heat
- loss of financial control

The space audit provides the opportunity to:

- re-visit the opportunities and constraints of the building stock available, and review the 'premises policy'
- review the changing demands of the organisation in the light of the take up of information technology
- test actual space usage against an effective space budget and planning concept
- assess the effectiveness of the facilities management process in planning and managing space and responding to change.

*The process of auditing space*

The objectives of assessing how space is being used are to:

- relate the amount of space used to norms that may exist for firms in a similar business. These norms, in addition to reflecting lettable, usable and workplace area per person, may also include a number of different grades, amount and type of enclosure provided, average ancillary space per person, and number of staff per meeting room (**FIG 4.1.N**).

- assess the way space is being used in practice against organisational guidelines

- identify discrepancies of space provision and usage between departments, grades of staff and working groups. Space planning guidelines formulated by the organisation may bear little relation to changes in patterns of work and the technology used in some groups; the space audit may help to identify these discrepancies.

FIG 4.1.N: *Preliminary assessment of existing space usage*

| | Professional consulting engineers | Contracting consulting engineers | Multi-national main-frame computer company | Multi-national mini-computer company | Local authority |
|---|---|---|---|---|---|
| **Managers:** | | | | | |
| Number of grades | 2 | 4 | 2 | 2 | 4 |
| Range of areas | 12 - 18m² | 12 - 20m² | 13.4 - 18.7m² | 15 - 18m² | 12 - 25m² |
| **Professionals:** | | | | | |
| Number of grades | 1 | 2 | 1 | 2 | 3 |
| Range of areas | 7.1m² | 7.0 - 10.6m² | 6.7m² | 9.0 - 12m² | 8.5 - 10m² |
| **Draughtsmen:** | | | | | |
| Number of grades | 1 | 1 | - | - | - |
| Range of areas | 7.0m² | 6.5m² | - | - | 8.5m² |
| **Clerical:** | | | | | |
| Number of grades | 1 | 4 | 2 | 1 | 1 |
| Range of areas | 5.1m² | 4.0 - 10.2m² | (4.2)* - 6.7m² | 9m² | 7m² |
| **Conclusions:** | | | | | |
| Number of grades | 5 | 11 | 5 | 5 | 8 |
| Range of areas | 5.1 - 18m² | 4.0 - 20m² | 4.2 - 18.7m² | 9 - 18m² | 7 - 25m² |
| Ammount of cellurisation | 2 Grades | 4 Grades | 2 Grades | 2 Grades | 2 Grades |
| * Salesman | | | | | |

The quickest way of making an initial assessment of how effectively space is being used is a plan survey. This first hit, with the minimum of input, allows an assessment to be made of:

- the proportion of space being used for circulation; support and 'people' space which can be compared with company standards and accepted practice

- average workplace area per person in different departments

- size and number of cellular offices.

Using existing floor plans of the building, a 'walk round' survey of the building can be made to note the following information:

- numbers of people (desks) in each room (space)

- numbers of staff per VDU/peripheral (printer) in each space

- easily identifiable ancillary activities

- rooms with specialist support functions.

The 'walk round' should be undertaken with the location manager or a representative from each department who can answer questions concerning number of staff per room, designated group boundaries, usage and responsibility for ancillary areas, and clarify usage of special space. A review of 50,000SF of normal office space should take from three to five hours. From marked up plans an assessment can be made of variations in density and distribution of space usage (**FIG 4.1.P**).

**FIG 4.1.P:** *Preliminary sketches indicating density and nature of space usage*

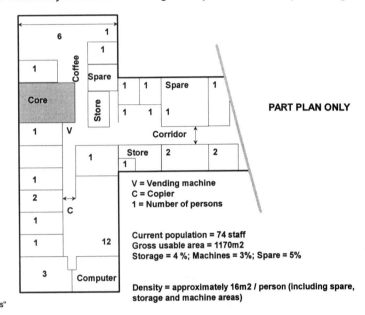

Source: "Premises Audits"

A more accurate analysis of space allocation may be undertaken as a building use survey. Such a survey provides invaluable data before beginning a major replan; it identifies accurately how space is being used in practice, helps in setting future guidelines and maps areas of wastage to be concentrated on in future replans (**FIG 4.1.Q**). Note that the area of common support and ancillary usage on the single floor in this example may not be typical of the overall pattern.

**FIG 4.1.Q:** *Building use survey - a more accurate pre-planning analysis*

|  | (ft²) |
| --- | --- |
| Net Internal (lettable) area | 7,590 |
| Primary circulation | (1518) |
| Common support space | (1140) |
| Ancillary space | (1330) |
| Redundant space | (570) |
| Gross workplace area | 3032 |
| Core |  |

Managerial/professional 130 ft²

Senior Manager 280 ft²

Professional 4 person office 500 ft²

Source: "Premises Audits"

Such a survey is undertaken by drawing in freehand the situation as observed on every floor. In the office, later, more thorough take-offs may be made of space distribution (possibly using CAD as in the example). A building use survey of 50,000SF of normal office space will take two to three man-days.

The final evaluation that may be undertaken is a furniture and equipment survey to ascertain whether there is more or less furniture and equipment being provided than is needed for the job and whether the amount of screening provision or shared furniture - such as meeting tables, filing cabinets and book shelves - is compatible with company objectives.  Such an assessment may be made by random sampling, by first identifying areas of varying styles of work and then taking a 10% sample. Actual patterns of space usage may vary dramatically from planned standards.  In fast-growing organisations the distribution of space and demand may change even as the planning process proceeds.

## *Reviewing the demands of information technology*

The impact of office automation on the office environment has been in retrospect dramatic.  Its effect is pervasive, influencing:

- the ergonomics of the workplace

- the amount of worksurface required for personal screens, as well as the additional floor space required to accommodate printers, and central processing units

- the levels of lighting and the design of light fittings to reduce glare and reflection on screens

- the capacity of the building and furniture to cope with wires and cables

- the need to extract heat from equipment

- the need for acoustic barriers to reduce the clatter of machines

- the pattern of work, and eventually the distribution of space

- the desire for a visual language that can cope with the proliferation of equipment and cables

- the cost of operating the building and

- the cost of a new building, refurbishment and fitting out.

A review of the demands of information technology on the building and space usage should cover:

- take up of both personal and central computing, and predicted future developments

- an assessment of adaptations that have already been made and the expenditure.  Main frame and central  telecommunications installations tend to be budgeted as capital items, but the installations of minor systems, such as word processing systems and personal micros, may well be revenue items, purchased by individual departments, and additional furniture, extra wiring and even a local air handling system may come out of the revenue and maintenance budget.  The result is that operating costs appear to increase, which could be the result of a 20-30% add-on for adapting to information technology

- a visual survey of pinch points where the unplanned take up of information technology has resulted in a deterioration of the working environment.

To understand trends in IT take-up, a small group consisting of the DP manager, telecommunications manager and facilities manager may be brought together to map past experience and predict future trends.  This information should act as a basis for predicting additional space needs and a building adaptation policy for dealing with additional equipment.

A 'walk round' survey of the building may be used to identify areas where the environment is deteriorating with excess office automation. Simple indicators are:

- the number and length of trailing wires, which will suggest the need for more outlets at close centres

- surface mounted wiring (either along skirtings, or across floors) with a tape covering, reflects problems of cabling

- fan on desks to take off heat; paper over windows to reduce heat gain, and glare on screens

- density of terminals (both VDU's and printers) which may be measured as floor area per terminal or as a ratio of terminals to staff. These measures may then be used to calculate heat gains, and thresholds for installing mechanical air handling/cooling

- the number of VDU workstations with cardboard hoods or home-made adjusters to reduce reflection on the screen.

Of course, current Health and Safety legislation is addressing many of these issues - see Chapter 8.2.

*Ensuring effective space usage*

The most effective evaluation is achieved when standards exist against which to measure performance. Effective monitoring may be undertaken against a planning concept and workplace guidelines that should be prepared at the stage of a move in, and act as the basis for space management.

A planning concept (**FIG 4.1.R**) identifies:

- **capacity**: the number and size of individual offices it is possible to provide on each floor, and the total number of staff that could be accommodated using a minimum and maximum density

- **zoning**: the most suitable areas to locate offices so as not to compromise the effective use of space. The location of activities requiring special servicing (machine rooms, copiers)

- **servicing**: a strategy for cable distribution and zoning of high intensity cooling requirements to use the building most effectively

**FIG. 4.1.R:** *Planning concept*

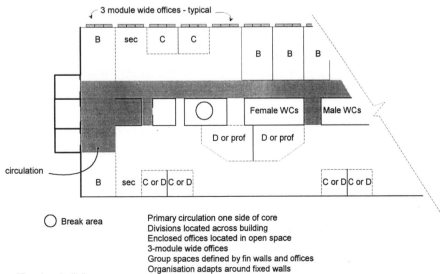

Source "Premises Audits"

### 4.1.4 MANAGING SPACE

*Space
standards*

Space standards are a necessary tool for optimising and managing the effective use of space. To ensure that standards are easily managed and economical to apply they should be:

- modular, so that partitions do not have to be moved continuously, but an intermediate partition can be installed in a large office to make two smaller units

- in the minimum number of sizes to reduce arguments and minor adaptations

- guidelines (**FIG 4.1.S**) which can be adjusted to individual building configurations and grids, and reflect style of work and the need for privacy, or interaction.

**FIG. 4.1.S:** *Space planning guidelines - net workplace area*

| 300 ft² Senior managers * | 150 ft² Managers * 2 x secretaries * | 100 ft² Professionals * Supervisors * Secretaries * | 75 ft² Senior professionals * Supervisors * | 50 ft² Clerical and other similar functions * |
|---|---|---|---|---|

* Note: these are functional descriptions **not** grades

Source: "Premises Audits"

**However, the golden rule for space standards is that they must relate to the functional needs of the occupier rather than his or her grade/status within the organisation.** That is not to say that a person who needs to be seen to be important should not have an appropriate workplace - just that the decision must be made on an individual rather than global basis.

As was shown in Chapter 1.1 the **space standards must stem from the business plan and will determine the total cost of premises. For this reason they constitute the most critical decision an organisation has to make in connection with premises economics apart from location.**

*Space planning*

Space planning is a part of architecture and interior design, but it certainly is not true to say that every architect or interior designer is able to do it effectively and efficiently. Before employing full-time space planners or consultants do make sure that references to successful projects are available in good numbers. Getting the furniture supplier to do it - even for a fee - will lock the organisation into a plan to suit the system or range rather than vice versa. Space planning can have a fundamental effect on facilities economics and worker productivity so should benefit from high quality professional input rather than being done cheaply by third-raters or, worse, carried out in-house with untrained personnel.

**FIG 4.1.T** shows the sort of typical costs per capita which might be saved over and above a more conventional approach in terms of reduction in the cost and rate of 'churn' (see Chapter 7.8) and a 10% reduction in space standards (without loss of environmental quality) showing an annual saving of over £150,000 in a building of 100 or so employees. The relatively small cost of a competent space planning exercise to achieve this result, even on this relatively small scale operation, is clearly well worth the investment.

**FIG 4.1.T:** *Potential premises cost savings through careful space planning*

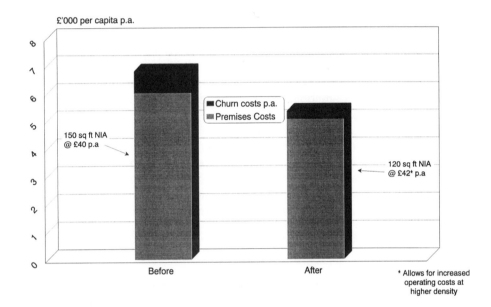

## Administration

On larger organisations it is probably worthwhile dedicating personnel to space management and planning. Where CAD facilities exist there is an overwhelming argument for using a space management program for tracking relocation of personnel and equipment about the premises as well as for the planning of revised layouts. Simply scanning in drawings rather than re-drawing from scratch is probably adequate to get the system up and running; spot checks on the accuracy of key dimensions in support of the scanning is, nevertheless, a prudent precaution.

If using a consultant's CAD program it is essential that the facilities manager has access to it at all times, and essentially on his own premises.

## 4.1.5 OPTIMISING SPACE USE

### Main objectives

The two principal objectives in re-planning space – from any day to day modifications at one end of the scale, or departmental moves at the other, are:

- to improve efficiency at the workplace
- to reduce costs

– in that order.

*Planning
options*

Changes in the way space is used can be classified as

- de-cellularisation

- 'non-territorial'

- a combination of both

The changes should aim to reduce the amount of space needed for the work whilst improving the quality of the facility. Successful changes have redistributed space from workplace to support functions, often accompanied by improved management of communications, data handling and more comfortable formal and informal meeting areas.

The move away from cellular offices continues as a trend which, if handled sensitively and with full user 'ownership' of the concept, usually meets the approval of all but those lower grade middle management staff who see their own private room as paramount in their efforts to establish or maintain some status within the organisation.

Open-planned areas can be economical with space as illustrated by the example at **FIG 4.1.U** where the cost of the reconfiguration at £4m generated another 300 workplaces, a saving of £1750 per capita pa across the board. In this example the employer was able to release for sale, surrender or sub-letting a freed-up building, which is, of course, not always the case – certainly in the short term.

**FIG. 4.1.U:** *Conversion of office space from cellular to mainly open plan*

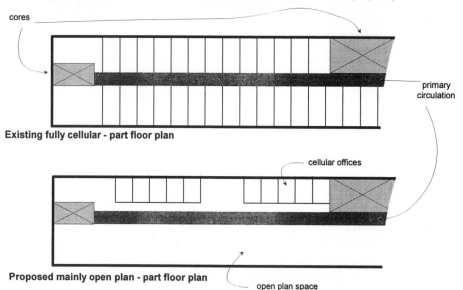

*Non-territorial
space planning*

The 'just-in-time' non-territorial approach to space planning has now been established in a number of major organisations worldwide including IBM, Arthur Andersen and Ernst & Young. Otherwise known as: **hot desking, free address, virtual workplace, sharing** and **hoteling**, the principle of non-territorial space allocation involves giving up the right to a personally designated workspace for other than a short period. The concept reflects the fact that in some occupancy patterns workplaces are unoccupied for up to 70% of the time. So the 'non-territorial approach' plans undesignated workplaces which may be booked as required (or just used as available) and are able to service the occupant, one way or another, with his or her own computer and telephone connection (possibly wireless as looks increasingly viable - see Chapter 7.5), filing and access to a local meeting area/ refreshment centre.

The IFMP[1] has documented a number of these studies, and the details of the projects and the post-occupancy appraisals make fascinating reading. For present purposes, **FIG 4.1.M** above indicates the  premises costs savings possible for the JIT approach;  note that the lowest option involves partner/directors offices being used (by arrangement) when empty, which is a feature proving difficult to introduce in many of the projects initiated to date.

Most of the feedback from these projects is positive in terms of staff approval - which implies some impact on productivity, or at least no adverse effects - except in one or two cases where the changes were made without transferring 'ownership' of the concept to the users or consulting with them sufficiently throughout the piece. The latter approach not only alienates the user but also risks a failure properly to understand the way the group or department actually works.

Space reduction for cost's sake is an incredibly damaging strategy.  Implementing it without proper consideration of, or consultation with, the users will merely exacerbate the economic folly.

---

[1]      International Facility Management Program – Cornell University

# PART C

# PREMISES OCCUPATION

# SECTION 5

# PREMISES
# OPERATING COSTS

# CHAPTER 5.1 – OPERATING COSTS IN CONTEXT

## 5.1.1 OPERATING COST CENTRES

'Operating costs' is a term relating to the cost of the physical activities required in running and maintaining the building and its services; at one time the terms 'running' costs or 'running and maintenance' were in conventional use but their lack of precision led to confusion, hence the adoption of this more generic term.

The cost centres under this heading are:

- Maintenance
- Cleaning and housekeeping
- Energy
- Water and drainage
- Waste disposal
- Interior landscaping
- Exterior landscaping

The authors' own rules of classification of the contents of each of these cost centres are given in Section 12 at **FIG 12.2.A**

## 5.1.2 OPERATING COSTS AND PERFORMANCE

Like all supposedly non-core expenditure the operating costs are constantly under pressure from those responsible for overall financial management. They are perceived as an overhead which can be turned on and off like a tap without undue adverse implications for the overall service provision.

Sometimes the financial managers are right in this supposition. Too often facilities managers defend their quarter using warnings of failure which will inevitably result from deprivation or deferral of funds and which turn out to be unsubstantiated; like the boy who kept crying 'wolf' the facilities manager who makes his case badly by exaggeration puts the business at risk of real harm when the rubber band really does break.

Defence of one's budget is made much easier if the premises policy and the strategies supporting them are formally accepted as part of the business plan as propounded in Chapter 1.1. This relationship is considered again in **FIG 5.1.A** which illustrates also that although the costs of operating the premises are predominantly linked to the **physical performance** of the buildings the latter is itself influenced by the **functional** demands of the business plan.

For example, the figure indicates that 'quality' and 'space standards' are established by functional requirements thereby influencing the costs of operating the premises which stem from the resulting physical performance.

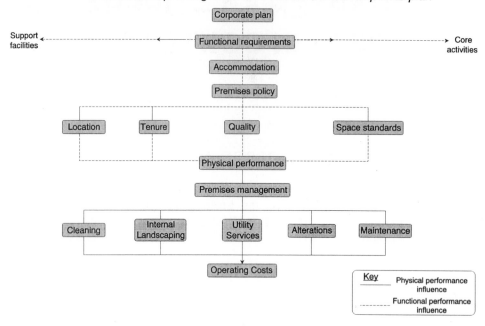

FIG. 5.1.A: *Operating costs in the context of the corporate plan*

One of the biggest problems facing facilities managers is an almost complete lack of hard evidence as to the true consequences of failure in any of the components of physical performance. If the lifts in a 4-storey building are out of action for 2 days the occupants might complain bitterly - unless they are training for the London marathon, trying to slim or away from the premises on productive business. Just like the CBI's calculation that the UK economy is £15bn p.a. worse off as the result of traffic-related delays, loss of productivity is very difficult to prove conclusively.

Anecdotes abound, but hard facts are scarce.

Such evidence as exists supports the view that a 'caring' facilities management regime funding less than perfect premises on a shoestring will foster a bigger contribution to the bottom line profit realisation than a disinterested set-up running better premises badly with more funds available. Possibly it is the 'pulling together' team spirit syndrome which has the biggest implication.

Nevertheless, the building which stops supporting vital business is a nightmare situation which few core managers would contemplate if they were reliably and credibly informed of its imminence.

Designers sometimes tempt providence in this respect. A bespoke building in the South-East of England housing a computer installation servicing over 500 organisations in that region has a 3-layer felt roof. Water penetration through this cheap and notoriously unreliable material is as inevitable as the consequences will be catastrophic. Funds to prevent such a disaster are an essential business provision and must be made available whatever other cost centres the business may have to plunder.

The facilities manager's role in identifying such performance characteristics within the premises policy and strategies is absolutely critical - a strategy based on crying 'wolf' could eventually result in the business being decimated.

## 5.1.3 OPERATING COSTS AND TOTAL REVENUE EXPENDITURE

Operating costs as defined above are unlikely to represent more than about 1%-1.5% of an organisation's total annual revenue expenditure (see **FIG 5.1.B**)

If they do the chances are that they are over-provided and are in need of re-appraisal unless the core activity is unusually low cost eg: mainly low-grade clerical.

**FIG.5.1.B:** *Operating costs in context of turnover*

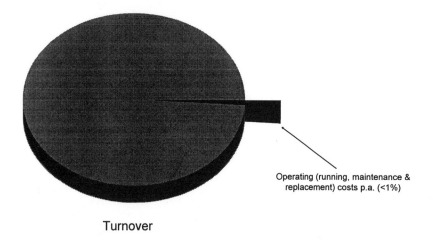

Operating (running, maintenance &
replacement) costs p.a. (<1%)

Turnover

Even in the latter case, the level of premises performance and costs would normally be graduated downwards with a decrease in the operating costs per capita more than compensating for the operating costs per unit of floor area increasing (see **FIG 5.1.C**).

**FIG. 5.1.C:** *Effect of density on operating costs per unit of area and per capita*

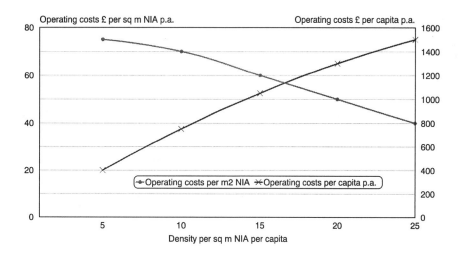

**FIG 5.1.D** shows even more vividly how the savings in property costs increased by intensity of usage far outweigh any consequential impact on the operating costs.

There is a dichotomy between the relative insignificance of the operating cost expenditure (in the context of both investment option appraisal and proportion of total annual expenditure) and the potential risk to vital business from long-term under-provision of funding for these essential tasks.

**FIG. 5.1.D:** *Effect of density on operating and property costs per capita*

Density (sq m NIA) per capita

- Property costs (rent, rates & insurance) per capita p.a.
- Operating costs per capita p.a.
- Total premises costs per capita p.a.

£'000 per capita

To overcome the worst exigencies of deprivation of funds facilities managers should develop a coded warning procedure linking control of funds for priority operating expenditure to potential harm to vital business. Financial control programs such as *prem*FINANCE incorporate such a feature (see **FIG 5.1.E**).

**FIG 5.1.E:** *Effects of operating cost decisions on core business efficiency*
*- premFINANCE warning codes*

| REQUESTS FOR FUNDS - premFINANCE STATUS CLASSIFICATIONS | |
|---|---|
| **Priority status** | A. Not applicable<br>B. Mandatory<br>C. Business Requirement<br>D. Recommended<br>E. Desirable<br>F. Advantages |
| **Consequence of deferral** | A. Not applicable<br>B. Harm, Vital business<br>C. Harm, Ancillary business<br>D. Harm, Business profile<br>E. Harm, Non-business<br>F. Risk, Vital business<br>G. Risk, Ancillary business<br>H. Risk, Business profile<br>I. Risk, Non-business<br>J. No consequence |

# CHAPTER 5.2 – MAINTENANCE

## 5.2.1 MAINTENANCE AND BUILDING PERFORMANCE

*The importance
of maintenance*

BS 3811 defines maintenance as: 'the combination of all technical and associated administrative actions intended to retain an item in, or restore it to, a state in which it can perform its required function'.

A car may continue to work without servicing but its performance will deteriorate through two phases: first it will begin to consume more resources, such as fuel and minor repairs, accompanied by failing efficiency, and then it will require major repair and/or replacement of components in response to imminent or actual breakdown.

The impact of inadequate maintenance of buildings will be felt in due course in both the profit and loss account and the balance sheet. Business efficiency will reduce and output fall as a result of time wasted and the psychological consequences of an apparent lack of care or pride on the part of top management (however hard the facilities manager may try to minimise the damage); resultant hostility may cause abnormal absence through sickness, and genuine ill-health may also be a direct result of inadequate maintenance especially with regard to the mechanical and electrical services. Legionnaires Disease is living testimony to such failure and the so-called 'Sick Building Syndrome' is also frequently blamed upon inadequate maintenance.

On the balance sheet building values will be down-graded as the asset depreciates physically through lack of investment in its preservation.

*The
components of
maintenance*

Maintenance is required in respect of three main aspects of premises:

- the fabric
- the services
- the grounds.

Modern buildings are more likely to suffer early deterioration of the fabric than the hardier and simpler masonry structures prevalent in the first half of this century. Nevertheless, the problems - mainly the result of a greater proliferation of materials and components having no historic performance credentials - do not normally manifest themselves until sometime into the building's life-cycle.

In any event, maintenance of the fabric is normally a smaller component of the maintenance cost centre. In a modern air-conditioned office building the annual maintenance expenditure, including replacement of minor components, is typically as illustrated in **FIG 5.2.A**.

**FIG. 5.2.A:** *Typical distribution of maintenance expenditure in a modern air-conditioned office building*

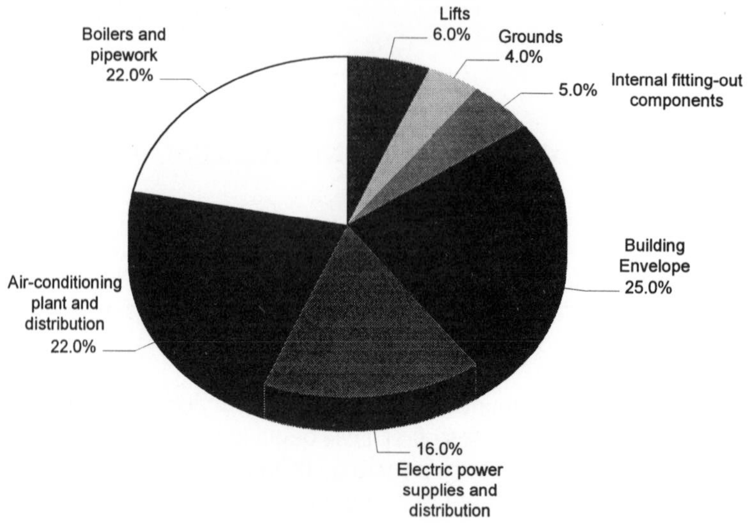

## 5.2.2 MAINTENANCE MANAGEMENT

*In-house v out-sourcing*

Because of its technical complexities the use of contractors to carry out maintenance of services in air-conditioned buildings was commonplace long before the core v non-core arguments considered in Chapter 2.1 had surfaced.

With respect to the building fabric 'Term' maintenance contracts nowadays often replace the in-house DLO operation.

Frequently the facilities manager will have professional in-house surveyors and engineers to specify, procure and monitor maintenance contract services and sometimes the professional function will itself be out-sourced either as advisory in support of a technically qualified manager or seconded full-time in an in-house capacity working to a 'lay' facilities manager.

The concept of the direct labour organisation looking after maintenance is fast disappearing as the specialist contractors sharpen their act - and their pencils -and benchmark comparisons generally tend to show the DLO operations to be a less cost-effective solution.

In theory there is no reason why a well-run DLO should not be as cost-effective as the out-sourced alternative; **in fact, the 'best of breed' in the authors' extensive facilities cost data base is an internally managed almost totally DLO regime**. However, the historic complacency of the DLO is hard to eliminate in the short-term and the tide of conventional opinion of core business management is firmly in favour of the out-sourced option for this supposedly non-core activity.

The in-house team may offer greater flexibility in terms of response to change. The contractual claims thereby avoided in pursuit of the optimum business solution have to be carefully weighed against the conventionally more cost-effective out-sourced alternative.

*Maintenance
policy and
strategies*

BS 3811 describes the various maintenance strategies as follows:

- **Planned maintenance**

  The maintenance organised and carried out with forethought, control and the use of records to a pre-determined plan.

- **Preventative maintenance**

  The maintenance carried out at pre-determined intervals or corresponding to prescribed criteria and intended to reduce the probability of failure or the performance degradation of an item

- **Scheduled maintenance**

  The preventative maintenance carried out to a pre-determined interval of time, number of operations etc.

- **Condition-based maintenance**

  The preventative maintenance initiated as a result of knowledge of the condition of an item from routine or continuous monitoring

- **Corrective maintenance**

  The maintenance carried out after a failure has occurred and intended to restore an item to a state in which it can perform its required function

- **Emergency maintenance**

  The maintenance which it is necessary to put in hand immediately to avoid serious consequences

- **Unplanned maintenance**

  The maintenance carried out to no pre-determined plan

These strategies may be required in total or in part. Their presence and implementation should be encapsulated in a maintenance policy forming an integral part of the operating costs component of the Premises Policy (see **FIG 5.1.A**). The policy and its strategies should take account of potential changes to the stock of buildings - especially incorporation of improvements within major capital projects (see **FIG 2.2.3.C** in Chapter 2.2) and have regard to the stage attained in the life-cycle of each property. It should also highlight areas where neglect or failure could be positively harmful to vital business.

BS810: 1986 Section 2 defines a maintenance policy thus:

- The maintenance policy should ensure that value for money expended is obtained, in addition to protecting both the asset value and the resource value of the buildings concerned and the owner against breaches of statutory and legal obligations.

Planned preventative maintenance is a strategy which sets out to control performance in terms of day-to-day function, health & safety, longevity and investment value. In the harsh economic climate of the 1990's the strategy has come under close scrutiny and much criticism. Insofar as it presumes the need to maintain and replace components at pre-estimated stages in their life-cycle it permits two serious breaches of sound economics:

- contractors or DLO operatives may fail to check or maintain mal-functioning parts which are not on their work schedules

- components may be replaced before their useful working life has been exceeded.

Many organisations adopting a planned maintenance strategy are beginning to suspect that their buildings are 'over-maintained' to the detriment of funds for core business activity.

Perhaps the best solution is based on 'planned inspection' and reporting followed by essential repair and replacement.

## Alterations disguised as maintenance

FIG 5.2.B shows an analysis of 'maintenance' produced in the course of a premises audit. On inspection it was found that only about one-third of the items included under the cost centre were truly maintenance (the services and fabric); the balance was made up of upgrading, alterations, and the dreaded 'churn' (see Chapter 7.8). In spite of rigid Inland Revenue interpretation of what constitutes revenue as opposed to capital expenditure, it is not unusual to find a lot of capital works included in the maintenance cost centre.

**FIG.5.2.B:** *Incorrect analysis - upgrading and 'churn' disguised as maintenance*

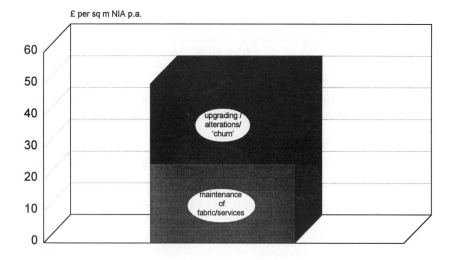

That may be good for Income Tax relief (although you can still get Capital Allowances on those items of plant improvements) but it does not help revenue budgets or assist management to understand the problems which are presented by an inadequate building and/or poor space management.

## Prioritisation

The need to prioritise maintenance is heightened by the pressure of funds available. It is doubtful whether any economic or political regime has ever over-funded maintenance of property and the 1990's version is certainly no exception - worldwide.

Unarguably first priority must always be given to health & safety – inside or outside of the statutory requirements – and avoidance of adverse effects on business will follow closely on the tail of the statutory needs.

Any funds left over after dealing with the exigencies of these two main drivers will be fought over by:

- any statutory building preservation requirements
- the significance of any element needing attention in terms of
    - its contribution to asset life and value
    - potential malfunctioning or failure causing harm to vital business activity.

Performance indicators should be geared to the priorities which should, in turn, be incorporated in the premises policy.

Subjectivity in prioritisation is to be avoided at all costs. If the chairman's carpet has a coffee stain under his desk it ought to take its place in the queue behind the threadbare safety hazard on the floor of the main reception.

*Performance indicators*

The maintenance provider will be expected to be targeted and monitored in respect of

- response to emergency call-out
- down-time of essential plant & equipment
- physical inconvenience to occupiers
- quality of repair
- costs of operations.

PI's relating to the percentage of planned to unplanned maintenance are meaning-less unless

- they are clear as to whether it is cost or number of events which is being targeted
- the proportion of planned v unplanned maintenance has been previously subjected to risk and cost/benefit analysis and set accordingly
- the items of unplanned maintenance have been prioritised in accordance with the maintenance policy.

*Maintenance management programs*

There is an increasing number of software packages available for assisting with the management of maintenance - particularly the planned preventative type. Some of these are linked into CAD for a visual effect and also to exchange information between the CAD drawn data and that in the data-base. These systems and their economics are described in greater detail in Chapter 2.2 - 'Facilities management functions'.

### 5.2.3 MAINTENANCE OF THE FABRIC

*Typical*
*expenditure*

In a modern office building the typical annual expenditure on maintenance and repair of the fabric is between £5.00 and £10.00 per sq m. of the gross floor area (see Chapter 4.1 for definition) per annum - see **FIG 5.2.C**. The cost drivers, in no particular order of significance, are:

- the age of the building and its current state of repair
- the quality of the materials and workmanship
- its shortcomings with reference to Health & Safety at Work regulations
- the quality of cost control applied in the design, procurement and implementation
- the inclusion of non-maintenance items within the cost centre
- the intensity with which the premises are utilised (eg: increased densities of personnel per sq m. of the usable floor area will reduce lives of carpets, doors etc.)
- any listing in respect of building preservation

**FIG. 5.2.C:** *Typical spread of fabric maintenance costs p.a. for modern office buildings with suggested impact of key cost drivers*

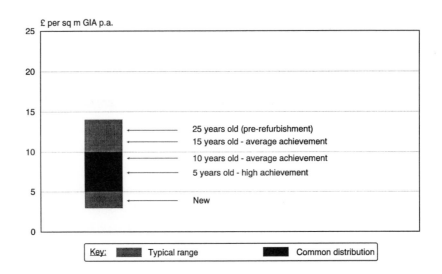

### 5.2.4 MAINTENANCE OF THE BUILDING SERVICES

*Typical*
*expenditure*

In a modern air-conditioned office building the costs of maintaining the building services per annum is typically between £10.00 and £20.00 per sq m. of gross floor area - see **FIG 5.2.D**.

The cost drivers are:

- whether or not the building has a mechanical ventilation/cooling/air-conditioning system
- the age of the M+E installation, its unexpired life and current state of repair
- the quality of workmanship and materials in the installations
- the Health & Safety implications

**FIG. 5.2.D:** *Typical spread of services maintenance costs p.a. for modern office buildings with suggested impact of key cost drivers*

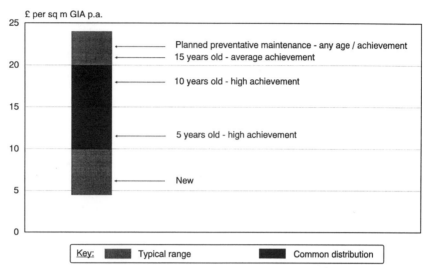

- the quality of cost control applied to the design procurement and installation

- the inclusion of non-maintenance items within the cost centre

- the intensity of usage eg: increased density will increase operating intensity and wear and under-usage may cause a system to fail through failure of the building to achieve the conditions it was designed to alleviate; over-specified power-loadings causing VAV boxes to fail to respond to minimum temperature changes are believed to be a primary cause of the 'sick building syndrome'

- the existence of a planned maintenance programme not accompanied by a planned inspection programme

The comparative maintenance costs pa for some of the more common cooling and heating systems are given at **FIG 5.2.E** together with their typical energy consumption.

**FIG. 5.2.E:** *Total energy and maintenance costs p.a. (HVAC only ) office building 4,250 sq m NIA*

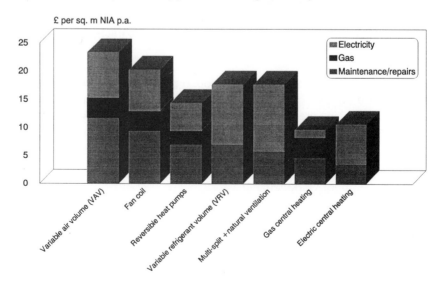

### 5.2.5 LIFE-CYCLES

*Building life*

Whole-life building economics is considered and illustrated in detail in Chapter 10.4. One vital issue particularly affecting the maintenance cost centre is the design policy in respect of the planned life of components.

Indeed, there is much controversy over the total life span to which building design should be aimed. Commercial buildings are generally expected to have a useful life of 60 years. The concept of 'long life, loose-fit, low energy' was promulgated in the 1960's and reinforced by Dr. Frank Duffy's analysis of 'Shell, scenery and services' [1] in the 1970's.

Although the economics of low-cost short-life purpose-built buildings are powerful in business terms they do not marry with the view of the investment institutions that a building life should coincide with the terms of the favoured long lease.

However, radical change in the functional requirements of buildings has tested much of our commercial building stock in the past decade. Perhaps surprisingly some of the older pre-war properties have proved more robust in the face of change than their modernist and post-modernist successors. This has probably less to do with architectural style than the meanness of post war property developers in seeking to minimise storey-heights to save money and increase site coverage within planning height restrictions.

Ironically, the 'meanness' of these latter-day buildings, which earned them the unwanted tag of 'prematurely obsolescent' in the 1980's as they failed to accommodate the information technology explosion, is now being forgiven as the technology itself becomes more sophisticated and less demanding of its accommodation. The impact of depreciation on property values is explained with worked examples in Chapter 3.7.

*Component life*

The life-spans of building and services components is poorly documented. However anecdotal evidence exists aplenty and examples of life-cycles of some of the more significant building and services components are given in Chapter 10.4.

A contemporary Research Project under the LINK/CMR/SERC scheme has developed the concept of the 'Performance-and-cost-managed building [2]. This concept illustrated at **FIG 5.2.F** relates to the process whereby the cost and performance of a building are managed throughout every phase from inception, through design, construction and occupation to refurbishment and, finally, demolition. The technical instrument for delivery of the concept entails a building data-spine supported by, and linked to, a data-base of building component lives and costs of maintenance and replacement.

In time, when commercially developed and exploited, the process will yield much better data than exists at present. Nevertheless, the external influences on component life are so varied as to make it unrealistic to expect **absolute** values to emerge from such a system. Issues such as

- incompatibility of materials
- poor workmanship
- variable levels of maintenance
- variable exposure to the elements
- different conditions in use

will all need to be reflected in any attempt to forecast how long a material, component or system will last.

**FIG. 5.2.F:** *The 'performance-and-cost-managed building' - the building data spine*

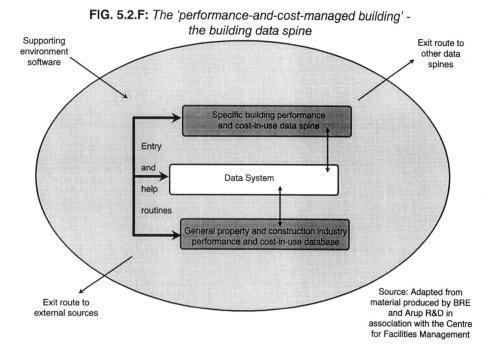

Also, given the time it takes components to complete their life-cycle, some may become obsolete in advance of total failure leaving designers to choose once again from new, untried components.

———————————

(1)    Planning Office Space (Architectural Press)

(2)    Centre for Facilities Management (U. Strathclyde) / Arup R&D / BRE

# CHAPTER 5.3 – CLEANING AND HOUSEKEEPING

## 5.3.1 CLEANING AND BUILDING PERFORMANCE

*Definition*

The scope of the cleaning service varies quite considerably from one office building to another; the premises auditor who does not analyse the cost centre into sub-elements - such as external, internal, housekeeping, laundry, carpet, fabric - will quickly founder in financial mis-analysis.

The split between 'housekeeping' and cleaning is frequently confused - and the term 'housekeeping' itself is not a particularly meaningful or helpful title for cost analysis purposes: it can embrace many items which are often included in the cleaning budget such as changing towels, renewing soap and soap substitutes, and cleaning toilets. And, of course, accounting for any cleaning costs forming part of the service charge is a major item on the auditor's list of initial things to concentrate on.

Although it is quite common for 'housekeeping' to be shown as a separate cost centre it is included within this chapter for convenience.

For purposes of logical comparison the following generic headings are therefore proposed:

- internal surfaces, fittings and equipment
- external building surfaces
- grounds and outbuildings
- housekeeping.

Details of the items comprising these sub-elements are given in **FIG 5.3.A**.

**FIG 5.3.A:** *The 'cleaning' cost centre - definition of contents*

| Sub element | Principal contents | Exclusions | Cross - reference |
|---|---|---|---|
| Internal surfaces, fittings and equipment | Office waste collection/disposal<br>Surfaces<br>General office areas<br>Special areas<br>Toilets<br>Lift cars<br>Cleaning and disinfecting<br>Sanitary fittings<br>Office furniture<br>PC's and monitors | Deep-clean kitchens<br>Special plant cleans | Catering maintenance |
| External building surfaces | Windows<br>Cladding<br>Atria<br>Roofs and integral gutters | Clearing out fitted gutters and drain pipes | Maintenance |
| Grounds and out - buildings | Litter collection<br>Sweeping<br>Hosing down pavings/roads<br>Clearing pools/fountains etc.<br>Graffiti removal | | |
| Housekeeping | Toilet consumables<br>Towels and laundry<br>Maintenance of appliances<br>Pest control | | |

*Quality and performance*

The quality of cleaning is a reflection of the aspirations of the organisation and its employees. The number of cleaners employed may influence the speed of the cleaning operation but the brown stains in the bottom of the coffee mugs will speak volumes for the inability of management to achieve an appropriate level of performance.

Management must set objectives for the facilities manager in terms of cleanliness as well as the other operating cost centres. How best to achieve those objectives within a sensible budget must be the facilities manager's decision. The facilities manager must also have a strong say in what is a 'sensible budget' and what the objectives ought to be.

The scope of the service will normally be a constant in terms of what has to be cleaned: the only variable is the division of responsibility in a leasehold situation between the landlord and tenant - that is, the extent to which the service charge covers cleaning of common parts such as reception areas, staircases and toilets.

So, with the scope constant, the frequency of cleaning, the materials used and the supervision are the major determinants of the quality of performance.

The frequency of such cleaning operations as polishing desk tops, washing down partitions, vacuuming carpets and cleaning sanitary fittings has a marked effect on the cost of the service; it also has a marked effect upon the observed functioning of the system. E.g.: a facilities cleaning policy may entail having the lavatories cleaned four times a day. Apart from the obvious desirability of extra hygiene the policy may well be supported by core management on grounds of good PR. Perhaps in no other cost centre - even taking energy into account - is the diligence and efficiency of facilities management more open to comment (favourable or otherwise) than in cleaning. This PR feature is an integral part of the performance requirement: the premises policy must identify this feature and point out to management the cost implications of the policy.

It is worth noting that the co-operation and empathy of staff is extremely important to successful and economic facilities management. In that context a 10-20% addition to the cleaning budget in an attempt to improve relationships between management and employees will not normally result in an overall increase of more than, say 2.5% in a typical operating cost budget.

## 5.3.2 MANAGEMENT OF CLEANING

*Supervision*

The effect of good or bad supervision is felt in terms of cost and quality. It is, of course, a human factor and, despite the arguments often advanced to the contrary, is not directly related to the debate over contract v in-house cleaning. The buck stops with the facilities management who will be concerned to see that standards are in line with costs. If performance is below standard for the price paid (and assuming market rates are being paid), it will come down to a question of whether or not the in-house or external supervising staff are being diligent in insisting upon adherence to the specification.

*Contract*
*Cleaning*

The main cost difference between contract cleaning and direct labour is that the contract cleaner carries his own supervision, charges for his overheads and profit and carries a contract risk. Strictly speaking, direct labour costs, being minus profit and risk, should be lower than contract cleaning. However, this will depend on the ability of facilities management to exercise good cost control and quality supervision - which must include regular cost checks against the external contractor. Regular tendering of the cleaning is, of course, necessary, but too rigid a policy on selection by price alone can be counter-productive. By all means keep the existing contractors on their toes but do not jump out of the frying pan into the fire for the sake of 1p or 2p/sq.ft. pa.

The use of contract cleaning is an easy option for facilities management. It can ease an administrative burden but this ought to show in reduced administration costs, not simply in a quieter life and having the luxury of someone else to blame.

*Cleaning and*
*component life-*
*cycle*

The frequency and specification of a cleaning operation will not only effect revenue expenditure, but also the depreciative consequences of the policy on the treated surfaces.

The life of carpets, furniture and so on is influenced by the nature of the cleaning cycle. Although it is likely that decay is reduced and the life of materials lengthened by frequent cleaning and treatment, this saving must be set against the extra revenue cost, to see if the extra specification is really justified on grounds of pure economics. The chances are that it will not be. However, once the argument spills over to functional as opposed to physical performance the true economic case will take a different turn.

*The cost of*
*cleaning*

**FIG 5.3.B** shows a range of cleaning costs taken from a sample of 25 prestige office buildings. The upper and lower extremes of the range are partly due to inconsistency of analysis but the mean figure is consistent with buildings re-analysed into the classification at **FIG 5.3.A**.

FIG. 5.3.B: *Sample range of cleaning costs for office buildings*

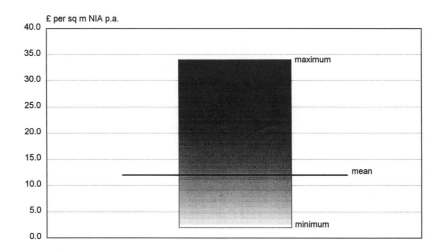

A typical sub-analysis of the norm in terms of both type of operation and distribution of resources is suggested at **FIG 5.3.C**.

**FIG. 5.3.C:** *Typical distribution of normal cleaning costs in terms of type of operation and resources*

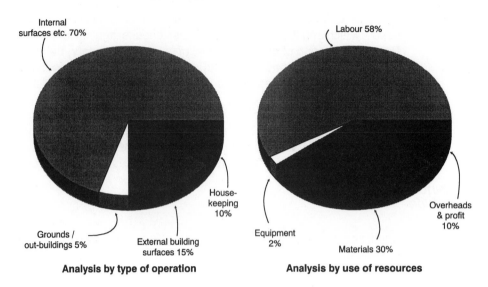

**Analysis by type of operation**          **Analysis by use of resources**

The principal cost drivers in general terms are:

*   the labour rate - see **FIG 5.3.D** for typical cross-regional analysis and for breakdown of cost components

*   the nature and frequency of cleans - see **FIG 5.3.E** for typical analysis

*   adequate storage and access for optimum equipment - a cleaners cupboard on every floor and wide doors to lifts and toilets can make a world of difference to the cost

*   precision in the specification

*   health & safety provisions

**FIG 5.3.D:** *Cleaning labour and supervision - analysis of hourly rates*

| Duties | Hourly rate analysis | Region - £ per hour | | | |
|---|---|---|---|---|---|
| | | Central London | Outer London | Home Counties | N W England |
| **Domestic cleaning staff** | Basic rate | 3.50 | 3.40 | 3.40 | 2.90 |
| | Labour on - costs plus OH + P mark-up | 0.62 | 0.57 | 0.54 | 0.45 |
| | **Contract rate** | **4.12** | **3.82** | **3.94** | **3.35** |
| **Janitorial staff** | Basic rate | 3.40 | 3.45 | 3.65 | 3.10 |
| | Labour on - costs plus OH + P mark-up | 0.85 | 0.60 | 0.58 | 0.48 |
| | **Contract rate** | **4.25** | **4.05** | **4.23** | **3.58** |
| **Supervisory** | Basic rate | 5.25 | 3.70 | 4.20 | 3.95 |
| | Labour on - costs plus OH + P mark-up | 1.37 | 0.65 | 0.67 | 0.61 |
| | **Contract rate** | **6.62** | **4.35** | **4.87** | **4.56** |
| Source: Premises and Facilities Data | | | | | |

**FIG 5.3.E:** *General cleaning specification task frequency comparison*

| Group category | Cleaning item | Description of task | Cost band descriptions | | |
|---|---|---|---|---|---|
| | | | A | B | C & D |
| | | | High standard | Average standard | Low standard |
| **Externally** | Windows | Wash and polish | weekly | monthly | quarterly |
| **Generally** | Windows | Wash and polish | weekly | monthly | quarterly |
| | Glazed partitions | Wash and polish | daily | monthly | quarterly |
| | Furniture (desks) | Dust/polish | daily | monthly | quarterly |
| | Other furniture | Wash and polish/vacuum clean | weekly | quarterly | half yearly |
| **Lifts** | Doors | Clean and burnish | daily | monthly | quarterly |
| **Toilets** | Partitions and walls | Thorough wash and clean | daily | daily | weekly |
| | Floors | Machine clean | weekly | monthly | quarterly |
| | WC's and urinals | Wash, clean and disinfect | daily | daily | weekly |
| **Office spaces** | Floors | Vacuum clean | daily | daily | weekly |
| | Bins etc | Empty and fit liners | daily | daily | alt days |
| | Doors | Dust and polish | weekly | quarterly | half yearly |
| | Other furniture | Dust clean | daily | quarterly | half yearly |
| | Reception desk | Clean/polish | daily | weekly | monthly |
| **Tea points** | Walls | Wash and polish | daily | weekly | monthly |
| | Floors | Machine clean | weekly | monthly | quarterly |
| **Staircases/landing** | Handrails | Wipe clean and polish | daily | monthly | quarterly |
| | Glazing | Clean/polish | daily | weekly | monthly |

Other general issues to note are the provision of ventilation to rooms where charging of battery packs can take place and the careful control of the chemicals to be used - both for safety, long term effects on materials and possible damage to equipment and artifacts.

*The cost drivers*

The general cleaning sub-element is the largest component and is almost exclusively about getting rid of dust, dirt and standard office waste. 80-90% of the dirt entering a building arrives on people's feet. If the facilities manager can devise an effective means of ridding those boots and shoes of their dirt before they enter the heart of the building (preferably in at least two strides) then his cleaning operation will be both quicker and more efficient and probably cheaper. Together with an improved life-span for some of the surface materials, these are the essential ingredients of the value for money which the facilities manager is seeking in every cost centre.

The other main cost drivers are:

- the nature of surfaces to be cleaned
- number of 'special' cleans
- flooring around wet areas
- wet or dry carpet cleaning
- clear desk policy
- tidiness of local storage arrangements
- time available for cleaning function
- the existence of an atrium
- openable windows
- quality of air-filtering (if any)

Dry cleaning of carpets is known to be more effective than wet cleaning, avoiding discolouration and colour bleeding, shrinkage, stretching or splitting. Nevertheless, regular wet cleaning is essential to the control of microbes and reduction of static electricity.

Carpet tiles, with their stiff backings, are difficult for vacuums to suck air through; a light adhesive pat in each corner will help the use of a more powerful vacuum (but run the risk of disqualification for capital allowances -see Chapter 11.2).

Avoidance of too many changes of flooring surface can also speed the cleaning process. 'Track off' areas (where people drag dirt on to carpets from smooth surfaces and 'funnel areas' (where people congregate or traverse in intensive numbers) should be carefully controlled and minimised. Easily pitted surfaces should be avoided at all costs.

*Special cleans*

Cleaning of acoustic ceilings is probably best carried out by specialists to avoid discolouration and damage to the acoustic properties - painting the tiles is not a good preventative measure on both those grounds.

Lighting losses of up to 50% can result from inadequate lamp cleaning. Venetian blinds are a real dirt trap and the use of ultra-sonics in the cleaning process will ensure a thorough result.

The specification should also cover the IT services, keyboards and telephones (in the latter case a regular hygiene service is highly desirable), especially where operators are allowed to eat food at the workstation!

## 5.3.4 CLEANING EXTERNAL SURFACES

*Window cleaning - the cost drivers*

Apart from the obvious point about the proportion of glazed areas, adequate mechanism to permit cleaning from cradles or boats is clearly paramount. Abseiling from ropes is becoming increasingly popular and can be facilitated at a low capital cost. Reversible windows are appropriate in some environments and obviously save time and cost in the window cleaning process.

Windows cleaned with the wrong, abrasive, cleaner will become 'shot' over time making the process difficult and unrewarding in visual terms.

Again the proportion of walls to windows will impact - but not as much as the specification of surfaces requiring frequent treatment eg: power-jet washing down every 3 months - a requirement recently discovered by a facilities manager for the first time at handover of his new building. In this example the process was essentially a 'maintenance' item and the cost of that operation should have been analysed into that cost centre rather than 'cleaning'.

Graffiti may be a problem in certain areas. Leaving it just encourages more artistry but it can be hard to remove. A preventative treatment using a polyurethane finish has been found to ease this serious cleaning problem.

### 5.3.5 CLEANING THE GROUNDS

*The cost
drivers*

Litter will accumulate wherever it gets the chance. Cobbled areas are a nightmare for litter attraction and collection; unfortunately, terrorist activity sometimes precludes adequate provision of receptacles which, incidentally, makes the anti-litter legislation almost impossible to enforce evenly and fairly from one location to another. Terrorist threat can sometimes mean that keeping external grounds free from litter etc. can become part of the security operation.

Water features can create an excellent image and ambience but may present health hazards if not properly maintained and cleaned. Again, there is a fine line to be drawn between cleaning and maintenance of water features.

### 5.3.6 HOUSEKEEPING SERVICES

*Consumables
and appliances*

The housekeeping facet of cleaning is of course fraught with problems, not least being the impact of Health & Safety legislation on the levels of hygiene to be achieved in toilets and washrooms.

Worthwhile economies can be found on a small scale. Products such as large roll theft-proof paper dispensers, sensor-triggered automatic flushing systems etc. will not only save a few pounds a week; much more importantly they will ensure that the facilities provided are always properly provided and in a hygienic state.

Vandalism is more easily controlled where decor and lighting are of good quality; a well planned tidy facility will not only enhance the image of the owner but also, again, discourage wilful damage.

Warm-air dryers are also vandal-resistant and cheap to maintain but not suited to general office toilet areas - roller towels (linen fed) are best for the administrative areas with paper towers in the blue-collar loos and food preparation areas. However, proper disposal of waste toiletry paper and sanitary towels is not only highly desirable but required by statute.

Other main requirements are for good ventilation, as well as hot and cold running water, the wherewithal to dry off and a general state of cleanliness.

# CHAPTER 5.4 – ENERGY

## 5.4.1 SOURCES

*Delivered
energy*

Energy arrives in business premises in the form of:

- gas
- electricity
- oil
- coal and coke
- steam.

Insofar as they provide a heat load in the building the following are also sources of energy:

- energised equipment
- human beings
- radiation, conduction and convection.

*Gas supplies*

Gas derives from fossil fuels, and in this day and age comes direct from natural sources such as the sea-bed or land-based sub-terranean sources. This latter-day development replaces the process prevalent until the early 1970's in which fossil fuels such as coal and coke were burned to produce 'town gas'.

This environmentally unfriendly (with hindsight) process produced an efficient fuel which was able to be delivered in relatively small bore pipes; the process of converting to natural gas eliminated the need for fuel-burning gas-works but required the wholesale re-adaptation of manufacturing and domestic plant and equipment to accept the rougher, if not entirely raw, product.

The investment in this change having been amortised gas has emerged as a comparatively cheap environmentally-and-user-friendly fuel source, particularly appropriate to central heating.

In economic terms it has a number of deficiencies, in that it requires local combustion with consequent loss of efficiency and giving rise to a need for:

- local provision of exhaust emission
- fire precautions
- precautions against asphyxiation
- cleaning of equipment
- servicing of equipment
- relatively early replacement of equipment.

However, the cost per unit of delivered energy is competitive with the other fuels making total comparison of energy-dependent systems - including capital, running and maintenance costs - essential in consideration of any service where energy source is optional.

## Electricity supplies

Electricity arrives at its destination in a dynamic state ie: in an incombustible form in which it can instantly be converted into a driving force, lighting or heat source.

It requires rigorous safety provisions, but is less likely to be the cause of major catastrophe than the combustible fuel alternatives. Electricity is the only fuel which can provide all the energy requirements of a building.

Its derivation may be similar to the old gas regime ie: coal-fired power station, or it may be generated by nuclear reactors or the elements eg: water-or wind-driven dynamism. Both coal-fired and nuclear derivations are subject to environmental criticism -the former in terms of the 'greenhouse effect' of burning fossil fuels, the latter because of the potentially disastrous consequences of radioactive contamination due to escape of nuclear waste during and after reaction.

Nuclear power generation is considered to be the most efficient form of electricity generation, and has made the fuel competitive across the world; however, the technique has yet to stand the test of time in environmental terms, and is particularly dependent upon man-made solutions and implementation in respect of waste disposal.

Naturally driven dynamism such as is available from hydroelectric dams is dependent upon massive investment, whereas 'windmill' technology is only appropriate on a relatively minor scale.

The process of providing and distributing electricity is expensive, environmentally unfriendly and indispensable; the only choice we have is how much of it we use and, since April 1994, where we purchase it.

## Oil supplies

Like gas, oil requires secondary combustion on site with all the attendant problems described for gas.

Additionally it requires a storage provision on site, secondary distribution to, and careful maintenance of, the point of combustion and, probably most significantly, tanker deliveries not only to the site by road/rail but also to the country by sea from foreign powers to supplement pipe-line deliveries from the adjacent UK sea-beds.

Oil is a comparatively 'dirty' fuel in its combustion phase. This, together with the risk of price and availability identified with overseas supplies, has rendered it very much an also-ran in the race for energy supremacy in all but the major industrial plant and combustion engine vehicle markets.

## Coal and coke

Coal and coke products are now an anachronism in respect of energy supplies to modern office buildings in the UK. Their use is obviously restricted to on-site combustion heating; like gas and oil heating sources they rely upon electric power to supplement the process by way of pumps, fans and exhaustion of fumes; in common with oil they require on-site storage and are apt to be particularly dirty and labour-intensive in operation and maintenance.

## Steam

Steam as a primary source of energy to-day only exists in locations where steam is a by-product of a manufacturing process. Modern safety requirements prohibit anything other than central calorification and the source has little application to modern office buildings in the UK except where there may be access to a district heating arrangement.

*Energised
equipment*

A major contributor to levels of discomfort in office buildings in recent times has been the invasion of a plethora of electric and electronic equipment which has revolutionised not only methods of working but the performance required of the building and its services.

In particular, the heat emitted by PC's, photocopiers, printers and the like have added considerably to the required cooling load, and reduced the mechanical heating load proportionately.

A building wherein IT take-up is around 1:1 will probably be generating additional heat of around 15-20 watts per square metre of floor area. **FIG 5.4.1.A** shows the typical heat gain from various sources in a large office building.

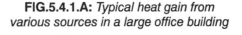

**FIG.5.4.1.A:** *Typical heat gain from
various sources in a large office building*

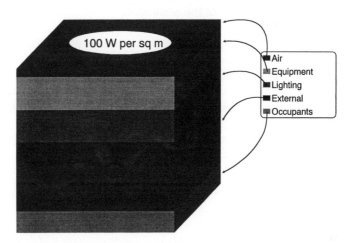

Ironically, just as the world has come to terms with the problems - with engineers inventing enormously expensive and quite inappropriate systems of dealing with the cooling requirement - some of the main manufacturers have redressed the problem by introducing 'low energy' pc's and other equipment absorbing only 10% - 20% of the small power required by the older models with proportional reduction in heat gain. As many of the existing cooling systems are already designed to cope with two/three times the actual heat gain from equipment the move towards down-sizing of such plant will be further encouraged. Of course the heating capacity will have to be watched but extra energy costs in heating will be offset several times over if the process of handling the cooling load can be reduced to suit the actual needs.

*Body heat*

Everyone knows that human beings generate significant heat via their bodies as a waste product from the energy used up in the processes of simply being and doing. Just how much this contributes to the required cooling load was shown at **FIG 5.4.1.A** above.

The main problem with handling body heat is that it is less static and predictable in terms of location and concentration than equipment and solar radiation; six people gathering in a small meeting room will quickly generate a cooling problem which may or may not have a ready solution.

Identification of 'hot spots' involving people and equipment and designing for them in terms of both planning and services allocation is a key aspect of interior design and, indeed, building architecture as a whole.

## Radiation, conduction and convection

Heat gain from outside the building can be delivered by radiation (from the sun or a process), conduction (via the fabric from a warmer environment) or by the air supply (forced or infiltrating).

Of these factors solar radiation is probably the most significant especially when arriving direct through windows; its warming effect on the fabric can also be important, although much of the heat retained in the fabric may well be returned to the ambient exterior at night time in the cooler northern climates. Careful attention to design and specification both to prevent the sun's rays penetrating the glass or fabric and/or to reflect or absorb them can make a big impact on the gain and are of particular importance where a building is on the threshold of requiring mechanical cooling. Eg: shading of windows with blinds (preferably external) or overhangs/ projections are effective and special glazing and window design can reject/absorb up to 70-80% of the solar gain.

The 'all-air' systems such as variable air volume (VAV) are quote profligate when it comes to sucking in warm air from outside which then has to be cooled before being pumped round the building - and repeating the process several times an hour; and in their own way the simple open windows provide an uncontrollable source of warm air to an un-cooled building when it least wants it.

Of course, there are also systems which collect and use solar energy to good effect, thereby eliminating (or minimising) the need for mechanical heating in a highly cost-effective and environmentally friendly manner.

## Combined heat and power (CHP)

CHP is the simultaneous generation of useful heat and electricity. In one single process it takes the heat produced in electricity generation and puts it to use as a source of useful heat rather than wasting it to the atmosphere.

CHP can operate at up to 90% efficiency compared with the 35% offered by the old power stations or 50% available in the combined cycle gas turbine stations. It therefore has the potential to kill two birds with one stone; lower energy costs and reduced $CO_2$ emissions.

It can use any fuel; gas is most common but systems using oil, coal and waste are also to be found.

Because of its relatively high capital cost the system is really only viable where buildings are in constant use - 17 hours a day seems to be the breakpoint. Since buildings operating for this length of time are able to use cheap night rate electricity - eg: keeping the computer rooms cooled - the application to offices is somewhat limited. However, where stand-by generation is an essential component CHP may be worth considering because CHP plant, whether driven by diesel, dual fuel or gas turbines, coal or waste, can double-up this stand-by function.

There are various ways of reducing the onus of capital cost, whether by shared or district schemes, innovative financing or using various forms of contract hire. Hotels, hospitals etc are increasingly changing over to CHP and it may be that office buildings may become viable targets as the technology develops and wherever stand-by generation becomes essential.

## 5.4.2 ENVIRONMENTAL IMPLICATIONS

*Burning of*
*hydrocarbons*

The effects upon the ozone layer of excessive burning of fossil fuels are well documented and widely accepted.

The generation of electricity by the traditional coal-burning process has been identified as a serious contributor to the 'global warming' process, out-weighing the side-effects of combustion of gas and oil at the point of energy consumption.

However, the fact that all modern office buildings require a supply of energy which can only be sourced by electricity is a major reason for looking at ways in which that product can be generated and used efficiently - especially given the potentially finite supply of natural gas and oil as alternatives for heating.

*Embodied*
*energy*

Electrically powered heating and ventilating appliances have no intrinsic need for the energy storage facilities, gas emission flues, water pipes or ducts demanded by the 'liquid' alternatives. They therefore save not only in mechanical components but also in space to accommodate them, and consequently consume less energy than other systems in their manufacture and installation.

For example, a variable air volume (VAV) air conditioning system using a gas-fired boiler for heating plus all the ventilation trunking, fans and pumps and extra storey-height in the building to deliver 10 air-changes an hour (see below) will consume considerably more energy in manufacture than a chilled ceiling system with supplementary electric heating. The embodied energy in the more expensive system must be considered alongside the remaining costs; perhaps revelationally the energy consumption of the maintenance and running of the simpler all-electric systems is much less than that of the more complex systems based substantially upon the cheaper, more environmentally friendly natural gas fuel - and that is before embodied energy in manufacture, installation and accommodation for plant, ducts etc. is taken into account.

**FIG 5.4.2A** compares undiscounted values of the whole life costs of five heating and cooling systems and two heating-only systems the detailed analyses of which are considered later in this chapter.

**FIG. 5.4.2.A:** *Comparative whole-life costs of heating and cooling systems in an office building 4,250 sq m NIA*

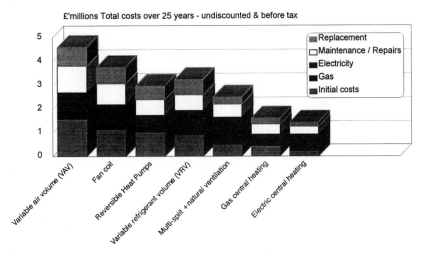

£'millions Total costs over 25 years - undiscounted & before tax

Legend:
- Replacement
- Maintenance / Repairs
- Electricity
- Gas
- Initial costs

Systems: Variable air volume (VAV), Fan coil, Reversible Heat Pumps, Variable refrigerant volume (VRV), Multi-split + natural ventilation, Gas central heating, Electric central heating

The initial and replacement costs may be taken as a crude indicator of the embodied energy in the provision of each system; alongside these figures the consumptions represented by the annual fuel bills (see **FIG 5.4.7.A** below) is of rather less significance than the environmental scientists would have us all believe.

The science of terotechnology is insufficiently advanced - or credible - to give us much reliable data on embodied energy. However, such data as is available suggests that the embodied energy in manufacturing physical energy conservation measures such as insulation, double glazing etc may take a long, long time to pay back from energy savings on location - regardless of the fuel cost savings and any reduction in plant sizes.

## 5.4.3 MEASUREMENT OF ENERGY

Energy delivered to site is measured in various forms.

**Electricity** (always) and **gas** (usually) are billed in terms of kWh - kilowatt hours - which in simple terms reflects the number of kilowatts consumed on the site per hour multiplied by the number of hours for which the supply is billed. This is of course an average, for the consumption varies continuously and the meter automatically computes it to the common kWh unit.

Oil, which does not get instantly converted to energy on delivery, is billed in litres or tonnes, while coal, coke etc are all billed by the tonne; gas is still occasionally billed by the therm.

**FIG 5.4.3.A:** *Conversion of fuel to kWh*

| Fuel | Typical unit of supply | Conversion factor Gross Calorific Value to KWh |
|------|------|------|
| Electricity | KWh | 1.00 |
| Natural gas | therm / KWh | 29.31 / 1.00 |
| Propane | tonne / litre | 13,888 / 6.96 |
| Butane | tonne / litre | 13,694 / 7.85 |
| Domestic heating oil | tonne / litre | 12,778 / 10.22 |
| Gas oil 'D' | tonne / litre | 12,519 / 10.58 |
| Light Fuel Oil 'E' | tonne / litre | 11,942 / 11.22 |
| Medium Fuel Oil 'B' | tonne / litre | 11,617 / 11.28 |
| Heavy Fuel Oil 'G' | tonne / litre | 11,644 / 11.42 |
| Coal | tonne | 7,140 to 8,333 |
| Coke | tonne | 7,750 to 7,883 |
| Air dried wood (burnt as waste) | tonne | 4,395 |

NB: Gross Calorific Value includes the latent heat of condensation of all water vapour in the products of combustion
Source: These factors are taken from 'The Business Energy Saver' edited by the NIFES consulting group

Conversion of therms, litres and tonnes of fuel to kWh based on the 'Gross Calorific Value' can be made using the computed factors given in **FIG 5.4.3.A**. For benchmarking energy consumption it is useful to calculate energy billed in terms of kWh per $m^2$ of the 'treated' floor area per annum; the treated floor area is that part of the building having the direct benefit of the heating or cooling energy supplied and billed. So, a tenant's energy supply should be geared to his net internal (lettable) area - as defined in Chapter 4.1 - unless he also pays the energy bills for the 'common parts', which would normally be part of the landlord's service charge in a multi-tenanted building.

In either case the plant room areas, stores, covered car parks etc should be deducted; where possible the cost of any energy supplies to such areas should be identified and omitted from the comparisons.

The DOE Energy Efficiency Office's guide to 'good practice' energy consumption per $m^2$ of treated area pa is given over.

## 5.4.4 WHERE THE ENERGY GOES

*'Energy efficiency in offices'*

The DOE's energy Efficiency Office has publicised an excellent guide to 'Energy Efficiency in Offices' - No. 19 in its Best Practice Programme (October 1991) - the figures and abridged text of which are reproduced below with their permission.

The information in the guide is based upon data collected form some 200 office buildings which were considered for inclusion in the Energy Efficiency Office (EEO) series of good Practice Case Studies, and another 200 buildings from which energy survey information was available.

*Variations in annual consumption*

Annual delivered energy consumption can range from under 100 to over 1,000 kWh/m² of treated floor area, costing from £4/m² to £40/m² or more at 1990 prices. Of this fossil fuel (normally gas) averages 200 - 250 kWh/m² and £3/m².

In contrast to fossil fuel use, electricity use varies more widely, the most significant influences being:

•    open plan designs, which normally make more use of artificial lighting

•    air conditioning: fans and pumps usually need almost twice as much as refrigeration

•    mainframe computer rooms and their air conditioning

Energy use by general office equipment is significant, but seldom as high as people expect, and never as high as the load specified on the actual equipment.

Larger offices often contain more equipment and operate for longer hours, adding to energy use. However, their higher consumption and better load factors can give them more advantageous tariffs which lower their unit fuel costs.

Ideally each office would have its individual energy consumption and cost target, but that is beyond the scope of the guide. Instead average and good practice patterns of energy use and cost are outlined for the four typical office types described in **FIG 5.4.4A**.

Energy costs in Good Practice offices are usually 30-50% below average levels, as Case Studies and other publications in the EEO Best Practice programme demonstrated (**FIG 5.4.4.B**). Many savings measures are proven and cost effective when undertaken as part of ongoing new construction, refurbishment and alteration work. Some of them and particularly improvements to lighting, controls and management, are also often viable in their own right.

| Office Type 1:<br>Naturally Ventilated Cellular | Office Type 3:<br>Air Conditioned |
|---|---|
| A fairly small, simple building with largely individual offices, and perhaps a few group spaces. Daylight is good while artificial lighting is usually less intense than in the other three office types, and easily controlled by individual switches by the doors. There are few common facilities and catering is usually restricted to the odd sink and kettle. | Similar in occupancy and planning to type 2, but usually larger and with deeper floor plan and tinted or shaded windows which reduce the availability and use of daylight still further. The air conditioning system may be either all-air (for example variable air volume) or air/water (for example induction units or fan-coils). |
| Office Type 2:<br>Naturally Ventilated Open Plan | Office Type 4:<br>Prestige Air Conditioned |
| Largely open planned but with some cellular offices and special areas such as conference rooms. Light levels and lighting power tend to be higher, and with deeper plans daylight is less available. Lights also tend to be switched in large groups. There is often more office equipment, vending machines etc. | Larger still, and often a national or regional head office, with a computer suite, a restaurant serving hot lunches for at least half the staff, and a generally higher level of equipment, facilities and information technology. Hours of use are also extended owing to the more diverse pattern of occupation. |
| Data taken from: Energy Consumption Guide No.19 | |

**FIG 5.4.4.A:** *The four typical office types used in the EEO's Energy Consumption Guide No. 19*

**FIG. 5.4.4.B:** *Energy costs of typical and good practice offices*

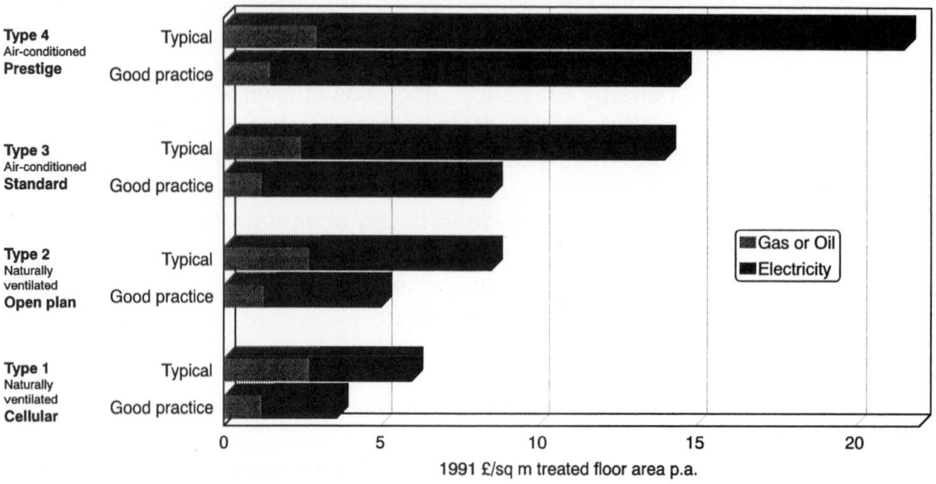

Data taken from: Energy Consumption Guide No. 19

## The four different office types

The patterns of energy use and cost in the four types of office give some reference points against which to judge individual buildings.

Individual offices may contain features of more than one of the four typical examples; in this case, comparisons can be made against a combination of figures from the different office types.

Annual electricity and fossil fuel use and costs are shown for:

- a 'typical' example near the middle of the consumption range for the national office stock as a whole, and

- a 'good current practice' building, well managed and using simple, readily available and proven technologies and design features.

The values given for 'good current practice' are drawn from energy consumption data in Case Studies of energy efficient offices. The buildings and refurbishments featured in the Case Studies, published under the EEO Best Practice Programme, are already several years old and would perform even better with today's plant, lights and controls. The examples do not deal explicitly with all-electric offices which, like for like, usually have rather lower annual energy consumptions but higher energy costs.

Savings are not only possible within a given building type: case studies demonstrate that in favourable circumstances one may also be able to achieve a less energy-dependent design by reducing the need for electric lighting and air conditioning in what could have been a fully air conditioned design, whilst still offering prestige offices. Instead, use of air conditioning and electric lighting is minimised through a 'mixed mode' approach, which uses natural ventilation and daylight when and where possible, with much of the building using full air conditioning only for limited periods of the year.

## Hours of use

Energy use is sometimes also standardised for hours of occupancy or plant operation, but linear corrections tend to introduce more discrepancies than they resolve. Most offices are intensively occupied for about ten hours a day, five days per week, with another hour or two at the beginning or end of the day for cleaning.

At other times, only a few people remain (except perhaps in special areas such as data processing) and only local heating and lighting should be required. If everything stays on, that is a problem to be exposed, not concealed by increasing the energy target. It is often more instructive to state the reasons why the intensity of use is high (eg: regular Saturdays or multi-shift operation) or low (eg: if the building is partly empty), than to make arithmetical corrections.

*Typical annual*
*energy use*

**FIG. 5.4.4.C:** *Typical energy consumption in office buildings*
*in kWh per sq m of 'treated floor area'*

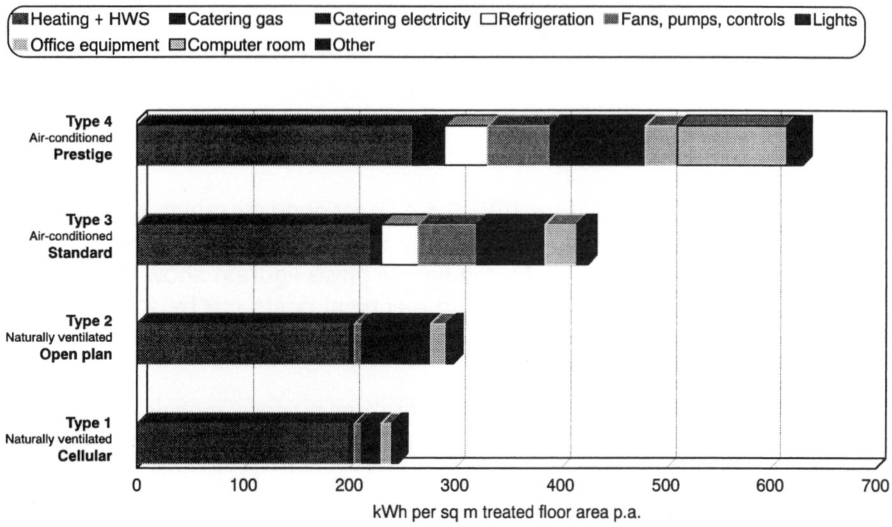

Data taken from: Energy Consumption Guide No. 19

Annual energy use in a typical office for each of the four types is shown at **FIG 5.4.4.C**

**Fossil fuel consumption** (in the diagrams for heating) hot water and catering only is similar for all four air conditioned buildings often requiring slightly more in type 4, owing to higher fresh air loads over a longer heating season and simultaneous heating and cooling from time to time. The prestige air conditioned (type 4) office also has longer operating hours and extra requirements for the kitchen and the associated hot water supplies.

**Electricity consumption** rises rapidly with increasing complexity from the simple to highly serviced office types. Heating system pumps, burners and controls in the simple naturally ventilated type 1 office use relatively little; they are likely to use rather more in the open plan type 2 office as mechanical ventilation for toilets, meeting rooms etc is more likely. In the air conditioned type 3 and 4 offices, fans, pumps and controls use considerably more electricity, particularly the fans in all-air systems, where refrigeration energy is often lower owing to 'free cooling' cycles using outside air. In air-water systems, for example fan-coils, fan energy is lower and refrigeration energy higher though not usually by quite as much.

**Lighting energy consumption** rises progressively across the range of offices as the use of daylight tends to fall, illuminance standards and hours of use rise, and internal rooms become more common. In open plan offices, light switching also becomes a more complex issue, and lights usually stay on much longer than really necessary unless well designed automatic and manual controls are fitted.

Electrical consumption by **office equipment** tends to increase across the range as operations become more sophisticated and intensive. Equipment loads are rising at present with growth in information technology, which also increases the perceived need for air conditioning. However, heat output is often less than expected and by the end of the decade it could fall as equipment becomes less demanding of power, particularly once levels of equipment reach saturation.

Electrical use by **lifts, telecommunications systems and ancillaries** such as car parks and external lighting is classed as 'other'. These all tend to grow with the complexity and sophistication of the building as a whole, as does the energy use for catering.

The **computer room** figure varies widely. Here an average is given from a number of surveys of offices with mainframe computer suites occupying perhaps 5% of net internal floor area. Dedicated computer centres use much more energy and are not covered here. Typical electricity consumption by computer air conditioning is 60-80% of that of the computer equipment etc.

*'Good practice' energy use*

The companion figures (**FIG 5.4.4.D**) for good current practice (which are based on the assumption that the electricity used by office equipment and mainframe computers is the same as for the typical office figures) show that heating costs overall can be more than halved and electrical costs cut by at least one-third by using readily available methods.

**FIG. 5.4.4.D:** *'Good practice' energy consumption in office buildings in kWh per sq m of 'treated floor area'*

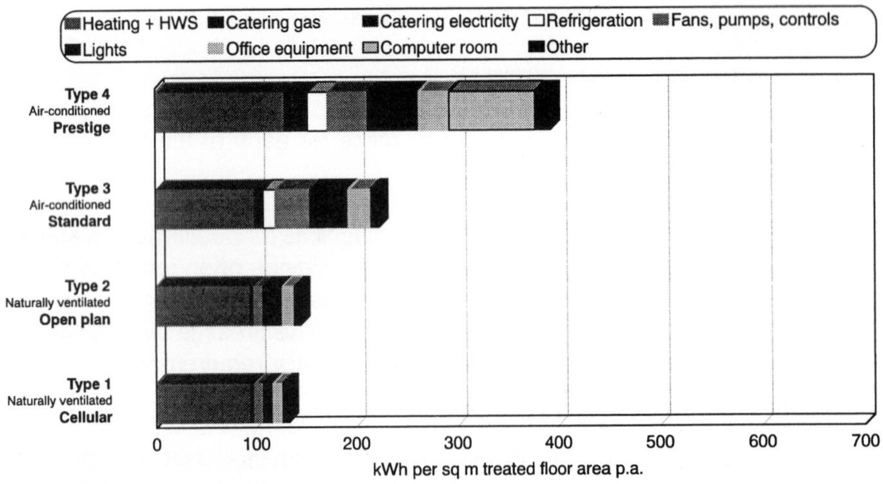

Data taken from: Energy Consumption Guide No. 19

These good practice levels are by no means the ultimate achievable, particularly in new buildings and major refurbishments. For example, most of the case studies indicate scope for further improvement, and few include condensing boilers and high frequency lighting, which can now be specified with confidence.

*Achieving 'good practice' levels*

The lower fossil fuel consumption is attributable to better insulation, more efficient boilers, improved control and management, and more efficient hot water systems. In existing buildings, substantial savings are often possible by attention to plant and management without necessarily improving insulation.

Lower electrical costs for HVAC systems arise not only from better control and management, but also from designing systems with low pressure drops and consequently low fan power. People often regard chiller efficiency as paramount. ;however, with all-air systems the fans usually cost more to run, and attention to fan power and control can be more rewarding. Excess running hours often lead to unseen - and often undetected - waste. Hours-run meters on important items of plant can be helpful and parts of the office which are regularly used outside normal hours should be separately zoned and controlled.

Lighting is often the largest individual item of energy cost, varying over a wide range depending upon installed power and hours of operation. In cellular offices people can easily use available daylight - as they do at home -and should be encouraged to do so. In open plan offices the situation is more complex and the lights often tend to stay on all day, whether or not they are required. Lighting has improved massively over recent years, and it is now often possible to light offices well at 2.5 Watts per square metre per 100 lux or less with modern fluorescent tubes, efficient reflectors, and electronic high-frequency ballasts. In the 1970's one would have needed two or three times the power for a similar result.

Electronic controls can also give more individual control through hand-held remote controllers for example. However, controls have to be well designed and in cellular offices switches by the door often do a good enough job.

In corridors, WCs etc and for many decorative purposes, compact fluorescent sources have made tungsten lighting superfluous, giving energy and maintenance cost savings for lamps which often burn for long hours.

Small savings have been assumed for computer rooms, with lower lighting loads and a tendency now to run computers in darkness with operators elsewhere. Unified control of packaged computer air conditioning is also assumed, avoiding stand-by units running autonomously under their own controls and cycling unnecessarily. Further savings can be made by using heat recovery or 'free cooling' systems, but they are not included here as it will not always be cost effective to go to such lengths.

Mainframe computer suites can sometimes account for more than half of the entire energy bill. Their air conditioning often runs inefficiently and offers scope for substantial savings through improved control and management. If possible, power supplies to the computer and its air conditioning should be separately metered and regularly monitored: if the ratio of air conditioning to computer consumption is more than 0.6, there may well be scope for improvement.

33% savings have been assumed in catering, where equipment is often operated very wastefully. An important reason for this is that energy supplies to catering contractors are usually provided 'free' by the customer. Sub-metering and re-charging is recommended to provide incentives.

No savings are assumed for office equipment etc although with careful selection and use some could be achieved.

Although office equipment often uses less energy than people expect, averaging perhaps one-third of the labels on the back, the common practice of leaving it on unnecessarily - and particularly overnight - should be discouraged. Purchasing decisions should take account of energy requirements: some brands and types of equipment are considerably more energy-efficient than others, and their lower heat output also helps to reduce both the need for air conditioning and the cooling loads it has to serve.

*Annual energy
costs*

**FIGS 5.4.4.E and F** show energy use data converted into money (at 1991 levels) for the typical examples and good practice cases. Only in the simple type 1 office are fossil fuel and electrical costs similar: in the others electricity predominates owing to its much higher unit price. Note that the costs of both lighting and electricity for HVAC systems often individually exceed the cost of heating.

**FIG. 5.4.4.E:** *Typical energy costs in office buildings per sq m of 'treated floor area'*

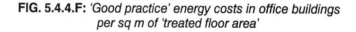

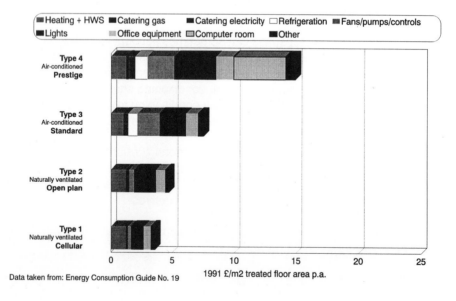

Data taken from: Energy Consumption Guide No. 19

**FIG. 5.4.4.F:** *'Good practice' energy costs in office buildings
per sq m of 'treated floor area'*

Data taken from: Energy Consumption Guide No. 19

*Factors
influencing fuel
costs*

Fuel costs vary with office size, type, region, contract and load profile. Unit prices tend to be lower for larger and more intensively serviced buildings. These are also more likely to be supplied at a higher voltage and have better load factors. The energy manager therefore has more bargaining power in negotiating with the energy suppliers (see below).

Correctly apportioned electrical unit prices also vary with end use. For example, lower than average rates will apply for computer rooms and communications equipment (with better load factors) and for comfort cooling chillers (predominantly a summertime load). Conversely, higher rates will apply for kitchens (with poor load factors and usually contributing to maximum demand peaks at lunchtime) and humidifiers.

## 5.4.5 ENERGY AUDIT

*Variations in energy costs*

**FIG. 5.4.5.A:** *Energy costs per sq m of NIA- a sample of 25 prestige office buildings*

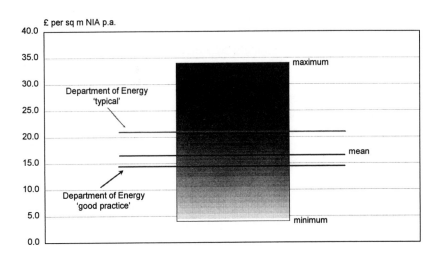

An interesting comparison with the EEO's figures of typical consumption is given at **FIG 5.4.5.A** which compares the results of a random sample of 25 prestige office buildings drawn from the authors' own audited data-base. The range of figures is far wider than Guide No.19 would indicate, but the average figure is only slightly higher than the 'good practice' level suggested for this building category in **FIG 5.4.4.B** above.

This confirms the EEO's assertion that good management could bring the average down even further. For instance, the figures at top and bottom of **FIG 5.4.5.A** are, in fact, misanalyses which were subsequently adjusted following a premises audit; the fact that the figures were submitted wrongly in the first place was indicative of a lack of control at level one. 'If you can't measure it you can't understand it' says Harrington - and the same goes if you can't measure it correctly!

An energy audit demands such measurement. Outside macroeconomic considerations, the main purpose of an energy audit is to investigate the quantity and type of energy used and to compare the results with the performance achieved. The concept of relating cost to performance is the basis of value engineering.

At first consideration (with the accountancy definition of auditing in mind) it might be thought that energy auditing would preclude the initial quantification of usage described below. However, the energy audit - in common with audits of all premises costs centres (see Section 12) - should always extend into diagnosis of faults and prescription for remedy. Energy management and control should arise naturally in the course of an audit.

The audit is usually carried out in two stages - a preliminary appraisal followed by a more detailed investigation ie: the energy audit proper. Preventative action normally follows each stage.

*The preliminary
energy
appraisal*

This is sometimes referred to as 'the first strike' - an initial assessment of the way the building and its occupants consume and generate energy and the cost-effectiveness of the organisation's overall energy policy.

The simple method of calculating the cost of energy per square foot (or square metre) of lettable or gross floor area is a useful first step to understanding the potential scope of the problems and the likely size of the benefits to be gained from the exercise. The accountancy-trained auditor will assess the cost implications in this way before probing for engineering answers; the engineer-auditor is more likely to start with megajoules and come back to cost later. The method of approach is relatively unimportant - what matters is that all the stages are properly identified and tackled.

Early on in the preliminary appraisal, the auditor will establish the total quantity of energy consumed from each energy source. This will be expressed in terms of units of energy - say kWh – and actual costs. Depending on the ease of accessibility to the appropriate base data, fairly accurate (probably partly extrapolated) data will become available, possibly identified to departmental or functional cost centres. By drawing initial comparisons with similar usages in other buildings, the energy auditor can start to isolate those areas in which cost-effective energy use is to be the subject of immediate investigation.

Savings of up to 20% are common (and far greater savings sometimes recorded) as a direct result of the preliminary appraisal through removal of some of the worst causes of energy wastage at the very outset.

In office buildings the opportunity for choice of energy type is normally restricted to the boiler fuel; how to use electricity in the distribution and outlets is the only major choice to be made. In production plant the choices are much greater, and the scope for the energy audit to effect striking improvements is correspondingly greater.

Normally, by the end of the first month of an organisation's first energy audit, certain fundamental energy management procedures will have been instigated and put into operation. These should include the appointment of a full-time or part-time energy manager, the nomination of a director with special responsibility for energy control and the establishment of interim 'consumption yardsticks' to be set against some of the more obviously profligate energy uses. Department managers will have been given an initial indication of the extent of their department's energy consumption, its cost-sensitivity relative to the total energy budget, and its apparent cost-effectiveness. The extent and effectiveness of metering and monitoring will have been established. The existence of a large number of estimated consumption levels is a sure sign that closer metering is needed, and the auditor will know where this should be set up.

As a rule of thumb, any consumption centre using more than 10% of the total will need to be individually metered; any consumption centre over 5% of the total should be put up as a case worthy of early analysis and investigation.

Certainly by the end of the preliminary appraisal the potentially most fruitful areas of investigation should have been identified and steps taken to rectify any obvious deficiencies.

Any obviously advantageous changes in the mix of energy types purchased arising both from basic cost-effectiveness and tariff considerations, should also start to be implemented in this early period.

*The audit
proper*

The preliminary appraisal is a part of the process in an initial energy audit; the necessary subsequent periodic audits will skip this phase apart from a quick scan of data compiled as a consequence of the initial audit. The 'first-strike' will have emerged as the interim consequence of a longer and more detailed build up of technical data about the building stock, its fabric, its occupants, and their activities, the internal and external environment, insulation gaps, leakages and idling of motors. The purpose and usage of all forms of energy entering the building are logged, the energy distribution outlets registered and, where necessary, metered.

It cannot be sufficiently emphasised that the preliminary appraisal is only a first move in the direction of energy management. It has been known for some organisations, having made quick early savings from the preliminary appraisal, to quit while still in front. However, others who have persevered and taken the value-engineering approach to energy management have been well rewarded for their thoroughness. The energy auditor's primary aim is to establish a system of energy management - that is, a method of planning and budgeting of energy consumption. The good auditor will set up an energy budget for the organisation as soon as possible, based on whatever data he can assemble in as short a time as possible.

Departmental heads will, at first, simply be made aware of the budgets set for them. Setting budgets presupposes that some will fail; attempting to reconcile tight budgets with loose data, inadequate control and general lack of interest is an occupational hazard for the energy auditor and the facilities manager who are responsible for accommodating this new discipline within the company's routines. An early, stated commitment by the chief executive to the principle of energy budgeting and control can represent the difference between success and failure in an energy management programme.

A long-term plan for energy should be established and have the same status as a business finance plan for any other part of the business.

*The energy
summary sheet
(ESS)*

The basis from which the energy auditor develops a management system is the energy summary sheet. This schedules, by department, key data including:

- actual/estimated consumption of each type of energy
- production output
- space use
- outside temperatures
- numbers of occupants

The ESS will also pick up the key energy consumers. For each of these key users efforts to save energy will be centred on changing methods of modifying plant and equipment, or both.

The outcome of the initial energy audit and the compilation of the energy summary sheet should be a solid basis for energy budgeting related to yardsticks of perform-ance per person, department, product, service and so on. Management will have been made aware of the opportunities to economise in an area of production overheads previously uncharted for then and thus now accessible to them for the first time.

Preliminary consumption forecasts over, say, a 12-month period geared to estab-lished environmentally conditioned and cyclical occupation or production proc-esses can be discussed and agreed with key consumers and management, as a forerunner to establishing targets based on properly monitored historic data.

These targets, given top management support for the energy manager, should soon attain the status of all other corporate finance plans. Each key-consumer manager should eventually be made formally accountable for his energy results - gently, at first, while data is still being gathered, but more positively (that is, within tighter parameters) as the energy management system, backed by further periodic audits, evolves and matures.

## Energy conservation programmes

The preliminary appraisal having eliminated some of the worst excesses of energy misuse, there will be other opportunities of improving the efficiency of many routines and procedures which, though not significantly wasteful on their own account, amount to major amounts taken overall. Changes in methods, equipment and energy type can be examined on a project basis geared to seeking any economic means of achieving reductions in energy consumption.

This detailed approach requires a thorough study of the energy used in the various production and environmental systems. It also requires of the auditor, facilities manager and energy manager a sound working knowledge of the principles of energy conservation and the available control and recovery techniques.

These optimising techniques should be taken as projects by the facilities manager and the energy manager - best carried out in consultation with the energy auditor. Remember that these projects from the basis of the value engineering approach to energy use; budgets may limit excesses, meters may record excesses but only positive action resulting from energy-saving projects can result in genuine conservation at all levels of usage.

## Building (energy) management systems (BEMS)

Energy conservation cannot be discussed these days without reference to the adoption or otherwise of Building (Energy) Management Systems B(E)MS.

These gather information about environmental conditions in a building and use the data to adjust the performance of the services to optimise both comfort and energy efficiency. They can respond to predicted external environmental conditions - and override the inevitable mis-forecasts - as well as controlling peak loading to contain maximum demand.

Improvements in building management and maintenance often accompany the energy savings, but maintenance of the BEMS itself can be a problem, especially if the specification of the controls is inadequate, operator training is sub-standard or performance is tested inaccurately, too seldom or never at all.

However, the biggest draw-back to getting the full benefits of a BEMS is undoubtedly the problems occurring at the Man-Machine Interface (MMI). Manning the controls can be a soulless task, and the monitoring facilities are often too complex for the operator and are not implemented.

Some of the latest BEMSs, particularly those arriving packaged in as part of the VRV (variable refrigerant volume) systems, can now run on automatic control response and diagnose their own operational efficiency; at a surprisingly low cost they cut out the bulk of the MMI problem.

An example of a pay-back analysis of a BEMS for an office building of 5,000m²GIA is given at **FIG 5.4.5.B**.

FIG 5.4.5.B: *Pay-back analysis of a B(E)MS for an office building of 10,000 sq m GIA*

| Typical example in a prestige air conditioned office building of 10,000 sq ft NIA | | £ | £ |
|---|---|---|---|
| Capital cost of B(E)MS | Full B(E)MS installed in a 'type 4' building having 'typical' energy consumption | --- | 100,000 |
| Annual costs | Monitoring -- 25% full-time:<br>Training -- 5 days pa:<br>Maintenance:<br>LESS existing manual control --<br>50% full-time: | 5,000<br>2,500<br>2,500<br><br>(10,000) | |
| | Net additional costs pa* | NIL | |
| Energy savings -- on lighting and HVAC only | 15% × 10,000sq m @ £12.50/sq m | (18,750) | |
| Net annual savings | | | (18,750) |
| * Excluding finance charges. | | | 18.75% ROI* |

The example is set at about the scale of operation when BEMS can show some kind of sensible pay-back. Some of the 20% energy saving suggested for lighting and HVAC might well be achieved by more conventional energy-saving measures. In fact a recent BEMS user survey gave a range of 15% - 30% savings - but whether on the whole energy bill or that which the BEMS controlled was not very clear.

The installation of a BEMS may well be justified by pay-back on energy-savings alone if the user starts from somewhere near the upper quartile of **FIG 5.4.5.A** above. In the end, it is most likely that the effects on the workforce of good or bad environmental conditions, or a good or bad perception of management's attitude towards it, which are likely to be the really significant factors in the equation (or, more probably left out of it!).

On the other hand, the costs of running and maintaining a BEMS properly may not always be adequately addressed when the appraisal is made.

## 5.4.6 LIGHTING SYSTEMS

Some ways of cutting back on energy consumption in lighting were discussed in the 'good practice' guide above. A summary of many common techniques for reducing lighting energy consumption is given at **FIG 5.4.6.A**.

FIG 5.4.6.A: *Some common sources of reduction in lighting energy consumption*

| Lamps and control gear | 26 mm fluorescent tubes in lieu of 38 mm (-8%)<br>Ditto, in luminaires + switch start control<br>Compact fluorescent + integral control gear - replace tungsten<br>Ditto, + separate control gear (NB plug-in adaptors)<br>Display - tungsten halogen lamps (-40%)<br>Metal halide lamps<br>High pressure sodium lamps<br>Low loss control gear (-10%)<br>High frequency electronic control gear (-20%)<br>Lamp cleaning and replacement |
|---|---|
| Luminaires | Apply reflectors |
| Design | Uniformity / localised |

**FIG 5.4.6.B** is an illustration of how a reasonable pay-back might be achieved on a lighting control installation.

The capital cost of a vast range of lighting solutions has been computed by Derek Mott. Some examples of these are given at **FIGS 5.4.6.C and D**. Of course, not only will the capital costs vary but the energy consumption and replacement levels will also be affected - not just for the lighting but the heating and cooling systems as well.

FIG 5.4.6.B: *A typical illustration of a pay-back period calculation - lighting controls*

| Lighting energy | Net internal area (NIA) - sq m | Cost / sq m NIA pa £ | Total pa £ |
|---|---|---|---|
| | 4,250    x | 5 | 21,250 |
| Lighting control system | | | |
| Capital cost | | | 10,000 |
| Saving on electricity pa | 10%  x  21,250 | | 2,125 |
| Saving on re-lamping pa | 10%  x  4,250 | | 425 |
| Total saving | | | **2,550** |
| £10,000 / 2550 = 3.92 i.e. approx 4 years payback on investment | | | |

## FIG. 5.4.6.C: *Typical lighting layouts, performance and capital costs - 1500mm square ceiling grids*

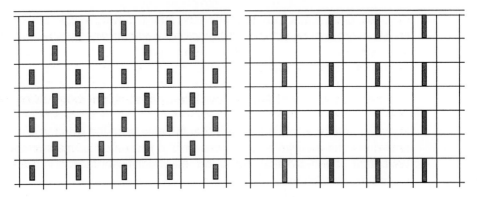

Layout 1:
1300 x 300 Luminaires with 2 No.
36W tubes
Open plan - 625 lux
Watts/m2 - 16.5

Cost (from riser cupboards)
- £40/44 per sq m NIA

Layout 2:
1500 x 300 Luminaires with 2 No.
58W tubes
Open plan - 590 lux
Watts/m2 - 12.8

Cost (from riser cupboards)
- £20/24 per sq m NIA

Source: Derek Mott

## FIG. 5.4.6.D: *Typical lighting layouts, performance and capital costs - 1800mm square ceiling grids*

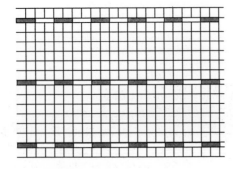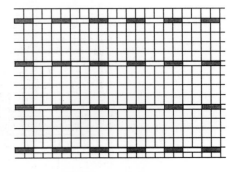

Layout 1:
1200 x 300 Luminaires with 2 No.
36W tubes
Open plan - 550 lux
Watts/m2 - 9.6

Cost (from riser cupboard)
- £20/22 per sq m NIA

Layout 2:
1200 x 300 Luminaires with 2 No.
36W tubes
Open plan - 660 lux
Watts/m2 - 13.2

Cost (from riser cupboard)
- £27/30 per sq m NIA

Source: Derek Mott

## 5.4.7 HEATING AND COOLING SYSTEMS

*Keeping cool - open v sealed windows*

A statistically significant number of controlled surveys now exist on the subject to environmental comfort. These all indicate, beyond doubt, that most office workers, given the choice, would open the windows to cool down an overheated office, or even to modify the condition of air which has been mechanically-controlled and treated other than to their liking.

Opening windows can sometimes alleviate over-heating but not without the ever-present risk of ingress of noise, airborne dust and fumes, felons (including squirrels pinching the sandwiches), wind gusts and sudden deluges of rain, hail, sleet or snow. Sometimes, in the summer, external temperatures are as high. or higher, than those internally and usually there is not enough of a breeze to bolster the work of a proliferation of desk top fans creating a transient but false illusion of coolth.

As discussed in detail in Chapter 8.2 - Health and Safety at Work - air-conditioning engineers like to seal the building completely from direct contact with the mixture of microbes, pests and carcinogens accompanying the carbon dioxide through open windows and natural air vents. Unfortunately, the protection afforded by their filters seems to be counter-balanced by strong evidence of a correlation between the so-called sick-building syndrome and sealed buildings. Furthermore, the droplets of water from the humidifiers and cooling towers in air-conditioned buildings have a propensity to hasten the growth of bacteria and fungi; and microbes and other noxious organisms carried in by the workers themselves find plenty of room to colonise in ventilation ducts.

*Whole-life costs*

Although air-conditioning bumps up the energy bill considerably it must not be forgotten that air-conditioning is a significant cost centre in terms of capital as well as revenue expenditure. **FIG 5.4.7.A** shows graphically the outcome of a whole-life cost comparison between two generic forms of central heating and five popular air cooling/conditioning systems. The example is of a provincial city centre office building of 4,250m² lettable (net internal) floor area and considers the services over a 25-year life-cycle.

**FIG. 5.4.7.A:** *Whole-life analytical cost comparison of heating and cooling systems in an office building 4,250 sq. m NIA*

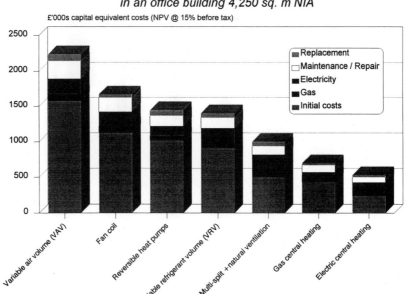

The capital costs include not only the cost of the services but also any additional structure required to accommodate them. Eg: whereas an all-electric central heating system will need no space for boilers or pipes the VAV system needs:

- boiler plant room
- refrigeration plant room
- floor space for riser ducts
- height for distribution ducts.

In fact, a VAV system typically will require 325mm more storey height than any of the other heating and cooling systems due to the size of ducts and the need to accommodate light fittings beneath rather than in between them.

To the capital costs of services and structural on-cost in the analysis have been added fees and construction finance charges. Energy and maintenance projections are benchmarked from the author's own audited operating cost database covering over 24m square feet of occupied office buildings; data on the VRV systems is, however, still a bit sparse and so the costs of energy attributed to them may prove to be somewhat exaggerated.

Equally there are few buildings of this size 100% electrically centrally-heated and both the maintenance and energy costs would almost certainly turn out to be less than shown.

Of course, this analysis of generic systems is only intended as a guide to some general principles; individual installations will vary significantly. Nevertheless, capital costs of this order do find their way into the rent (or mortgage for the owner/ occupier) and the revenue expenditure into the facilities manager's operating costs budget. Taking the latter first, **FIG 5.4.7.B** extracts merely the annual energy and maintenance costs from the examples to show how the different systems impact.

**FIG. 5.4.7.B:** *Annual energy and maintenance costs for heating and cooling systems in an office building 4,250 sq. m NIA*

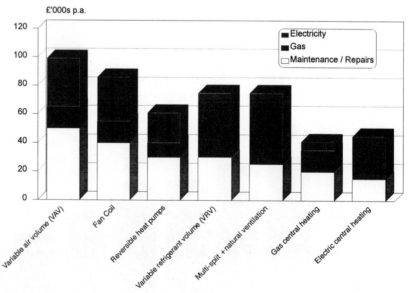

As for the capital costs, **FIG 5.4.7.C** shows the typical building cost analysis of the same office block with the 'extra-over' cost of the mechanical cooling services (ie: the cost over and above that of central heating) separately hatched. The 'extra-over' cost is not that significant, and when one considers the cost of the building in the context of the whole development equation it is even less significant.

**FIG. 5.4.7.C:** *'Extra-over' capital cost of cooling services in the context of the construction budget*

£ per sq m GIA

*The energy costs in perspective*

In fact, as **FIG 5.4.7.D** illustrates, this 'extra-over' figure when rentalised is rarely more than 5% of the rent. Taking into account also that the costs of maintenance and energy specifically in respect of comfort cooling are little more than 30% of total operating costs (**FIG 5.4.7.E**) one has to question what all the fuss is about. If the development equation is not sensitive to the capital costs of comfort cooling and the extra running costs are but a drop in the revenue ocean, surely we should opt for the best cooling systems available in terms of ergonomics and the environment - not necessarily for the highest cost systems just for the sake of it.

**FIG. 5.4.7.D:** *The rentalised 'extra-over' capital cost of cooling in a prestige building*

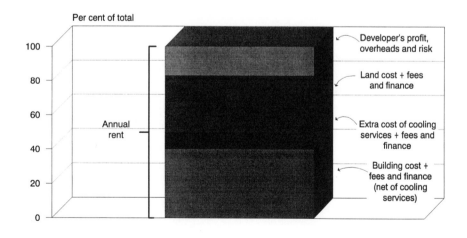

Unfortunately neither developers, investors, surveyors advising them or the facilities managers choosing and running their buildings really know the difference between a good and bad system or, indeed, the real effect of discomfort, sick building syndrome and lack of individual environmental control on the productivity of the occupier.

**FIG. 5.4.7.E:** *Energy and maintenance for heating and cooling a prestige building in the context of total operating costs*

£ per sq m NIA p.a.

Additional costs due to HVAC

- Maintenance - other
- Maintenance - HVAC
- Energy - HVAC
- Energy - Other
- Cleaning
- Alterations
- Administration

**FIG 5.4.7.F** puts these issues into perspective. In a typical organisation where staff costs represent up to 75% of turnover and the comfort cooling component of premises is no more than ½% of turnover the adverse effect on productivity of a poor environment (or, worse, a perception that management does not care) must outweigh any premises cost implications of the comfort cooling syndrome in a ratio of at least 150:1.

**FIG. 5.4.7.F:** *Energy and maintenance costs of heating and cooling a prestige building in the context of annual turnover*

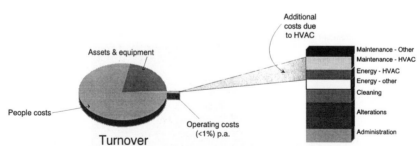

*Environmental considerations*

Green issues are serious and must be taken on board. Naturally-cooled buildings do save energy but they cost about the same to build as air-conditioned buildings and have to contain provision for mechanical cooling at some time in the future (at extra unwanted cost) to have a chance of being funded and/or purchased by the investing institutions.

The biggest environmental threat from energy consumption is in the by-production of carbon dioxide ($CO_2$) in the generating process (on or off site).  The relative efficiencies of the principal fuels in this respect are given at **FIG 5.4.7.G**.

**FIG. 5.4.7.G:** *Estimated CO² emissions from energy consumption by type of fuel*

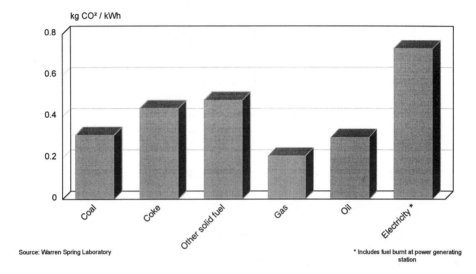

Source: Warren Spring Laboratory

\* Includes fuel burnt at power generating station

The $CO_2$ emission from each of the systems analysed above is estimated at **FIG 5.4.7.H** and shown in the context of the **overall** building energy consumption.  Even though the embodied energy in those systems which are more expensive in capital and maintenance terms is not taken into account, it can be seen that the **economical** use of electricity to perform these functions is not necessarily as damaging as many pundits make out, especially when considering that some 50% of electric energy consumption is unavoidable and that commercial buildings create no more than about 15% of the $CO_2$ emissions of all UK end users.

**FIG. 5.4.7.H:** *Estimated CO² emissions from the HVAC systems and other energy uses in the building analysed*

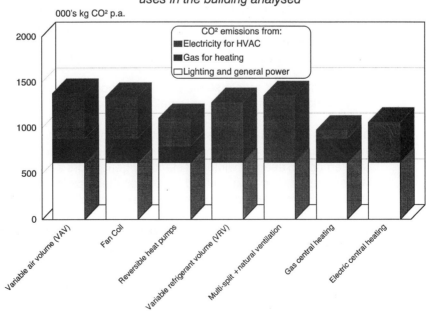

## 5.4.8 PURCHASING ELECTRICITY

*Electricity
supply
franchises*

Since the 1980's it has been possible for users of more than 1000KW of maximum demand to negotiate with any of the electricity supply companies (including their own regional electricity company - REC) for supplies of electricity. This withdrawal of the franchise market was further extended from 1 April 1994 when the minimum level of maximum demand at which an alternative supplier could be sought was reduced to 100KW - typical of an air-conditioned office of say 25,000 sq.ft GIA.

Maximum Demand is generally set on the basis of that achieved in three out of the previous 12 months (see below). Obviously joined buildings on the same complex may be aggregated in calculating the demand figure.

*Components of
the price*

Even where the new supplier is not the REC the latter still has responsibility for the provision and maintenance of the local distribution system, transformers etc. The new supplier deals directly with the REC, paying them direct.

They get the money for this from the component of the customer's bill relating to the system charges from the REC; the supplier's charges for energy are separately shown in the bill, the whole of which is, however, payable direct to the supply company.

Each component relates to:

*   standing charges

*   availability charges

*   maximum demand charges

*   kWh charges.

On top of the normal charges there is a levy (10% for 1993/94) in respect of subsidies towards development of non-fossil-fuel-burning generation technology. The all-in price for the supply should be stated to include an allowance for all losses occurring in the course of transmission and distribution and the bill should make clear which points of supply are being charged either individually or aggregated as discussed above.

*The 'Pool'*

The RECs in the UK purchase the power at a 'pool' price which varies as between the generators and the RECs on a half-hourly basis.

Consumers of negotiating size may opt for a 'pool price' contract, especially if they have the capacity to control their loading at times when pool prices are high - eg: late afternoon in deepest winter. If stand-by generators are needed for commercial reasons they may be programmed to cut in at these peak times; some companies, particularly in manufacturing, can either close down plant or work around the peaks.

Of course, not all surges in pool price are predictable, so some risk always attaches to this particular strategy.

*Load factor*

The load factor is a measure of the efficiency with which power is used. The calculation of this figure as a percentage of average to maximum demand is shown at **FIG 5.4.8A**

**FIG. 5.4.8.A:** *Calculation of the load factor*

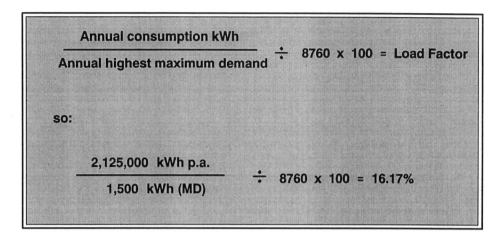

Where the load factor is high customers should strike a better deal in the market - a point to look out for at the next bidding phase if the factor is escalating since the previous contract.

*Rates of charging*

There is a **standing charge** to cover the supply company's fixed costs of connecting and metering supply, invoicing and collection of payments. This is constant, regardless of unit consumption but variable by tariff.

Unit charges per kWh are variable depending upon the time of consumption. Typically there are separate unit charges for different times of the day and night at different times of the year. Depending on the tariff the customer may also get billed for **Maximum Demand charges**; these are usually computed by taking the largest number of units supplied in any half-hour in the billing period and doubling it to give the maximum Kw demand per hour. Price for each kWh of the maximum demand unit charge is variable by season.

Accompanying the standing charge for the maximum demand rate if an **Availability Charge** for each kVA (kilovoltampere) of **chargeable service capacity** made available in accordance with the customer's **Maximum Power Requirement** in the billing period and relates to the costs of the REC's distribution system as opposed to consumption of the supplier's energy. Any excess kVA required over and above that predicted for the tariff is subject to a **reactive power charge** for each hour of the excess supply, measured at kVArh.

## 5.4.9 PURCHASING NATURAL GAS

Gas was privatised before electricity but is only slowly being liberated. At present independent suppliers hold over half of the business in **firm supplies** of gas ie: where consumption is in excess of 25,000 therms (732,678kWh) per annum. In the larger industrial user market of **interruptible supplies** ie: over 200,000 therms (5,861,420kWh) per annum the independents are struggling to make an impact; the abolition of the lower monopoly threshold of 2,500 therms per annum sought by the independents would enable them to use the interruptible market as a buffer against the seasonal swings in domestic gas loadings.

Most offices work off the Firm Supply schedule, which is simply a **block price** for the first 25,000 therms in each **block year**, and a **scheduled reference price** for those therms consumed in excess of the block; the scheduled reference price comprises a monthly standing charge and a unit price (per kWh).

Customers have the option of either fixed price or indexation, and may also opt for seasonal pricing variations.

The purchasing of gas supplies by some independent electricity suppliers may well see the development of a collective energy market in years to come.

## 5.4.10 OTHER FUELS

There is a free market in **heating oil**. As for **coal, coke** and the like there is free competition between the coal merchants who do, however, have to purchase from the coal-fields at the government-subsidized price. Neither oil nor coal/coke are serious contenders as fuel for heating in modern office buildings, mainly due to the high costs of delivery, storage and maintenance.

## 5.4.11 TYPICAL FUEL PRICE COMPARISON

**FIG 5.4.11A** gives an average range of prices overall per unit delivered of the major generic fuels for the four types of office buildings used in the above examples.

**FIG 5.4.11.A:** *Average ranges of fuel price per unit of energy delivered to office buildings*

| Office type as EEO guide No 19 | Typical price per unit of energy delivered | |
|---|---|---|
| | Fossil fuel | Electricity |
| Type 1 | £ 0.015 | £0.07 |
| Type 2 | £0.015 | £0.065 |
| Type 3 | £0.0125 | £0.06 |
| Type 4 | £0.0125 | £0.055 |

## 5.4.12 CONTRACT ENERGY MANAGEMENT (CEM)

*The concept*

CEM is based on the principle that energy savings can be made using out-sourced specialist contractors without the client having to interrupt his core activities to get involved with the energy conservation process. Services are usually paid for on the basis of a fixed management fee or a share of the savings of both.

*The credentials*

The CEM contractor's expertise will cover the basic energy assessment techniques together with a thorough knowledge of the systems available to provide a good pay-back from the savings generated. He may also provide the financial investment for the conservation methods adopted.

*Types of contract*

There are about 10 companies providing CEM on a large scale in the UK at present, an indication that clients are getting a perceived benefit from the approach. The principal contract arrangements are:

- shared savings contract
- fixed fee
- fixed fee plus shared savings
- heat service contract.

In the **shared savings** type of contract the CEM contractor may well be responsible for specifying, providing and installing the equipment free of direct charge to the customer. Depending on the deal he may also take over the running and mainte-nance of the equipment. He bears the risk of his energy saving assessments being inaccurate, although to some extent this will be limited if the user does the sensible thing and gets an independent professional opinion on the preliminary calculations presented by the CEM contractor in support of his contract proposal.

Of course there is always the problem with any type of shared-savings contract of defining the base line sufficiently clearly to measure the improvements while organisational change is constantly undermining the basic parameters.

The **fixed fee** arrangements do not provide the 'one-stop-shop' of some of the sharing deals and inevitably draw the facilities manager into contact with the issues and decision-making processes.

The charges under **heat service** contracts are based on a special tariff which is variable depending on the amount of energy delivered to the site - the less delivered the higher the charge from the contractor, but a good deal for both parties overall.

Government departments may now take up certain types of CEM, provided that they are not seen as mechanisms for securing 'soft loans' to get around public spending restrictions; as long as the contract involves a significant service element from the CEM company it should pass muster.

# CHAPTER 5.5 – WATER AND SEWERAGE SERVICES

## 5.5.1 SOURCES OF SUPPLIES AND SERVICES

*The utility companies*

Fresh water supply and sewerage services in the UK are franchised to the privatised water companies. All modern office buildings are entitled to a fresh water supply from the utility companies and all buildings so supplied are connected, directly or indirectly, to the public sewers for which they are responsible.

## 5.5.2 CHARGES

*Basis of charging*

Charges for both water supply and sewerage are calculated separately in respect of any property having the benefit of these services, directly or indirectly.

Both water and sewerage can be charged on either a **metered** or **unmetered** rate. The utilities have to move completely away from the unmetered basis by the year 2000. Their policy has therefore generally been to ensure that all new and converted properties have meters installed, in which case the customer has no option but to pay on a metered basis.

Where there is no meter installed the customer may elect to continue to pay on an unmetered basis; on the other hand, if the premises have a high rateable value (upon which the charges for unmeasured supplies are based) but are a low consumer of the water and sewerage utilities, the user may find it beneficial to have a meter installed at his own expense and opt for the metered supply.

*Metered supplies*

The metered supplies comprise two components:

- a standing charge
- a volume charge

In the case of commercial buildings the **standing charge** is calculated by reference to the size of the meter, graduated according to size. A current standing charge tariff from one of the companies is included at **FIG 5.5.A**. The **volume charge** for the sewerage as well as for the water is based on the **volume of water supplied** - logical enough, because most of it will be discharged from the premises; if less than 90% of water supplied is discharged from the premises the utility company may be requested to abate the sewerage charge. The rates for volume charges are currently around 45 to 50p per cubic metre for the water supply and slightly lower at 40-45p per cubic metre for the sewerage services.

**FIG 5.5.A:** *Current standing charges for metered water supplies and sewerage services*

| Meter size | | Standing charge | |
|---|---|---|---|
| mm | inches | Water £ pa* | Sewerage £ pa* |
| Up to 12 | 0.50 | 22 | 34 |
| 20 | 0.75 | 49 | 77 |
| 25 | 1.00 | 88 | 136 |
| 30 | 1.25 | 137 | 213 |
| 40 | 1.50 | 198 | 306 |
| 50 | 2.00 | 352 | 544 |
| 65 | 2.50 | 550 | 850 |
| 80 | 3.00 | 792 | 1,224 |
| 100 | 4.00 | 1,408 | 2,176 |
| 125 | 5.00 | 2,200 | 3,400 |
| 150 | 6.00 | 3,168 | 4,896 |
| 200 | 8.00 | 5,632 | 8,704 |
| 250 | 10.00 | 8,800 | 13,600 |
| * VAT may be chargeable in addition. Source: Thames Water | | | |

**FIG 5.5.B:** *Current standing charges for unmetered water supplies and sewerage services*

| Supply pipe size | | Standing charge | |
|---|---|---|---|
| mm | inches | Water £ pa* | Sewerage £ pa* |
| Up to 12 | 0.50 | 15 | 24 |
| 20 | 0.75 | 33 | 55 |
| 25 | 1.00 | 60 | 96 |
| 30 | 1.25 | 93 | 151 |
| 40 | 1.50 | 135 | 216 |
| 50 | 2.00 | 240 | 384 |
| 65 | 2.50 | 375 | 600 |
| 80 | 3.00 | 540 | 864 |
| 100 | 4.00 | 960 | 1,536 |
| 125 | 5.00 | 1,500 | 2,400 |
| 150 | 6.00 | 2,160 | 3,456 |
| 200 | 8.00 | 3,840 | 6,144 |
| 250 | 10.00 | 6,000 | 9,600 |
| * VAT may be chargeable in addition. Source: Thames Water | | | |

*Unmetered supplies*

Some older and/or remote commercial buildings may not have a meter, in which case the basis of charging comprises:

• a standing charge

• a rate-based charge.

The **standing charge** again is geared to the size of the water supply pipe and is separately calculated for water and sewerage as shown in the current tariff at **FIG 5.5.B**.

The **rate-based charge** is calculated by applying an annual rate in the £ to the chargeable value (normally the rateable value) of the user's property. The annual rate varies from one location to another reflecting the fact that similar types of premises - that is in terms of their designated use and consequently consumption of the supplies - will have lower chargeable value away from the main centres, so the water rate has to be adjusted upwards to compensate. So, for example, the rate-based charge for water supplied in Central London is currently about 18p in the £ compared to South Oxfordshire where it is nearly double that. Similarly, sewerage charges in these two locations vary from around 14p to 31p in the £.

*Typical annual out-turn costs*

**FIG 5.5.C** shows a range of total annual water and sewerage charges per square metre of gross internal area (GIA) from a selected sample of office buildings across the UK. The average cost is around 10% of the typical cost of the energy consumed in these buildings.

**FIG. 5.5.C:** *Typical range of total annual costs of water supplies and sewerage services for UK offices*

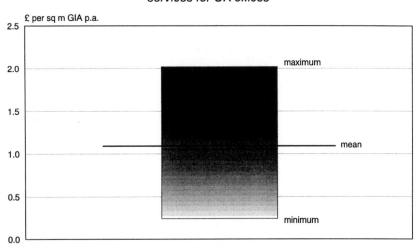

*Conservation measures*

Simple measures to save water and sewerage charges do exist and can pay back quickly - albeit that the sums involved in this cost centre are not especially large.

One of the more popular systems is one in which the operation of automatic flushing toilets cuts off outside of normal hours, being then triggered by either a light-sensor, body-sensor or light switch when anyone enters the area outside of these hours.

Generally speaking, however, there are more important costs for most facilities managers to worry about.

# CHAPTER 5.6 – WASTE MANAGEMENT

## 5.6.1 THE PROBLEM

*Facilities waste*

As far as the facilities manager's responsibilities are concerned the term 'waste' encompasses residual:

- paper and paper-based products
- computer/printer/copier consumables - toner cartridges etc
- discarded furniture and equipment
- food
- cans, bottles and other receptacles
- toxic effluents
- etc.

The paperless office has not arrived - on the contrary over the years more and more waste paper has accumulated for disposal from office buildings - plus a whole host of new nasties - leading to serious environmental problems as well as adding to bottom-line costs enhanced by increasing need to comply with statutory controls.

*Legislation*

Leaving aside the problem of toxic effluents, which is predominantly an industrial building issue, the office facilities manager now not only has to cope with the internal collection, storage and disposal of waste material but also with a weight of new legislation -as usual emanating mainly from the EU.

These new restraints quite legitimately set out to stop man from destroying his environment by abuse of natural resources - both by using them profligately and then disposing of them dangerously.

The Environmental Protection Act 1990 (EPA) is the principal legislation and in fact this is a domestic piece of law, albeit that it is strongly influenced by similar regimes emanating from Brussels - eg: the EC Framework Directive on Waste 1992 - 'the Waste Directive' under the EPA.

All producers of waste are held legally responsible for its safe handling and disposal. Failure to adhere to the 'Duty of Care' could result in **company directors or senior management facing criminal proceedings**.

Under the 'Duty of Care' it is up to the facilities manager to ensure that all waste is:

- handled in the correct manner by trained staff aware of environmental and public health risks
- correctly described, documented, with quantities recorded and analysed if necessary
- secure, contained in appropriate storage containers and presenting no risk to employees or the environment.

When the facilities manager chooses a waste contractor he **must** comply with legal obligations and satisfy himself that

- the waste management company he chooses is fully licensed

- all waste is disposed of in a suitably licensed disposal site

- all sites used comply with new environmental legislation and carry out environmental audits

- all vehicles carrying waste are suitable for the type of waste being transported

- the contractor is fully aware of the waste type and quantity and has an efficient documentation system

- all contractor's employees are fully trained to handle the waste, especially in emergencies.

When the facilities manager is also the landlord to a tenant or sub-tenant then he may also find himself liable for any default of his paying guests in respect of the provisions of the new legislation.

## 5.6.2 WASTE MANAGEMENT POLICY

*Government policy*

The British Government's policy in respect of waste management is laid down in DoE circular 11/94 (para 9) as follows:

'A. Subject to the best practical environmental option in each case, waste management should be based on a hierarchy in which the order of preference is:

(i) **reduction** - by using technology which requires less material in products and produces less waste in manufacture, and by producing longer lasting products with lower pollution potential;

(ii) **re-use** - for example, returnable bottles and re-usable transit packaging;

(iii) **recovery** - finding beneficial uses for waste including:

   (a) *recycling* it to a usable product

   (b) *composting* it to create products such as soil conditioners and growing media for plants; and

   (c) *recovering energy* from it either by burning it or using landfill gas

(iv) **disposal** - by incineration or landfill without energy recovery.

B. Each of these options should be managed and, where necessary, regulated to prevent pollution of the environment or harm to human health.'

*Facilities policy*

The facilities policy in respect of waste management must embrace:

- compliance with legislation
- sympathy towards the objectives
- control mechanisms
- economics.

*Control
mechanisms*

There are a few simple actions the facilities manager can take to ensure that he stays on the right side of the law and does the right thing by the environment. Briefly these are as follows:

- be aware of the presence of waste materials - incoming and outgoing

- check the need for any licences or registrations of exemptions

- label for identification

- write a description - by name, process or source of production, legal status

- note special considerations - separation, special enclosures/containers, transfer and disposal requirements

- ensure safety in collection, storage and transfer

- use officially sanctioned carriers/managers

- check their activities and credentials

- document all transfers.

In terms of social responsibility the facilities manager can do much to encourage an economically viable approach to environmentally friendly waste disposal:

- **recycling** of waste paper can be encouraged by the installation of a second waste-paper basket - for recyclable materials only, particularly the high-grade waste paper

- **special collections** or depositories for low-grade general waste such as newspapers and parcel wrappings

- **purchase** of paper products produced from low-grade waste

- **purchase of washable**, not disposable, cups, saucers and plates

- **cross-charging** of waste disposal to departments where such a generic policy is in place

- **pro-active stock control** procedures checking consumption of paper against value-engineered and environmentally-friendly targets

- **staff awareness** programmes and campaign - 'save-a-tree' posters and other accumulation models may well do for the environment what the 'Save the Black Babies' fund-raising campaign of the 1940's did for the world population.

### 5.6.3 ECONOMICS

*Recycling of
paper*

The economic gains from recycling low-grade paper are only marginal commercially, so any additional costs incurred in its separate collection within the office may be hard to justify. If it can be saved without extra cost the low-grade material, such as newspapers in large enough quantities, can be effectively recycled to produce writing paper and even toilet paper both of which are conventionally made from high-grade waste. One company is doing extremely well manufacturing disposable bedpans and specimen jars - for hospital use - out of old newspapers.

Computer print-out is probably the most valuable recyclable paper due to its lighter and regular printing rather than its quality.

*Recycling other materials*

The public-at-large has now become accustomed to the use of bottle banks and other waste segregation opportunities; the larger organisations can help the environmental and economic cause by providing similar facilities on site.

*Storage and disposal*

The cost of **compaction** may be a worthwhile investment if space is at a premium, although waste disposal costs are relatively small in the scheme of things. Money saved on container hire and waste transfer may not justify an on-site compaction process, even though volumes can be reduced by as much as 90%.

*Collection*

Unless the organisation is located way outside of normal collection zones there will be no premium to pay for collection unless the waste is of a hazardous nature where disposal facilities are remote.

Where large volumes of waste are involved the design of the vehicle access and loading bays will have a significant effect on the contract process which will be dependent upon speed of access, collection and departure. The use of large, purpose-designed waste-bins which can minimise the number of collections in a regime which optimises the time of the collection/transfer cycle will clearly have an impact on the bottom-line costs.

*The costs of waste disposal*

**FIG 5.6.A** gives the range of costs of waste disposal per annum across a wide range of office buildings in the UK. The sums involved, as with energy costs, are comparatively insignificant in the scheme of things but belie the importance of the subject area which they quantify.

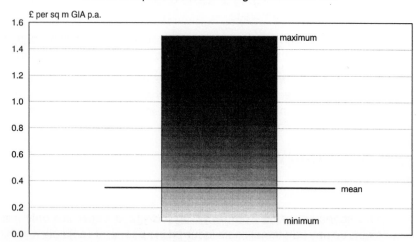

**FIG. 5.6.A:** *Typical range of costs of waste disposal from a sample of office buildings across the UK*

**In the end the environmental impact of inadequate waste disposal policies will rebound on everyone, regardless of their profits, income or legal liabilities.**

# CHAPTER 5.7 – INTERIOR AND EXTERIOR LANDSCAPING

## 5.7.1 LANDSCAPING IN CONTEXT

*The costs of landscaping in context*

**FIGS 5.7A and B** indicate the sort of annual expenditure range encountered in audits of the internal and external landscaping cost centres. Apart from the 'country house' settings represented at the top of the external landscaping sample the costs are generally minimal for commercial office users, barely meriting a small chapter to themselves alongside facilities expenditure of infinitely greater magnitude.

**FIG. 5.7.A:** *Typical range of annual expenditure on internal landscaping*

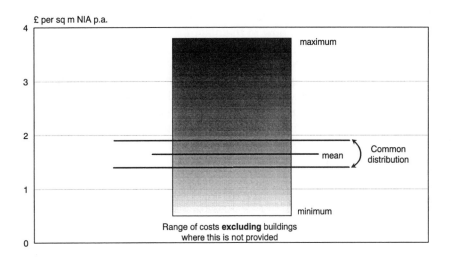

**FIG. 5.7.B:** *Typical range of annual expenditure on external landscaping*

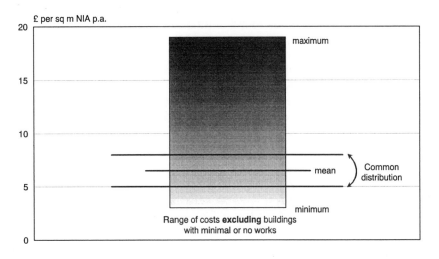

However, cost and added value are frequently quite disproportionate - in both directions - and in this case the balance is definitely heavily in favour of the beneficial effects of small but wise expenditure.

These benefits evidence themselves predominantly in terms of improvements in

- ambience
- health & safety
- public relations.

## 5.7.2 INTERNAL LANDSCAPING

*Options*

The provision of interior landscaping can be either domestic or managed, natural or artificial, structured or unstructured and the consequences of these alternative policies are quite varied in their impact.

*Domestic provision*

Provision and control of plants by the organisation or individual members of staff is really only appropriate in the smaller offices where staff are allowed to control what their environment looks like and take responsibility for buying, locating and maintaining their own plants; sometimes in larger offices someone with an interest will take special responsibility for advising either staff or management on types of plants to buy and how to maintain them.

However, rarely will a 'domestic' policy be satisfactory in a well-planned office and the inevitably haphazard solutions will most likely produce an unsatisfactory visual ambience to the visitor and many of the in-house personnel. Nevertheless, the feeling of being **in control** of the environment which seems to be so important in the case of comfort cooling and heating is also a factor to be taken into account before telling the amateur gardeners that the nurserymen are taking over.

*Outsourced services*

The **externally managed** interior landscape may merely involve provision and maintenance of artificial plants or, as is more and more common, a full-blown exercise in horticultural planning, planting and maintenance.

Where space is concealed/defended by the 'domestic' provider anarchy is likely to prevail. However, properly designed and managed internal planting schemes can provide a highly cost-effective solution to functions such as screening and visitor-direction/guidance.

Installations on any sort of scale should always be part of the interior design contract - or at least under the designer's direction - and large naturally-grown installations such as found in atria are best left to qualified landscape architects.

*Artificial plants*

These cost about the same to buy as the natural variety - about half the price is in the container anyway - but obviously maintenance is much lower, only a regular dusting and freshening (possibly even replenishing artificial fragrance) and occa-sional repair to replacement due to damage being required.

The better quality artificial plants, made from polyester silk, are really quite difficult to tell from the real thing on casual inspection but add nothing to the physical as opposed to the visual environment. Nevertheless they are a vast improvement on nothing at all, and can be used to good effect in darker or cooler parts of the building where the natural varieties might struggle to survive. Asthma and hay-fever sufferers as well as well-intending but cash-strapped management may also show a preference for artificial plants on totally practical grounds and the lack of any need for watering means that designers have a much wider range of containers from which to choose.

## Natural planting

Natural plants are almost universally preferred to the artificial variety but owners do need expert advice on provision and maintenance; where provided domestically, they have a tendency to grow out of control - or not at all - especially where the species has not been matched to the required climatic conditions. Eg: tropical plants need a lot of light (some up to 1000 lux) and warmth, whereas some of the smaller species prefer, and look best, in the darker corners. Maintenance is needed about twice a month - dusting, cleaning, pruning and feeding - and watering, unless the containers are set up to be self-watering, a system which is possible for compost-grown plants at a capital cost of between 10% and 20% of the cost of the containers.

Depending on whether the contract is full-rent-and-maintain or maintenance-only the contractor will replace plants as required within the annual charge or seek approval and funding to any reinstatement.

In **atria**, where tall varieties such as palms and weeping figs can reach 8m, there is a problem of damage by natural pests. Some companies' environmental policies prohibit chemical spraying in which case (and why not in any case?) predator-pest-control systems, whereby non-harmful insect varieties are introduced to see off the nasties, can be successfully implemented and are totally 'green'.

**FIG 5.7.C** considers the alternative life-cycle costs of an artificial and natural plant which is typical of the generic economic argument.

## Health and comfort benefits

**FIG. 5.7.C:** *Comparative annual equivalent costs of artificial and natural plants*

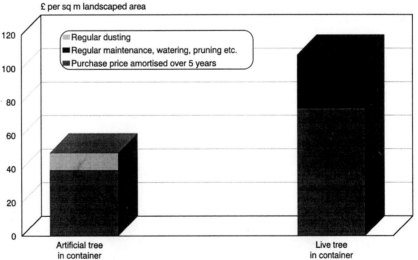

Apart from the psychological benefit of working in a pleasant, green environment recent research in the USA has shown that certain pollutants commonly found in the office atmosphere can be countered and abated by various species.

Additionally, static electricity can be controlled and reduced by the presence of moisture in the live plants. As well as the filtering and oxygenating properties of the plants themselves many horticulturists and environmental scientists also hold that the **soil** from plants in well-maintained containers has a beneficial effect upon air quality within the office.

### 5.7.3 EXTERIOR LANDSCAPING

*Locational issues*

Most city centre offices have only a minimal requirement for exterior landscaping provision and maintenance; where annual costs do arise they are usually in the service charge from the landlord managing a complex of buildings such as found in some parts of Central London or the provincial office parks.

Grounds maintenance is a low cost item even where it is extensive as in the office parks or 'country house' offices. Nevertheless the importance of greenery around an office building cannot be over-stressed in terms of its impact on an organisation's public relations - to both customers and employees - not to mention the contribution to the natural environment.

The initial costs of hard landscaping is a lot greater than soft landscaping but the maintenance costs of the latter are often much smaller than people imagine. A simple example illustrating this point is at **FIG 5.7.D** which shows that although a paving solution to landscaping a public area will save the costs - and hassle - of maintenance, its overall life-cycle costs do not provide any economic justification for the investment. The landscape architect may argue that, if the area is subject to wear and tear, maintenance of the soft area to peak condition may not be possible therefore making the hard solution desirable on aesthetic grounds. Nevertheless, it is important to recognise that, in spite of its maintenance requirements, soft landscaping is probably the architect's most cost-effective design tool in terms

**FIG. 5.7.D:** *Comparative annual equivalent costs of hard and soft landscaping*

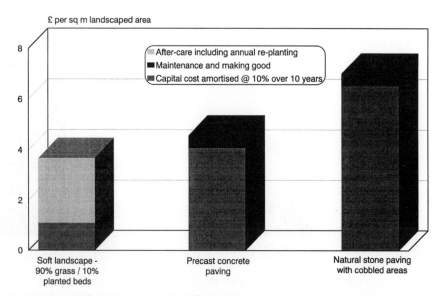

£ per sq m landscaped area

Legend:
- After-care including annual re-planting
- Maintenance and making good
- Capital cost amortised @ 10% over 10 years

Categories:
- Soft landscape - 90% grass / 10% planted beds
- Precast concrete paving
- Natural stone paving with cobbled areas

of generating aesthetic acceptance and pleasure within low overall costs, and one which many are reluctant to introduce due to inadequate appreciation of the total economics.

# SECTION 6

# FITTING OUT
# AND
# ALTERATIONS

# CHAPTER 6.1 – THE NATURE OF FITTING OUT AND ALTERATIONS

## 6.1.1 DEFINITIONS

*Shell, scenery and services*

It was Dr. Francis Duffy[1] who first highlighted the comparison between an office building and the theatre stage. He likened the theatre building enclosure to the office building shell, the scenery sets and props to the office interior and furniture, and the services to..... well, the services.

*'Shell and core'*

Perhaps spurred on by this analogy – and also by the costs of pulling down and replacing unwanted items of scenery and services provided by the developer – some developers in the UK took a leaf out of the American, Japanese and some European entrepreneurs' books and opted to produce speculative buildings to 'shell and core' finish.

This meant that the office interiors to be leased had no finishes to floors, wall or ceilings and the HVAC and electrical services were capped off at each floor ready for the incoming tenant to do his own thing. This would avoid the waste accompanying the ripping out of the inappropriate finishes and services usually put in at the letting agent's insistence. Most letting agents believe passionately that marketing of a speculative development is severely prejudiced without carpets, false ceilings, wall coverings, fluorescent light fittings and VAV boxes in place from the outset. In practice, the number of fully fitted speculative offices that could accommodate the incoming tenant's layout without serious, expensive and time-consuming modification is so small as to be statistically insignificant.

However, the shell and core developer's posture is not entirely philanthropic; by saving the 3-6 months needed for his fit out stage the developer, if he is lucky enough to have a tenant at 'shell-and-core' stage, will save the interest charges on the whole development cost which would otherwise have been incurred in the conventional rent-free fitting out period at commencement of the lease.

Some developers offer a 'shell-and-core' deal but if no tenant is secured at that stage, progress to developer's fit out without delay. This rather strange decision is motivated by the belief – fostered by many letting agents – that prospective tenants will be unable to commit to a building without seeing what it will actually look like!

It is hard to conceive that facilities managers of large organisations in the 1990's would prove to be so incompetent.

*Alterations and adaptations*

These terms mean the same thing, though they are frequently used together to describe the process whereby the shell, scenery and services designed to be a permanent fixture of the freeholder's premises are modified to perform their function differently – or to perform a different function.

Examples are extension, conversion or improvements to fabric and services. Frequently alterations form part of fitting out projects but it is very important to separate the costs both for the purposes of accurate estimating from benchmarked comparables and for asset tracking and recovery of capital allowances. Alterations to items of 'scenery' such as demountable partitions, carpets and suspended ceilings can influence the recovery of capital allowances whereas holes in walls do not.

## Refurbishment

Refurbishment describes the process whereby an existing building is substantially upgraded in quality either through restoration or improvements, or both. The process usually involves works to the fabric and services and is accompanied by increased investment value – unlike fitting out which becomes a depreciating asset on the balance sheet from day one.

## 6.1.2 CATEGORIES OF FITTING OUT

### Developer's fit out

This is often referred to by developers and their agents as Category 'A' fit out and has already been discussed above in the context of alterations to 'shell and core'. Basically it comprises carpet/carpet tiles, plastered and decorated walls, a tiled suspended ceiling and air-conditioning outlets and light fittings positioned in presumption of an open-plan layout. Prime locations will normally boast a fully accessible raised floor complete with floor boxes.

Any cellular space, be it for private workplace, meetings or conferences, will have to be provided at the expense of substantial modifications to finishes and services; preservation of privacy and operation of HVAC services at point of compartmentation usually present a problem on all perimeters – floors, walls and ceilings.

### Open plan

This term implies an absence of private rooms. Nevertheless, 'definable space' is acknowledged in most open plan solutions with screens and/or storage cabinets demarcating ownership. In some space 'management' regimes users are allowed to build up their own 'defence' but the inherent unstructured nature of such regimes leaves them prey to attack from the rigours of economic reality.

100% open plan offices are a rarity, although the open plan concept is sufficiently accepted as to be conventional for large parts of many organisations' premises. In economic terms the space saved at the open plan workplace is often re-allocated to meeting areas, which often need to be cellular.

The success of an open-planned working environment is mainly dependent on the furniture system adopted. In many cases the cost of a successful furniture system may outweigh the savings in partitioning costs; however, the inefficiency inherent in cellular space plans normally means that, on a cost per capita basis, the more open plan layout is more cost-efficient taking all the premises costs into consideration.

### Cellular layout

100% cellular layouts are now an anachronism, restricted to small firms working out of small premises. Modern cellular solutions are based on the concept of demountable partitions; these systems are much more expensive than builders' stud partitions which are actually just as demountable as their highly-engineered cousins, and rarely get moved anyway.

*Part open/part
cellular*

This is the most common space-use strategy, usually based on open plan for clerical workers - or possibly money or share dealers working in close proximity for cultural (surely not productivity!) reasons. Where tenants go into a previously fitted out space the cost of providing this part-and-part accommodation is usually quite expensive. Not least of the problems is adapting the HVAC systems to the new layout.

Older buildings with perimeter induction air-conditioning cannot cope with cooling loads beyond the originally planned room-depth so partial decellularisation will become costly in respect of the open areas. On the other hand, VAV boxes positioned evenly for open plan will require major reconfiguration or supplementation to ensure equivalent comfort in the cellular spaces; lighting and switching points may also be inconveniently placed relative to the required room and partition layout.

*Non-territorial*

The concept of multi-use workstations allied to enhanced common support areas was touched on briefly in Section 4. Clearly the balance of the facility as between general and special areas changes with this arrangement but the dramatic increase in density of space use more than compensates for the cost of this change, and indeed any higher level of quality which may be provided as an inducement to acceptance by staff.

### 6.1.3 SPECIAL AREAS

This term is used to define any part of the fitting-out which is not to general office areas such as:

- reception

- post room

- dining

- kitchen

- conference room

- computer room

- library

- central storage

- etc.

---

[1]     'Planning Office Space' (Architectural Press)

# CHAPTER 6.2 – FITTING-OUT COSTS

### 6.2.1 FITTING-OUT COSTS IN CONTEXT

*Fitting-out costs over time*

Although fitting-out qualifies as capital rather than revenue expenditure, and the value of the work becomes a business asset on the balance sheet, the regularity of the expenditure and/or the rapid rate of depreciation means that many organisations annualise the costs for benchmarking purposes.

Typically, larger organisations refit their whole space on average every 5 years, although not necessarily all in one go. Those with excessive 'churn' (see Chapter 7.8) without a planning strategy to handle it will find the fitting-out cycle rather shorter than 5-years; those who do not need to refit other than for cosmetic purposes may sometimes have to prolong the life of a fit-out on economic grounds. One way of 'annualising' the capital costs is to calculate a loan-purchase rate for the given period. In **FIG 6.2.A** a typical range of fitting out costs is shown at a mortgage rate of 10% over 5 years and as a straight-line depreciation over the same period for balance sheet purposes.

| Fitting-out costs (including fees) [1] | Pre-tax cost of 5-year 10% mortgage | Straight line depreciation over 5-years |
|---|---|---|
| £ per sq m NIA | £ pa | £ pa |
| 300 | 79 | 60 |
| 400 | 106 | 80 |
| 500 | 132 | 100 |
| [1] Excludes VAT, Corporation tax. | | |

**FIG 6.2.A:** *Alternative methods of expressing fitting-out costs in annual equivalent terms*

**FIG. 6.2.B:** *Fitting-out costs in the context of premises costs per annum*

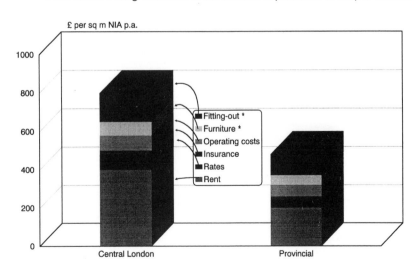

£ per sq m NIA p.a.

Central London     Provincial

Fitting-out *
Furniture *
Operating costs
Insurance
Rates
Rent

* 5 year amortisation @ 10%

**FIG 6.2.B** takes the mid point of those figures in **FIG 6.2.A** and expresses it in the context of Central London and provincial premises costs while **FIG 6.2.C** shows how the same figure sits in the context of a typical organisation's turnover.

**FIG. 6.2.C:** *Fitting-out costs in the context of annual turnover*

Turnover

Amortised
fitting-out costs
(1% turnover)

## 6.2.2 GENERAL OFFICE AREAS

*Fit out from
shell and core*

**FIG 6.2.D** shows the typical costs resulting from a fit-out involving modifications to the so-called 'developer's finish' for two alternative layouts. Compare this with a fit-out from 'shell-and-core' (**FIG 6.2.E**) where the higher costs would be abated by the developer's allowance for the finishes as a contribution to the deal. Note that most developers insist on making a cash contribution rather than discounting the rent; this is because of the effect on the investment value as well as the impact on market rents generally.

**FIG. 6.2.D:** *Fitting-out general office areas from developer's finish - costs for 10,000m² (NIA) building*

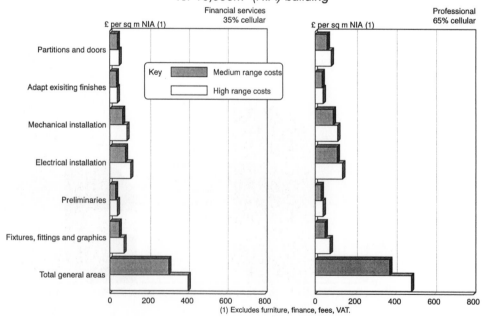

**FIG. 6.2.E:** *Fitting-out general office areas from 'shell and core'- costs for 10,000m² (NIA) building*

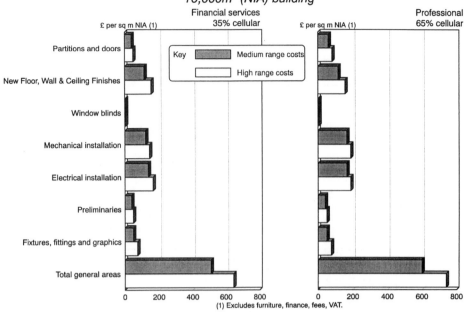

Where the developer does make a contribution to the tenant's fit-out the tenant should make sure he pays against work-in-progress, thus saving, in this example, maybe £100K in interest charges on the finishing works.

*Open plan v cellular layout*

In the examples above the overall costs of fitting-out the less cellular option is marginally cheaper. However the true economies are in the amount of space used in that largely open plan option where savings of up to 30% in space per capita will be the critical factor. A worked example of this thesis is given at **FIG 6.2.F** which also considers the total premises cost implications of the 35% and 65% cellular options - taking the fit-out from developer's finish.

**FIG. 6.2.F:** *Total premises costs per capita per annum for varying degrees of open-plan layout*

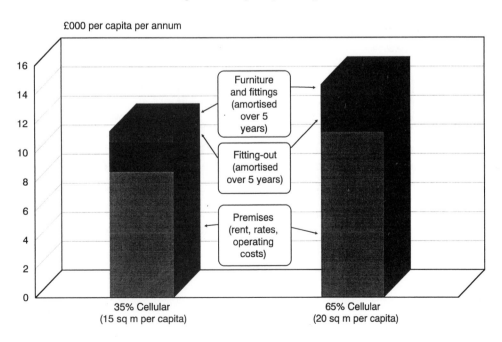

Capital allowances on demountable partitions, which used to be available as a matter of course from the Inspector of Taxes, are now subject to question under the latest legislation (see Chapter 11.2). An organisation bent on a cellular solution might well consider the 'builder's option'; a comparison of the two alternatives, after tax and with and without capital allowances, is given at **FIG 6.2.G**. Note how the

**FIG 6.2.G:** *Capital cost comparison of fixed and demountable partitions*

| Specification | Quantity sq m | Unit Rate £ / sq m | Total before tax relief (1) £ | NPV(2) of relief through capital allowances (3)(4) £ | Total net of discounted tax relief £ |
|---|---|---|---|---|---|
| Metal panel demountable partitions | 1,000 | 75 | 75,000 | (19,000) | 56,000 |
| Fixed stud partitions faced with plasterboard and decorated | 1,000 | 35 | 35,000 | nil | 35,000 |
| (1) Excluding: Fees, VAT, finance, periodic relocation costs, cleaning. | | | | | |
| (2) See Chapters 2.2 and 10.4 for explanation of discounted cash flow. A 10% discount rate was used. | | | | | |
| (3) May not be recoverable - see Chapter 11.2. | | | | | |
| (4) Assumes adequate taxable profits available. | | | | | |

large cost differential, even if tax relief is available, clearly goes nowhere near justification of the demountable solution in terms of savings in use, unless only a short life is envisaged for the fitting-out layout.

*Fitting out special areas*

**FIG 6.2.H:** *Fitting-out to special areas*
*- typical costs*

| Function | Fitted-out area £ / sq m (1) |
|---|---|
| Kitchen | 1,500 |
| Dining | 500 |
| Board Room | 1,500 - 2,000 |
| Conference | 350 - 500 |
| Computer Room | 1,500 |
| Reception | 1,000 |
| Vending | 1,800 |
| Post Room | 500 - 1,000 |
| (1) Excludes VAT, Fees, Loose furniture. | |

**FIG 6.2.H** considers the cost of fitting out 'special' office areas, and support areas such as restaurants, reception etc. in an existing building. In the 'non-territorial' office planning strategies particular attention is usually paid to the common areas eg: some of the meeting areas may take the form of comfortably furnished coffee lounges and the reception area has to be highly efficient as well as containing emergency 'waiting' accommodation for the occasional over-subscription of workplaces.

As is shown in Chapter 4.1 the common support may be as much as 10% - 20% of the total space to be fitted out. So, where the fitting out costs of the support space are significantly higher than the general office areas the impact on the overall cost of fitting out may be significant.

Against this, however, common support areas tend not be chopped and changed around as often as the general areas, so may have a longer life-cycle.

# CHAPTER 6.3 – PROCURING THE PROJECT

### 6.3.1 THE PROJECT PROCUREMENT PROCESS

*Objectives, responsibilities and project management*

The facilities manager's task is to deliver up fitted-out space to accommodate the business requirements.

The objectives will encompass the intentions regarding quality, cost and time and the degree of risk exposure which is acceptable for all three aspects of the project.

The principles of project management and the tools available for the job are considered in detail in Chapter 2.2. The decision as to whether the facilities manager handles the project or out-sources its management should depend on the scale of a fitting-out project and the experience of the in-house team.

Whether or not the facilities manager or a member of his team acts personally as the project manager is irrelevant with regard to his ultimate responsibility for the project. If he undertakes it himself there is an assumption of responsibility and a presumption of competence; if he out-sources it he will be responsible for the selection of the project manager, agreeing his brief and monitoring performance. Effective procurement is one of the three facets of cost control described in Chapter 2.2. Its place in the trinity is shown in **FIG 6.3.A.** Note that the term 'project' as used here relates to the whole process from inception to completion; a fitting-out project embraces a number of stand-alone procurement procedures.

**FIG. 6.3.A:** *Competitive procurement as one facet of cost control*

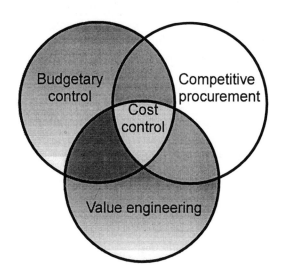

*The stages of project procurement*

The stages of project procurement are:

- feasibility study
- briefing
- procuring the design
- procuring the works
- procuring the furniture (where appropriate).

Fitting out projects involve both design and construction; often the two processes are the responsibility of one person or company, but the main design work is most commonly the responsibility of an interior designer or architect independent of the principal constructor.

At this early point in the consideration of the process it is necessary to review the stage at which the designer should be introduced and the manner of his appointment. Since the designer should be expected to contribute to the feasibility and briefing process there is often a conflict where the intention is to adopt a 'single-point-of-responsibility' (design-and-build) route of procurement.

The need for this early involvement at concept stage means that the design-and-build contractor cannot be selected competitively for this work on the basis of a finite scheme. There are two ways around this: the first is to involve an independent designer at the briefing stage who may or may not be novated to (ie: his contract assigned to) the contractor at a later stage; the second is to select the design-and-build contractor by means of a preliminary 'two-stage' tendering process (see below) which will determine the relative competitiveness of the companies offering their services and incorporate a mechanism for ensuring that the level of competitiveness established in the first-stage bid flows through into the pricing of the work as finally designed and specified.

## 6.3.2 THE FEASIBILITY STUDY

*The objective*

The feasibility study is the process whereby changes in the organisation's space requirements are reviewed in the context of the available space (existing or new) and potential solutions. In its most fundamental form it will embrace all the accommodation options including those involving total or partial relocation (see Section 9). However, here we are only concerned with the process from the project brief stage ie: the point at which the fitting-out strategy has been finalised and agreed and the location and extent of the works identified.

The feasibility study must consider a sufficient number of generic solutions in terms of planning and quality together with their approximate costs, time-scales, risks and constraints to ensure that management is given the opportunity to make a well-considered decision with respect to formulating the design brief.

*The study team*

Ideally, the team assembled for the feasibility study will include:

- the facilities manager
- a space planner
- a designer
- a cost consultant
- structural, M+E and other engineers (as required).

Subject to the caveat regarding design-and-build appointments discussed above, the team for the study should ideally be the design team in embryo. This will avoid the dangers of key points in the concept falling between two stools and also the loss of time and productivity resulting from a re-learning curve facing a new team.

It is usual to reimburse consultants on a time-charge or lump sum fee. In hard times, some consultants may work this stage for nothing in anticipation of being instructed to undertake any project which emerges. However, since it is at this stage that all the major influencing issues are explored and determined it is far better to pay consultants something - not necessarily a full fee, but enough to encourage them to approach the study seriously in the knowledge that some or all of the cost of their time is being recovered.

On large feasibility studies consultants should always be paid a full fee for their services. Popular idioms about getting 'owt for nowt', 'paying peanuts and getting monkeys' etc. owe their existence not to disillusioned consultants but to the bitter experience of clients whose projects have failed because the feasibility stage was wrongly addressed and inadequately resourced.

## The appraisal process

It may be that the generic layout is pre-determined by the organisation's premises policy, in which case it should only be necessary to carry out a quick check on any constraints which may prejudice a satisfactory design solution. For example, if a partly cellular layout is to be the basis of the scheme the M+E engineer should check that there are no insuperable problems in terms of the nature and location of cooling system components, floor access boxes etc. and any performance problems such as acoustic transfer above ceilings or below floors should also be investigated. A quick check-over by the cost consultant either confirming previously achieved cost levels or identifying sources of extra expense will then enable the decision to be taken.

If constraints do pose a risk to cost then it is very important that the value-engineering process (see Chapter 2.2 and below) should be instigated in the evaluation of more cost-effective solutions - either at specific locations or by wholesale rearrangement. The importance of commencing the value engineering process at this stage is stressed in **FIG 6.3.B** which shows all the stages of financial control.

**FIG. 6.3.B:** *Stages of cost control in building projects*

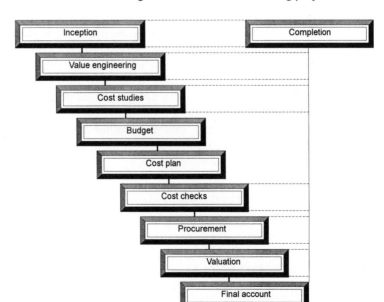

The cost consultant's estimate may be on a cost per square metre of the fitted-out area or, if there are a number of alternative layouts, he may produce estimates using more detailed measurement and synthesis of contractor's prices (see below). It may not be necessary for the designer to plan floors in detail for each generic solution being considered, provided that he can indicate his intentions sufficiently for the facilities manager, engineers and cost consultant to conceptualise and report on the likely impact in the context of their own specialist discipline.

The importance of having team members who can think conceptually cannot be over-stated; too often time and resources are frittered away as a result of detailed layouts being prepared only to be discarded on account of constraints which might easily have been foreseen by professionals of the right calibre and experience. A truly conceptually-competent team should be able to do much of the study without any drawings whatsoever.

Many designers prefer to 'go away on their boat for a weekend' to produce the early schematics. However, this practice denies the opportunity for any creative contribution in terms of building economics, services or structure from the other specialists before the designer has become emotionally and irretrievably wedded to the solution he believes is 'right'! Getting the constraints and potential economics on the table at the outset for all to see is the only way to ensure that the feasibility study achieves its main objectives ie: to produce optional solutions whilst ensuring that performance optimisation is an inherent consequence of the process.

### 6.3.3 BRIEFING

*The contents of
the brief*

It has already been indicated above that there are two types of brief - the project brief and the design brief.

The project brief comes from the core management usually in consultation with the facilities manager. It identifies the problem to be addressed and may have been the result of a conceptual feasibility study. It will dictate the policy in terms of who, where and how; it may also pre determine how much by way of space and cost, and the generic planning style to be tested; in other situations these detailed considerations may be left to development of the design brief.

The design brief will confirm the requirements of the management brief and will also be concerned with such issues as quality of finishes, space norms or guidelines, workplace configuration, locations and extent of ancillary facilities such as storage and meeting spaces, and any special provisions of common support (see Chapter 4.1 for definitions of space use). The design brief will contain any policy on signs and graphics, colour schemes, furniture systems, information technology, etc. together with any critical guidelines emerging from the feasibility study which informs it. Usually there will be a target cost although sometimes the brief and the project programme will allow for a client response to a fully costed solution without pre-judging the cost levels; this is a rather archaic approach which usually evidences a faulty or non-existent feasibilty study and flies in the face of any serious attempt at a value-engineered solution.

*The importance
of the brief*

Having a properly documented brief is a condition precedent to a successful project. Too often the designer is left to elicit the client's requirements – a sure sign of sloppy or non-existent project management and also a guarantee that the designer will run the project his way; this often entails the 'weekend-on-the-boat' design syndrome discussed above, which is anathema to the value engineer.

Of course, the design team will have to interpret - probably improve - the brief but they should not have to write it by default.

*Performance specification*

It would be most unusual to find a design brief which specified the client's functional performance requirements with such precision that all the design team had to do was to choose layouts, materials and systems which, efficiently integrated, would demonstrably achieve the required efficiency.

Nevertheless, it should be possible for the facilities manager to define his major requirements in terms of physical performance characteristics eg: type, quality and quantity of space, acoustics, temperature, stability and durability so as to challenge the design team to find cost-effective value-engineered solutions. Whilst this may be asking a lot from the occasional user of the construction/shop-fitting industry the regular customers really ought to hone down their performance requirements to non-product-specific specifications to encourage creative and cost-effective solutions.

*Life-cycle implications*

The brief must have regard to the expected life of the particular fit out and ensure that materials chosen properly reflect this requirement. Most commonly designers over-specify materials and furniture, having insufficient regard to the realities of modern building usage.

A way to avoid this wastage and also to encourage designers and facilities managers to consider the consequential effects of design and specification decisions is to incorporate in the brief a set of cost benchmarks for all the operating cost centres. It then behoves the design team to demonstrate the impact of their choice in respect of each element on these running cost targets. **FIG 6.3.C** shows a low-cost fitting-out example of this technique and is similar in principle to the new building example of a life-cycle cost plan given in Chapter 10.4. The point of the exercise is not so much to reduce running costs per se (although that is obviously a worthy goal) but more to ensure that the impact of the choice of materials and services on facilities management is properly thought through at the early stages of design thereby helping to avoid impractical solutions.

**FIG 6.3.C:** *Life-cycle cost analysis - low cost fitting-out components (before tax)*

| Cost centre | Capital cost £ / sq m NIA | Annual Costs per sq m NIA | | | | |
|---|---|---|---|---|---|---|
| | | Amortised capital cost over 5 years @ 10% £ | Cleaning £ | Maintenance £ | Energy £ | Total £ |
| Partition and Doors | 40 | 14.56 | 0.50 | 2.00 | - | 17.06 |
| Wall finishes | 15 | 5.46 | 2.00 | 1.00 | - | 8.46 |
| Floor finishes | 20 | 7.28 | 4.00 | 1.00 | - | 12.28 |
| Ceiling finishes | 20 | 7.28 | 1.00 | 1.00 | - | 9.28 |
| Window blinds | 10 | 3.64 | 0.25 | 0.10 | - | 3.99 |
| Adapt HVAC | 50 | 18.20 | - | 10.00 | 7.00 | 35.20 |
| Lighting | 30 | 10.92 | 1.00 | 5.00 | 4.00 | 20.92 |
| Adapt Power supplies | 20 | 7.28 | - | 2.00 | 2.00 | 11.28 |
| Fixtures, fittings and graphics | 25 | 9.10 | - | 1.00 | - | 10.10 |
| Builder's work and preliminaries | 20 | 7.28 | - | - | - | 7.28 |
| **Total** | **250** | **91.00** | **8.75** | **23.10** | **13.00** | **135.85** |

### 6.3.4 PROCURING THE DESIGN

*Selecting the vehicle*

The facilities manager must decide from the outset the process by which he intends to procure the fit-out design. In all but the most minor alterations he will be expected to engage an experienced, qualified person to design the project; the only decisions will then be with regard to the vehicle by which the design is delivered.

Unless suitable designers are on the establishment the design will have to be outsourced. The homes in which designers might then be found are:

- consultancies
    - architects
    - interior designers
    - space planners
    - multi-disciplinary practices
- contractors
    - general building
    - shopfitters
    - furniture suppliers.

Contractors undertaking design services may have their own in-house specialists - usual where design-and-build is a major feature of their business -or may engage consultants on a project-by-project basis; sometimes the client's scheme designer may be novated to the contractor when the design-and-build contract is struck.

The merits or demerits of the design-and-build approach are discussed below. Suffice it here to say that a client is entitled to, and has no reason not to, obtain the services of good designers of his choice without paying a premium. The staff architect, however talented individually, is likely to suffer from lack of design ambition and innovation through his anonymity; he may also miss the cross-fertilisation of ideas which should inform his independent counterpart who is likely to be working across a broader spectrum of clients and building types.

While it would be wrong to be too categorical in this respect, the facilities manager should take extra care to explore the experience, credentials and track record of any design team proffered by a contractor. That is not to say that he should not vet any consultants just as thoroughly, only that his control over the contractor's designer will be one step removed and therefore defence of quality will be more dependent on the stuff of which the latter is made.

The independent or in-house designer will be the client's man and will also probably be the quasi-arbitrator for the works contract. Although in a perfect world this should not be a consideration the client will probably take some comfort from the fact that the designer has the building employer's interests primarily to heart when matters of quality, cost and time are at risk.

There are, nevertheless, powerful arguments in favour of design-and-build; eg: it is an important feature of the Japanese construction industry which is perceived to be rather more efficient than Europe's. However, a sea-change to this method within our present industry culture is by no means certain to produce the benefits which its proponents would have us all accept.

Better project management encouraging the full introduction of value engineering activity from the earliest stages should bring its rewards without the client sacrificing control of the design process.

*Selecting the
team*

Choice of designer has already been considered from the point of view of his contractual status. The only other considerations are the background and qualifications most appropriate to the project. As with all the consultants this must be a key feature of the selection process to be fully considered alongside the fee bid.

Few individual architects can offer a portfolio of projects embracing building design, interior design and space planning although some of the larger firms may have a reasonable range of experience across the board. At this time, and since forever, architects have conventionally been pre-occupied with the exterior of buildings to the detriment of their usefulness to the occupiers. This is the result of the almost universal treatment of architecture as one of the liberal arts for educational purposes. This process tends to produce 'prima donna' architects whose reputation for distinctive design belies their inability to interpret clients' ergonomic requirements; these individuals have to be avoided by facilities managers at all costs, not least because of the intransigence which normally accompanies their affiliation to their idiosyncratic design solutions.

Interior designers by dint of qualification, or those few qualified architects who have moved into that field, are more likely to understand the client's fitting-out brief and the particular sector of the construction industry which will deliver it up in its built form. They may be less well versed in the management of the design process, building services, costs, and contract procedure than 'regular' architects which means that project management will have an important bearing on the outcome.

Interior designers also have a propensity to say what they want rather than specify or even draw it, and the shop-fitting industry which responds to them is geared up to accommodate this style of practice. Not surprisingly such an approach can play havoc with cost control; a good cost consultant familiar with the 'seat-of-the-pants' fast-track financial control necessitated by the employment of such designers – and the nature of most fitting out projects – will be a major bonus to the team.

Mechanical and electrical engineers can usually adapt from new building to fitting out work without adverse effects; their knowledge of life-cycle implications of M+E design should be thoroughly explored by the project manager in advance of appointment. The estimated costs should be produced by the cost consultant with the engineer being invited to comment upon them. Some services engineers have a reasonable knowledge of costs, especially if they have worked for contractors and their input can be valuable. Equally, a lot of cost consultants are weak on M+E services costs and design principles; if one such consultant should slip into the team by default the engineer's ability or otherwise to help may prove critical.

The cost consultant should always be independently appointed, even if he is nominated by the designer, as is not infrequent. Teams of designers and cost consultants who have worked together regularly can often bring a smoothness to a project which is missing from ad hoc teams set up for specific one-off projects . If the project manager is satisfied that this established team will benefit his project he is strongly advised to have the cost consultant appointed direct. The cost consultant should continue to wear his 'team hat' and report through the designer - this is essential to avoid misinterpretation of cost reports - but is still available to give independent cost advice on design proposals direct to the project manager if required.

Most important of all, the project team must really be a team. The project manager must take great care in his selection that he not only gets the calibre of professionals he needs to do the job but also the personalities which will determine whether or not the unit will function efficiently.

**It is people, rather than systems or firms, which make or break any project.**

*Contract
arrangements*

Many consultants are quite happy to enter into a contract based on a simple exchange of letters. The professional institutions have recommended standard conditions of engagement which may help to clarify the extent of services being offered and any rights and liabilities of the parties. The design-and-build contracts will nearly always be based on a formal document.

In the event, if things go wrong the most important thing is not who pays for them - which is what most formal contracts are about - but how to rectify the problems before they do irrevocable damage. This will probably be down to people and personalities as much as any written clauses, so carefully choosing players who know the rules will be more likely to influence the result than relying upon the rule book to control a nondescript misassortment of inadequately experienced professionals.

*Reimbursement*

Until recent years the professional bodies published fee scales which were mandatory for their members on pain of admonition or dismissal. These were outlawed one-by-one by the Monopolies Commission, so now they exist only as a point of reference, sometimes as a basis from which discounts are bid or negotiated. If these scales are used as a discount base it is very important to clarify whether or not the discounted fee relates to all the services listed, and to the full service in respect of each facet.

Sometimes fees are bid on a percentage of the cost of the works, enabling the consultant to claw back the extra costs of administering post-contract changes to the scheme; that is fine, but only if it is the client who has changed his mind, not the designer. A more usual method these days is the lump sum related to a specific project brief. This leaves the consultant free to claim extra costs for his client's scope changes and vice-versa. The lump sums may be built up from a resource schedule with related time-charges and, exceptionally, clients may accept open-ended time-charges where the scope of work is indeterminable at the outset. This is not usual with fitting-out projects unless accompanied by extensive refurbishment of old buildings.

Payments are either at pre-agreed stages or, more commonly in these hard economic times, on a regular monthly or bi-monthly basis, again on a pre-set schedule.

The design component of design-and-build is normally subsumed into the cost of works and paid monthly on valuations of the fitting out works. The VAT implications of such arrangements do, however, need to be carefully assessed - Chapter 11.4 refers.

### 6.3.5 PROCURING THE WORKS

*Selecting the
procurement
route*

As for getting the works built, the employer has only two generic choices;

- lump sum

- cost reimbursement.

However, within these categories there is a bewildering variety of tendering procedures and contract arrangements which are now discussed in detail.

It is important to distinguish between the processes of obtaining bids for the work and the execution of the contract under which they will be built.

*Lump sum contracts*

Traditionally for major building works lump sum contracts based on the industry's standard (JCT) forms were bid in open competition. Any builder could get hold of a copy of the tender documents - possibly drawings and bills of quantities or simply specification and drawings - and put in a bid which, if accepted, would be the contract price. This system implied two conditions ie: independent design and adequate definition of the work to be built. (see **FIG 6.3.D**)

**FIG. 6.3.D:** *Traditional JCT lump sum contract with independent design*

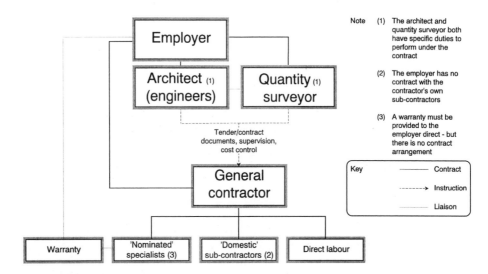

Bills of quantities are not used very often for fitting-out works - more so in refurbishment. Where bills of quantities are available the prices for measured work become contract rates for adjusting the contract sum for any changes in design or specification. Also, if the quantities are found to be wrong post-contract the contract sum is revised following corrected measurement. Of course, the designers never complete the drawings on time so the quantity surveyors often make up the specification, measure it in the bills and hope the cost of the eventual detailing will be covered by the hypothetical measured work. In practice, there is the danger that if the final detail is more expensive the contractor will claim extra, whereas as if it is cheaper the matter may be left to lie quietly unless the QS is diligent.

A bill of quantities or specification may contain provisional sums for work not yet designed - the costs are calculated post-contract by the quantity surveyor who, subject only to arbitration, is the sole determiner of how much the builder is entitled to be paid for any variations and on monthly valuation. Works by specialists such as air-conditioning or proprietary fittings are often included in the contract as prime cost (pc) sums to be expended in due course against a nominated sub-contractor's quotation - the sub-contractor being contracted to the main contractor following the architect's instruction.

The JCT contracts (with or without quantities) have never been particularly popular for fitting-out works which at one time were often carried out by shopfitting contractors on a simple lump sum basis. However, with the advent of a much greater degree of sophistication and technology in fitting-out works the JCT forms came to be used much more frequently, with general contractors taking over from the shopfitters; usually the contracts were 'without quantities' although from the 1980's most clients have usually employed a quantity surveyor in the dual role of cost consultant and financial manager for the contract

A new type of lump sum contract has entered the picture imported via international construction managers (see below) This has been adopted by the British Property Federation in their own form of contract devised to replace the JCT versions which they deemed to be unfairly biased against the employers. Although BPF contracts are not common in fitting out works the concept of the 'scope' contract has been used in some larger construction management projects. The object is to invite the contractor (main or trade) to estimate the cost of carrying out all the works indicated and implied by the designer's performance brief. In fact, it is to some extent the extension of the concept of performance specification which has been used for many years to obtain lump sum bids for specialist works requiring contractor's design and guarantee.

Bidding for lump sum works can be by

- open tender
- selected list tender
- straight negotiation
- competitive negotiation / 2-stage tender.

Open tender, where anyone may pick up the bid document and submit a tender, is rarely used nowadays for reasons which must be self-evident.

Straight negotiation is really only beneficial in special circumstances, such as where the client wishes to extend the works under construction, or the works are of a highly specialist nature. The cost consultant should be able to negotiate a competitive price but sometimes lack of a viable alternative limits what he can achieve.

In most cases it is possible to get the project under way quickly by holding the competition on a **two-stage** basis eg: by measured approximate quantities, simple profit margins on hypothetical trade values and any number of ingenious methods devised by quantity surveyors. The object is to make sure that the builder selected in advance of design development can be seen to be demonstrably the most competitive and be held to that pricing level in the negotiation of prices for the work as finally designed.

Given that designers rarely specify adequately in time for proper tender documentation, and also the wasted resource of contractors pricing 5 or 6 projects in full for every one that they get, there is, in fact, a very good argument for all lump sum projects being tendered in this way. The process also gives the employer and his design team the potential benefit of the builder's experience in the design development phase; he can also advise on material availability and the cost consultant can develop the cost plan in the context of the chosen contractor's pricing and commercial regime rather than forecasting them as he normally must - sometimes with embarrassing inaccuracy.

The main problem with this clever technology is that unless it is properly explained it may lead both designer and client into a false sense of security with regard to the adequacy of the information available to the contractor when he starts on site. This can lead to very serious problems once the contract gets under way.

## Cost reimbursement contracts

Again, traditionally, works which could not be defined sufficiently to enable lump sum bids to be sought and/or which needed to start ahead of design were sometimes let on a 'cost-plus' basis - the 'plus' being either a percentage or a fixed lump sum fee and the cost being the authenticated 'prime cost' of all the labour, materials and plant used up in the process.

This type of contract (even though enshrined in a JCT form) in the hands of any contractor worth his salt was a licence both to print and to waste money and has long been discarded as a serious procurement route.

Partly as an alternative to this approach the concept of professional **'management contracting'** grew up in the UK from the late 1960's. Originally based on the prime cost reimbursement process denounced above but laced with a philosophy that the client was there to be served rather than fleeced, the system was expanded into a process whereby the 'professional' contractor managed the work of sub-trades who were in sub-contract to them but on an 'open-book' basis; the client only paid the sub-contractor's agreed price with the management contractor taking a lump sum or percentage fee (see **FIG 6.3.E**)

**FIG. 6.3.E:** *Management contracting procedures*

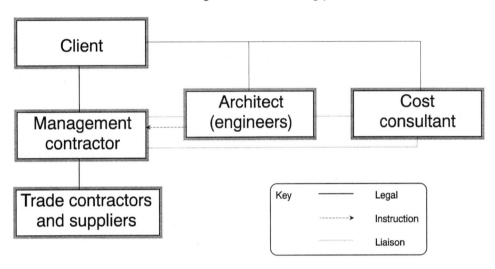

Although the principle was much the same as the original 'yellow peril' JCT prime cost contracts the pioneers of management contracting tried hard, and with a certain degree of success, to instil unto their managers that their main bias was towards helping the client deliver his project to time, quality and budget rather than look for opportunities to claim extras every time a hiccup threatened to disrupt the basis of the client's projections.

The system has lost some ground in recent times for several reasons, including:

- highly competitive lump sum bids concealing hidden profit margins have made the management fee seem expensive by comparison

- construction management has presented an even more professional, client-orientated image

- the problem of recruiting and training managers who could readily aspire to a totally different philosophy

- the 'bandwagon' syndrome in which may contractors sought to cash in on the vogue without properly understanding, or caring about, the underlying philosophy.

- 'paid when paid' clauses affecting the level of trade contractors' prices

**Construction management** came to the UK in a big way from the USA and parts of Europe in the 1980's (see **FIG 6.3.F**). A more purist approach than that of management contracting it sets on a totally professional footing the person who will organise and procure the work of trades contractors. The construction manager has no contract with the trade suppliers or sub-contractors, all of whom are put into direct contract with the building employer. The construction manager draws a fee - again, a lump sum or percentage. Like the management contractors and unlike the professional consultants, this fee normally includes only overheads and profit, with the costs of all site managers and dedicated head office personnel reimbursed at prime cost.

**FIG. 6.3.F:** *Construction management procedures*

Among the many potential benefits from construction management are the dedicated approach accompanying the pioneering of a cause they really believe in, which leads to a greater contribution on the client's behalf at all stages from feasibility stage (where they would and should be involved) to completion.

Although the best of the new breed of construction managers now suffer from most of the problems of 'pale imitation' facing management contracting as discussed above there is a sufficient number of regular and large-scale building employers using construction management to guarantee its continued position as a credible alternative to lump sum contracting for any project where scale, complexity and time constraints merit bearing the perceived risk of being contractually liable to reimburse all the prime costs incurred.

This said, construction management in the UK has been spectacularly successful at lowering project cost levels, particularly through better organisation, improved buildability, avoiding middle-man sub-contractors and encouraging prompt or otherwise beneficial payment terms to the trade contractors. In particular many clients have appreciated the opportunity to get 'hands on' the project through the construction manager being able to make strategic changes to scope and time with minimum exposure to risks of disruption and claims.

Construction management is a particularly appropriate vehicle for procuring fast-track, fast-build fit-out projects. However, cost control should be overseen and all costs audited by a competent independent cost consultant, even though the construction managers like to persuade their clients they can carry out this critical function themselves. In the final event it is the time and quality of the construction which motivates the construction manager and his natural aggression in achieving these goals needs the support of sophisticated, **independent** financial monitoring.

Bidding for construction managers and management contractors usually seeks separate fees for the pre-commencement period (anything from feasibility to start on site) and for managing the works on site.

*'With-design'*
*contracts*

All of the above variants of lump sum and cost reimbursement can be based on the 'with design' principle ie: the designer is part of the contractor's or manager's team as illustrated in **FIG 6.3.G**. Whereas such arrangements make a lot of sense for simple projects such as industrial sheds requiring little special design input, they are harder to justify for 'quality' projects where the client might be expected to benefit from having the designer directly answerable to him at all stages.

**FIG. 6.3.G:** *Design-and-construction - lump sum and construction management alternative procedures*

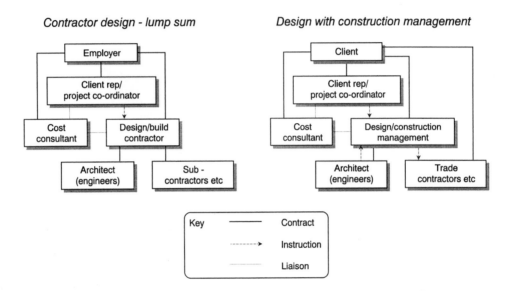

In fact the current vogue for design-and-build springs from the inability of conventional design teams to get their act (and their clients') sufficiently together to avoid frequent and serious overruns of time and cost. Too often there are justifiable complaints from contractors that they are being impeded by poor design and inadequate project management in their genuine efforts to build to a good standard.

The attraction of single-point responsibility, with the contractor or manager cracking the whip over the designers with respect to the provision of adequate and prompt information for building, is not difficult to appreciate. Nevertheless, contractors do have a tendency to be philistine in their approach to business and there is an ever-present risk that the unwitting design / build client runs the risk of exposure to second-rate design and heavy punishment should he change his mind.

As has been mentioned more than once in this text **it is the people who minimise risk** and optimise solutions - not the systems or regimes under which they operate.

## 6.3.6 BUDGETARY CONTROL

*Definition*

The principles of budgetary control are described in Chapter 2.2 where it is defined as **'the process whereby an appropriate and acceptable budget is established for the works envisaged at the commencement of, and at any later stage in, a project and the proposed and actual expenditure monitored against forecasts to avoid unplanned over- or under-expenditure'.**

*The
applications*

Budgetary control is another of the three facets of cost control (see **FIG 6.3.H)** so necessary to the financial success of any project.  As with the other two facets - effective procurement and value engineering - budgetary control is applicable on two levels ie: overall project costs and construction costs.

**FIG. 6.3.H:** *Budgetary control as one facet of cost control*

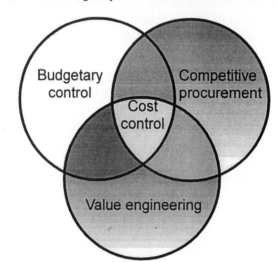

The principles and processes are no different at either level.  However, in fitting-out projects of any size the budgetary control of the works will usually be exercised by a specialist (consultant or in-house) whose work will be concerned with much detail;  he normally reports on cost of the works to the project manager who will feed that information into the overall project budgetary control system which may include design, legal and agent's fees, equipment, furniture and other non-building supplies.

*The estimating
process*

The stages of cost control are shown in **FIG 6.3.B** above.  The estimating process up to the time of appointment of contractors is usually carried out by the specialist cost consultant.  In the feasibility stages he may be providing 'ball-park' estimates - possibly per unit of the area to be fitted out - based on his experience of similar projects.  Historic cost data has to be constantly updated for inflation, market conditions, quality and changes in statutory requirements.  Once the scheme gets outline approval the cost consultant will usually present his cost studies by standard cost centres, using either extrapolation of data, approximate quantities, budget quotations or, most probably, a combination of all three.  Before considering these methods in more detail note the paramount contribution of the initial budget to the value engineering process described in principle in Chapter 2.2 and, in more detail, below.

'Extrapolation' will be from the cost consultant's database eg: from the limited information available he may only be able to forecast the total cost of partitions on a cost per square metre of floor area basis; this need not necessarily be unreliable for sometimes whole preliminary estimates are produced by simple modification and transportation of the elemental costs of a previous similar project.

Nevertheless, as scheme design gets underway the cost consultant will soon be in a position to assess the quantities and specification of the major cost items. In this case he will use the technique known as 'approximate estimating' in which he attempts to forecast the unit prices the future contractor (or sub-trader) will be applying to quantities of work deduced by measurement from the designer's contract drawings. The approximate estimating technique involves rough measurements of the item in question, eg: the length or area partitions to which is applied a unit pricing rate drawn from his data-base of similar work on similar projects..

Unit prices for the specification items making up a contract bid – the level of which will have to be forecast by the cost consultant ahead of the bid process – are usually established by estimating the time needed to carry out an operation, the cost of the operatives' time, the cost of materials (allowing for waste including breakage or theft) and delivery, plus an allowance for overheads and profit. A simple example of this for carpet laying is shown at **FIG 6.3.J**. It should be noted that many of these prices per unit of parameter are familiar to builders' estimators in the form of labour 'constants' which the more sophisticated of them will vary to suit forecast conditions.

**FIG 6.3.J**: *Typical analysis of prices per unit area*
*- supplying and laying carpets*

| Work Item | Sub-total | Total |
|---|---|---|
| **Materials** | £ | £ |
| Carpet & underlay 1,000 sq m @ £20: | 20,000 | |
| Waste @ 5%: | 500 | |
| Trims, etc say: | 500 | |
| **Sub-total:** | **21,000** | 21,000 |
| **Labour** | £ | |
| 0.25 hours / sq m @ £10 x 1,000 sq m: | 2,500 | |
| Travelling & expenses: | 100 | |
| **Sub-total:** | **2,600** | 2,600 |
| **Overheads and Profit** | £ | |
| OH + P @ 10% x £23,600: | 2,360 | |
| **Sub-total:** | **2,360** | 2,360 |
| **Total:** | | **25,960** |
| **Unit Rate (£25,960 / 1,000 sq m)** | | £26 / sq m laid |

Sometimes builders' estimators will build up a price for a complete task and may then be required to break the price back to cost per parametric unit for a bill of quantities or schedule of rates. These prices will be the basis of any variation requiring re-measurement; usually they are taken as read, but contracts often have provision for the rate to be modified if the forecast conditions on which a rate was calculated are materially different in the work as varied.

So, the preliminary estimate for partitions which was, say £x per square metre of the lettable floor area will now be replaced by a calculation - say 100 square metres of partitions (measured across doors and glazing) @ £y per square metre of the partition components. The cost consultant doing an early estimate will normally 'round up' the rate to provide a contingency to cover more expensive or additional work coming to light in the detailed design development of that cost centre.

At the early stages, and indeed throughout a project, the cost controller may have to include forecast costs of items not yet depicted on drawings or specifications. When doing so it is critically important that the location and extent of such items is flagged up when costs are reported. The importance of communicating to the design team and the client in this way the basis of any forecasts cannot be overstated; the whole team must own the budget and its composition, albeit that the cost consultant takes special responsibility for the level of costs forecast and the accuracy of the measurement.

Examples of a preliminary and scheme design budget report are shown at **FIG 6.3.K and 6.3.L**. Sometimes it is prudent to obtain budget quotations for specialist work or if market conditions are uncertain. These should be treated with caution as they may be under-or-over-estimated depending on the trader's strategy and his view of the estimating risk.

**FIG. 6.3.K:** *Preliminary budget report 'Ceramic Tiling' Cost Centre - EXTRACT*

PROJECT: *Example*

COST STUDY No.2    DATE: October *1994*

WORK PACKAGE : *Ceramic Tiling*
WORK PACKAGE No.: *7100*

| LOCATION | SPECIFICATION | SOURCE | QUANTITY | UNIT | RATE | TOTAL |
|---|---|---|---|---|---|---|
| | **Wall Tiling** | | | | | |
| Servery / Finishing Kitchen | White ceramic tiles in epoxy grout | Meeting 2.5.94 | 300 | m² | 60.00 | 18,000 |
| Servery | Ceramic tiles PC £40/m² supplied, in epoxy grout | Meeting 2.5.94 | 65 | m² | 95.00 | 6,175 |
| Generally | Cut and fit around switches etc. | Allowance | 100 | No. | 5.00 | 500 |
| Generally | Expansion joint | Allowance | 50 | m | 10.00 | 500 |
| Generally | Mastic pointing at all junctions | Allowance | 100 | m | 5.00 | 500 |
| Generally | Stainless steel corner guards to tiling | Arch 7/7/94 | | Item | | 1,500 |
| | | | | Rounding Factor | | (75) |
| | | WORK PACKAGE TOTAL TO SUMMARY £ | | | | 101,000 |

**FIG. 6.3.L:** *Scheme design budget report 'Ceramic Tiling' Cost Centre - EXTRACT*

PROJECT: *Example*

PROJECT COST PLAN    DATE: November *1994*

WORK PACKAGE : *Ceramic Tiling*
WORK PACKAGE No.: *7100*

| LOCATION | SPECIFICATION | SOURCE | QUANTITY | UNIT | RATE | TOTAL |
|---|---|---|---|---|---|---|
| | **Wall Tiling** | | | | | |
| Servery / Finishing Kitchen | White ceramic tiles in epoxy grout | Dwg 1/2/004C | 500 | m² | 50.00 | 25,000 |
| Servery | Ceramic tiles PC £40/m² supplied, in epoxy grout | Dwg 1/2/004C | 50 | m² | 80.00 | 4,000 |
| Generally | Cut and fit around switches etc. | Allowance | 100 | No. | 5.00 | 500 |
| Generally | Expansion joint | Allowance | 50 | m | 10.00 | 500 |
| Generally | Mastic pointing at all junctions | Allowance | 100 | m | 5.00 | 500 |
| All areas | Stainless steel corner guards to tiling | Arch 7/7/94 | | Item | | 3,000 |
| | | | | Rounding Factor | | (100) |
| | | WORK PACKAGE TOTAL TO SUMMARY £ | | | | 85,000 |

Once the works are let, either on a main contract or in sub-trades, then the cost consultant's forecasts of quantities and rates are replaced in the budgetary control system by the contract estimates - hopefully not too far different. It is not at all unusual for the cost consultant's overall forecast to be close to the contract total whilst there are significant variations, on a cost centre by cost centre basis, between forecast and contract price. This need not imply luck or ineptitude on the cost consultant's part: different contractors have their own special areas where they can procure particularly efficiently but the competitive total bidding process sees that the discrepancies cancel themselves out.

Post-contract changes will be forecast by the cost controller using the contractor's rates and pricing structure as described above, often with the forecasts being made jointly with the contractor's surveyor and ideally negotiated and agreed as contract prices at that stage. Note that in the JCT lump sum contracts it is the quantity surveyor who states the value of a variation; the contractor must give him sufficient information to do so, but his only recourse on disagreement is to arbitration. In practice the two surveyors normally sort it out by negotiation.

## Cost reporting

In building projects there are various generic stages and types of cost reporting:

- feasibility study
- cost studies
- project cost plan
- pre-contract financial statement (sometimes called the cost check)
- report on tenders
- post-commencement financial statement
- final account.

A detailed examination of the process is beyond the scope of this work. However, the principles to be observed, in common with all systems of financial control, are that at all stages of cost reporting:

- the basis of any cost projection must always be communicated to client and design teams
- the project manager must get the team to ratify the basis of all cost-change projections and establish whether they are requesting to have them incorporated in the project
- the status of any projections presented in a cost report in terms of client acceptance, contractual commitment, legal obligations, risk etc. must always be made explicit, with projections categorised by prior agreement between the client and/or his project manager.
- departure from the agreed basis of the budget should only be permitted with the client's prior approval.

## Cost monitoring

In order to maintain budgetary control the following provisions will have to be securely in place:

- the basis of the budget must be published, disseminated, understood and accepted by client and design teams, including, not least, the cost controller himself
- the presentation of the data must be in such a way that the information becoming available concerning potential change can readily be identified as such by reference to the latest amplified cost report
- the cost controller must have a pro-active approach to identifying and reporting the possibility that any potential action, activity or event may impact upon the planned cost
- the client and/or his project manager must have the opportunity and time to consider any change proposals; in the event that cost increases are unavoidable - eg: unforeseen structural problems - cost damage limitation techniques such as revision of specification or omission of non-critical works should be given as much time as possible to be implemented.

With these disciplines in place the cost controller has a better than 50/50 chance of ensuring that unforeseen extras or savings do not turn up in the budget without prior warning or common ownership or an opportunity to consider them properly before their 'window of opportunity' has been closed irrevocably.

Influences outside of the obvious ambit of a specific project must also be monitored. For instance, reliable reports of significant changes in market conditions should be brought to the table for consideration by the design team in the pre-contract phase. Of course, such a report will only be of use if the budget contains a coherent statement as to the conditions projected at the time the budget was agreed. One way this might be done is to quote the relevant point on any reputable published price index which may be applicable to the project estimate.

Many people fulfilling the role of cost consultant hold back from the soul-baring philosophy advocated here. They do so through lack of confidence in their conceptual and physical estimating ability, failure to understand the reasons why budgetary control breaks down and lack of an antidote to it.

*The 'Journal'
system of
financial control*

FIGS 6.3.M and 6.3.N give a typical example of a cost plan and a pre-contract financial statement and FIG 6.3.P shows a post contract cost report. On a 'fast track' project, where some of the work is unlet post contract and still the subject of the cost controller's predictions of future contract prices, the cost report must be expanded to identify each category of prediction so as to reflect the level of price certainty in each cost centre.

**FIG. 6.3.M:** *Cost plan - 'Journal' system summary report - EXTRACT*

PROJECT: *Example*  —  **WORK PACKAGE SUMMARY**

PROJECT COST PLAN  —  DATE: November *1994*  —  GROSS INTERNAL FLOOR AREA = 8,788 m² 94,639 sf

| WORK PACKAGE No. | WORK PACKAGE TITLE | WORK PACKAGE COST £ | WORK PACKAGE COST £/M² GIFA | WORK PACKAGE COST £/SF GIFA | % |
|---|---|---|---|---|---|
| 2500 | GENERAL BUILDER'S WORK | 150,000 | 17.10 | 1.60 | 3.13 |
| 2900 | FIRE STOPPING | 20,000 | 2.30 | 0.20 | 0.42 |
| 3000 | SUSPENDED CEILINGS | 242,000 | 27.50 | 2.60 | 5.04 |
| 4000 | RAISED FLOOR | 100,000 | 11.40 | 1.10 | 2.08 |
| 5000 | PARTITIONS & OFFICE FRONTS | 925,000 | 105.30 | 9.80 | 19.27 |
| 5490 | LAN ROOM PARTITIONS | 10,000 | 1.10 | | |
| 5600 | SPECIALIST JOINERY | | | | |
| | | | | | 0.42 |
| | | 130,000 | 14.80 | 1.40 | 2.71 |
| 7100 | CERAMIC TILING | 85,000 | 9.70 | 0.90 | 1.77 |
| 7500 | CARPETS & VINYL FLOORING | 270,000 | 30.70 | 2.90 | 5.63 |
| 7725 | STONEWORK | 5,000 | 0.60 | 0.10 | 0.05 |
| 7760 | BLINDS & DRAPES | 5,000 | 0.60 | 0.10 | 0.05 |
| 8200 | DATA & VOICE CABLING INSTALLATIONS | 160,000 | 18.20 | 1.70 | 3.33 |
| 9222 | PRELIMINARIES | 340,000 | 38.70 | 3.60 | 7.08 |
| 9500 | MANAGEMENT CONTRACTOR'S FEE | 80,000 | 9.10 | 0.80 | 1.67 |
| 10000 | DESIGN & CONSTRUCTION CONTINGENCIES | 218,000 | 24.80 | 2.30 | 4.50 |
| | | £ 4,800,000 | £546.00/m² | £51.00/sf | 100% |

These examples are from the computer program called the **'Journal' system of capital cost control** [1]. The 'journal' system was devised in 1967 and was the first cost control system to introduce a **proactive** approach to the management of financial change. In its manual form it was highly labour-intensive which proved a discouragement to most quantity surveyors to run with a methodology which would potentially give a considerable lift to the calibre of the service offered to their clients. The computerised system developed in the late 80's has overcome these objections.

**FIG. 6.3.N:** *Pre contract cost check - 'Journal' system financial statement of 'Ceramic Tiling' Cost Centre*

PROJECT: *Example*                                    COST REPORT NO: *08*

REPORT: *WORKS CONTRACTOR 7100 - CERAMIC TILING*          DATE: *March 1995*

| Change Order No. | Included in Cost Report No. | Subject | Financial Effect ADD £ | OMIT £ |
|---|---|---|---|---|
| **Procurement** 04/70 | 04 | Omit: Cost Plan; Add: White & Black's tender | 56,290 | 66,175 |
| | | Add: Allowance for additional work | 5,000 | 0 |
| **Client Requirements** 03/31 | 03 | New WCs to L5 Dining Rooms | 4,000 | 0 |
| 05/104 | 05 | 25 x 25mm tiles in lieu of 50 x 50mm tiles to Fitness Centre, & addition of ceramic tiles to shower area ceiling | 15,177 | 0 |
| **Co-ordination between budgets** 04/86 | 04 | Re-allocation of Fitness Centre finishes, Joinery in lieu of Tiling | 0 | 20,000 |
| **Design Development** 06/171 | 06 | Air freight tiles from USA to suit programme | 2,000 | 0 |
| | | | £82,467 | £86,175 |
| | | | | £3,708 |

**FIG. 6.3.P:** *Post contract cost check - 'Journal' system financial statement*

PROJECT: *Example*                                    COST REPORT NO: *08*

REPORT: *Executive Summary*                               DATE: *March 1995*

| COST CENTRE | AUTHORISED COST PLAN £ | ADJUSTED COST PLAN £ | ANTICIPATED FINAL ACCOUNT £ | SHIFT FROM ADJUSTED COST PLAN £ +/(-) | PREVIOUS ANTICIPATED FINAL ACCOUNT £ | SHIFT SINCE PREVIOUS REPORT £ |
|---|---|---|---|---|---|---|
| CONSTRUCTION COSTS | 4,582,000 | 4,463,000 | 4,136,000 | (327,000) | 4,327,000 | (191,000) |
| BUDGET COSTS FOR COMPRESSION OF CONSTRUCTION PROGRAMME | 300,000 | 300,000 | 284,000 | (16,000) | 284,000 | 0 |
| CONTINGENCIES | 300,000 | 300,000 | 300,000 | 0 | 300,000 | 0 |
| TOTAL CONSTRUCTION COSTS | 5,182,000 | 5,063,000 | 4,720,000 | (343,000) | 4,911,000 | (191,000) |
| CLIENT DIRECT CONTRACTS | 1,876,000 | 1,876,000 | 1,876,000 | 0 | 1,876,000 | 0 |
| TOTAL PROJECT COSTS | 7,058,000 | 6,939,000 | 6,596,000 | (343,000) | 6,787,000 | (191,000) |

The key feature in this system is the Estimate Note (**FIG 6.3.Q**) which triggers not only the cost controller's forecast of a projected change to the planned expenditure but also provides information on a number of other key issues and required actions such as

- who instigated the notion and how
- what it is
- how much it will cost
- its potential effect on programme
- whether the client has an option
- if so, how long it will remain open
- which contingency sum, if any, is to be adjusted.

If the architect wants the client to accept the alteration he signs the Estimate Note accordingly and passes it to the client with a formal request;  only if the client confirms acceptance will the proposal go ahead.  This principle, enshrined in the 'Journal' system, applies equally to pre-contract change proposals where the cost plan is treated as 'pseudo-contract' pending the establishment of a works contract.

**FIG. 6.3.Q:** *The 'Estimate Note' feature of the 'Journal' system*

| COST PLAN / CONTRACT SUM | |
|---|---|
| **ESTIMATE NOTE** | |
| **PROJECT:** *Example* | |

| | |
|---|---|
| **Work Package:** Ceramic Tiling | **Reason for origination:**<br>1 Client Requirement |
| **Number:** 7100 / 9 | |
| **Source:** Architect | **Authorisation Status:**<br>Potential Change Order –<br>Identified |
| **Information Received:** 10 Jul 95 | |
| **Issued to Architect:** 12 Jul 95 | **Issued to Client:** |

**Subject:** Revised specification to walls of staff toilets

**Notes:** Telephone conversation 10 Jul 95

| Work Package Programme Implications | EXTEND | REDUCE | Contract Programme Implications | EXTEND | REDUCE |
|---|---|---|---|---|---|
| | 5 days | | | Nil | |
| | ADD | OMIT | Method of assessment: | | |
| Financial Effect £ | 1,500 | | 2 – Approximate Estimate | | |

| | Signature | Date |
|---|---|---|
| **Requested by Architect on behalf of Design Team:** | _____ | _____ |
| **Authorised by Client:** | _____ | _____ |

| | |
|---|---|
| **Incorporated in Cost Report:** 08 | **Classification:** Optional |
| **Contingency Fund to be Adjusted:** Design | |
| **Architect's Instruction:** | **Latest Decision Date:** 19 Jul 95 |
| | B W A |

**The 'cost study' is sometimes erroneously called the cost plan but it should not attain that status until the client and design team have collectively 'signed off' the bottom line figure and its detailed basis.**

*Risks to budgetary control*

The risks to efficient budgetary control are

- inadequate outline and/or detail design resulting in excessive change

- estimating error in terms of quality, market conditions and thoroughness of the cost control process

- re-active cost reporting

- inexperience - individually and collectively

- poor communications

- not enough time to consider alternatives

- poor or non-existent authorisation procedures

- inadequate contingency fund

- poor procurement

- lack of value engineering.

The inter-relationship between the three facets of cost control in this context can be demonstrated by reference to a budget set for a project by a cost consultant envisaging the appointment of a team skilled in procurement and value engineering; in the event an inferior or less experienced team is appointed (possibly the result of low fee-bidding) resulting in all the budget assumptions about cost control being invalidated. It is a constant source of amazement to those who understand cost control of building and fitting-out works that clients and their project managers fail to grasp the bottom-line consequences of appointing a design team and cost consultants unfamiliar with or not motivated by these principles.

### 6.3.7 VALUE ENGINEERING

*Definition*

In Chapter 2.2 the contribution of value engineering to the process of facilities management was discussed in principle. The authors' definition is repeated here ie: **'the process by which the required performance of a product is defined and the product developed to achieve such performance in the most cost-effective manner'.**

*The applications*

**FIG. 6.3.R:** *Value engineering as one facet of cost control*

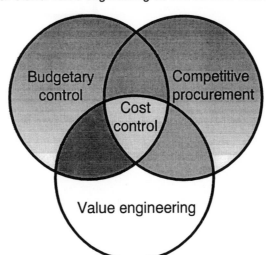

Figure **6.3.R** is a further reminder of the interdependence of the three facts of cost control of which value engineering is by far and away the most significant in terms of achieving overall competitiveness in a project.

In fitting out terms, value engineering can influence the initial (and possibly running) cost of a wasting asset which does not contribute long-term investment value to a company's balance sheet; so, whereas the cost of a new building or refurbishment can be quickly side-lined in importance by gearing up of asset values the same can certainly not be said in respect of fitting out.

In fitting-out there are therefore three main objectives and applications for value engineering:

- selecting the scheme which contributes most to health, well being and productivity of the occupants and the optimum use of the premises

- choosing designs and specifications which meet these requirements for the least capital cost

- choosing capital cost solutions which do not invoke unreasonably high running and maintenance costs.

**FIG. 6.3.S:** *The introduction of value engineering in the cost control process*

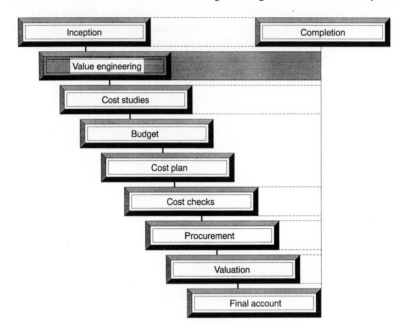

## The processes

As shown in **FIG 6.3.S** the value engineering process should begin in the inception phase, being an integral part of the procedures for establishing the brief and testing design options.

Probably 80% of the impact of the process will be made in this phase but the activity must be diligently pursued pre- and post-contract until all the important decisions have been taken.

The process will be greatly encouraged and improved if a 'challenging' but achievable budget limit is introduced at an early stage, bearing in mind always that it may need to be reconsidered once the cost studies are completed. Such a target cost may be derived from a reliable statistical base, initially by application of experienced conceptual estimating and then by cost studies of apparently appropriate design solutions.

A process which is gaining in popularity is that of the zero-based budget. An application of this technique illustrated at **FIG 1.3.B** in Chapter 1.3 shows how both functional and physical performance may be submitted to the rigours of cost/benefit analysis without over-complicating the decision-making process.

## Minimising costs

The scope for minimising costs is rather less in fitting-out than it is in the construction or refurbishment of a complete building. This is because one of the major determinants, ie: the geometrical aspects of design economics, have limited application in the fitting-out design process.

Specifically, in a construction project, the initiatives which may be brought to bear in the process of eliminating redundant performance are:

- design economics -

    - geometry

    - specification

    - spatial efficiency

- construction economics -

  - 'buildability'

  - speed

It is also important to be aware of the influence that the size and shape of the building may have upon the quantities of different components of cost centres.

**FIG 6.3.T:** *Cost sensitivity of partitions/doors element*

| Examples | | Ratio of area of partitioning / doors to NIA | Element unit rate £ / sq m | Elemental cost £ / sq m NIA |
|---|---|---|---|---|
| Case A | Mainly cellular layout | 2:1 | 60 | 120 |
| | Floor-to-ceiling height 3.7m | | 100 | 200 |
| Case B | Mainly open plan layout | 1:2 | 60 | 30 |
| | Floor-to-ceiling height 2.8m | | 100 | 50 |

In particular, the effect of the building's configuration on the quantity of elements or components has to be taken into account in the context of the 'cost sensitivity' of that element or component. This refers to the relationship between the quantity of the element or component relative to the floor area or some other measure of the total scope of the project. Eg: where there is a very high floor-to-ceiling height and a mainly cellular layout is proposed the ratio of partitions to floor area will be particularly large. **FIG 6.3.T** compares the ratio of partitions to floor area in such a situation, as also in a relatively open-plan layout. In the first case the choice of specification for the 'cost-sensitive' partitions will be important as they may represent between 15% and 20% of the total fit out cost. Applying two alternative unit rates to the area of partitions the potential cost differential is highlighted.

Understanding these ratios is a very important key to understanding the effect of design on cost. The ratio of the element area to net internal area is called the **'Element Quantity Factor' (EQF)** and **the Element Unit Rate (EUR)** is the total cost of the element divided by its overall area. As **FIG 6.3.U** shows and explains, simply multiplying the EQF and the EUR will give the cost of the element per unit of floor area - a very handy way of quick appraisal of alternative proposals.

**FIG 6.3.U:** *Using the element quantity ratio factor for rapid appraisal of cost and cost-sensitivity*

| Full Calculation | | | | |
|---|---|---|---|---|
| A. Element Quantity sq m | B. Element Unit Rate (EUR) £ / sq m | C. Element Cost (A x B) £ | D. Net Internal Area (NIA) sq m | E. Elemental Cost (C / D) £ / sq m NIA |
| 1,000 | 50 | 50,000 | 2,000 | 25 |
| Simplified Calculation | | | | |
| | F. Element Quantity Ratio Factor (EQF) (A / D) | B. Element Unit Rate (EUR) £ / sq m | E. Elemental Cost (F x B) £ / sq m NIA | |
| | 1,000 / 2,000 = 0.5 | 50 | 25 | |

**'Buildability'** is defined as **'the extent to which the inherent characteristics of a building design and specification influence the efficiency and hence cost of the construction process'.** The phenomenon of 'buildability', when it does manifest itself, usually falls to the benefit of the building contractor. Provided the 'buildability' was appreciated (probably designed in) by the client's design team this

In value engineering terms design for fitting-out should address the following 'buildability' goals:

- reduce complexity
- minimise 'learning' time
- optimise on-site time
- optimise site-based assembly
- reduce return visits
- reduce sequential criticality
- improve workmanship
- minimise damage
- minimise waste
- reduce capital costs
- reduce maintenance costs.

## Risks to value-engineering

One of the easiest ways to lose the opportunity to value engineer a scheme is to permit the development of the design concept in an economic vacuum. Good designers are perfectly well able to express themselves creatively within economic constraints and should be made to do so.

Other risks to the success or existence of the process are

- over-stated performance requirements
- excessive budget
- poor design management
- too little time - to consider alternatives
- intransigence - of the designer wedded to his concept
- poor procurement
- poor budgetary control
- inaccurate estimating.

Good project management can overcome most of these risks. The first two simply allow the emergence and retention of redundant performance. The design management must allow proper time for considering change options while poor procurement and budgetary control can frustrate the most diligent value engineering effort.

The problem of inaccurate estimating can be particularly serious. Any architect who has been denied the use of a component on the basis that another is cheaper only to find the out-turn cost was greater, will resist the value engineering process at future stages - and with good reason.

A major fillip to value engineering is a budget which is set as close as possible to the minimum required to achieve the required performance. However, it is often necessary to use typical specification to imply or define performance requirements with the danger of built-in redundancy.

If the risks can be overcome, the financial advantages of strategic value engineering can be quite startling for both capital and revenue expenditure.

## 6.3.8 QUALITY CONTROL

*Quality of design*

The control of design quality is the project manager's responsibility. Getting the quality of the concept right is an elusive goal full of subjectivity and not necessarily influenced to any degree by the way the design process is carried out. That said, concept quality will be the better for having all the known constraints, such as cost or availability of materials, on the table at the initial briefing stage with the concept development process guided by the appropriate specialists.

Design development through to working drawings may be improved by the application of standard quality control procedures such as BS EN ISO 9000 or TQM as described in Chapter 2.2. However, the performance of most consultants is probably best assessed from their track record rather than their commitment to paper pushing. The project manager must make his quality control requirement known at the fee-bidding stage and then ensure that he chooses a designer who patently understands what is required of him.

Both project manager and designer must make sure that there is adequate time in the design programme to do the job properly. Fast-tracking techniques as described below can make a programme look feasible on paper but the designer must defend his corner and the project manager should not pressure him unduly to accept the risk.

*Quality of the works*

Normally the architect or interior designer is responsible for supervising the quality of works on site. The project manager sometimes has this job, (for instance in certain central government projects) in which case he will usually engage an architect or interior designer as sub-consultant in respect of quality control.

On some, possibly larger, projects a Clerk of Works may be engaged to keep an eye on detail but economic constraints have seen a gradual disappearance of this noble discipline from the scene of the action. However the NEW ENGINEERING CONTRACT reintroduces the function in the form of a 'supervisor' who is named in the contract.

Of course, the facilities manager should make it his business to visit the site regularly (and officially) and keep everyone on their toes by looking for obvious deficiencies and praising good performance.

The use of 'sample' panels, areas etc. to set the standards is a worthwhile investment and will be rather more useful than woolly specification terms such as 'workmanship shall be of the highest quality'. Asking for it is one thing, but defining it is another.

## 6.3.9 THE PROGRAMME

*Time and the fitting-out process*

Almost without exception fitting-out projects are required to be carried out in the shortest possible time-frame. Most tenants have a 'rent-free' period at the commencement of a lease affording them sufficient time to fit out to their requirements. Obviously this acts as a spur to the organisation to get up and running before the rent and the service charge begin clocking up.

Once in occupation, re-fitting an area is even more time-critical, given that the organisation is

- paying rent on the 'dead' space

and/or

- possibly paying rent on temporary space

or

- overcrowding the remaining stock.

Whilst allowing too much time for the process will not necessarily result in added value the converse is certainly not true - ie: too little time will guarantee a bad job.

Any premises cost savings through looking to save too much time in the fitting out stage will probably be eroded in the short term by contract claims arising out of inefficient design and contract management. In the post-project era the loss of productivity resulting from a poor quality, ill thought out scheme will be many times more significant than any premises cost savings.

*The time drivers*

Principles and applications for programme management are fully considered in Chapter 2.2.

Apart from the scope of works, factors which will determine the overall length of a project are:

- **pre-construction**
  - early involvement of the constructor - to advise on 'buildability', availability of materials and labour and sequencing of drawings
  - time allowance for thorough development of the brief
  - time allowance for value engineering
  - time allowance for the design development and working drawings
  - experience of the team
    - collectively
    - individually
  - previous working relationships between team members
  - the bidding process - particularly time allotted to interviewing bidders and explaining the scheme to them

- **post contract**
  - the knock-on effects of the pre-construction phase
  - the time allowed for construction
  - the calibre of the constructor's team
  - the extent and timing of changes to the works
  - degree of insistence on quality
  - contractor's financial status - those in trouble may not get credit for the resources they need for the job.

There are legitimate ways to shorten the overall process whilst keeping the risk low - or maybe lessening it. The easiest targets are:

- omitting the single stage tender period which conventionally has to await completion of the working drawings and specification

- overlapping the design and procurement processes

- shortening the construction period by better front-end planning.

# FIG. 6.3.V: Effect of the procurement process on time

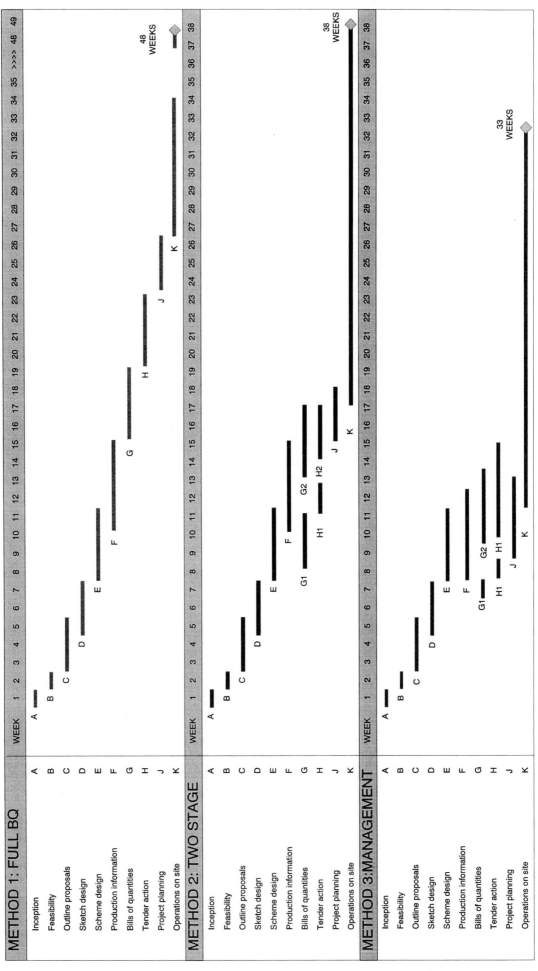

N.B: ASSUMES OPERATIONS ON SITE = 21WEEKS IN ALL CASES

These targets can only be achieved by involving the constructor at an early stage in the project, either by a two stage tendering procedure, management contracting, or construction management or some forms of design/construct arrangements.

**FIG 6.3.V** shows the generic processes of single stage lump sum, two stage tender lump sum and management. Note how the two stage tender pinches time by allowing negotiation of the price of the works as the scheme design, specification and possibly bills of quantities are being developed. In this process, as with the management route considered below, the contract time should also be reduced below that indicated through the constructor's opportunity to plan the work more efficiently and also influence the specification, buildability and drawing production sequence.

The management route saves even more time through appointment of the manager on a fee without the need for a two stage tender document. His even earlier involvement and his client-orientated interest will be of particular benefit as trade contractors are brought in for discussions about their contribution to the works and the programme. The professional manager will also be trying hard to impress and his familiarity with the front end process in which he is asked to participate may well be greater than that possessed by a traditional builder.

Provided that the fast-track programmes allow enough time for each activity and the cost control is sharp the management type of procurement process will not produce higher costs. In fact, the fast-building opportunities generated may save direct costs through simplicity of operations as well as cutting down project time.

In the event it will be the calibre of the team, its members, its personnel and its management which will produce fast projects at reasonable cost to the required quality. Snappy systems and procedures can help but in the wrong hands all the potential benefits will turn into unmitigated disasters.

**Fast projects are more difficult and need better people.**

## 6.3.10 PERCEPTIONS OF RISK

**FIG. 6.3.W:** *Procurement process v risk of price certainty*

The risk in a fitting-out project is in respect of cost, time and quality. It has been proposed above that it is not systems which, of themselves, reduce these risks, but people of the right calibre working within the appropriate regimes under competent management.

For example, many clients get concerned that they are at higher risk of cost over-run the further they move away from the single-source-responsibility procurement route. **FIG 6.3.W** illustrates how the early certainty of price declines as the client gets more involved in the selection and reimbursement of suppliers of services and goods for the project. As seen earlier the ultimate in uncertainty of price is where the employer accepts liability for the cost of the work down to the number of packets of nails delivered to site. In fact, good contractors make good profits from undertaking projects for a fixed price in the face of similar cost uncertainty them-selves; it is therefore logical that, given the same calibre of management available to the aforesaid good contractor, the client would save the profit, risk and over-heads margin otherwise attendant upon a lump sum contract price. At the other end of the scale, making the designer answerable to the constructor affords the employer one point of redress if things go wrong but makes the designer one step removed from the client's authority and allegiance.

The design and construction management process may not bring earlier price certainty; however, the close involvement of the construction manager with the design process should reduce the risk of inadvertent over-expenditure against pre-agreed budgets, and is shown as equivalent risk to the lump sum contract.

A hypothetical comparison between the cost of procurement of a project via either a good lump sum process or construction management is shown at **FIG 6.3.X**. This proposition was offered in support of a recommendation to a client to proceed along the construction management route on 'time' grounds; the 'lump sum' forecast was readily predictable from close and current comparables. In the event both client

**FIG. 6.3.X:** *Effect of procurement process on cost*

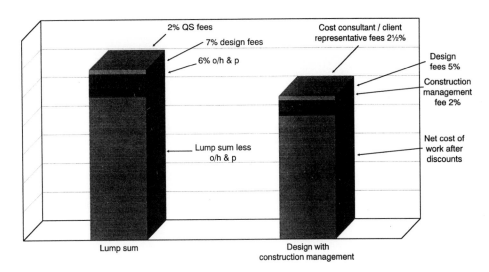

and project manager were rewarded by delivery of the project under a process of **design-with-construction-management** at 10% less than the predictions in **FIG 6.3.X** to an incredibly tight programme; the contingency fund was handed back to the client intact.

## 6.3.10.2 RISK AVOIDANCE

If a fitting out project goes wrong in any respect, for whatever reason (and many are suggested above) proving whose fault it was is never going to be easy; no-one ever wins in building litigation so the best way to avoid losing is to go for excellence in every function needed to deliver the project. If that means paying a little more than peanuts to obtain such services then the extra should be the insurance needed against man-made disaster.

However, if the facilities manager does not thoroughly understand the process or consults a man who undeniably does, how can he possibly take the decision as to which procurement route will deliver the **appropriate quality** at the **right price**, in **time** with the least **risk** to any or all of these critical factors?

[1]    The 'Journal' system of capital cost control – BWA

# PART D

# SUPPORT SERVICES

# SECTION 7

# BUSINESS SUPPORT

# CHAPTER 7.1 – SECURITY

## 7.1.1 RISKS TO SECURITY

*The meaning of
security*

A dictionary definition of 'security' implies a state of freedom from danger, damage, fear, care, poverty - and the precautions taken to ensure against such disbenefits.

In facilities management all these threats can apply - including poverty as a result of failure!  But 'security' can also embrace other activities ie: the by-products of the availability of personnel and technology engaged predominantly on prevention of one or other form of damage to the business.

So, security guards in the main reception area may double as receptionists and 'smart' cards for electronic access/egress may contain the holder's medical history for use in case of accident.

Doubling up of business security with other key visitor and personnel services can be a key determinant in the economics of a security regime as also in the success, or otherwise, of its implementation.  If visitors, staff and management all feel comfortable (or uncomfortable in appropriate circumstances) with, and supportive of, the security facilities which are provided the chances of getting value for money will be enhanced by a large factor - not least because individual awareness of risks to security and the importance of reporting them are probably the single most important determinant of achieving secure facilities.

*The risk
centres*

Typically an organisation is exposed to risk in six categories:

- Premises
- Personnel
- Equipment
- Data
- Informative systems
- Public relations.

In each category the threat is both external and internal to the organisation.

The significance of that threat will also vary depending upon the nature of the business activity, the height of its profile, its location and other specific factors.

The issue is further complicated by the fact that the physical design and perform-ance of a building will itself both present and prevent threats in a way which does not readily afford cost analysis.  Eg: a building over-provided with access points will require a greater degree of security but automatic access control may minimise the on-cost when compared to physical guarding by security personnel.

*Risks to
premises*

The principal risks to premises are:

- Natural disasters
    - fire
    - flood
    - subsidence
    - earthquake
    - tornadoes / hurricanes
- Malicious damage
    - explosion
    - vandalism
    - fire.

Whereas it is normally possible to take out insurance cover against natural disaster it is becoming increasingly difficult to obtain cover against malicious damage, particularly the consequences of terrorist activity.

Chapter 7.10 – 'Disaster recovery' deals with the special measures needed to make buildings secure from terrorist damage and their associated costs.

Other risks to property such as failure of mechanical components, power supplies etc. are maintenance problems which should not be the direct responsibility of the security manager - except insofar as they may be caused by vandals.

*Risks to
personnel*

Apart from the risks to personnel arising out of the damage to premises described above, there are the following threats:-

- theft of personal property
- assault
- health and safety.

Risks to health and safety are considered in Chapter 8.2 and, again, are not the responsibility of the security manager other than protection from tampering with essential supplies such as water and air.

Theft of personal property may be covered by insurance but its impact on staff morale and trust goes way beyond the actual cost of replacement.

*Equipment
security*

Theft and malicious damage in respect of items of equipment such as computers, fax machines, office furniture etc., may be covered by building contents insurance - not that anyone should use this protection as other than a back-stop. In large organisations particularly, the loss of items of equipment is surprisingly common, frequently aggravated by the absence of proper inventory controls; very often theft of equipment is insidious and will go undetected over long periods if such control is lacking.

*Risks to information*

Most organisations possess data which is either

- essential to their own production process
- confidential to their business
- confidential to their personnel
- confidential to their clients.

Some may also possess government classified data.

Loss of or damage to this data will, one way or another, hurt the business either through loss of output, removal of business, benefits to competitors or mere replacement costs. Insurance cover may be available against some of these risks but it is difficult to establish the potential consequential loss when placing the risk - and often even harder to justify it to the loss adjustor after the event.

*Risks to information systems*

Anyone who has ever caused the network to 'crash' through faulty application of a program will know that this is an enormous risk which can only be controlled by a really high level of training for all who do, or might, load up a program.

Just as serious, and increasingly problematical, are the computer 'viruses' which find their way into a system via one program or another and infect it such that the whole system may malfunction with file structures on hard disks being destroyed, floppy disks contaminated and data lost irretrievably. These 'viruses' are maliciously introduced and are undetectable until triggered by a pre-determined event. The best way to protect against viruses is to produce regularly maintained anti-virus software and also to draft contracts of employment forbidding copying of unauthorised software on to office systems.

Backing up data is another well-understood but frequently overlooked risk management technique. Routines must be thoroughly drafted, understood and religiously observed. Once a day - at lunchtimes - is a good practice in most situations. Automatic recovery and 'mirroring' software are further sophisticated options to guarantee retrieval of 'lost' files - but not protection against corruption from faulty power supplies.

Power supply variations - surges or reductions - can cause the power supply to fail with particularly serious consequences to data inputted but not backed up and also corruption to the data file header records. A line-conditioner is an economical first line of defence by maintaining the voltage level. However, to prevent loss of power at the computer as well as maintaining the voltage, an uninterrupted power supply (UPS) is necessary. This entails a large store of batteries which are automatically available to pick up a failed power supply. **The capital cost of a UPS might range from £500 to £1000 per KVA depending on the extent of the computer installation and the size of the building giving a cost of around £10-15 per m² of gross internal area.**

In critical installations a dedicated 'clean' line can be supplied direct from the main distribution board to the processor. The capital cost of such a provision is not excessive - **eg in a building of 5,000m² gross internal area, clean supplies to one sub-distribution board per floor - including sub-main cabling, earth boundary and final cable runs – will cost less than £3 per m² gross internal area.**

The risks to systems discussed above - plus unauthorised access to files by unauthorised system users - are the responsibility of the system manager, not the security manager.  The risks the latter will have to guard against are:

- access by unauthorised personnel
- theft of software and hardware
- malicious damage to software and hardware.

*Risks in public relations*

External public relations - ie impact on the passer-by, visitor or casual observer - will be affected by:

- quality of reception
- exposure of any inadequacy or inefficiency eg unsuccessful disaster prevention
- apparent efficiency
- courtesy
- delays or inconvenience.

Apart from the above external issues, internal public relations will be prejudiced by personal debilitation, theft and regular vandalism.

In this, as in so many operating cost centres, the consequences of a building's physical and functional performance on the performance of the occupiers can often be disproportionate to the amount of actual expenditure involved.

## 7.1.2 SECURITY MANAGEMENT

*The security policy*

The decision to provide security to one degree or another can only be taken by corporate management;  the principles and objectives should, however, be stated positively in the organisation's premises policy statement.

The facilities manager's job is to make sure that the efficiency and cost of the security strategy is reasonable relative to the agreed policy, the potential loss and the degree of exposure to risk.

The grades of security have been defined by Grahame Underwood [1] as:

Grade 1 –  Deterrence of vandals and casual criminals (opportunists); reservation of minor confidentiality (for example, personnel files).

Grade 2 –  Protection of low values against the deliberate criminal; preservation of high confidentiality;  protection of high values against vandals.

Grade 3 –  Protection of moderate values against the deliberate criminal.

Grade 4 –  Defence of high values against organised crime.

Grade 5 –  Defence of terrorist targets (may be added to any of the above)

## 7.1.3 SECURITY METHODS AND SYSTEMS

*Security control activities*

Management of the security risk must address the following activities:

- external access/egress control
- internal access/egress control
- surveillance of activities
- reporting of events
- immediate and long-term remedy.

Most security systems use a combination of human, mechanical and electronic resources. They will seek to detect and/or deter intruders and to detect and prevent natural disasters.

Human resources take the form of

- dedicated security personnel
- the general staff - through their alertness to dangerous situations and willingness to report promptly and clearly.

Mechanical resources include physical barriers such as doors, grilles, smoke detectors, sprinklers etc. and electronic resources include means of opening and closing access points, detectors, video cameras and so on.

Each of these resources has a different measure of sophistication, cost, risk and effectiveness as is discussed below.

*Dedicated security personnel*

In all but the smallest or lowest-risk premises it is essential that security staff be properly trained and carefully selected. In practice this condition is almost universally met by the use of security firms, which supply properly trained, uniformed staff on periodic contracts to an extent of provision agreed with the employer.

A security officer should be used to accepting responsibility, observant, resourceful and have good presence of mind. For special assignments he may need to be specially trained but in the normal course of events he will have been trained under the syllabus set up by the British Security Industry Association (BSIA) - **FIG 7.1.A**. He will also have received on-site practical training under supervision and at the security firm's expense.

A key factor in choosing the security firm - apart from the quality and training of its employees - is the extent of management support available to the man on site on mobile patrol. Security firms are normally set up on a regional basis. Each region will have a hierarchy of managers and inspectors. Operations are controlled through a 24-hour, heavily protected control room which usually doubles as a central alarm monitoring station. Managers and inspectors should make frequent visits to the site and these visits should be logged; any points noted by inspectors should be followed up immediately by the management.

It is quite easy to assess the quality of the security service from first impressions when calling at a site; it is particularly common for the service to fall away after the first few weeks of the contract.

**FIG 7.1.A:** *Training syllabus - British Security Industry Association*

| | |
|---|---|
| Uniform | a) Maintenance and importance of the companies' uniform and accoutrements |
| Standing orders | a)Standing orders regarding pay, sickness benefits, grievance procedures.<br>b)Standing orders regarding reporting for duty and performance of duties.<br>c)Reporting on/off duty, check calls. |
| Security duties | a)Powers of uniformed security officer<br>b)Security of keys, maintenance of key register<br>c)Patrol activities<br>d)Cash-in-transit procedures<br>e)Key points - use of clocks and other key point systems |
| Static duties | a)Reception, access/exit control<br>b)Security of keys, maintenance of key register<br>c)Patrol activities<br>d)Key points - use of clocks and other key point systems |
| Verbal communication | a)Methods of approach to staff at all levels, visitors and members of the public<br>b)Use of telephone, radio, clarity of speech and 24 hr clock |
| Written communication | a)Use of daily occurence/vehicle log book<br>b)Other site books<br>c)Incidence reports |
| Fire<br>first aid<br>bomb alerts practical | Fire drills, use of basic appliances<br>Basic knowledge plus 'when not to touch'<br>Report and evacuation procedures<br>a)Visiting sites - various types<br>b)Site training - supervised training specific to site detail |
| Exercises | a)Radio exercise, voice procedure<br>b)Report writing exercises<br>c)Fire exercises |

Depending on the degree of risk, cover may be:

- day time only - static guard

- 24-hours - static guard

- day time only - static guard plus mobile patrol

- 24-hours - static guard plus mobile patrol.

On an office building of up to, say, 10,000m², the typical costs for security cover for five days a week would be as in **FIG 7.1.B.** Cover at the lower levels would only be acceptable in either a grade 1 or 2 risk or where there was a high level of security system back up.

**FIG. 7.1.B:** *Typical costs of guarding a 10,000 sq m GIA building 5 days a week*

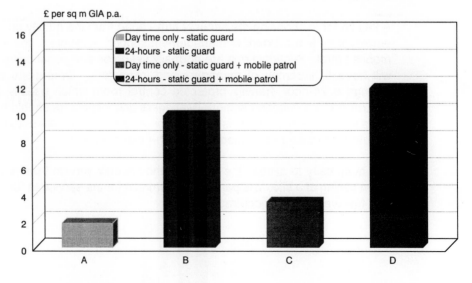

£ per sq m GIA p.a.

Legend:
- Day time only - static guard
- 24-hours - static guard
- Day time only - static guard + mobile patrol
- 24-hours - static guard + mobile patrol

Across the board security ranges from the low levels indicated above to as much as £30per sq.m GIA for high risk buildings such as data-centres. Use of security personnel for commissionaire duties or as receptionists can help to keep costs down but this will not always suit the company's desired image.

Contracts are normally tendered and are for a one-year period. The full range of supporting systems available under the contract eg central alarm monitors, key-holding, radio network, should be set down clearly. There should be adequate insurance for:

- Public liability - £5m is common
- Employer's liability - unlimited
- Efficacy and contractual liability - £5m is common
- Fidelity bond - £10K is common
- 'Loss of key' insurance - £2.5K is common.

*General staff awareness*

However thorough or sophisticated the security personnel and systems may be, no organisation will have satisfactory security unless the general staff are fully aware of and willing to apply the necessary level of alertness, surveillance and speed and clarity of reporting required of them.

A simple real-life example of how important this attitude may be is where a multi-tenanted provincial office building opens directly on to the High Street with only a part-time security guard/receptionist and a proximity card reader/entry telecommunication system. At lunch-time, after the guard has gone home, the office staff come and go; some of them, on exiting, will hold the door open for those outside (whom they may not know!) to come in out of the rain. This is a very common situation in smaller buildings where external management leaves much to be desired.

The worst excesses of this type of breach can be avoided by including simple procedures not only for preventing illegal entry but also for challenging unauthorised personnel and/or alerting management to their presence. The same goes for training in respect of reporting fires, water ingress and other sources of natural or mechanical disaster.

Although it is the non-core visiting staff such as cleaners and guards who are the first to come under suspicion for petty theft or vandalism, it is surprising how often the culprit turns out to be a regular - sometimes popular - member of the core staff. Although Personnel can avoid the employment of undesirables the whole staff must always be aware of the need to leave their workplace and their personal belongings in a secure state; wallets in breast pockets of coats over chair-backs are just asking to be stolen!

*Intruder detection systems*

Systems normally contain a combination of some of the following features:

- alarms
- detectors
- door viewers
- surveillance mirrors

- central control

- personnel devices

- closed circuit tv (CCTV).

In addition to specialist systems, the design of buildings, and in particular external and internal lighting, can be important aids to detection. **FIG 7.1.C** reproduced from the manual, *Design Economics for Building Services in Offices (DEBS)* [1] shows a typical initial security control installation.

**FIG. 7.1.C:** *Generic security control installation*

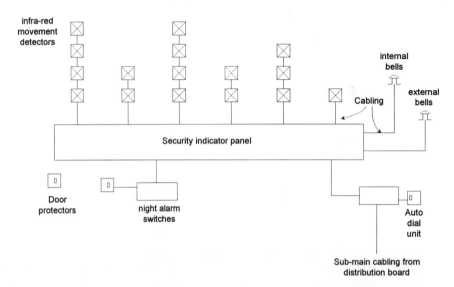

The system analysed is for the whole building and provides protection to all exits and entrances to the building with visual or audible alarm during periods of non-occupancy. There would be one security indicator panel at ground level connected direct to the internal/external security bells, infra-red movement detectors, door protectors, night alarm switches and auto-dial unit - all at ground floor level.

**Capital costs range from as little as £0.50 per sq.m of GIA in very large buildings to around £2.50 per sq.m of GIA on buildings of 2,000 sq.m or less.**

**FIG. 7.1.D:** *Generic closed circuit television (CCTV) installation*

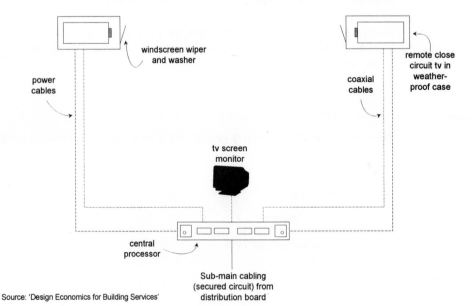

Source: 'Design Economics for Building Services'

**FIG 7.1.D**, from the same source, looks at external CCTV. This system is usually used to supplement conventional systems particularly where there is a high 'foot-print' area or a large level of external area requiring surveillance. The central control processor will include camera control positions and zoom facility, video recording and screen monitor. This is connected to remote, closed-circuit tv cameras by power and co-axial cable; in the example in **FIG 7.1.D**, a building of 2,000m² might need four cameras whereas one of 30,000m² might need 10/12. **Here again, the capital cost of security is many times cheaper per m² GIA in the larger buildings dropping as low as £1 per m² of GIA from the level of £8-10 per m² GIA in the smaller premises.**

Sometimes systems are added which could enable the personnel complement to be reduced but, particularly where security staff are in-house, there is a tendency for management to turn a blind eye to the consequent over-manning. This is also often the case where the risk in a building changes as a result of departmental relocation.

*Intruder deterrence systems*

Barriers, barbed wire, plain or electrified fences and extensive external lighting are a highly effective first line of deterrence. Close-up and internal security, door viewers, entrance telephones and entrance video systems are again very effective at putting off would-be intruders.

Protection of designated areas from intrusion by members of staff as well as outsiders is usually controlled by some form of card-key system. Such systems have various levels of complexity and can be zoned to provide many levels of status or graded access.

Access control, with the aid of modern technology, is more and more concerned with controlling movement of people about a building rather than merely discouraging unauthorised entry. Systems will be either

- self-contained ie: electronically programmed to accept or deny access - cheap but relatively effective for low-grade risk

- on-line ie: card-readers feeding information to a central computer

- networked ie: provision of 'intelligent' readers on a network, the number and location being variable as user requirements are modified; this is the most sophisticated, but is cost-effective in larger buildings and estates, especially where 'churn' and change are prevalent features.

In each case the type of access card or token will be a critical decision. The type of 'key' will affect the cost of the reader as also ease of use, copying, issuing and up-grading and the speed and number-limitations of access.

The access control is normally either

- proximity-based

- card-based

- remote.

The proximity-based cards or tokens can be kept on a key-ring and, as they are only held close to the reader, do not wear out or get damaged. They are more expensive than the plastic 'swipe' cards. The remote systems work like the 'proximity' keys but can be operated from a distance - just like the electronic door-locking devices on cars.

'Smart' cards can double as a medical records, 'phone cards or even as credit cards! They hold the data themselves, not the computer as in traditional card-access systems.

Another newish development is of biometric devices which can 'read' personal characteristics - expensive but 100% secure.

An analysis of the initial cost of a high-security proximity system in a building of 10,000 sq.m GIA is given at **FIG 7.1.E**. If the cost were to be annualised the ensuing figure would be midway between the high and low levels for day-time only human guarding given at **FIG 7.1.B** above.

**FIG. 7.1.E:** *High security proximity based access control system - capital costs for 10,000 sq m GIA office building*

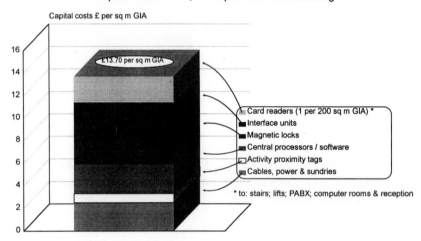

**FIG. 7.1.F:** *Conventional intruder deterrence system - generic layout*

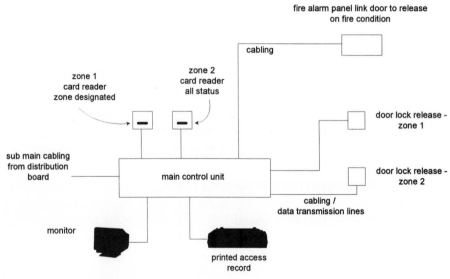

Source: 'Design Economics for Building Services'

The example from *DEBS* at **FIG 7.1.F** is of a far simpler conventional system with two levels of access and costing between £1.00 and £3.00 per sq.m GIA. The main control unit has a VDU screen and maintains a printed access record. It is linked by power cable/co-ax to fire alarm, card readers and door lock release. In this example, smaller buildings would have the whole of each floor independently zoned, whereas the larger ones would only be zoned to protect the main core.

Building components such as security grilles, locks and enclosures together with 'strong' features like anti-bandit glass all make their contribution to deterrence and prevention. The technique of cost-benefit analysis should be applied to all these add-on design features rather than their being provided at whim. Also, the effect of the introduction of security features on the insurance premiums must always be investigated.

## *Fire protection*

Fire and flood detection is normally solely a mechanical function comprising sensors and alarms. Control and/or extinction may be manual or automatic or both. The security staff should be trained to deal with the fire problem although often it will be the staff themselves who have to take initiatives. Larger premises usually have a dedicated fire officer - his costs should be allocated to security.

**FIG 7.1.G** shows how the capital cost of the fire protection by different means varies between the four generic office types in *DEBS*.

**FIG. 7.1.G:** *Capital costs of alternative fire protection installations - range of building sizes*

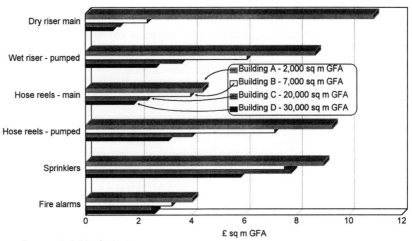

Source: 'Design Economics for Building Services'

## *Conclusions*

Security is a highly specialised field and one in which the cost of provision of personnel, components and systems varies considerably. Generally speaking, buildings suffer from too little rather than too much security. Nor can the level of security be easily gauged or interpreted from taking benchmarks from other organisations. In the sample given at **FIG 7.1.H** the range is very considerable and is obviously variable by many factors including, grade of risk, the mix of human and mechanical systems and procurement routes. When appraising alternatives the capital and operating costs must be compared eg: as in **FIG 7.1.J** which compares a mainly human guarding resource with a 'mixed' human and electronic control system.

**FIG. 7.1.H:** *Security costs - representative sample of prestige offices*

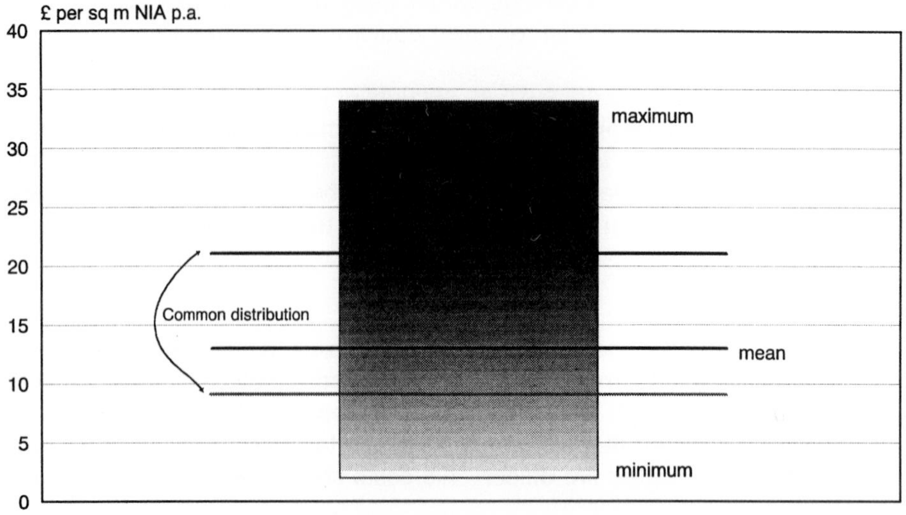

Cost-benefit analysis in respect of all three types of provision - personnel, components and systems - should be encouraged and when new buildings are on the drawing board the facilities manager must get the design team to set an **operating budget** for security in the context of their built-in **capital cost provisions** for security. He should always encourage them to think about the security implications of their design; a great deal of capital and operating costs can be saved - and disasters prevented - by talking to security experts before finalising design proposals.

**FIG 7.1.J:** *Comparative costs of electronic and human guarding for access control*

| 1. High security access control system as 7.1.E | | |
|---|---|---|
| Capital cost | £140,000 | |
| Amortise over 10 years - say | £20,000 pa | |
| Maintenance | £1,500 pa | |
| Replacement tags | £1,000 pa | |
| Central monitoring - security personnel - say | £20,000 pa | |
| Total costs pa | £42,500 / 10,000 sq m = | £4.25 sq m NIA |
| 2. 100% Human guarding | | |
| Say 1 per 1,000 sq m : 10 guards @ £12,500 pa (inc O / H + P) | £125,000 | |
| Total costs pa | £125,000 / 10,000 sq m = | £12.50 sq m NIA |

[1]  'Design Economics for Building Services' – (Building Economics Bureau Ltd, Bromley Kent)

# CHAPTER 7.2 – STORAGE

## 7.2.1 RECORDING AND DISTRIBUTING INFORMATION

*Paper in the office*

In spite of the prophesies to the contrary the 'paperless' office is no nearer than it was a decade ago. 90% of documents are still held in paper form - all that new technology has done is increase the amount of data which can be generated by computer operators in a working day; office paper is expected to double in volume in the next five years. Many letters are faxed prior to posting and the volume of redundant word-processed amended drafts lying around in files is bordering on the criminal.

Against this background employees' aspirations regarding the quality of the working environment have put pressure on space planners to reduce the clutter of filing cabinets at and around the workstation, while the same employees are in receipt of the greater volume of data referred to above.

Office space grows ever more expensive - a prime target for cost reduction - and efficiency of the storage operation is at risk through the human factors ie: mis-filing, and the cost of manual filing per se.

A recent estimate by the International Records Management Council indicates that the average document is copied 19 times and costs £14 to keep stored. Worse, the cost of mis-filing a document is an average of £84 including time spent trying to find it and/or replacing it.

Local on-site storage can absorb up to 5% of gross usable area, with archive space on-and-off-site sometimes as high as 15% of an organisation's total space requirement - although the off-site space will be a lot cheaper per unit of area. Consequently more and more documentation is being transferred away from the office filing cabinet - either to remote storage or on to microfilm or electronic disk.

The economics of storage and retrieval are extremely complex especially when the productive output of the user is taken into account - as of course it must be to make any sort of economic sense of the decision-making process.

## 7.2.2 STORAGE AND RETRIEVAL OF PAPER DOCUMENTS

*The business requirement*

Paper documents provide information to which reference may have to be made on many occasions. The decision as to whether the document should be on the desk, in the desk, adjacent to the desk, remote from the desk, or remote from the building should be dictated primarily by the needs of the user to access it, rather than the facilities actually available to contain it.

Documents obviously vary in importance. The routine business correspondence tends to have an active life of 5-7 working days before being relegated to its place in the file where it may well live on or near the workstation for up to 2 years. Once the project is completed it may be shredded or, as in the case of legal documents, building projects etc., stored remotely in one form or another either in perpetuity (as a last will and testament) or for a term of years to comply with the Statute of Limitations.

It is no longer necessary to generate or keep most documents in paper form - only legal records cannot sensibly be put to the risk of irretrievable electronic corruption. Nevertheless most people still correspond and record on paper and the facilities manager needs to find the optimum solutions for controlling access and storage.

*On - and off - site document filing*

Wherever practical in business and premises terms documents should be kept in the cheapest appropriate space available. Archiving in low-cost basement areas and/or off-site premises must be found for all but those files in regular use which have to be kept locally on site (unless available electronically or on microfile).

There are 3 main categories of local filing:

- drawer-based floor cabinets / lateral filing
- cupboard style wall units
- mobile track units.

Floor cabinets occupying 'dead' space under a work surface do not incur a premises cost penalty; where free-standing cabinets form a boundary within an open plan scheme this cost is mitigated but each unit still consumes several times the space of a free-standing screen.

Wall cabinets in theory do not take up floor space but care must be taken not to create dead space beneath them.

Mobile shelving systems running on floor tracks are relatively expensive to buy but save on circulation space associated with banks of group filing cabinets.

There are various ingeniously planned storage systems which can increase the volume of documents stored within the capacity of a storage unit and various types of filing systems can also impact on this form of space efficiency.

If the documents are needed locally on site for regular access then all these options need to be thoroughly evaluated in the context of space consumption and the commercial deals available on the products.

Where such access is not required then the on/off site storage equation needs to be worked through.

**FIG 7.2.A** shows how the physical (as opposed to image) document storage equation may be calculated. Note that there is an allowance against the remote storage for the theoretical extra cost of re-fitting the floor space to achieve the more intensive use of the space freed by the outing of the floor cabinets; however, in practice this might well be achieved by simple re-arrangement of furniture and the provision of screens (not included in the calculation).

In the example a serious under-estimate of the numbers of retrievals would, in practice, erode the remote storage saving. On the other hand, if existing filing arrangements are inadequate then the cost per item retrieved by staff in-house could well be much higher than the estimate given.

If the extra space freed up by the elimination of the storage furniture avoided the upheaval of moving or taking on more space that might be a big bonus. Of course, a sensitivity test of various rental levels would also have a major impact. The example presumes a provincial town; Central London costs could triple the on-site penalty with no counter-effect on the off-site alternatives. Equally, if you cannot use the extra space efficiently there is no advantage to be gained other than better planning.

FIG 7.2.A: *Typical appraisal of on-site v self-managed off-site storage*

| On - site | £ / pa | Off - site | £ / pa |
|---|---|---|---|
| Leasing costs - say 100 × 4-drawer filing cabinets for group storage | 1,000 | Say 200 boxes @ £5 pa (including sorting and boxing) | 1,000 |
| Retrieval by staff: 500 items @ £3/each | 1,500 | Retrieval by staff: 500 items @ £5/ each (excluding any charges) | 2,500 |
| Space occupancy costs (including circulation) 1,000SF @ £20/SF NIA | 20,000 | Re-planning & fitting out 1,000SF NIA @ £20/SF: £20,000 over five years say | 5,000 |
| **Total costs** | **22,500** | | **8,500 \*** |

## 7.2.3 MICROFILMING

When records are in regular use, being continually referred to, amended, annotated and circulated it is really better to keep them on paper until they achieve 'passive' status. At this point off-site storage of the paper documents may be a viable option. The physical option has been examined above but another common solution is microfilming.

Microfilming, as the name implies, is a photographic process using either 16mm or 35mm rolls - roll microfilm - or 100mm flat microfilm which is called microfiche. The latter is most commonly used in normal day-to-day business.

Microfiche consumes only a tiny fraction of the space occupied by documents. Because the initial set up costs are high the system comes into its own when large volumes are involved. Equally, the less retrieval required the better although 'active', as opposed to 'inactive' or 'passive systems', can be economical where retrieval at the speed of a paper system is necessary.

Here sophisticated indexing is the key, possibly linked to a data-base in the larger systems. However, since it is the cost of indexing which is the most critical factor in microfilming the level of detail to which it extends must be considered most carefully. Microfilm rolls can store up to 2,500 pages without indexing whereas a fiche can hold as few as 60 pages - expensive but indexable to that level of detail.

For most microfilm users, however, it is the inactive or passive system which is in use. Simple indexing systems can separate those files which are most likely to be retrieved from those, such as important legal deeds, which may need to be accessed from time to time. The legal profession has taken quite extensively to microfilm (usually the microfilm rolls containing many more documents and being comparatively tamper-proof) and there is now a British Standard (BS 6498:1984) dealing with its use in evidence.

As **FIG 7.2.B** shows the cost implications of using microfilm when the example at **FIG 7.2.A** is raised to a different volume of documentation.

Where documents are required to be kept for a long time the amortisation period can be extended with a consequent large reduction in the annual equivalent cost of the initial filming ; microfilm is expected to remain usable for up to 80 years.

Microfilming is shown managed off-site by a Bureau in the example. On-site processing and storage means that the documents never leave the site which may be important where active papers are involved. Nevertheless in-house training costs - and, of course, the non-core activity argument (see Chapter 1.1) - must be taken into account at option appraisal.

**FIG 7.2.B:** *Comparative costs of microfilming*

*and physical off-site storage*

| Off-site storage | £ pa |
|---|---|
| Say 10,000 boxes @ £3 pa including sorting and boxing | 30,000 |
| Retrieval by staff say 25,000 items @ £0.20/ each (excluding any charges) | 5,000 |
| Total | 35,000 |
| Microfilm bureau | £ pa |
| Initial filming say 20M pages @ 1p each = £200,000 - amortised | 50,000 |
| Film storage on-site say 1,000 sq ft NIA @ £20/sq ft | 20,000 |
| Staff training - say | 5,000 |
| Bureau management charge - say | 50,000 |
| Total | 125,000 |

In business efficiency terms microfilm provides a safe, well-organised, permanent, easily duplicated and distributed means of dealing with and avoiding losing/misfiling records. It is a well-established medium supported by sound bureaux and well-tried and tested technology.

Clearly it saves an enormous amount of space and is hard to fault in terms of both facilities and production economics once the volume border-line for viability has been crossed and users have come to accept its rigours, slow rate of retrieval and enforced changes of habit.

The change-over can, however, cause an enormous hassle; many organisations leave the backlog in physical storage and apply the microfilming process to new records only. Modern processes also permit direct filming from computers; a system known as Computer Output Microfilm (COM) replaces the line printer with a COM recorder.

## 7.2.4 ELECTRONIC FILING

These systems are variously termed:

- document image processing (DIP)

- electronic data (or document) management systems (EDMS)

- optical informational systems (OIS)

- electronic information and image management (EIIM).

They all save a digitised copy of paper on a storage medium - usually an optical disk. The documents are readily retrievable at a pc or workstation and can, if required, be printed out.

One optical disk can hold up to the equivalent of two fully-loaded four-drawer filing cabinets - about 13,000 A4 pages. The pages can be scanned and stored up to a rate of 40 pages per minute. However, this rate does depend heavily upon the condition of the documents. Eg: if there are a lot of staples, clips and other attachments which have to be removed prior to scanning/digitising the rate will drop and preparation costs increase accordingly.

There are three categories of system:

- stand-alone

- distributed

- integrated.

Stand-alone systems contain all the components needed to carry out image capture, processing, retrieval and display. Their economic use is limited to low volume or undemanding applications.

Distributed systems can have multiple personal computers networked with several servers. Resources of a system are distributed to provide the optimum file/facility performances and workstations for viewing and retrieval.

Integrated systems are large scale systems in which database and application software is run on a computer that will control the file server linked to workstations via local area networks (LANS).

Any purchase of an integrated system must be considered a long-term investment and have the expansion and overall growth potential built in.

Two types of disks are available for this application.

WORM (write once read many) - the files stored on here cannot be altered or erased; it is the cheapest form of electronic filing and is ideal for archiving.

RE-WRITABLE - allow files that are stored to be updated when needed; it is ideal for files in current use and can also be used to transfer directly into store documents which have been viewed on E-mail. However the hardware costs quite a bit more and the storage disks are that much more expensive than, say, CD's which are not re-writable. Even with re-writable disks, the contents of the document itself cannot be re-written; the page is viewed only as a picture and that page may only be removed and replaced with another.

Some companies tend to use the re-writable optical disk to store their live records, financial details etc. and at year end convert these files to the cheaper CD storage format.

With some systems it is possible to retrieve an archived filmed page and convert it into digital format if it is needed more frequently. This serves to provide a convenient bridge between fast access electronic media and low cost archival film media, in many cases providing an ideal solution to document management.

At present the initial cost of this system limits its use to large, fast moving offices where information is needed very quickly. As more systems are developed and the supply goes up the costs will come down and the electronic systems will be available to the smaller business user.

These systems, once installed, can dramatically increase the productivity of the staff as well as saving considerable space. However, a great deal of these productivity gains rely on correct indexing and filing along with good systems management, especially where optical disks are used to store and manipulate live records such as invoicing. If the system is not thoroughly thought through in terms of indexing, cross-referencing etc., then the premises goal of achieving a cost reduction in terms of storage costs may well be totally outweighed by a dramatic loss of productivity.

The legal profession, that great consumer of document space, does not accept electronic filing due partly to the risks of security but also through a general mis-trust of the technology and the perception that irretrievable corruption could bring about disaster.

Its speed of retrieval, computerised indexing, multi-user access and low operational costs make the system compare favourably with microfilm, which does begin to look a dated process in this age of IT. Nevertheless the set-up costs both in terms of capital investment, digital scanning (one page at a time though still a lot faster than microfilming) and system conversion again make the system best suited economically to the larger volumes of documentation. The state of the organisa-tion's IT culture will obviously make a big difference to the ease of introduction and implementation of an electronic system.

**FIG 7.2.C** shows the costs of a typical electronic filing system for comparison with the physical and microfilm examples at **FIGS 7.2.A & 7.2.B.**

FIG 7.2.C: *Typical calculation of large-scale electronic filing system costs*

| Cost Breakdown | £ pa |
|---|---|
| Initial data entry 20M pages @ 2.5p each = £500,000 - amortised | 125,000 |
| Staff training | 5,000 |
| 'Re-writable' software | 2,000 |
| Maintenance - say | 5,000 |
| **Total** | **137,000 \*** |
| N.B. Speed and frequency of retrieval may be a critical factor justifying the slightly higher annual expenditure.<br>* Excludes any additional costs of IT support installation. | |

**Of course, as with all the examples in this text, the actual levels of cost in these theoretical calculations will always depend upon the market conditions at any one time; the figures used to illustrate the issues must not be taken as categoric evidence of the economics of the various approaches.**

# CHAPTER 7.3 – STATIONERY

### 7.3.1 THE CONTENTS OF THE COST CENTRE

*Definition*

The term 'stationery' originally meant writing materials such as paper, pens, ink, blotting pads and rulers. Over time the true meaning has been distorted as a result of vendors - be they retailers, wholesalers or direct distributors - extending their activities across a whole range of consumer-related products.

So, for example, stationery retailers now also sell newspapers, tobacco and confectionery - and some provide a sub-post-office function. With regard to offices the suppliers of pens and paper long since grasped the opportunity to sell in everything conceivable in terms of small workplace consumables, plus, in many cases, larger items of office equipment from waste-bins and filing cabinets to desks, photocopiers and pc's. Some will also plan the space and fit it out!

Consequently, the cost centre is one which, not having been subjected to the same sort of benchmarking rigours as its premises counterparts, **is likely to be found analysed on the basis of the category of supplier rather than the nature of the items making up the bills.**

The classification at **FIG 7.3.A** is therefore suggested as a means of introducing a semblance of order into a cost centre which, though not particularly large, is still just as important financially as cleaning or building maintenance and often outstrips them for cost without a terribly good reason.

**FIG 7.3.A:** *Suggested classification for the 'stationery' cost centre*

| Sub-category | Contents | |
|---|---|---|
| General office paper products | Bespoke stationery - <br><br> Plain paper products - | • letterheads & continuations<br>• envelopes<br>• business cards<br>• forms/memos etc<br>• photocopier paper<br>• pads & notelets |
| Personal desk stationery | Writing materials & - accessories | • pens, pencils, erasers<br>• staplers, hole-punchers<br>• calculators |
| Storage stationery | Document holders - <br><br> Filing systems - | • filing envelopes<br>• ring binders<br>• filing trays<br>• suspension systems |
| Presentation materials | Document presentation - <br><br> Display presentation - | • report cover sheets & backings<br>• binding machines & materials<br>• overhead projectors & foils |

However in the first instance it may be more practical to separate what is called 'stationery' in this classification from all the rest of the goods coming through on the office supplier's bills.

Taken across the board, and excluding those maverick items, paper-based goods are by far the biggest component of the bill. Even where the hardware items (including computers and furniture) are left in the analysis, the costs of paper goods still outweigh the general consumable items by about 2:1. **FIG 7.3.B** is one office supplier's estimate of the percentage value of goods supplied across the board. The lowish percentage of items of furniture in the table reflects the fact that major purchases of office furniture are generally made direct with the manufacturer.

**FIG 7.3.B:** *Percentage value of goods supplied to all customers by a typical office supplies company*

| Goods supplied | Percentage | Comments |
|---|---|---|
| Consumables | 20% | * |
| Books, paper & pads | 14% | |
| Envelopes | 10% | |
| Computer supplies | 9% | * |
| Bespoke stationery | 9% | |
| Filing & storage | 8% | * |
| Machines & consumables | 6% | * |
| Office furniture | 6% | ** |
| Desk accessories | 4% | |
| Office accessories | 3% | * |
| Writing & graphic supplies | 2% | |
| Presentation & planning | 2% | |
| Diaries | 2% | |
| Personal accessories | 1% | * |
| Packaging | 1% | |
| Washroom supplies | 1% | ** |
| Catering equipment | 1% | ** |
| Safes & fireproof cabinets | 1% | ** |

NB: * Includes some items excluded from the 'stationery' cost centre
** All to be excluded form the 'stationery' cost centre

Source: Office Plus Ltd (Union Street, London SE1)

## 7.3.2 THE USE OF PAPER

The paperless office refuses to materialise. Continuing growth in the consumption and waste of what is now recognised as the product of an environmentally un-friendly use of raw materials, has meant mounting bills for paper in tandem with the increased cost of the technology which was expected to replace it.

Such is the demand worldwide for paper products that the pulp manufacturers' prices have risen well above general inflation, these prices now finding their way into the end-users' bills. The biggest cause of the accelerating demand is the increase in production of printed and photocopied material as laser printers and high-speed photocopiers have become more and more an integral part of the office output process. Not only are users producing more copies -they are also matching the paper quality to the high quality of the graphic and printed output made possible by the modern equipment.

### 7.3.3 STATIONERY COSTS

*Costs per capita*

**FIG 7.3.C** gives a range of stationery costs from a wide sample of organisations of all shapes and sizes. Although the data is not as finely sifted as some other cost centres analysed in this text there is a solid consistency about the common distribution which reinforces the level of some of the better-analysed statistics forming the core of the sample.

**FIG. 7.3.C:** *Typical range of stationery costs per capita across a wide sample of disparate organisations*

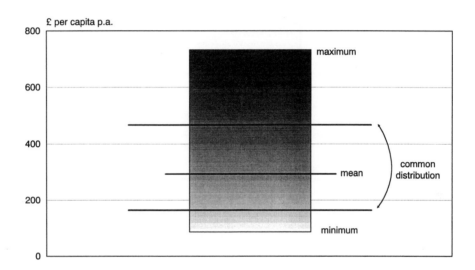

*Economy measures*

There are several ways to cut down on excessive expenditure under this cost centre. The first, and most cost-effective, is to **dedicate** one person to **cost control** of 'stationery' - the 3 facets of cost control as described in Chapter 2.2 and not just procurement or budget reconciliation. At the average cost of £300 per capita in the sample an organisation of 500 employees would be spending £150,000 pa on stationery. An employee dedicated for 1 day of his/her time per week to controlling the costs would need only to effect a 2.5% saving to justify the role - and pro-active control of an otherwise unpredicted upwards spiral could be even more beneficial. In larger organisations the payback for the same investment would be even greater.

Critical measures to achieve effective cost control would be to:

- analyse the cost centre at budget stage into the categories suggested above or as practically convenient for benchmarking and budgetary control purposes

- prepare the budget analytically and by reference to benchmarks in a form such as suggested in **FIG 7.3.D** – this will provide both justification for the estimate and a base from which to track change pro-actively

- set up a stock control system and monitor key categories on a regular basis; this will not only avoid running out of stock but also indicate areas where change in processes or type of project or numbers of personnel, or inherently wasteful practices are likely to break the budget

- dispense consumables from a central source - do **not** leave then to be picked up from an uncontrolled stock area (Editor's note: I have just counted 85 biros in my dressing-table drawer - there are about another 100 in a bag under my desk, retrieved guiltily two year's ago from the same source!)

**FIG 7.3.D:** *Preparation and presentation of the stationery budget*

| | Category | Components | Budget per capita £ | Number of employees | Total £ |
|---|---|---|---|---|---|
| 1. | General office paper products | A Headed notepaper<br>B Copier paper<br>C Fax paper<br>D Envelopes & labels<br>E Books and pads<br>F Business forms<br>G Packaging materials<br>H Sundries | 180 | 850 | 153,000 |
| 2. | Personal desk consumables | A Writing equipment<br>B Typing accessories<br>C Collating and adhesive accessories<br>D Sundries | 60 | 850 | 51,000 |
| 3. | Storage stationery | A Ring binders and files<br>B Filing systems<br>C Visible record systems<br>D Storage boxes<br>E Sundries | 30 | 850 | 25,000 |
| 4. | Presentation materials | A OHP foils and storage<br>B Slides and storage<br>C Presentation equipment<br>D Seminar / conference incidentals<br>E Sundries | 15 | 850 | 13,000 |
| 5. | Administration | Clerical assistant 1/1.5 days / week | - | - | 5,000 |
| | Totals | | | | £ 247,000 |
| | Total per capita | | | | £ 290 |

- check the prices of a key sample of goods on a regular basis against the supplier's competitors

- make sure that quantity discounts are always applied where applicable

- check each bill thoroughly and query **any** discrepancy, however trivial - it will keep the suppliers on the ball and your interest may draw a better service out of them

- take an interest in the processes consuming the stock, and look for ways to **value engineer** the way stationery is used in **every activity**

- do not waste time trying to recycle waste paper in the office as scrap pads;  it takes a lot of effort and people will not use them anyway.  It is better to concentrate on recycling the waste paper externally; at least that way a token contribution will be made to the overall cost of paper from recycled sources

- try to purchase as many products as possible from **low-grade** recycled material - this will help to make its collection and re-processing commercially more viable

- always match the quality to the need - Conqueror left in the photocopier paperfeed from the last report is apt to be host to many images not worthy of the quality it offers

- always remember that exceeding the stationery budget may be the result of increased or more profitable business compared with that forecast; the key to cost control is in identifying the changes in advance of un-budgeted excesses (budgetary control) and being all the time on top of the relationship between the business requirement and efficient use of the consumables supporting it

- remember the lesson from 'Pareto's principle' - that 80% of the cost will be in 20% of the goods purchased - and pick out the key cost drivers for particular and constant analysis and monitoring.

If a dedicated cost controller cannot be resourced then there are firms who specialise in doing that job for no cost - just a share of the saving they will surely make from anyone's average spend on stationery.

# CHAPTER 7.4 – PRINTING AND REPROGRAPHICS

## 7.4.1 HARD COPY REPRODUCTION

*The processes*

At one time printing was what book publishers and newspapers did and photocopying was something the office junior did in the occasional idle moment.

In the mid 1990's printing is done on high-speed, high quality photocopiers in the office from graphic material produced by computer from in-house laser printers. Meanwhile external printing is cheaper than it ever was through the development of presses which can produce excellent and inexpensive full colour copies - as easily as black-and-white - from a disk supplied direct from the office without the expensive process of colour-separated artwork.

The term 'printing' to the office worker is now as synonymous with the ink-jet on the end of his pc 'print' button as with production of the Daily Mirror. Both processes stem from the same technology but **bulk** printing and **graphics** printing are not yet differentiated correctly in the minds of those who analyse office services costs.

Just to confuse the issue the so-called 'industrial' photocopiers are capable of producing 'printed' quality mono-colour documents in small quantities at a low cost reflecting the absence of a need for the plate-making and set-up time which made the printing process so costly for short-run work.

So, not only are the economics of the process changing - the location is also varying, not just the point of reproduction but also the origination.

*Origination*

A wide range of graphic and desk-top publishing software packages gives the organisation the opportunity to produce in-house those important prestige documents and visual aids which used to go out to the graphic design house for manual artwork. Those same houses these days use much the same software as the in-house originator; the difference is in the design skills of the professional which may not be available in-house unless dedicated graphic designers can be afforded and kept busy on a full-time basis.

For a special publication such as a company report and accounts or a product operating manual, the cost of origination will be anything from 15% to 50% of the total cost; at the lower end are found the low-circulation slim reports where printing costs of a small publication tend to be high due to 'make-ready' time, and vice versa.

*Reprographics*

Modern photocopiers are judged on six issues:

- quality
- productivity
- creativity
- reliability
- size
- price.

High quality is more or less taken for granted, with the increasingly sophisticated built-in electronic controls able to monitor performance and, in many cases, adjust the operating settings to correct any fall-off in the pre-set quality. Eg: variation in drum toner deposition, temperature, humidity and exposure may be picked up by a sensor and automatically re-adjusted to suit, and advanced all-digital machines can be connected to the maintenance monitoring team by modem for 'remote diagnosis'.

This improved performance does mean more capital cost but on the other hand can significantly reduce 'down time' as well as guaranteeing quality and producing copies more quickly.

Two-sided copying obviously saves 50% on paper, which can reduce by up to one-third the total cost of producing a photocopied report. This process has been speeded up by better document-feeding and paper-handling: paper paths are now shorter and can handle a large range of different paper sizes including re-cycled stock. 50-100 gsm copier paper can usually be accommodated in cassettes, stackers and trays while manual by-pass feeders will cope with acetate film for transparencies as well as paper up to 200 gsm.

Operator time is a big feature of photocopying, especially where long repetitive runs are involved. Internal memory in the latest copiers enable complex sequels of instructions to be memorised, freeing the operator for other tasks. This is particularly important in smaller 'top heavy' businesses where senior and expensive specialists sometimes tend to do their own copying to cope with rush jobs.

On some machines commonly used sequences can be programmed by inserting a credit-card sized memory card or remotely using a desk-top editor which may be a battery-operated portable. The all-digital copiers are now making inroads into the mid-range market. Their increased productivity through digitally once-only-scanned images stored in memory, two-sided copies being produced without a duplex tray, electronic storage of pages in the correct order, plus creative features such as wide zoom range, merging of images, addition of text and comprehensive editing make them attractive to organisations highly dependent upon high resolution, high speed domestic copying.

The facility to interact photocopiers with the computer network is an added bonus with some of the latest models.

FIG 7.4.A shows a generic range of photocopiers together with typical capital costs while FIG 7.4.B works out on a theoretical base the cost per copy (excluding paper) in a typical copy run. It is interesting to see how the machine cost per copy remains relatively constant as the runs get bigger, whereas the staff time in attendance reduces to a less insignificant figure. This is partly due to the programmable routines of the larger more sophisticated machines but also to the fact that the set up and retrieval time per copy are much less as the runs get longer - just like the old 'make-ready' time in traditional printing. Of course, where two sided copying is concerned the larger fast machines can halve the paper and machine cost with little penalty in terms of attendance time; with large quantity discounts this means that the paper costs will come down by about 0.25p per page of the document saving almost 0.4p per copy overall.

Colour photocopying at the rate of 10 copies per minutes in full photographic colour is typical of the high end of an increasingly sophisticated market which has yet to develop at the rate anticipated.

**FIG 7.4.A:** *Typical capital and running costs for various grades of photocopier*

| Reference | Generic Features | | | | Capital cost £ |
|---|---|---|---|---|---|
| | Paper supply - sheet | Copies per month | Basic speed - A4 | Duplex speed | |
| 1 | 1,000 | 8,000 | 15 / min | 1 / min | 2,500 |
| 2 | 2,000 | 20,000 | 30 / min | 10 / min | 7,500 |
| 3 All-digital | 4,000 | 50,000 | 50 / min | 20 / min | 15,000 |
| 4 All-digital | 5,000 | 75,000 | 60 / min | 45 / min | 19,000 |
| 5 All-digital | 6,000 | 100,000 | 80 / min | 50 / min | 22,000 |

**FIG. 7.4.B:** *Typical machine and operating cost per copy of each generic type of photocopier*

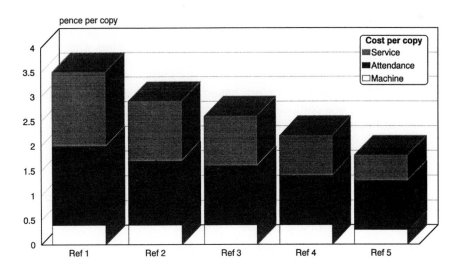

*Machine printing*

This process which was traditionally based on printing presses using hand-set lead characters was overtaken in the late 1960's by the off-set lithographic process. This has remained in place as the principal system with the machines developing in sophistication, particularly electronically, and now able to print direct from disks.

More economical than reprographics over long runs there is yet little difference discernible to the lay person between off-set litho and state-of-the-art 'industrial' photocopiers in terms of quality.

Few companies contemplating bringing their printing in-house (bucking the trend nowadays) would consider other than high-quality reprographics given issues of cost, quality and simplicity of operation and quality control.

*Computer printing*

The object of the computer printer is to produce the 'artwork' from which pages can be reproduced by photocopier or lithographically.

The generic printing types are:

- dot matrix

- ink jet

- laser

- l.e.d.

The **dot matrix** printer is the cheapest in terms of capital cost although letter quality can only be achieved on the top 24 pin machines.  Most organisations having dot matrix printers will use them only for internal reporting.

Output speeds are quite good, paper handling is flexible and some of the better quality machines can handle graphics and connect up to ink-jet colour printing. They tend to be a bit noisy and are rapidly losing out in the market to the laser printers.

The **ink jet (bubble jet)** machines are the middle of the range with quality higher than dot matrix and approaching that of laser.  They are the slowest process and the ink is smudgable for a minute or two after printing.  Small, lightweight, quiet machines they have good colour options at a reasonable cost and are particularly efficient for putting graphic images on to paper.

**Laser printers** have taken the market by storm with prices getting lower and more competitive all the time.  They can produce professional looking documents at high speed, have excellent paper-handling capabilities and can produce high quality colours.

A new breed of printers based on light emitting diodes (**l.e.d's**) matches laser quality at a competitive capital price.  They are noisier than lasers but considerably cheaper to maintain.

## 7.4.2 PROCUREMENT

Important matters to consider when choosing a copier or printer are:

- monthly volume

- the expected growth of the company

- requirements for colour copies

- the main need for photocopier

- how much space is available for the copier

- quality

- extent of collating

- speed of output

- extent of use of mainly A4 copies

- frequency of need to enlarge/reduce/two-sided copying.

Photocopiers and printers are all available with a full range of procurement options. They can be purchased outright or leased with a variety of plans and tax benefits similar to that described in detail for motor vehicles in Chapter 7.9 below.  However, lives of the printing and reprographic machines are normally only about 3 years, so depreciation and rental are comparatively high.

The majority of copiers are leased and only ones used for low volumes are bought outright. The types of lease/rentals available are:

**Copy Plan** - a rental is paid for the machine and then a charge is paid for the number of copies made

**Service Plan** - a rental is paid for the machine and a quarterly charge is paid to cover any services necessary for the machine

**Straight rental** - a fee is paid for the rental of the machine only, any call-out charges being invoiced at cost.

There has been concern in recent years about copyplan and leasing contracts which has led to a number of major suppliers to issue codes of practice. The problems occur because most manufacturers deal at arms length with the end users of the machines. When getting into a copier contract it is important to know the monthly volume of copies.

A Marplan survey recently revealed that 63% of UK companies were paying too much for their copying services.

Things to consider before entering into a contract are:

- monthly volume of copies

- length of contract desired

- type of contract wanted eg: copyplan, service plan

- future company needs

- the full contract implications eg: some contracts can only be changed by paying 45% of the remaining rentals, so getting the contract right at the start is essential

- many companies get taken in by 'X000 copies free' - this has usually already been added to the capital cost of the machine.

## 7.4.3 THE IN-HOUSE PRINT DEPARTMENT

It is a fact, that along with the 'first impression' of a company portrayed by the telephonist/receptionist, the quality of the printed material emanating from a company either by way of marketing/publicity material, mail-shots, annual reports, presentations, general correspondence, and even architect's drawings speaks volumes in to-day's highly competitive market place.

With the technology now available, the days of the dark and dingy printroom, billowing clouds of ammonia from the dye-line machines somewhere in the basement, are over.

The printroom now is very much an integral part of the business, working in close co-operation with every department in an organisation with a need for one.

Generally speaking, photocopiers are still to be found on every floor for use by all employees as required, but the printroom is manned by specialist personnel with machines capable of producing high quality material.

However, the large industrial photocopiers capable of producing direct copy (mono or colour), enlarging/reducing, trimming, collating, folding, stapling/binding documents at high speed, need to be sited where the resultant noise will not invade the general ambience of the organisation.

The innovation of CAD in recent years, has largely made obsolete the need for dyeline printing in those organisations with the necessary technology to enable the information to be sent direct to a plotter sited in the printroom from a pc anywhere in the building.

Given the requisite volume of business and relevant expertise there is no reason why the in-house print-room should not be just as efficient as the outsourced version. All other things being equal it is all down to the quality of management, the funds available to fund the inevitable and relentless upgrading of technology and the vigour with which the core versus non-core issues are raised and contested.

## 7.4.4 THE ANNUAL COSTS

Costs for a wide variety of organisations per capita pa are given at **FIG 7.4.C**; although the larger companies have more expensive equipment the economies of higher volumes even it out. They also tend to go for a consistently higher quality - to an extent inadvertently, for the productive high speed copiers generate the quality automatically.

**FIG. 7.4.C:** *Sample range of reprographic and printing costs per capita p.a.*

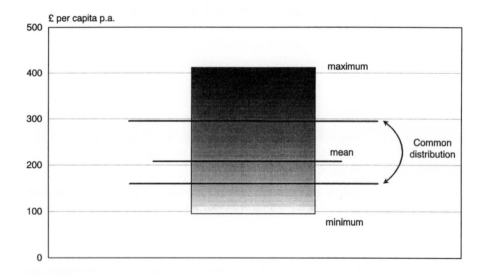

Overall, as with 'stationery' in Chapter 7.3, there is no discernible pattern of difference in the wide-ranging sample of large and small organisations - however there are some critical differences in the way the cost centre is analysed. The principal issues are whether or not paper and attendance are included; this analysis **excludes** paper and **includes** attendance.

Where printing is outsourced the cost of the paper should be asked for separately to enable the costs to be analysed comparably with an in-house cost **excluding** paper. Most printers quote for large jobs on a separated basis anyway, so it should present them with no problems.

# CHAPTER 7.5 – INFORMATION TECHNOLOGY

### 7.5.1 IT AND THE BUSINESS

*The origination
of IT*

The term 'information technology' - IT - was culled in the 1970's when the first main-frame computer installations were installed to supply computing power to carry out simple functions like calculation of wages and salaries, preparation of fuel bills etc. These early computers had limited processing power and only a tiny memory, unlike the computers now almost universally available to every office worker. Eg: an IBM mainframe running 50-100 terminals in the '70's probably had no more than 4Mb of random access memory (RAM - see below); in fact the same power is now available on the desk-top at 0.1% of the cost.

The advent of wholesale cheap computing and information exchange facilities has been made possible by the development of **transistors** manufactured out of tiny wafers of semi-conductor material such as germanium or silicon. Transistors have the ability to use a small current to switch on or off a large current. Several transistors can be integrated into a circuit to perform logic functions such as addition and subtraction. The technological advances in integrated circuit fabrica-tion over recent years have enabled these transistors to become progressively smaller and perform more complex logical functions at higher speeds; known commonly as (micro) chips they form the central processing function (micro-processor) in a small computer.

*The effect of IT
at the
workplace*

Modern developments described below such as local area networks, telecom and wide area networks and satellite communications have made possible not only tremendous improvements in the quality and output of the computer-user but also the conditions and location in which the operation takes place. In many cases keys pressed in one country can deliver a message to a screen in another, and simpler developments enable the operator to function from home or a 'satellite' office in his or her locality - so changing the traditional office-based regime.

The IT facilities and the premises and other support services are so closely inter-related both physically and financially that there is a very strong argument for linking them more closely, if not totally integrating them under one facilities man-ager.

Although it is nowadays quite common for the data-cable management to be under the facilities manager's supervision the other components of systems management are often beyond his control. One reason for this may stem from a lack of familiarity with some of the principles of the technology and the equipment and installations

**FIG. 7.5.1.A:** *Turnover, profit and facilities costs*

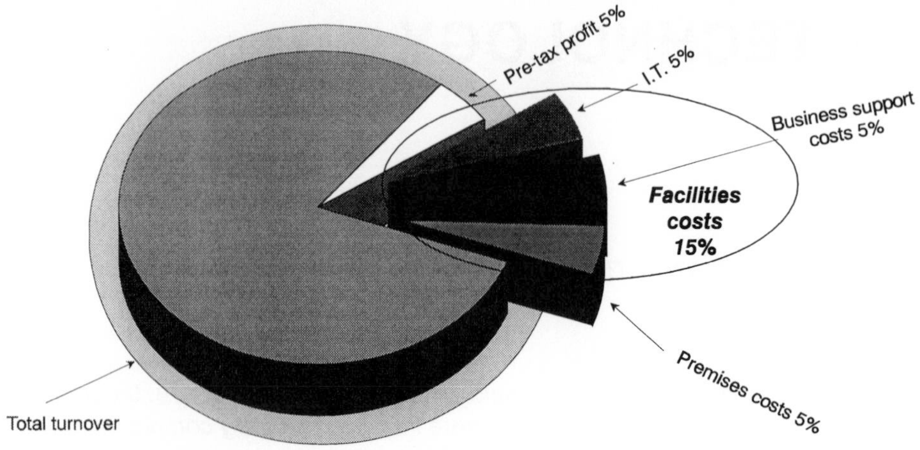

Pre-tax profit 5%

I.T. 5%

Business support costs 5%

**Facilities costs 15%**

Premises costs 5%

Total turnover

e.g. Turnover p.a. = £50m (profit p.a. = £2.5m / facilities costs p.a. = £7.5m)

driving it to the top of everyone's list of non-core financial commitments. **FIG 7.5.1.A** indicates a typical relationship between the costs of IT and the other facilities in the context of annual turnover.

## 7.5.2 BUSINESS COMPUTER INSTALLATIONS

*Types of installation*

In simplest terms installations are either

- mainframe

- mid range

- fileserver & pc.

**FIG.7.5.2.A:** *Mainframe computer installation*

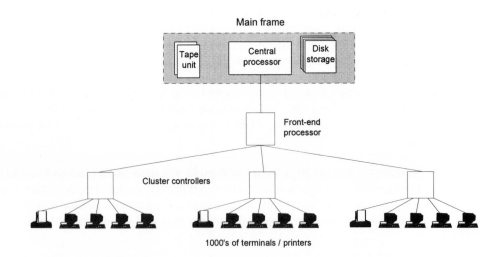

Illustrations of typical arrangements for each of the three generic networked layouts are given in **FIGS 7.5.2.A-C** (inc).

**FIG.7.5.2.B:** *Mid-range type installation*

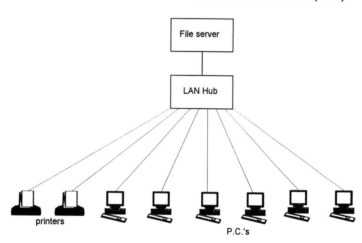

10's or 100's of terminals, printers or P.C's 'emulating' terminals

**FIG.7.5.2.C:** *File server and local area network (LAN)*

Stand-alone PC's still have a minor role to play where, for example, security requires that data is not held on the network, or requires a guaranteed response time which the network cannot deliver if overloaded. However, as they need a dedicated printer and cannot connect to another terminal or program they have become something of an anachronism in the modern office.

The mainframe central processor is conventionally linked to terminals dedicated to specific functions. Development of the concept of client/server systems, in which the processing is divided between the client (for display functions) and the server (for data access and processing) has heralded the beginning of the end for the mainframe, potentially relegating it to the role of little more than a large file server. At half the cost of a mainframe some client/server distribution systems can support hundreds of pc's for sophisticated applications. However mainframes continue to be used for really large applications like airline reservations and cash dispensing networks.

### 7.5.3 NETWORKS

*The function of
a network*

The purpose of a network is to enable information to be relayed to and from a number of terminals which may be 'dumb' ie: having a keyboard and screen but no processor or disk - as in a dedicated mainframe situation - or intelligent, operated by a micro-processor accessing the network and a local hard or floppy disk. The network enables each PC workstation user to share the programs available, giving rise to the concept of a 'multi-user licence' for most widely distributed programs such as word-processing, spreadsheets, data-bases, electronic mail and CAD.

Networks may be either:

- Local area networks (LANs)

- Wide area networks (WANs)

*Local area
networks
(LANs)*

These, as the name implies, apply to an individual office, or a locally grouped collection of offices.

**FIG. 7.5.3.A:** *Ethernet network arrangement*

Traditional Ethernet bus

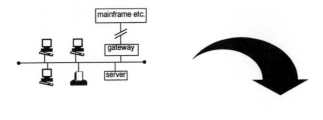

Typical realisation

10MBps Ethernet with a fibre backbone and twisted pair copper distribution is the market leader. Token Ring which today uses similar cabling methods and can achieve 16MBps is favoured by IBM customers. The conventional system arrangement of both types of LAN are given at **FIG 7.5.3.A and B**.

A new technology called 'Asynchronous Transfer Mode' (ATM) is forecast to become the standard in due course. It is capable of deriving image and voice - as well as data - economically in real time and can run at 155 MBps

The fast version of Ethernet and Fibre Distributed Data Interface (FDDI) both run at 100 MBps but are comparatively expensive; ATM has the advantage that it can use existing data grade category copper wiring. Also ATM is quickly becoming standardised, a problem for the earlier systems, and is expected to be the catalyst for the spread of multi-media communications to the workplace.

Meanwhile LAN users will have to continue to rely upon intelligent hubs, bridges and routers to try to overcome performance deterioration due to congestion.

**FIG. 7.5.3.B:** *Token ring network arrangement*

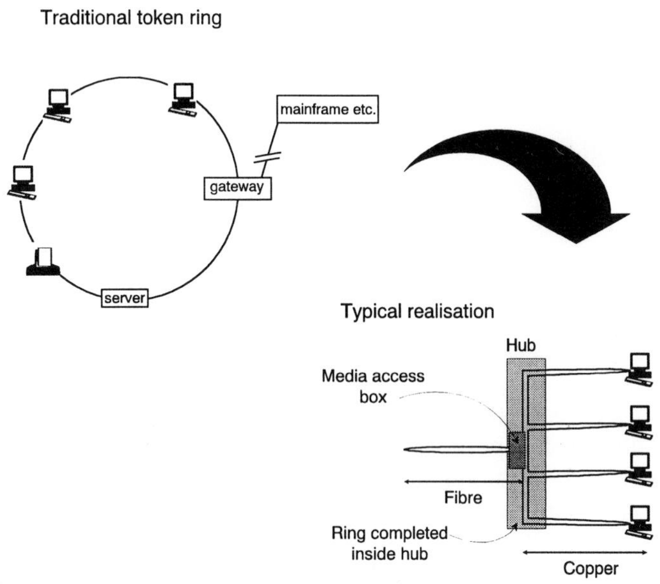

Radio LANs are commercially available, and possess the potential to cut down the cost of the enabling physical accommodation - false floors etc. The bandwidth for the current generation is limited to 1-2MBps and it is hard to see how they will ever replace wired LAN's which are already capable of 100-155MBps.

*Wide area networks (WANs)*

These systems enable inter-office communications by public network over longer distances nationally and internationally.

In the past WAN's have been associated with relatively low-speed data lines connecting branch offices to mainframe data centres. Recently there has been growth in demand for inter-connecting LANs at data rates of 2-8MBps.

*Value added networks*

Network operators are increasingly offering 'value added' network services such as electronic data interchange (EDI) which is the descriptor for the exchange of business documents, like invoices and orders, in a structured form between computers. There are going on for 10,000 EDI users in the UK alone, and the technology is developing and expanding all the time.

## 7.5.4 THE HARDWARE

*The main components*

The principal kit in a system comprises:

- processing unit
- hard disk
- disk drive
- random access memory (RAM)
- monitor
- printer/plotter.

The **processor** is the 'chip' in the pc or mini-computer which does all the hard work.

The **hard disk** holds all programs and data. However, the computer has its own built-in operating system linking the processor to the **Disk Operating System (DOS).** Both built-in operating system and the DOS have to be on if the machine is to work. Hard disks in DOS usually have a capacity from 70 to 250 megabytes - plenty of space for data and text but image applications can use up to 1Mb per colour A4 page.

**Floppy disks** or **diskettes** are portable disks which are easily transportable, but carry only a relatively small amount of data. Disks are coated on one side (SS) or both sides (DS) with magnetic film which holds the encoded data.

Diskettes of the 3½" 'high density' variety are now the norm for handling daily routine data, with a capacity of 1.4 megabytes. A new range of removeable hard disk cartridges is now available capable of sorting up to 21Mb but their formats are not yet fixed as standards. **CD ROMS** (compact disk read only memory) have a much greater storage (a 3½" CD-ROM can hold up to 128 Mb of data) but require availability of expensive hardware to 're-write' them. As discussed earlier in Chapter 7.2 - 'Storage'; they are particularly suitable for keeping large volumes of information for reference only or distributing application software.

**Random Access Memory (RAM)** is the facility used by programs to hold the data in store while in operation. Every program's requirement varies according to the degree of complexity; DOS-based systems need a minimum of 4Mb, autoCAD requires 12Mb and UNIX 16+Mb. Any hardware running a **'graphic user interface' (GUI)** such as Microsoft Windows must have at least 8Mb available.

**Monitors** or **Visual Display Units (VDUs)** may be monochrome or colour (ie: 8,256 or 16.7 million shades according to the price paid!) and need to be carefully specified if eye-strain (and possible contravention of Health & Safety legislation) are to be avoided.

**Printers and plotters** should be able to transfer output either to paper or direct to film. The earlier 'dot matrix' printers are still used extensively for mass generation of data but monochrome high-resolution laser printers can now cope economically with high volumes of output for presentation.

**Plotters** originally relied upon fibre tipped pens but this has been superseded by inkjet technology which can produce reasonable quality text and graphics; colour inkjet printing is not suitable for high quality presentation where thermal colour printing can provide a high quality, but expensive output.

## 7.5.5 SOFTWARE

*Principal
processing
applications*

**The operating system** is responsible for low level functions such as reading and writing data to disk, responding to the keyboard and displaying characters on the screen. All application software uses these low level functions to drive the hardware.

**Graphic user interfaces** are becoming an almost universal feature of all operating systems. The 'windowing' applications using 'point-and-click' icons are taking over all forms of program access including the note-book type of portable equipment. Windowed access shortens the learning curve by presenting a logical user interface.

Apart from the operating systems the principal categories of software applications in everyday use are:

- word-processing programs

- spreadsheets

- data base handling programs

- presentation graphics

- accounting

- desk-top publishing

- computer-aided design/draughting (CAD)

- image processing.

Most of these are familiar and CAD is discussed in the context of computer-aided facilities systems at Chapter 2.2.

**Image processing** programs enable storage and reproduction of photographics quality monochrome and colour images.  The images require considerable storage space on disk in 'bitmap' files.  In contrast CAD graphics require less disk space than bitmap images.

The advent of multi-media including live video at the desk-top is further revolution-ising the graphic output of the pc.

## 7.5.6 SYSTEM COSTS

*The cost
centres*

IT system costs are usually presented per capita per annum

The cost sub-centres suggested for more detailed analysis are as follows:

- **Personal computing including local area network and departmental file servers**

    - Depreciation

    - Hardware maintenance

    - Purchase of pc software and software upgrades

    - Staff costs of supporting hardware and software including help desk etc.

- **Main-frames, mid-range systems and corporate fileservers**

    - Depreciation

    - Maintenance

    - Annual licence fee for operating system, database software and corporate applications eg: electronic mail, Lotus Notes.

    - Wide area network charges

    - Staff costs of supporting main-frames, mid-range systems and fileservers.

- **IT management**

    - IT management and administration staff costs

- **Disaster recovery**

    - Back-up hardware, software etc

- **Exclusions**

  - It is normal to exclude from the above licence fees and staff costs associated with developing/enhancing business application soft-ware.

*Annual costs analysed*

**FIG 7.5.6.A** gives a typical range and analysis of costs for IT installations at a density of 1:1.

**FIG. 7.5.6.A:** *Typical range of IT costs per capita p.a. at a density of 1:1*

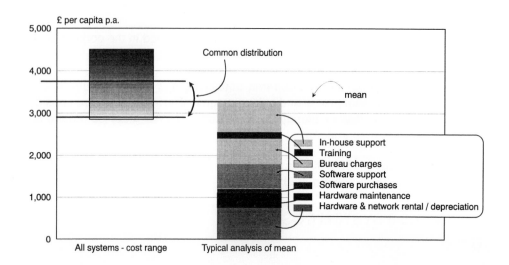

Because of the wide range of alternative configurations, it is neither feasible nor wise to provide typical costs against specific types of installation.

*Hardware maintenance and support*

The costs are fairly consistent with the complexity, and hence capital costs of the hardware. **Depending on the exigencies of the call-out requirements the annual costs will normally be between 5% and 10% of the original purchase price.**

*Software maintenance and support*

The better programs have a 'help desk' facility to guide the user through operating difficulties. The main cost driver is the continual need to update; in many cases the purchase price will include for a certain number of updates, and/or offer them at large discounts.

*Software licences*

The licence is for a given number of users of the software and is a component of the price paid. Use of a program in excess of the licensed number is a breach of contract and copyright and is more easy to detect than many transgressors realise.

*System management*

The management of the system embraces

- cable management

- condition and loading monitoring

- backing-up strategy

- application training

- proactive advice on availability, performance and price of new hardware and software.

In a large installation a number of personnel will be dedicated to this function, possibly working to a director or senior manager with special responsibilities in the field. As a rough guide an organisation of 1,000 employees with a 1:1 terminal:user regime might need one dedicated systems manager for four assistants - say 0.25% of turnover. The ratio would be lower in a larger organisation and vice versa

However, much depends on the complexities of a system, its age and the flexibility of the cabling system. **Structured cabling** requiring only one type of cable to support all commonly available voice and data systems is a major bonus to the systems managers, especially given the usual proliferation and availability of useful equipment and systems and high 'churn' rates.

Some of the latest systems are designed with a special 'hub-based' connector enabling repositioning of workstations to be carried out in a fraction of the time required to relocate a conventional floor box.

## 7.5.7 INTELLIGENT BUILDINGS

*'The intelligent building in Europe' study*

The research project under this title on which this section is based was undertaken by DEGW and Technibank together with their European group-related subsidiaries.

The main goals of the project were to define a new European user-focused model of building intelligence and to produce a competitive analysis and forecast for the European intelligent building marketplace.

*The costs and benefits of intelligence*

There is a lack of comparable data on the costs and benefits of building intelligence, particularly data that relates these technologies to the overall effectiveness of organisational performance in the workplace. Even before such data can be made available, it is necessary to define an approach to understanding and measuring the cost and benefits of intelligence.

The approach of the research project in defining intelligence in buildings moved away from technical definitions of intelligence towards understanding intelligence in terms of what an organisation is trying to achieve within a building or workplace.

Three goals of an intelligent building have been defined:

- building management:

  the management of the building's physical environment using both human systems (facilities management) and computer systems (the building automation system)

- space management:

  the management of the building's internal spaces, such as space layout, location of partitions, terminals and the management of cables, over time. The overall goals of effective space management are the management of change, the minimisation of operating costs and the satisfaction of the end user

- business management:

the management and support of the organisation's core business activities and working patterns. In most cases this is characterised as a combination of ideas and information in many forms.

These three goals have then been translated into a number of key tasks or activities which technologies are designed to support.

The three tier model of the goals of intelligence in buildings is obviously geared to the ways in which an organisation will perform its activities in the workplace. The critical problem of measurement is then how to understand the relationship between these goals and what the technologies offer.

The researchers proposed that measurements of costs and benefits that capture the link between organisational performance and intelligent technologies have to distinguish between *efficiency* and *effectiveness* benefits.

This concept, but related more generally to building performance as a whole, has been discussed in detail earlier under 'The performance of buildings' at Chapter 1.2

## Efficiency productivity

Efficiency benefits are understood to be straightforward cost reductions in the physical provision of a service or activity within the intelligent building. These are operational cost savings. The benefits would include savings, for example, on energy, maintenance, and re-configuration costs. They are cost savings that are relatively straightforward to identify and measure in a before-and-after time period. They allow for hard numeric targets to be set, against which savings can be measured. Such targets can be established on the basis of benchmark comparisons, internal experience and following the use of commercial/sales information. These cost savings are easier to measure than effectiveness gains, and may be less important in terms of total business impact, but are essential as part of making a business case for intelligent systems.

## Effectiveness productivity

**Effectiveness productivity is understood as benefits associated with increases in work output and quality for the organisation within the intelligent building**. This may include increases in turnover, higher quality performance, or improved levels of staff and customer satisfaction. Effectiveness improvements will be measured against the particular kinds of business being undertaken by the tenant or user. In general, it is likely that the more dynamic, fluid and changeable the work processes of an organisation, the higher the expectations and demands for support and contribution from the building. Individual companies will set their own objectives relating to their expectations of the building and its performance. Assessing this performance in financial terms is very difficult.

Assessment will depend on the definition of objectives of the organisation to be set against building performance characteristics. **Suppliers should develop models for organisations to attempt these kinds of measurements**.

## Additional costs or disbenefits associated with intelligence

In addition, an organisation may also experience additional costs associated with intelligent systems, for example for the constituent technologies themselves and for their maintenance. They may also experience real disbenefits from building environment or over-dependency on technology, or problems in staffing and managing the technologies.

Neither efficiency nor effectiveness benefits have been widely measured by suppliers of technology or by users of intelligent buildings, so the problems of measuring effectiveness gains continue to obstruct informed design-decision-making.

Efficiency gains, understood as cost savings in operation, have been identified by suppliers and users for many kinds of intelligent products and services. The problem is that these cost savings alone cannot always justify the capital investment which brings about the wider qualitative benefits of building intelligence for organisational performance.

The greatest added value for organisational performance from building intelligence will be from the hardware and software that will allow the redesign of the work processes and heighten the quality of work performance. The measurement of such gains will necessitate suppliers and users collaborating on measurements of the integrative effects of these technologies on the overall performance of the user's organisation.

However, it is clear that there are gaps in our understanding of the total effect of intelligent systems on overall organisational performance.

# CHAPTER 7.6 – COMMUNICATIONS

## 7.6.1 INTRODUCTION

The world is shrinking, so the cliché says, not just physically because of increased speed of physical transportation, but also because of the ready transfer of voice, image and data via radio, telephone, television and fax.

The previous chapter on information technology considered some aspects of audio-visual communications; the specific economics of telephone, fax and video and the physical activities and costs involved in moving hard copy externally and internally are considered here in greater detail.

## 7.6.2 TELEPHONE COMMUNICATIONS

*Services available*

Voice communication is available via:

- public switched telephone network (PSTN)
- cellular radio telephone
- cordless telephone.

Additionally, paging and voice-mail systems, including those linked with a **pabx** (private automatic branch exchange), can alert users to the need to make contact when they are away from their desk.

Within the past decade the old **analogue public exchanges** have been gradually replaced with **digital technology**. The latter convert analogue speech into numerical code and send a stream of 'binary' numbers. This 'digital' transmission can be regenerated over long distances without introducing noise or distortion. In addition digital signalling provides almost instant call set-up and connection.

Most exchanges in the UK have now been converted, and it is expected that 1995 will see 100% country-wide coverage. On the back of this digital switching and transmission capability network operators have introduced Integrated Services Digital Network (ISDN). There are two ISDN facilities available:

- ISDN2 is appropriate for smaller-scale business activities such as branch offices of large organisations, or small/medium-size businesses and provides two 64MBps voice/data channels
- ISDN 30 is aimed at medium-large firms and provides up to 30 x 64MBps voice/data channels.

Current connection and rental charges for the two systems are given at **FIG 7.6.2A**. Call charges within the UK are at the normal analogue tariff.

**FIG 7.6.2.A:** *Telephone connection and rental charges for ISDN*

|  | Connection charge | Quarterly rent | Minimum period |
|---|---|---|---|
| **ISDN 2** | £400 | £84 | 12 months |
| **ISDN 30** | £99 per channel - min 15 channels | £34 | 12 months |

*Public
Switched
Telephone
Network
(PSTN)*

The PSTN is the universal global telephone system operated in the UK by BT, Mercury and new companies like Energis and internationally by co-operative agreement under the guidance of the ITU (International Telecomms Union).

For business purposes, PSTN services are accessed via a **pabx** or **key system**. These systems comprise:

- central control box - handling call traffic and connecting to individual extension users

- telephone instrument

**Key systems** allow any extension user to answer and redirect incoming calls from the nearest available telephone; they are only used on smaller installations up to say 72 exchange lines and 180 extensions.

On the other hand, **PABX's** have a centralised operator position with a capacity to inter-connect hundreds of lines and thousands of extensions.

At one time, PABX's were dependent upon switchboard operators for connecting all incoming calls. However with facilities like Direct Dial In (DDI) and voice-mail it is possible to reduce the number of operators required and provide service outside the normal working day. **FIG 7.6.2.B** gives examples of the purchase costs of various systems available.

**FIG. 7.6.2.B:** *Typical range of purchase price of various telephone systems of different size - per incoming line capacity*

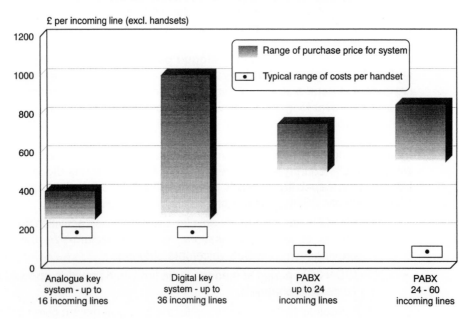

The range of features available on modern systems is well beyond the need and understanding of most users. Careful set-ups and user-training are essential. Some of the features aimed at speed of connection can pay back in terms of better public relations. The latter in particular is a fundamental criterion of choosing and manning a telephone system: for instance **any 'phone not answered before the fourth ring is liable to be the source of lost business. However, that is a feature of good facilities management which applies regardless of the type of system installed.**

Telephone systems can be purchased or rented from the network operator or independent suppliers. All require a pre-connection inspection before they can be connected to the public network.

As with the other utilities, telephone bills are based on a standing tariff related to the number of lines plus metered call charges based on a matrix involving distance of calls, duration and time of day. Calls are subject to a minimum charge.

Apart from any savings to be made by calling long distances at cheaper times - and for as short a time as possible - the various telephone companies offer discounts for such features as:

- volume of calls,
- 'regular number' calls ie: the numbers a subscriber calls most frequently.

Such is the competition between the telephone companies that the incentives are constantly changing as the companies find new chinks in the other's promotional armour. For this reason it is not proposed to discuss current tariffs here, but only to consider some principles of using the business telephone efficiently and economically. Because the pricing structure and circumstances of mobile telephones are quite different from the PSTN the economics of the latter are considered here prior to discussion of the other modes.

There are some simple disciplines which can be introduced to economise on the call-charges, most of which are actively promoted by the companies as they are intended to ease the pressure on peak-time usage of the network.

Economy measures include:

- time-barring
- number-barring
- distance-barring
- least-cost routing
- call logging
- cross-charging
- break out
- education and training.

The three barring options simply stop the staff from making calls either at expensive times (time-barring), or to non-business numbers (number-barring) eg: the 0898 range of consumer telephone services, or to subscribers outside of a certain call-charge band.

**Least cost routing** is a system programmed to identify called numbers and take the most cost-effective route available from the carriers at the time.

**Call logging** is an in-house 'Big Brother' analysis of the destination, duration or originating extension of each call. **In general if staff know call logging is in use the annual phone bill will fall by some 15%.** Most call logging can produce a summary of call costs per department per month or quarter which allows cross-charging.

**Cross-charging** - both externally as expenses and internally via the internal market - are both extremely effective mechanisms for saving money on calls. The customer being charged abnormally high expenses will soon complain and get his way, and the internal cross-chargee will quickly get his mind around how to avoid running up a bill to a level which can easily equate to **more than the annual building and services maintenance per capita.**

**Break out** is a facility whereby organisations with private leased lines between offices can use their private network to reach a distant node and then 'break out' onto the public network. In this way they only pay a 'local' rate for a long distance call.

In the end, educating the staff (and directors) to use the telephone economically is an essential part of the facilities manager's role. Nevertheless, in spite of the high cost of the overhead it is a small proportion of the cost of employing the workforce; as such **the savings regime must never be allowed to impede the efficiency of key staff going about their essential core business.**

## Cellular radio phones

These are very popular for business users - and for the more efficient private individuals - in spite of being rather expensive and offering a level of performance and quality somewhat inferior to the fixed network. Although the capital costs have come way down, the standing and call charges make its use highly uneconomical except for those employees or directors whose mission is sufficiently important to justify being accessible and/or able to dial out at all times.

For the busy executive on the move the mobile phone can be a good way of using the journey time - by train, cab, car or even on foot - to catch up with calls which would otherwise be accumulating in the office awaiting his return. Sometimes dealing with 'hot' enquiries as they arise will secure business that otherwise might not materialise.

**A feature of mobile phones that is often under-rated in its importance is the facility to let people know that one's arrival will be delayed. However valid may be the reason for delay, unnotified lateness often causes frustration and disaffection of the party waiting; a 2-minute chat from the 8.15 stranded by a points failure will eradicate hostility and induce sympathy, paving the way for a satisfactory - though late - meeting.**

**FIG 7.6.2.C** shows a comparison of the total cost of calls from a mobile phone by an occasional, regular and constant user in conjunction with conventional static telephone calls.

**FIG. 7.6.2.C:** *Typical mobile' phone bills for an executive compared with PSTN*

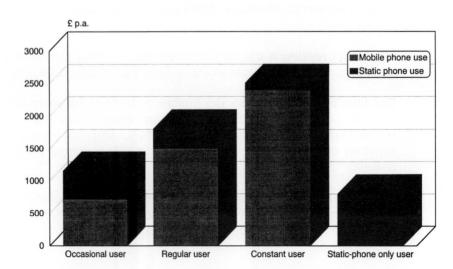

*Cordless
telephone*

Individual cordless telephones can be operated within 100-200 metres from base station units directly connected to the public telephone system. In the office the cordless PABX can support a number of personal handsets. The key feature of this technology is that the extension number becomes mobile meaning that people can move from their desk or indeed become entirely freed from dependency upon any territorial space requirement, so affording economies of space-use. However the range limitation of 100-200 metres limits the technology to 'in building' users.

Other economies of the cordless telephone stem from the obviation of any need for rewiring or changing of extensions when the inevitable 'churn' takes place. Furthermore the cordless system can be fully integrated with a company's local, national or international network and call charges are the same as for fixed phones.

*Paging and
voice-mail*

**Paging** is a cheaper alternative to a mobile phone - provided the recipient of a call has access to a telephone. Service providers offer regional or national coverage with either a simple alert tone or, more usually, 29-98 character messages.

**Voice-mail** has gone a long way in the USA. This technology, which links the recipient to a PBX, gives an answering-machine-plus service, with a record of messages awaiting, and affording the caller the facility of connecting direct to an extension - which could be of the cordless variety. This can save a lot of time in trying to contact someone who needs - and wants - the call; it is estimated that two-thirds of business calls do not hit the target first time, and voice mail is credited with cutting the number of re-calls by as much as 50% - not to mention waiting time spent by switchboard staff.

*System
maintenance*

The maintenance of the lines is included in the line rental charge for either analogue or digital connections. For around £35 pa extra BT will provide a 24-hour back-up service for ISDN 2 lines. The operators aim to repair lines within one working day.

Maintenance of all PABX and key systems is mandatory from a BSI-approved contractor where there is more than one exchange line. Qualification of a suitable contractor (apart from his BSI qualifications) should include:

- length of time in business
- current and historic customer references
- contracts in the immediate area
- numbers and deployment of service technicians
- sub-contractor references

The system maintenance will cover:

- central equipment including operator consoles
- wiring (although this can now be subcontractor's)
- handsets (if required)

**Depending on the call-out response time required the 'maintenance' will cost between 5% and 10% of the installed cost after the first year.** This is very profitable business for suppliers since new digital electronic systems are very reliable and require no preventative maintenance at all.

*Total costs of telephone services*

A wide range of telephone service costs is incorporated in the sample range at **FIG 7.6.2.D** which includes PSTN, cellular radio and cordless communications media but **not** facsimile transmission charges which are separately billed and deserve distinct analysis and cost control

**FIG. 7.6.2.D:** *Sample range of telephone costs per capita p.a.*

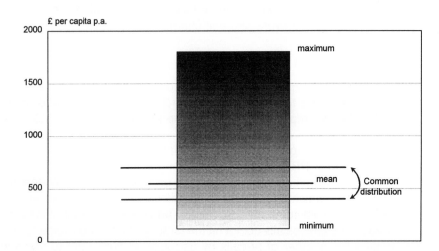

## 7.6.3 FACSIMILE

*Use of fax*

Around one half of all UK businesses are now regular users of a fax machine. Like all new toys they tend to be used with care at first but abuse soon sets in as they become a permanent feature of the workplace.

Fax machines have, in a few short years, become more sophisticated, user-friendly and cheap. Nevertheless it is not the cost of the equipment, or the paper, or the back-up photocopies or the calls which drive the economics of fax - it is the time taken by senior staff preparing and processing them which is critical, coupled with the **unnecessary use of what is the most expensive form of communicating simple messages or letters.**

Fax should really only be used where speed of communication is of the essence. However, the undisciplined user of the facility will also use it because no typist is available to send a formal letter (or he cannot be bothered to write one) - and because handwritten notes are still generally considered to be acceptable to the receiver of a fax message. Some will also use fax so they can deal with a matter while it is on their desk, rather than let it slip through following a conventional office services route.

*Generic equipment*

Fax machines are categorised broadly in terms of certain characteristics ie:

- CCITT grouping

- type of printing process

- memory availability

- image scanning
- paper-feeding
- photocopying capability.

Faxes are either **CCITT group** 3 or 4.  Group 3 faxes communicate via analogue telephone lines whereas Group 4 must have an ISDN line to operate at full speed.

Group 4 fax is of no benefit unless the counter party also has a Group 4 machine. It is unlikely that the number of Group 4 machines will exceed that in Group 3 for a number of years.

The **printing processes** in every day use are:-

- thermal fax paper
- plain paper laser
- plain paper l.e.d.

The **thermal** fax machines are the original concept which have the benefit of cheap paper costs but lowish quality - 200 dots per inch maximum - and difficulty of handling and filing caused by the 60gsm paper curling up in the thermal process and fading in 1-2 years.

**Plain paper** faxes overcome the quality problem both in terms of clarity (being on a white as opposed to a grey background) and paper substance.  Printing may be either by ink-jet or laser; when working to a laser printer of 400 or even 600 dpi (dots per inch) resolution quality will be as high as the transmission carrier permits.

**LED** fax printers are cheaper than laser to purchase and maintain because they do not have a lot of moving parts.  Although the quality is lower than that available on the laser printer the machines print on to plain paper, are smaller and lighter and more reliable in use.

A new higher quality 80 gsm brand of thermal paper may prove popular if it successfully counters the inherent problem of the old variety wherein photocopies are taken of the received document for ease of handling at the desk.

Fax machines are either **memory** or **non-memory**.  One with a memory may be able to do just simple jobs like automatic re-dialling, through remembering important, regularly used numbers (100 or more in the most sophisticated) to having scanners which can hold up to 1,200 pages in memory to be transmitted at off peak times or held in the bank while paper is being replenished.  Image scanning speeds of 30/A4 pages per minute are now achievable.  Another important **memory** feature is the **dual-access** function which allows a fax to be processed for outward transmission while an incoming call is being accepted; a mailbox facility will distribute copies to pre-set extensions.

Even the low-cost machines now have automatic paper feed as standard, only the capacity of the document feed-tray and paper storage in the machine being largely variable.  The biggest machines have paper trays holding 750 sheets with automatic feed of 50 originals for faxing

Apart from the lower quartile of the range all good fax machines have a photocopier facility as standard.

*Economic considerations*

Although memory features are useful in terms of flexibility of operation and use of cheap call-charge rates (all good machines now have a 'Mercury' button for 'least cost routing') it is the **speed** of transmission which is the overall most critical economic factor.

Whereas the bottom end of the market will take about 20 secs to transmit an A4 sheet, the top of the range Group 4 faxes can go as fast an 1.5 secs per page when linking to another ISDN subscriber. The effect of the low call-time and operator time of the fast machines in overall economic terms is quite startling.

FIG 7.6.3.A: *Comparative purchase price of a generic range of fax machines*

| Generic type | Memory | Key features | | | | | Cost £ |
| --- | --- | --- | --- | --- | --- | --- | --- |
| | | Paper | A4 document feed | Paper storage - A4 sheets | Scanner speed | Transmission speed | |
| Group 3 - low cost | no | thermal fax | 5 sheets | 5 | - | 20 secs | 300 - 500 |
| Group 3 - high cost | yes | plain A4 | 10 sheets | 20 | - | 12 secs | 700 - 1000 |
| Group 4 - low cost | yes | plain A4 | 25 sheets | 250 | 3 secs | 6 secs | 1250 - 2000 |
| Group 4 - high cost | yes | Plain A4/A3 | 50 sheets | 1200 | 2 secs | 1.5 secs | 2000 - 2500 |

**FIG 7.6.3.A** compares the capital costs of generic systems; typical costs per A4 page (based upon a conventional mix of call distances) are postulated for these options at **FIG 7.6.3.B.**

**FIG. 7.6.3.B:** *Typical costs per faxed page for the four generic machine types*

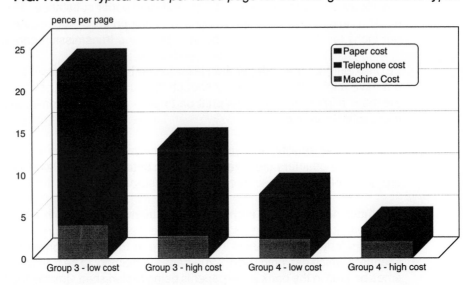

The figure excludes attendance time which is obviously considerably less for the faster machines; if included it would have a far more dramatic effect on the differential than the figure indicates. Of course, the cost of time taken to prepare a fax for transmission is a constant and, again, an infinitely greater number than the combined total of operational and attendance costs.

Some useful additional features available depending upon the price paid are

- error correction

- broadcast fax - for p.r. announcements to a regular list

- itemised billing of calls

- direct-to-accounts cost notification

- network integration - for direct-from-pc faxing

- mobile (including car-based) machines

- remote diagnosis and re-setting.

Finally, a sample from a large number of varied fax users at **FIG 7.6.3.C** gives the cost per capita **excluding paper**. This is a legitimate analysis convention given that the paper is not necessarily dedicated to fax in the growing number of plain paper models.

**FIG. 7.6.3.C:** *Sample range of fax costs per capita for a variety of users*

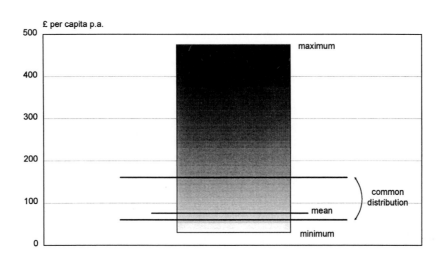

Nevertheless, it is important to analyse the paper **separately under stationery**, if possible by collecting and analysing the individual fax reports over the year for both annual budgeting and monthly cost monitoring. Of course, anyone who feels happier about including the paper in the cost centre may do so; as long as one knows the cost of a sub-component it does not, to a point, matter too much where it is finally deposited.

Faxes are not to be relied upon contractually. For this reason it is still normal practice for 'hard copies' of important correspondence to be separately mailed. Not only is this a particularly expensive practice - it also leaves the decision about contractual significance to the sender, who may not be qualified to make the judgement.

Modern use of the fax frequently results in expensive employees spending time over the fax machine which would be better spent at the workplace with a dictaphone; and just because faxes can now be sent direct from the pc to a receptive machine in another office does not make them any more reliable in legal terms, even it if were to prove to be economical for expensive executives to type their own letters.

## 7.6.4 CONFERENCE

Meetings can consume up to 15% of an organisation's resource. Of that figure frequently more than half is spent in transit to and from the meeting incurring time costs and travelling expenses and often debilitating the travelling attendees to the extent that they under-perform at the event.

Meetings are expensive events which may not always be necessary, or even desirable. The dichotomy primarily revolves around who should attend the meeting rather than whether it should actually take place. One point of view says that anyone who might have a contribution to make or need to hear the facts first hand should be there. The opposing view says to keep it small and make sure it is fully and accurately minuted.

If the former view prevails then the cost of those travelling will obviously be in direct proportion to the numbers.

Various forms of tele-conferencing are available to ease this problem but are considerably under-utilised, quite surprisingly so since they are invariably highly cost-effective.

## Audio-conferencing

The simple ploy of gathering in a room to share a telephone conversation is little used. Many people would rather keep the conversation personal and relay a precis to whomever they deem appropriate rather than plan the call ahead and invite those who should really be participating in the discussion to sit around the phone for 10 minutes or so - listening and contributing.

Conference adaptors costing less than £100 have been available for years, albeit that some of the pioneering models - designed primarily for hands-free use of the 'phone - made the speakers sound as if they were calling from the bathroom! However, the modern hands-free phones, especially those linked to the ISDN, provide excellent sound quality for audio-conferencing.

So audio-conferencing has two main advantages:

- it enables colleagues to share a conventional telephone conversation
- it can help avoid travel to a formal meeting.

On the downside, the 'whites of the eyes' cannot be seen, which may, or may not, be relevant and opportunities for social contact may be passed over to the general detriment of the marketing function.

**To put the matter into economic perspective, two senior personnel travelling across a city for an hour-long meeting will possibly cost the organisation up to 4 man-hours (excluding the meeting time) plus two lots of travelling expenses - say £100 -£500 in total depending on the time-costs and distance. Against this, one hour on a 'phone, even at peak time, would cost less than £10.00.**

## Video-conferencing

The advent of multi-media cable together with lowish-priced desk-top video converters means that the need for extensive and expensive national and international travel for meetings will come under closer and closer scrutiny.

The bureaux who specialise in visual tele-conferencing facilities - originally via two sets of TV studios but now using sophisticated video-conferencing facilities - can make a strong economic argument for their services; from the adequately equipped desk-top the case is infinitely stronger.

A typical bureau installation might comprise:

- two colour monitors - to show both incoming and outgoing signals
- table camera with full pan, tilt and zoom facilities
- fixed table camera for larger groups (say up to 6 people)
- presenter camera to pick up projected presentations or group personnel overview
- document presenter camera mounted at ceiling level
- microphones
- control panel.

The system works by **Codec** which compresses pictures received by the cameras then digitises them before transmitting only the moving parts in order that they can be sent over the ISDN telephone networks at conventional speeds of between 128 and 384 Kb per second, although some systems can operate on speeds as high as 2Mbs. The receiving equipment reverses the procedure. Quality of picture will be higher where calls are to a similar proprietary system, although standard protocols exist which make acceptable visual communication between dissimilar systems feasible.

**'Point-to-point'** conferences are between two stations; the optional second monitor and the document camera enables one station to preview a document prior to transmission and also while it is being reviewed at the receiving station.

**'Multi-point'** conferences usually engage a 'switching house' to link together a number of office stations. Only the station talking is transmitted but long periods of 'butting-in' to the conversation will automatically cause the transmission to switch to the interjecting station.

The audio-conference example of cross-town travel would also work very favourably for the video-conference - just a few such trips saved would pay for the desk top facility.

If the example is extended to inter-city travel taking a whole day plus two shuttle tickets then a cost of up to £2,000 for the meeting is quite likely. The cost of a bureau video-conference for a 3-hour meeting would be little more than £400 - £500 including time and expenses incurred travelling to and from a City Centre bureau. The further the distances the more economical it becomes, particularly when international trips are involved. It also makes it possible for more people to attend the conference - which may or may not be beneficial.

If the whites of the eyes need to be seen they can be in video-conference - though perhaps not as clearly, or everyone's at the same time! Equally, **the scent of fear is definitely not transmittable - even on ISDN!**

## 7.6.5 MAIL DISTRIBUTION

The process whereby letters and other packages are distributed internally and externally has not changed as radically as might have been expected given advances in information technology which threatened a paperless office by the late 1990's.

In spite of E-mail and the direct computer linkages between customer and supplier considered in the previous chapter, the biggest effect of IT on distribution has been to get people to produce more and more data which is too bulky to fax yet too late to be of use unless carried physically by courier.

In many ways the office has twin communications engine-rooms - the switchboard and the post-room - each of which has a critical part to play in the way the organisation makes and maintains contact with its customers. But, whereas the switchboard has grown in sophistication at the expense of all but one or two operators, the army of people physically carrying letters and packages in and out of buildings has decreased but slightly - even in recession.

*The post room*

Post-room staff have a dual role:

- opening, collating, referencing and distributing incoming mail
- collating, packaging (if required) stamping, recording and posting/dispatching outgoing mail.

Depending on the size of organisation, post-room staff will either be dedicated - as in most medium/large business - or part of the secretarial function in the smaller organisation.

Typically one post-room employee should be able to service the mail of between 250 and 400 employees, the lower end being where there is a substantial element of mechanised handling internally, or electronic mail - both internally and externally.

The design of the post-room is very important with mail sorting well arranged to facilitate handling by dwarfs and giants alike. Sturdy yet lightweight mail-and goods-handling trolleys should be in plentiful supply (with room for standby parking), plus electric letter openers, intelligent weighing machines which alert the user to under-or over-stamping (but franking in preference to stamping, please) and direct envelope printers for regular volume mailings.

Bomb detector screens in 'letter' and 'parcel' sizes cost only a few hundred pounds and are really an essential accessory for the more 'public' organisations.

Most of all a neat, tidy, decor backed up with a rigorous on-going 'keep clean and tidy' campaign can go a long way to making sure that an often under-rated task is not perceived to be under-valued by the management.

## Internal distribution

The small-to-medium sized facility will probably rely upon the foot-soldier to fetch and carry, almost certainly doubling up with secretarial or security duties. However, once mail is passing to and from more than say 150 staff then dedicated self-motivated personnel will become viable, especially if set performance targets.

Sorting of incoming mail is a straightforward task in a well-ordered mailroom, so the efficiencies will be made in the distribution. Here much will depend upon the horizontal and vertical transportation systems in the premises.

Larger buildings designed with facilities management in mind may well have special delivery services built in. Eg: a transit-box system working on the principles of a continuously moving paternoster-type elevator can be designed so that the mail can be distributed vertically direct from the mail-room. One such system involves proprietary tough plastic containers pre-coded for the various destinations by the mail-room staff; electronic devices scan the codes and mechanically deposit the boxes as required at each floor. Speed of operation, with box weights of up to 20kgs can make big inroads into delivery times and costs of messenger services, as well as allowing a steady flow of outbound mail to trickle down to the post room on a regular basis during the day.

**FIG 7.6.5.A:** *Payback on a dedicated document conveyor system serving 750 staff on 4 floors - 120,000 sq ft NIA*

| | | |
|---|---|---|
| **Capital costs** | Installation including builder's work, fees, finance and accessories: | £ 30,000 |
| | Loss of built floor area 120 sq ft GIA @ £50 sq ft say | 6,000* |
| | **Total** | **£ 36,000** |
| **Annual reduction in messenger staff** | 1 @ £15,000 pa gross: £36,000 ÷ £15,000 = | **2.4 years payback** |
| \* If the conveyor is inserted into an existing building, then the loss of rented floor space must be deducted from the annual saving. Eg. @ £20 sq ft NIA this might amount to some £2,500 pa - and the capital costs would be about 20% higher | | |

As **FIG 7.6.5A** shows, pay-back on the capital installation cost of such a service in an organisation of, say, 500 personnel could be as little as 2 to 3 years with increased efficiency to boot.

*External distribution*

Typical external distribution costs per capita based on a broad-based sample are given at **FIG 7.6.5.B**. These show that the common-or-garden post-office service is being challenged as never before by the 'overnight' carriers (who offer good delivery performance at excellent prices for the larger customers) and the 'mad-mo-biker' services who can deliver locally at high speed - as long as the forwarding address is written in large capital letters and located within 50 metres of a trunk road!

**FIG 7.6.5.B:** *Typical external distribution costs per capita pa*

| Component | Typical range of cost £ pa | Mean £ pa |
|---|---|---|
| Postage: Home and international stamps | 80 - 250 | 180 |
| Overnight carriers | 10 - 30 | 15 |
| Courier/despatch riders | 50 - 200 | 125 |
| Totals | 140 - 480 | 320 |

The cost of these express deliveries comes to about 50% of the external distribution costs. **At the more expensive end of the range costs of express delivery are about the same per capita as energy costs per annum in an air-conditioned building**. All this suggests that the organisation can ill afford to leave delivery of its outgoing product to the last minute.

Afford?

In the event, the value of the product must surely always make the costs of conveyance to the customer fade into insignificance. If it does not, then either the mode of conveyance must be out of sync with the product or the product is not appropriate to the mode of delivery.

In other words, low value goods must be transported in bulk or via the letter box, whereas really valuable products can go by whatever means can ensure their timely (and secure?) delivery.

**Facilities must always support, not hinder, the product**; however the right balance must be struck, for bad product managers often fail to understand how **unnecessary** overheads can impact on profitability. **FIG 7.6.5.C** illustrates this point, showing the balance between distribution, office services, turnover and profitability.

**FIG. 7.6.5.C:** *Distribution costs in the context of turnover, profits and office services*

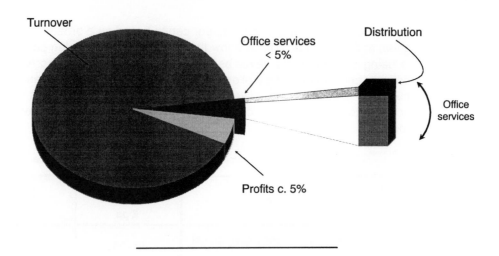

# CHAPTER 7.7 – OFFICE FURNITURE

## 7.7.1 THE COMPONENTS

*Basic requirements*

Office furniture may be provided for the purposes of

- routine working
- storage
- meeting
- waiting
- dining
- display
- space division.

It comprises:

- work surfaces
- seats
- screens (division and/or display)
- storage units
- signs & graphics

A full categorisation of the contents of these generic furniture components is given at **FIG 7.7.A**.

**FIG 7.7.A:** *Office furniture classification*

| Category | Component | Category | Component |
|---|---|---|---|
| Work surfaces | · drawing boards<br>· desks (ie: work surfaces with integral storage capacity<br>· workstations (ie: designed for accomodating VDUs<br>· tables<br>· workbenches | Storage units | · pedestal units<br>· cupboards (with or without shelves)<br>· open shelving<br>· mobile storage units<br>· rotundas<br>· rotators<br>· credenzas |
| Seats | · workplace chairs<br>· stools<br>· conference chairs<br>· easy chairs<br>· settees | Signs and graphics | · organisation name<br>· personnel names<br>· group / department names<br>· room functions<br>· exit / ingress routes |
| Screens | · dining chairs<br>· freestanding units or<br>· facings to backs of storage units | | · apparatus<br>· floor numbers<br>· location pointers<br>· artwork<br>· etc... |

*Performance*

The physical and functional characteristics of furniture are very much driven by an amalgam of basic needs, life-span and initial cost.

The impact of each of these factors is discussed within the category sections below.

Typical points to be considered are (in no particular order of significance):

- material
- form of construction
- strength
- weight
- appearance
- simplicity
- complexity
- appearance
- wear resistance
- size
- comfort
- adjustability
- statutory compliance
- cable management (for workstations)
- multi-purpose
- availability (replacement etc.)
- space consumption
- durability
- cleanability
- sound integrity
- net cost (after discounts)
- after-sales service

## 7.7.2 THE FUNCTIONAL OPTIONS

*The functions
examined*

The best way to consider furniture options and their economics is to consider each function in turn ie:

- the workplace
- the reception/waiting areas
- conference/meeting areas
- dining rooms.

However, in categorising thus it must be remembered that an increasingly important feature of office furniture is the need to standardise as much as possible **between** functions to improve the bulk order prices and to reduce the problems of storing and/or purchasing replacement units.  So, for instance, there may well be a case for the chairs around the meeting table in the director's office to be the same as those in the main conference areas.

*The workplace*

The workplace may comprise simply a workstation or it may also accommodate storage and, in some cases, a meeting area.  Whether it is in a cellular or open plan location will not necessarily determine the performance or quality, although if cellular equals higher status then this can permit higher quality without permanently flaunted exposure of that policy.

The workstation itself will always have a working surface and a seat, in its simplest form a table and chairs; engineers and other designers will have a drawing board, normally accompanied by an adjustable chair.   Most workplaces will have local storage either under the work surface (as part of a desk or a separate pedestal unit) and some may have additional storage nearby – on the floor or on the wall/screen or both.

The workstation itself may be designed specifically to accommodate information technology:  desks may be designed to contain and manage cables, and worktops for the screens may be adjustable for tilt and height.  EC Directives on Health & Safety at Work (see Chapter 8.2) require the adjustability for tilt in all workstations brought into use on or after 1/1/93 and in any case after 31/12/96; similarly, seats at VDU screens must be capable of height adjustment under the new regime.

Fully adjustable tables and chairs are available, some beautifully engineered, for those organisations who recognise that staff over 2m tall cannot get their legs under a table by lowering the seat height without leaning backwards at 15°.

Many modern workstations are modular ie: they can be varied in their layout to suit a planning arrangement - particularly useful in open plan designs.

Depending on the job function (please **NOT the job grade**) personnel will require some measure of meeting support adjacent to the workstation.  In modest cases this may mean a couple of chairs for visitors (internal or external), at higher levels a table and chairs and maybe easy chairs/settee for those clinching the big deals.

The market will determine the actual price paid for furniture - sometimes in a good deal one can purchase high quality fully adjustable workstations at less cost than the pretty but RSI-prone designer-favoured alternatives.  Nevertheless, it is useful to compare the typical costs of workstations for various grades (the term used loosely here to define job function) across the broad spectrum of quality ranges - see **FIG 7.7.B**.  The higher end of the range may represent style, engineering excellence, uniqueness and just plain 'Kings suit of clothes' syndrome so value for money must be established by cost/benefit analysis;  the performance characteristics given above may form a useful base for such an appraisal.

**FIG 7.7.B:** *Furniture and fittings requirements and budget capital costs per workplace*

| Grade | Furniture requirements | Cellular office | | | Furniture requirements | Open plan office | | |
| | | Quality rating | | | | Quality rating | | |
| | | 1 £ | 2 £ | 3 £ | | 1 £ | 2 £ | 3 £ |
|---|---|---|---|---|---|---|---|---|
| Secretary | Chair, desk, return, storage cabinets (2), pedestal | 1,500 | 2,250 | 3,375 | Chair, worktop, return, screens (3), cabinets (2), pedestal | 1,875 | 2,450 | 3,600 |
| Professional/ executives | Chair, desk, storage cabinets (2), visitors chairs (2) | 1,300 | 2,000 | 3,000 | Chair, worktop, return screens (4), screen storage, storage cabinet (1). visitors' chairs (2) | 1,675 | 2,250 | 3,750 |
| Manager/ Director | Chair, desk, storage cabinet (1), meeting table, visitors' chairs(4), settee | 2,250 | 3,000 | 4,500 | Chair, worktop, screens (5), screen storage, storage cabinets (2), meeting table, visitors' chairs | 2,600 | 3,400 | 6,600 |

## Special areas

**FIG 7.7.C** again looks at budget costs for three current levels of quality for 'special areas'.  The comments above concerning value for money equally apply.  In areas such as Board Room and Main Reception many organisations seek to indulge and impress by commissioning bespoke furniture such as the boardroom table and the reception desk.  The latter investment is more likely to produce an appreciable return on investment by dint of its marketing implications (out of the marketing budget?!) than the former.

FIG 7.7.C: *Furniture and fittings requirements and budget capital costs for 'special areas'*

| Feature | Quality 1 | £ | Quality 2 | £ | Quality 3 | £ |
|---------|-----------|---|-----------|---|-----------|---|
| Computers | Audio / visual workstation | 2,250 | Audio / visual workstation | 2,850 | Audio / visual workstation | 3,750 |
| Kitchen/dining | Table, chairs (6), average of 3 sittings - cost per place | 45 | Table, chairs (6), average of 2 sittings - cost per place | 110 | Table, chairs (6), average of 1 sitting - cost per place | 285 |
| Meeting room | Table, chairs (8), 1 room per 80 staff - cost per employee | 20 | Table, chairs (8), 1 room per 60 staff - cost per employee | 40 | Table, chairs (8), 1 room per 40 staff - cost per employee | 75 |
| Plants & graphics | 1 plant per 20 employees, graphics £20 per employee - cost per employee | 45 | 1 plant per 10 employees, graphics £30 per employee - cost per employee | 100 | 1 plant per 5 employees, graphics £65 per employee - cost per employee | 150 |
| Accessories | Filing, general storage, etc. - cost per employee | 100 | Filing, general storage, etc. - cost per employee | 140 | Filing, general storage, etc. - cost per employee | 185 |

However, in truth, the amortised cost of the Boardroom furniture (however apparently wanton) as a proportion of the directors' remuneration is so small that it is either irrelevant or may indeed generate a return on investment by encouraging recruitment of better directors and/or helping them to be more efficient.

**FIG 7.7.D** looks at the cost of 3 qualities of Reception Area and Boardroom furniture in the context of an organisation occupying a Head Office building of 50,000SF net internal (lettable) area.

FIG 7.7.D: *Furniture and fittings - budget capital costs for reception and boardroom areas*

| Feature | Quality 1 (£) | Quality 2 (£) | Quality 3 (£) |
|---------|---------------|---------------|---------------|
| Reception area | 5,000 | 10,000 | 20,000 |
| Boardroom area | 10,000 | 25,000 | 50,000 |
| N.B. Examples relate to a head office building - 50,000 sq ft NIA | | | |

## 7.7.3 PROCUREMENT

*Design*

Section 4 - 'Space Management' - and Chapter 7.8 'Churn' discuss the relationship between furniture, layout and the efficiency and flexibility of space use. Here we must consider the fact that, in open plan space, the furniture does form part of the dividing function conventionally carried out by partitions in cellular space.

For this reason, the cost of furniture should always be included in any comparative study between cellular and open-planned space and the comparison must also address the cost per capita because of the differences in space-use efficiency between the layouts.

A typical range of fitting-out costs per capita for cellular and open plan office areas including alternative qualities of furniture is given at **FIG 7.7.E**.

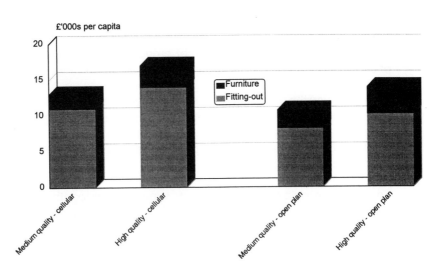

**FIG. 7.7.E:** *Total furniture and fitting-out costs per capita (cellular and open plan arrangements)*

It is essential to have independent advice when procuring furniture in large quantities, or in small quantities as part of an incremental programme. There are many excellent interior designers whose experience of the pros and cons of the myriad generic types of furniture components and systems and their effect upon the working environment can be invaluable. However their recommendations should be supported by an independent cost consultant.

Unfortunately, 'hidden' discounts are sometimes made available to impoverished interior designers by unscrupulous distributors desperate for sales, so any undue bias by a designer in respect of one particular system may have to be viewed with some degree of scepticism; the facilities manager ought to be given a full appraisal of performance vs cost to enable him to be the final arbiter.

For the same reason - only more so - leaving the design and specification to individual suppliers is really asking for trouble unless a reasonably sophisticated 'single-point responsibility' tender process (see Chapter 6.3) has been instigated and properly managed.

## Specification and purchasing

Inviting large-scale bids from furniture suppliers should always be done on a thoroughly prepared performance specification. Unless bids are also requiring space planning (not a very good policy - far better to pay to have the planning done by independent designers) the precise quantities of each unit should be stated. As with all bidding processes it is always better to eliminate as many variables as possible; the consequence of contractors mis-calculating their estimates never works to the client's advantage.

The performance of each generic unit should be described in such a way that tenderers can identify one or more of their products to fit the bill; exact compliance is not essential and suppliers will often offer more than one product type, drawing attention to any major departures from the given performance level. Eg; modular workstations may be offered in a choice of finish; however, if cable-carrying is part of the brief, then alternatives which cannot carry cables will obviously not be considered. Most reputable suppliers know the rules of the performance specification process and will bid sensibly.

It is important to identify the job functions of the intended users, the delivery requirements, and any statutory compliancies (eg: Health & Safety at Work). The tenderers should be asked to show all discounts from list price and to confirm that all available discounts are being made to the client alone - this to guard against conceded discounts to third parties.

Care should be taken to ensure that product ranges offered are not likely to be phased out in the near future - or if so that the price reflects this obsolescence.

Before placing the order, samples of each product should be inspected and labelled as a check against quality of the bulk deliveries. Where possible, products should be tested on site over a reasonable period, particularly workstations where the comfort of the user and his/her approval need to be established in advance of a major investment.

There is currently a trend back towards simpler, push-together styles away from the fully extensible systems. Legislation on provisions for VDU operation can be accommodated without excessive mechanical adjustment eg: height adjustment by the use of wall brackets and slotted angles. Although the 'better engineered' solution will definitely be valuable to some organisations, if the users themselves do not want it there is absolutely no point in parting with the extra cash.

However, the issue of 'adjustability' should be thoroughly examined with the 'staff side' before any major new acquisition programme; the users' comfort and convenience should be paramount in any furniture choice, for the effect on their productivity, one way or another, will far outweigh the cost of the furniture itself.

Finally, the decision as to whether to lease or purchase outright will be down to the finance director who will take into account the funds available plus the taxation considerations. Leasing costs go straight against profits whereas bought items of furniture are subject to claims for capital allowances (see Chapter 11.2).

# CHAPTER 7.8 – 'CHURN'

## 7.8.1 THE MEANING

'Churn' is the facilities manager's jargon for the movement of personnel, groups and departments as a direct result of changed operational requirements.

At its worst incidence it involves wholesale reconfiguration or even new construction but in a highly controlled state may be restricted simply to the movement of people.

The 'churn rate' is the ratio between the number of workstation moves made in a year to the number of personnel working in the premises. The rapid growth and change of the eighties caused 'churn' to get out of control in some organisations, both in terms of frequency and the cost of implementation. The lack of any previous experience of the phenomenon - or at least within the context of highly technologically-serviced workspace - caught many firms by surprise and 'churn' rates as high as 2:1 - ie: an average of two moves per person per annum - were reported.

## 7.8.2 THE COST

A recent analysis of churn in a number of medium and large organisations indicated a cost per capita (excluding loss productivity) of between £60 and £900 pa. The cost per SF of NI(L)A ranged from £0.41 to £8.20pa and averaged £2.13. As such it was in many cases higher than any of the other operating cost centres - see **FIG 7.8.A.**

**FIG. 7.8.A:** *Average cost of 'churn' within a typical premises operating budget*

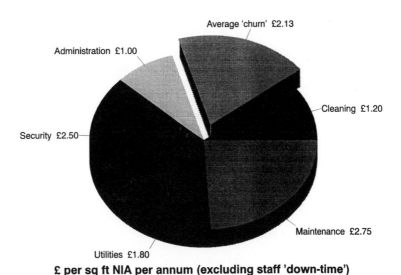

**£ per sq ft NIA per annum (excluding staff 'down-time')**

*The cost drivers*

The cost of churn is driven by the following factors:

- the rate of churn

- the preparation of the new workstation and its facilities

- the preparation of the vacated workstation and its facilities

- the time taken to move the employee's equipment, papers and personal effects

- the time at which the move is carried out

- the grade of personnel effecting the move.

The down-time of employees as a result of the move is not usually counted into the cost, although it can be a significant component, eg a churn rate of 2:1 can result in a 5% loss of productivity per employee pa.

Many reports are of costs higher than this sample; **FIG 7.8.B.** suggests how the cost components of 'churn' might range in a wider sample from £60 to £1,700 per move.

Note that any cost per move must be seen in the context of the rate of churn; an example of the effects of this interaction on the total annual cost is given below.

**FIG. 7.8.B:** *Analysis of range of costs of 'churn' per move*

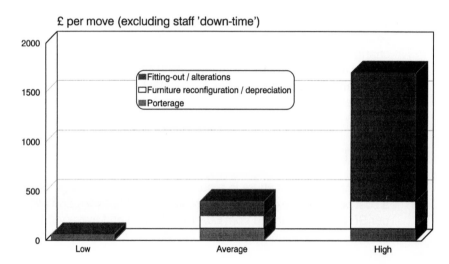

£ per move (excluding staff 'down-time')

*The rate of churn*

While in most cases churn cannot be avoided it is certainly possible, by good planning, to minimise its incidence.

Churn is caused by some or all of the following factors:

- staff increases

- staff reductions

- business re-structuring

- bad space planning

- management whim.

Whereas the facilities manager cannot influence the first three above unless they are catered for in the premises policy, he certainly can and should be able to impact on the latter two.

### 7.8.3 MANAGEMENT AND CONTROL

*Control*
*Mechanisms*

Chapter 4.1 describes the space planning function, so here it is only necessary to consider two aspects of that science relevant to churn - keeping records and planning flexibility.

It is vitally important to keep account of the number of moves -in other words to track the rate of churn. Not for the first time in this work Lord Kelvin's quote 'if you can't measure it you can't understand it' and Harrington's 'if you can't measure it you can't improve it' are used to make a point.

Many of the worst churn rates in recent years crept up on facilities managers by surprise; once they identified the scale of the problem, and began to plan avoidance, the rate dropped back to manageable levels.

In the example, at **FIG 7.8.C** a financial services company was experiencing a steep increase in churn compared to its growth in staff numbers. A space planning initiative introduced in Year 2 brought the rate of churn down to about 1 per annum in Year 4. At the same time they reduced the costs per move in stages from £600 to £200 to £70 per person. The higher costs included departmental time, crates and modifications to electrical services, data, telecommunications, furniture, decor etc. The low-cost moves involved only the actual moving cost and an absolute minimum of local adjustment/replanning.

**FIG. 7.8.C:** *Reduction in annual cost of 'churn'*
*through analysis and improved planning*

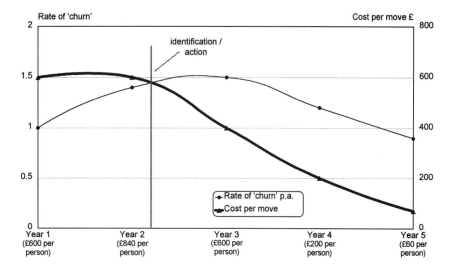

The provision of new furniture systems giving the key to the savings was planned to coincide with natural obsolescence of the older variegated and less flexible units and did not introduce a cost penalty. As shown in **FIG 7.8.C** the saving worked out to £700 per person for the 2,500 staff -a massive £2m and over £9 per sq.ft. of the lettable floor area per annum.

Recording moves is obviously much easier on an electronic database - CAD can be helpful too, especially when it comes to testing re-configuration. Computerised inventories of personnel, their location, job requirements and equipment will also help the fight against churn.

Standardisation of workstations, easily re-configured furniture, good cable management all serve to reduce or avoid the need to carry out alterations in support of a move. Well thought out stacking plans with overflow space built in for expansion will also help to keep the worst scenario - the departmental change around - at bay; a total refit can cost up to £10,000 per capita and protection must be provided against premature exposure to this risk albeit at the cost of a little slack in the space allocations within the system.

## Managing the move

In the ideal situation all that will be necessary will be a team of porters coming in at the weekend to move the employees' personal belongings and equipment to a new location and just plug in. This gives the £70 move - porters are cheap, even at weekend/overtime rates. However one suspects that many facilities managers are around to help at these times and that their unpaid extra hours are not costed into the data provided.

The more expensive moves often involve the transportation of the employees' furniture (usually the result of non-standardisation or variations in quality) and, in the worst cases, substantial re-configuration of the old and new workstations and accompanying alterations to decor, cables, services etc. It must always be borne in mind that in most cases one move equals two ie: the place vacated will be filled at some time in the future.

## Management policies

Finally, the issue of management whim. One organisation used to reward its sales force by up-grading them as they achieved financial milestones. In the good times some of the better salesmen got upgraded twice in a year. The only bad thing was that the management's policy was to match accommodation space and quality to grade with the consequence of a really high penalty on each upgrade, especially when the work place entitlement grew from open plan to cellular office. **There are better and more cost-effective ways of rewarding staff than taking £5,000 or so out of profits every time they do particularly well - and giving it to a building contractor!**

# CHAPTER 7.9 – MOTOR FLEET MANAGEMENT

## 7.9.1 THE COMPANY TRANSPORT POLICY

*Individual staff transport*

Until recent years in the UK the use of a motor vehicle provided and maintained by the firm was an accepted and almost indispensable perquisite, being added into salary for computation of earnings for mortgage transactions - but not for tax purposes. In 1971 this all changed in the UK when the government introduced personal income tax on private motoring mileage; since then the government has levied increasing levels of personal taxation from the beneficiaries of a company car policy. The point has now been reached where there is scarcely any financial advantage at all to the beneficiary while the employer still has all the hassle of financing and managing or contracting a car fleet.

There are few benefits to the employer other than a reasonable certainty as to the safety and reliability of the mechanical medium for its employees' inter-site travel. In terms of national economics there is no doubt that the motor industry gets more business via company cars than it would otherwise; and although roads should be safer with better maintained, more reliable vehicles on them the human factor, whereby drivers treat their employers' property with rather less respect than their own, probably outweighs the benefits of fleet care.

*Goods vehicles*

Those organisations whose businesses depend on physical distribution of goods will probably have a dedicated fleet manager rather than relying upon facilities management; control of driver hours, safety of loading/unloading, the sheer size of the vehicles and complexity of their mechanisms demand highly qualified and motivated management. Where a fleet contains just a few heavy goods vehicles, fully maintained contract hire or even complete out-sourcing of such transport is probably the best solution.

Because HGV fleets are an intrinsic part of industrial and retail activity as opposed to administration facilities they are not considered further in this chapter.

## 7.9.2 PROCUREMENT

*Choosing the vehicles*

As a general rule it makes sense to stay with one manufacturer for all the vehicles, or at least for the generic categories such as used by sales reps, executives and directors. Not only will a better deal be struck on the purchase/lease but service charges will be lower than for a plethora of different machines.

Choice of colours may affect the price - fads have swung literally between black and white over the years.

Some foreign cars distributed in the UK do have difficulty replacing parts - especially on the older models - and component costs are frequently higher than on the mass-market UK models. However, since there are now no wholly-owned major UK motor manufacturers this bias is rapidly being eroded.

Low mileage nearly-new cars - usually ex-car hire vehicles sold at auction after just a few months - can be up to 30% cheaper than new and will run just as well.

The simpler the car is the less can go wrong with it and the cheaper the replacement parts. Nevertheless executives doing high mileage between high profile appointments ought to be afforded automatic gearboxes and power steering, even on smaller cars, but run-about-town reps may not benefit much from such added comfort, much as they might lobby otherwise.

There is patently a lot of choice, and not just in terms of makes and models but also of deals from particular companies and methods of purchase.

## Procurement options

A purchase scheme, as defined by the Finance Act 1971, is one in which the company spends money under a contract which permits eventual ownership.

**Purchase** can take the form of:

- outright purchase
- hire purchase
- lease purchase
- contract purchase
- purchase of private cars by employees.

**Leasing** does not envisage eventual ownership. The contract may be for either:

- finance lease

  -open-ended lease

  -Close-ended lease

or

- operating lease

  -contract hire

  -purchase and leaseback

Identifying the most appropriate vehicle funding strategy for your company is a complex and confusing task. The fleet operator is faced with the job of choosing cars that are most suited for the company's current tax and balance sheet position.

## Outright purchase

A large initial expenditure is involved with this type of purchase which deprives potential profit-making core business of funds. The day-to-day management of the fleet can be a time-consuming task. Very careful consideration of purchasing costs and maintenance costs needs to be made to ensure that the best deals are obtained. It will be the responsibility of the company to get the best price for the vehicles when their useful life is over. Outright purchase really only makes sense for the organisation having the cash to spare and the time and resources to devote to fleet management.

## Hire purchase

With this arrangement the user is effectively the owner but may not have title to the vehicles until the loan is paid off and the option to purchase is exercised. An initial deposit is paid and the balance of the capital sum and interest is paid back in monthly instalments over a specified period. The cost of the vehicle is spread over its useful life.

*Lease
purchase*

This is not, strictly speaking, a lease but a hire-purchase scheme. Again, an initial low deposit is made and then monthly payments set at a level to cover just depreciation and interest. The option is then available of paying part of the capital amount at expiry and then paying or receiving a lump sum depending on the proceeds of sale, or having a normal full payout agreement. The cost of the vehicle is spread over its useful life; with hire and lease purchase the options do not attract VAT on the capital and finance elements and writing down allowance in respect of Corporation tax are available.

*Contract
purchase*

This type of contract combines the service and operational benefits of contract hire with the tax advantages of outright purchase. The main advantage to the customer is that the capital and finance elements are completely exempt from VAT. Part of the vehicle cost is depreciation over the life of the agreement and the balance is paid as a lump sum at the end. Title passes to the customer when the lump sum is paid.

*Purchase of
private cars by
employees*

Some companies still operate the option of reimbursing employees for the business travel that they undertake in their own car. This payment usually comes in the form of mileage allowance in pence per mile and may include a fixed monthly sum to assist with the running of the car. A few companies even provide low interest funding to assist employees with the initial purchase of the vehicle.

*Finance lease*

In this type of lease the lessor company is the legal owner of the vehicles and can claim capital allowances while the vehicle user has possession and use of the car and can offset rental costs against profits.

Finance lease agreements come in two forms - open-ended and close-ended

With **open-ended leases** - equal monthly payments are made over a pre-determined period to recover the capital. Sale of the vehicle is usually undertaken by the leasing company who keep the profits in the first instance but then return them to the lessee company as a rebate on rentals. Subject to status VAT charges are recoverable.

**Close-ended leases** - recognise the residual value of the vehicles in the funding calculations. This residual value is anticipated in the contract and the renting company will be charged with any shortfall and/or credited with any surplus when the vehicles are sold. Subject to status VAT charges are recoverable.

In both the above agreements the operation and administration of the fleet remains with the lessee company.

*Operating
lease*

In these types of lease the risks and rewards in operating the vehicles will remain with the lessor company. The vehicles will not show on the lessee company's balance sheet as assets. The lessee company will retain the vehicles at the end of the lease and can then sell or re-lease them. Operating lease agreements also come in two forms - contract hire and purchase-and-leaseback

**Contract hire** vehicles are leased for a fixed monthly rental for a specific time and mileage and the operational and financial risk remains with the lessor company. The majority of leases include a fixed price maintenance package or a vehicle maintenance programme operated by a fleet management company.

**Purchase and leaseback** contracts are useful when a company which has initially purchased a fleet wishes to inject some cash back into the organisation. The company's fleet is wholly or partly sold to the leasing company and is then leased back on an agreed time and mileage parameter. This will then take on all the financial and operational aspects of conventional contract hire. It is a useful alternative source of re-financing core business activity if funds become short after the original non-core investment.

*Taxation considerations in procurement*

In the purchase schemes the tax regime may permit Writing Down Allowances against a statutory computation of depreciation to be offset against corporation tax. When the vehicle is sold a balancing allowance or charge is computed by reference to the comparative values of the sales proceeds and the Tax Written Down Value. Eg: a car purchased for £15,000 may be written down to £7,000 after four years: if it is then sold for £4,000 the Balancing Charge of (£7,000 - £4,000) £3,000 is further allowable against profits, thereby allowing the whole depreciation, albeit part-deferred. Usually the interest component of purchase schemes is fully allowable as operating expenses except in certain categories of contract purchase where there is a sales option on completion.

On lease transactions both the depreciation and interest element of the rental may be allowable to the lessor subject to upper levels established in the tax regime.

In all cases of purchase and lease the service and maintenance charges built into the rental or contract (or directly incurred) are fully allowable as operating expenses.

Where employees are paid a mileage allowance by their employers in respect of business use they may be entitled to recover capital allowances themselves; alternatively they may obtain relief for the actual cost incurred in the business mileage - but only one or the other, not both.

Whereas VAT is payable on both capital and finance elements of a finance lease, a lease purchase, contract purchase or hire purchase transaction does not attract VAT on those elements.

*Effect on trading accounts*

In some organisations the value of motor vehicles may represent a potentially sizeable asset - provided they are purchased outright or on one or other of the purchase schemes discussed above.

In a leasing situation the test of whether the vehicle asset belongs to the lessor or lessee is 'who has substantially all the risks and rewards associated with the ownership of the asset, **other than the legal title**'. Thus, a finance lease and a hire purchase should be shown as the lessee's asset whereas an operating lease will not. Outstanding finance lease payments must be capitalised on the lessor's balance sheet.

Sometimes it will suit a company to minimise its book assets - possibly to improve its return on capital employed (ROCE) or other performance ratio. This may influence the procurement route in favour of leasing - and vice versa where a patently strong capital base is sought.

A point to note is that where, in contract purchase, the customer has an option to sell vehicles back to the Fleet Service company for a guaranteed price they must always appear on the customer's balance sheet unless he can prove that he always has - and presumably always will - exercise his option.  In the latter case an opportunity to go 'off-balance-sheet' may be available and attractive to the high-ROCE aspirants.

## 7.9.3 FLEET MANAGEMENT

*In-house v out-source*

The decision is no different from any other cost centre - partly an issue of core v non-core and particularly one of availability of relevant skills.  Even the contract operators mainly use the distributors' service agents for maintenance, but using in-house qualified engineers to vet their performance.

'Fleet management only' contracts are widely available and may be a viable solution where the user has strong purchasing power and cash flow but has a policy of contracting-out non-core activities.

*Management reporting*

Management reporting on operating costs, values, condition, mileages, rental levels, tax efficiency, safety, insurance etc is needed on a regular basis tailored to the company's needs (including any cross-charging) and is time-consuming, even when computerised.

Other issues to take on board for regular review are insurance, replacement strategy, accident support, driver training (for HGV's) and mobile communications.

## 7.9.4 FLEET MANAGEMENT ECONOMICS

*The cost drivers*

The key cost drivers in a motor fleet operation are:

- initial cost of vehicles
- finance costs
- rate of depreciation
- wear & tear
- reliability
- servicing costs
- replacement costs
- mileage
- type of fuel
- insurance
- accident repair
- re-sale value
- taxation implications.

**FIG 7.9.A** shows a typical analysis of the mileage cost for three different size models assuming a well-established manufacturer.

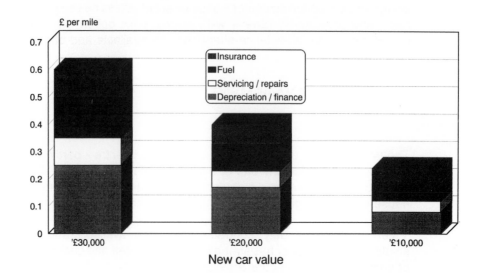

**FIG. 7.9.A:** *Typical costs per mile for a range of private cars*

## Initial cost

Most people think they know about how to get the right deal on a new car, though the professional fleet operators have the financial muscle to do better than their potential customers. However, when dealing with an operator any 'hidden' discounts and short-term special offers should be squeezed out of the system to the customer's advantage - though this may only be possible through the exigencies of competition.

Beware cheap foreign cars with poor reliability and spares availability, and poor second-hand value retention; which is not to say that most established imported models are likely to be any less satisfactory than the UK 'trusties'.

Except in the case of the least reliable foreign imports, cheaper, simpler cars have lower life-cycle costs in every cost centre and hold their value well so good discretion should be used in making the final choice.

'Nearly new' discounts of up to 35% may prove a good bargain, provided the users will tolerate the 'second-hand' stigma.

## Finance charges

Unless the borrowing for purchase is made directly by the customer the rate offered by the lender must be viewed with some scepticism. Most contract operators either have their own finance companies or have a close association with one. In either case it is common to put forward an attractive finance rate which is in fact to be subsidized out of some other profit centre. In terms of the total deal, and tax efficiency, this may not alter the overall cost, provided that the purchasers do not ignore the opportunity for competition believing that the finance deal is too good to pass over.

## Rate of depreciation

Most fleet motor vehicles are written off over 4 years, usually representing 80,000 to 100,000 miles. The residual value is realised by the user company in the purchase arrangements and also in the 'open-ended' lease. The 'closed-end' lease may return a residual value to the lessees if there is a surplus over that originally anticipated by the agreement.

## Wear and tear

Where the residual value is to the benefit of the user the choice of vehicle and the standard of maintenance and driver-care are issues to take seriously into account. In the contract hire or some lease arrangements the supplier will insist on a 're-conditioning' charge for vehicles delivered up in a poor state of wear and tear on expiration of the agreement. In such cases the definition of 'poor' should be defined and bench-marked for the avoidance of dispute. Also, users should insist that rental payments do not have to continue through any 're-conditioning' period.

## Reliability

Though not a cost centre in itself, the reliability of the fleet will drive not only the maintenance and replacement costs and residual values but also the productive output and morale of the users - probably a much more significant factor than any apparent saving by purchasing cheaply.

## Servicing costs

Regular maintenance of the fleet is a fairly significant annual cost which can vary enormously between models and their manufacturers - see **FIG 7.9.B** . As well as looking at the bottom-line whole life cost comparisons the user should also look to secure absolute reliability in terms of quality and minimising time off the road.

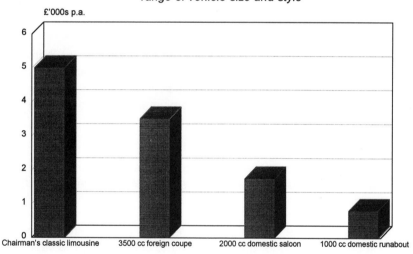

**FIG. 7.9.B:** *Annual servicing and maintenance costs - range of vehicle size and style*

Some service agents now operate a drive-in/drive-out service system where the car is only off the road for the hour or so it takes for routine maintenance or (by prior arrangement) major repairs. Facilities are available for the driver to have a snack, watch the tv or, even better, catch up with some overdue paperwork. Waiting times are guaranteed subject to the need for repairs.

## Replacement parts

Again, availability and costs vary greatly between makes and models. Major fleet owners can insist on minimum levels of dedicated spares in the service agent's stock or may carry them themselves, at the same time reaping the economies of bulk direct purchasing.

The contract hirer should satisfy himself as to the suitability of the contractor's replacement parts strategy prior to entering the agreement; although most hire contracts offer a fixed maintenance/replacement price, the time off the road will probably be a far more critical risk to bottom line profits than the price of a spare part.

## Mileage

Contract hire agreements often incorporate an 'excess mileage' condition, whereby the user has to pay a premium for every mile driven over the prescribed minimum. How accurately this level is assessed can make or break the economics of contract hire and needs to be the subject of thorough investigation - not only of historic mileage but of future requirements based on giving business trends. The facilities manager must be pro-active on this issue as in all management tasks!

Where possible the user should negotiate a universal mileage rather than taking each vehicle separately, thereby offsetting under-mileage against excesses.

Modern vehicles, even the smaller cheaper ones, conscientiously driven and maintained, can often go over 100,000 miles before ending their useful life; vehicles using diesel fuel can be expected to outlive their petrol-driven counterparts by as much as 10-20%.

## Type of fuel

As well as the above-mentioned longevity diesel-fuelled cars may save up to 1.5p to 2.5p per mile depending on the model. There is a big question mark over the environmental impact of diesel fumes which may become the focus of legislation in due course. Meanwhile, the economics in running, maintenance and resale (at present diesel cars have a better residual value) have resulted in a steady increase in the numbers of diesel vehicles on the UK's roads - up from 18% of the market in 1993 to 25% in 1994. It is therefore probably just as well that there has been a comparable increase in the proportion of petrol-driven vehicles using lead-free petrol over the same period.

The grade of fuel chosen also needs to be put under thorough scrutiny. Many drivers are under the false impression that higher grades mean higher performance regardless of maker's recommendations. On the contrary, using Super grade where the maker recommends Premium will simply add to the mileage cost with no increased performance whatsoever.

## Insurance

The user will almost always have to provide his own insurance cover, and the terms will have to be acceptable to the financier or hirer where the vehicles are not purchased outright.

Always test the market at each renewal, and, where appropriate, give the fleet supplier or manager the opportunity to bid; they have a vested interest in the risk and its effect on their interests and will almost certainly have a far greater knowledge of the motor insurance market than does the facilities manager.

## Accident repair

All motorists know that once a vehicle has been repaired after collision damage it is never quite the same again. 'I like the two-tone' says the smart second-hand car salesman when the discussion about trade-in value of your monotone pride and joy gets under way. Nevertheless, modern technology in skilled hands can achieve good repair results. Much more important than appearance is any structural damage caused by serious mishaps. The loss adjustors for the less scrupulous insurance companies will often resist a write-off claim; where this will obviously result in a loss of residual value the decision should be vehemently contested, if necessary with a threat of legal action to recover any loss.

Again, time-off-the-road will be a critical economic factor, and the fleet manager should ensure that his relationships with insurers and repairers are established in such a way as to minimise the time-lapses between:

- accident and estimate
- estimate and visit by loss-adjustor
- inspection report and repair works.

Some insurance policies and hire contracts will cover replacement vehicles for some or part of the time off the road. Otherwise 'down-sizing' of vehicle as well as simple daily hire as required are recommended ways to avoid the worst of the financial impact of the need for temporary replacement.

**Better still, good up-to-date records of cars not in use through illness, holidays or business circumstances can throw up a pool of available cars at no cost at all.**

## Re-sale values

The implications for the user of re-sale values depending on the procurement route are discussed above.

Sometimes users are tempted to sell fully written-down cars to the employees at the written down price in the accounts. Where the true re-sale figure is substantially greater the Inspector of Taxes may take an interest in the transaction with a view to treating the employee's gain as income to be taxed.

The fall-off of sales of new cars during the recession of the early 1990's has left a shortfall of residual vehicles due to come to the market from 1993-96. This has enhanced the prospects for the re-sale value of such vehicles, a benefit which has been further boosted by the new tax regime for personal use of company cars which favours vehicles of four years old or more.

## Taxation implications

The consequences of the various procurement routes with regard to Corporation Taxation and VAT are discussed above.

The benefits to employees of having a company car are also now almost eroded through personal taxation. The current tax regime links the personal 'benefit in kind' directly to the original purchase price (35% of the list price to be precise) rather than engine capacity. Mitigation is available to major business users and drivers of older cars - but not much is on offer to the vintage car buffs.

'Perk' drivers doing less than 2,500 miles per annum will now pay a lot more tax, so a smaller or older car could suit them better.

New car prices for tax purposes are based on list price before discounts, and fleet contractors are now looking for new ways of presenting prices while maintaining the profits arising from the discounts of up to 40% they can elicit from the manufacturers.

**FIG 7.9.C** shows the taxable benefits from 6/4/94 of a company car under 4 years old against the list price. The provision of a company car is still considered by employees to be a bonus for many reasons including status, condition and availability on the road

The employer can obtain tax relief on the depreciation, finance and running costs and possibly show the asset on his balance sheet to good effect.

Taxation implications aside, the most important benefit to an employer of providing a company car is that he can be reasonably sure that - human frailties aside - transport of his employees to and from potential profit centres is safe and reliable.

**FIG. 7.9.C:** *Taxable benefit of a company car against list price*

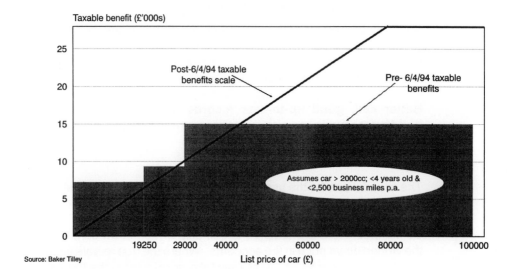

# CHAPTER 7.10 – DISASTER PREVENTION AND RECOVERY

## 7.10.1 THE NATURE OF DISASTER

*Definition*

In its broadest context 'disaster' refers to any situation the totality of which could threaten the ability of an organisation to carry on its business in an effective manner.

A series of unfortunate events, possibly a combination of natural and man-made incidents, lies behind many disasters.

Man-made disasters may be accidental or intentional. Intentional disasters are motivated by war, politics or other causal dedication, malevolence or insanity - the latter arguably being at the root of all the atrocities committed under the guise of one or other of the above excuses for indiscriminate death and destruction.

Chapter 7.1 considers **security** in general and the problems facing the organisation deprived of its electronic communications facilities. This chapter therefore deals specifically with the risks of deprivation of the **use of premises** on a large scale, the costs of disruption and the costs of protection and recovery.

*Natural disaster*

In the UK purely natural disasters such as earthquake, hurricanes and flooding are not generally considered a threat to major properties although the 1989 persistent flooding in the West Country was a worrying omen of what might happen one day anywhere in the country. The flood risk to the City of London posed by the River Thames relies upon the Woolwich flood barriers for its antidote; one hopes that the full implications on flood levels of the global warming identified in recent years was taken into account by its designers.

Equally, earthquakes on a high point of the Richter scale are not known in the UK, so we do not have foundations designed specifically to counter seismic activity. But there is always a first time.

Hurricanes are not a threat to the stability of modern city centre commercial building structures, but could cause a problem to some of the more lightweight structures sometimes found on the outskirts of provincial centres.

A major cause of disaster - fire - is a natural phenomenon which can be brought about by accident or deliberately - either way it is a crippler.

*Man-made disaster*

The principal cause of man-made disaster in peace time is the terrorist bomb. The terrorist attempts to advertise and enhance his cause by bringing public attention to his disastrous activity. It is often an insidious process, occasionally a one-off gesture. In every case severe personal or physical damage is sought or threatened. The whole activity is dependent upon each event -and its dire consequences - being broadcast to those parts of the world where it might be expected to be of concern, and, through fear, influence public opinion to turn against the stance of authority on a particular issue.

## 7.10.2 DISASTER RISK

*Media
responsibility*

Given that publicity of the threat to human life and well-being is the sole cause of terrorist incidents, whether in the form of explosions or contaminated fish-paste, it does seem blindingly obvious that denying such publicity would eliminate the majority of incidents overnight.

The inherent risk to the perpetrator of a terrorist attack is such that it could not be justified in the absence of extensive media coverage of the incident. So, why international governments cannot collaborate in outlawing *all* media-reporting of claims made as to the responsibility for an incident is beyond the comprehension of most intelligent people giving the matter serious consideration.

It is only the **claim to responsibility** which needs to be quashed – the incident will publicise itself or, as in the case of food-contamination, require to be broadcast. However, a simple statement referring to 'a terrorist bomb' or 'intentionally contaminated fish-paste' without identifying the protagonist would surely satisfy the general public's curiosity; in fact, since the corollary would be to make such atrocities irrelevant to the various causes, there would soon be few, if any, incidents to report.

The media will not regulate itself in this regard, so every life lost and every business seriously disrupted is, inadvertently, as much their responsibility as the perpetrators'!

Only very tough and wide-ranging anti-broadcast measures will remedy this late-20th century phenomenon whereby TV, radio and press commentators almost fall over themselves to be first to convey the terrorists' propaganda message and unwittingly (or carelessly) encourage the next incident.

*Human
response*

Although flood barriers, anti-seismic structures, seismic readings and climatic analysis can mitigate against or warn of potential natural disaster man cannot actually stop the elements from behaving in such a way as to cause widespread destruction.

It would seem that it is not possible to guarantee total security against disaster, whether natural or man-made, so what can the facilities manager offer his company by way of protection against the risks?

*Terrorist
explosion*

The usual means of creating physical havoc are improvised explosive devices (IED's) which are easily manufactured domestically, and carry little risk to the assailants either in the making, carrying or planting.

IED's are either incendiary or explosive. Incendiary devices are easily concealed and are usually planted in groups in and around combustible materials and furniture. They have a simple timer mechanism which is normally set to go off out of hours when the ensuing fire will do most damage before detection.

Staff must be trained to be observant and report unusual or unfamiliar objects although the installation of sprinklers may, in the end, be the best way of avoiding too much damage. Obviously sprinklers can themselves cause damage, so it is particularly important for all important papers and equipment to be stored or otherwise protected outside of normal working hours. The initial cost of sprinklers is considered in Chapter 7.1

Explosive devices comprise the explosive, its detonator and a timer - all enclosed in some form of container. Placed close to its target a properly functioning device can, as we have all seen far too often, create havoc, death and destruction.

Explosive devices are unpredictable in the scale, direction and spread of the destruction and are particularly varied in the form of their containment and concealment eg: boots of cars, litter bins and parcels are but a few disguises commonly adopted by terrorists to conceal their weapons of destruction.

IED's can also be launched from a distance rendering external anti-terrorist security for a specific building almost impossible other than in the immediate location.

Physical anti-explosive construction is very expensive and is not yet a normal feature of design briefs for mainland UK commercial buildings. However, it is possible to plan to mitigate the threat of explosion and its immediate physical consequences as also the disaster recovery package.

## 7.10.3 PLANNED PREVENTION

*The threats*

Establishing the exposure of the organisation to risk of terrorist attack is the essential first step in planning prevention. Critical factors will be:

- the significance of the organisation and/or its business as a target
- proximity to such organisations
- any history of terrorist activity in the locality
- ease and extent of public access to the main part of the building
- apparent security measures.

Having determined the nature and level of any identified risk the plan can then be drawn up. The plan will embrace protection and response, no different in principle from any other security plan as discussed in Chapter 7.1.

As with other security measures, anti-terrorist protection comprises deterrence and detection; however, some construction and planning measures can be taken to reduce the effect of explosion on fabric and personnel.

*Physical protection*

**FIG. 7.10.A:** *Typical cost ranges of alternative means of protection against flying glass*

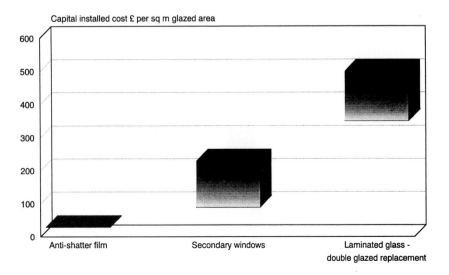

Existing buildings are not easily altered to provide protection. However, anti-shatter film (ASF), secondary windows or laminated glass will all limit the internal hazard of flying shattered glass. **FIG 7.10.A** shows typical comparative initial costs for these measures. Of course, partitions give more protection than screens so locating cellular offices on the vulnerable perimeters may be popular with those in the open plan interiors – possibly less so with the occupants of the cellular space who might normally be pleased with the privilege.

Many city centre buildings could benefit in investment value through a face-lift, so re-cladding or over-cladding with a blast-absorbent non-fragmenting material could perform a dual function; **FIG 7.10.B** gives some typical costs.

**FIG. 7.10.B:** *Capital cost ranges of alternative re-cladding / over-cladding options*

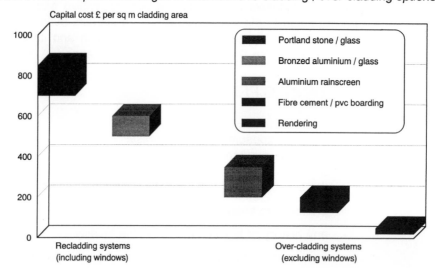

FIG 7.10.C shows how, by taking the opportunity to extend the floor area during re-cladding, the protective exercise will most probably pay for itself and leave a profit. **The example is of an office building of 5,000 sq m GIA (4,250 sq m NIA) valued before re-cladding on the basis of £300 per sq m NIA and 11 YP (9% initial yield)**. If only the added value of the extra floor space were to be taken into account at the same rent and yield the costs would not be justified. However, because such an extension could not be carried out without altering the services and replacing the finishes the investor might expect that the improved image and perceived quality would generate either an improved yield or a better rent – or more likely both. **The effects on the investment value of first a lowering of the yield to 8% (12.5 YP) and then a rental increase to £350 per sq m NIA show how the exercise begins to stack up.**

**FIG. 7.10.C:** *Cost / value appraisal of re-cladding and refurbishing while increasing floor area by 14%*

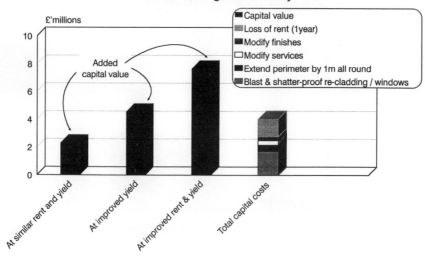

It is interesting to note that the loss of a year's rent costs nearly as much as the re-cladding works. However, such works are normally carried out at the end of a lease when a void might in any case have been anticipated and equally the investor may well have a sinking fund provision for the refurbishment. Either or both factors will make the profitability of the venture even greater.

Nevertheless, the location must be capable of sustaining a higher valuation otherwise any such improvements will have to rely solely upon an occupier's business case – possibly a problem if the asset is to support the financing of the project.

Planning the car parking away from buildings will make detection of plants easier and also reduce the impact of any explosion.

The effects of blast can be contained in new building design by:

- use of homogeneous energy-absorbent materials such as reinforced concrete which do not easily deform or fracture and give warning signs of impending failure
- use of anti-shatter glazing materials as described above
- planning important areas away from the immediately vulnerable disaster zones
- simplifying perimeter shape to avoid blast-wave reflection.

Detection and deterrence can be helped by:

- light-coloured elevations to aid detection on dull days and at night-time
- floodlighting.

and other deterrent and detection methods relevant to basic security as discussed in Chapter 7.1

*Alertness*

Many organisations have coded states of alert which are useful for keeping the staff, visitors and potential assailants aware of the existence of a planned and manned security regime.

Natural disasters are frequently accompanied by broadcast warnings. The main security companies permanently monitor the radio and TV for such omens. Where the security manning is in-house there is a good reason to allow, even encourage, at least one security guard to stay tuned into the appropriate wavelength.

## 7.10.4 RESPONSE

*Response to a threat*

The team designated to deal with the threat, its duties and communications processes must be well established. Bomb-response procedures should be written down and regularly rehearsed. Where appropriate, safe areas should be designated; blast-proof areas should be:

- internal
- away from primary circulation routes
- enclosed by solid, preferably reinforced concrete, structures
- equipped with communications media.

Liaison with the police during a confirmed incident is essential and their advice must be sought on evacuation.

## Recovery plan

The procedures recommended in the wake of a disaster affecting vital business are now well documented in all organisations where terrorism is even remotely a risk. It should not be forgotten, however, that natural disaster can present just the same consequences as the man-made variety and needs just the same recovery procedures. The facilities manager may have a front line role in the recovery plan or just be a member of the core team. In any case he will certainly have to take up responsibility for reinstatement of all facilities and operating services and have a back-up pool of accommodation and suppliers to support the pre-identified key recovery job functions.

Security post-disaster will have to be particularly tight, especially with regard to malevolent supplementary damage by disaffected staff and also looting. A clear-desk policy is not only highly desirable with respect to cleanliness - it also provides major protection against one of the worst consequences of disaster - lost or damaged documents.

Photographic evidence of one form or another must be produced for negotiations with the insurance lost adjustor; for the same purpose all costs of the recovery and reinstatement must be carefully maintained by the facilities manager. A particular point to note is that the cost of immediate post-disaster construction work may not be allowed in full by the loss adjustor if the procurement route has not been planned and negotiated in advance to avoid 'blackmail' charging.

The question of insurance against disaster is considered more fully in Chapter 3.6.

**FIG. 7.10.D:** *The guide to disaster recovery action planning*

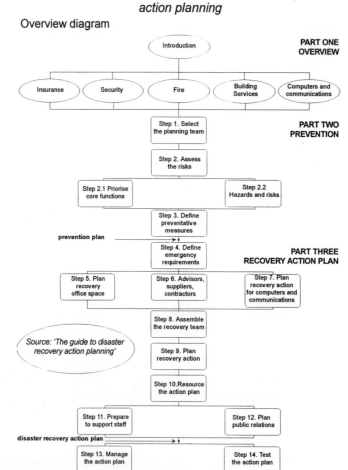

An excellent book by David Hyams [1] on the subject of 'Disaster Recovery Action Planning' contains the overview diagram reproduced at **FIG 7.10.D.**

[1] MRC Business Information Group Ltd, Oxford Tel: (0865) 200202

# SECTION 8

# STAFF SUPPORT COSTS

# CHAPTER 8.1 – CATERING

## 8.1.1 THE CATERING POLICY

*Catering and the corporate plan*

As with all facilities management cost centres the decision as to whether, why, who, what, when, how and at what cost to provide catering must stem naturally from the organisation's facilities policy (see Chapter 1.1)

The principal reasons for providing industrial catering are:

- employee satisfaction
- hospitality.

Employee satisfaction will become an issue for one or more of the following reasons:

- an isolated location offers limited or no alternative
- a 'perk' is needed to encourage recruitment and retention of staff
- time away from the workplace may be critical to the function of particular tasks
- to discourage poor eating habits where 'junk' food outlets and sandwich bars are the only alternative in a short lunch period
- to discourage lunch-time visits to public houses or wine bars
- as a philanthropic gesture of social responsibility to ensure staff are properly fed, especially in shift situations where lunch may have to be the main meal of the day.

In-house hospitality catering is not just a highly cost-effective alternative to dining-out for it also can be a great time-saver appreciated by to-day's time-pressured business visitor as much as by the host.

Hospitality dining is usually in a separate but adjacent facility, although the directors' areas are usually away from the staff dining and may have dedicated service. Alcohol is still served in most hospitality areas, but its provision in staff dining is still almost universally taboo; this ban harks back to the Victorian abstentionists but now has a foundation in plain common sense.

*Policy decisions*

Having decided, on one or more of the above grounds, to provide an on-site catering facility the organisation will have to make decisions in the following key areas, all of which will have important cost implications:

- catering numbers
- style of service
- range of menu
- price structure
- speed of service
- opening hours
- decor

- space
- food preparation technology
- location of catering facilities.

## 8.1.2 CATERING NUMBERS

*Proportion of staff dining*

Where formal catering is provided on site the proportion of staff availing themselves of the opportunity varies from around 50% - 80%. Really remote sites may achieve 100%.

The minimum number to make formal catering viable in an organisation is usually considered to be 100 - also the number at which out-sourcing of the facility becomes of interest to the contractor.

Generally speaking an organisation which has a policy of catering provision will want to optimise its use, partly for reasons of economies of scale but mainly to get as much good internal public relations as possible out of the provision.

*Size of sitting*

How many of the diners participate in one sitting obviously impacts on the space provision, but it is unlikely that space use considerations will drive the policy in this respect; time available for lunch will be the key determinant of the size and style of the facility.

## 8.1.3 STYLES OF SERVICE

*The choices*

The catering options available are many and varied, due to the advances in technologies for preparation, storage, cooking, serving, clearing and disposal.

In ascending order of sophistication (and cost) the principal serving styles are:

- self-catering
- self-service
- part self-service/part waitress service
- waitress service only
- 'remote' service.

In each case a decision will also have to be made as to whether the facility will be single - or multi-status.

*Self-catering*

The simplest form of self-catering is the snack/drinks vending machine. These are considered later in the Chapter.

Few modern self-catering facilities now depend on gas/electric ovens with the associated pots and pans and domestic kitchen clutter. However, microwave technology has offered an acceptable quick and 'clean' alternative which can suit the smaller organisation.

It is important for the smaller organisation to know that the use of 'domestic' microwaves on business premises contravenes the Food Safety Acts. The reason for this stipulation is primarily that domestic units lose their capacity with continuous use thereby failing to meet the 70°C needed for proper cooking and putting the consumer at risk of food poisoning.

**'Commercial' grade units up to 1,000 Watts are easily available in most localities at a cost of up to £1,000 for ovens ranging from 700 - 1,000 Watts.**

The commercial models have a greater capacity, better controls and sometimes alternative cooking processes. The degree of sophistication will depend upon whether the catering regime is truly self-catering or will have some assistants in attendance. Avoidance of queuing is particularly important, especially as staff operating the ovens may become flustered under the scrutiny of their impatient (real or imaginary) colleagues.

Ready-made dishes can be sold or stored on the site and clearing away is usually left to the diner; disposable 'crockery' and cutlery are often provided free of charge.

## Self-service

Self-service is now almost universally adopted for staff catering. Apart from the obvious saving in manpower and cost, the main advantage is speed of service - so important to staff wanting only a short break so as to take advantage of a flexi-time bonus, or just to leave time for social gathering, shopping etc. Options are becoming more and more innovative, catering for hot and cold food and sometimes 'fast' food.

The traditional self-service arrangement of one long counter with chef's assistants serving all menu items has largely been replaced by 'free-flow' service points eg: islands serving (or offering for self-serving) such menu variants as salads, hot dishes, sandwiches, fruit and drinks. Some restaurants have delicatessen-style refrigerated dispensers.

The principal advantage of the 'island' type of layout is speed of service as also the prevention of queuing which is a counter-productive (sic!) irritant. Of course, speed of service must be accompanied by speed of check-out.

A speed benchmark for really sophisticated self-service is 3 minutes from entering the cafeteria to becoming seated at the dining table.

Methods of payment are also becoming more sophisticated mainly, again, with a view to increased speed and avoidance of queuing. Coins are out, being replaced by tokens or sometimes pre-encoded cards. Tokens may either be purchased to cover two or three course meals or provided free of charge if that is the catering policy. Cards can identify the user's tariff rating and either be 'loaded' by cash pre-payment into validation units or deducted from salaries by linking to the payroll program. Digital displays on the tills or vending machines indicate the current financial status of the card.

The payment point and beverage dispenser are usually the bottle-necks in the system. Payment can be speeded up by the various token/card arrangements and also by siting the cashier in such a manner as to permit calculation of the cost of down-queue meals pending settlement of the one immediately at the check-out.

Hot beverage service can be speeded up by attendant service, or by siting the facility outside of the main dining area, say in a coffee lounge; in this way only those wanting a hot drink with their meals will have to queue before check-out.

## Waitress service

Such indulgence is only merited when neither speed nor cost is the main consideration. It is possibly appropriate to those organisations where a high proportion of employees frequently have cause to introduce visitors - in other words not a typical commercial company or public department.

Where waitress-service is deemed appropriate it is usually separate but adjacent to the main self-service restaurant using the same kitchen, but some Boardroom areas have dedicated catering.

Service may be 'plated' ie: suitable for middle-management with higher standards and great variety than in self-service, or 'silver-service' for senior management or any aspirants who can afford it.

*Remote Catering*

Satellite offices or special locations within a campus may be served by smaller kitchens and dining areas, with meals delivered in heated trolleys or by hand or vehicle. Some organisations provide a trolley service of mainly cold snacks to the workplace; however, the provision of vending machines is now making this practice redundant.

*Single or multi-status*

The decision as to whether to go single or multi-status is relevant to all but 'silver-service' catering. Within the range to which multi-status is appropriate the golden rule is to set standards to the highest common denominator, which will have implications for the cost per meal, but mitigated by the increased usage and better internal public relations.

## 8.1.4 THE MENU

*The factors influencing the range*

Among the most important factors affecting catering policy with regard to what is available are:

- perceived importance of provision in respect of employee satisfaction
- length of lunch-break
- social and cultural groupings
- predominant age and sex of employees
- need to provide the main meal of the day
- dietary policy.

Apart from the long-distance commuter and singletons most employees prefer to have the main meal of the day at home, a trend which has led the demand away from heavy meals towards lighter lunches and snacks.

Where main meals are served, caterers try to avoid the sauces and trimmings of the private restaurant, to grill rather than fry and to encourage consumption of salads, pasta and other low calorie, low cholesterol products. Not only is peppered steak with french fries expensive, it also breaks a lot of healthy diet rules and, in any case, the glass of wine ideally to go with it is probably not available due to company policy - except maybe in the 'function' or 'silver-plate' dining rooms.

The range of food available will also depend on the location of preparation which, in turn, may depend on the size of the catering facility. Full site-preparation is usual in the largest kitchens, and does require a delivery point separate from any waste disposal operation; kitchens need to be laid out with separate areas for preparing and cooking each type of food to avoid cross-contamination.

Simpler provision is where the food is delivered, chilled for same-day service or frozen for consumption sometime in the future. Kitchens for such provision are smaller but the range of meals available need not be less than in the full-preparation regime.

Again, required speed of service need not result in less choice of menu items.

### 8.1.5 THE PRICE

*The pricing
policy*

Two factors influence the price of the meal to the consumer:

- the cost of providing the meal
- any subsidy

The cost of providing the meal is discussed below. The policy with regards to subsidy is a matter for personnel rather than facilities management. A common policy is for the diner to pay the cost of food plus VAT with the company picking up the cost of management, preparation, equipment and service. Such an arrangement is normally considered by HM Inspector of Taxes as falling outside of the realm of taxable benefit, whereas 100% subsidy certainly does not.

Other policies require the employee to pay a full price for 'special' dishes, beverages etc.

In the final event, the investment per capita in terms of provision and subsidy will turn on the benefit accruing to the organisation deriving from it, whether measured by recruitment, retention, wealth or health of the employees.

Of course, if management gets any of it wrong then it would, in every economic aspect, be better not to have introduced the facility at all.

### 8.1.6 OPENING HOURS

*Availability
requirements*

The range of time for formal catering availability is from two hours at lunch-time, through breakfast, coffee, lunch and afternoon tea-time to 100% full availability ie: where full 24-hour shift-work is in operation.

The commonest provision is lunch-time only with vending areas catering for other requirements during the day.

A short unstaggered lunch-break necessitates a large facility with extremely sophisticated management; such an arrangement is not normal and is obviously expensive. More typically, an average of between two and three 'covers' in a two hour lunch period applies to most self-service facilities.

### 8.1.7 DECOR

*Design
requirements*

It is most important that the dining area should feel distinctly different from the main working areas. Lighting must be softer, colours warmer, servery counters and furniture (see also Chapter 6.7) crisp (and seats not so comfortable as to encourage a long stay!) and easily cleaned, and areas screened to provide a feeling of identity and possibly some privacy.

Changes of floor level are discouraged by the operators but can add considerable amenity; provided the main dining area is on the same level as the kitchen most operators will accept this feature, particularly in the self-service areas where diners clear their own tables.

Because of the space occupied by dining areas some organisations like the facilities to double as meeting areas outside of dining hours. Although this puts pressure on cleaning staff and is also very demanding in terms of compliance with the Food Safety Act, it does make economic sense. The designer's brief will therefore require the decor to be appropriate for the alternative function. For this reason, and also to facilitate cleaning, the level of lighting must always be adjustable in dining areas.

*The cost of fitting out*

**FIG 8.1.A** gives indicative costs for fitting out a range of dining area styles and configurations per unit of area and per capita. The actual space required is discussed below.

**FIG.8.1.A:** *Costs of fitting-out and equipping dining areas - various catering styles*

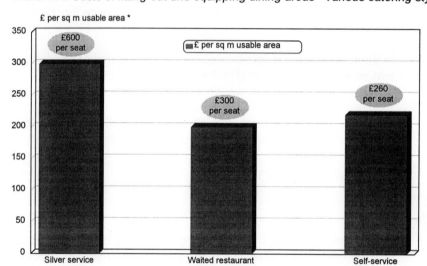

£ per sq m usable area *

* Excludes kitchen, loose furniture, fees, finance, VAT.

## 8.1.8 FOOD PREPARATION

*Types of processing*

As discussed in the 'Menu' paragraphs above, preparation may be

- full preparation
- cook/chill/re-heat
- cook/freeze/thaw/re-heat.

*Space and equipment*

Each process has a different space requirement and health and safety restrictions.

In particular, the delivery of fresh meat is only permissible during normal hours where there is a dedicated service access.

Modern kitchen equipment is multi-functional, space-saving, faster, energy efficient and mobile to facilitate both general cleaning of the rooms and specialist cleaning of the equipment itself.

The surfaces must be easy to clean and hygiene generally scrupulous. eg: lighting control should be by means of sensors to avoid spreading germs from one food to another via the light switches.

## 8.1.9 SPACE REQUIREMENTS

*Space per meal*

The space per 'cover' required in the dining area ranges from around 2m² in smaller establishments where there is waitress service down to 1.2m² for a for a self-catering area. The coffee area is typically 0.7-0.8m² per cover.

Space in the kitchens will depend upon how much preparation takes place and whether it contains an active servery. Typically a large full-preparation kitchen supporting a free-flow operation needs about 0.4m² per meal compared with 0.65m² for a 200-meal operation; cook/chill or cook/freeze operations can save substantially on space in some situations.

## 8.1.10 LOCATION OF CATERING FACILITIES

*Geographical location*

Ideally dining facilities should be provided in space not otherwise dedicated - or worse rented as - offices. Some larger premises have catering dedicated in basement or lower-ground floor areas with rental values adjusted accordingly. As **FIG 8.1.B** shows, if it is not possible to use non-office space the space costs per meal, especially in high value locations, can be very considerable, even prohibitive.

**FIG 8.1.B:** *The impact of premises costs on catering costs where prime office space is dedicated to dining*

| Premises costs † £ per capita gross pa * | | | |
|---|---|---|---|
| Location | 200 Meals | 500 Meals | 750 Meals |
| City of London | 700 | 650 | 600 |
| West End | 650 | 600 | 500 |
| Greater London | 390 | 360 | 300 |
| Provincial City | 260 | 240 | 200 |
| Out of Town location | 250 | 200 | 150 |
| Premises costs † £ per meal per person dining * | | | |
| Location | 200 Meals | 500 Meals | 750 Meals |
| City of London | 5.50 | 5.40 | 5.00 |
| West End | 5.40 | 5.00? | 4.17 |
| Greater London | 3.25 | 3.00 | 2.50 |
| Provincial City | 2.17 | 2.00 | 1.67 |
| Out of Town location | 2.08 | 1.67 | 1.25 |

+ Rent, rates and operating costs but excluding fitting-out and furniture.
* Based on 50% of staff taking one meal per working day pa
i.e. double these costs per regular daily diner.

*Location in premises*

At an operational level, dedicated access to the kitchens/food storage areas is critical in avoiding the need for out-of-hours delivery of fresh foods, so provision of goods lifts may be necessary if the facility is above ground floor.

Where premises are formed in a local cluster it may be beneficial to use the least operationally strategic space for dining rather than that most convenient for the more senior staff. Much will depend on the time available for lunch, the desirability or otherwise of a short walk in the neighbourhood and how important the provision is in personnel terms.

As a general rule it is best for catering to be in the building containing most potential diners. However, if the 'flag-ship' is smaller but reasonably accessible then many satellite staff will make a short trek, just to be 'seen'. Again, if the cost of space in the flagship is high the decision must be made particularly carefully taking all costs and benefits into consideration.

## 8.1.11 THE COST OF CATERING PROVISION

*Typical costs
per capita*

**FIG 8.1.C** gives unabridged figures from a sample of 12 office catering analyses per unit of floor area and per capita.

**FIG. 8.1.C:** *Catering costs per capita from a representative sample of data*

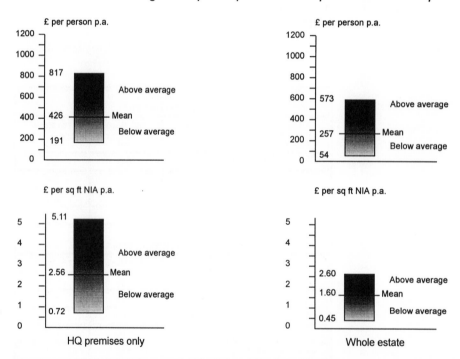

Income from sales and subsidies is excluded from the figures. The numbers of diners is not given in the data so the costs per capita reflect the total workforce - possibly a better benchmark. As previously shown the ratio of diners is typically from 60-80% of the workforce. Several of the specimens in the example are locally clustered offices; in all cases the catering is provided in the Head Office building. For this reason the costs per unit of area and per person have been calculated on the basis of the whole building stock and workforce in the clusters as well as just for Head Office.

*Typical meal
cost analysis*

**FIG 8.1.D** shows typical costs per meal for self-catering, self-service and waitress service facilities indicating adjustments to be made for quality of menu and location.

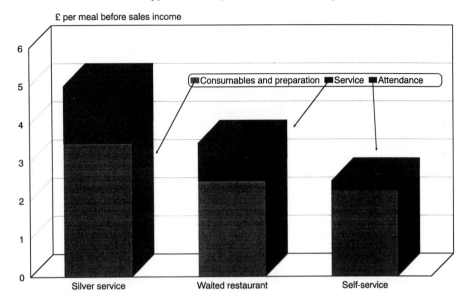

**FIG. 8.1.D:** *Typical costs per meal - excluding premises costs*

## 8.1.12 MANAGEMENT

*In-house v out-source*

The core/non-core argument takes on significance once the catering numbers rise above 100; below this the contractors do not find the work profitable or must charge excessively to achieve the desired return on investment.

In-house catering can be effective and efficient just as in provision of any other specialist service. Nevertheless the purchasing power, labour resources and commitment to hygiene, health & safety of the contractors are powerful arguments in their favour

*The catering contract*

Choosing and monitoring the contractors is critical; reputation alone will not necessarily guarantee quality, so the in-house liaison person must insist on the letter of the agreement, in particular with regard to:

- availability and calibre of trained staff
- diet balance
- management reports (monthly is preferable)
- cost accounting (up to date and accurate)
- management audit.

Sometimes contractors will design the facilities and organise construction, purchasing and funding; they will always insist on controlling cleaning and maintenance.

There are two principal mechanisms for paying the catering contractor:

- cost-plus
- single fee.

In both cases the catering contractor runs the whole operation, with all costs (net of all trade and cash discounts) being reimbursed to the contractor plus an agreed percentage or sliding scale fee.

In the case of the cost-plus arrangement the client has potentially more control over what is provided in terms of quality, cost, portions etc. whereas in the single fee arrangement the level of provision is fixed subject only to inflation of raw materials and labour.

A variation on the theme relates final reimbursement to performance against performance indicators - much as in some types of maintenance agreement - including financial and management as well as quality targets.

Care must be taken to ensure that, where different styles of catering such as 'self-service' and 'silver-plate' are being sought under the same contract, the caterer has the experience and staff levels necessary to provide both services efficiently.

In all cases, as well as in-house provision, regular, independent questionnaire surveys must be conducted in the interests of staff, caterer and business management alike.

## 8.1.13 VENDING MACHINES

*Services available*

Vending machines can these days provide each and every refreshment requirement from a cold drink to a hot meal.

The range of consumables available through vending machines comprises:

- cold drinks
- hot beverages
- confectionery
- snacks
- hot meals.

Cold drinks come refrigerated in cans and cartons bearing 'well known' brand-names. Hot beverages (in-cup or fresh brew) include tea, coffee (cappuccino, espresso, au lait), savoury drinks, fruit cup etc. The confectionery merchandisers selling chocolate bars, crisps, nuts etc. are operated on a commission basis to the employer, which should return a profit after rental payments and maintenance.

The chilled merchandisers operate on a similar basis offering packaged snacks (eg biscuits and cheese) and sandwiches and pies etc. or whole meals for microwaving. The latest models can now incorporate a microwave oven, thereby offering a complete, if limited-menu, on-site catering service.

*Quality and maintenance*

Nearly all goods purveyed are quality name brands. The hot beverages can be freshly brewed and the ingredients mixed to taste; most users of good machines consider that the taste is about as good as that produced in the kitchen via the kettle. Upkeep such as keeping the machines stocked can be contracted-out if necessary. Troublesome coin-in-the-slot machines are fast being replaced by the far more efficient token - or electronic-card - operating equipment.

The 'in-cup' and sachet systems avoid release of ingredients amongst the working parts, so dramatically improving efficiency of performance, and reducing down-time maintenance costs; such systems also avoid the need for filling on site by contractors.

*Vending-
machine policy*

The decision to use vending machines will normally be covered by the need to:

- provide a minimum on-site convenience
- augment a primary catering or snack facility in 'remote' locations
- provide a drinks and beverages facility about the site in lieu of, or to augment, a central facility
- to make a profit.

The latter is not a serious consideration since by far the over-riding purpose of the provision is for staff convenience, internal public relations and hygiene/safety.

*The economics
of vending*

All the services can provide a return to the employer by way of commission on sales, rebates, or free maintenance or even free rental. It all depends upon the numbers of machines, volume of sales and any subsidies available.

In some situations the need for an on-site catering facility can be avoided, without loss of face, by providing a combination of beverage dispenser and chilled merchandisers.

Machines take up less space than kitchens, are easier to keep clean, keep the Health and Safety Officer happy (or less miserable) and may subsidise or eliminate the rental cost of this facility.

**Monthly rentals currently range from £10 per month for in-cup beverage dispensers to £7000 per month for hot/cold fresh brew machines and chilled meal merchandisers with built-in microwave.**

When considering the time spent by employees making tea/coffee from the kettle, vending machines do provide a good return on investment. Surveys have shown that on average 45 minutes a day is spent (outside of formal breaks) per capita on making tea and coffee. Even at a low average time-charge of £15 per hour this means an average loss of output of over £10 per day per capita. Perhaps for this reason alone the Americans and Japanese now have one machine per 25 head of population; given that this phenomenal development is largely the result of electronics replacing the old coin-in-the-slot and dispensing mechanisms now available in the UK, no doubt our present modest one machine per 100 head of population will soon whittle down.

As it is, over 5bn cupped drinks are sold in UK vending machines each year, yielding around £2 bn of sales. This average of 40p per cup can be as little as 10p in the lower quartile so, taking the £10 per day time-loss calculated above, the economic argument does seem to fall in favour of the machine see **FIG 8.1.E**.

FIG 8.1.E: *Theoretical calculation of self-catering v vending for break-time beverages*

| Cost Breakdown | Free beverages - self catering | £ per capita per day | Free beverage vending machine | £ per capita per day |
|---|---|---|---|---|
| Lost output per capita per day | 5 x 10 min @ £15 per hour | 12.50 | 5 x 5 min @ £15 per hour | 6.25 |
| Ingredients and maintenance | 5 beverages per capita per day @ £0.20 per beverage | 1.00 | 5 beverages per capita per day @ £0.40 per beverage | 2.00 |
| Total | | 13.50 | | 8.25 |

The only thing not quite certain is how the time spent around the machine equates to the kitchen time, or whether people would otherwise be productive in the time saved - perhaps they need frequent breaks to function efficiently the rest of the time.

Nevertheless the arguments in respect of availability, cleanliness, space and convenience, probably win the day for the automatons.

# CHAPTER 8.2 – HEALTH & SAFETY AT WORK

## 8.2.1 RISKS TO HEALTH AND SAFETY AT WORK

*Who is at risk?*

Considerations of health & safety at work are not just restricted to the employees of one organisation working from its premises.  Just as much at risk are:

- visitors to the premises on official business from other firms (including contractors and suppliers)
- visiting relatives and social acquaintances of employees
- members of the general public affected by activities, emissions and waste associated with the premises.

The consequences of disaster resulting from failure to afford adequate protection will fall upon both the individuals affected and the organisation responsible for the event;  responsibility may be passed onto a third party in certain circumstances.

*Risk to the afflicted person*

The individual is at risk from

- viral infection
- physiological disorder
- postural injury
- psychological injury
- physical impact damage
- asphyxiation
- burning
- electrocution.

Personal injury, illness and debility will be accompanied by financial loss which may or may not be recouped by insurance cover or civil action.

*Risk to the organisation responsible*

Whereas the individual may suffer death, disability or illness the perpetrator may also suffer in several ways eg:

- criminal prosecution under statutory provisions against:
  - the organisation
  - its directors
  - its employees
- civil action under the laws of contract or tort against:
  - the organisation
  - its directors
  - its employees
- expense and loss of employee productivity through

- sickness

- re-recruitment

- loss of morale

- absenteeism.

In fact **absenteeism** used to be, and in many cases still is, a very highly significant factor in lost productivity. Local authorities used to have the worst record in this respect;  however, a report by the Audit commission [1] in 1990 highlighted the problem as a result of which many authorities responded with considerable success (**FIG 8.2.A**).

**FIG. 8.2.A:** *Improvements in the rate of absenteeism in local authorities - 1990-94*

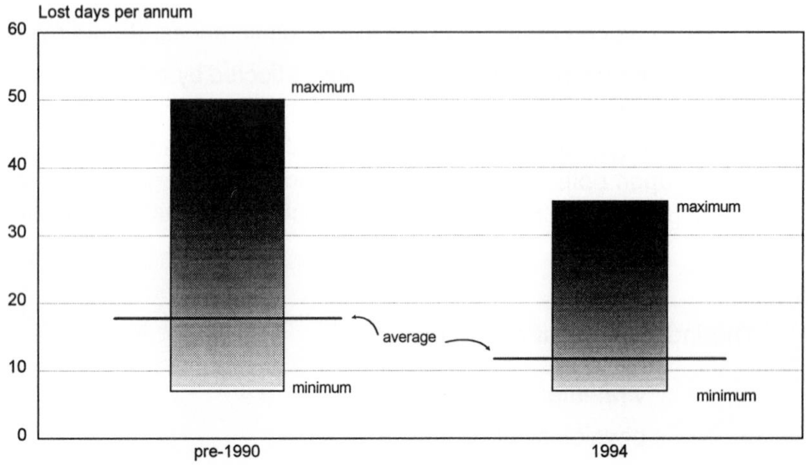

Source: Audit Commission / The Times

Private sector absenteeism on average is currently estimated by the CBI as 3.2% (8 working days lost p.a.) compared with 3.5% to 4.5% in the public sector and 2.4% in the Japanese private sector.

How much of this lost time is due to genuine illness and how much to malingering cannot be accurately assessed. However, it has been shown that where management has taken up an inquisitive and caring approach to employees' absenteeism, days lost have often fallen significantly.

Pre-return interviews have sometimes identified situations where the employee is in fact not ready for work (or possibly ready for part-time only) and provide a useful record for reviewing staff performance and health statistics.

The CBI survey in fact concludes that those who keep computer records of sickness suffer 30% less absenteeism from sickness than those who do not keep any at all.

It may of course be the fact that management seems to care which encourages better attendance, though whether the response is motivated by appreciation or fear almost certainly varies from one employee to another.

## 8.2.2 SOURCES OF RISK

*Bacteria and
fungi*

Poorly designed and/or maintained HVAC systems can provide a breeding ground for such agents of infection. The problem is often heightened when simple ventilation is extended to provide cooling and humidification. The contribution of wet cooling towers to legionella is now well documented; in fact, any system based on water droplets - of which humidification is one example - contains a high risk of infection and must have scrupulous preventative attention. Sterile steam humidification is believed to minimise or eliminate the risk.

Obviously the health and safety officer cannot prevent the introduction of naturally air-borne viruses to his premises but he can prevent contamination of water supplies and also ensure that hygiene in toilet, catering and vending areas is thorough.

*Contaminants*

Tobacco smoke and fuel vapours are known to contain many potentially harmful substances including carcinogenic agents.

Tobacco smoke can certainly be (and should be) banned from the office; 'passive smoking' as a cancer risk is now well documented and is bound in due course to involve litigation against employers permitting smoking.

The location and emission levels of concentrated vehicle movement should be carefully planned to prevent ingress via windows or 'fresh-air' intakes. Anyone who has ever waited in the taxi queue in the sub-basement at Euston Station will not need warning that diesel exhaust fumes are extremely unpleasant and a potential health hazard.

Most contaminants affect the respiratory system in one form or another, but usually bring on an allergic reaction such as asthma or hay fever.

The organic solvents are particularly virulent even in small concentrations; they come from adhesives and foams. Gases and vapours, such as formaldehyde as used in insulating products and bonded chipboard, are a problem when the materials are new, whilst photocopiers and many cleaning compounds are also sources of harmful vapour emissions.

'Particulates' describes the group of contaminants which are breathed-in in the form of tiny particles such as man-made fibres from carpets, curtains and other fabrics including many of the more common insulation materials. While there is as yet no positive evidence of long-term adverse effects of such inhalation, common sense suggests that it is unlikely to do anyone any good. Tests from the US Environmental Protection Agency accepted by the World Health Organisation have cleared mineral products from charges of being carcinogenic; fortunately the particulate contamination emanating from asbestos has now been identified and the product banned.

*Micro-
organisms*

As well as the disease-causing bacteria which can flourish in moist, and poorly-ventilated areas it is common for microbial activity to take place anywhere that dirt is allowed to accumulate. In particular, the dust mites whose droppings in a domestic environment have been discovered to be a cause of asthma, may well be a danger in the office, although the extent of this risk is probably less in the modern well-cleaned offices. The most likely area of risk is in areas where papers are left lying around untouched for long periods allowing dust to accumulate, especially where near open windows.

## Lighting

Lights which are inadequate for the task in hand can cause eye strain and inner tension. Additionally (and less obviously) high frequency flickering which is not actually noticed by the worker may yet cause headaches, as will excessive glare from surfaces and screens.

## Workstation arrangements

Apart from visual fatigue the arrangement of the workstation, particularly one with a computer display screen, can cause physical disabilities to the occupier. The repetitive strain injury (RSI) has already been the subject of successful civil action against hapless employers not aware of the emergent problem. Although this phenomenon is as much to do with ergonomic control as with furniture and equipment the newly-defined 'work-related upper limb disorders' (WRULD) have also been picked out by a recent EC Directive as requiring attention to the tilt of the work surface and adjustability of chair height.

Some furniture, being fully adjustable for desk-height as well as tilt, can cater for the below-average height worker without the risk of being unable to find the statutory foot-rest when required. Of course, a foot rest will not be of any use to the 6'4" operator who needs to lower the chair to get his knees under a non-height-adjustable table - he then needs a hole in the floor! In practice it is possible to raise work surfaces without making them adjustable, just as it is possible to provide footrests. Nevertheless, since some 20% of the workforce will be sufficiently above or below average height to require special provision, fully adjustable furniture for them is a viable risk-reduction option.

One problem is that designers like to stay with the visual order of one system; they may not like the visual appearance of the adjustable design and argue against it on those grounds, abetted by the suggestion that the employees do not use the facility anyway. However, the employee who develops muscular-skeletal problems not having used the adjustable facility (or having mis-used it) will have no claim against the employer provided proper training has been given.

Regardless of adjustability, the work surface must be large enough to permit a flexible desk-top layout.

## Equipment

Computer equipment may become a source of risk to the person operating it who should be able to move its position to suit his particular needs. Screen images and their presentation should be clear and adjustable and the keyboard separate from the screen.

Among the problems generated by computers and other office equipment are noise, heat, radiation, electrical charges, fumes (discussed above) and static electricity. The latter can be avoided by control of humidity; nevertheless, humidity control itself has been seen to be a potential source of threats to occupants' health - winning the health and safety war depends upon manoeuvring through many mine-fields.

As well as the physical implications for equipment operators the psychological consequence of coping with the employer's imposed computer-based applications have to be carefully monitored. Problems of psychological stress are increasingly common where operators are involved in prolonged and concentrated inputting of data. In such cases performance indicators can be an aid to monitoring employee's health as well as their productivity - well, George Orwell would have approved anyway!

*Space*

The Offices, Shops and Railway Premises Act 1963 subsumed into the Health & Safety at Work Act 1974, gave minimum area in a room per employee as 40SF. As this is below even the worst of modern practice, and since the parameter is not properly defined or even relevant to the modern workplace it does not present a threat to the facilities manager.

However, the practice of increasing space planning densities to levels not provided for in the design of HVAC, lighting, fire escapes and floors can inadvertently put the employer into breach of statute - not just the Health & Safety legislation - as well as inviting civil action for negligence.

Deep open planned space is also suspected of being a cause of psychological stress, and a windowless environment may be a cause of claustrophobia.

*Heat*

Bodily comfort can be affected by direct radiation from radiators and/or equipment, local air temperature and exposure to draughts. HSE regulations embodying EC Directives now stipulate air ambient temperature of 19-22 degrees celsius for offices with air-conditioning. Where there is no air-conditioning a maximum of 28 degrees C is laid down; prior to these changes only minimum temperatures were statutory, but the heat-gains from the modern office environment have made this upper level control essential.

The dehydrating effect of excessive dry heat can only be countered by humidifying air treatment which is not always a feature of the 'comfort cooling' systems proffering a low-cost alternative solution to 'all-air' cooling systems.

Many of the symptoms ascribed to the so-called 'sick-building syndrome' (see below) are caused either by lack of humidity or lack of proper maintenance of systems which provide it.

*Electricity*

The danger posed by exposure to electrocution is instilled into most people as soon as they are old enough to crawl. This does not stop people changing lamp bulbs with the switch still at 'on' or touching light switches with wet fingers. Although most office appliances could not see the light of day without thorough anti-shock protection, equipment which is designed to be moved around is said to cause 25% of all reportable electrical accidents. Examples of such equipment include pc's, cooling fans, electric kettles, photocopiers and printers. Problems usually emanate from the post-manufacture human treatment of the equipment: incorrect wiring of plugs, wrong replacement fuses, damaged insulation to leads, loose connections are typical. These portable appliances now have to be tested formally and regularly under HSE regulations.

Apart from appliances the principal dangers of electrocution arise from those responsible for maintaining the electrical supplies to and around the premises. Switchboards and motors are usually the risk centres, as it is often necessary to maintain or repair them in a 'live' condition to avoid disrupting production.

Most electrical accidents are caused by inadequate working practices with inadequate maintenance responsible for some 20%. Over 3% of all reported electrical accidents are fatal and the circumstances leading to a fatality are rarely different from those in a non-fatal accident. One cannot always see an electrical fault, and the importance of qualified personnel dealing with work to live loadings cannot be over-stated. Perhaps of all the cost centres the 'benchmarking' of maintenance to electrical services, equipment and portable appliances must be carried out from first principles with but a passing reference to the peer-group norm.

*Fire*

The Fire Precautions (Places of Work) Regulations 1994 cover procedures for:

- risk assessment
- emergency plans
- means of escape
- fire-fighting equipment
- warnings
- instruction and training.

Causes of fire include:

- faulty electrical equipment, appliances and (wiring)
- faulty gas appliances
- lighted cigarettes
- incendiary devices
- boiler explosion
- overheating of chemicals.

Fire conditions can be aggravated by the materials comprising the building and its contents eg: furniture, fabrics etc. Careful attention to the relevant regulations should ensure the containment of all but the most persistent of fires. It is, however, important to note that in the course of a fire **asphyxiation from smoke is a far more common cause of death or injury than burning.**

*Physical impact*

This can be the result of any one of a wide range of incidents from bomb explosion to articles falling from shelves. The Health & Safety Inspectors take a poor view of free-standing shelving, and builders' shelving screwed to old walls is just as likely to get the thumbs down sign. Several incidents are on record of injuries caused by employees hurrying about their work not looking where they are going - some involving piping hot beverages being thrown over unlucky fellow employees who happened to be in an unlucky place at the time. These things will happen, but if internal corridors fail to afford sight-lines at junctions their incidence will be encouraged.

## 8.2.3 SICK BUILDING SYNDROME

*Definition*

This condition has received considerable media attention in recent times, as much because of the 'mystery' nature of the issue as for the consequences to employees and their employers. It relates to ill-health symptoms which manifest themselves during time spent at the workplace but which tend to reduce or disappear completely once out of the office environment.

Typically such symptoms comprise many or all of the following:

- runny nose, sneezing and blockage of the nasal passages
- sore, dry throat
- eczema and other skin irritations
- itching, reddening and watering of the eyes
- nausea
- headaches
- dizziness
- a general and uncharacteristic lethargy at, or disaffection with work.

*The causes*

As these symptoms are transient they are unlikely to be caused by infection; rather the source of affliction will be some local irritant, allergen or toxic substance. No single factor has been identified as the primary cause of 'sick building syndrome' (SBS) although causes of other occupational-related diseases such as asthma, humidifier fever and legionella are now well documented.

SBS is of concern because it not only causes great personal distress but also results in loss of productivity, absenteeism and, sometimes, enforced retirement. It is quite likely that some employees may be hyper-sensitive to the causative conditions but that does not let the employer off the hook.

Air-conditioning systems can be a source of the problems and also a protection. For example all-air systems are thought to improve air quality and humidity but require a high level of maintenance. The induction type of system where air introduced at the point of heat exchange is often not humidified creates a deficiency which is a commonly held cause of SBS. However, 'sealed' air-conditioned buildings have been found to give more exposure to SBS than other simply (mechanically or naturally) ventilated buildings.

One building fitted with an induction-based air-conditioning system in the London area in the 1970's was a constant source of complaints from its government employees. On refurbishment in 1981 it was discovered that none of the duct joints had been properly taped: the system had never worked since 'commissioning'!

Other inadequacies in factors such as temperature, airflow and lighting may encourage employees to complain when they otherwise might not have bothered. In particular the opportunity to control local environmental conditions and the apparently caring (or otherwise) attitude of management towards maintenance and environmental conditions have been found to have a significant effect on the incidences of lost productivity and absenteeism.

## 8.2.4 PROTECTION

*The legislation*

A set of six EC Directives - known as the 'EC Six-pack' - became part of UK statute law on 1 January 1993. They derive from article 118A of the Treaty of Rome and have now been incorporated into the following regulations:

- Workplace (Health, Safety & Welfare) Regulations 1992
- Manual Handling Operations Regulations 1992
- Management of Health & Safety at Work Regulations 1992
- Personal Protective Equipment at Work (PPE) Regulations 1992
- The Provision and Use of Work Equipment Regulations 1992
- Health & Safety (Display Screen Equipment) Regulations 1992.

Most of these merely augment the provisions of the Health & Safety at Work Act 1974 – but there are new concepts, especially concerning how health and safety should be managed and dealing with hazards at the computer workstation. A particular requirement now is for management to assess the health and safety risks in their premises, devise antidotes and put them into effect, measure their effectiveness and appoint competent persons to be engaged on these activities.

Further directives have brought about new requirements in respect of consumer products, fire precautions (see above), pregnant women and new mothers, and construction sites.

In addition to the formal Health & Safety at Work regulations the following statutes are also relevant to the subject:

- Control of Substances Hazardous to Health Regulations 1988
- Electricity at Work Act 1989
- Food Safety Act 1990
- The Environmental Pollution Act 1990

## Protective procedures

Obviously strict compliance with the requirements of the law is essential if optimum risk control is to be achieved. Inclusion of specific requirements in this respect in all external supply or service contracts is also of the utmost importance.

Some very important precautions which may not necessarily be covered specifically by the regulations are:

- overcrowding should be resisted

- standards of cleaning and maintenance observed relative to the possible risks in the buildings' design, function and population

- use of indoor planting to absorb pollutants in the air (also considered in Chapter 5.7)

- some natural lighting and an external view from the workstation are highly desirable while avoiding the introduction of noise and traffic fumes via open windows in City areas.

- choose all materials for fitting out with great care, particularly avoiding - or at least respecting - those which give off toxic gases in their newly installed state

- provide a measure of personal control over the environmental conditions and demonstrate care for the health, safety and comfort of the occupants

- ban smoking everywhere, including the Chairman's suite!

- do not seal offices unless there is a good supply of natural ventilation

- avoid excessive re-circulation of return-air

- keep air humid but take great care to maintain the humidifying plant free from chemical and bacterial contamination

- watch out for all symptoms of stress

- make protective clothing, footrests and other statutory props readily available at all times

- make sure that fire and smoke alarms, any sprinkler systems or other mechanical precautions are regularly tested.

- the list could go on and on.

## Economics

**The current stage of health & safety at work can be summed up as having two phases - the project and the monitoring.** Many organisations have by now completed the project phase ie: they have appraised the risks, and devised and implemented the precautions.

The resource to achieve this in a large organisation may be one or two man-years.

Other costs will involve new or modified furniture, enhanced maintenance and cleaning budgets and some re-planning of the workstations and their environment.

The on-going monitoring need not be a major draw on resources, and in fact some companies have been sharing the services of experienced health & safety executives.

Procedures and checking thereof are going to be a way of life for future health & safety and there is at least one company offering a complete one-stop process of:

- check list and explanation of legislation
- risk assessment of whole site
- list of defects and non-compliance
- specific recommendations
- clarification of responsibilities
- contractor documentation
- written reporting on the monitoring & actions taken to ensure compliance
- training
- certification of compliance
- updating legislation.

**There is a one-off charge per capita to set up the first year with a rather lower annual fee for maintaining and certification thereafter. It is also available as a specific service in respect of the landlord's areas.**

The economic benefits to an employer of having a fit, healthy and respectful workforce must certainly far outweigh the additional costs of complying with the new statutes; in any case, better financial management of facilities should enable the funds to be found out of previous budget levels.

# CHAPTER 8.3 – SPORTS, SOCIAL AND WELFARE FACILITIES

## 8.3.1 STAFF SUPPORT FACILITIES

*The nature of
the investment*

The types of facilities considered in this Chapter are generally optional and not to be confused with the 'special areas' discussed under fitting-out in Chapter 6.2 - although they do come into that category with regards to costs. Unlike 'special areas' such as reception, meeting areas etc., staff support facilities are provided either as a philanthropic gesture aimed at better public relations with the staff side and to impress visitors, or genuine investments geared directly to perceptible improvements in productivity. Sometimes both benefits may arise, but, like so many other attempts to add value by enhancing the functional performance of the facilities, the measurement of any payback is usually highly dependent upon subjectivity.

*Categories of
staff support
facilities*

The range of facilities within this category encompasses:

- catering and vending
- restrooms and lounge-rooms
- residential accommodation
- workplace nurseries
- fitness centres
- changing rooms/showers
- indoor sports facilities
- banking facilities
- travel agency
- retail outlets
- club room (with/without bar)
- playing fields
- club house

Catering and vending has already been fully discussed in the previous Chapter 8.1.

## 8.3.2 REST ROOMS AND LOUNGE AREAS

**Rest rooms** for staff are not mandatory under the Health & Safety at Work regulations. However, organisations of a size sufficient to warrant a first-aid room may find it beneficial to provide sufficient space for a bed for the employee feeling unwell.

**Lounge** areas are usually part of the catering facilities but may be provided specially as part of the 'non-territorial' space arrangements considered in Chapter 4.1. Sometimes the reception area may extend into a coffee lounge though this is a difficult format to control both with regards to tidiness and security.

## 8.3.3 RESIDENTIAL ACCOMMODATION

This may be in respect of a resident caretaker or, alternatively, offer overnight-stay facilities for senior executives who may need to make frequent overnight stops near the office locality (possibly to meet early-morning travel times) or due to long spells of late night/early morning headquarters-based activities.

Unless it turns out to be a business perk without a foundation in productive benefit, a residential facility in City centres will usually pay back quite quickly. An example of such a valid proposition is given in **FIG 8.3.3.A** which assumes that residential accommodation may be provided above commercial offices in a situation where the space thereby created would not otherwise attract planning permission for office use; the land value hypothesized therefore relates to residential rather than commercial values which, in important locations, would be substantially higher.

**FIG 8.3.3.A:** *Payback on residential accommodation through savings on hotel bills*

| | | £ |
|---|---|---|
| **Residential accomodation costs (including siteworks)** | 1 - bed flat 60 sq m GIA @ £600 per sq m | 36,000 |
| | Fees, finance and other development costs | 12,000 |
| **Total building costs (excluding land costs)** | | **48,000** |
| 'Notional' residential land values | | 20,000 |
| Fees, finance etc. on notional land value | | 5,000 |
| **Total development costs** | | **73,000** |
| Commercial mortgage @ 10% for 10 years × 0.163 | | 11,880 pa |
| Running and maintenance costs | | 2,120 pa |
| **Total annual costs** | | **14,000** |
| **Payback analysis** | | |
| **Number of overnight stops pa to cover hotel bills (room-only charges)** | @ £200 per night : 70 No. | |
| | @ £100 per night : 140 No. | |
| | @ £50 per night : 280 No. | |

## 8.3.4 THE WORKPLACE NURSERY

*The social case*

Women constitute about one-half of the total labour force in the UK. However, the number of British mothers with toddlers under 5 years old in employment is well below the EC average.

Because the extent of daycare facilities in nurseries is negligible British mothers who want to go to work are generally restricted to a part-time occupation.

The equal opportunities case for providing nursery care to make it easier for young mothers to get straight back to work – and possibly a career – as soon as they are ready and able is overwhelming. Nevertheless, the welfare of the children is equally if not more important, both for their own wellbeing and the benefit of a society which will suffer at large if children are not given an appropriate and fair start in life.

The Children Act 1989 lays down standards for the accommodation and provision of childcare facilities. It is now generally recognised that having the childcare at the workplace is preferred by families on grounds of:

- avoidance of additional travel to and from work/childcare centre
- better monitored care quality
- better facilities
- easy access by mother to child.

The biggest demand is for places for babies under 12 months, a fact that has caught out more than one workplace nursery provider forcing them to re-fit the facilities to suit. On the other hand, much depends on the location. For example, a mother with a 3 month old baby may not be attracted by a nursery in the City Centre workplace given the problems of peak-hour travel; for that matter she may not be too keen about traipsing a two and four-year old pair through the metropolis. In both situations, however, the alternative may well be a difficult circuitous journey around town to work via the carer's address. The strength of demand for the facility together with the performance requirement should be tested by interview and questionnaires to avoid getting it wrong on the back of the personnel director's hunch.

## The business case

According to a survey conducted by the national voluntary organisation 'Working for Childcare' in May 1994 there are nearly 500 organisations in the UK providing childcare facilities for their employees. Rather less than half this number are provided at the actual workplace; the balance are 'partnership nurseries' ie: places at day nurseries allocated to, or taken by, one or more employers for use by their staff.

Among other important statistics unearthed by the 'Working for Childcare' survey were that:

- less than one pre-school child in every 250 has access to an employer-sponsored nursery place
- the average fee for a full-time place in such a nursery is £76.00 per week
- the public sector subsidises more nurseries for its staff than the private sector
- the greatest concentration of identified nurseries is in London and the South East
- over half of all identified nurseries are provided for use by staff (and students) in hospitals, colleges and universities.

So what are the business arguments in favour of providing or sponsoring childcare facilities for employees?

Probably the strongest case revolves around the loss of productivity plus the recruitment costs in the process of losing and replacing a valuable employee who wants to return to work after having a child, but cannot manage to find a suitable childcare facility to enable her to do so.

It costs employers quite a lot of money to train an employee in particular clerical skills; at the high-end of the business structure women in senior positions often carry their share of the business' goodwill which is lost on premature and avoidable retirement.

The combination of training time, learning curve, decline of productivity on an employee's permanent retirement, plus recruitment costs, training time and learning curve for the replacement, obviously add up to a large financial loss in each case - not to mention the inevitable increase in absenteeism where mothers experience temporary difficulties in securing adequate childcare facilities.

Various independent studies have concluded that the costs of replacing a member of staff average out at £100,000 p.a. or more.

One employer introducing nursery facilities recorded a near doubling of staff returning to work after taking maternity leave; an example of how the economics of a case built up from these statistics is given later in the Chapter, drawing from the costs and income data discussed in the following text.

Apart from the 'hard-nosed' direct returns the facility will also do wonders for the morale, concentration and enthusiasm of the beneficiary and will also promote a good public image externally, so it should present a bonus to personnel recruitment on more than one count.

## The facilities required

Childcare provision for the under-eights is governed by the Children Act 1989 which lays down standards in respect of the staffing and premises, and there are also guidance notes issued by HMSO.

The premises should ideally afford access to the open air, which may present problems in the more expensive inner city complexes - though access to an atrium may effect a suitable compromise.

The accommodation should afford both structured and play activities as well as providing for the disabled. It should have a 'friendly' ambience (not particularly easy to achieve in a commercial building) giving children and their parents a sense of security and confidence.

FIG 8.3.4.A: *Minimum workplace requirements for a nursery*

| Age of child | Minimum overall open floor space (excluding hallways, toilets and kitchen) | |
| --- | --- | --- |
| | sq ft | sq m |
| Under 2 years | 40 | 3.7 |
| 2 - 3 years | 30 | 2.8 |
| 3 - 5 years | 25 | 2.3 |

The minimum space requirements under the Children Act 1989 are given at **FIG 8.3.4.A**. About 25-30% should be added to provide space and storage for equipment, furniture etc. Where possible a room should be made available where older children can get down to concentrative activities in peace and quiet.

Facilities must be 'user-friendly' and, in addition to the nursery area itself will need to provide space for administration, a staff-room and a kitchen or other catering area. The recommended use of industrial microwave ovens for reasons given in the previous chapter on 'catering' is equally applicable in the childcare catering facility.

The Act specifically requires separate toilet facilities for adults and children - one WC and wash-hand basin per 10 children - plus a 'mother's room' for changing nappies.

Provision of the facility in a commercial building will require the acquisition of all the usual licences including planning consent, fire and building regulations approval and registration with the local authority's Social Services department. All furniture and equipment should meet BS safety standards and pictures, books, and graphics should portray multi-cultural activities by both sexes in many and varied roles.

*Managing the facility*

The quality of the service will depend upon

- the ratio of staff to children
- the qualifications of the staff
- staff remuneration
- the facilities available.

**FIG 8.3.4.B** gives the minimum staffing levels laid down in the Children Act. Note however that additional staff will be required

- at the Local Authority's discretion (1:1 may be required for children under 1 year old)
- for nurseries open longer than 10 hours per day
- for overall supervision - where there are more than 20 children
- for catering, administration and cleaning.

**FIG 8.3.4.B:** *Minimum staff : children ratios according to the Childrens Act 1989*

| Age of children | Ratio of staff : children |
|---|---|
| Under 2 years | 1 : 3 |
| 2 - 3 years | 1 : 5 |
| 3 - 5 years | 1 : 8 |

Ideally, at least half of the staff should have a suitable qualification - either for nursery or sick nursing. Any employment of trainees on ET schemes should always be properly structured and supervised, supernumerary to staffing levels and with adequate allowances being made for staff-time in training and monitoring on top of basic duties.

Under the Children Act 1989 local authorities are obliged to inspect every nursery at least once a year to check on standards of facilities and care.

*The cost of providing and operating workplace nursery*

Unless the facility is to be new-built the capital costs will relate to

- conversion
- fitting-out
- equipment.

Typical costs for these components are given at **FIG 8.3.4.C**.

FIG 8.3.4.C: *Typical capital cost of providing fitting-out and equipping a workplace nursery*

| Space requirement | | sq ft |
|---|---|---|
| Free area : Say 20 children @ an average of 30 sq ft per child | | 600 |
| Add : storage, furniture & equipment space, catering, circulation, admin etc. 100% | | 600 |
| **Total dedicated area** | | **1,200** |
| **Capital costs** | | **£** |
| **Building costs** | Conversion of existing space 1,200 sq ft NIA @ £20 sq ft | 24,000 |
| | Fitting-out of existing space 1,200 sq ft NIA @ £30 sq ft | 36,000 |
| | Fees @ 10% | 6,000 |
| **Total conversion and fitting-out cost** | | **66,000** |
| **Equipment and furniture** | say 20 @ £1,000 per child | 20,000 |
| **Total capital costs** | | **86,000*** |
| **Annual equivalent @ 10% pa over 10 years : × 0.163** | | **14,000** |
| * Excludes VAT and any bridging finance costs | | |

*The annual costs*

**FIG 8.3.4.D** estimates the cost per child per annum taking the amortised capital cost of the 20-child example used above and including a notional rent, operating and staffing costs. The rent assumes that space is taken from a fairly expensive commercial area and that any open-areas are part of the common areas and not rentable.

FIG 8.3.4.D: *Typical annual costs of a 20-child workplace nursery*

| Premises costs | Amortised capital costs as Fig. 8.3.4.C | £14,000 |
|---|---|---|
| | Notional rent, rates & operating costs - 1,200 sq ft NIA @ £30 sq ft pa | £36,000 |
| **Operating and management costs** | Support services / consumables @ £600* per child × 20 | £12,000 |
| | Staffing @ £4,500* per child × 20 | £90,000 |
| **Total annual costs before tax and fees** | | **£152,000** |
| **Total cost (at 100% occupancy) per child** | pa | £7,600 |
| | pw | £146 |
| * based on figures provided in the booklet 'A practical guide to workplace nurseries' by Sue Finch | | |

*Fees, funding sources and taxation factors*

Employers usually subsidize the costs, often on a sliding scale according to income. So, for example, a cost per child place of say £110 (in a lower-rental area than the example and after the employer has claimed tax relief on any plant/ machinery content of the works and all the revenue expenditure) may be charged to the working parent at say £50 per week.

There is no tax payable by the recipient of the subsidy. It is important to note that the provision of **childcare allowances** and **vouchers** are still regarded as taxable benefits whereas the **subsidized fee** is not!

Further tax concessions are available to employers in the industrial sector - more if they have the benefit of a remainder of an Enterprise Zone concession. The supply of childcare is **exempt** from VAT provided it is registered under the Children Act.

*The business*
*payback*

The £60 or so residual figure per child per week which is down to the employers has to deliver a payback: this can only be in terms of saving the cost incurred in staff retiring prematurely due to lack of convenient childcare facilities.

For the 20-child facility in the above example, a taxable organisation would be spending a net £60,000 or so (£3,000 per child) each year. Given that the cost of one premature retirement costs an average £100,000 it is clear that, if only one of the 15-20 mothers of the children in the group is back to work because of the provision, the facility should quickly pay for itself.

Looked at another way, if the latest statistics are to be believed the number of premature retirements is halved by access to a workplace nursery. In that case in an organisation of say 500 employees of whom 250 were women including 75 existing and 75 potential caring mothers, between 5 and 10 premature retirements might take place annually in the absence of the facility: that figure halved would save between £250,000 and £500,000 per annum (ie: 2.5 to 5 times £100,000) so justifying a nursery subsidy of £3000 per child for between 75 and 150 children - obviously well in keeping with what is needed for the 75 existing mothers and the few joining the club each year.

### 8.3.5 THE PHYSICAL FITNESS CENTRE

*The medical*
*case*

'Healthy body, healthy mind' goes the adage but does it have any foundation in fact?

Physical fitness represents the achievement of an optimal state of both physiological and psychological performance with low health risk factors, thus increasing our overall well-being. Exercise stimulates the production of endocrines in our bodies with a net result of improved neuro-muscular motor skills, eg improved concentration, speed of response, clarity of mind etc. In addition, adequate cardiovascular exercise is also known to relieve stress and also lower and regulate our blood pressure levels. As a major contributor to the prevention and combat of CHD (Coronary Heart Disease), cardiovascular exercise reduces the risk of artherosclorosis (furring of the arteries) due to its effect on our liptoprotein profile, by the production of high density liptoprotein (HDL) cholesterol and the reduction of low density liptoprotein (LDL) cholesterol.

Adequate exercise is generally acknowledged to be a major contributor to health-related fitness in terms of our overall well-being and all round performance.

**Adequate** exercise - yes, but there are question marks over many aspects of physical exercise of a violent or repetitive nature such as the heart-muscle extension resulting from exacting activities like squash and long-distance running - the latter especially damaging to back and limbs when perpetuated on punishing hard surfaces.

A general description of physical fitness is defined by Dr Kevin Sykes of Liverpool University as "the ability to carry out daily tasks with vigour and alertness without undue fatigue and with ample energy to enjoy leisure-time pursuits and to meet unforeseen emergencies".

It would therefore be reasonable to assume that physically fit individuals would perform better than average in their day-to-day tasks

## Fitness and productivity

Whereas there is some logic in the assumption that regular participation in fast-reaction sports such as squash, badminton and (to some extent) tennis make executives sharper about their work (unless they have played 1½ hours at lunch-time and pushed themselves to near exhaustion) the case for non-competitive fitness routines is a little less clear-cut.

Body-building per se develops muscles and reduces fat (in the short-term) without sharpening the reactions - although education of the flow of oxygen and adrenaline to the brain may well be a beneficial by-product of fighting against the spring-loaded paraphernalia now finding its way into corporate expenditure on facilities.

According to a report in 'The Times', Fitness for Industry (FFI), who own and run some 30 corporate fitness clubs in the UK, claim that regular use of the facilities available in the gymnasium can make the difference between an executive who stays the course of the day sharp, and one whose performance falls off over the last hour or so. They point to a NASA exercise control programme in the USA which showed that regular exercising produced a 12½% increase in productivity.

Another company reported a cut of about 50% in absenteeism over the course of a six-year corporate fitness programme. Whether this was due to fitness or because people were keen to come to work to indulge in the fitness routines may need further research to clarify and the findings may not of themselves be too relevant.

It may just be the fact that Management seems to care (a common theme running through many of the cost centres in this text) or it may be some physically beneficial consequence which generates the increased productivity; either way, it does not really matter as long as it works - not just in the short term but over time.

## Capital and running costs

A typical corporate gymnasium will be about 3,000SF including an area for aerobics plus changing/shower/toilet facilities in the proportions shown at **FIG 8.3.5A**. The cost of converting and fitting out the space together with the equipment is predicted at **FIG 8.3.5.B** and the extension of this calculation of the annual equivalent cost (before tax) to the total annual cost of the fitness centre is given at **FIG 8.3.5.C**

**FIG. 8.3.5.A:** *Fitness centre*
*- distribution of area by function*

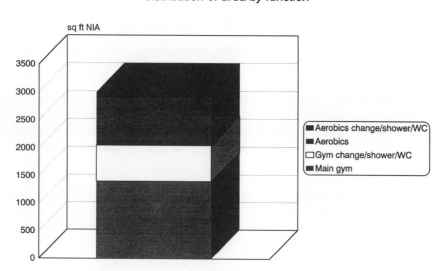

FIG 8.3.5.B: *Fitness centre - capital costs of conversion, fitting-out and equipment*

| Capital costs | £ |
|---|---|
| Conversion costs 3,000 sq ft NIA @ £20 sq ft | 60,000 |
| Fitting-out costs 3,000 sq ft NIA @ £30 sq ft | 90,000 |
| Fees and finance @ 10% | 15,000 |
| **Total conversion and fitting-out costs** | **165,000** |
| Equipment gym area: 1,400 sq ft NIA @ £70 sq ft | 98,000 |
| **Total capital costs** | **263,000** |
| **Annual equivalent @ 10% pa over 10 years × 0.163** | **42,869 pa** |

FIG 8.3.5.C: *Typical annual costs of a corporate fitness centre*

| Annual costs | £ |
|---|---|
| Amortised capital costs as Fig. 8.3.5.B - say | 43,000 |
| Notional rent, rates and operating costs - 3,000 sq ft NIA @ £30 sq ft pa | 90,000 |
| Equipment maintenance / replacement | 10,000 |
| Supervision | 30,000 |
| **Total annual costs before tax and fees** | **173,000** |
| **Assuming 200 club members** | **£865 per capita pa** |

## The business case

Clearly the cost per capita is such that, even if after tax relief by way of capital allowances and revenue expenditure the cost is reduced to say £650 per capita p.a., subsidized membership may not be easy to justify as an investment.

On the other hand, if but one quarter of the 200 members of the club benefit to the extent of increasing their productivity by the suggested 12½% (see above) then the annual saving might well amount to (say) £20,000 x 50 x 0.125 = £125,000.

Compared with the annual cost of £173,000 and given that the saving of £125,000pa might well be enhanced by reductions in absenteeism and recruitment costs as well as a small improvement in productivity of the remaining 150 members, then the facility might well be seen as washing its face in commercial terms with a public relations bonus in attendance.

## Sports facilities

Few organisations these days can afford the luxury of providing and maintaining sports facilities either at the place of work or remotely based.

Most major centres have local public or private facilities for squash, badminton and (sometimes) indoor tennis, so the need for special provision does not often arise.

Nevertheless, many of the bigger organisations which have had the capital investment in a sports facility written-off over time still consider the public relations benefits to outweigh the not inconsiderable costs of running and maintaining grounds and clubhouse for the use of only a small proportion of their workforce who either -

- live near the centre, or
- prefer not to join a private club.

Because of the wide range of facilities available and given that provision of new facilities on a grand scale is a feature of another economic era, details of capital and running costs are not provided in this section.

However, it is significant that facilities management in this sector is now prey to the outsourcing route just as much as the workplace facilities. It may well be that such a policy will provide a further degree of acceleration to the pace at which staff sports clubs are disappearing from the scene.

# PART E

# RELOCATION

# SECTION 9

# RELOCATION

# CHAPTER 9.1 – LOCATION AND BUSINESS PERFORMANCE

## 9.1.1 LOCATION AND THE PREMISES POLICY

*Premises and the corporate plan*

**FIG 9.1.A** replicates **FIG 1.1.C** in Chapter 1.1 which considered the essential linkage between the business requirements to be accommodated and the premises performing that function.

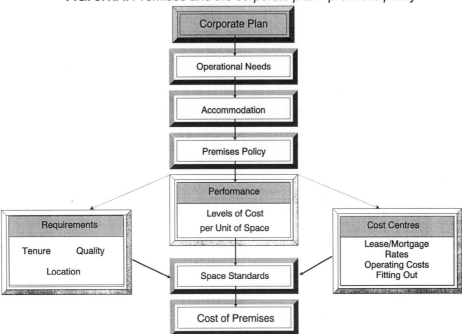

**FIG. 9.1.A:** *Premises and the corporate plan - premises policy*

That the location is a critical factor in the business plan from the point of view of production, sales, marketing or personnel is undeniable. However, it is not unknown for top management, under embarrassing scrutiny in their attempts to improve bottom-line efficiency, to use cheaper premises costs as the excuse for a relocation which will reduce staff costs by a factor of at least 10 times the saving on premises costs. The relationship between premises costs, support services and total turnover at **FIG 9.1.B** illustrates this point graphically.

**FIG. 9.1.B:** *Turnover, profit and facilities costs*

Pre-tax profit 5%

I.T. 5%

Business support costs 5%

**Facilities costs 15%**

Premises costs 5%

Total turnover

e.g. Turnover p.a. = £50m (profit p.a. = £2.5m / facilities costs p.a. = £7.5m)

However, politics aside and looking at the matter of accommodation purely from a premises perspective, what issues should a facilities manager consider when the ability of the existing premises stock to accommodate the business requirement comes into question?

*Fitness of premises for purpose*

The circumstances which will require the organisation to review the suitability of its accommodation will be triggered by any or all of the following underlying issues:

- shortage of space
- too much space
- inefficiency of space
- inadequate internal environment
- image
- location
- corporate centralisation
- corporate de-centralisation
- flexibility
- premises costs
- staff costs
- redundancy policy
- real estate factors
- accountancy policy.

The solutions available to overcome these problems boil down to just a handful of generic options:

- stay and make alterations as necessary
- move away to new location(s).

A combination of these options and some further sub-options is considered below.

## 9.1.2 THE PREMISES OPTIONS

*Make do and
mend*

This option may be dictated by economics, and probably means effecting some compromise. The scope and quality of the alterations together with any tenure factors will determine the extent to which this option is economically viable; sometimes, in the case of over-supply of space, part of the existing premises may be prepared for leasing or sub-leasing. The effect of making radical and expensive alterations to the leasehold property - for example, upgrading for IT - must be carefully weighed up in the context of the terms of the lease. It is not at all unusual for tenants to have their rents revised to a level reflecting the improvements they have paid for themselves.

It is far better to do a deal with the landlord and sign a new agreement whereby some or all of the costs are rentalised on the basis of a low institutional investment yield. This will normally be a better bet than the organisation funding it out of cash-flow or on a commercial mortgage (see **FIG 9.1.C**) even though there will, of course, be normal reviews on the extra rent in the rentalised option. The risks inherent in refurbishment are discussed in Section 6 - Fitting out and Alterations.

**FIG. 9.1.C:** *Alternative funding options for refurbishment of a leased building*

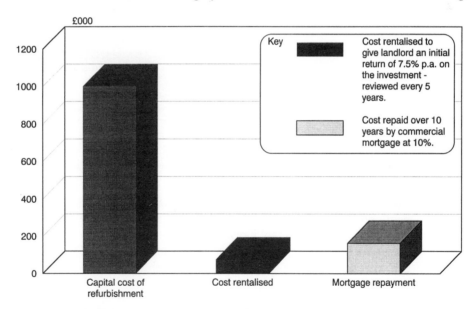

The taxation implications are similar in principle in respect of revenue expenditure (but **not** for capital allowances – see Chapter 11.2 except that obviously the relief on the mortgage will be greater earlier )although only on the interest component for the duration of the loan whereas the rental is deductible in full throughout the tenancy.

*Total relocation*

There is a rich variety of sub-options.

The tenure may be:

- leasehold

    -newly built speculative development

    -existing building

    -proposed speculative development

    -bespoke development on sale and leaseback terms

, • freehold

-newly built speculative development (outright purchase from developer)

-existing building

-bespoke development

The decision on freehold v leasehold is discussed in Section 3.1 and will be dictated by such issues as availability, accountability, financial status, flexibility, image, location or, probably, a combination of all or some of these factors.

There can be advantages in getting into a development early enough (either as a tenant or owner) to have the building tailored to suit one's requirements - often without a cost penalty.

**FIG. 9.1.D:** *The fitting-out cost penalty for works to buildings with existing scenery finish*

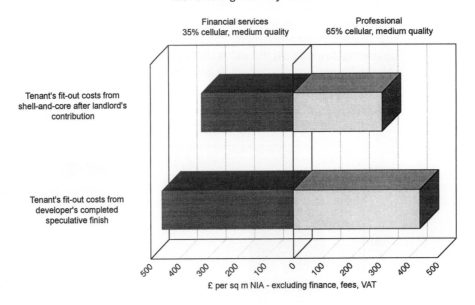

**FIG 9.1.D** draws from **FIGS 6.1.A** and **6.1.B** in Chapter 6.1 to show the potential cost penalty to be paid in speculative development where it is necessary to adapt a finished building to meet individual requirements. Up to 40% of the cost of a re-fit can be spent on ripping out and/or altering what is put there by a developer or a former tenant - one reason why the 'shell and core' type of development has gained favour.

Note that although the costs from 'shell-and' core' at **FIG 6.1.B** are higher than from the 'developers' finish the cost of the latter should be allowed to the tenant by the developer if he lets the building on a shell-and-core basis. The tenant then incurs a lower fitting-out cost net of the contribution and is able to co-ordinate both sections of the work to his best advantage.

The temptation to optimise the real estate benefits - particularly for balance sheet purposes -is often very strong. However, the purpose of the premises is to accommodate the corporate plan; unless itself a property development or investment company an organisation would do best to think of premises as *plant* to aid the business function. The real estate implications should not be ignored but equally should not dictate the decision.

The location will have a big impact on:

• premises costs

• cost of staff

• turnover of staff

- availability of staff
- image
- travel times to, from and during work.

Ways to assess the benefits or disbenefits alongside actual premises costs are considered below. It is quite common for major decisions about location to be based on the personal convenience of the decision makers and/or their spouses. The best way to scupper such appallingly bad practice is to make a watertight financial case for the best strategy.

The performance of the new premises against which the cost is assessed should be looked at under the following main headings such as:

- efficiency of design, layout and specification
- comfort
- convenience
- image - external PR, internal PR
- flexibility
- resilience
- capacity.

Although it is not usual for these factors to be valued in monetary terms there are techniques for bringing them into the financial equation to help consider the issue of value for money. An example was given at **FIG 1.2.B** in chapter 1.2. Alternatively they can be considered in judgemental mode as illustrated in **FIG 9.1.E** which is taken from the Building Quality Assessment (BQA)[1] program which 'scores' buildings via a sophisticated system of market-tested weighted evaluation of 137 quality criteria factors.

**FIG. 9.1.E:** *Performance comparison of two buildings using the BQA method*

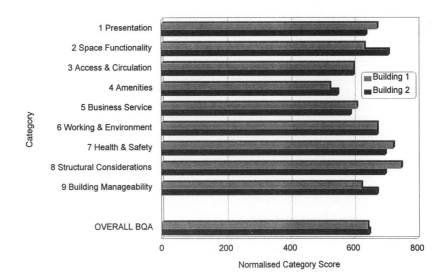

**Partial relocation**

Frequently the existing office is retained as a 'flagship'. In this case it is often best for the satellite premises to be a good distance away where both premises and staff may come a lot cheaper.

Where there are a number of offices in a cluster the tendency is, over time, for either all-embracing corporate premises to emerge or, alternatively, for the 'flagship - plus scattered back-office premises' policy to be adopted.

### 9.1.3 TECHNIQUES OF EVALUATION

*Degrees of sophistication*

There are many ways of looking at the costs and benefits of a premises strategy and for comparing one with another. These range from the simplistic 'annual premises costs' calculation to highly sophisticated techniques of cost benefit analysis.

*Annual cost method*

Here the cost centres are calculated for a given point in time (normally current) and a simple comparison made. This is normally only a 'first strike' process to aid discussion and to eliminate obvious non-starters. **FIG 9.1.F** illustrates this technique where Building X is the current tenancy to which the annual cost of essential improvements is added to the passing rent for comparison with alternative rented options at Buildings Y and Z.

**FIG 9.1.F:** *Alternative premises strategies - preliminary appraisal by comparison of annual costs per unit of area*

| | Building X 7th floor (16,994 sq ft NIA incl. mezzanine storage) | | Building Y 10-14th floors (15,750 sq ft NIA) | | Building Z 3rd & 4th floors (16,645 sq ft NIA) | |
|---|---|---|---|---|---|---|
| | £,000 | £ / sq ft NIA | £,000 | £ / sq ft NIA | £,000 | £ / sq ft NIA |
| Rent (analysed over first five year review period) | 360 | 21.18 | 440 | 27.94 | 616 | 37.01 |
| Rates (current) | 45 (Borough A) | 2.65 | 135 (Borough B) | 8.57 | 133 (Borough B) | 7.99 |
| Operating costs (including service charge) | 105 (non a/c) | 6.18 | 144 | 9.14 | 150 | 9.01 |
| Fitting-out costs † (includes building works, professional fees and bridging finance) | 195 | 11.47 | 100 | 6.35 | 100 | 6.01 |
| Additional cost for comfort cooling | 70 | 4.12 | Inc. | Inc. | Inc. | Inc. |
| Furniture † (includes fees) | 70 | 4.12 | 70 | 4.44 | 70 | 4.21 |
| Total annual costs | 845 | 49.72 | 889 | 56.44 | 1069 | 64.22 |

† Amortised over a seven year period at 13%
N.B. The above figures exclude any allowance for: VAT; Work to landlord's wcs and sublet areas; Data cabling and telecommunications; Decanting.

*Life-cycle cost analysis*

This is a more sophisticated technique the principles of which are described in Chapter 10.4. The appraiser must attempt to forecast such things as:

- extent of rent reviews
- changes in rates
- premiums on leases surrendered
- re-active and pro-active maintenance
- service charges and operating costs
- 'churn' alterations
- inflation.

The resultant cash flow projections will normally be discounted at a rate (or rates) indicated by the user. The user may wish to introduce certain additional quantifiable costs such as:

- moving
- replacement
- redundancy payments.

He may also wish to consider certain indirect costs of a move -loss of productivity caused by the move, say, both during the move itself and through loss and recruitment of staff. In more sophisticated appraisals he may wish to look at changes in the level of organisational productivity as a consequence of the move - for example, shorter journey times for employees moving around the premises, for key executives travelling locally and abroad, and genuine improvements in productivity at work.

**FIG 9.1.G** shows how such a cost/benefit analysis may be prepared. In this case the productivity change assumptions are calculated by simple percentage addition to (or deduction from) total costs of the staff affected. As discussed further at **FIG 9.1.4** below such an appraisal is most useful when sensitivity testing of the assumptions is employed. This particular example is adjusted for inflation and it should be noted that inflation in the rent is calculated at the estimated (mid-year) rent review figure for the 5 succeeding years, whereas other costs are inflated annually. Discounted cash flows and the pros and cons of including inflation are considered in detail in Chapter 10.4

FIG 9.1.G: *Cost/benefit analysis of a premises strategy taking account of potential impact on productivity - inflated and discounted*

| Cost centre | | 1995 £,000' | 1996 £,000' | 1997 £,000' | 1998 £,000' | 1999 £,000' | 2000 £,000' | 2001 £,000' | 2002 £,000' | 2003 £,000' | 2004 £,000' | Total £,000's |
|---|---|---|---|---|---|---|---|---|---|---|---|---|
| Premises | Rent | (2979) | (3211) | (3211) | (3555) | (3555) | (3555) | (3555) | (4278) | (5000) | (5000) | (37899) |
| | Rates | (2372) | (2491) | (2615) | (1247) | (1322) | (1401) | (1499) | (1604) | (1717) | (1837) | (18105) |
| | Operating costs | (1392) | (1462) | (1535) | (1247) | (1322) | (1401) | (1499) | (1604) | (1717) | (1837) | (15016) |
| | Routine alterations | (290) | (305) | (320) | (210) | 223 | (236) | (253) | (271) | (290) | (310) | (2708) |
| | Total | (7033) | (7469) | (7681) | (6259) | (6422) | (6593) | (6806) | (7757) | (8724) | (8984) | (73728) |
| Fitting-out | Fitting-out | 0 | 0 | (5226) | 0 | 0 | 0 | 0 | 0 | 0 | 0 | (5226) |
| | Furniture | 0 | 0 | 0 | (3102) | 0 | 0 | 0 | 0 | 0 | 0 | (3102) |
| | Total | 0 | 0 | (5226) | (3102) | 0 | 0 | 0 | 0 | 0 | 0 | (8328) |
| Real Estate | Premiums | 0 | 0 | 0 | 2000 | 0 | 0 | 0 | 0 | 0 | 0 | 2000 |
| | Disposals & Aquisitions | 0 | 0 | 0 | (180) | 0 | 0 | 0 | 0 | 0 | 0 | (180) |
| | Total | 0 | 0 | 0 | 1820 | 0 | 0 | 0 | 0 | 0 | 0 | 1820 |
| Productivity | organisational | 0 | 0 | 0 | 2477 | 2614 | 2758 | 2909 | 3069 | 3238 | 3416 | 20481 |
| | physical communications - internal | 0 | 0 | 0 | 2319 | 2447 | 2581 | 2723 | 2873 | 3031 | 3198 | 19172 |
| | physical communications - external | (335) | (353) | (373) | (552) | (582) | (615) | (648) | (683) | (721) | (760) | (5622) |
| | Total | (335) | (353) | (373) | 4244 | 4479 | 4784 | 4984 | 5259 | 5548 | 5854 | 34091 |
| Relocation | Removals including general temporary loss of productivity | 0 | 0 | 0 | (3218) | 0 | 0 | 0 | 0 | 0 | 0 | (3218) |
| | Replacement of staff | 0 | 0 | 0 | (3130) | 0 | 0 | 0 | 0 | 0 | 0 | (3130) |
| | Total | 0 | 0 | 0 | (6348) | 0 | 0 | 0 | 0 | 0 | 0 | (6348) |
| Total | | (7368) | (7822) | (13280) | (9645) | (1943) | (1869) | (1822) | (2498) | (3176) | (3130) | (52553) |
| Net present value factor * | | .0.87 | 0.76 | 0.66 | 0.57 | 0.49 | 0.43 | 0.38 | 0.33 | 0.28 | 0.25 | |
| Net present value pa | | (6407) | (5915) | (8732) | (5515) | (966) | (808) | (685) | (817) | (903) | (774) | (31520) |
| * Rounded to 2 decimal places | | | | | | | | | | | | |

### 9.1.4 RELOCATING THE BUSINESS

*The influential factors*

As discussed above the decision to relocate can result from a wide range of pressures. Common examples include company growth and change, shortage of space, financial pressures, organisational inefficiency, the need for company rationalisation and operational problems.

Thus, the motivation can be seen as corporate led (that is, by business factors) or premises led (that is, by accommodation issues). The distinction is important because it is likely to dictate the stage at which the facilities manager becomes involved in the decision-making and, therefore, his ability to influence the parameters of the relocation project.

Whichever is the cause, however, a 'to move or not to move' appraisal is appropriate as it will help to clarify the issues, set the objectives and involve the facilities manager with the board in developing a plan of action. In this way, premises management and the corporate plan will become more inter-dependent.

The early development of a plan highlighting the key decisions necessary for the relocation project and its presentation to the board will help to address the pre-conceptions and priorities of those concerned with managing the move. Moreover, detailed tactical plans to deal with specific stages, such as site finding, cost-benefit analysis or building appraisal can be addressed within the framework of an agreed masterplan. This approach affords the facilities manager much needed flexibility through the relocation project.

*The use of consultants*

The complexity of relocation is such that many companies hand over responsibility for day-to-day planning and implementation of relocation to specialist consultants. This frees the facilities management team to meet existing responsibilities; it can be more objective and it will provide a buffer for resolving internal disagreement. Other companies, particularly those with large and experienced facilities management teams, will choose to handle the project internally. This approach avoids the learning curve needed by consultants, and it centralises project management.

A compromise between these two extremes is often favoured, whereby an internal team is given responsibility for the management and implementation of the relocation plan, while appointing consultants at key stages to provide expert help where necessary. This approach fits into the two-tier strategic and tactical plan model outlined above.

Thus, once locational criteria, operational imperatives and budgetary considerations have all been decided internally, outside help may be sought as and when necessary to evaluate a short-list of locations, undertake cost-benefit appraisals, cost development options and assess space planning options.

The identification of available sites of buildings is but one example of the necessity for specialist advice at particular stages of preparing detailed plans. A company cannot hope to cover all lines of enquiry. In appointing specialists, time will be saved and more comprehensive appraisals will be made. The recommendations of the specialist can then be absorbed into the overall relocation strategy.

*Planning*

Relocation will involve exhaustive planning and co-ordination. Once the master plan has been approved by the Board, a series of tactical plans can be drawn up to address specific issues.

These will work within the framework of the master plan, forming discrete packages of work. A relocation management team, with individuals responsible for sets of tactical plans, will simplify the complexities of planning.

Detailed programmes and costings of the studies needed, together with the collection of all relevant internal information and data at this stage, will pay off at later stages of the project.

Each tactical plan will form an element of an overall critical path network (see Chapter 2.2), which provides a schedule of actions and decisions. This schedule will run through until after occupation of the new premises allowing for post-relocation assessment. Such a schedule tightens overall control of the project.

The detailed studies necessary for the relocation will revolve around three main areas. It is in addressing these that the priorities of the business plan again overlap with premises management.

The first main area involves organisational issues. Can the organisation operate effectively in the new location and what factors will enhance this effectiveness? Flows of information between parts of the organisation, inter-departmental communication, the uptake of information technology and functional space requirements may all be relevant considerations here. The ability of the organisation to meet its customers' needs has to be central to the relocation process.

The most efficient and well designed building will ultimately become a non-productive cost factor if its location, function or use fails to meet operational needs.

The second key area of concern here is personnel. Is the relocation inspired by a need to shed staff? How many staff are likely to be lost, and how many is the company prepared to lose? On the positive side, the tactical plan can recommend ways of informing staff of key decisions and setting up 'internal PR'. Most companies move only short distances, and the shorter the distance, the fewer staff are lost. However, in a move from, say, a low cost to a high cost area, the difficulties encountered by staff may need to be addressed by the company itself. In some instances, particularly with qualified or skilled staff, incentives may be necessary.

The third and final area for detailed studies is the premises themselves - the type of building required (how big, what level of specification, what image, and so on), the servicing requirements, the space available. A review of the existing space will make an invaluable contribution to refining requirements.

The extent to which these and other significant factors are taken in to the economic evaluation depends on the appraiser's belief in the merits of cost/benefit analysis. Below we will consider in more detail the pros and cons of this sophisticated approach.

*Economic*
*appraisal*

Even where the need to consider a relocation option derives from the inadequacy of the premises to accommodate the business activity it should never be considered in the light of premises costs alone. Indeed, as was in shown in **FIG 9.1.B** the cost of the premises in the context of the cost of the operations going on inside them is relatively insignificant. Therefore, the simple 'annual costs per sq.ft..' appraisal of rents, rates and running (operating) costs can only be of use as a background for further and more sophisticated evaluation. The same applies to the life cycle cost analysis technique which, though more sophisticated, through the use of discounted cash flow still preoccupies itself with premises costs rather than the real issue - the operational efficiency of the user.

**FIG 9.1.G** gave an example of how certain consequential 'non premises' effects of relocation could be introduced into the life cycle cost plan to provide a cost/benefit analysis. The effect on productivity within the organisation was projected by applying a percentage reduction to staff costs, to take into account easier communications internally (movement around the premises) and easier communications externally (such as movement to and from the premises, as affected, say, by a closer proximity to the airport).

Although such analyses are subjective and open to valid criticism they do have the effect of focusing the mind on issues which, though cost significant, are not easily quantified. Premises costs can be calculated easily but is that a good reason for leaving other, probably more important and cost-sensitive values out of the argument? Most certainly not. Cost-sensitivity analyses - that is, taking a range of values for the assumptions on productivity increases and so on - will normally enable management to take these issues into account without the need to argue the case for and against a specific value judgement: 2.5% or 10% may not tip the balance of the appraisal. If it does, then everyone will have found something important to look at.

On the subject of tenure, the cash flow analyses can be quite distorted by the decision as to whether to rent or buy (and if to buy, whether to develop or purchase) and in either case whether to lease back, mortgage or fund out of cash flow.

The effect of different options is illustrated in **FIG 9.1.H and 9.1.J.** In a discounted cash flow (DCF) calculation, the reducing effect on up-front capital expenditure is much less significant than on future revenue costs, especially at the highish discount rate (15%) used in this example, so renting always comes out looking much better economically on paper. Note that because the example is not based on inflation there is no increase in the rent after year 5.

In **FIG 9.1.H** the rented option therefore has a discounted net cost over seven years of some £7.22 million less than the freehold development option costed in pure management accountancy protocol. This is for two reasons: first, the capital cost occurs at the beginning of the cash flow so is not discounted by a very large amount; second, the existing building cannot be sold until the new one is built, so the income is discounted over the 2 years elapsed time.

Under the freehold development option the annual expenditure on 'new premises' is reduced to merely the operating costs.

**FIG 9.1.H:** *The penalising effect of DCF appraisal on options involving early capital investment and delayed sales income*

| Rented option | | Year 1 £,000's | Year 2 £,000's | Year 3 £,000's | Year 4 £,000's | Year 5 £,000's | Year 6 £,000's | Year 7 £,000's | Total £,000's |
|---|---|---|---|---|---|---|---|---|---|
| Annual expenditure | New premises | (1,750) | (2,500) | (2,500) | (2,500) | (2,500) | (2,500) | (2,500) | |
| | Existing premises | 0 | 0 | 0 | 0 | 0 | 0 | 0 | |
| Capital expenditure | | (2,000) | 0 | 0 | 0 | 0 | 0 | 0 | |
| Capital income from sale | | 6,000 | 0 | 0 | 0 | 0 | 0 | 0 | |
| Net annual cash flow | | 2,250 | (2,500) | (2,500) | (2,500) | (2,500) | (2,500) | (2,500) | |
| NPV @ 15% | | 2,250 | (2,174) | (1,890) | (1,644) | (1,429) | (1,243) | (1,081) | (7,211) |

| Freehold development option | | Year 1 £,000's | Year 2 £,000's | Year 3 £,000's | Year 4 £,000's | Year 5 £,000's | Year 6 £,000's | Year 7 £,000's | Total £,000's |
|---|---|---|---|---|---|---|---|---|---|
| Annual expenditure | New premises | 0 | (500) | (1,000) | (1,000) | (1,000) | (1,000) | (1,000) | |
| | Existing premises | (800) | (400) | 0 | 0 | 0 | 0 | 0 | |
| Capital expenditure | | (9,500) | (6,500) | 0 | 0 | 0 | 0 | 0 | |
| Capital income from sale | | 0 | 6,000 | 0 | 0 | 0 | 0 | 0 | |
| Net annual cash flow | | (10,300) | (1,400) | (1,000) | (1,000) | (1,000) | (1,000) | (1,000) | |
| NPV @ 15% | | (10,300) | (1,217) | (756) | (658) | (572) | (497) | (432) | (14,432) |

**FIG 9.1.J** shows what happens to the same example if the effect on the company's assets is superimposed on the cash flow - note how the result in **FIG 9.1.H** is stood on its head.

FIG 9.1.J: *The effect of introducing created asset value to a discounted option appraisal*

| Freehold development option (including capital value) | | Year 1 £,000's | Year 2 £,000's | Year 3 £,000's | Year 4 £,000's | Year 5 £,000's | Year 6 £,000's | Year 7 £,000's | Total £,000's |
|---|---|---|---|---|---|---|---|---|---|
| Annual expenditure | New premises | 0 | (500) | (1,000) | (1,000) | (1,000) | (1,000) | (1,000) | |
| | Existing premises | (800) | (400) | 0 | 0 | 0 | 0 | 0 | |
| Capital expenditure | | (9,500) | (6,500) | 0 | 0 | 0 | 0 | 0 | |
| Capital income | | 0 | 6,000 | 0 | 0 | 0 | 0 | 0 | |
| Net annual cash flow | | (10,300) | (1,400) | (1,000) | (1,000) | (1,000) | (1,000) | (1,000) | |
| Net capital value | | 0 | 19,005 | 0 | 0 | 0 | 0 | 0 | |
| Net total | | (10,300) | 17,605 | (1,000) | (1,000) | (1,000) | (1,000) | (1,000) | |
| NPV @ 15% | | (10,300) | 15,309 | (756) | (658) | (572) | (497) | (432) | 2,094 |

Of course, because the asset value is not cash income it has no logical place in a discounted cash flow example. Nevertheless the expenditure incurred in creating the asset is not money down the drain as **FIG 9.1.H** implies and, of course, the asset can be used as security for borrowing money. However, to be correct management accountants would show the asset value at the end of the life-cycle, possibly discounting it back over 40-60 years.

A further method of appraising rent v buy options is to treat the capital cost as funded out of external borrowing at a commercial rate, maybe allowing for a down-payment of 10%- 20% of the total. This is probably the best way to do it, and **FIG 9.1.K** shows how its adoption affords a much fairer comparison with the rented option in **FIG 9.1.H**

FIG 9.1.K: *Option appraisal as FIG 9.1.H but expressing capital expenditure as a commercial mortgage @ 10% over 15 years*

| Rented option | | Year 1 £,000's | Year 2 £,000's | Year 3 £,000's | Year 4 £,000's | Year 5 £,000's | Year 6 £,000's | Year 7 £,000's | Total £,000's |
|---|---|---|---|---|---|---|---|---|---|
| Annual expenditure | New premises | (1,750) | (2,500) | (2,500) | (2,500) | (2,500) | (2,500) | (2,500) | |
| | Existing premises | 0 | 0 | 0 | 0 | 0 | 0 | 0 | |
| Capital expenditure | | (2,000) | 0 | 0 | 0 | 0 | 0 | 0 | |
| Capital income | | 6,000 | 0 | 0 | 0 | 0 | 0 | 0 | |
| Net annual cash flow | | 2,250 | (2,500) | (2,500) | (2,500) | (2,500) | (2,500) | (2,500) | |
| NPV @ 15% | | 2,250 | (2,174) | (1,890) | (1,644) | (1,429) | (1,243) | (1,081) | (7,211) |

| Freehold development option | | Year 1 £,000's | Year 2 £,000's | Year 3 £,000's | Year 4 £,000's | Year 5 £,000's | Year 6 £,000's | Year 7 £,000's | Total £,000's |
|---|---|---|---|---|---|---|---|---|---|
| Annual expenditure | New premises | 0 | (500) | (1,000) | (1,000) | (1,000) | (1,000) | (1,000) | |
| | Existing premises | (800) | (400) | 0 | 0 | 0 | 0 | 0 | |
| Capital expenditure | | (9,500) | (6,500) | 0 | 0 | 0 | 0 | 0 | |
| Development loan (100%) | | 0 | 16,000 | 0 | 0 | 0 | 0 | 0 | |
| Loan repayments | | 0 | 0 | (2,100) | (2,100) | (2,100) | (2,100) | 0 | |
| Loan repayments years 7 -17 inc. NPV @ 15% | | 0 | 0 | 0 | 0 | 0 | 0 | (10,500) | |
| Capital income | | 0 | 6,000 | 0 | 0 | 0 | 0 | 0 | |
| Net annual cash flow | | (10,300) | 14,600 | (3,100) | (3,100) | (3,100) | (3,100) | (11,500) | |
| NPV @ 15% | | (10,300) | (12,702) | (2,343) | (2,040) | (1,773) | (1,541) | (4,968) | (10,263) |

Management accountants dancing on the point of a needle will argue forever about the imperfections of such presentations. However, in order to understand economic arguments a bending of traditional rules (provided the logic behind both rule and deviation is understood) can often be a big aid to management in decision-making.

*Implementation*

Once the studies have been completed, the results will have to be co-ordinated and re-cast as a strategy for implementation. Again, the importance of the critical path will be underlined, because it will provide the continuity for moving from planning to implementation.

If findings seriously question elements of the master plan, these will have to be resolved within the context of the business plan. The critical path, however, should allow for this period of reconciliation as the company pauses for breath.

Where construction of a new building is involved, the company will need to prepare for relocation during the building programme. Rationalisation of leases, organisational changes and moving-in strategies can all begin. Relocation to an existing building will telescope these stages so that they can proceed simultaneously.

The actual move can be an extremely disruptive exercise, but if the earlier stages have all been completed successfully, disruption can be minimised. Thorough consultation with user groups through formal channels can pre-empt many problems. Needless to say, involving a skilled and reputable removals contractor in the plans from an early stage is essential.

*Post-occupancy*

The relocation exercise does not end with occupation of the new building. Inevitable teething problems will need to be ironed out. The relocation team will be required to respond to the problems and worries of staff as well as ensure the smooth running of the organisation as a whole.

## 9.1.5 PARTIAL RELOCATION

*Reasons for splitting locations*

Fundamental issues activating the suggestion to move part of an organisation away from the single place of operations include the following:

- shortage of space coupled with
    - lack of extension capacity
    - high cost of extension
    - no particular need for centralisation
    - desire to reduce overall level of premises costs
    - ready availability of suitable location space
    - desire to reduce staff costs
- desire to maximise existing central space by
    - improving space standards, or
    - generating income from valuable space freed up by partial relocation,

or

- desire to move part of the organisation to a better location in terms of
    - image
    - staff recruitment
    - salary levels
    - customer access

The solutions to all of these issues have implications for the cost of premises. However, they should not stem initially from the desire to make or save money on the real estate side.

All the better if it can be done without impairing business efficiency. That calculation needs to be thoroughly investigated and a good attempt made to express all the 'knock-on' effects in money terms - not just those which are easily and traditionally quantifiable - such as rent, rates and operating costs.

*Partial relocation - reduced premises costs*

There is a wide difference in the cost of premises nationwide and internationally. The total cost of premises in a typical selection of UK and other European centres at present is given in **FIG 9.1.L**.

**FIG. 9.1.L:** *Prime office costs - regional variations*

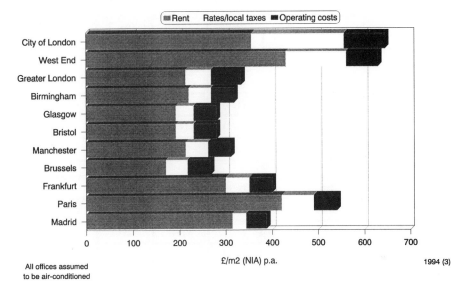

All offices assumed to be air-conditioned

1994 (3)

High premises costs in the metropolis often cause management to think seriously about relocating those staff who do not need to be in such prestigious accommodation. Of course, staff costs can also be saved in provincial locations, but the following examples address both sets of considerations.

Thus an organisation of 400 employees occupying 6,000 sq.m of net internal (lettable) floor area in the West End of London electing to relocate 320 staff to a back office on the South coast might calculate its prospective premises costs as shown in **FIG 9.1.M**. which presumes that the required back-office space is immediately available to rent.

The amount of lettable space taken on board in the new location allows for similar space standards to those previously adopted for clerical grades in the West End but there is an addition for improved space standards for supervising grades. Also provision is made for 5% p.a. growth in the back office over a five-year period with partial recovery of the extra costs through short-term leasing out (see 'Rental income' in the Figure). Head office space and quality standards are also improved.

All costs have been inflated at 5% p.a. but there are no rent reviews for the 5 - years period in the example. Due to the high discount rate costs and income beyond the first 5 years have been excluded from this and the following related examples.

**FIG 9.1.M:** *Premises cost appraisal of partial relocation (rented) option by comparison with status quo*

| Option 1 - Status quo | | Year 1 £,000's | Year 2 £,000's | Year 3 £,000's | Year 4 £,000's | Year 5 £,000's | Total £,000's |
|---|---|---|---|---|---|---|---|
| West End | Rent | (1,800) | (1,800) | (1,800) | (1,800) | (1,800) | (9,000) |
| | Rates | (750) | (788) | (827) | (868) | (912) | (4,145) |
| | Operating costs | (480) | (504) | (529) | (556) | (583) | (2,652) |
| | Fitting-out | (300) | (315) | (331) | (347) | (1,800) | (3,093) |
| | Rental income | 0 | 0 | 0 | 0 | 0 | 0 |
| Total £,000's | | (3,300) | (3,407) | (3,487) | (3,571) | (5,095) | (18,890) |
| Present value factor @ 15% pa | | 1.0000 | 0.8696 | 0.7561 | 0.6575 | 0.5718 | |
| Present Value | | (3,330) | (2,963) | (2,637) | (2,348) | (2,913) | (14,191) |

| Option 2 - Partial relocation | | Year 1 £,000's | Year 2 £,000's | Year 3 £,000's | Year 4 £,000's | Year 5 £,000's | Total £,000's |
|---|---|---|---|---|---|---|---|
| West End | Rent | (1,800) | (1,800) | (1,800) | (1,800) | (1,800) | (9,000) |
| | Rates | (188) | (197) | (207) | (218) | (228) | (1,038) |
| | Operating costs | (120) | (125) | (132) | (139) | (146) | (662) |
| | Fitting-out | (375) | (75) | (79) | (83) | (450) | (1,062) |
| | Rental income | 1,350 | 1,350 | 1,350 | 1,350 | 1,350 | 6,750 |
| South Coast | Rent | (675) | (675) | (675) | (675) | (675) | (3,375) |
| | Rates | (225) | (236) | (248) | (260) | (273) | (1,242) |
| | Operating costs | (270) | (284) | (298) | (313) | (328) | (1,493) |
| | Fitting-out | (1,013) | 0 | 0 | 0 | 0 | (1,013) |
| Overall total £,000's | | (3,316) | (2,042) | (2,089) | (2,138) | (2,550) | (12,135) |
| Present value factor @ 15% pa | | 1.0000 | 0.8696 | 0.7561 | 0.6575 | 0.5718 | |
| Present value | | (3,316) | (1,776) | (1,579) | (1,406) | (1,458) | (9,535) |

## Benefiting from a successful location

An important point about the premises costs of relocation - and one which is often missed in appraisal - is the effect of successful judgement on the cost of premises in the area of relocation, and the further influence of the rent/buy decision on that appraisal.

For example, an organisation locating in the M4 corridor ten years ago might well now be paying a rent 100% higher due to the popularity of the area in subsequent years.

The leaseholders will probably be picking up five-yearly upwards only rent reviews, so they will at regular intervals be open to the vagaries of the market - at present not a detrimental prospect but one to watch out for in the future. For example, the discounted (that is deflated) rental growth is still well above the 1984 figures; and disproportionate to the much slower growth in the original central location. The hoped-for saving in annual premises costs is effectively reduced following this calculation so the organisation is penalised for its successful judgement of the quality of the new location.

**FIG 9.1.N:** *Partial relocation appraisal as FIG 9.1.M but with owner-occupied development for the 'South Coast' option*

| Development option | | Year 1 £,000's | Year 2 £,000's | Year 3 £,000's | Year 4 £,000's | Year 5 £,000's | Total £,000's |
|---|---|---|---|---|---|---|---|
| West End | Rent | (1,800) | (1,800) | (1,800) | (1,800) | (1,800) | (9,000) |
| | Rates | (750) | (788) | (225) | (236) | (248) | (2,247) |
| | Operating costs | (480) | (504) | (132) | (139) | (146) | (1,401) |
| | Fitting-out | (375) | (75) | (79) | (90) | (95) | (714) |
| | Rental income | 0 | 0 | 1,350 | 1,350 | 1,350 | 4,050 |
| South Coast | Land Purchase | (1,000) | 0 | 0 | 0 | 0 | (1,000) |
| | Construction | (1,200) | (3,000) | 0 | 0 | 0 | (4,200) |
| | Fitting-out | 0 | (1,013) | 0 | 0 | 0 | (1,013) |
| | Rates | 0 | 0 | (248) | (260) | (273) | (781) |
| | Operating costs | 0 | 0 | (293) | (307) | (322) | (922) |
| Overall total £,000's | | (5,605) | (7,180) | (1,427) | (1,482) | (1,534) | (17,228) |
| Present value factor @ 15% pa | | 1.0000 | 0.8696 | 0.7561 | 0.6575 | 0.5718 | |
| Present value | | (5,605) | (6,244) | (1,079) | (974) | (877) | (14,779) |

**FIG 9.1.P:** *Partial relocation appraisal as FIG 9.1.N but incorporating the capital cost of development by way of annual loan repayments*

| Development option | | Year 1 £,000's | Year 2 £,000's | Year 3 £,000's | Year 4 £,000's | Year 5 £,000's | Total £,000's |
|---|---|---|---|---|---|---|---|
| West End | Rent | (1,800) | (1,800) | (1,800) | (1,800) | (1,800) | (9,000) |
| | Rates | (750) | (788) | (225) | (236) | (248) | (2,247) |
| | Operating costs | (480) | (504) | (132) | (139) | (146) | (1,401) |
| | Fitting-out | (375) | (75) | (79) | (90) | (95) | (714) |
| | Rental income | - | - | 1,350 | 1,350 | 1,350 | 4,050 |
| South coast | Development loan | 5,200 | - | - | - | - | 5,200 |
| | Loan repayment | (846) | (846) | (846) | (846) | (846) | (4,230) |
| | Land | (1,000) | - | - | - | - | (1,000) |
| | Construction | (1,200) | (3,000) | - | - | - | (4,200) |
| | Fitting-out | - | (1,013) | - | - | - | (1,013) |
| | Rates | - | - | (248) | (260) | (273) | (781) |
| | Operating costs | - | - | (293) | (307) | (322) | (922) |
| Overall total | | (1,251) | (8,026) | (2,273) | (2,328) | (2,380) | (16,258) |
| PV factor 15% | | 1.0000 | 0.8696 | 0.7562 | 0.6576 | 0.5718 | - |
| NPV | | (1,251) | (6,979) | (1,179) | (1,531) | (1,361) | (12,841) |

On the other hand, if they had bought and developed a site or bought a freehold, the capital value of their asset would have benefited substantially from the same market in real terms even allowing for temporary rises in yields. As all the financial services commercials now have to say, prices can go down as well as up. The freeholder faces exactly the same problems as the tenant - but in reverse for in the rent-increase example described above he will improve his asset base as rental levels rise.

**FIG 9.1.N** shows how the sums in **FIG 9.1.M** would be varied using a development option. Because of the development period the move and subsequent benefits are not shown until year 3. Note that a continuance of 'churn', albeit at a lower level, is included in 'fitting-out' in the West End office but written out – maybe rather optimistically – in the newly planned South Coast building.

The option is shown financed out of the business cash flow which both penalises the heavy up front expenditure and discounts down the income from sub-letting in the West End.

**FIG 9.1.J** showed how the inference of such a calculation would be reversed if the effect on assets were to be shown in the DCF appraisal. However, expressing the capital costs by way of instalments of a commercial mortgage as in **FIG 9.1.P** makes the back office development option look fairly attractive in this case especially given that the company owns the south coast asset .

## 9.1.6 TOTAL ECONOMICS OF RELOCATION

*The premises argument*

The premises cost argument should never be paramount. The costs and benefits should always be gathered into one equation to find the true picture.

In the case of partial relocation the advantages of such savings as premises costs and possibly staff costs have to be read against possible increase of overheads in supervision, travelling between offices, disruption and so on. **FIG 9.1.Q** shows how the South coast example might look in the context of a cost-benefit analysis

**FIG 9.1.Q:** *Partial relocation appraisal as FIG 9.1.P but as a cost/benefit analysis introducing personnel costs and improvements in productivity*

| Development option | | Year 1 £,000's | Year 2 £,000's | Year 3 £,000's | Year 4 £,000's | Year 5 £,000's | Total £,000's |
|---|---|---|---|---|---|---|---|
| Premises costs - West End | Rent | (1,800) | (1,800) | (1,800) | (1,800) | (1,800) | (9,000) |
| | Rates | (750) | (788) | (225) | (236) | (248) | (2,247) |
| | Operating costs | (480) | (504) | (132) | (139) | (146) | (1,401) |
| | Fitting-out | (375) | (75) | (79) | (90) | (95) | (714) |
| | Rental income | - | - | 1,350 | 1,350 | 1,350 | 4,050 |
| Premises costs - South Coast | Development loan | 5,200 | - | - | - | - | 5,200 |
| | Loan repayment | (846) | (846) | (846) | (846) | (846) | (4,230) |
| | Land Purchase | (1,000) | - | - | - | - | (1,000) |
| | Construction | (1,200) | (3,000) | - | - | - | (4,200) |
| | Fitting-out | - | (1,013) | - | - | - | (1,013) |
| | Rates | - | - | (248) | (260) | (273) | (781) |
| | Operating costs | - | - | (293) | (307) | (322) | (922) |
| Business costs - both Facilities | Direct moving cost | | | (50) | | | (50) |
| | Indirect moving cost | | | (500) | | | (500) |
| | Productivity benefit - West End | | | 32 | 64 | 67 | 163 |
| | Productivity benefit - South Coast | | | 64 | 128 | 134 | 326 |
| | Dual location costs | | | (150) | (158) | (165) | (473) |
| | Salary saving | | | 450 | 473 | 496 | 1,419 |
| | Total | | | (154) | 507 | 532 | 885 |
| Overall total | | (1,251) | (8,026) | (2,581) | (1,314) | (1,316) | (14,488) |
| Present value factor @ 15% pa | | 1.0000 | 0.8696 | 0.7561 | 0.6575 | 0.5718 | |
| Present value | | (1,251) | (6,979) | (1,951) | (864) | (752) | **(11,797)** |

incorporating these factors. Of course, forecasts of productivity changes are always going to be challenged, so a sensitivity testing of these assumptions is absolutely essential. The easiest way to calculate figures for such analysis is by taking percentage savings (or increases) in the total salaries bill for all the staff whose productivity is likely to benefit (or otherwise) from the change.

**FIG 9.1.R** summarises the results of the various strategies. In this case the rental relocation option looks more favourable than owner-occupation.

FIG 9.1.R: *Partial relocation study - summary of alternative appraisal calculations*

| | Premises costs only | NPV cost £,000's |
|---|---|---|
| Fig. 9.1.M | "Do nothing" (West End) option | (14,191) |
| Fig. 9.1.M | Part relocation (South coast) rental option | (9,535) |
| Fig. 9.1.N | Part relocation (South coast) development option | (14,779) |
| Fig. 9.1.P | Part relocation (South coast) development option - loan repayment option | (12,841) |
| | **Premises plus business costs** | NPV cost £,000's |
| Fig. 9.1.Q | Part relocation (South coast) development option (including cost / benefit analysis) | (11,797) |

The introduction of business efficiency/cost assumptions from **FIG 9.1.Q** indicates a further beneficial effect which would, of course, similarly influence the other appraisals if applied.

The 'front and back offices' premises policy does usually make economic sense, and in the example has helped to avoid the worst symptoms of the 'churn' disease. However, not a few organisations have found to their cost that the second centre has been more trouble than the expected saving was worth and either re-relocated or re-centralised at further expense.

If the business logic is sound, the premises advice well informed and the appraisal technique flexible and comprehensive then the right decision will be made - **but only if the business decision drives the premises policy** and not vice-versa.

### 9.1.7 MOVING OFFICE

*Project
management*

Whether it is just another piece of internal 'churn' or a major premises relocation the actual move needs to be meticulously planned and executed if the organisation is not to suffer from delays and disruptions leading to extensive loss of productivity.

In major moves a dedicated project manager will almost certainly be needed, possibly externally appointed but in close liaison with the facilities manager.

Issues relating to staff notifications, relocation allowances etc., are down to the personnel department but the project manager must liaise closely with them to ensure that the date and time of the operation are agreed well in advance – changes of plan can be disastrous in terms of employer/employee relationships at these times.

*Preparing to
move*

The following is a checklist of key issues to be addressed by the project manager in preparation for the move once the relocation decision has been taken:

- the budget

- staff/facilities requiring special treatment eg: the handicapped, key executives, pabx system

- lead times for installation of new or relocated facilities such as: security systems, telephones, IT networks, power supplies

- permissions and licences eg: loading/unloading, parking, skips, liquor licence (for the caterers)

- identify equipment and/or substances requiring special handling (by external suppliers or contractors) such as photocopiers, toxic materials

- design production and delivery of new headed stationery

- advice to customers and suppliers of the move date and new address etc. and also any temporary arrangements pertaining to the period of the move.

*Choosing the
contractor*

It will be advisable to tender the work on a fairly specific document; however, because the best way to handle dealings with removal contractors is in fully co-operative mode it is well worth making the appointment as early as possible getting his input to the logic of the process from the outset of planning. This dichotomy can be solved by the sort of two-stage tendering process described for selection of a building contractor at Chapter 6.3, leaving the tying up of a comprehensive contract to be negotiated at the second stage by reference to key competitive factors established in the first-stage bidding process.

*The
programme for
the removals*

Depending on the nature of the business it may be possible to carry out the whole operation at one go. However, some organisations cannot afford a complete shut-down - even for 24/48 hours - so for them a staged programme, or weekend operation will be essential. Although weekend and out-of-hours working may be more expensive (this can be determined at the first-stage bid) the cost of the move per capita will normally be insignificant in the whole financial scheme of things when the effect on employee productivity is brought into the equation.

Every good programme has a float and a contingency. The float may be concealed but the contingency, both in terms of time and recovery plan, must be made known to all key managers.

*Moving out and in*

Key issues to be addressed relating to the actual move are:

- the insurance of both new and existing properties

- availability of all utility services and disconnecting as appropriate

- security and fire protection services in place and fully operational at both locations

- a condition survey completed and agreed by the landlord/assignee of the old premises and the new landlord if applicable

- washroom and catering facilities must be up and running for the work-force and any 'pioneering' staff

- only move goods and equipment which are needed in the new location - it is surprising how reluctant people are to 'out' rubbish and the move is a perfect time to insist on it

- make sure of the times at which legal possession and relinquishment actually take effect to avoid the embarrassment of being locked out of one or both properties while the contractor's vans wait in the road outside

- the contractor must take full responsibility for the protection of both buildings during the move - specify the performance rather than the method, and check his insurance cover for damage to goods and property, as well as loss in transit

- thoroughly check the inventory on leaving and arrival; companies with bar-coded equipment for asset tracking will find this easier, but remember that the code-readers are not usually intelligent. Someone with a live pc (possibly a lap-top computer) should be able to keep well on top of the inventory from beginning to end - also checking accuracy of drops to various floor levels and locations in the new buildings

- with the contractor check out the access points (again) before commencing to unload; in particular, dimensions of openings, lift and floor loading capacities must be reviewed in case last minute changes to the arrangements prove to be illegal or impossible or both

- the contractor will have his own modus operandi for labelling crates, mechanical handling and transportation and marking up the drawings. Always check it, but make sure that he takes full and sole responsibility for its accuracy and efficiency.

*Post-move activity*

The commissioning of any new or modified services needs to be reset once the building is ready for occupation, and a 'deep clean' is essential prior to any staff taking up their posts.

Finally, a new telephone/fax directory needs to be in place and distributed from day one - it is amazing how often this simple but critical operation is overlooked risking the goodwill of the staff at a time when plaudits are potentially there for the taking.

## The cost of moving

**FIG 9.1.S** gives an approximate guide to the cost of removals per capita across town and to a remote location. Note that if the move were to take place over a weekend the costs would be from 15-30% higher - a drop in the ocean compared with losing 2 man-days output per member of staff!

**FIG. 9.1.S:** *The approximate cost of weekday removals per capita*

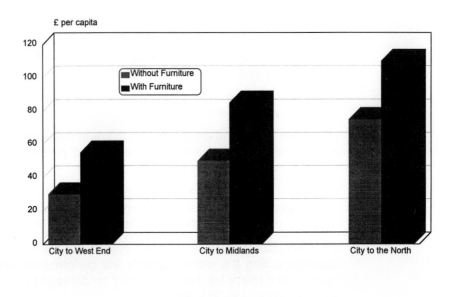

(1) Available from QAI (Europe) Ltd – c/o DEGW, London

# SECTION 10

# THE DEVELOPMENT OPTION

# CHAPTER 10.1 – THE FACILITIES MANAGER'S ROLE IN A NEW DEVELOPMENT

## 10.1.1 THE DECISION TO BUILD

*The facilities manager's involvement*

In the previous Chapter on 'relocation' the issue of whether to rent or build was explored and the financial implications of both options considered in detail.

Once the management board has made up its mind for a new-build project the facilities manager can expect to be pushed into the front-line role in the commissioning and managing of the project. If he is not, then he ought to volunteer; not just because it is a fascinating process - which it is - but because the facilities manager's constructive involvement is essential to the success of the venture.

*The project management decision*

Whereas the facilities manager may be capable of managing fitting out projects - albeit possibly on a smaller scale - without external assistance, project management of the development process is strictly for the professionals. Few facilities managers will have the background in real estate finance and construction to be able to deliver a project of any size to time, quality and cost without exposing the organisation to an unacceptable level of risk.

However, there are two facets of project management; the **delivery** process referred to above ie: the **development project management**, and the **liaison** process - which is the role the facilities manager must carry out to ensure that the requirements of the **premises policy** are met in full and that the organisation is fully and properly involved and informed about the whole process from start to finish.

*Project liaison management*

The **project liaison manager** (sometimes called the **project sponsor**) is ideally an in-house appointment although it is not unusual for consultants to be appointed to this role where a suitable candidate is not available internally.

The role is quite distinct from that of the development project manager in that it entails forging that critical link between the client and the development process.

The liaison manager will probably be involved from the early stages of developing the brief, commissioning the feasibility study, guiding and informing the decision-making process. Once the process begins in earnest he should take up his role at the interface between the participants as depicted at **FIG 10.1.A**.

Internally he will need to be the organisation's focal point with regards to

- developing and refining the brief
- reporting on progress

- advising on client decisions required

- issuing instructions

- authorisations eg: payments etc.

- dealing with other consultants - eg: agents, solicitors, valuers, funding agents (possibly in conjunction with the development project manager)

- liaison with personnel management concerning the move and staff requirements, approvals etc.

- management of the move - or liaising with a dedicated move manager.

It is important that the liaison manager and the development project manager work closely together; really a side-by-side structure should be established in practice, although the liaison manager is theoretically superior in the hierarchy. In spite of this it must always be totally clear as to who carries what responsibility, and that clarity must prevail in-house as well as to the outside world.

**FIG. 10.1.A:** *The role of the project liaison manager*

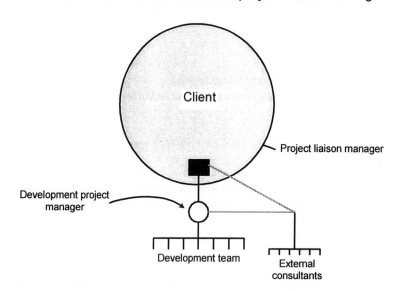

## 10.1.2 PROJECT ACTIVITIES AND PARTICIPANTS

*The qualities required of the development project manager*

The development project manager will have many tasks to control and many disparate people, companies and authorities to manage by whatever means available to him. He needs experience, intelligence, nouse, vision, tact, tenacity, patience, charm and resources to list but a few of the qualities essential to successful delivery of a project. Very importantly he should have a **thorough understanding** of the philosophies and strategic roles of the key consultants, contractors and authorities with whom he must work.

## The development activities

The key processes coming under his direction, more or less in consecutive order are:

- brief
- feasibility study
- site finding
- planning permission
- bridging finance (possibly)
- land acquisition
- design
- cost control
- change
- asset management plan
- handover
- removals
- occupation
- long-term finance (possibly).

Depending on the arrangements which best suit the project and the relevant experience and skills of both the liaison and development project managers, some of these activities may be carried out direct by the client or by the two managers in tandem.

## Participants in the process

In the course of these extensive and often overlapping activities the project manager will have to deal with (again possibly in conjunction with the liaison manager) any or all of the professions who are essential to various stages of the process such as:

- solicitors
- letting agents
- funding brokers
- valuers
- architects
- structural engineers
- mechanical engineers
- civil engineers
- highway engineers
- quantity surveyors
- planning consultants
- landscape architects
- building control officers
- planning officers

and so on.

## Buying the land

Once the location has been decided the hunt for a site begins - unless the whole concept has been initiated by the availability of a piece of land which meets, or has kindled the idea of, a relocation strategy.

The worst thing a prospective owner-occupier can do is try to compete for land with the professional developers in a seller's market. Apart from the obvious lack of commercial 'nouse' - even if supported by the expertise of a real estate agent - there are the 'hidden agendas' of the developers and investors which can turn the true value of an individual site on its head eg: where it has a 'marriage value' with adjoining sites making the whole worth infinitely more than the sum of the parts.

It is most important to understand that **development land has no intrinsic value; its value is a residual figure** the calculation of which is explained in Chapter 10.2. Furthermore, although the residual figure has to be projected prior to purchase the true residual will be whatever turns up in the post-project reconciliation statement. **FIG 10.1.B** is a graphic representation of the calculation given at **FIG 3.3.2.B** in Chapter 3.3 but showing the 'true' residual land value after allowing for a 'normal' development profit rather than the 'windfall' profit portrayed in that example. This is another good illustration as to why no-one should ever buy land on the basis of some 'comparable' transaction which may be founded on a completely different set of cost/value parameters.

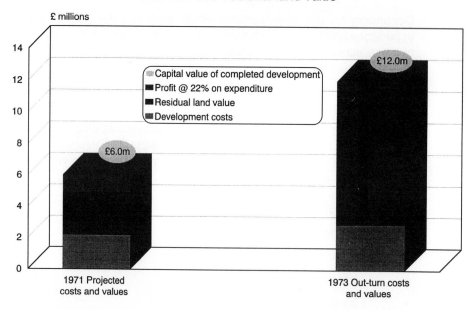

**FIG. 10.1.B:** *Development budget out-turn compared to forecast - effect on 'true' residual land value*

## The planning process

The process of putting a site together from disparate but adjacent land components is excruciatingly complicated and frustrating; it can also be rewarding for the speculator, but rarely for the serious owner-occupier. Ironically the 'cleverness' of speculators in this respect has led to some of the least appropriate facilities imaginable.

The Centre Point office building at the junction of Oxford Street and Tottenham Court Road was a triumph of man over the planning process, but rather less successful in terms of provision of a useful facility; 10,000 sq.ft per floor in a skyscraper in the heart of London's West End was never going to excite a major occupier at the sort of rent its owner's strenuous efforts might have justified and it remained unlet for several years after completion.

Whether the chosen site is green- or brown-field the prospective owner-occupier may well be able to use his pulling-power as an employer – or attractor of employment opportunities – to obtain a valuable planning consent which the planning authority might be loath to award to a speculator. The process is not as pure as the 1948 legislators probably intended; job prospects may sway the views of worthy town councillors who might otherwise throw up their hands in horror at the idea of their rate-payers' environment being offended by the new high-tech building on the edge of town.

In the end, 'politics' will determine the fate of sensitive planning sites, and the best strategy is to try to recognise them and then avoid them like the plague -unless the political bias is strongly and patently supportive.

## The finance

Unless the developing owner is cash-rich he will have to look externally for funding. There are two distinct phases in funding:

- bridging finance
- long-term finance

**Bridging finance** is short-term borrowing - sometimes from the bank or out of cash deposits - for the land purchase and the execution of the project to handover. It is usually paid for at a commercial rate and is expected to be repaid on completion, by which time the owner should have secured the **long-term finance**, usually by a sale-and-leaseback arrangement or a medium-term commercial mortgage. Both these routes will require payment at a lower return than the bridging loan reflecting the fact that the **risk** of carrying out the development to successful completion has disappeared from the equation.

How to estimate the cost of bridging finance is shown in the following Chapter 10.2 while the various methods of short-and-long-term financing for a property develop-ment are discussed in greater detail in Chapter 10.3.

An essential feature in obtaining the long-term finance to pay back the bridging loan is that the value of the completed development must be significantly – say 25% - 30% – greater than the original amount borrowed. Indeed, the initial funds cannot normally be raised unless the development equation stacks up in that way.

Where there is some form of leaseback arrangement from an investment institution it is quite common for the bridging finance to come from that same source.

**FIG 10.1.C:** *Development cash flow (simplified)*

| EXPENDITURE | 1st quarter | 2nd quarter | 3rd quarter | 4th quarter | 5th quarter | 6th quarter | 7th quarter | 8th quarter | Totals |
|---|---|---|---|---|---|---|---|---|---|
| | £000 | £000 | £000 | £000 | £000 | £000 | £000 | £000 | £000 |
| • Land acquisition | (2,000) | | | | | | | | (2,000) |
| • Legal & agent's fee | (35) | | | | | | | | (35) |
| • Pre-contract design etc. fee | (50) | (150) | | | | | | | (200) |
| • Construction works | | | (250) | (1,000) | (1,000) | (500) | – | (250) | (3,000) |
| • Post-contract professional fees | | | (20) | (20) | (20) | (20) | (10) | (10) | (100) |
| • Marketing / agent's fee | | | | | | | | (50) | (50) |
| Sub-total per quarter | (2,085) | (150) | (270) | (1020) | (1020) | (520) | (10) | (310) | (5,385) |
| Cumulative balance | (2,085) | (2,287) | (2,614) | (3,699) | (4,811) | (5,454) | (5,603) | (6,056) | |
| INCOME from sale | | | | | | | | 8,000 | 8,000 |
| • Interest on balance @ 2½% per quarter | (52) | (57) | (65) | (92) | (123) | (139) | (143) | – | (671) |
| TOTALS | (2,137) | (2,344) | (2,679) | (3,791) | (4,934) | (5,593) | (5,746) | 1,944 | 1,944 |

However the bridging finance is raised the project manager will be responsible for producing a development cash flow showing the rate of expenditure, the amount required to be borrowed at any one time and the forecast interest charges. A simple example of what is often a highly complex calculation is given at **FIG 10.1.C**. In practice interest would be calculated monthly or even daily rather than quarterly as shown here for simplicity. **The final figure of £1,944,000 is the profit.**

## The construction project

The various participants in, and stages of, a new-build project are all similar to those examined in detail under the fitting-out process in Chapter 6.3. However, the nature of the beast is such that there is a far greater scope for error and default than in the simpler interiors projects and the designers and constructors tend to specialise in one field or the other - in a normal market!

The whole new-build process is infinitely more complex than fitting-out so any decision to push the pace of the design or construction process (eg: as suggested in **FIG 6.3.V** in Chapter 6.3) needs to be considered most carefully and particularly in the light of the calibre of firms and individuals likely to be available to participate.

The facilities manager is particularly vulnerable at this decision-point and has to take his project manager very much on trust if he agrees to the fast-track route which may be needed to meet the organisation's accommodation requirements.

The professionals must all carry indemnity insurance (discussed in Chapter 3.6) and the constructor's 'latent defects' insurance needs to be most carefully scrutinised.

## The asset management programme

The best time to produce an asset management programme is when the cost plan has been 'signed off' at Stage C (outline proposals) of the design and construction programme; in fact the asset management plan eg: as shown in **FIG 2.2.3.B** in Chapter 2.2, should emanate directly from the **life-cycle cost plan** which informs the decision-making process prior to the cost plan being adopted by all sides.

The property being developed may well form an important component of the organisation's asset base and requires to be planned and designed with its physical performance under thorough - though not dominant - consideration; remember, it is people and their equipment who are the biggest assets and **their** functional interface with the property must always be at the forefront of the facilities manager's mind when dealing with the project manager over matters of building quality and performance.

## The handover

Once the client has taken physical possession of the building there is a period - normally 6 months - during which time the builder has to make good any defects arising out of the works but not evident at the handover stage. Usually the architect, with the project manager's consent, will allow the builder to potter around after handover making good the items on a practical completion 'snagging list' of a relatively minor or decorative nature. However, once the 'final certificate' is issued the contractor is liable only for a period of 6 years (12 years where contract is under seal), although there is a longstop of 15 years under the Latent Defects Limitation Period.

Insurance against latent defects is a highly specialist area and one in which there are currently some interesting new approaches available which the facilities manager should insist upon being fully explored by both his own and the contractor's insurance broker well before the project is commenced.

# CHAPTER 10.2 – THE DEVELOPMENT PROCESS

## 10.2.1 THE NATURE OF PROPERTY DEVELOPMENT

*Introduction*

Property developers fall into two categories:

- developer/dealers
- developer/investors.

The facilities manager will only be likely to come across the developer/dealer in the course of approaches or negotiations to sell part of the organisation's estate to the dealer for the purposes of development or redevelopment.

On the other hand the developer/investor may well become the organisation's landlord - even its partner in the provision of new-build facilities leased or leased back to the organisation on completion of the project as described in Chapter 10.3.

A cynic once defined a property developer as 'someone who follows you through a revolving door and comes out in front!' Although this is grossly unfair to very many of the legitimate old-establishment developers who generate a goodly slice of our national wealth, the facilities manager should be aware that the apparent rich pickings from development attracts some inexperienced but shrewd 'fly-by-night' characters who may act unscrupulously in any dealings.

It is essential to use a reputable and experienced consultant in **any** property dealings but particularly in dealings with developers.

*Property dealing and development*

An individual or other 'person' who buys and sells land and buildings as a way of trade is known as a property dealer and is broadly similar in function (for taxation purposes at least) to a property developer who trades by buying land, building on the land and selling the completed properties. Both may act as landlords or even occupy the premises during the period of ownership; nevertheless the intention is trade rather than to invest, and the 'badges of trade' will be apparent in most instances, leading to taxation under Schedule D Case I, whereby income tax or corporation tax is charged on profits under the Income and Corporation Taxes Act 1988.

Builders of residential property for sale also fall into this group.

For taxation, it is usually clear when a person is trading and hence liable under Schedule D Case I but in some instances recourse to law will require a review of the 'badges of trade' to determine the objectives of the taxpayer. It is outside the scope of this work to examine the subject in detail. It may be noted that case law provides guidance on the nature of dealers and others – investors, house-owners, and so on.

A developer/dealer does not pay capital gains tax on the disposal of land which is stock-in-trade; any profits will be caught under Schedule D Case I. However, disposal of any capital asset, eg the premises from which the business is run, may give rise to capital gains tax, although roll-over or retirement relief may be available - see Chapter 11.3.

Note, however, that a landowner undertaking development of his own land for business use or dealing will not be classified under this tax regime unless he restructures his organisation accordingly.

Clearly the skills required by the successful developer will be far more extensive than those needed by the dealer; nevertheless both will survive and flourish only by having a 'nose' for a good deal and the 'savoir-faire' to bring it to fruition.

As the prime purpose is trading or dealing, the duration of borrowing the funds required for this purpose is likely to be both short-term and medium-term.

Commercial, industrial and other developers, eg for offices, shops, and industrial premises, who intend to sell are likely to use short-term borrowing for the duration of construction, obtaining funds from merchant banks, joint stock banks and other 'short-term' providers of funds. Whilst agreeing such finance, long-term arrangements will be explored so that repayment may be at the end of the development period. This may be by way of outright sale of the freehold or headlease held by the developer.

Sometimes one of several forms of sale and leaseback (see Chapter 10.3) may be arranged, so enabling the developer to retain an interest for a longer period; but this implies an investment policy rather than dealing.

*Property
development
and investment*

An individual or other body may buy land, develop it, and hold the completed building as an investment for letting. There are numerous ways in which funds may be made available for this operation.

In the main direct property investment outside the institutional sector has been by property investment companies with shareholders' funds sometimes being relatively highly geared (ie with a high ratio of borrowings to initial investment value) by debentures and loans. Sometimes in the past the institutions would lend on a long-term basis but this has not generally been the case in the last twenty years, with equity participation tending to supplant such loans.

In the past, the property investment companies have also adopted project funding arrangements by mortgages or by sale and leaseback arrangements of various kinds. In more recent times bank lending, debentures or rights issues have become prevalent, particularly as the institutions have tended to move into direct development.

Generally, the traditional mortgage and sale-and-leaseback may be described as the most popular means of funding for long-term retention of the property. The attraction of each to the seeker of funds will depend on the views held on the relative advantages and disadvantages of these methods. The commercial mortgage, subject to interest rates, may seem more attractive in times of high inflation but the sale-and-leaseback enables the retention of realised capital profits (once short-term borrowing for the construction period has been repaid), provided the extent of the loss of profit-rent equity is appreciated.

A property investment's net income is taxed under one of several taxation schedules of the Income and Corporation Taxes Act 1988.

Section 75 of the Income and Corporation Taxes Act 1988 provides that expenditure on management of an investment company is allowable for corporation tax purposes. Also, the taxpayer may be able to offset against taxable income interest on loans provided there is a 'qualifying purpose', eg the purchase of land, or improving or developing land or building on the land. Generally, interest on debenture stock is deducted against profit.

For a company, dividends paid to shareholders are not tax deductible. However, the dividends are paid net of the basic rate of income tax under Schedule F of the Income and Corporation Taxes Act 1988 and the company pays the tax under the advanced corporation tax system.

Disposal of an asset results in liability to capital gains tax, subject to any exemptions or reliefs which may be available. The charge is the current corporation tax rate applied to the chargeable gain as far as companies are concerned, unless the company is a small one. Individuals pay capital gains tax at standard and top rate income tax as appropriate, but an annual relief is available.

**Organisations developing their own land as investment, whether for owner-occupation or letting-out in whole or part, will have the same liabilities to and relief from corporation and capital gains tax in respect thereof as the developer/investor.**

*Property development activities*

Property development requires several activities to be undertaken. In this section they are only given in a general sequential order: in practice they are not likely to be so regular! Given the objectives and vehicle, the activities might include:

- marketing research to evaluate the appropriate market segments in a particular property sector

- the formulation of the 'mix', once the segments have been identified, to satisfy their requirements

- search for land, effecting options, and the acquisition of interests in property for dealing, investment or occupation, ie once appropriate planning enquiries have been made and any necessary consents obtained

- management of acquired land, obtaining possession, demolition, fencing and clearance

- the procurement of new buildings using one of the many approaches, eg 'design and build', 'traditional', and 'construction management'

- raising funds, either by a 'corporate approach' or by 'project funding' as described above

- promotion and agency, either to let or sell the completed building or to commission for owner-occupation

- evaluating taxation consequences of proposed transactions, development, funding or other activities.

The objectives of the land owner may influence the approach adopted in terms of joint venture projects or partnership arrangements.

## 10.2.2 DEVELOPMENT ECONOMICS

*The
development
equation*

Like economic appraisal of any other product the development equation says simply that:

Value less Costs = Profit

Although a simple concept the difficulty in making a successful project lies in the fact that not only are the end value and demand difficult to predict but also the level of costs tends to be volatile at every stage from inception to completion.

The development process starts with a synthesis of the out-turn costs, values and profits from a development of a specific building type (or complex) and a predicted size - usually described by floor area. This appraisal is based on what is commonly termed the 'development budget'; its first practical application will be to calculate how much the developer can afford to pay for the land.

*Components of
the
development
budget*

The developer will have to take account of four main groups of factors in preparing his development budget, and they can be briefly summarised as follows.

1. Factors related to the capitalised or market value of the development on completion.

- For any type of property the value of which is not conventionally geared to its income potential (eg residential property for sale with vacant possession to owner occupiers) these factors comprise:

    - selling price.

    - annual ground rent (eg from flats).

    - expected market yield (of ground rent) - see Chapter 3.3.

    - selling costs.

- For income or investment property (commercial, industrial or residential for leasing) these factors comprise:

    - rentable floor area

    - achievable annual rent from rentable floor area

    - non-rental income

    - annual operating expenses

    - expected market yield (or market capitalization rate)

    - leasing costs and commissions.

2. Factors related to the cost of the land:

    - basic cost of the land

    - acquisition costs (agency and legal)

    - finance charges on the land and acquisition costs.

3. Factors related to the Developer's building cost:

- basic cost of building and site development

- professional fees (architect, quantity surveyor, structural, mechanical and electrical engineers, soil analysts etc.)

- finance charges on the building cost and professional fees

4. A margin to cover the developer's overheads, profit requirement and development risk.

The commercial facilities manager is unlikely to be concerned with any form of residential development, so the chapter concentrates solely on the 'commercial' category of property development. However the principles are applicable to any category of user.

*Applications of the development budget*

The development budget has three principal applications. Most commonly it is used by the developer to calculate the residual land value, ie the maximum amount he can afford to pay for the land given specific assumptions on development costs and a required profit margin.

In this case referring to the four budget components above - the Building Costs (BC) and required Development Profit (P) are subtracted from the Capitalised Value of the completed Development (CV) to arrive at the Residual Land Value or Land Cost (LC). Thus:

$$CV - (BC + P) = LC$$

Secondly where the developer knows the land cost and has estimated the building cost he is able to calculate his profit margin or return on investment. Thus:

$$CV - (LC + BC) = P$$

Finally, where the developer has been offered a plot of land at a fixed price and has decided on the minimum profit he requires for the development, he is able to calculate a target building cost ie the maximum he can afford to spend on the building. Thus:

$$CV - (LC + P) = BC$$

*Explanation of the components and factors*

The following are brief explanations of the above components (or their factors) as they would normally appear in a development budget.

**The capitalised value of completed commercial development** is the net annual income from the development (gross rental income plus 'other' income), capitalised by use of an appropriate 'multiplier' (or 'years purchase' figure) to reflect the interest rate required to attract investors to purchase the property (ie: expected market yield). Thus if investors expect initial net earnings to show an 8% return on investment (100) then the investment (or capitalised) value of the property is the years purchase ($100 \div 8 = 12.5$) x net earnings; this calculation is considered in detail in Chapter 3.3.

This method is the one most widely used in the property industry for assessing investment values and corresponds to the simple 'rate of return' formula where initial or current net income is expressed as a percentage of the purchase price to calculate the investment yield. The capitalization rate is then the reciprocal of the yield.

**Leasing, selling costs and commissions** include any Estate Agent's commission and advertising or any costs of a direct sale; legal costs in respect of the sale of the completed dwellings are normally met by the incoming tenant although there is a growing trend for landlord and tenant to meet their own legal costs. Costs here normally constitute up to 10% of the initial gross annual rent, ie between ½% and 1% of the capital value of the completed development

At initial feasibility study the **basic cost of building and site development** will normally be calculated per square foot or square metre of the gross internal area. The unit price must include the cost of any demolitions and site development work. On schemes of any size the works will normally be costed in some detail prior to committing to land purchase, but in a 'bull' market speculators may take a chance on the unitary rate method.

**Professional fees (building work)** include the costs of services provided by the architect and quantity surveyor and in many cases, the services of a structural, mechanical and electrical engineer, soil analyst etc. Fees are conventionally expressed as a percentage of the building costs, and the appraiser should round the percentage figure upwards to allow for incidental expenses - such as printing etc. Fees should be calculated separately even where a design-and-build contract is envisaged.

**Acquisition costs** include any agent's fees for introducing the site and the legal costs of establishing title, preparing contracts, payment of stamp duty, effecting indemnity insurance and the like.

The allowance for **developer's overheads, profit and risk** provides a return to the developer for devoting his skill and time to the development, for the risk that he undertakes, and to offset the overhead costs of his organisation.

**Finance charge** covers the interest chargeable on the loan or equity capital required to carry the costs of the land, building and professional fees, during the period of the development. An interest charge should always be imputed for the equity capital element since, by using his own capital, the developer forfeits the opportunity of gaining a return from an alternative investment - 'the opportunity cost' in management accounting parlance.

Chapter 11.4 examines **Value Added Tax (VAT)** in some detail. For present purposes it is sufficient to note that VAT is generally chargeable on construction cost and all fees in connection with commercial development and refurbishment.

The tax may also be chargeable on the sale of freehold or leasehold land if the vendor so elects; otherwise it is exempt.

The same applies to the onward sale of the completed building. However, once the land has been charged VAT through 'election to waive exemption' all subsequent transactions must be charged at standard rate.

The tax is ultimately recoverable providing the developer is registered for VAT, since he is then considered to be the builder for VAT purposes. Thus the only costs incurred by the developer are the extra finance charges on the tax until recovery, and some overhead and administration costs.

Therefore when calculating the building cost when VAT is standard rated, or selecting a percentage to cover professional fees or acquisition costs, the cost of VAT should be included so that the finance charges will automatically be included as well. The recoverable amounts should then be deducted as appropriate. However, it is quite common for VAT to be excluded from preliminary development appraisal unless the developer is unable to recover it.

*The development budget in use - example*

Although the development budget is normally worked through a detailed cash flow appraisal programme most developers still tend to appraise schemes at an early feasibility stage using simple arithmetical calculations with rule-of-thumb calculations for interest charges. The following examples are therefore worked on these simple principles.

The practical use of the development budget can best be demonstrated by considering the following examples. The first example shows how a developer would normally set about estimating his profit margin (or his annual return on investment) on the construction of an investment property, on the basis of known land and building costs [Equation as above: CV - (LC + BC) = P]

Example:

An office development with a gross internal floor area of 10,000 sq.ft. (930m²) is to be built. What profit can the developer expect to make, assuming a sale to an investor, if the following factors are expected? (Nb: since imperial measurement is still often used in the property development and investment world this particular example is worked accordingly).

- Non-rentable floor area is expected to be 15% of gross internal area (ie: net internal area is 85% of gross)

- Annual rent will be £20.00/sq.ft. of net internal (rentable) area

- The expected market yield (or market capitalization rate) will be 8%

- Total building costs (including demolitions, site development etc.) will be £80 per square foot of gross internal area (ie: £861/m² of gross internal area)

- Professional fees will be 10% of the total building cost

- Construction contract period will be 1 year

- Finance charges on building costs and associated professional fees will be 11% pa compound

- Purchase price of land is £650,000

- Land acquisition costs will be 3½% of the land cost

- Development period will be 1½ years (assuming immediate letting)

- Finance charges on land and acquisition costs will be 11% pa compound

- Initial leasing commissions will be 10% of first year's gross rental income

- Value added tax is omitted for simplicity

From the above data the developer would normally estimate his before-tax development profit as shown in **FIG 10.2.A**

**FIG 10.2.A:** *Development appraisal - calculation of profit on capital expenditure*

| Capitalised value of completed development | | | | | | |
|---|---|---|---|---|---|---|
| Gross internal area GIA | Less non-rentable area : 15% GIA | Rentable floor area NIA | Rent / pa NIA | Total rent pa | Capitalisation factor @ 8% initial yield | Capital Value £ |
| 10,000 sq ft | (1,500 sq ft) = | 8,500 sq ft x | £20 sq ft = | £170,000 x | 12.5YP | 2,125,000 |
| **Development cost** | | | | £ | | |
| Land costs | Purchase price | | 650,000 | | | |
| | Acquisition costs (3½%) | | 22,750 | | | |
| | Finance charges @ 11% pa compound over 1½ year development period on £672,750 (Note 1) | | 111,000 | | | |
| Building and site development costs | 10,000 sq ft gross floor area (930m²) @ £80/sq ft (£861/m²) gross internal area | | 800,000 | | | |
| | Finance charges (monthly cash flow basis) ½ x 11% pa for 1 year construction contract period (Note 2) | | 44,000 | | | |
| Professional fees | 10% of building cost | | 80,000 | | | |
| | Finance charges (monthly cash flow basis) ¾ x 11% pa for 1 year construction contract period (Note 3) | | 6,600 | | | |
| Other costs | Initial leasing commissions (10% of gross rent for first year) | | 17,000 | | | |
| **Total development cost** | | | **1,731,350** | | **( 1,731,350 )** | |
| **Residual profit (before tax)** | | | | | **£ 393,650** | |
| **This represents a profit of 22.74% on capital expenditure (total development cost)** | | | | | | |

### Notes to FIG 10.2.A:

**Note 1:** Because the land is usually purchased before the building contracts are produced it is necessary to add a period on to the building contract period to cover this elapsed time.

If it is anticipated that there may be a 'void' between completion and rental income then a further period should be added to the development period and a similar allowance made in respect of the **full amount** of the building and site development costs for the **whole amount** of the elapsed time.

**Note 2:** Most building contracts provide for monthly payments to the Contractor based on valuations of the work carried out in the particular month; for the purpose of calculating finance charges on the building cost, it is sufficiently accurate at the first feasibility study to assume that the monthly payments are equal throughout the building contract period for each phase of the development. Since the employer will only borrow money to make the monthly payments as they become due, it follows that his finance charges will average out at the full interest rate over half of the building contract period. This rule-of-thumb therefore approximates the results of a cash flow forecast and probably is as accurate as a full cash flow analysis given that all figures are normally only predictions anyway.

**Note 3:** The fee scales of most professional bodies connected with the building industry provide for the greater proportion of fees (though not so much now as in days gone by) to be paid on completion of the contract documents (ie: drawings, specifications, bills of quantities etc). The remainder of the fees are then paid in instalments over the building contract period.

As with the building costs the employer will only borrow to make the payments as they become due; practice has shown that it is sufficiently accurate, at the first feasibility study, to assume that the finance charges on the professional fees, for each phase of the development, will average out at the full interest rate over three quarters of the building contract period.

The second example at **FIG 10.2.B** is of the same project but illustrates how the developer can calculate how much to offer for the land given that he must make a given capital profit of 20% on his development expenditure.

The resultant figure is slightly higher than the figure of £650,000 used in the first example; this is because a minimum profit figure of 20% is used here whereas the actual profit in example 1, based on the lower land price, is 22.74%.

The residual method of land valuation described here is preferred for development appraisal. The merits and demerits of other approaches such as the 'comparative method' are discussed below.

**FIG 10.2.B:** *Development appraisal - calculation of residual land value*

| Capitalised value of completed development | | | | | | |
|---|---|---|---|---|---|---|
| Gross internal area GIA | Less non-rentable area : 15% GIA | Rentable floor area NIA | Rent / pa NIA | Total rent pa | Capitalisation factor @ 8% initial yield | Capital Value £ |
| 10,000 sq ft (1,500 sq ft) = 8,500 sq ft x £20 sq ft = £170,000 x 12.5YP | | | | | | **2,125,000** |
| **Development cost** | | £ | | | | |
| **Profit** | | 20% of expenditure, i.e. 16.67% capital value (Note 4) | 354,238 | | | |
| **Building and site development costs** | | 10,000 sq ft gross floor area (930m²) @ £80/sq ft (£861/m²) gross internal area | 800,000 | | | |
| | | Finance charges (monthly cash flow basis) ½ x 11% pa for 1 year construction contract period | 44,000 | | | |
| **Professional fees** | | 10% of building cost | 80,000 | | | |
| | | Finance charges (monthly cash flow basis) ¾ x 11% pa for 1 year construction contract period | 6,600 | | | |
| **Other costs** | | Initial leasing commissions (10% of gross rent for first year) | 17,000 | | | |
| **Sub-total** | | | 1,301,838 | | | ( 1,301,838 ) |
| **Gross residual land value** | | | | | | 823,162 |
| **Land finance and acquisition costs** | | Eliminate finance @ 11% pa over 1½ year development period ÷ 1.165 (Note 5) | | | | 706,577 |
| | | Eliminate acquisition costs 3½% of land costs ÷ 1.035 (Note 6) | | | | 682,683 |
| **Net residual land value** | | | | | | £ 682,683 |

### Notes to FIG 10.2.B

**Note 4:** The allowance for developer's overheads, profit and risk is normally expressed as a percentage of his capital expenditure. However, when preparing a 'residual land valuation' the capital expenditure is not known to start with, since the cost of the land (to be found) is part of that capital expenditure. It is therefore necessary for the amount to be reserved for profit on capital expenditure to be expressed as a percentage of the expected capital value of the completed development.

The principle behind the calculation of that percentage can best be demonstrated by considering a development budget to calculate developer's profit, expressed in the simplest possible terms:

|  | £ | £ |
|---|---|---|
| Capital value of completed development |  | 120,000 |
| **Less** |  |  |
| Total cost of land | (50,000) |  |
| Total building cost | (50,000) |  |
| Total capital expenditure |  | (100,000) |
| Developer's overheads, profit and risk |  | £20,000 |

ie: 20% of Capital expenditure $\dfrac{20,000}{100,000}$ = 20%

or:  $\dfrac{£\ 20,000}{£120,000}$ = 16 2/3% of Capital value of completed development

To convert profit as a percentage of Capital expenditure (P/E) to Profit as a percentage of Capital Value of completed development (P/V) the formula is:

$$\frac{P/E}{100 + P/E} \times 100 = P/V$$

**FIG 10.2.C** illustrates this concept graphically.

**FIG. 10.2.C:** *Graphic illustration of mathematical relationship between development cost, profit and value*

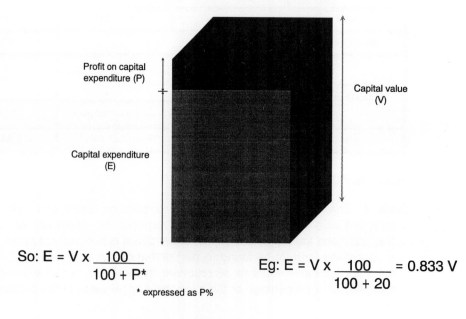

So: $E = V \times \dfrac{100}{100 + P^*}$

\* expressed as P%

Eg: $E = V \times \dfrac{100}{100 + 20}$ = 0.833 V

**Note 5:** The gross land value which has been calculated at this stage of the valuation includes the net cost of the land, land acquisition costs and finance charges. The simplest way to eliminate the finance charges is to multiply by the appropriate 'Present Value Factor' for the particular interest rate over the development period. Discount or Valuation Tables can be used to obtain the 'PV Factor'. Since the Present Value is the reciprocal of the compound interest the example shows how to make the adjustment if discount tables are not to hand - in this case 1½ years @ 11% gives a compound interest multiplier of 1.165.

(Nb: regardless of the various patterns which developments take, the development period in this context is deemed to be between the date of purchasing the land and the selling or letting of the completed development; therefore since the land acquisition and fees must be paid for at the start of the development period, it then follows that finance charges must be allowed for on the whole amount over the whole period - see also Note 1 to **FIG 10.2.A** above).

**Note 6:** The figure now arrived at, say Z, includes the net cost of the land and land acquisition costs. Land acquisition costs are expressed as a percentage of the net land cost (A%).

Therefore to eliminate land acquisition costs:-

Deduct $Z \times \dfrac{A}{100 + A}$

Example: £

Say Z = £100,000
A = 3½%

| | | | |
|---|---|---|---|
| Net cost of land but including acquisition costs @ 3½% | | = | 100,000 |
| Deduct land acquisition costs: | $£100,000 \times \dfrac{3.5}{100 + 3.5}$ | = | (3,382) |

Therefore Residual Land Value = 96,618

(3½% of £96,618 = £3,382)

In the calculation in the example at **FIG 10.2.B** a short cut has been taken, eliminating the acquisition costs by dividing by the factor representing the inclusive figure ie: 100 + 3.5 = 103.5; therefore

$\dfrac{103.5}{100}$ is the dividing factor

The visual representation of this calculation at **FIG 10.2.D** may help the less mathematically minded to understand this calculation, as also the profit elimination described in Note 4 above.

*Guide to selection of development budget factors*

When calculating the 'Residual Land Value', 'Residual Profit' or 'Residual Building Cost' for a particular development it will often be the case that not all the values of the development budget factors are known. However, in such circumstances it should always be possible to make a reasonable assessment and non-experts may find this guide to the selection of the various factors helpful.

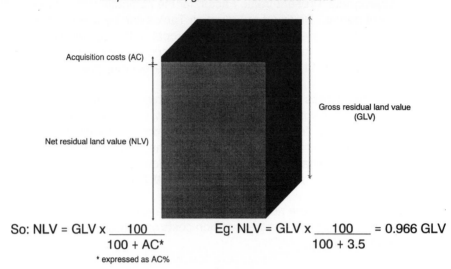

**FIG. 10.2.D:** *Graphic illustration of mathematical relationship between acquisition costs, gross and net residual value*

So: $NLV = GLV \times \dfrac{100}{100 + AC^*}$

\* expressed as AC%

Eg: $NLV = GLV \times \dfrac{100}{100 + 3.5} = 0.966\ GLV$

**Non-rentable floor area percent of gross internal area:** generally, it will be the Architect's aim to create the maximum permissible rentable floor area. As shown in Chapter 4.1 this area is calculated in the UK by measuring between the inside faces of the external walls (this calculates the gross internal area) and then, in the case of offices for instance, omitting staircases, landlord's (ie: public) circulation spaces, toilets and amenity areas, plant rooms and any other non-usable space.

Unfortunately the term gross floor area (or gross floor space) is also used in town planning to calculate plot ratio. When used in this context it is the total area of the building measured from the **outside** edge of the external walls. The actual area of external walls will normally be between 2% - 6% of the 'gross' depending on the thickness of the wall construction and the shape of the building (ie: the wall/floor ratio).

In blocks of offices and flats the proportion of non-rentable floor area to gross floor area can be expected to increase with the height of the building. The variation is such that in a typical 4-storey block the non-rentable floor area might be approximately 20% of the gross floor area, whereas in an 18-storey block it could even be as much as 35%. Much depends also on the amount of plant and riser space required for any air-conditioning system.

In shops, warehouses and factories it can generally be assumed that the whole gross floor area will be rentable (ie: non-rentable floor area is 0% of gross internal area). The productive floor area of hotels and restaurants should be assessed by inspection.

**Minimum profit required on capital expenditure:** the amount of profit to be included in the development budget will be determined by such factors as risk, overheads and competition. Assuming that all items of capital expenditure (including 'opportunity costs') are taken into account, most developers (and their financiers) will require a minimum profit of between 15% and 33 1/3% of capital expenditure.

**Expected initial yield** will undoubtedly be the single most important factor to assess in any budget for a commercial or industrial development. To arrive at a realistic result this factor should be assessed by an experienced valuer. At the height of the boom in 1988 investment yields on prime office buildings were as low as 5% whereas at the time of publication such transactions as are taking place are rarely bettering 6½% and it has been worse.

Rent reviews at intervals of less than 5 years will cause the expected initial yield to drop and conversely reviews at longer intervals will cause it to rise, perhaps by as much as 1½%.

Investors and developers do not always consider the provision of a sinking fund as part of the outgoings but adjust the expected market yield to allow for it.

Discount and Valuation tables include a dual-rate table for calculating the necessary adjustment - see also Chapter 3.3.

Some of the larger firms of commercial property agents publish tables of 'current' investment yields from time-to-time. It must be stressed however that any such 'rules-of-thumb' as stated above should only be used for preliminary appraisal and only when the services of an experienced valuer are not readily available.

**Annual rents** recently commanded by prime properties (generally new buildings in good locations) in various UK locations and some international examples are given in **FIG 10.2.E**. For investment appraisal purposes, it may be deemed prudent to inflate the figures presented in making an assessment of future rental growth.

**FIG. 10.2.E:** *Office rents across the EU*

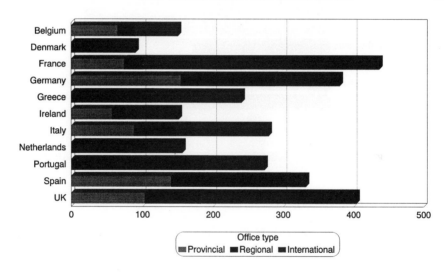

Source: 'Building & Development Economics in the EC'

**Construction contract period** this is a factor which will obviously vary considerably depending on the type of building, form of construction, size, site conditions, etc. Various methods of speeding up the construction/development period are available but often carry a higher risk; this should be reflected in the construction cost forecast, the required profit margin - or both.

**Professional fees on building cost** payable to the architect, quantity surveyor, structural engineer and mechanical & electrical engineers etc usually amount to between 5% - 12½% of the building cost for commercial and industrial development. Developers can get a very good price from construction professionals at the time of publication - time alone will show whether the savings made will be offset by expensive problems down the line.

**Finance charges - rate of interest pa compound:** bridging finance charges for property development can normally be obtained at standard commercial rates of interest.

If the developer intends to invest his own capital he should base his calculations on the 'opportunity cost' of an interest rate equivalent to his company's internal rate of return.

**Building costs:** quite clearly, a realistic estimate of the likely final building costs of any particular building, can only prepared by an experienced quantity surveyor/cost consultant from drawings and specifications. However, this is not always possible and for the purposes of a preliminary feasibility study it is not necessary to be so precise.

**FIG. 10.2.F:** *Typical international office building costs per sq m GIA across the E.U.*

Source: 'Building and Development Economics in the EC'

With the advancement of cost data-bases and cost planning techniques it has become possible to state with a reasonable degree of certainty that, at any given time, a particular type of building could be built within a given cost limit.

**FIG 10.2.F** gives a range of prices per sq.m of gross internal area for building an 'international standard' office building in the UK and abroad.

All the prices in **FIG 10.2.F** exclude external works, furniture, equipment and professional fees and assume a basic set of conditions:

- that the prices reflect the national average (nb: due to market factors such as demand and supply of labour and materials, workload, taxation, and grants, a location factor should be applied to allow for abnormal regional variations.

- that no exceptionally difficult site conditions pertain

- that the building will have 'normal' foundations relative to local conditions

- that the contract prices will be obtained on the best terms available

- that adequate cost control will be exercised during the design and construction stages

- that a normal building period will be available

- that the prices are as tendered by contractor to developer - they may not be applicable to builder/developers (ie builders undertaking development also sometimes subsume their **net** building costs into the budget before development profit is calculated).

**Land acquisition costs (agency & legal):** professional fees for acquiring land are charged by the letting agent and solicitor in respect of the following services:

- agent's fee - for introducing the site and negotiating the sale
- solicitor's fee - for establishing title, preparing contracts, payment of stamp duty and effecting indemnity insurance and the like

Fees and costs together usually amount to a total of between 3½% and 5% of the land cost.

**Development period:** regardless of the various patterns which developments take, it is assumed in the examples above that the development period is between the date of purchasing the land and the date of selling or renting the completed development.

As discussed briefly in Note 1 to the worked example above the development period can be considered in three parts: (i) between the purchase of the land and the start of the building contract period, (ii) the building contract period; (iii) the 'void' between the end of the building contract period and the selling or renting of the completed development. It will obviously be in the interest of any developer to restrict the development period to a minimum to keep down the costs of finance and overheads.

Between the date of purchase of the land and the start of building it may be necessary to obtain planning permission (except, of course, where there is an option or conditional contract subject to planning permission and other statutory consents). Designs have to be developed, tenders obtained and building contract documents prepared. For most developments this should take between 3 months and 9 months.

Depending on the economic climate, quality etc, it can sometimes take several months after completion of the building to sell or let the completed development. Therefore in the absence of details 6 months to 1 year might reasonably be added to the building contract period in estimating the development period to cover for this risk.

**Selling costs on sale price** include any Agent's commission and advertising or any costs of a direct sale; legal costs in respect of the sale of the completed dwellings are normally met by the purchaser. Agency and promotional costs normally constitute up to 2½% of the sale price.

## Methods of land valuation

The most common form of valuation of land for development is the 'Residual Method' described above. However, another common form of valuation is the 'Comparative Method' and it will be useful to consider the two different approaches.

The 'Comparative Method' consists of making a direct comparison with prices paid in the open market for similar pieces of land which are available for similar development, or redevelopment.

Although the 'Residual Method' is used extensively by valuers and property developers to assess the value of land for development, it is the 'Comparative Method' which is favoured by the Lands Tribunal in the majority of its compensation cases. The Tribunal has said that:

'...it is a feature of the residual valuation that comparatively minor adjustment to the constituent figures can have a major effect on the result...' and '...once valuers are let loose on residual valuations, however honest the valuers and however reasoned their arguments, they can prove almost anything'.

Such criticism is no doubt entirely justified when considering a residual valuation which has been prepared by the valuer to support the representations of his client to the Tribunal. However, it is not necessarily justified when considering a completely realistic valuation - prepared for the personal use of the valuer's client. In fact, as already mentioned, the 'Residual Method' is used extensively by valuers and has certain definite advantages over the 'Comparative Method':-

- it is related to a particular property to be developed in a particular way by a particular developer. It is of far more use to the developer to know that, given a definite building cost, fees, finance charges etc, and allowing for a definite profit margin, then the land is worth £x to him, than merely to know that another developer has paid £y for a similar property

- a plot of land being considered for development may have received planning permission for a particular density. It is of little use comparing the value with prices paid for similar properties, if those properties have received planning consent for higher or lower densities – whatever the similarities may be in other respects

- sometimes the price paid for land is based on assumptions or information known only to the purchaser, eg: he may wish to enhance the value of his own adjoining property in some way, or he may have been given some verbal encouragement by the planning authority. On the other hand land prices are sometimes higher than they should be due to lack of knowledge of the problems of the site

- the 'Residual Method' can be applied to any plot of land, whereas the 'Comparative Method' must by definition rely on the open market value of similar properties. In certain cases the circumstances of the available comparables differ in important respects from the land under consideration, so the 'Comparative Method' becomes virtually impossible. The Lands tribunal has itself been faced with such situations and has accepted valuations based on the 'Residual Method'.

## Land-use economics

Even the most casual observers of the activities of property developers will be aware that there are three principal ways in which a developer, land-owner or land-speculator can make a killing out of development land:

- to obtain valuable planning consent on land bought cheaply

- to get an improved planning consent on land bought on the basis of an earlier approval

- 'marriage value' ie: assembling two or more sites cheaply then merging them into one site for development purposes.

Generally speaking most landowners are wise to these machinations and it is unusual for developers these days to 'beat the system' in the spectacular manner of some of their predecessors. However, sometimes land can have a negative residual value as is shown in **FIG 10.2.G**

**FIG 10.2.G:** *Negative residual land value resulting from changes in the cost and value assumptions at FIG 10.2.B*

| Capitalised value of completed development | | | | | | |
|---|---|---|---|---|---|---|
| Gross internal area GIA | Less non-rentable area : 20% GIA | Rentable floor area NIA | Rent / pa NIA | Total rent pa | Capitalisation factor @ 10% initial yield | Capital Value £ |
| 10,000 sq ft | (2,000 sq ft) = | 8,000 sq ft x | £14 sq ft = | £112,000 x | 10YP | **1,120,000** |
| **Development cost** | | | | **£** | | |
| **Profit** | | 16.67% x £1,440,000 | | (240,048) | | |
| **Building and site development costs** | | 10,000 sq ft gross floor area (930m²) @ £80/sq ft (£861/m²) gross internal area | | (800,000) | | |
| | | Finance charges (monthly cash flow basis) ½ x 11% pa for 1 year construction contract period | | (44,000) | | |
| **Professional fees** | | 10% of building cost | | (80,000) | | |
| | | Finance charges (monthly cash flow basis) ¾ x 11% pa for 1 year construction contract period | | (6,600) | | |
| **Other costs** | | Initial leasing commissions (10% of gross rent for first year) | | (11,200) | | |
| **Sub-total** | | | | (1,181,848) | | (1,181,848) |
| **Gross residual land value** | | | | | | (61,648) |
| **Land finance and acquisition costs** | | Eliminate finance @ 11% pa over 1½ year development period: ÷ 1.165 (Note 5) | | | | N/A |
| | | Eliminate acquisition costs 3½% of land costs: ÷ 1.035 (Note 6) | | | | N/A |
| **Net residual land value** | | | | | | **Negative** |

**FIG 10.2.H** indicates how the impact of lower development values in recent times has affected land values across the range of UK locations. Note how the 1993 reduction in rent and increase in initial market yield reduced the City of London capital value (and hence land value) from the 1989 level in this example. In spite of lower construction costs the residual land value is less than one-third of its boom figure.

**FIG. 10.2.H:** *Changes in the development equation in the City and a provincial centre between 1989 & 1993*

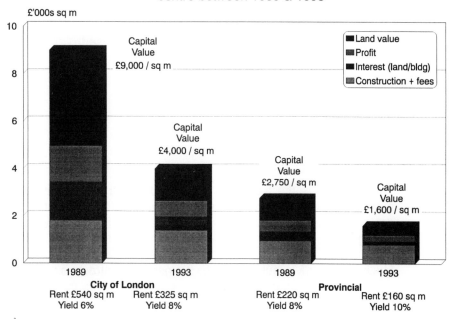

The land value has reached rock bottom in the provincial centre in the example, even with a lower building performance and cost and easier finance rates – if available at all for such a project. The problem is that the capital values are decimated by the high yield of 10% which gives only 10 years' purchase of the lowish rent. Of course, when supply dries up through lack of a decent price structure pent-up demand will coax it back to the market just by the 'weight of money' available to drive the price up in a short market.

Late 1994 reports are of yields returning to the pre-recession levels for really prime investments. However, rental levels are only slowly turning the corner so there is still quite a shortfall in overall values compared with 1989 boom levels.

One problem of low land and total property values is that security for borrowing for development finance is eroded; currently it is estimated that the gross value of security held by financiers is only about 70% of development funding advances.

Funding of property development is considered in more detail in Chapter 10.3.

## 10.2.3 THE CONSTRUCTION PROCESS

*The construction industry*

The various contract arrangements available for design and construction in the fitting-out process as described in Chapter 6.3 are equally applicable to new construction works and are not further elaborated upon here. Nevertheless it should be remembered that there is a big difference in the complexity of the new construction process compared with fitting-out; not only are the large contracts considerably larger, they also take longer and are subject to much greater risk in terms of quality and cost as well as time.

The new-build construction process is surprisingly complicated, especially when one considers that many of the works activities themselves are comparatively straightforward. The problem seems to lie with the peripatetic nature of the industry where every site is a new production plant involving new teams, new techniques, often new materials and equipment - and one which is normally disbanded on completion, never to be reconvened in the same form again.

Worse still, every brief is perceived as a design challenge; consequently the learning curve is always in evidence, particularly being exacerbated by the fact that designers (especially of the independent variety) seem to relish the opportunity to create a bad new detail to replace the better old one which the industry had just about got to grips with.

In the UK the design team has traditionally comprised:

- architect
- structural engineer
- mechanical engineer
- electrical engineer
- quantity surveyor.

The architect is the traditional team leader, with the other consultants usually appointed direct by the client but under the architect's direction. Sometimes the design team is part of the contractor's organisation in the design-and-build type of arrangement.

Much of the work is 'outsourced' by the general contractors to sub-contractors who will often again sub-contract without people further up the line knowing about it - in spite of contract conditions strictly forbidding that situation.

Builders' merchants supply the materials and plant for smaller contracts but the larger contractors usually deal direct with the suppliers, taking advantage of bulk order discounts which do not always get declared in those cost-reimbursement contracts – including various forms of construction management - where the customer pays all the suppliers' bills direct.

*The efficiency of the UK construction industry*

The UK industry is particularly inefficient by comparison with most of its overseas counterparts. **FIG 10.2.J** shows (at current rates of exchange) how the various EC countries compare in the total costs of building offices, with the relative hourly labour rates superimposed. **FIG 10.2.K** gives the same data but adjusted for 'purchasing power parity' ie: the factor which links the cost of production to the amount of goods which can be bought domestically with the currency.

**FIG. 10.2.J:** *Relative EU construction industry productivity at current rates of exchange*

**International Offices, 1993**

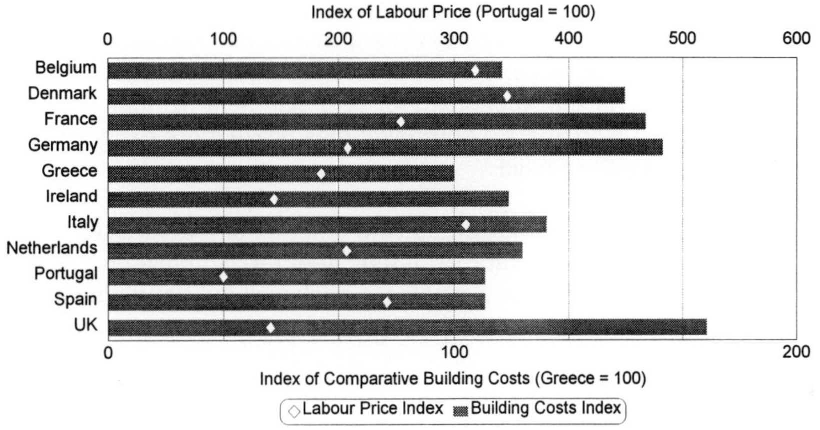

Source: based upon data originally published in "Building & Development Economics in the EC"

**FIG. 10.2.K:** *Relative EU construction industry productivty at purchasing power parity*

**International Offices, 1993**

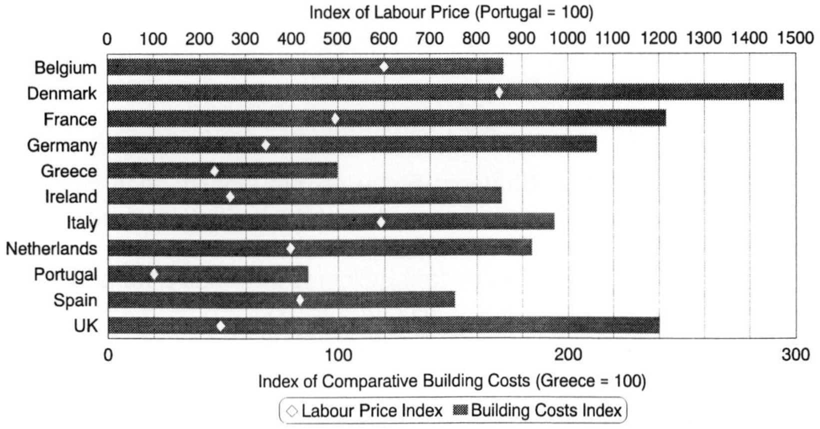

Source: based upon data originally published in "Building & Development Economics in the EC"

The reasons for the UK's poor performance are many and varied. However, according to the report 'Building and Development Economics in the EC' [1] the worst features are to be evidenced in the more sophisticated 'one-off' buildings - eg: prestige headquarters offices - where the re-invention of every construction detail, the specification of every component from a multiplicity of catalogues, combine to make it impossible to build economically - although some of the better construction managers work wonders in narrowing the gap between the typical UK and other EU costs given in the figures.

Other influential studies such as the 'Secteur' [2] report commissioned by the European Commission have corroborated the general trend of the authors' Financial Times report.

Strong project management is essential if the industry is not be to allowed to take the British client for a ride. More and more the architects are losing this role to the professional project managers - sometimes to the construction managers themselves - much to their chagrin and resulting in even more players on an already over-crowded pitch.

## Refurbishment

The 'cut-and-carve' process is fairly cyclical, alternating with new construction at times when money is scarce and/or new development is not financially viable in the context of current property investment valuations. The economics of refurbishment are generally not well understood. John Desmond [3] highlighted and analysed the critical factor in the economics of refurbishment ie: that unless the building is modern or in a good state of repair it may prove more expensive to refurbish than to demolish and re-build.

Apart from that key consideration the other feature of refurbishment which is often overlooked is the **risk factor.** It may seem reasonable on paper to show a door opening being formed in a plastered brick wall but not unusual for the whole wall to need re-plastering once the first coal-chisel has been applied to the ageing surface.

Any facilities manager contemplating or being involved in a refurbishment project should be insistent upon a **contingency sum** appropriate to the nature of the base building and the extent of alterations proposed.

In certain circumstances a contingency of up to 25% may be prudent - and may possibly tip the scales against that process as an option. A fundamental rule for any feasibility study involving refurbishment as an option is that **a thorough structural and condition survey** must be carried out professionally in advance of any financial appraisal.

---

[1]     'Building and Development Economics in the EC' – by Bernard Williams Associates (Financial Times Management Reports, 1992)

[2]     'SECTEUR – Strategic Study on the Construction Sector' – W.S. Atkins International Ltd. in association with CSSC (University of Reading) et al

[3]     'The Re-use of Redundant Buildings for Small Enterprises' – Peter Eley and John Worthington (Architectural Press)

# CHAPTER 10.3 – PROPERTY FUNDING

## 10.3.1 TYPES AND SOURCES

*Equity and debt*

The scope for property funding is growing and it is likely that innovative means to meet novel funding problems will continue to emerge. The subject is too wide to be dealt with adequately in this section, which gives a general overview of 'corporate' and 'project' funding.

It may be noted that an important distinction is that of 'debt' and 'equity' funds, the latter implying ownership in enterprise. Thus, equity is the use of one's own funds to buy and develop for investment, dealing or owner-occupation, by owning shares or units in some business, property or intermediary. Debt funding involves borrowing eg: by mortgage or by issuing interest bearing bonds. The relationship between the proportions of equity and debt ie: 'gearing', which underpin the ownership of property may have important implications on obtaining the next tranche of monies. The gearing will also affect the returns to the equity portion in times of changing rental levels or interest rates or both.

Also, it may be noted that the various ways and means of funding have different taxation implications. In any appraisal, taxation is likely to be a material factor affecting the outcome of the proposal being considered.

*Types of funding*

Funding for property acquisition, development or rehabilitation may be grouped into the following:

- corporate funding;  and

- project funding.

The status of the 'person' seeking funds may influence the outcome of the search. Thus, corporate bodies may seek both corporate or project related funds. On the other hand an individual intent on maintaining control may seek project funding. However, the individual wanting to plan for taxation, say inheritance tax, may wish to create a company for future property holding or dealing.

Similarly, the 'objective' of a landowner as an investor will tend to long-term funding (similarly for business ownership), whereas a dealer will tend to short-term finance. Of course, both may operate in corporate guise.

Thus, corporate funding seeks to provide or raise funds through a corporate vehicle, such as a company, a charity or a trust. Devices or means of such financing cover:

- creation of a private company

- the flotation of a company on the International Stock Exchange

- the issue of debenture stock

- the issue of preference shares, which are, perhaps, convertible to equity capital

- the issue of paper scrip; and

- the issue of bonds of some particular type eg: a Eurobond or a deep discounted bond.

On the other hand, project funding seeks to raise funds by virtue of the project itself. In practice it is likely that the use of project funding would have an impact on the capital structure of the fund user. Examples of project funding include:

- mortgage

- sale and leaseback; and

- forward funding.

The essence of project finance by borrowing is the repayment of the loan from income – ie: from the business to be conducted or rental income. This will enable funds to be repaid over a period of medium duration.

It may be noted that joint ventures or 'partnership' arrangements may be regarded as vehicles for funding development projects.

## Private sector sources of funds

A host of private sector funding sources may be identified; many are considered in later sections. They include:

- the clearing banks for overdraft and other short-term facilities and for mortgages

- the merchant banks for short-term funds and mezzanine finance

- the finance houses for equipment and plant leasing arrangements

- the insurance companies for sale and leaseback arrangements, mortgages, forward funding arrangements with ultimate purchase

- mortgage houses.

## Public sector sources of funds

In the public sector numerous local, regional and national bodies are sources of grants or loans or both. Some such bodies may be seen as underpinning development with powers of land acquisition, planning powers, provisions of infrastructure and, perhaps as a catalyst, providing grants and loans in prescribed policy areas. In some instances, the authority of involvement with public cash generates a substantial injection of private sector funds, of the order of, say, 1 to 4.

With their grants or loans from the various government initiatives public bodies tend to be project-oriented funders. They may have powers in a given instance to enter into 'partnership' either as lessor, eg: of a ground lease for a development site, or as a shareholder in a corporate body.

The European Investment Bank of the European Community may make loans or guarantee loans for private or public projects involving development.

## Duration of funding arrangements

Generally, the duration of funding is described as 'short', 'medium' or 'long-term'.

Those who require short-term funds eg: funding a development which will be sold (such as a speculative office development), may only need funds to cover the construction and disposal period.

The sources include overdrafts from banks, trade credit from suppliers, stage payment arrangements with the purchaser's funders and loans from contractors employed to carry out the work.

Loans from banks, the building societies and similar bodies which are made available for periods which range from, say, 5 to 10 years are regarded as medium period. They may or may not be secured on property. The kind of borrowers will be those wanting to buy or improve property, eg: proprietors or owners intent on running a small hotel, guest house, restaurant and the like. Also, dealers in property may seek such funds, sometimes on a 'flexible' or 'revolving' basis.

Long-term project funds are upwards of 10 years and may be as long as 60 years, eg: for agricultural property, but 20 or 30 years is common.

Large projects may need funding for a long term, say 25 years, and mortgages suit this need. However, in these cases the relative risk the parties face tend to result in different forms of funding ie: other than the mortgage. Leases, sale and leaseback and other devices are used in this context.

## 10.3.2 CORPORATE FINANCE

*Flotation of company*

The flotation of a company requires several months of intense work for its directors and senior staff. In a sense every issue of shares is a test of the board and management of a company in the eyes of the public. It is also a test of the advisers to the issue in that they must prepare the board and senior management in the presentation made in the prospectus. The matters likely to require detailed consideration are:

- the taxation position of existing shareholders
- the taxation position of future shareholders
- control of the new company
- the disposal of surplus assets
- the settling of debts and taxation liabilities
- board representation on the company; and
- the status of any occupational pension scheme.

The kind of issue selected is important. It may involve a quote on the International Stock Exchange.

Various approaches to the flotation may be considered including an 'offer for sale', and 'offer for sale by tender', a 'placing' or a 'share introduction'.

A number of criteria are used, such as:

- the cost of the issue in money terms and in terms of management involvement
- the loyalty of shareholders in terms of holding the shares
- practical support of the shareholders in providing further funds
- the degree of control given by the existing proprietors or shareholders; and
- the support of shareholders in times of difficulties.

## Rights issues

For any existing company, another way of raising funds is an approach to existing shareholders with a rights issue in equity or stock.

The advantage to the issuing company is that the company's gearing is reduced, as no extra borrowing is incurred. Some dilution of earnings may follow and this may result in a drop in the value of shares, much to the consternation of the shareholders.

## Preference shares

Preference shares rank ahead of other equities for dividends, taking a fixed dividend. They are, therefore, relatively less risky than ordinary shares but do not usually take further profits/dividends.

## Debentures

A debenture is a type of long-term corporate borrowing which may take one of several forms, eg: mortgage debentures and convertible debentures. Interest is normally paid on the capital of the loan (which may be secured as a fixed or a floating charge). A particular advantage of debentures is that the interest, like mortgage interest, is allowed against profits for corporation tax purposes; in contrast, dividends are not allowed, since they are a distribution of profits subject to tax.

Debentures 'gear' a company's financial structure and almost all are redeemable (unlike equity shares). Debentures have featured in property company financing since the 1980's.

## 10.3.3 PROJECT FINANCE

## Leasing

As described in Chapter 3.1 the most readily available means of funding the use of commercial property is a lease which enables the lessee to acquire and use a capital asset without immediate outlay (unless a premium is paid to the landlord or a capital sum is paid for an assignment of the lease). The landlord's capital asset is used by the tenant; the rent being paid represents the return to the lessor, and in effect interest to the lessee. The terms and conditions upon which the grant of a lease are made will partly determine the capital worth of the asset to the lessor. Where premiums are taken the net-of-tax outcome may need to be evaluated, including any relief to the tenant.

## Leaseback arrangements

In a **sale-and-leaseback** an owner of property sells the freehold or a long lease and the purchaser grants a lease to the vendor at a rent and on terms and conditions which are mutually acceptable. As well as a means of releasing non-core finance to bolster liquidity sale-and-leaseback has been a fairly common means of funding development for owner occupation in recent times.

Typically a developer/investor will build to the user's requirements, financing the project on a short-term basis with interest charges built in to the total cost upon which the user's rental income is wholly or partly related.

A similar arrangement known as **lease-and-leaseback** is where the holder of a long lease assigns it at a premium - again in return for reasonable leaseback terms.

Care should be taken to evaluate the taxation consequence, if any, of such transactions.

*Mortgages*

The nomenclature of mortgages, like most property finance areas, has developed with such expressions as 'term mortgage'. 'droplock mortgage'. 'bullet mortgage' and 'participating mortgage'. Basically, the mortgagor (the one borrowing) offers the mortgagee the property as security for a longish term loan. The loan may be repaid during the term as an annuity (interest and capital) or at the end of the term (interest only being paid during that period).

A mortgagee's 'measurement' of the mortgagor's ability to cover the security of the investment is likely to include:

- references from bank or trade suppliers

- accounts of business

- level of earnings or joint earnings

- collateral offered by the mortgagor or others

- published information eg: Dunn & Bradstreet

- deposit or equity share held by the mortgagor

- profession or occupation.

The mortgagee will have the property valued at the mortgagor's expense. The valuer will provide a report on its suitability for a loan, and, perhaps, some aspects of the terms and conditions upon which the loan might be made (as a matter of policy for the mortgagee to determine).

It is likely that the mortgage agreement will be subject to most, if not all, of the following:

- period of loan
- rate of interest, variable or fixed
- insurance of the property
- mortgage protection or endowment provisions for the life of the mortgagor
- putting the property into good condition
- maintaining the good condition of the property
- repayment of the loan by instalments, or at the end of the loan period.

Where property is used as a security for a loan SVAP17 of the RICS Statement of Asset Valuation Practice and Guidance Notes, 3rd edition, covers aspects of valuation practice.

## 10.3.4 FUNDING BY CONTRACTORS

Building contractors employed on development projects sometimes provide funds for a client developer as part of the contract for the scheme. The loans may, for instance, be on deferred payment terms and secured by mortgage arrangements. Such arrangements are, however, fraught with difficulty in situations where the contractor's building performance falls below standard with regard to cost, time or quality since onerous protective clauses are not acceptable to the contractor/ funder.

### 10.3.5 FRANCHISE

A growing sector of business enterprise is the franchise. A successful entrepreneur with a suitable type of business (frequently, but not exclusively, retail) can become a 'franchiser'. In essence the franchisee buys a package which enables him to run an already proven business. The franchiser is able to build up a network of businesses each generating initial acquisition capital and a stream of 'royalties' and sales in the provision of supplies. An added advantage for the franchiser is the likely keenness of self-motivated entrepreneurs who carry the business risk in the venture. The franchiser offers a marketing mix which may include many of the following: the name, house-style, specification for premises, detailed manuals on trading systems and operations, advice on the selection and fitting out of premises, supplies of stock and equipment, promotional services and advice, access to funding arrangements, and training of staff.

The impact of franchise operations has become apparent, especially in town centres. Already names such as Sketchleys, Thorntons, and Tie Rack are seen in numerous locations and the trend is likely to grow in the next few years. In a sense, the franchisees indirectly fund the growth of the franchised business through the borrowing they are able to make in support of their operation of the franchise.

The cost of a franchise to the prospective franchisee could be from,, say £3,000 to over £500,000. Several of the clearing banks have created specialist departments to deal with applications for loans with which to fund the acquisition of a franchise and to proffer advice in this respect, eg: by providing information packages.

The British Franchise Association represents this growing field of business where employment has grown rapidly.

### 10.3.6 INSURANCE COMPANIES

*Investment role*

The nature of the business of an insurance company will affect the general strategy for investment. If the company is in endowment assurance a steadily growing fund may be expected. If annuities are its main business, the fund is established and earns income but the payment of annuities will gradually diminish it over the years. Finally, a whole life fund will gradually grow, peak and eventually decline.

Several kinds of insurance companies exist but the important property related type is the life insurance company, which insures individuals who take up policies on their expectation of survival. The premiums are geared to calculated rates of mortality for males or females and it is the aggregate of the premiums, together with the proceeds of disposals and investment income, which is available for long term investment at any time (after meeting claims and management expenses).

Like the pension funds, the life insurance companies spread their investments to include equities, gilts, mortgages and property. In recent years mortgages being inflation prone have lost favour; nevertheless companies still offer mortgages, perhaps as an adjunct to obtaining insurance business, but this does not usually amount to a substantial part of their business. Gilts and other interest-bearing dated stock provide a measure of certainty in meeting actuarial estimations of future liabilities and obligations to clients.

On the other hand, direct and indirect investment in property is substantial reflecting, perhaps, a somewhat more bold policy than pension funds in that the larger companies have grown into direct development and redevelopment of land and buildings in recent years. Thus, the emphasis on investment seems to be in new building, with divestment of older properties.

The spread of investments reflects all the property sectors ie: shops, offices, industrial and agricultural; residential property tends not to be favoured because of statutory controls on rents below certain rateable value limits. Similarly, the marked drop in agricultural land values in recent years suggests that the rural sector is less favoured in the current climate; over-supply of agricultural land is now a significant factor in low values.

Innovation in investment policy tends to develop slowly, reluctance to recognise the early retail warehouses being but one example. In the UK many of our standards in respect of structural capacity stem from out-dated requirements of the institutional investors. The imposition of these exacting standards for investments in new developments has resulted in buildings which are unnecessarily expensive or design which does not properly address the real needs of occupiers.

*Role as a financial intermediary*

The insurance companies have an important role as providers of funds to developers and investors. As mentioned above, mortgages are sometimes available, perhaps as a package, with the prospect of offering insurance business to the recipient. Much more substantially, the insurance companies provide funds by way of equity participation in companies, either existing or on new issues, and in the field of sale and leaseback and similar devices. Of course, their role as financial intermediaries is always linked to their investment objectives unless they are investing directly in property on their own behalf.

## 10.3.7 INVESTMENT TRUSTS AND PROPERTY

*Trust status*

The shares of investment trusts are bought and sold on the Stock Exchange with the usual fees, charges and taxes. Thus, despite their name, investment trusts are not trusts but limited liability companies in which individuals and others may invest in the shares of the company, receiving dividends net of income taxation under Schedule F. (There are, however, many investment trust 'products', eg: PEPs and warranties).

In most cases the companies invest in equities, either in a specialist sector or with other explicit policies. In effect their shareholders invest indirectly in property to the extent that the investment trust holds any shares in property investment or dealing companies.

Generally, investment trusts may obtain funds by borrowing eg: debentures, and by issuing preference shares.

*Objectives*

The principal aim is to spread the risk for the shareholders who receive dividends and may sell their holdings on the Stock Exchange in the usual way, the price being determined by the market.

One feature of the investment trust is the 'discount' the shares frequently have, ie: the aggregate worth of the shares is usually less than the net asset value of the shares held.

Some investment trusts are set up on a limited life basis with either a fixed termination date or a determinable date. Once the date has arrived, and the shareholders so decide, the company realises its assets and the net proceeds are distributed to the shareholders. If the shares were purchased at a discount such a distribution has obvious advantages to the shareholders.

*Investment policy*

An investment trust may invest in property and assets other than listed equities eg: unquoted shares, although the majority are in the investment field of equities which are quoted. Borrowing of funds is permitted so they are able to 'gear' their investment portfolio with loans.

## 10.3.8 PENSION FUNDS AND PROPERTY

*Role*

The pension funds, like the life assurance offices, hold a somewhat privileged position in society, eg: in taxation matters. They invest as a financial intermediary on behalf of a large proportion of the employed and self-employed population. There are nearly 1,100 pension funds and they cover the funded schemes of the public sector, superannuation schemes in the private sector and the local authority schemes.

The role of pension funds as one of several kinds of 'financial institution' is the accumulation of pension contributions from individuals and employers. A capital fund producing income is created over a long term with the view to meeting pension rights at a later date. **This obligation must, of course, be regarded as imperative to the role.**

The pension fund has a particular and privileged status as a trust.

*Investment policy and management*

As far as investment policy is concerned the pension funds' range of longer-term investments include equities, gilt edge stocks, mortgages (to a very limited extent) and direct property for the larger pension funds. The smaller funds tend not to invest directly in property but use the avenues of property company equities and, in particular, the property unit trust, a vehicle which has been 'designed' for small pension funds and charities. The property unit trust enables the pension fund to spread the risk of property investment over a range of properties depending upon the policy adopted by the unit trust managers.

Given the **imperative obligation** mentioned above, the trustees must seek a degree of risk which will not fault it.

Pension fund managements should be properly conscious of selecting quality investments and safeguarding that quality subsequently. Apart from a few who have in-house estate management those that invest in property will seek the services of professional real estate consultants for acquisitions, management and disposals. The pension funds have currently reduced markedly the rate of investment in property compared with previous years.

## 10.3.9 BONDS AND PROPERTY

*Introduction*

A bond enables the investor of relatively small means to make a single payment in a fund which is invested in a spread of investments. The 'property bond' is an example of this kind of single premium bond, the other is the managed fund.

The purchaser buys a 'bond' for, say, £1,000 or £5,000 and the managers invest the aggregate of bond sale net proceeds directly into property and a life policy for each individual purchaser.

*Property bond*

A property bond is a form of insurance policy where the payments made by an investor are invested directly into a spread of property sectors or a particular sector, eg: agricultural property.

*Managed fund*

A managed fund is a similar device but is not exclusive to property; its spread may also include equities, gilts and other securities. The management may switch from one investment to another to take advantage of any relative changes in the investment sectors.

*International bonds*

An international bond, eg: a Eurobond, is a means by which governments, international companies and others may raise funds on the international market, much of it centred in London and other major cities. A company issuing a bond usually does so to raise funds for an overseas project or the acquisition of a foreign business. The cost of such funds depends on the prevailing strength of that currency in terms of supply and demand which is affected by such factors as the political, economic and social stability of the 'home' country.

A bond may be issued in one of several currencies including sterling, the dollar,, the yen, and the deutschemark. The European Currency Unit (ECU) is also used.

Some bonds are convertible into the issuing company's equities, which has the effect of bypassing the traditional way of issuing shares by the Stock Exchange.

Prospectuses as such are not issued but the bonds are dealt with by licensed bond dealers eg: a merchant bank. Generally, dealers are regulated by the Securities and Futures Authority with powers to suspend, reprimand or expel members.

*Deep discount and deep gain bonds*

A device which some property development companies and others have used in recent years is the 'deep discount bond'. Schedule 4 of the Income and Corporation Taxes Act 1988 defined such a bond as a security which is issued at a discount of more than ½% for each year of the life of the bond or more than 15% of the amount payable on redemption. A 'deep gain bond' is one where these measures are exceeded.

# CHAPTER 10.4 – WHOLE-LIFE ECONOMICS

## 10.4.1 THE BUILDING LIFE-CYCLE

*Introduction*

The building life-cycle is from birth (first occupation) to death (demolition). Its gestation period ie: conception (design) thru pregnancy (construction) is, totally analogously, responsible for most of the factors contributing to its performance throughout its life.

As in human life, neglect, accident, care, attention will impact on the performance of the product but its intrinsic physical qualities will be the overriding factor in the usefulness of its contribution to those depending on it.

During its life a building will undergo many changes. Apart from the washing and scrubbing to keep it clean, the repair and replacement of parts which go wrong, the redecoration to keep it looking smart, the building will also be subjected to considerable change throughout its life - mainly due to obsolescence either in terms of how it is geared up to handle the business requirement or, more fundamentally, if the basic design is not totally appropriate to the basic needs of the user.

To carry the human analogy further than is probably advisable a building emulates the re-training and redundancy phases of a working life and tends to be similarly indiscriminate in the timing, location and extent of those phases.

The concept of 'shell, scenery and services' was discussed in Chapter 6.1. The shell, comprising the structure and the envelope, will remain unchanged throughout the building's whole life (subject to extensions, change of use, re-cladding etc).

The scenery, ie: the components applied to the interior to make it fit for a specific purpose, might have a life of say 5-7 years before becoming redundant through change of one sort or another and subsequently replaced.

The building services have a longer life-cycle - say 10-20 years - conditioned by the physical capacity of the components and natural obsolescence in a fast-changing business/technology environment.

Of course, these phases and time forecasts are only indicative: a lift motor, well maintained, might last 30 years in a building just growing old gracefully whereas the scenery might get altered within a couple of years due to 'churn' or simply change of user.

Nevertheless, the ephemeral nature of this regime tends to compound even medium-term prediction and is a nightmare in terms of depreciation and asset valuation - issues discussed in Chapters 3.3 and 3.7 respectively.

*Attitudes towards whole-life economics*

When Dr Stone [1] introduced the principles of cost-in-use to the UK (and possibly worldwide) construction industry in the early 1960's his efforts were greeted with well-merited academic recognition and complete apathy from the industry's practitioners.

The reasons for this apathy - then as now (or until quite recently) are quite simple:

- the data is not generally available to make the appraisals realistic

- even if it were, the sums involved are relatively minor in the whole financial scheme of things

- the effects of discounting on future cash flows makes the impact of future expenditure even less significant in the investment appraisal

- relief from Corporation Tax on revenue profits is available for all the costs of running and maintaining buildings.

So, with clients interested in the bigger fish, consultants unlikely to command an additional fee for this clever new technique and the constructors not in the slightest bit interested, the principles and techniques of cost-in-use were left to be considered mainly in the lecture room.

Two things have occurred in the past decade to cause this apathy to be challenged. First, the increasing complexity of the modern commercial building has caused the whole level of the life-cycle costs to rise significantly. This has led not only to greater pressure on budgets but also engendered a much higher profile for the way the building performs in physical terms - especially if under-performance has adverse consequences in terms of the business operation. In tandem with (and mainly because of) this sea-change is the advent of a new breed of facilities managers, with a greater influence on the way their buildings are put together, and under constant pressure from the finance director to contain expenditure on premises.

However, one very important factor to be taken into account when considering whole-life economics is that the user is frequently not the owner. Therefore, when buildings are designed speculatively on behalf of developers and/or investors there is no immediate incentive to improve the life-cycle performance above the conventional norm because the investor cannot be certain of directly benefitting from it. Unless and until building performance is adequately reflected in rents and value - as discussed in Chapter 1.2 - pressures will continue to be on designers to pare capital costs at the expense of the ultimate physical performance.

Possibly the days of completely speculative development are nearly through, to be replaced by buildings with bespoke design for the owner or pre-let occupier. If so then the techniques considered here will become more relevant. However, as we shall see, their application may be in a different economic context than that envisaged by Dr Stone and the educational pundits who have slavishly promulgated his valid but anachronistic logic over the past 30-odd years.

*Constituent parts*

The whole-life cost of a building comprises

- its initial construction cost

- the cost of operation, maintenance and repairs

- the replacement costs

- costs of fitting-out, alteration, adaptation and extension

- demolition costs.

As discussed above the fitting-put, alteration, adaptation and extension costs are not normally predictable in terms of time or cost so most life-cycle forecasts ignore them unless they are part of a phased programme. The fitting-out is cyclical and, if accommodated in the appraisal, will be hypothesized.

The initial construction cost will include all fees and finance charges. Land is not normally included since it is not deemed to be a wasting asset; the cost of demolition clears the way for re-use of the land, presumed to be still useful at the end of the physical construction's life-span.

The cost of managing the premises should be allocated to the operating and replacement costs. The operating cost centres themselves are as discussed in Section 5. Note that Business Costs as incorporated in the cost/benefit appraisals in Section 9 are not usually included in life-cycle appraisal since they reflect specific aspects of the user's business rather than the inherent performance of the building. Nevertheless, some overlap is inevitable and end-of-needle inspection can take over from practicality. For example, the need for security depends largely on the user's business; sometimes buildings have adequate security precautions and/or 'securability' designed in, so lessening the demands of security personnel on revenue expenditure.

However, in most cases whole-life appraisal is a 'personal' issue and the appraisers may include whatever they deem to be appropriate - provided they observe consistency in any cross-comparisons.

*Building performance*

The concept of building performance, discussed earlier in Chapter 1.3, suggests that the costs of providing and operating premises reflect their physical performance.

Conventional life-cycle cost analysis will therefore only be concerned with the physical - ie: 'invoiceable' aspects of the premises over the life-cycle; however, as previously stated there is no reason whatever why the life-cycle cost analyses should not be extended into cost/benefit analysis for purposes of option appraisal on behalf of an occupier, thereby bringing both physical and functional aspects of building performance into the equation.

## 10.4.2 LIFE-CYCLE COST ANALYSIS

*Appraisal techniques*

There are three principal methods of evaluating the life-cycle costs of buildings:

- Simple aggregation

- Net present value (NPV)

- Annual equivalent (AE).

Each of these methods can be calculated with or without inflation and with or without tax.

The Aggregation method simply adds the total capital costs to the total of all expenditure on operating, repairs, maintenance and replacement over the building's life. This calculation is usually expected to show up in a good light proposals to spend more on the capital cost in order to reduce annual expenditure.

However, as the histogram in **FIG 10.4.A** illustrates (ignoring inflation) this is by no means usually the case, which is due to the fact that although the better quality building 'B' is slightly cheaper to run and maintain per annum, the cost of replacing the more expensive components is rather higher - though deferred.

A more compelling argument for focusing attention on the operating and replacement costs is that (as **FIG 10.4.A** shows) the aggregated annual costs (excluding inflation) will be many times the initial costs - even before costs of fitting-out and alteration have been taken into account. **FIG 10.4.B** depicts the cyclical effect of operating and replacement costs.

**FIG. 10.4.A:** *Aggregated life-cycle cost analysis of options 'A' and 'B' - undiscounted*

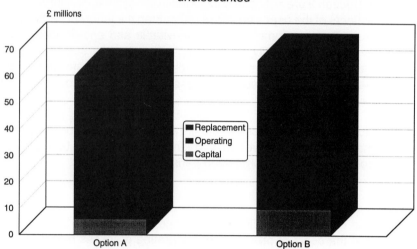

**FIG. 10.4.B:** *Life -cycle cost analysis of options 'A' and 'B' - undiscounted*

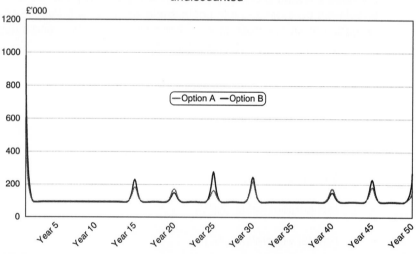

Although sometimes used to make a point, (in this case that it is important to get the life-cycle costs right because they are so much greater than the initial costs) the 'Simple Aggregation' method has no standing in management accountancy terms; this is because it ignores the highly significant effect of Discounted Cash Flow (DCF) on the real value of deferred expenditure. DCF, considered in more detail below, takes into account the interest potentially earned on capital invested pending deferred expenditure.

In the case of the Net Present Value method, the aggregation of initial and annual expenditure is modified by deduction of the interest (at the chosen rate) theoretically earned on the money invested during the period from inception of the project to the actual date of payment for the component. The effects of this calculation, using a discount rate of 6%, on the previous Aggregation examples are shown at **FIGS 10.4.C** and **10.4.D**.

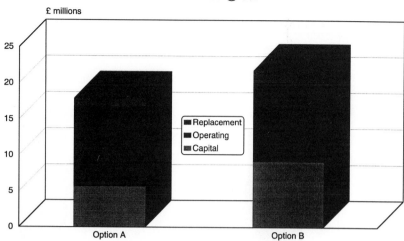

**FIG. 10.4.C:** *Aggregated life-cycle cost analysis of options 'A' and 'B' - discounted @ 6%*

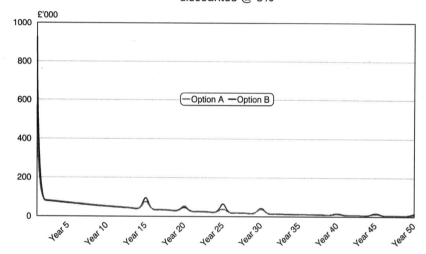

**FIG. 10.4.D:** *Life -cycle cost analysis of options 'A' and 'B' - discounted @ 6%*

Note how the order of the comparative costs of the two options remains unchanged; this situation holds good in the example whatever the discount rate because the annual operating costs are similar in both options. The low discount rate of 6% still exaggerates the NPV of the operating and replacement costs; at 15% they would show less than the capital cost (see **FIG 10.4.H** below).

Taking relief from corporation tax in the year end following this expenditure and adding tax on the interest earned during the deferred expenditure period will obviously change the figures again, as would the inclusion of inflation; both these aspects are discussed more fully below.

The third method, the Annual Equivalent Cost expresses the aggregated amounts in terms of the 'mortgage payable' on the initial cost added to the typical annual costs of operating, repair and replacement usually related to the unit of floor area. This same quick method which provides a 'snap-shot' at a point in time can also be used for comparison of rental options – see **FIG 10.4.E**.

**FIG. 10.4.E:** *Life-cycle cost analysis of options 'A' and 'B'*
*- annual equivalent cost per sq ft NIA*

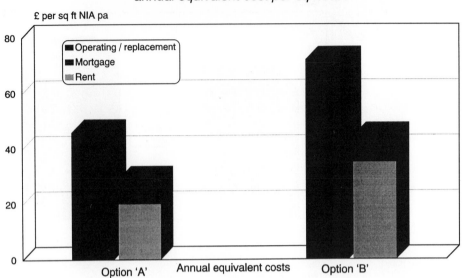

*Discounted cash flow*

The effect of interest earnings on the calculated worth of deferred expenditure as described above is, in practice, calculated from tables of factors produced for the purpose or from first principles. Eg: the calculation of the interest earned on the expenditure deferred until year 1 of the example at **FIG 10.4.A** can be calculated from the formula:

$$PV = (1 + i)^{-n}$$

where:

. PV = Present Value

. i  = Rate of interest

. n  = number of years

so, at 6% interest over 50 years

$$PV = (1 + 0.06)^{-1} \quad \text{or} \quad \left(\frac{1}{(1.06)}\right)^{1} = 0.9433$$

By the same formula the factor becomes 0.8899 at year 2, 0.8396 at year 3 and so forth - applied to the net amount of the cash flow for the period. Note that this same formula can be used to calculate factors for any period eg: monthly, quarterly etc.

The annual equivalent of the initial cost is calculated rather like a mortgage instalment table ie: it is the annual interest rate per £ added to the sinking fund required to be set aside to replace £1 capital by the end of the period.

So, the annual equivalent factor applied to the initial cost is calculated from the formula:

(i + s) where

- i = the remunerative rate of interest

-      s = the sinking fund for a 50 year life accumulating @ 6%.

In this case (0.06 + 0.0034) = 0.0634

The sinking fund, also used in the calculation of depreciation (see Chapter 3.7), is calculated from the formula:

$$\frac{i}{(1 - i)^n - 1}$$

ie: it is the amount required to be invested annually at a given rate of interest (before/after tax) to repay the initial sum borrowed by the end of the period. It is the reciprocal of the amount of £1 pa at the remunerative rate.

Given that tax relief may be available in the form of capital allowances and against most revenue expenditure the effects of such savings need to be calculated prior to discounting.

The effects of inflation on DCF are at one and the same time a problem of forecasting and an argument against the whole process.

Although DCF will whittle away at the future cost of deferred expenditure, inflation will be compounded and will counteract and outweigh the effects of discounting in most cases - ie: money spent up front may well result in an apparently satisfactory return on investment through future savings. Nevertheless the standard procedure has been to ignore inflation entirely - as in the examples above.

This overcomes the argument that it cannot be readily predicted but this is not the strongest case for leaving inflation out of the equation. Some text books on the subject claim that, when discounting, one must take account of the actual inflated sums which will have to be paid **at the time payments are due;** nevertheless, it must surely be the case that the real value of money will have appreciated by a similar amount, meaning that when payments are made they are in a similar relationship to the company's finances as if no inflation had taken place.

An example of **FIG 10.4.C** taking inflation at 5% pa is shown at **FIG 10.4.F**.

The calculation is simple - just add the inflation percentage, in this case 5%, to the discount factor for the period in question, giving the formula:

$PV = [1 + (i + inf)]^{-n}$ where

**FIG. 10.4.F:** *Aggregated life -cycle cost analysis of options 'A' and 'B'- inflated @ 5% p.a.(compound) & discounted 6% p.a.*

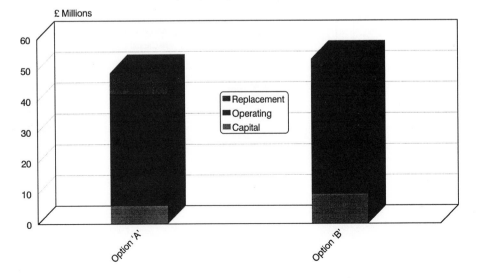

'inf' = the inflation per £ pa - ie: 0.05 is the figure for inflation at 5%pa

A summary of the Net Present Values of the two schemes for two rates of interest, tax and inflation are given at **FIG 10.4.G and H**. One could be forgiven for being cynical about the consequences of letting two management accountants loose in support or opposition of a proposal. Nonetheless, it is submitted that the process, like any other predictive exercise, encourages proper consideration of the issues.

In any case, a sensitivity analysis - of which the latter is but one example - can be extremely useful in knocking out spurious objections to the benefit of consideration of the real issues.

**FIG. 10.4.G:** *Aggregated life -cycle cost analysis of options 'A' and 'B'- inflated @ 5% p.a.(compound) & discounted @ 6% p.a. - after tax (30%)*

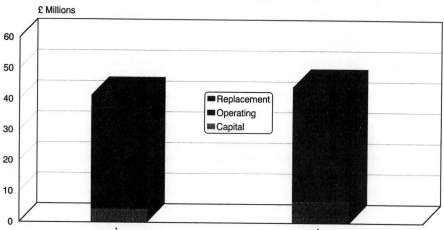

**FIG. 10.4.H:** *Aggregated life -cycle cost analysis of options 'A' and 'B'- inflated @ 5% p.a.(compound) & discounted @ 15% p.a.*

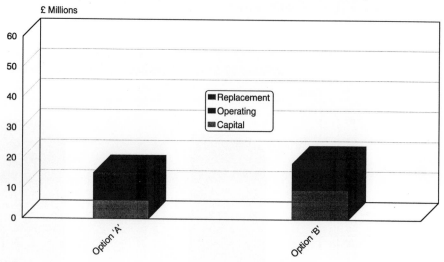

## Data capture

As if the machinations and manipulations of the choice of DCF factors were not enough a further major obstacle to the acceptance of life-cycle cost analysis in practice is the perception that data about the life of buildings and their component parts and the associated costs-in-use is unreliable - even in the relatively few cases where it can be found at all.

Good records of life-cycles are not kept publicly although several good private data-bases are known to exist. There are also published sources [2] based on anecdote which are probably as good as one could want given that actual life-cycles can be influenced by all sorts of factors outside of the intrinsic qualities of the individual component, eg: design, workmanship, maintenance, modification, use etc. **FIG 2.2.3.C** in Chapter 2.2 gives some guidance in respect of typical materials and components.

A research project [2] funded under the LINK/CMR scheme resulted in proposals for data capture which, if commercially adopted, would, in time, not only improve the quality of data available to life-cycle predictors but also better inform designers as to the life-cycle consequences of their selection and application of materials and systems.

Other computerised techniques now used in facilities management will also gen-erate more information on physical performance, eg: maintenance management data-bases, properly kept up to date will provide good data for the future. Better still, the pro-active financial management control systems now coming to the scene can provide not only ready access to actual life-cycles and costs but also an audit trail back to the original predictions - passing the maintenance and performance history en route.

In summary, data is required under the following categories:-

- the life of buildings
- the life of systems
- the life of components
- the cost of maintenance
- the cost of repair
- the cost of replacement
- the causes of deterioration and failure
- the consequential effects of deterioration and failure

Until better data is available we have to use the best evidence we have; better an intelligent prediction than no thought at all - which seems to be the present convention.

### 10.4.3 LIFE-CYCLE COST CONTROL

*Application of cost control principles*

The three facets of cost control - **budgetary control, procurement and value engineering** (see Chapter 2.2) are, of course, totally applicable to the process of life-cycle cost control.

However, the emphasis between the various components of the equation, ie: initial, operating and replacement costs, will shift depending on the financial interest of the building developer. The developer/trader (see Chapter 10.2) is likely to be more concerned with minimising capital costs at the expense of revenue cost which will be incurred by another party; this is a historic tendency which is, thank goodness, starting to be changed due to the advent of a buyer's market and a more discerning and powerful user lobby.

The owner-occupier will probably be seeking a better balance between initial and running costs than is conventionally available in speculative buildings to rent. Concentrating on the owner-occupier's equation, let us consider how cost control principles should be applied from inception to completion.

*Budgetary control*

The principles and application of budgetary control described in Chapters 2.2 and 6.3 apply to new-build and refurbishment schemes in just the same way as to fitting-out. In such projects, as with major fitting-out work, the budgetary control will nearly always be carried out by in specialists - either independent consultants or part of a packaged team.

The facilities manager should be closely involved with the development of the budget cost plan and he, or his project manager, must have power of veto over any proposal to diverge from the cost plan agreement; specifically, he has **three critical functions** to carry out.

**First**, he must make sure that the cost plan is right for the performance required of the building ie: its physical, functional and financial performance. This will not be easy, given the conventional wisdom (or lack thereof!) in this area. It is also (as has been discussed in Chapter 2.2) an integral part of the value engineering process to set the budget at this optimum level.

Although analysing the functional value of a scheme design is undeniably difficult, the **second** task of the facilities manager, ie: correctly balancing the initial expenditure of a scheme against the revenue cost implications of its physical performance, is achievable - but only within a discipline which he must impose on the design team from the outset.

Turning back to the life-cycle cost analysis at **FIG 10.4.A** let us assume for present purposes that this is the forecast out-turn from a cost plan proposal put forward by the design team at sketch design stage. The facilities manager should require the design team to demonstrate in detail the basis of their forecasts for building and component life-cycles and costs of operating, maintenance, repair and replacement.

Given the state-of-the-art in terms of culture philosophy and lack of data this will undoubtedly stretch them. Nevertheless, it will make them think through the consequences of their proposals in a way which should avoid the worst excesses of the traditional process. A recent anecdote concerns the case of a facilities manager taking over his brand new bespoke building and discovering, for the first time, that the external cladding required to be power-jet cleaned every three months!

In reality the relatively insignificant impact of running costs on the overall business finances, coupled with the effect of discounting on deferred expenditure, means that the most important reason for this exacting process of appraisal is the avoidance of such unexpected problems. It is, however, as well to remember that the facilities manager who inherits a building which is difficult or expensive to operate and maintain will face a running battle over the years with his customer or the finance director - or probably both.

Although these revenue costs are never likely to sway the option appraisal one way or another, to the facilities manager 5 years down the line on the inevitable tight budget it can be a matter of life or death to have enough funds to run the building properly. In any case, if there is no good reason to build a problem for the future then it should not be allowed to happen.

An example of calculations which might be offered in support of the cost plan proposed at **FIG 10.4.A** is given at **FIG 10.4.J**. This examines the proposals for the lift installation and the estimated consequences in terms of maintenance, replacement and energy consumption.

**FIG. 10.4.J:** *Comparative life-cycle cost analysis of alternative lift installations in options 'A' and 'B' - undiscounted*

| Lift A - low specification - 8-person | | Life cycle costs - 50 year period | | | | | | 0.0182267 |
|---|---|---|---|---|---|---|---|---|
| Cost centre | | Year 1 | Year 5 | Year 10 | Year 15 | Year 20 | Year 25 | Total |
| Initial installation | 0 | 63,000 | 0 | 0 | 0 | 0 | 0 | 63,000 |
| Energy | | 2,700 | 2,700 | 2,700 | 2,700 | 2,700 | 2,700 | 67,500 |
| Maintenance | | 12,000 | 12,000 | 12,000 | 12,000 | 12,000 | 12,000 | 300,000 |
| Cleaning | | 6,000 | 6,000 | 6,000 | 6,000 | 6,000 | 6,000 | 150,000 |
| Overhaul every 5yrs | 0 | – | 4,435 | 4,435 | 4,435 | 4,435 | 4,435 | 112,500 |
| Total | | 83,700 | 25,135 | 25,135 | 25,135 | 25,135 | 25,135 | **693,000** |
| Assumptions | | Floor to floor height of 3.5m<br>Standard finishes to cars, doors and gates<br>Electrically operated 8 or10 person lifts<br>Serving 6 levels at a speed of 1 m/s | | | | | | |
| Lift B - high specification - 10-person | | Life cycle costs - 50 year period | | | | | | 0.0182267 |
| Cost centre | | Year 1 | Year 5 | Year 10 | Year 15 | Year 20 | Year 25 | Total |
| Initial installation | 0 | 72,000 | 0 | 0 | 0 | 0 | 0 | 72,000 |
| Energy | | 2,500 | 2,500 | 2,500 | 2,500 | 2,500 | 2,500 | 62,500 |
| Maintenance | | 13,000 | 13,000 | 13,000 | 13,000 | 13,000 | 13,000 | 325,000 |
| Cleaning | | 7,900 | 7,900 | 7,900 | 7,900 | 7,900 | 7,900 | 197,500 |
| Overhaul every 5yrs | 0 | – | 2,383 | 2,383 | 2,383 | 2,383 | 2,383 | 58,750 |
| Total | | 95,400 | 25,783 | 25,783 | 25,783 | 25,783 | 25,783 | **715,750** |
| Assumptions | | add £4,000 for -<br>add £4,000 for -<br>add £1000 for - | Stainless steel finishes to cars<br>Enhanced efficiency motors and energy saving controls<br>Serving 6 levels at a speed of 1.25 m/s | | | | | |

The **third** function which the facilities manager must carry out in budgetary control is to set up from the outset a fully pro-active budgetary control system for the operating, maintenance, repair and replacement costs. Such a system should be linked into an asset management program and, ideally, will contain the following features:

- automatic end-of-year accounts reconciliation

- pro-active budgetary control forecasts of potential commitment

- reports on contractor exposure and performance

- audit trail through all pre/post budget activity

- risk appraisal of budget change proposals

- automatic VAT liability computation

- option to transfer excesses to contingency budget

- record of contract and contractor details

- built-in benchmarking parameters and performance indicators
- record of leases, rents and service charges
- option to specify one's own cost centres and risk categories
- graphic and tabular outputs.

The important thing to observe is that any control system is only as good as the people charged with operating it. A budgetary control system requires the basic assumptions underlying the budget estimates to be recorded in such a way that potential changes can be identified by simple reference back. This takes expertise, and the process of picking out events or proposals which will lead to cost over-runs (or under-spends) requires a discipline which does not come naturally to line managers. Even in the finance departments themselves it is rare to find genuinely pro-active financial management; most are content with budget control by reference to committed expenditure. The corollary of such a reactive approach is that once the budget for one cost centre is spent reductions must be made in other works to recover the position.

Ironically, the state-of-the-art financial control systems now becoming available to cope with the dynamic processes of construction and facilities management may well be the forerunner to changes in the financial management of core business activity.

## Procurement

The role of efficient procurement of both capital and revenue works is considered in Chapters 2.2 and 6.3. One specific issue perhaps worth considering in the whole-life economics context is the concept of 'one-stop-shop' building provision and management.

This is a recent innovation and involves developers offering a life-cycle cost plan as part of their contract - provided they are retained to manage the facilities for a given part of the life-cycle.

Clearly, the risks to both parties are quite high and both need to provide adequate contingency against deficiency of performance in both building and premises management terms.

As an exercise in risk management it does have a high cost penalty and is more likely to be to the advantage of the contractor - who gets a lot more work out of it - than the user, who may lose control of the vital management information. Nevertheless, it should have the effect of encouraging the sort of holistic approach to project appraisal recommended above as an integral part of design development.

## Value engineering

Properly equating initial and deferred expenditure is an essential part of value-engineering the building through its whole life.

Presuming that the life-cycle budget has been set at an appropriately 'challenging' level it will remain for the many components, systems and elements to be tested individually for economic efficiency.

Each capital cost centre should have its life-cycle costs forecast in a format such as suggested in **FIG 10.4.J** which compares the undiscounted whole-life costs of the alternative lift proposals. This is depicted graphically in **FIG 10.4.K** and the results are compared with the discounted appraisal at **FIG 10.4.L**.

**FIG. 10.4.K:** *Aggregated comparative life-cycle cost analysis of alternative lift installations in options 'A' and 'B' - undiscounted*

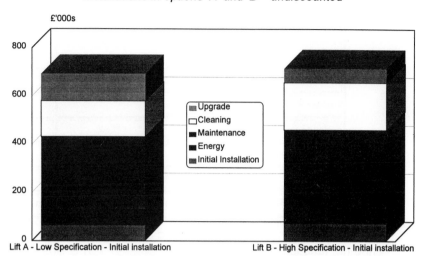

**FIG. 10.4.L:** *Comparative life-cycle cost analysis of alternative lift installations in options 'A' and 'B' - discounted @6%*

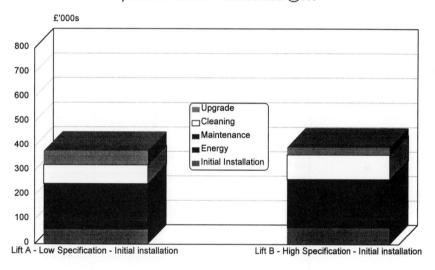

In both these examples the incidence of corporation tax relief on revenue expenditure and via capital allowances will impact on both examples proportionately so may be ignored; however, some sensitivity analysis testing of various tax rates and depreciation regimes could be valuable on larger items of expenditure (see also Section 11).

Note also that a comparison of two design options, (eg: builder's partitions, which do not carry capital allowances against 'demountable' partitions which may (see example in Chapter 6.3), will always need to be tested for tax as well as construction efficiency.

A further example of value engineering computation based on the simple 'pay-back period' is shown in the example of energy conservation of lighting installations at **FIG 10.4.M**.

The three-year pay-back shown on this lighting control proposal (before tax) is, of course, equivalent to a 33% return on initial investment (ROI). Although this looks very good many organisations will not commit management time and resources to such improvements if the pay-back is more than 3 years. Because the pay-back period is short DCF is not normally applied to such calculations.

FIG 10.4.M: *Lighting energy payback period on conservation measures*

| Lighting energy | Net Internal area (NIA) - sq m | Cost per sq m NIA pa £ | Total pa £ |
|---|---|---|---|
| | 4,500      x | 5 | 22,500 |
| Lighting control system | | | |
| Capital cost | | | £10,000 |
| Saving on electricity pa | 10%      x | £22,500 | £2,250 |
| Saving on re-lamping pa | 10%      x | £4,250 | £425 |
| Total saving | | | £2,675 |
| £10,000 ÷ 2,675 = 3.74 i.e. approx 4 years payback on investment | | | |

A step in the right direction with regard to value engineering the 'whole' performance (ie: functional and physical - see Chapter 1.3) is illustrated at **FIG 10.4.N**.

FIG 10.4.N: *Performance evaluation - alternative lift installations in office building - options 'A' and 'B'*

| Subject: | Lift installation | Estimated capital cost |
|---|---|---|
| Location: | Main core | |
| Zero-base | Option A | £ 63,000 |
| Proposal: | Option B | £ 72,000 |
| Subjective Evaluation | | |
| Effect of proposal on functional performance | Perceived quality | Better |
| | Visual ambience | Better |
| | Comfort | Better |
| | Ergonomics | Better |
| | Flexibility | Better |
| | Safety | - |
| | Speed | Better |
| | Waiting time | Better |
| | Capacity | Better |
| Effect of proposal on operating costs | Cleaning | Worse |
| | Energy | Better |
| | Maintenance & repairs | Worse |
| | Security | - |
| | Insurance | - |
| | Replacement | Worse |
| | Management | Better |

This example was originally developed in the context of a value engineering exercise where the client wished to challenge the design team's principal 'cost drivers' in terms of both functional and physical performance. In the example, as with a long list of items suggested by the whole team collectively, the provision of the higher quality lift installation was considered in a round-table discussion by the facilities manager and the design team against the criteria listed. Quite rightly, the client knew he could not easily value the functional criteria but equally realised that the physical performance cost consequences would be much smaller - so did not request detailed financial appraisal.

As a value-engineering tool for all major design decisions this method has much to commend it. Not only does it make sure that all 3 facts of performance are properly considered by the facilities manager at design stage -it also meets the requirements for the team properly to consider the performance consequences of their proposals in principle, even in the absence of good data for finite appraisal.

## 10.4.4 LIFE-CYCLE COSTS IN CONTEXT

*Initial costs in context*

Because initial costs, viewed as a one-off payment, would present a non-viable investment option for most organisations they are invariably amortised over a medium or long term - either by way of commercial mortgage for the owner-occupier, or in the rent for the tenant.

Taking two current examples of commercial offices in a City Centre and Provincial location, costs of development and amortisation over 15 years might be as shown in **FIG 10.4.P**.

**FIG. 10.4.P:** *Development costs and amortisation - front-and-back-office examples*

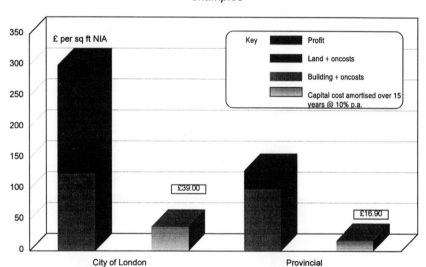

Building 'A' with an annual amortising cost of £39/SF of net internal area (NIA) including land, finance, fees etc, costs £3.9m pa. In the context of an organisation of 400 employees the turnover generated in the building might be say £120m pa.

Similarly, Building 'B' with annual amortising costs of £16.90/SF NIA ie: £1.69m pa might be set in the context of a 'back office' turnover/business costs of £70m pa.

**FIG 10.4.Q** shows both these as pie diagrams, graphically and perhaps dramatically highlighting the relatively small impact of the initial costs on the whole financial scheme of things - building 'A' is about 3.25% and Building 'B' 2.4% of turnover.

Rentalised by a developer the cost pa would actually be less. **FIG 10.4.R** shows the previous example but with capital costs adjusted to include for developer's profit and initial rental being based on initial investment yields of 7% for Building 'A' and 9% for Building 'B' - the latter representing the out-of-town nature of the investment - although a first-class covenant attached might well pull this back nearer to prime (see Chapters 3.3 and 9.1 for detailed consideration of investment yields and the effects of location thereon).

In fact after taking business rates and operating costs into account the total cost of premises is rarely more than 5-6% of turnover unless the space is being under-utilised or there is a need for extremely high premises quality in a specific location.

**FIG. 10.4.Q:** *Amortised development costs in context of annual turnover*

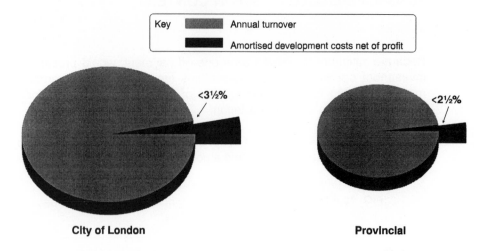

**FIG. 10.4.R:** *Developer's budget rentalised - front-and-back-office examples*

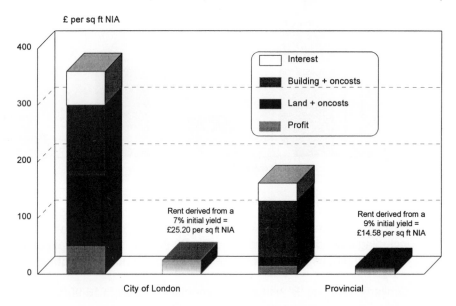

**FIG. 10.4.S:** *Amortised building and associated costs (fees, interest etc.)*
*in context of annual turnover*

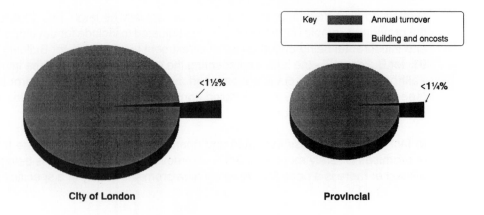

Note also that when the land and ancillary costs are removed from the equations at **FIGS 10.4.P** and **Q** the 'building only' component drops to around 1½% of turnover in all cases - see **FIG 10.4.S** - much less when rental values rise with demand and rent reviews.

This is very important when considering the cost/benefit of buildings in relation to functional performance (see Chapter 1.3).

## Operating costs in context

Taking the same examples the typical operating and replacement costs pa are shown in **FIG 10.4.T**. The total running costs are no more than about 1½% of turnover at maximum; it is interesting to recognise how little significance such items as important to facilities managers as maintenance and energy have in this overall context - though not wise to belittle the importance of getting them right in terms of performance and cost.

**FIG.10.4.T:** *Operating and replacement costs in the context of amortised building costs and annual turnover*

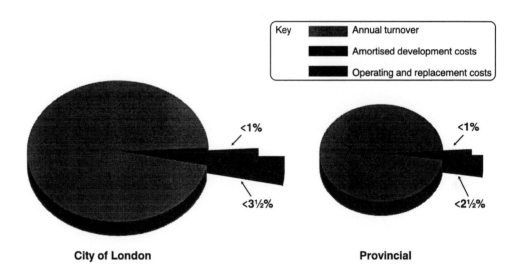

| Key | Annual turnover |
| | Amortised development costs |
| | Operating and replacement costs |

City of London          Provincial

## Whole-life costs v 'people' costs

Since the greater part of revenue expenditure making up turnover in a commercial organisation is staff-related the significance of these statistics is the help they give in comprehension of the likely consequences on profitability of attempting to reduce premises costs at the expense of performance.

**FIG 10.4.U** looks at the 'City' situation showing pre-tax profits at 5% roughly equating to the premises costs. Clearly any saving in the premises costs which might be effected without loss of performance should go straight to the bottom line profit.

**FIG. 10.4.U:** *Premises cost in the context of typical corporate turnover and profit*

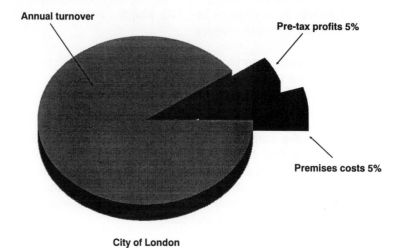

City of London

On the other hand, impairment of the functional performance either as a result of inadequate initial cost/performance and/or operating delays, breakdowns or other inefficiencies will clearly have a highly geared effect on the output cost of the occupiers. Research is now on-going [3] to investigate such relationships in some detail; until those results filter through it is necessary just to understand this gearing and thus avoid costly mistakes through ill-conceived cut-backs in the comparatively minor premises cost centres.

**It is axiomatic that business operational requirements must always drive the premises budget - not vice versa!**

---

[1]     'Building Design Evaluation, Costs in Use' – Dr. P.A. Stone (E & FN Spon, 1968)

[2]     'The Performance and Cost Managed Building' – (CFM / Arup R&D / BRE)

[3]     'The Functional Performance of Buildings' – (BWA / Oxford-Brookes University / BRE)

# PART F

# TAXATION

# SECTION 11

# TAXATION CONSIDERATIONS

# CHAPTER 11.1 – TAX EFFICIENCY

## 11.1.1 TAXATION AND THE FACILITIES MANAGER

Even in the best organised companies, the dialogue between the accounts department and facilities management may become perfunctory and negative; as a result facilities managers all too often fall into the trap of controlling expenditure against the budget without planning, or at least considering, the most tax-efficient solution to a problem, whether it is maintenance, fitting out or any other operational cost.

Equally, some accounts departments split costs and budgets for taxation accounting purposes without letting the facilities manager know the implications of the methodology. In every area of expenditure on premises there is an alternative solution or strategy which has different exposure to one tax or another. Very often the decision is not made by the facilities manager; choices such as whether to lease or buy, rent or mortgage will almost certainly be taken with the benefit of the advice of the company's tax specialist.

However, such is the range of choice of specification solutions to premises problems that it is quite easy for the facilities manager unwittingly to choose solutions to day-to-day problems which are not tax-efficient. Facilities managers do not need to be tax experts but they must have a sound working knowledge of the basic principles of taxation and allowances to avoid making decisions which lead to loss of valuable tax allowances and so optimise the tax efficiency of the operation.

## 11.1.2 PROPERTY OWNERSHIP AND TAXATION

Ownership of interests in property is inseparable from property taxation and the importance of taxation on property cannot be over-stressed - and not only with regards to expenditure on fitting-out and operating the premises. Before implementing any proposal for a transaction or a development, an evaluation should be made of the prospective tax burden arising from investment in property; from construction of certain buildings and structures; and from certain ways of disposal or occupation of property.

Generally, and at the risk of over-simplification, a person may arrange affairs to take advantage of the tax exemptions and reliefs which are available. However, statutory provisions which seek to counter avoidance of tax do exist eg: section 776 of the Income and Corporation Taxes Act 1988; also, case law has moved against avoidance of tax.

It follows that property taxation is an area where professional advice should be obtained before transactions or works are commenced. In the context of property this usually requires joint consideration by the accountant, lawyer and surveyor as well as the facilities manager.

### 11.1.3 NATIONAL TAXATION POLICY

Government policy over nearly two centuries has laid down the broad structure of national taxation, with increasing detail since 1945. The annual Budget and consequential Finance Act provides incremental changes each year, sometimes with wide-ranging effects. From time to time the legislation is consolidated as follows:

- the Capital Allowances Act 1990

- the Taxation of Chargeable Gains Act 1992

- the Value Added Tax Act 1983

- the Inheritance Tax Act 1984, and

- the Income and Corporation Taxes Act 1988,

Thus, there are three principal groups of taxes: income taxation, capital taxation and consumption taxation:

- income taxation covers income tax and corporation tax

- capital taxation covers capital gains tax and inheritance tax; and

- consumption taxation (for the purposes of this section) covers rates, value added tax and stamp duty,

### 11.1.4 INCOME TAXATION

The Income and Corporation Taxes Act 1988, as amended, provides for incomes to be taxed on an annual basis.

Generally, income taxation falls into two broad categories:

- income tax which is charged on the taxable incomes which individuals have each year

- corporation tax on the taxable income and gains of large companies.

The government's policy in recent years has been a general lowering of both income tax and corporation tax rates but this has been tempered by the need to redress the effects of excessive public borrowing.

Rents from leases in the United Kingdom and premiums on short leases (50 years or less) and certain other items are assessed under Schedule A. (Certain premiums and deemed premiums on the grant of short leases may also suffer capital gains tax).

The assessment of rents to income taxation is based on the gross rent receivable less permitted deductions. The chargeable amount of a premium is the premium reduced by 2% of the premium for each year of the lease except the first. Where a lease is let at a 'full rent' there are rules governing the right to carry forward losses during the currency of the lease or to offset in the same year a loss on one property against the profit from another (the so called pooling arrangements).

Dealing in property is assessed under Schedule D Case I of the Income and Corporation Taxes Act 1988, ie: on annual profit. Where a person is trading, expenditure on land and buildings or on the erection of buildings is treated as revenue expenditure and, where wholly and exclusively incurred for the purposes of trade, is brought into the computation of profit. Section 74 of the 1988 Act sets down the limitations on revenue expenditure.

Section 776 of the Income and Corporation Taxes Act 1988 provides a pitfall for those seeking to avoid tax in certain kinds of land transactions. Cases pertinent to section 766 include: *Yuill v Wilson* (1980); *Page v Lowther and Another* (1983) and *Sugarwhite v Budd* (1988).

Dividends from shares in property companies are assessed under Schedule F. The basic rate of income tax is deducted at source from dividends received by share-holders. It is then allowed as advanced corporation tax (ACT) against any liability the company has to pay that tax.

The list is by no means exhaustive and belies the technical minefield of taxation confronting the investor, dealer or business. It may be borne in mind that numerous exemptions, reliefs and concessions exist. For instance, capital allowances under the Capital Allowances Act 1990, as amended, may be available to the taxpayer whereby the cost of construction of a building or of plant and machinery may be set against rental income or business profits to arrive at taxable income.

## 11.1.5 CAPITAL TAXATION

Capital gains tax is chargeable to any capital gains accruing on a disposal which relates to a period of ownership since 1982 except where accruing to those who are in the business of 'dealing' eg: property developers, or who are eligible for some exemption or relief.

## 11.1.6 CONSUMPTION TAXATION

The Value Added Tax regime was introduced to construction and real estate in 1988 following sustained pressure from the European Union. Its effects are widespread and profound.

Aside from VAT, business rates and stamp duty also affect the cost of procuring and occupying premises.

## 11.1.7 EXPENDITURE ON PROPERTY

It is important to identify expenditure on property as either capital expenditure or revenue expenditure. It will then be allocated to the correct assessment for the purposes of taxation. For instance, investors tend to hold property for long periods and expenditure by the landlord on such matters as repairs, maintenance, insur-ance, management and services are generally set against gross income to find the profit or loss under Schedule A. A similar approach is adopted in determining the profit of trades, professions or vocations under Schedule D eg: for retailers, farmers and architects.

Generally, investor landlords (or businesses owning and occupying buildings) will find that the expenditure on acquiring them and on improving them will be treated as capital expenditure. Capital expenditure is not normally allowed against income as a revenue deduction, but may be allowable for capital gains tax.

The only depreciation of capital assets allowed to landlord investors or businesses for income taxation purposes is that given as 'capital allowances' by the Capital Allowances Act 1990 and various Finance Acts. Thus, for certain types of building and for qualifying plant and machinery, capital expenditure is deductible under the regime for capital allowances. Large sums may arise and it may be prudent to review all development projects where no claims have been made previously.

It should be borne in mind that, unlike the case with dealers in land, the cost of land and buildings occupied for commercial purposes is expenditure on capital assets and may feature in future capital gains tax computations on disposals, subject to roll-over relief or retirement relief.

## 11.1.8 MANAGEMENT OF TAXATION

Statutes lay down government policy as law which is applied and managed by the Board of Inland Revenue and the Board of Customs and Excise.

Assessments to income taxation are made by Inspectors of Taxes, demands for payment and collection are made by Collectors of Taxes and the District Valuer deals with much of the work of property valuation (or Valuation Office for rating).

Of course, VAT is dealt with by the Commissioners of Customs and Excise.

Appeals of various kinds are heard by the General or Special Commissioners of Inland revenue with appeals to the hierarchy of courts, ie: the High Court, the Court of Appeal, and the House of Lords. The Lands Tribunal deals with valuation appeals in most instances, but there is a local valuation court system to handle rating matters prior to the Lands Tribunal.

# CHAPTER 11.2 – CORPORATION TAX AND RELIEF

## 11.2.1 LIABILITY TO CORPORATION TAX

The tax regime for each accounting year is established in the annual Finance Act. Corporation tax is applied to the profits arising in a given accounting period after deduction of certain 'allowances' against items of capital and revenue expenditure as decreed by the current Finance Act and supported by case law.

The rate of corporation tax for the year ending 31/3/94 varied depending on the size of profits in the accounting year:

- profits up to £300,000 - rate applied 25%

- profits over £300,000 but no more than £500,000 - rate applied 35%

- profits over £500,000 - rate applied 33%.

**FIG 11.2.A** shows how the Corporation Tax is applied to a company with taxable profits (after deduction of all allowances) of £300,000 in the current accounting year. **FIG 11.2.B** shows what happens to a larger company with taxable profits of £2 million.

**FIG 11.2.A:** *Corporation tax computation - small company*

| Net profit before tax | | £500,000 |
|---|---|---|
| Corporation tax on profits | on £300,000 @ 25% CT | £75,000 |
| | on (£500,000 - £300,000) = £200,000 @ 35% CT | £70,000 |
| Gross corporation tax liability (that is, before capital allowances) | | **£145,000** |

**FIG 11.2.B:** *Corporation tax computation - larger company*

| Net profit before tax | | £2,000,000 |
|---|---|---|
| Gross corporation tax liability on profits | on £2,000,000 @ 33% CT | **£660,000** |

Deductions from profits before applying Corporation Tax fall under two quite distinct headings - revenue expenditure and capital expenditure

## 11.2.2 ALLOWANCES IN RESPECT OF REVENUE EXPENDITURE

As a general rule, all the premises costs incurred in the normal running of the business can be offset against income before calculating taxable profit. Allowable revenue expenditure is offset in full against profits for the accounting year in which it is incurred, whereas allowances for capital expenditure are normally spread over a number of years at varying rates depending on the current tax legislation. Revenue expenditure embraces routine premises costs such as rent, rates, cleaning, energy, routine maintenance, repairs and service charges.

## 11.2.3 ALLOWANCES IN RESPECT OF CAPITAL EXPENDITURE

*Government policy*

From time to time governments have introduced capital allowances as a means of recognising the consumption of assets by a business or more pertinently to encourage particular forms of investment, eg: thermal insulation in industrial buildings, safety at sports stadia, small workshops and development in Enterprise Zones.

The general reduction in the scope of such allowances in recent years probably signals the government's ability to bring finer tuning into the economic policy.

*Nature and amounts of capital allowances*

The capital allowances are as follows:

- an initial allowance, where the whole or a relatively large proportion of the expenditure is set against taxable income - generally, initial allowances have been abolished, except in Enterprise Zones and one or two special cases

- a writing down allowance, where a relatively small percentage is given against taxable income - they are either 'straight line', ie: a fixed percentage of the original cost, or 'reducing balance', ie: a fixed percentage reduction of the last calculated written down value

- a balancing allowance which arises when, on a disposal, the written down value is greater than the consideration attributable to the asset (or vice versa for a balancing charge).

For buildings, the eligible expenditure includes site clearance, cost of construction and associated professional fees. Care has to be taken that the building qualifies under the relevant statutes, ie: the Capital Allowances Act 1990 as amended by provisions in later Finance Acts. Also, a substantial body of case law has developed to interpret the Acts, particularly on the different types of qualification for buildings and on qualifying plant and machinery, eg: the latter must be 'functional' rather than part of the 'setting'.

Outside of the Enterprise Zones capital allowances are writing down allowances at 4% - eg: on industrial buildings.

Plant and machinery enjoys a writing down allowance on a reducing balance basis at 25%. Capital allowances are particularly important in Enterprise Zones where 100% of the cost of construction of industrial, retail and certain other buildings, but not residential buildings, is allowable against otherwise taxable income. In an Enterprise Zone plant and machinery enjoys capital allowances by an extra-statutory concession.

However, for the facilities manager the most significant aspect of capital allowances is the substantial amount of fitting-out and refurbishment works which can count as 'plant and machinery' making them eligible for off-setting against revenue tax.

Occasionally the service charge may contain items of capital expenditure which attract capital allowances. These may only be reclaimed by the landlord. **The tenant may claim the whole of the service charge as revenue expenditure.** The landlord receiving the service charge payment will have to add it to income and potentially some or all of it will be taxable as the landlord's profit. It is important to note that the capital allowance may now be claimed against actual expenditure and not, as in the past, delayed until the project is competed and operational.

There is at least one program on the market which enables the organisation to recover the capital relief on a monthly basis and to track the endless sequence of changes to the components being written down at any one time in the building's life.

The plant and machinery element is not defined by statute. However, it is commonly accepted that, in its ordinary sense, the term plant and machinery includes whatever apparatus is used by a businessman for carrying on his business - not his stock in trade, which he buys or makes for sale, but all goods and chattels, fixed or movable, live or dead, which he keeps for permanent employment in his business (1987 Yarmouth v France).

**FIG 11.2.C:** *Items of capital expenditure on buildings normally qualifying for capital allowances*

| Items of plant | Comments |
|---|---|
| Blinds | - |
| Demountable partitions | Where regularly moved in the course of trade |
| Carpet | Where readily removable in the course of trade (eg carpet tiles) |
| Suspended ceilings | Where acting principally as a plenum as part of the a/c system |
| Loose furniture & furnishings | - |
| Fittings & equipment | Tea points, credenzas inc. 'fridges, dishwashers etc |
| Office equipment | - |
| Sanitary appliances | Wash-hand basins, baths, urinals etc |
| Hot water system | Includes pipework, tanks, builders' work |
| Heating system | Includes pipework, builders' work |
| Control panels | Eg temperature controls - but not switchboards |
| Air-conditioning & ventilation systems | Includes ductwork, builders' work |
| Emergency generators & transformers / UPS | - |
| Task lighting | Where attached to furniture |
| Ambient lighting | Moveable fittings connected to a circuit not dedicated solely to lighting |
| Emergency lighting | - |
| Wiring from outlet to loose equipment | No other general electrical wiring included |
| Sprinkler systems | Includes pipework, tanks, builders' work |
| Fire alarms / fire fighting equipment | Includes builders' work |
| Security systems | Includes builders' work |
| Lifts & escalators | Includes electrical work and builders' work, but not lift shafts |
| Preliminaries | Proportion of preliminary costs (foreman, scaffolding, temporary work, insurances) |
| Professional fees | Proportion of total cost |
| Telephone & data | - |
| Cabling | - |

**FIG 11.2.C** shows common items of expenditure which may be deemed to be plant and machinery for tax purposes. The main borderline area is the one concerning repairs - when does a repair become refurbishment? Repair expenditure is generally taken as that sum spent on maintaining the original performance of an asset. It is regular expenditure, usually budgeted annually, and is required throughout the life of a building.

The impact of expenditure on certain new buildings which can also qualify for capital allowances at varying rates is shown at **FIG 11.2.D**. Capital allowances are available only to the person who incurs the expenditure. Capital expenditure is usually that which has a benefit that extends beyond a single accounting period.

**FIG 11.2.D:** *Capital allowances on new building work*

| Building type | | % of capital allowed against tax in each year | |
|---|---|---|---|
| | | **1** | **subsequently** |
| **1. Industrial** | **Expenditure before 1/1/95 if contract entered into between 1/11/92 - 31/10/93** | 24 | 4% p.a. until year 20 |
| | **Otherwise expended after 5/11/62** | 4 | 4% p.a. until year 25 |
| **2. Commercial, trade or professional** | | NIL | (Plant and machinery items only) |
| **3. Industrial, commercial, trade, professional, or hotels in an enterprise zone** | | 100 | |
| **4. Scientific research** | **Expenditure before 1/1/85 (or before 1/4/87 under a contract pre 20/3/85)** | 100 | on cost excluding land and any dwellings (Finance Act 1985 s.63) |
| | **Otherwise expended after 1/1/85** | 100 | |
| **6. Residential buildings (other than qualifying as scientific research)** | | NIL | |
| **7. Qualifying hotels of a commercial nature (e.g. at least 10 bedrooms, open 4 months a year, 25% ancillary offices)** | **Expenditure and in use before 1/1/95 if contract entered into 1/11/92 - 31/10/93** | 24 | 4% p.a. until year 20 |
| | **Otherwise expended after 11/4/78** | 4 | 4% p.a. until year 25 |
| NB Generally buildings must be in use by given dates to qualify for allowances | | | |
| Source: Up to and including Finance Act 1994 | | | |

The issue of items of capital expenditure which are disguised as revenue expenditure is discussed in an earlier chapter. Much of this concealed capital expenditure frequently goes on upgrading premises to accommodate information technology. If management were fully aware of this, they might reconsider the whole of their premises policy. Whether expenditure is finally allocated to capital or revenue it is important that all associated overhead costs such as consultants' fees and contractors' 'preliminaries' are identified and added to the net cost of actual work items.

An example of an ongoing assessment of the amount of plant and machinery in a fitting-out contract is given at **FIG 11.2.E**. Note that there is a distinction between what the team believes is certain to be acceptable by the Inspector of Taxes and those items where negotiation may need to take place; the Inspector may well take a much harder line on the 'grey' areas as a result of the 1993 statute.

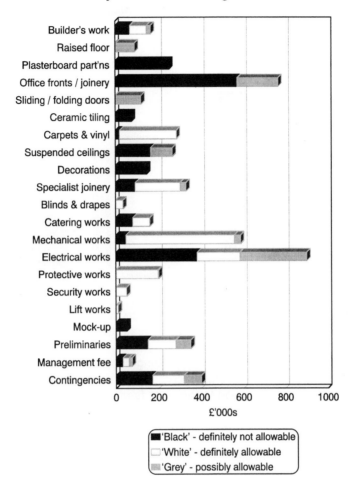

**FIG. 11.2.E:** *Preliminary appraisal of plant and machinery content of a fitting-out contract*

£'000s

'Black' – definitely not allowable
'White' – definitely allowable
'Grey' – possibly allowable

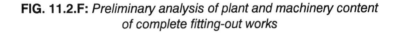

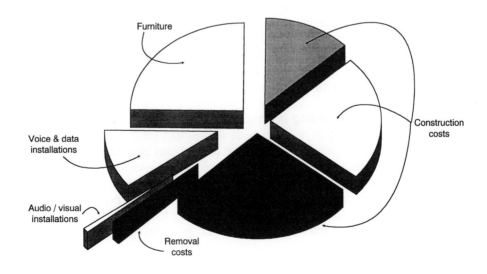

**FIG. 11.2.F:** *Preliminary analysis of plant and machinery content of complete fitting-out works*

Furniture

Construction costs

Voice & data installations

Audio / visual installations

Removal costs

The communications component of the fitting-out is allowable in full and **FIG 11.2.F** shows this in the context of overall fitting-out project costs.

**FIG.11.2.G:** *Potential contribution of capital allowances to funding complete fitting-out works*

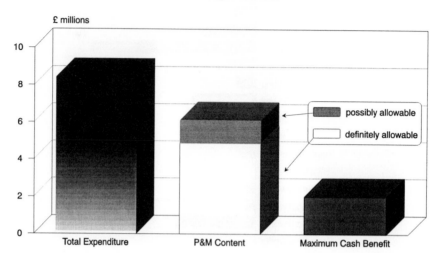

Capital allowances are an important source of funding for projects and can make a sizeable contribution as **FIG 11.2.G** illustrates.

In special circumstances a whole building designed for a one-off special use may be admissible as plant or machinery. However, it seems likely that this loophole in the regime will be closed in the near future.

## Corporation tax planning

Short of fudging the figures between capital and revenue expenditure, the organisation has little opportunity to control the amount of tax it pays. There are, however, three approaches to the use of tax allowances which can be fruitful. The first relates to the choice of specification, the second to the method of purchasing and the third to the timing of the expenditure. In all cases the facilities manager in consultation with the accountants and/or tax consultant, will need to establish the potential liability to Corporation Tax in the current and immediate future tax years. They can then exercise their choice to optimise efficiency.

The decision to create new rooms in an office building gives rise to **specification** options with variable tax allowances. For example, fixed solid plastered partitions are inexpensive but do not attract capital allowances nor do they rank as revenue expenditure. On the other hand, demountable partitions can cost two to three times as much but may rank as plant and machinery for tax purposes, bringing the appropriate capital allowances.

As far as **purchasing** is concerned the company may be able to enter either a contract-leasing or hire-purchase agreement for the demountable partitions; this gives the alternative of claiming the annual cost against revenue expenditure rather than claiming capital allowances against a one-off cash purchase. The facilities manager must try to discover the extent to which these issues are actually considered in depth in the facilities decision-making process. Where the methodology fails to meet his criteria, he should try to see whether it is apathy, ignorance or arrogance in the organisation which is at the root of the problem.

As for **timing** there is not much sense in acquiring tax allowances in excess of profits. In a bad year firms are usually keen to defer expenditure in any way so it makes sense to do so and get the tax allowances against next year's prospective return to profit.

# CHAPTER 11.3 – CAPITAL GAINS TAX AND RELIEF

## 11.3.1 LIABILITY TO CAPITAL GAINS TAX

Capital gains tax was introduced in 1965 but the legislation is found in the Taxation of Chargeable Gains Act 1992 and relevant Finance Acts. Essentially all pay capital gains tax on any capital gain accruing on a disposal which relates to a period of ownership since 1982 (hitherto 1965) ie: there has been a 'rebasing' of the tax.

Of course, the tax is not charged on persons whose business is dealing or who are eligible for some exemption or relief. For instance, exempt persons include local authorities and charities.

The tax is charged on net gains in the year at standard or higher income tax rates on chargeable gains made by individuals and at corporation tax rate on those made by companies, other than companies with low profits. Individuals enjoy an exempt slice of gain.

It is outside the scope of this section to look at the computations for tax. However, it may be noted that ownership from before 6 April 1965 requires particular calculations but this has been changed by rebasing, although calculations may still be appropriate. Similarly, special calculations are needed for part disposals eg: the grant of a short lease at a premium; and the disposal of wasting assets, eg: a short lease.

Until 1982 there was no specific provision for inflation under capital gains tax. However, as a result of the Finance Acts 1982 and 1985 two forms of 'indexation allowance' were given, reducing the taxation of 'inflation gains' for gains made prior to the 1988 Budget.

As a result of the Finance Act 1988, the gains were to be assessed from 1982 as the base year, ie: rebasing introduces the use of the market value of the asset as at 31 March 1982. Of course, rebasing does not apply to property acquired after that date although indexation for inflation will apply. These provisions continued on consolidation of the legislation in 1992.

## 11.3.2 EXEMPTIONS AND RELIEFS

The principal property exemptions and reliefs from capital gains tax include:

- an individual's sole or main residence, provided conditions are met

- 'roll over ie: where the proceeds of disposal of a business asset are used to acquire assets for business, subject to qualification

- 'retirement relief', a gain of up to £150,000 is exempt on retirement under prescribed circumstances together with 50% of the capital gain between £150,000 and £600,000

- 'roll over' on compulsory purchase, ie: sales under actual or prospective compulsory purchase of non-business land which is not the claimant's sole or main residence

- on the death of an individual, no liability to capital gains tax arises.

# CHAPTER 11.4 – VALUE ADDED TAX (VAT)

## 11.4.1 GENERAL PRINCIPLES OF VAT

*Introduction*

Value Added tax was first introduced into the United Kingdom in 1973. The regime from the 1 April 1989 is based upon the Value Added Tax Act 1984, as amended by the Finance Act 1989. The latter legislation severely affects the way in which development, construction, leasing and investment involving landed property is approached.

There are two principal aspects of any legislation - the wording of the law and the interpretation by its administrators.

In the case of the new VAT legislation on construction, land and property, it is Her Majesty's Customs and Excise who have the task of letting the taxpayers know what they believe the law really says.

The indications to liability etc. given in this section rely upon the legislation, HMC&E published notices and leaflets and the authors' interpretation of the data as a whole.

*Taxable persons*

The Customs and Excise charge VAT to a taxable person for the supply of goods and services which is a taxable supply, ie a supply which is not exempt.

The VAT legislation seeks to tax the final consumer. Curiously, although the final consumer is taxed, or may be said to be taxed on standard-rated or zero-rated supplies respectively, he or she is not the 'taxable' person.

A taxable person is one who in the course of business makes taxable supplies and is registered for VAT because he or she has a turnover of more than the statutory sum per year or per quarter (or expects to have these levels of turnover for such periods).

*Input tax and output tax*

The tax on a taxable supply is known as an '**output tax**', whereas tax paid on supplies received are known as '**input tax**'.

The taxable person's liability may be expressed as:

$L = To - Ti$

where L is the liability, To is the output tax and Ti is the input tax.

If the result is positive, VAT must be paid: if the result is negative, the taxable person is eligible to a credit or remittance of VAT. Sections 14 and 15 of the 1983 Act allow offsetting of input tax against output tax.

VAT is an invoice system of taxation with the 'tax from tax' feature of net liability or net credit.

## Kinds of rates and exemption

At present supplies are subject to VAT as follows:

- at standard rate

- at zero rate

- exempt.

## Standard rate

The taxable person who supplies goods or services which are standard rated must charge tax (output tax) – currently at 17.5 percent. However, any tax on goods and services received which are taxed to VAT (input tax) may be offset against the liability to pay the output tax to the Customs and Excise.

Zero rate

Section 16 and Schedule 5 to the 1983 Act provide that zero-rated goods and services are those where no tax is payable by the customer but the taxable person, ie the supplier, may recover any input tax paid in respect of goods and services provided. Zero-rated supplies are 'taxable supplies' despite the fact that no tax is chargeable to the customer.

As far as land and buildings are concerned zero-rated supplies were defined in Schedule 5 Group 8 of the 1983 Act. Briefly, and oversimplifying, construction works, demolition services and disposals of buildings by builders were at that time zero-rated, except for 'protected buildings'.

Under EC VAT Second and Sixth Directives, zero rating may only be used 'for clearly defined social reasons and for the benefit of the final consumer'. Hence the challenge in the European Court of Justice which was decided in June 1988.

Under the current regime the following buildings and works are zero-rated:

- new dwellings

- almost all new communal residential buildings

- new buildings for non-business activities of charities

- certain approved works to protected buildings.

However, new commercial buildings, certain self-supplies, certain demolition services and certain disposals of new buildings are standard rated.

## Exempt supplies

Exempt supplies are those where no output tax is charged on supplies to the taxable person's customers. However, unlike zero-rated or standard-rated goods or services, input tax cannot be recovered by the taxable person.

Examples of bodies who make supplies which are mainly exempt include:

- banks

- charities

- educational bodies

- hospitals in the private sector

- insurance companies

- pension funds.

An exempt supply is said to provide a hidden tax charge which is passed on to the consumer who cannot recover it. Under the old regime many disposals or grants in land were exempt. However under the new regime some are now standard rated or the supplier has the option to tax, eg rents under leases.

Where supplies are partly exempt and partly zero-rated or standard-rated, the taxable person may be required to only offset part of the input taxes incurred. In recent years the regime for this 'partial exemption' has been tightened to prevent avoidance.

## Treatment in accounts

Input tax which is irrecoverable, eg on exempt supplies for partially exempt business, is attributed to the cost of the property acquired.

Thus, under statement of Standard Accounting Practices, VAT on fixed assets is included in the capital cost of the item.

In the long term this may be relevant to any Capital Gains Tax computation and may feature in calculations for capital allowances.

For VAT purposes no substantive difference is made between capital and revenue. Thus a taxable person pays input tax on taxable supplies of a capital nature as well as those of a revenue nature. Similarly, output tax is charged on standard-rated capital items and revenue items.

## Taxes interaction

It may be useful to note that VAT may interact with other taxes in some circumstances. A brief indication is given here. Thus where input tax is completely recovered against output tax, the following computations should be made without taking VAT into account:

- Income Tax or Corporation Tax
- capital allowances
- Capital Gains Tax.

Where input tax is not recoverable by a trader, eg for an exempt business, it may be available for setting against income tax or corporation tax liability.

Input tax charged on a capital item which is not recovered by or credited to the taxable person, may be used in a subsequent computation for Capital Gains Tax purposes. Of course, any VAT charged as output tax is not included in the consideration on disposal.

Persons who are not taxable persons for VAT may compute profits for income taxation and gains for Capital Gains Tax by deduction of any VAT paid as an input tax. Capital allowances are treated in a similar way.

For a person who is partly exempt, VAT on inputs must be apportioned to taxable outputs and exempt outputs; only the former input tax is allowable. Generally, unrelieved input tax is allowed against income or capital as described above.

## Recovery of overpaid VAT

Where a person has overpaid the amount of VAT actually due to HMC&E there is now a separate mechanism for obtaining a refund of that amount (see Finance Act 1989 - Chapter II, part 1, section 24).

*Incorrect certificates as to zero rating etc.*

If, subject to the satisfaction of HMC&E, a person gives a certificate in the prescribed form to his supplier that the supply or supplies are to building qualifying for zero rating and that certificate is incorrect then that person shall be liable to a penalty. (See Finance Act 1989 - Chapter II, part 1, section 23).

*HMC&E amendments*

The new section 35A(2) of the Value Added Tax Act 1983 as inserted by the Finance Act 1989 allows the Treasury by order to amend Schedule 6A to the VAT Act 1983.

*Goods and services*

Where land is an asset of a company it is, generally, to be treated as if it were goods forming part of the assets (see also Finance Act 1989 - Schedule 3, refers to VAT Act 1983 - Schedule 2, paragraph 8).

*'Capital goods' scheme*

From 1 April 1990 a new scheme came into force applying to certain capital items which are used for non-taxable purposes. The scheme only applies to a very small percentage of companies which are not fully taxable. It will not apply to any capital items acquired or brought into use or costs incurred before 1 April 1990.

The capital items affected are:

- computers and items of computer equipment worth £50,000 or more
- 'land and buildings' (or parts of buildings) worth £250,000 or more.

'Land and buildings' includes both freehold and long leases of buildings, and extensions and alterations to buildings are included, also buildings which the owner constructs for his own use.

The scheme generally operates by making adjustments to the original input tax reclaimed by the business where the taxable use of the relevant goods changes.

The adjustments are made where a change in use occurs for:

- computers etc. (as above) within 5 years
- 'land and buildings' etc. (as above) within 10 years. (Subject to the adjustment being only 5 years for building interests of less than 10 years).

Various regulations and controlling principles have been included to govern changes of ownership of companies and the goods themselves, theft, damage etc., and special calculation rules in limited circumstances.

## 11.4.2 RELEVANT SUPPLIES

*Types of supply*

For VAT purposes relevant supplies in connection with premises are:

- disposals of interests in land and buildings
- construction services and goods
- professional and specialist services

*Disposal of*
*interests in land*
*and buildings*

Technically this only applies to the sale, or granting a lease, of land or buildings. However, for the sake of brevity, the term is used here in connection with 'disposal of interest' to embrace also grants of rights and licences.

In the legislation the term 'major interest' is used specifically to define long leases and freeholds.

All the interests and rights are described in Chapter 3.2, however, for purposes of the VAT legislation there is a special definition of a 'long lease' ie

- leases for over 21 years including those providing for:
    - periodic rent reviews
    - right for either party to terminate within 21 years
    - assignment by a person of his lease of the site on which he has begun to construct, or first constructed, a building provided that the lease has over 21 years to run at the time of assignment.

NB. Assured tenancies and the like are excluded

Perhaps not surprisingly a 'short lease' is any lease which is not a long one!

Land includes buildings, walls, trees, plants and other structures and natural objects attached to the land so long as they remain attached.

Fixtures supplied under the disposal of a freehold or leasehold interest in land are regarded as 'flowing' with the land. Their liability will follow that of the land, that is exempt, zero-rated or standard-rated.

*Construction*
*services and*
*goods*

Supply of services takes place when a person does something, other than supplying goods, for a consideration.

Reconstruction services need to be separately identified in respect of:

- construction - only of new building:

    the sole purpose of this term is to distinguish straight- forward building construction from the 'design-and-build' process. Procurement processes involving payment of separate fees to management contractors, construction managers and the like are included in this definition.

    The management contractor does not carry out any of the building work but directly engages 'works contractors' to do it. The client pays the management contractor his fee and the proper cost of all the works contracts the management contractor has entered into. This total is the consideration, it is zero-rated or standard rated according to the liability of the building construction work carried out.

    A construction or project manager's fees are treated as professional services as they are not considered to be part of the total consideration. Therefore the 'accountable sum' in these contracts for the purpose of this definition is the total of the works contracts exclusive of the construction or project management fee.

- design-and-construction of new building:

  a client may obtain the necessary design work for a building project from a contractor as part of a 'Design and Build' package deal with the contractor. Where the design, workmanship and materials are supplied by a contractor to his client under a 'Design and Build' lump sum contract without any separate identification of the part of the lump sum relating to the design element, the VAT liability of the design element will follow that of the building work.

  For example, where a new building project is concerned, if the building works supplied by the contractor are zero-rated the design is also zero-rated. This also applies where, within a lump sum design and build contract, the part of the sum for the design element is shown separately solely for internal analysis purposes by the two contracting parties. But if there is a separate supply of design or other similar professional services to a client, it is always standard rated.

- alteration - only works:

  the sole purpose of this term is to distinguish straight-forward building construction alterations from the 'design-and-build' process for alteration works, discussed below.

- design-and-construction in alteration works

- sub-contract services in new building:

  this refers to sub-contractors working to a main contractor or another sub-contractor. For VAT purposes it is not currently necessary to distinguish sub-contractors from 'works' or 'trade' contractors working to management contractors or under the direction of construction managers.

- sub-contract alteration - only works

- sub-contractor design and construction of new building:

  a client may obtain the necessary design work for a building project from a sub-contractor as part of a design and build package deal with the sub-contractor. The principles with regard to the taxation of the design element are as for the main contractor in design-and-build.

- sub-contractor design and construction in alteration works

- supply of goods without services:

  goods supplied to purchaser where the supplier does not provide services in connection therewith. Typically this would cover supplies of materials from Builders' Merchants to contractors and any supply where exclusive ownership passes round one person to another. It is interesting to note, in connection with real estate, that **'goods' includes a major interest in land, ie a freehold or long lease. Other disposals of interests in land, eg rights licences and short-leases are held to be supplies of services rather than supplies of goods.**

*Professional and specialist services*

These may be either independent or integral.

**Independent professional services** comprise work of a design, legal, surveying, engineering, agency or project management nature which are typically provided for a fee to clients by independent consultants in relation to land and property development.

**Integral services** are provided within the total consideration for the supply to which they relate. If they are separately billed then they will normally be treated as 'Independent Professional Services' for the purposes of this manual.

It must be noted that whereas this situation is expressly confirmed by HMC&E in their explanatory publications in respect of 'design-and-build' contracts there is no such statement in respect of other comparable situations, eg a property dealer employing his own conveyancing staff.

**Specialist services** are treated in the same way as professional services. They comprise such supplies as site investigations (prior to differing a building contract), concrete testing, site security, site cleaning, site catering and temporary lighting.

Supplies of certain specialist services in the course of zero-rated construction can be zero-rated if they come with HMC&E's definitions of 'demolition', 'site restoration', 'hire-plant with operator' or 'the erection and/or dismantling of scaffolding, formwork and falsework' (but not the hire).

## 11.4.3 STAGES OF DEVELOPMENT FOR VAT PURPOSES

*Primary conditions*

Liability for VAT and the rate to be charged on such supplies is primarily conditioned by the development stages of the site under consideration. In the manual 'Property Experts Guide to VAT' [1] the authors defined these stages as:

- non-development land
- land under development
- land with mature development.

Each of these stages as defined below, relates to 'trigger' points in the legislation which determines whether a supply will be exempt, zero-rated or standard-rated.

*Definitions of 'non-development land'*

All land which, at the time of disposal of an interest etc. is:

- not yet 'Land under development' as defined below, ie does not contain any new building construction that has progressed beyond foundation stage; and
- not 'Land with mature development' as defined below.

*Definition of 'land under development'*

Land with new building construction that has:

- progressed beyond foundation stage and
- has been completed and unoccupied for 3 years or less.

The term new building includes all work of building construction other than works to buildings which are part of 'land with mature development' as defined below. By definition it specifically excludes:

- conversion
- reconstruction
- alteration

- enlargement

- extension or annexation which provides for internal access to the existing buildings

- extension or annexation for which the separate use, letting or disposal is prevented by the terms of:

  -any covenant

  -any statutory planning consent

  -any similar permission.

For the purposes of this section it also includes civil engineering works such as roads, sewers, drains etc. carried out concurrently and in association with other new building construction.

## 11.4.4 THE STATUS OF THE SUPPLIER

*Status in
construction
and
development*

It is important to distinguish between developer and the contractor.

The significance of the difference lies in the fact that the disposal of an interest in 'land under development' by the developer as defined below must be distinguished from the provision of the construction services for VAT purposes.

In relation to a building or works developer means any person who:

- constructs it (person constructing)

- orders it to be constructed

- finances its construction.

with a view to granting an interest in, right over or licence to occupy it (or any part of it) or to occupying or using it (or any part of it) for his own purposes.

Where a body corporate is a member of a group and is a developer in relation to a building or work and it grants an interest etc to another body corporate which is a member of the same group, then that body corporate is also a developer in relation to that building to work. The above applies to any body corporate which:

- was a member of the same group as the body making the grant at the time of the grant; or

- has been a member of the same group at the same time as the body making the grant has an interest etc in the building or work (or any part of it); or

- has been a member of the same group as any other body corporate which had an interest etc in the building or work (or any part of it).

## 11.4.5 OPTION TO TAX INCOME FROM PROPERTY

*The principle*

From 1 August 1989, subject to certain exceptions, there has been an 'option to tax' (officially called an 'election to waive exemption' from) what would otherwise be exempt grant of interests in and rights over land, and licences to occupy land. (See Finance Act 1989, Schedule 6A, paragraphs 2-4).

From 1 August 1989 a company (or a body corporate or relevant associate) can opt to tax the - otherwise exempt - sale, assignment, leasing or licensing of any other type of building or civil engineering work, or part of it, any agricultural land, including a building on agricultural land in which it has an interest which is identifiable as separated from any other agricultural land in which it has an interest, or any other land it specifies. Once having opted to tax any supply of these, however, every subsequent supply must always be taxed. The option is irrevocable.

If premises are linked by a walkway or similar means, or groups of separate units within a parade, precinct or complex these are to be treated as a single building.

Where making an inclusive supply of qualifying accommodation (ie qualifying for zero-rating or exempt from the option to tax), together with other, commercial or industrial accommodation the supplier must apportion the consideration, eg if he lets a shop with a flat over it at an inclusive rent he must apportion the rent between the standard-rated element for the commercial premises and the exempt element for the residential accommodation.

If, having opted to tax a building it is subsequently completely demolished and another building is constructed on the site, the supplier is not bound by his option for the previous building.

On acquisition of a freehold interest in land or a building in which the purchaser in turn intends to grant an interest, he is not bound by the previous owner's option.

Similarly with acquisition of any other interest in land or a building or any part of a building in which the purchaser intends to grant a sub-lease or licence he is not bound by the option exercised by the freeholder or head lessee.

*Eligibility for 'option to tax'*

A potential eligibility to opt to tax in relation to a building/land so that the building or land is changed into a taxable supply (at standard rate) from an exempt one depends on the type of disposal and/or the category of use:

- qualifying building

  -any transaction

- freehold sale

  -of land with mature development

  -of all undeveloped land

  -of agricultural land or buildings thereon where elector has an interest, right or licence

  -of agricultural land or buildings thereon

  -of any other land or building

- leasing

  -of all land

  -of buildings on agricultural land where elector has an interest, right or licence

  -of any other buildings on agricultural land

  -of any other building

- grant

  -of any leasehold at a premium

- assignment
  - of any leasehold at a premium

## Consequences

Once the option has been made it cannot be revoked.

As a direct consequence of the option, a taxable person will then be able to recover any input tax attributable to his taxable outputs in respect of the building or land from the date of election only. The deadline for limited back-dating of allowable input tax passed on 1st November 1989.

In the long term input tax incurred before the option will not be recoverable. But transitional rules apply to a supply made by a taxpayer in respect of the period 1.4.89 to 31.7.89.

## Timing

For VAT purposes there is no imposed time limit within which a supplier must exercise the option to tax. His responsibility for accounting for tax on an 'opted' supply runs from the time that he exercises the option. Exceptionally, however, if he exercised the option to tax before 1 November 1989 he can make the option retroactive from any date - but not before 1 August 1989.

## Notification

The suppliers must give written notice of his option to tax to the local VAT office not later than 30 days after he exercises it. If he is not already registered for VAT, but will become registerable by exercising the option to tax, he must include his written notice with the application for registration. He need not, however, give written notice where he opts to tax and the total consideration for all the supplies for the buildings or land for which he has opted is expected to be less than £20,000 in the next 12 months.

Where he gives written notice, he can do this by:

- naming the individual buildings
- opting for all his buildings without naming them
- opting for all his buildings with specific named exceptions
- opting for his buildings, together with any that he may subsequently acquire.

He must be careful, however, when he makes any option which does not specify actual buildings. He will be bound by any option which he exercises to account for tax on all future supplies of the land or buildings concerned. Remember that the option is irrevocable.

## Tax point for chargeable leases

There are special provisions which determine the point ie the time when the supply is treated, for VAT purposes, as taking place.

## Existing leases

If the company making the supply is a lessor or licensor it has the legal right to add VAT to the rent agreed in the lease or licence unless the lease specifically says it cannot. If it has opted but cannot, under the terms of the lease, add VAT to the rent, it must still account for VAT which is deemed to be included in the rent.

## Input tax

The supplier cannot claim his input tax on supplies (or importations) attributable to his building or land if the supplies were made to him before the effective date of his option except where he has made not previous relevant exempt supply in respect of his building or land.

*Advice to
landlords and
tenants*

Landlords are advised to tell their tenants in advance if they plan to exercise their option. This could avoid getting enquiries from them when the rent demands go out and help maintain good relations. The VAT will be a new expense for them: not all will be able to claim it (or all of it) as their input tax, and even those that can may incur a cash-flow disadvantage. Any who sub-let would appreciate notice so that they can consider charging tax on the rents they receive.

They should check that the lease entitles them to require payment of the VAT by the tenant.

Tenants not currently being charged VAT on their rent should check with their landlord. He will probably tell them what his plans are as regards charging VAT on the rent, but if they do not hear they could get in touch with him.

How far a tenant can recover as input tax any VAT on the rent he pays will be governed by the normal rules on input tax.

If tenants sub-let they will particularly wish to know whether their landlord intends to exercise his option so that they can decide whether to do the same and so recover, subject to the normal rules, the VAT they will pay to him. Their own tenants would appreciate knowing what the plans are.

## 11.4.6 SELF SUPPLY OF LAND

A company falling within the above definition of developer may be liable to a special VAT self-supply charge on certain of the building or civil engineering works which he constructs or arranges to have constructed.

*Liability of
charge*

What this means is that even if he did purchase the land specifically for the development, he may have to account for tax and to value according to a formula.

**FIG 11.4.A** shows how to determine if there is a liability in this respect.

**FIG. 11.4.A:** *'Self-supply' of land - how to determine any liability to VAT charge*

Source: 'Property expert's guide to VAT' (BEB)

If liable the charge will arise on the first occasion of:

- the exempt supply of part, or all, of the building, work or the land on which it is to be constructed; or

- use of the building, work or any part of it when not a fully taxable person (or if the representative member of a group of bodies corporate is not a fully taxable person) during the period commencing with the day when the building or work is first planned and ending 10 years after completion of construction.

The value of the self-supply is the total of:

- the value of grants relating to the land on which the building or work is constructed, made or to be made to the developer, other than grants to be made for consideration in the form of rent the value of which cannot be ascertained by the developer when the supply is treated as made; and

- the value of all the taxable supplies of goods and services, other than any that are zero rated ie paid before 1 August 1989, made or to be made for or in connection with the construction of the building or work; which includes: professional and managerial services, demolition and site clearance services, security services, hire of equipment, haulage services, landscaping services, fitting out services etc.

**FIG.11.4.B:** *'Self-supply' of construction services - how to determine liability to a VAT charge*

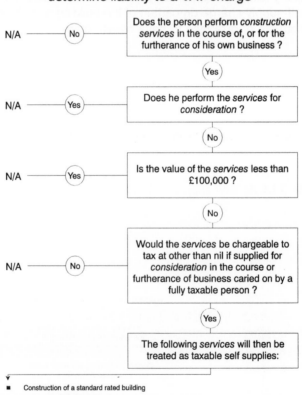

N/A —— No —— Does the person perform *construction services* in the course of, or for the furtherance of his own business ?

Yes

N/A —— Yes —— Does he perform the *services* for *consideration* ?

No

N/A —— Yes —— Is the value of the *services* less than £100,000 ?

No

N/A —— No —— Would the *services* be chargeable to tax at other than nil if supplied for *consideration* in the course or furtherance of business caried on by a fully taxable person ?

Yes

The following *services* will then be treated as taxable self supplies:

- Construction of a standard rated building

- Works to buildings such that additional floor area of not less than 10% of the floor area of the original building is created by:
  - extension OR
  - other alteration OR
  - construction of an annex.

- Civil engineering work

- Demolition work in connection with such services carried out:
  - contemporaneously therewith OR
  - preparatory thereto

Note    The value of the self supply is the open market value of the supply of an equivalent interest immediatley before construction commences.

### 11.4.7 SELF SUPPLY OF CONSTRUCTION SERVICES

If a company is using its own labour to perform construction services for its own occupation or use then there are various mechanisms which determine the level of tax to be paid, if any; the logic of these provisions is illustrated in **FIG 11.4.B**.

### 11.4.8 SERVICE CHARGES AND THE LIKE

*The provision of services*

It is common for leases between landlords and tenants to lay down that the landlord shall provide, and the tenants shall pay for, the services required for the upkeep of the building as a whole. The lease may provide for an inclusive rental, or it may require the tenants to contribute by means of a charge additional to the basic rent. These charges are sometimes called 'service charges', 'maintenance charges', 'further rent' or 'additional rent'.

Provided the services supplied in return for the charges are towards the general upkeep of the structure and common areas of the premises and grounds or for the services of a person such as a caretaker or warden they are regarded as part of the consideration for the grant to the tenants of their right to occupy the premises.

Therefore, where rent, including ground rent, is consideration for an exempt supply, then the service charge is **further consideration** for that exempt supply.

If the rent is consideration for a standard-rated supply - eg under the 'option to tax rent' then the service charge is further consideration for a standard-rated supply.

*The main supply*

The **main supply** is the main benefit passing under a disposal of interest etc to which the **main consideration** relates.

Where a person meets costs relating to premises which he shares with other persons the precise terms of the sharing arrangement will dictate whether such payments are a main supply as opposed to a **separate supply** or disbursements.

The main supply is one which is rendered in respect of the shared facility rather than one where the partner in the facility gains the whole benefit of the separately identifiable supply, ie a separate supply.

For example, a tenant recharging part of the rent invoiced to him will be making a main supply to the other occupier whereas cleaning of his room in the building is a separate supply.

*Separate supply*

Where a person sharing premises with other occupants makes a supply which is separately identifiable as being in respect of facilities he uses, he is making a separate supply. See also 'Main supply' above for further explanation of the distinction between the two categories.

### 11.4.9 OPERATING FACILITIES

*Facilities provided by the landlord*

Supplies which are **further consideration** are defined above.

The supplies by the landlord which may be described as **operating facilities** include the following:

- day-to-day maintenance

- general upkeep

- fixtures and fittings

- water and sewerage

- fuel and power

- cleaning

- telephones

- reception and switchboard

- administration

- management

- security

- office staff and services

- office equipment

- staff facilities

- car parking.

## 11.4.10 'NON-RELEVANT' CONSTRUCTION WORK

*Definition*

'Non-relevant' construction work is the definition used to describe construction goods or work that must always be **standard-rated** regardless of whether or not the building to which it is supplied otherwise qualifies to receive **zero-rated** supplies.

The following are examples of goods which are standard-rates because they do not fall within the general description of goods for which zero-rating is allowed - for instance, because they are not fixtures, or because the law specifically excludes them from zero-rating (most fitted furniture and domestic gas and electrical appliances):

- fitted furniture, both domestic and non-domestic, (other than units and work surfaces installed in the kitchens of dwellings or other qualifying buildings) whether supplied ready assembled or as materials, or part-assembled and finished-off on site. Examples in commercial buildings are:

    -desks

    -tables

    -chairs and other seating

- domestic electrical or gas appliances (but not space or water heating appliances), carpets and carpeting materials (including underlay and carpet tiles), even when stuck to the floor.

- other articles of a kind not ordinarily installed by builders as part of the construction work, eg: all trees, shrubs, flowers; and articles which are not fixtures, for example free standing equipment.

- any goods a company supplies for later use by a customer or for use by some other person supplying services to their customer.

- **goods supplied without construction services**, eg: by a builders' merchant.

- goods bought for the business but which are later used for work on a person's own home or property, even if the work would have been zero-rated if another builder had done it for them. But if they use such goods to build a complete new house for themselves, special arrangements may apply.

*Standard-rated work*

Standard rating will apply in the following examples:

- the conversion, reconstruction, alteration or enlargement of any non-qualifying existing building

- any extension or annex which has internal access to the existing building

- any extension or annex to an existing building, the separate use, letting or disposal of which is prevented by the terms of any covenant, planning consent or similar permission.

More specific examples of standard-rated work are:

- where the outer walls of an existing building remain even without floor or roof, any building operations in or around that shell

- the reconstruction of an existing building where internal features are retained in addition to any part of the external wall structure.

## 11.4.11 LIABILITIES TO VAT IN RESPECT OF COMMERCIAL BUILDINGS

*The principles of assessment*

All liabilities to charge VAT or otherwise in connection with premises fall within one or other of the three stages defined at 11.4.3 above

It is important to understand that land does not become 'development land' (as opposed to remaining 'non-development land' as considered below) merely on receiving the benefit of a planning permission for construction thereon. It only ceases to become non-development land when work is carried out to it to bring it within the second-stage category ie land under development.

Similarly, buildings may be complete and ready for occupation, but they still classify as 'land under development' until they meet the trigger point criteria for 'land with mature development' as defined above. The reason for this complicated set of definitions is that land, and the buildings under construction or built on it, are treated as inseparable for the purposes of VAT legislation – and, indeed, under the law of property.

Equally the supply of services such as construction or consultancy will potentially incur a different VAT charge depending on the stage in which they are provided.

*Liabilities in respect of the more common supplies*

**FIG 11.4.C** lists the liability to VAT in respect of the more commonly occurring transactions involving premises.

FIG 11.4.C: *VAT liability for some commonly occurring premises transactions*

| Nature of supply | Status of land / Tax rate | | |
|---|---|---|---|
| | Non-development | Under development | With mature development |
| Parking facilities | S | S | S |
| Most Licences to occupy | E/o | E/o | E/o |
| Most leases | E/o | E/o | E/o |
| Most freeholds | E/o | E/o | E/o |
| Professional services on S-rated disposal | S | S | S |
| Premium on S-rated disposal | S | S | S |
| Surrender | S | S | S |
| New Civil Engineering work | – | S | S |
| Construction work | – | S | S |
| Design-and-build | – | S | S |
| Independent Professional services (construction) | – | S | S |
| Material supplies | – | S | S |
| Specialist services | – | S | S |
| Rent | – | – | E/o |
| Further rent | – | – | E/o* |
| Separate supply of facilities | – | – | S |

| Notes. S = Standard-rated | * the tax-rate for the supply will follow that of the rent |
|---|---|
| E/o = Exempt within the option to tax | |

(1)    'Property Expert's Guide to VAT' – Bernard Williams Associates (Building Economics Bureau Ltd.)

# PART G

# BENCHMARKING

# SECTION 12

# THE PREMISES AND FACILITIES AUDIT

# CHAPTER 12.1 – THE OBJECTIVES

## 12.1.1 DEFINITION

A premises and facilities audit is an independent review of the costs of providing and operating premises and facilities, together with performance levels, management structures and systems.

Where appropriate the auditor will provide peer group benchmarks and indicate areas where a close scrutiny might be expected to lead to improvements.

Because the term 'premises audit' is now established in facilities management parlance the combination of **premises** and **facilities** in the title of this section is a compromise to accommodate this familiarity. However, as is shown in Section 1 the term 'premises' is subsumed within the wider definition of 'facilities'. For this reason the terms 'facilities audit' and 'facilities auditor' are used below with reference to the whole process.

## 12.1.2 THE CONCEPT AND ITS DEVELOPMENT

In the same way that some accountants have used their auditing role as a platform for development of business management consultancy, so some of the new breed of facilities management consultants can trace their roots directly back to the simple costs-benchmarking exercises first mooted in the mid 1980's. The modern-day facilities audit belies its title for the term 'audit' implies an arithmetical and procedural check of a company's financial position; the premises audit goes a lot further than that.

The concept of a formal **premises** audit was developed in the early 1980's by the authors. Its broad recognition as a discipline came finally through the publication of *Premises Audits*[1], first written as a series of articles for *Facilities*[2] and then produced in 1988 as a book.

Although space use audits, pioneered by the new breed of space planners in the UK from the early 1970's, had gained commercial acceptance by the time the series was written, interest in the operating costs of premises had remained firmly on an academic plane until then.

Ironically, it was the authors' close working association as building economists alongside these space planners which generated the base data so essential to effective auditing of premises costs. Alternative solutions for space problems, involving comparison on economic as well as ergonomic bases, were evaluated; whatever the options - refurbishment, redevelopment, green-field development etc - the present and predicted operating costs had to be fed into the financial equation and this meant ferreting them out of the organisation's usually inadequate records. Although the operating costs rarely influenced the outcome, the gathering of this data coincided with the IT boom of the early 1980's and its significant impact on both capital and operating costs of buildings and space utilisation.

Mounting costs saw facilities managers under increasing pressure to defend budgets which were wholly inadequate for demands being placed upon the premises by the business function. In most cases the defence presented against budget cuts was inadequate; this was partly due to inexperience of the facilities personnel, unable to appreciate the root cause of the problems, and partly due to the lack of any comparable cost data from their peer groups to give credence to their budget proposals.

With the growing database of premises costs, carefully sifted into cost centres by reference to their standard rules of classification, the authors were in a position to provide the cost 'benchmarking' which was, and is, so critical to facilities managers. The more premises audits carried out, the greater the depth of knowledge which was gained, not only of comparative costs but also, and more importantly, of the underlying performance, ergonomic and management issues which generated the cost levels which were uncovered.

In more recent times the audit base has been extended to cover all the issues addressed in this work, enabling the audit process to thrive on a wider as well as deeper database,

Even today **facilities audits** by consultants are by no means universally adopted. However, those organisations who have been brave enough to 'bare their souls' to a facilities auditor have, without exception, reaped considerable rewards.

---

[1]     'Premises Audits' by Bernard Williams (Bulstrode Press – out of publication)

[2]     'Facilities' (originally Bulstrode Press, and now MCB University Press )

# CHAPTER 12.2 – THE AUDIT PROCEDURE

## 12.2.1 THE STAGES

In most cases the audit will be in two stages: the 'first strike', and follow-up studies. The 'first strike' audit is a high-yielding investment which enables the facilities auditor, over a short period, to overview costs and procedures and give his opinions as to obvious or potential problem areas.

Normally steps can be put in hand immediately to stem obvious aberrations picked up from the 'first strike'. The consultant and client can then examine the costs and potential benefits of looking deeper into other areas identified as giving cause for concern.

## 12.2.2 THE 'FIRST STRIKE' AUDIT

*The process*

The term 'audit' implies an arithmetical and procedural check of a company's financial position; the facilities audit goes a lot further than that. Using the company's own cost data as a starting base, the auditor unscrambles it and puts it together again under cost centres (such as cleaning, energy, catering, communications and maintenance) which are directly comparable with those in his own database - which is drawn (in complete confidence) from auditing other organisations' facilities costs.

The auditor's next step is to analyse each cost centre per unit of floor area (square feet or square metres), per capita etc - so he can start to single out areas for further investigation. At the same time he will begin to establish what performance standards, if any, his client has set down for each element. These are checked against the work specifications for each element. The ultimate aim of this part of the audit is to see whether the firm's costs are more or less than average, whether they are appropriate to the level of specification and whether the level of specification is capable of securing the required level of performance. In plainer terms, is the firm getting value for money and achieving the standards it thinks it needs?

The attempt to answer these questions underlies each aspect of the facilities auditor's work - how he tackles his task, his standard method of elemental analysis, key economic features of each element, how he appraises the cost-effectiveness of work procurement, how design decisions influence operating costs, what management routines are most prone to abuse and the economic and performance consequences of any management failures.

*Cost centre definitions*

It is of course absolutely critical for the auditor to compare like with like when considering an organisation's costs against the database. The authors' classification system which has now been incorporated into the *'Premises and Facilities Data'*[1] service, is given at **FIG 12.2.A** Note that this covers only the 'premises' cost centres; the content of 'business support' cost centres, where needing definition, is given within the relevant chapters.

FIG 12.2.A: *Classification of premises cost centres*

| Operating cost centre | Components | Exclusions | |
|---|---|---|---|
| | | Cost component | Correct location |
| Services maintenance | Mechanical<br>• boilers<br>• chillers<br>• ductwork<br>• filters<br>• fire extinguishers<br>• humidifiers<br>• sprinklers<br><br>Electrical<br>• switchgear<br>• wiring<br>• internal lighting<br>• external lighting<br>• small power<br>• floor outlets<br>• fire-alarms<br>• generators<br>• UPS<br>• data cabling<br><br>Plumbing<br>• water supplies<br>• drainage<br><br>Lifts and escalators<br><br>Specialist plant cleaning<br><br>Service charge element | 'White-collar' administration<br><br>New installations<br><br>Alterations<br><br>Improvements<br><br>Environmental testing<br><br>Management time<br><br>Security systems<br><br>Churn<br><br>Premises costs | Management<br><br>Improvements & adaptations<br><br>Improvements & adaptations<br><br>Improvements & adaptations<br><br>Special<br><br>Management<br><br>Security<br><br>Improvements & adaptations<br><br>Property costs |
| Building maintenance | Fabric<br>• structural<br>• roofing<br>• partitions<br>• doors<br><br>Decorations<br>• finishes<br><br>Fittings<br>• furniture<br>• fixtures<br><br>External works<br><br>Service charge element | New installations<br><br>Alterations<br><br>Improvements<br><br>Management time<br><br>Churn<br><br>Office equipment<br><br>Premises costs | Improvements & adaptations<br><br>Improvements & adaptations<br><br>Improvements & adaptations<br><br>Management<br><br>Improvements & adaptations<br><br>Office services<br><br>Property costs |
| Cleaning | Internal areas<br>• stairs<br>• reception<br>• toilets<br>• atria<br><br>Windows & cladding<br><br>External areas<br>• car-parks<br><br>Service charge element | Deep clean kitchens<br>Toilet supplies<br>Management time<br>Cleans due to churn<br>Special plant cleans<br>Premises costs<br>Special computer clean | Catering<br>Special<br>Management<br>Improvements & adaptations<br>Services maintenance<br>Property costs<br>I.T. operation |

**FIG 12.2.A:** *Classification of premises cost centres (cont'd)*

| Operating cost centre | Components | Exclusions | |
|---|---|---|---|
| | | Cost component | Correct location |
| **Utilities** | Electricity<br><br>Gas<br><br>Oil<br><br>Water & sewerage<br><br>Waste disposal<br><br>Service charge element | Telephones<br><br>Management time | Office services<br><br>Management |
| **Security** | Staff<br>• reception<br>• patrols<br><br>Equipment<br>• appliances<br>• uniforms<br><br>Systems maintenance<br><br>Service charge element | Premises costs<br>Fire-alarms<br>New installations<br>Alterations<br>Improvements<br>Management time<br>Changes due to churn | Property costs<br>Services maintenance<br>Improvements & adaptations<br>Improvements & adaptations<br>Improvements & adaptations<br>Management<br>Improvements & adaptations |
| **Special** | Landscaping<br>Pest control<br>Supplies<br>Sundry<br>Service charge element | | |
| **Management** | Salaries<br><br>Benefits<br><br>Overheads<br><br>Senior management<br><br>Equipment<br><br>Service charge element | Office services management<br>Catering<br>Fleet<br>Communications<br>I.T.<br>'Blue-collar' / supervisors<br>Property management<br>Improvements | Office services<br>Office services<br>Office services<br>Office services<br>Office services<br>Operating category<br>Property costs<br>Improvements & adaptations |
| **Improvements & adaptations** | Churn<br>Extension to an existing system<br>Improvement to an existing system<br>Adapations to an existing system | Refurbishment<br><br>Statutory improvement | –<br><br>– |

The auditor must always try to establish categorically the content of any costs or space data provided by his client. For 'first-strike' purposes it may be adequate to focus on the principal 'cost-drivers' in each centre, leaving the minor detail to be flushed out at a later stage. Sometimes an initial difference between the client's costs and the auditor's benchmark will show up as an area for closer scrutiny; such scrutiny will often pick up misanalysis as the source of the apparent problem.

**FIG.12.2.B:** *Incorrect analysis - upgrading and 'churn' disguised as maintenance*

An example of mis-analysis distorting the figures is shown at **FIG 12.2.B.** Here the processes of upgrading and 'churn', being carried out by an in-house building and services unit, were merged under the heading of 'maintenance'. Not only were the figures misleading to the auditor, they were also misleading to the business' management who did not appreciate the obsolescence and 'churn rate' being concealed under the maintenance category. Of course, since the cost centre was not previously benchmarked they were not aware that a problem even existed.

*Space definitions*

Equally, the measurement of space must be in accordance with the accepted rules. The authors' definitions of space, based partly on the RICS definitions where available, are given in Chapter 4.1.

Using the wrongly defined parameter or, worse still, committing the cardinal crime of not stating precisely the parameter being used, can cause very serious errors.

No-one, consultant or his client alike, must ever use the term square feet or square metres without qualifying it appropriately eg: gross internal area, net internal (lettable) area, net usable area. To see how misleading the misinterpretation of the data can be, refer to **FIG 12.2.C** which shows how the cost of the maintenance of services will vary per unit of area depending on the choice of parameter. The same mistake also occurs frequently when estimates of costs of fitting out are given on a unit area parameter. For the revenue cost centres it does not particularly matter whether the gross or net internal area is used - so long as the user specifically states the denomination of square feet/metres he is using as the divisor.

**FIG.12.2.C:** *Effect of parameters on level of cost expressed*

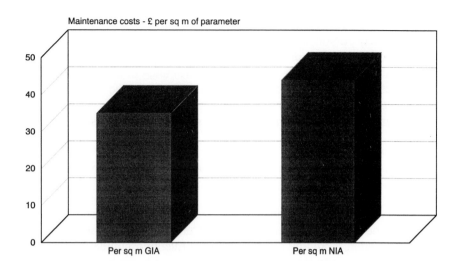

Maintenance costs - £ per sq m of parameter

*Performance evaluation*

The concept of performance is considered in detail in Section 1. For the purposes of this Section suffice it to say that the premises auditor should have due regard to the availability of any performance indicators from his client to inform any personal judgement he will make by talking to the client, the client's internal 'customers' and just using his eyes.

If the cleaning is being carried out for £7 per sq.m NIA and it is satisfactory then this fact should be stressed by the auditor - once having established that his view of 'satisfactory' matches the internal customers' needs and aspirations.

**Of course, the ideal arrangement is where the key performance indicators in the auditor's data-base can be used to quantify what must otherwise be a purely subjective performance comparison.**

*Management structures*

A facilities audit will usually be commissioned at the behest of upper management or facilities management. Whatever the motive, the management of the facilities function will certainly be scrutinised by the auditor for effectiveness and efficiency alongside the direct cost centres of the facilities budget. Although such a detailed process of analysis may be seen as threatening, in fact the results are almost always beneficial to the facilities management department, clarifying roles and often leading to the development of a formal facilities policy.

A simple check of the 'white collar' cost per unit of floor area managed can be a very useful starting point - but the extent of contracting-out works and consultant services must, of course, be among several factors to be fed into any comparative studies.

As discussed in Chapter 1.1 the relationship between costs and the business objective should be via a formal facilities policy.

The auditor's first job will be to seek out the existence or otherwise of such a policy to guide him towards benchmarks. Too often it does not exist, and becomes top of the list for follow-up studies. The level of communication within and from the facilities department will always be carefully scrutinised for potential weak points. Typical structures that can work well, given the appropriate calibre and attitude of the parties involved, are discussed in Chapter 2.1

*Management systems and controls*

Behind every instance of unwarranted or inadequate expenditure on facilities lies a faulty person, structure or system. Systems such as electronic communications, space management and financial control are discussed in detail elsewhere. It should, however, be noted that the presence of a system, even a good one, does not guarantee efficiency. Too often systematic application falls down under pressure of work or resources: the use – or abuse, misuse or non-use – of CAD systems is a particularly common example of deficiency in this respect.

The auditor will note these issues as he carried out his 'first strike' enquiries and analyse and flag them up for further more detailed investigation.

*Presentation*

The auditor will normally make an interim presentation of his 'first strike' findings to the facilities manager and other attendees as appropriate. That presentation should iron out any discrepancies or misunderstandings about the data, performance etc., and leave the auditor a week or two to modify his findings prior to final presentation which should end in distribution of the full report to facilities and top management, with recommendations, and an executive summary.

## 12.2.3 THE SECOND STAGE

Sometimes deficiencies, and the reasons therefore, are glaringly obvious and can be put to rights without further ado. However, in most cases it will prove necessary to commission a more detailed investigation of any anomalies - either internally or with the help of consultants. For example, unusually high energy costs will normally be corrected following an energy audit, abnormal use of space may be reviewed by a space planner and generally high levels of operating cost explored and value-engineered by a building economist.

The second stage can also be used to benchmark future expenditure and develop 'performance indicators'. The need to continue to keep a watch on levels of cost, space use etc is paramount for it is all too easy for the facilities efficiency to lose the sharp focus which always follows the audit procedure. It is a good discipline to invite the auditor in every year for a day or so to double-check that things are going in the chosen direction.

[1]     'Premises & Facilities Data' – (a joint venture between IML Group Ltd. – publishers of 'Premises & Facilities Management' – and BWA)

# CHAPTER 12.3 – BENCHMARKING

## 12.3.1 DEFINITION

Benchmarking is the process of comparing a product, service, process - indeed any activity or object - with other samples from a peer group, with a view to identifying 'best buy' or 'best practice' and targeting oneself to emulate it.

## 12.3.2 PROCURING THE DATA

*Alternative sources*

These are three principal sources through which an organisation can benchmark any of its facilities activities

- published data

- facilities auditor's database

- peer-group consultation

*Published data*

Published data on occupancy and support costs tends to be too general for benchmarking purposes because each organisation has its own individual requirements which cannot be identified from the anonymous sample. Frequently the data is collected by questionnaire, with respondents left to their own devices to determine how to fill in the answers; of course, there is no way of knowing how a firm's systems and procedures affect the cost levels without investigation, which is not possible using this data.

The biggest problem with published data, however, is that it tends to represent average cost performance rather than 'best practice'. As such it may be a first warning to the really wayward, but cannot be a basis for benchmarking to excellence.

Data-exchange services, such as the 'Premises & Facilities Data' service described in Chapter 12.2, which enable subscribers to contact and interrogate the other subscribers can lead to another type of arrangement discussed below.

*Facilities auditor's database*

The cross-fertilisation of ideas and cost-effective solutions facilitated by the experienced auditor is a highly efficient source of benchmarking data. Provided that he can demonstrate that the data is consistently analysed and can identify (anonymously of course) the nature of the organisations, buildings, locations etc, of the comparators then his client should have cause to be confident of his recommendations as to cost, space and performance levels.

*Peer-group
data exchange*

Sometimes peer groupings of facilities managers get together to compare notes about the costs etc of running and maintaining their premises, performance levels etc. Such groupings are to be much encouraged since they can only result in aspiration to the best of practice emanating from the discussions. Nevertheless busy schedules do have a tendency to cause structured benchmarking exercises to flounder and most facilities managers do not have the analytical skills or the database of a specialist consultant.

*Peer group
plus facilities
auditor*

A good alternative is to involve an auditor as the catalyst for the exercise, sharing his fees and tasking him to obtain the data from each company, to call, minute and possibly chair meetings, and produce a common report. This not only guarantees that the impetus will be maintained but also that analyses will be consistent and in accordance with standard rules of measurement; a most important bonus is, of course, that the auditor's experience and data base will be available alongside the group's results for additional comparison.

Groups of firms previously the subject of facilities audit by the same consultant and coming together to compare notes will also get a large added value for a relatively small additional and shared fee.

Another variation on the theme is for one organisation to offer to provide specific benchmark information to another currently being audited, on the basis that both might get something out of the exercise on a specific topic. An example of such collaboration is given at **FIG 12.3.A** where a local authority was afforded a comparison of the space standards of a 'hard-nosed' financial services company.

**FIG. 12.3.A:** *Space standards comparison
- local authority v financial services company*

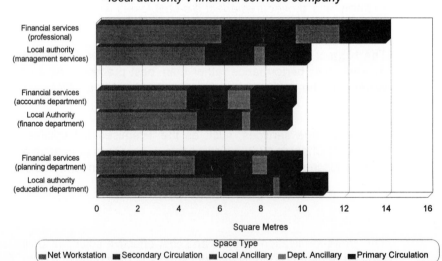

### 12.3.3 THE PROCESS

In some circumstances benchmarking is simple eg: a retailer comparing his wares for quality and price with his High Street competitors.

Some facilities benchmarks fall into this simple category eg: stationery, motor fleet etc. But others, especially those which are premises-related, are really quite difficult to establish with any degree of confidence.

For example, the cost of maintenance of building services depends on many factor such as:

- quality of original workmanship
- systems provided
- hours in use
- age
- preventative maintenance policy
- premises policy.

In such cases only a really large and well-structured database can throw up sufficient and accurate comparables to make cross-reference truly beneficial.

The best way for a company to use the auditor's benchmarks is to test them with a value-engineering study (see Chapter 2.2) incorporating a review of budgetary control and procurement procedures as well as the design and specification options and required performance levels.

Having set the targets it is very important for the facilities manager to explain the process to his team, get their support for the levels chosen, and set up the procedures, management and monitoring structures by which they may be achieved.

### 12.3.4 USING THE COMPARATORS

*The pitfalls of using 'second-hand' benchmarks*

Whatever parameters are chosen, the resulting cost benchmark still needs to be read against every factor bearing upon it. For this reason the practice of taking cross-references to costs per square metre or per capita either from published data, by anecdote or via exchange groups unsupported by specialists is to be avoided at all costs.

The example at **FIG 12.3.B** illustrates the simple fact that eg: the operating costs per unit of floor area will rise as the density increases but that the cost per capita of the same cost centres will fall.

**FIG. 12.3.B:** *Effect of density on operating costs per capita and per unit of floor area*

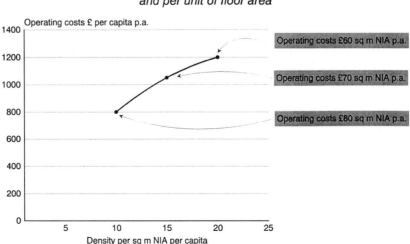

Equally, if the operating costs alone were being benchmarked to this comparator the point might well be missed that the improved space use would have a much more dramatic impact on the total premises costs per capita once the rent/rates etc come into the equation - see **FIG 12.3.C.** and note that this is to a much smaller scale than **FIG 12.3.B**

**FIG. 12.3.C:** *Effect of density on premises costs per capita*

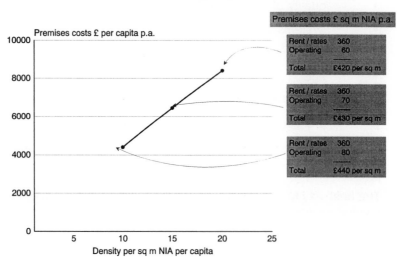

# CHAPTER 12.4 – THE BENEFITS OF AN AUDIT

## 12.4.1 AN INDEPENDENT OVERVIEW

A facilities audit carried out by an experienced consultant with an extensive, well-constructed and appropriate database will not fail to bring economic benefits to even the best-run facilities operation. Post-audit improvements, even from well run businesses, are frequently startlingly effective; a 10% improvement is quite common and savings of over 100% in some cost centres are regularly reported.

**FIG 12.4.A** and **FIG 12.4.B** are examples of the graphic conclusions of a facilities audit in respect of annual expenditure on premises and support services respectively.

**FIG. 12.4.A:** *Audited premises expenditure - conclusions shown graphically*

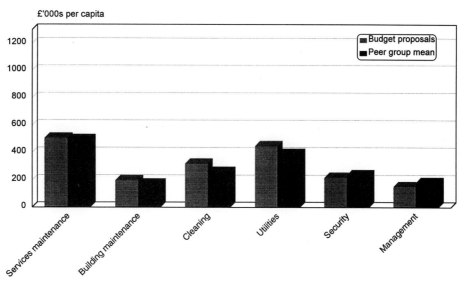

**FIG. 12.4.B:** *Audited support services expenditure - conclusions shown graphically*

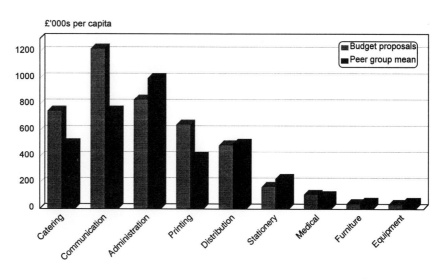

The independent facilities cost consultant will invariably find at least one aspect of the facilities costs or management where the adoption of peer group standards and procedures would bring immediate benefit in costs or performance - and most probably both.

## 12.4.2 BENCHMARKING TO 'THE BEST OF BREED'

At the present stage of development of facilities management most organisations will settle for just being as good as the median in the sample. However, good management demands that everyone should be benchmarking to 'the best of breed', so striving to beat 'the norm' and adding - directly or indirectly - to efficiency and bottom-line profitability.

# PART H

# INDEX
# AND
# LIST OF
# FIGURES

# INDEX

# LIST OF FIGURES